Real Estate Valuation
Principles and Applications

THE IRWIN SERIES IN FINANCE, INSURANCE AND REAL ESTATE

Stephen A. Ross
Sterling Professor of Economics and Finance
Yale University
Consulting Editor

FINANCIAL MANAGEMENT

Block and Hirt
Foundations of Financial Management
Eighth Edition

Brooks
PC FinGame: *The Financial Management Decision Game*
Version 2.0 - DOS and Windows

Bruner
Case Studies in Finance: *Managing for Corporate Value Creation*
Second Edition

Eun and Resnick
International Financial Management

Fruhan, Kester, Mason, Piper and Ruback
Case Problems in Finance
Tenth Edition

Helfert
Techniques of Financial Analysis: *A Modern Approach*
Ninth Edition

Higgins
Analysis for Financial Management
Fourth Edition

Levich
International Financial Markets

Nunnally and Plath
Cases in Finance
Second Edition

Ross, Westerfield and Jaffe
Corporate Finance
Fourth Edition

Ross, Westerfield and Jordan
Essentials of Corporate Finance

Ross, Westerfield and Jordan
Fundamentals of Corporate Finance
Third Edition

Stonehill and Eiteman
Finance: *An International Perspective*

White
Financial Analysis with an Electronic Calculator
Second Edition

INVESTMENTS

Bodie, Kane and Marcus
Essentials of Investments
Second Edition

Bodie, Kane and Marcus
Investments
Third Edition

Cohen, Zinbarg and Zeikel
Investment Analysis and Portfolio Management
Fifth Edition

Hirt and Block
Fundamentals of Investment Management
Fifth Edition

Lorie, Dodd and Kimpton
The Stock Market: *Theories and Evidence*
Second Edition

Morningstar, Inc. and Remaley
U.S. Equities OnFloppy
Annual Edition

Shimko
The Innovative Investor
Version 2.0 - Lotus and Excel

FINANCIAL INSTITUTIONS AND MARKETS

Flannery and Flood
Flannery and Flood's BankMaster: *A Financial Services Simulation*

Rose
Commercial Bank Management: *Providing and Selling Financial Services*
Third Edition

Rose
Money and Capital Markets: *Financial Institutions and Instruments in a Global Marketplace*
Sixth Edition

Rose and Kolari
Financial Institutions: *Understanding and Managing Financial Services*
Fifth Edition

Santomero and Babble
Financial Markets, Instruments, and Institutions

Saunders
Financial Institutions Management: *A Modern Perspective*
Second Edition

REAL ESTATE

Berston
California Real Estate Principles
Seventh Edition

Berston
California Real Estate Practice
Sixth Edition

Brueggeman and Fisher
Real Estate Finance and Investments
Tenth Edition

Lusht
Real Estate Valuation: *Principles and Applications*

Smith and Corgel
Real Estate Perspectives: *An Introduction to Real Estate*
Second Edition

FINANCIAL PLANNING AND INSURANCE

Allen, Melone, Rosenbloom and VanDerhei
Pension Planning: *Pensions, Profit-Sharing, and Other Deferred Compensation Plans*
Eighth Edition

Crawford
Law and the Life Insurance Contract
Seventh Edition

Crawford
Life and Health Insurance Law
LOMA Edition

Hirsch
Casualty Claim Practice
Sixth Edition

Kapoor, Dlabay and Hughes
Personal Finance
Fourth Edition

Kellison
Theory of Interest
Second Edition

Skipper
International Risk and Insurance

Real Estate Valuation
Principles and Applications

Kenneth M. Lusht

IRWIN

Chicago • Bogotá • Boston • Buenos Aires • Caracas
London • Madrid • Mexico City • Sydney • Toronto

IRWIN Concerned about Our Environment

In recognition of the fact that our company is a large end-user of fragile yet replenishable resources, we at IRWIN can assure you that every effort is made to meet or exceed Environmental Protection Agency (EPA) recommendations and requirements for a "greener" workplace.

To preserve these natural assets, a number of environmental policies, both companywide and department-specific, have been implemented. From the use of 50% recycled paper in our textbooks to the printing of promotional materials with recycled stock and soy inks to our office paper recycling program, we are committed to reducing waste and replacing environmentally unsafe products with safer alternatives.

© Richard D. Irwin, a Times Mirror Higher Education Group, Inc. company, 1997

All rights reserved. No part of this publication may be reproduced, stored in a retrieval system, or transmitted, in any form or by any means, electronic, mechanical, photocopying, recording, or otherwise, without the prior written permission of the publisher.

Irwin Book Team

Publisher: *Michael W. Junior*
Sponsoring editor: *Gina M. Huck*
Associate editor: *Maureen M. Harrington*
Marketing manager: *Katie Rose*
Project supervisor: *Lynne Basler*
Production supervisor: *Dina L. Genovese*
Designer: *Matthew Baldwin*
Prepress Buyer: *Charlene R. Perez*
Compositor: *Weimer Graphics, Inc.,
    Division of Shepard Poorman Communications Corp.*
Typeface: *10/12 Times Roman*
Printer: *R. R. Donnelley & Sons Company*

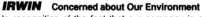

Library of Congress Cataloging-in-Publication Data

Lusht, Kenneth M.
    Real estate valuation : principles and applications / by Kenneth M. Lusht.
        p. cm.
    ISBN 0-256-19059-3
    Includes index.
    1. Real property—Valuation. I. Title
HD1387 .L87 1997
333.33′2—dc20   06-35439

Printed in the United States of America
1 2 3 4 5 6 7 8 9 0 DO 3 2 1 0 9 8 7 6

To my wife, Libby, and to my parents, Evelyn and Stanley Lusht

Preface

The appraisal profession and the appraisal process look very different than they did a decade ago. Some of the changes have come in reaction to problems in property markets, others the result of institutional evolution. Appraisers are now state licensed or certified, the Appraisal Foundation is increasingly influential in shaping policy, and in response to both federal legislation and advances in data processing technology, there is a rapid (and to some, threatening) move toward computer-assisted appraisals.

There is concern about international property markets, the valuation distinctions between "public" and "private" real estate, and how real estate as an asset class contributes to portfolio performance. A decade ago these were interesting topics for speculation; today, they are at the core of many investment and valuation decisions.

These kinds of changes impose a greater technical burden on those who provide the information and analysis to help others make the decisions, including in particular the appraiser. As a result, there is a renewed interest in real estate as an academic area at colleges and universities, as well as an increased sophistication of offerings at the professional level.

Intended Audience

Real Estate Valuation: Principles and Applications is intended to meet both academic and professional needs. There is sufficient rigor to challenge the student, while care is taken to develop applications that help to analyze and address marketplace problems. The text is written at the advanced undergraduate or introductory graduate level, meaning that it is also suitable for professional courses such as the Appraisal Institute's residential and income property series.

Some math and economics background would be helpful, but isn't necessary. Those whose algebra skills have eroded over time should not be concerned. There are chapters on statistical analysis, including regression, but there the emphasis is on application and interpretation, not mathematical foundations. In total, the book has sufficient depth and breadth to provide the reader with both a solid conceptual foundation and a guide to applications sufficient to handle most valuation problems.

Philosophy

The text is written from the perspective that principles are more important than processes. While detailed solutions are included for a wide variety of appraisal problems, the emphasis is always on the principle, not on how to crunch the numbers through a "formula." The goal is to teach students to think about valuation in a logical, intuitive way, so that they are able to creatively solve real-world problems.

Before appraisers can *estimate* value, they must understand what *determines* value in the marketplace. Thus, prior to beginning the detailed discussion of value estimation, the better parts of several chapters are devoted to the theory and evidence of value determination.

Features

Reliance on Empirical Evidence

Paradoxically, while the appraisal process is anchored firmly in the use of market information, one characteristic of most appraisal texts is the lack of reference to market evidence to support the principles and techniques being taught. This text has taken advantage of the work of real estate academics and practitioners who during the past couple of decades have produced an increasingly rich body of literature. In some cases the evidence supports, and in other cases challenges, traditional appraisal assumptions and practices. Wherever possible, this evidence is used to support the intuition and applications presented in the text.

Appraisal Options and Appraisal Reporting

At one time not so long ago, an appraisal was an appraisal—there was one set of guidelines that had to be followed, as well as a more or less standard reporting format. Few if any departures were allowed.

This has changed radically in the mid 1990s. The menu of appraisal process and reporting options has been expanded, and terminology such as "limited appraisal," "summary report," "departure provision," and "evaluation" must be familiar to both clients and appraisers. A clear and concise discussion of these new developments and how they may impact appraisal practice is provided.

Extensive End-of-Chapter Questions and Problems

Students learn best with a hands-on approach. Currently, most appraisal texts have few or no problems for students to solve. *Real Estate Valuation: Principles and Applications* provides not only extensive end-of-chapter problems, but carefully incorporates short-answer questions that require thinking and synthesis of important ideas. Detailed solutions to selected end-of-chapter questions and problems are found in Appendix A, while comprehensive solutions to all questions and problems are included in the Solutions Manual.

Liberal Use of Exhibits

Students tend to learn more quickly and to retain information better when a chart, graph, or table is used to support the discussion. These learning tools are sprinkled liberally throughout the text.

Extensive Referencing

In *Real Estate Valuation: Principles and Applications,* the discussions are extensively referenced, particularly those chapters that focus on value determination. Every attempt is made to reference both original sources as well as modern treatments. This provides the student with a guide to accessible supporting and supplementary materials.

Organization

Real Estate Valuation: Principles and Applications is designed to be as flexible as possible. If, for example, residential appraisal is the focus, the sales comparison and cost approach chapters can be covered while the income approach chapters are skipped, without damaging the integrity of the course. The same approach can be taken in reverse if the focus is income property appraisal.

The text is divided into seven parts. Part I has two chapters that introduce appraisal and the appraisal process, and discuss the characteristics of the markets in which property rights are exchanged. The question of *why* appraisals are needed is answered with a focus on the efficiency of real estate markets.

Part II deals with expected use analysis and property analysis, with separate chapters on location and property-specific characteristics. This is where value determination receives the most attention, beginning with the basic bid-rent model in perfect markets, then adding real-world complexities. There is extensive reference to empirical work. The expected use chapter compares the competing concepts of highest and best use, most probable use, and expected use.

Part III contains the sales comparison approach, with separate chapters on traditional (small sample) direct sales comparison, basic statistical analysis, and econometric (regression) analysis. Coverage is given to questions such as the number of comparables necessary, the appropriate search area for comparables, the use (and potential misuse) of cash equivalency, and the proper use of supporting evidence such as trend analysis. The chapters on statistical and econometric (regression) analysis focus on the proper use of these techniques, and in particular the interpretation of results. The last chapter covers special considerations when valuing land and sites.

Part IV includes three chapters that cover the cost approach. Time is spent on the relationship of the cost approach to the sales comparison and income approaches, and on the main issues with respect to the utility of the cost approach. For example, there are discussions of how the highest and best use of a property affects the applicability of the cost approach, and how market disequilibrium is reflected in the cost approach.

Part V covers the income approach. This is the largest part of the text due to the wide range of topics under the income approach umbrella. There are three sections in Part V, and they move generally from basic to more sophisticated models. Section A begins with a chapter devoted to estimating income, then covers direct capitalization techniques. Section B is devoted to discounted cash flow models, and Section C to discussions of various relationships among income approach models and issues related to their proper use. Again with the objective of flexibility, you will find that the three Sections of the Income Approach can be taught independently.

In addition to traditional income approach topics, there are extensive discussions on estimating the discount rate and on estimating terminal value (reversion), and a separate chapter on how the various models under the income approach umbrella relate to each other. The focus throughout is a general model that can be used to value any income stream, regardless of its pattern. Models such as Ellwood are treated as special cases, and are discussed together in a chapter titled "Shortcuts." A separate chapter addresses the question of whether the sum of the parts equals the whole, with specific reference to the relationships between financing and value, and securitization and value, and to the circumstances in which the value of the unencumbered fee equals the value of the leased fee plus the leasehold. The last chapter in Part V discusses investment analysis and its relationship to appraisal. Part VI addresses reconciliation and appraisal reporting.

Acknowledgments

Special thanks go to many colleagues and individuals for their efforts and assistance during the creation of this text; Roger Cannaday, University of Illinois; Richard Green, University of Wisconsin–Madison; Jim Vernor, Georgia State University; Elaine Worzala, Colorado State University; and Val Pasquarella, Jr., V. H. Pasquarella Company, provided valuable reviews and helpful comments; David Harrison offered a critical eye to all quantitative aspects of the text and Solutions Manual; Tom Geurts, California State University–San Bernardino, and Wei Song diligently checked all the problems and solutions in the text and in the Solutions Manual; Heather Asendorf and Janet Reese carefully prepared the manuscript. A special thanks to my editors, Gina Huck and Maureen Harrington, who offered feedback and support throughout the process.

Kenneth M. Lusht

Brief Contents

PART I
The Appraisal Process and Real Estate Markets
1. Real Estate Appraisals and the Appraisal Process   2
2. Price and Value in Real Estate Markets   13

PART II
Property Analysis: The Determinants of Value
3. Property Analysis: Location   24
4. Property Specific Characteristics: The Site and the Improvements   47
5. Expected Use Analysis   67

PART III
Estimating Value: The Sales Comparison Approach
6. Direct Sales Comparison   83
7. Sales Comparison With Basic Statistical Analysis   119
8. Sales Comparison Using Regression Analysis   139
   Appendix   A More Precise Confidence Interval   165
9. Special Considerations When Valuing Land and Sites   167

Part IV

Estimating Value: The Cost Approach

- **10** The Cost Approach: An Overview 179
- **11** Estimating Building Costs 187
- **12** Estimating Depreciation 199

Part V

Estimating Value: The Income Approach

Section A: Direct Capitalization

- **13** Estimating A Property's Productivity: Net Operating Income 234
- **14** Estimating Value Using Directly Extracted Multipliers and Rates 264
- **15** Estimating the Overall Capitalization Rate Using a Weighted Average of First Year Returns to Debt and Equity 277
  Appendix An Alternative Model Based on the Debt Service Coverage Ratio 289

Section B: Discounted Cash Flow Models

- **16** Discounting and Present Values 292
- **17** Completing the Basic DCF Model: Estimating Future Value (Reversion) 312
  Appendix Replacing the Estimate of Future Selling Price with an Explicit Forecast of Income 321
- **18** Finance and Tax Explicit DCF Models 323
  Appendix Using the Debt Service Coverage Ratio to Estimate the Loan Amount 348
- **19** Residual Models: Leased Fee/Leasehold and Land/Buildings 352
  Appendix Using a Finance-Explicit Model for Residual Valuation 368
- **20** DCF Model "Shortcuts" 370

Section C: Income Approach Model Relationships and Conceptual Issues

- **21** Relationships Among Income Approach Models 383
- **22** Estimating the Discount Rate 392

Brief Contents

23 Does the Whole Equal the Sum of the Parts? 403
24 Investment Analysis 412

PART VI

Reconciliation and Appraisal Reporting

25 Reconciling Value Estimates 432
26 Appraisal Reporting and Professional Practice 441

Appendix A: Detailed Solutions to Odd-Numbered End-of-Chapter Problems 451
Index 473

Contents

PART I
The Appraisal Process and Real Estate Markets

1 Real Estate Appraisals and the Appraisal Process 2

Introduction 2
Who Uses Estimates of Value? 2
Why Real Estate Appraisals Are Needed: Theory 3
Why Real Estate Appraisals Are Needed: Evidence 4
Estimating Value: An Introduction to the Appraisal Process and the
    Three Approaches 6
    The Sales Comparison Approach 7
    The Cost Approach 8
    The Income Approach 9
The Three Approaches and the Final Value
    Estimate: Reconciliation 10
Another Perspective on the Appraisal Process: A Mix of Results
    and Process 10
Summary 11

2 Price and Value in Real Estate Markets 13

Introduction 13
A Market Value Definition 14
    "Most Probable Price" 14
    "Reasonable Exposure" 15

"... Competitive Market ..." 15
　　Market Characteristics Associated with Relative Efficiency 16
　　Real Estate Markets 17
Implications for the Market Value Definition 18
A Modified Definition 19
Other Kinds of Value 21
　　Investment Value 21
　　Use Value 21
　　Assessed Value 22
　　Insurable Value 22
Summary 22

Part II

Property Analysis: The Determinants of Value

3 Property Analysis: Location 24

Introduction 24
Accessibility and Land Value 25
Accessibility and Land Value: Empirical Evidence 27
　　Why Cities Grow in "Circles" 29
The Land Value Gradient and Transportation Improvements 30
Refining the Land Value Gradient: Other Sources of the Lumps 32
Neighborhoods and Value 33
Components of "Neighborhood" 33
　　Special Accessibility (Proximity) 34
　　Stability 36
　　Environmental and Governmental Influences 37
　　Demographics 39
　　Neighborhood Life Cycles 40
The Land-Value Gradient Revisited: Neighborhood Effects 40
Non-Single-Family Neighborhoods: Districts 41
　　Apartment Multifamily Residential Districts 41
　　Commercial Districts: The Central Business District and
　　　Shopping Centers 41
　　Industrial Districts 41
The Use of "Neighborhood" in Appraisal:
　　Categorizing Neighborhoods 43
Neighborhoods and Appraisal Reports 44
Summary 45

4 Property-Specific Characteristics: The Site and the Improvements 47

Introduction 47
Identifying the Physical Property: The Property Description 47
Non-Ownership Impacts on Property Value: Government Regulation
 and Private Contracts 48
 Zoning and Deed Restrictions 49
 Assessed Values and Property Taxes 50
 Easements and Encroachments 50
 Leases 50
Factors Associated with Site Value 50
 Components of a Site 51
 The Size of a Site 51
 The Shape of a Site 53
 Corner Lots and Cul-de-Sacs 55
 Plottage and Plattage 56
 Topography, Contour, and Soil 56
 Excess Land 56
 The "Micro-Neighborhood": A Property's
  Immediate Surroundings 57
 Environmental Laws and Regulations 57
Building Characteristics Associated with Value 58
 The Size of the Building 58
 Building Materials and Their Quality 59
 Design 60
 Proportion and Adequacy 61
 Condition 62
 Proxies for Condition: Age and Effective Age 62
 Compatibility and Conformity 63
Other Property Types 64
Summary 64

5 Expected Use Analysis 67

Introduction 67
Criteria in Expected Use Analysis 68
Appraising Land as if Vacant 69
 The Highest and Best Use Premise 69
 When Comparables Are Available 70
 The Expected Use Premise 70
 When Sufficient Comparables Are Available 70
 When Sufficient Comparables Are Not Available 71

An Example of Expected Use Analysis 71
The Most Probable Use Premise 73
Appraising a Property Already Improved 73
Which Expected Use Premise Is Best? 74
Other Expected Use Issues 75
  Interim Uses 75
  Land, Improvements, and Consistent Use 76
  Mixed Uses 76
  Excess Land 77
  More Efficient Use, Renovation, and Additions 77
Summary 78

PART III

Estimating Value: The Sales Comparison Approach

6 Direct Sales Comparison 83

Introduction 83
Valuing Houses Using Direct Sales Comparison 84
  Selecting Comparables 85
  Where Should You Look? 85
  The Question of Time 86
  Physical Characteristics 86
  Age 88
  Time on the Market 88
  How Many Comparables Are Enough? 89
  The Use of Asking ("List") Prices 90
Adjusting the Prices of Comparables 91
  An Example 91
  Weighting the Adjusted Prices 92
  Using Percentages Instead of Dollars for Adjustments 93
  The Order of Adjustments 94
Sources of Adjustments 94
  Matched Pairs 94
  The Process of Matching Pairs 95
  An Example 96
  In Practice 98
  Regression Analysis 99
  Cost 99
  Survey 100
Adjusting for Financing: The Cash Equivalency Model 100
  The "Cash Equivalency" Model 101
  Other Financing Issues 103

Is There a Business Value Component? 104
Units of Comparison 105
Income Properties 106
   Selecting Comparables 106
   Units of Comparison 106
   Units of Comparison: An Office Building Example 107
   Units of Comparison: An Apartment Example 110
   "Bracketing" Prices to Estimate Value 111
   An Example 111
   Future Prospects and Comparability 112
Sources of Information 113
Supporting a Value Estimate: Other Indicators 113
   Using Value Trends 113
   Assessment Ratios 114
Summary 115

7 Sales Comparison with Basic Statistical Analysis 119

Introduction 119
Populations and Samples 119
   Describing a Population 120
      Frequency Distributions: The Pattern of the Population Data 121
      Graphing Relative Frequencies 122
Common Shapes of Frequency Curves 122
   Describing a Frequency Distribution 123
Measures of Central Tendency 124
Measures of Dispersion 126
   The Average Absolute Deviation 126
   Standard Deviation 128
Using the Mean and Standard Deviation 129
Using a Sample to Make Inferences about the Population Mean 131
   A Sample of the House Sales 131
Confidence Intervals with Small Samples 132
   Using the t-table 133
The Standard Error of the Mean 134
Using the Confidence Interval Around the Mean 136
Does the Population Have to Be Normally Distributed to Use
   Confidence Intervals Around the Mean? 136
Summary 137

8 Sales Comparison Using Regression Analysis 139

Introduction 139
Simple Regression 140
   A Scatter Diagram 141

Obtaining Greater Precision: Calculating the
Regression Line 142
The Regression Equation for Size and Selling Price 142
The Standard Error of the Estimate 143
Making Inferences Using Regression 143
Correlation Analysis 144
Making Inferences About the Slope (b) of the Regression Line 145
Limitations and Pitfalls Using Regression and
Correlation Analysis 146
Regression Measures Association, Not Cause and Effect 146
A Lack of Theory and Spurious Relationships 147
Extrapolation and Trending 147
A Summary Example of Simple Regression 147
Multiple Regression 149
A Multiple Regression Example 149
Interpretation and Analysis 150
The Significance of the Independent Variables 151
The Adjusted r^2 151
Using Qualitative (Dummy) Variables 152
Predicting Rent 153
Interpreting the Coefficients of Dummy Variables 153
Improving Regression Results 154
Multicollinearity 154
Does Multicollinearity Matter? 155
Other Strategies to Reduce Multicollinearity: Principal
Components and Ridge Regression 156
Missing Variables 157
Symptoms of Missing Variables 157
A Low r^2 157
Surprising Coefficients 157
Regression Residuals 158
The Effects of Narrow Stratification 159
Nonlinear Relationships 160
Summary 162
Appendix A More Precise Confidence Interval 165

9 Special Considerations When Valuing Land and Sites 167

Introduction 167
Site Versus Land 168
Highest and Best Use and Value 168
The Determination and Estimation of Site and Land Values 168
Methods of Estimating Site Value 169
Direct Sales Comparison 169

Making Adjustments to Comparable Price 169
A Completed Adjustment Grid 170
Plottage and Excess Land 171
The Land Residual Approach 172
Allocation and Tax Assessment Ratios 172
Capitalization of Land Rent 173
Site Value When the Improvements Should Be Demolished 173
Sources of Data 173
Summary 174

PART IV

Estimating Value: The Cost Approach

10 The Cost Approach: An Overview 179

Introduction 179
   Limitations of the Cost Approach 180
   Other Uses of the Cost Approach 180
   Steps in the Cost Approach 181
Reproduction or Replacement Cost 182
   Estimating Reproduction or Replacement Cost 183
   Estimating Accrued Depreciation 183
   Estimating Land Value 184
A Brief History of the Cost Approach 184
Summary 185

11 Estimating Building Costs 187

Introduction 187
   Sources of Reproduction Cost Data 188
   Cost Estimation 189
   The Comparative Unit Method 189
   General Description of the Subject Building 190
   Cost New of the Subject Property Using the Comparative Unit Method 191
   Unit-in-Place (Segregated) Method 192
   Cost New of the Subject Property Using the Unit-in-Place Method 192
   The Quantity-Survey Method 192
   Estimating the Cost New of a Commercial Property 193
   General Description of the Subject Building 194
   Bank and Mezzanine 194
   Offices 194

Penthouse   194
Quality   195
Indirect Costs and Developer's Profit   195
Improvements to the Site and Secondary Building Costs   195
Cost Trending   197
Summary   197

12 Estimating Depreciation   199

Introduction   199
The Cost Approach and Accrued Depreciation:
   Some Misconceptions   200
   The Cost Approach Produces Long-Run Equilibrium Value, Not Market Value   200
   The Cost Approach is Always (or Never) Useful   201
   The Cost Approach is Valid Only if the Current Improvements Are the Same as the Highest and Best Use as if Vacant   202
Categories of Accrued Depreciation   203
   Physical Deterioration   203
   Functional Obsolescence   203
   External Obsolescence   204
An Overall Perspective: Depreciation and Age   205
Conclusions to this Point   206
Estimating Accrued Depreciation   207
Estimating Depreciation in a Lump Sum: Age/Life Methods   208
   The Effective Age/Economic Life Variation   208
   An Example   210
   Modified Effective Age/Economic Life   211
   Using Age/Life Methods: Conclusions from Research   212
   Estimating Age/Depreciation Relationships in Local Markets   213
Market Disequilibrium and the Depreciation Estimate:
   Economic Obsolescence   214
   Disequilibrium and Depreciation on Residential Properties   215
   Disequilibrium and Depreciation on Income Properties   216
The Breakdown Method for Estimating Accrued Depreciation   217
   Applying the Breakdown Method   217
   Curable Versus Incurable Depreciation   219
   Short-Lived Versus Long-Lived Items   219
   Deficiencies, Defects, and Superadequacies   220
An Estimating Sequence   220
   An Example   220
   Estimating the Effects of Physical Curable Depreciation (Step 3)   222
   Estimating the Effects of Functional Curable Depreciation (Step 4)   223

The Deficiency   223
  The Defect   224
  The Superadequacy   224
  Estimating Incurable Depreciation   225
  Estimating the Impact of Physical Incurable Depreciation on Short-Lived Items (Step 5)   225
  Estimating the Impact of Long-Lived Incurable Physical Deterioration (Step 6)   226
  Estimating the Impact of Functional Incurable Obsolescence (Step 7)   228
  Estimating the Impact of Incurable External Obsolescence (Step 8)   228
  Estimating Total Accrued Depreciation (Step 9)   229
  The Value Estimate   229
Summary   230

PART V

Estimating Value: The Income Approach
Section A: Direct Capitalization

13 Estimating A Property's Productivity: Net Operating Income   234

Introduction   234
Estimating Net Operating Income   234
Potential Gross Income   235
  Estimating Potential Gross Income from Competitive Properties   235
  Published and Private Surveys   237
  Using the Subject Property as Its Own Comparable   237
  Units of Comparison   238
  Mixed Uses and Mixed Sizes   238
  The Search Area for Comparable Rents   238
  Quoted Versus Effective Rent   239
The Vacancy Allowance   239
  Estimating the Vacancy Allowance for Mixed Use Properties   240
Other Income   240
  How Much Other Income Should Be Counted?   241
Operating Expenses   242
  Fixed Operating Expenses   242
  Variable Expenses   243

Maintenance and Repair 244
Reserve for Replacements 244
The Complete *NOI* Statement for the ABC Building 245
A More Detailed Example 245
The Operating Expense Ratio 246
Two Expenses Are Not Operating Expenses: Depreciation and Interest 247
Using the Seller's Records 247
Market or Actual Net Operation Income? 249
Estimating Multiyear Income 249
Lease Analysis 250
Flat Rental 250
Periodic Revaluation 250
Indexed 250
Graduated Rental 251
Percentage Leases 251
Other Important Lease Clauses 251
Division of Expenses 251
Escape Clause 251
Renewal and Purchase Options 252
Tenant Improvements 252
An Example of a Multiyear Income Forecast 252
Forecasting the Future Income from the Property 253
The Rent Forecast 255
The 10-Year Forecast 255
Inflation Expectations and Income Forecasts 256
Adjusting Rents for Market Disequilibrium 259
Estimating Sales Proceeds at the End of the Holding Period 260
Summary 260
Appendix Estimating Potential Gross Income Using Regression Analysis 262

14 Estimating Value Using Ratio Models: Gross Income Multipliers and Overall Capitalization Rates 264

Introduction 264
The Gross Income Multiplier *(GIM)* 265
Mechanics of Using the *GIM* 265
The Logic of *GIM*s 266
How Many Comparables Are Enough? 267
Property Size 268
Potential Versus Effective Gross Income 268
*GIM*s and Inflation 268
Real Changes in the *GIM* 268
Applying the *GIM* Consistently 269

The Effect of Financing on *GIM*s 269
Moving from *GIM*s to Overall Capitalization Rates (R_0s):
The Operating Expense Ratio 269
The Overall Capitalization Rate 270
R_0s and Price/Earning Ratios 272
Why R_0s Differ Among Properties 272
Directly Extracted R_0s Are Widely Used 273
A Special Problem with Property Taxes 274
Reserve for Replacements 274
Summary 275

15 Estimating the Overall Capitalization Rate Using a Weighted Average of First-Year Returns to Debt and Equity: The Band of Investment Model 277

Introduction 277
The Band of Investment Model 278
An Example 278
The Relationship of R_m and R_e 279
More About the Rate of Return to the Lender (R_m) 280
The Band of Investment as an Equity Residual Model 281
Estimating R_m and R_e for use in the Band of Investment Model 282
The Reliability of the Band of Investment Model 283
Multiple Mortgages 284
An Example 284
Financing and Value 285
How Useful Is the Band of Investment Model? 285
Summary 287
Appendix An Alternative Band of Investment Model Based on the Debt Service Coverage Ratio 289

Section B: Discounted Cash Flow Models

16 Discounting and Present Values 292

Introduction 292
The Popularity of Discounted Cash Flow Models 292
The Concept of Present Value 293
Present Value is Market Value 294
Risk and the Expected Rate of Return 295
Time and the Discount Factor 297
Compound Interest and Simple Interest 298
Valuing More Than One Cash Flow 300
Another Example 301

Lenders, Loans, and Discounting   302
Two Shortcuts   303
   Shortcut One: When Annual Cash Flows Are Level   303
   Shortcut Two: Perpetuities   304
The Discounted Cash Flow Model   306
   Adding Detail to the Model   307
The Internal Rate of Return and Net Present Value   307
Summary   309

17   Completing the Basic Discounted Cash Flow Model: Estimating Future Value (Reversion)   312

Introduction   312
An Example Property   312
Estimating the Proceeds of Sale (The Reversion)   313
Future Selling Price: Theory   313
Estimating Future Selling Price: Practice   314
   Capitalizing NOI_{n+1} 314
   Estimating the Future Value Based on the Present Value   314
Estimating Value Using the Discounted Cash Flow Model   315
   An Example with Declining NOI 316
Is the Value Estimate Correct?   317
The Relationship of Income Change and Value Change   317
Summary   319
Appendix   Replacing the Estimate of Future Selling Price with an Explicit Forecast of Income Beginning in Year $n+1$ 321

18   Finance and Tax Explicit Discounted Cash Flow Models   323

Introduction   323
Model 1: Discounting Net Operating Income and the Net Selling Price   324
Model 2: Finance-Explicit (Mortgage-Equity) Models   325
Valuing the Apartment (Again) Using the Finance-Explicit Model   326
Another Example   329
The Utility of the Finance-Explicit Model   330
Constructing the Resulting Cash Flows   331
   A Computer Solution   332
Income Participation and Interest Only and Variable Loan Rates   334
Property Taxes   334
   An Example: The Apartment Property   334

The Relationship Between Equity Yield (Y_e) and Equity
    Capitalization (R_e) Rates   335
The Relationship Between the Overall Capitalization Rate (R_o) and
    the Overall Discount Rate (Y_o)   336
Model 3: Tax-Explicit Models   336
    The After-Tax Model   337
Valuing the Apartment (Again!)   338
Choosing Which Model to Use   340
    When Estimating Market Value   341
    Discounting *NOI* and *NSP*   341
    Discounting *BTCF* and *BTER* (Finance-Explicit)   341
    Discounting *ATCF* and *ATER* (Tax-Explicit)   342
What Investors Tell Us   342
What Appraisers Use   344
A Comment   344
Estimating Investment Value   344
Summary   345
Appendix Using the Debt Service Coverage Ratio
    to Estimate V_m 348

19 Residual Models: Land Building and Leased/Fee Leasehold   352

Introduction   352
The Building and Land Residual Techniques   353
    An Example of Building Residual Valuation   353
    The Same Example in Reverse: Land Residual Valuation   354
Raising the Analysis on Residual Income   354
The Reason for the Income Residual Technique: Split Rates   355
    A Conceptual Problem with the Land Residual Technique   355
    Residual Analysis for Land Development   356
    Residual Analysis and Highest and Best Use   357
Leased Fee/Leasehold Residual Techniques   358
    An Intuitive Explanation of Leasehold Value   358
    An Example   359
The Use of Split Rates   360
Sandwich Leases   361
Lease Options   362
    Does V Always $= V_{LF} + V_{LH}$ 364
Other Considerations   364
Summary   365
Appendix Using a Finance-Explicit Model for
    Residual Valuation   368

20 Discounted Cash Flow Model Shortcuts 370

Introduction 370
  Land Perpetuities 370
  Growing Perpetuity 370
  Annuity with a Finite Life 371
  A Perpetuity with an Escalation Clause 371
  "Ellwood" 372
  When Income and Value Remain the Same 373
  Using Ellwood: An Example 374
  When Annual Income Remains the Same, but Property Value Changes 375
  Changes in Both Income and Property 376
  How Precise Is Ellwood? 378
  Why Not a Simple Band of Investment? 378
  DSCR Model Shortcuts 379
Limitations of Shortcuts 379
Summary 380

Section C: Model Relationships and Conceptual Issues

21 Relationships Among Income Approach Models 383

Introduction 383
A Short History of Income Approach Models 383
The Relationships Among Models: A Numerical Example 385
  The Discounted Cash Flow Model 385
  The Band of Investment 386
  The Directly Extracted Overall Capitalization Rate 387
  The Gross Income Multiplier 387
Selecting a Model 388
  Direct Capitalization and Discounted Cash Flow Models: A Final Comparison 389
Summary 390

22 Estimating the Discount Rate 392

Introduction 392
Estimating Y_o: Theory 392
Estimating Y_o: Practice 394
  Using the Summation Approach to Estimate Y_o 394
  Using the Capitalization Rate to Estimate Y_o 396
  Estimating Y_o by Using Yields on Alternative Investments 397
  Using Surveys to Estimate Y_o: What Do Investors Expect? 398
  Estimating Y_o: The Impact of Financial Risk 398

Estimating Y_o: The Impact of Taxes   399
Summary   400

23 Partial Interests and Value: Does the Whole Equal the Sum of the Parts?   403

Does the Whole Equal the Sum of the Parts?   405
When the Whole Does Not Equal the Sum of the Parts   405
   The Grocery Store and Real Property   406
When the Whole Does Equal the Sum of the Parts   406
Financing and Real Estate Value   407
   Optimal Financing and Market Value Definition   408
   Valuing Creative Financing   409
   Valuing Limited Partnerships   409
Allocating a Change in Value: Property or Financing?   410
Summary   410

24 Investment Analysis   412

Measures of Return   412
Measures of Return Based on First-Year Expectations   413
Measure of Return Based on Expectations Beyond the First Year   415
   Discounted Cash Flow Models: Net Present Value and the Internal Rate of Return   416
A Summary of the Rate of Return Measures   418
Risk Analysis   419
   The Breakeven Point   419
   Breakeven Points and Cash-on-Cash Returns   421
   The Debt Service Coverage Ratio (*DSCR*)   422
   Risk Absorption Capacity   422
   Comparing *RAC*s   423
   Partitioning the *IRR*   424
   Partitioning the *IRR* of the Example Property   425
Sensitivity Analysis, Scenarios, and Simulation   426
Summary   427

PART VI

Reconciliation and Appraisal Reporting

25 Reconciling Value Estimates   432

Introduction   432
   Part One: The Review   433

Part Two: The Final Value Estimate, General Considerations 434
Part Two: The Final Value Estimate, Choosing the Number 435
Other Reconciliation Issues 437
    Rounding 437
    A Range of Values 438
Some Misconceptions About Reconciliation 438
Summary 439

26 Appraisal Reporting and Professional Practice 441

Professional Practice 441
    The Appraisal Foundation 442
    Licensing and Certification 442
Appraisal Reporting 443
Types of Appraisal Reports 444
    Complete and Limited 444
    Written and Oral 445
    Types of Written Reports 445
Other Types of Reports 445
Form Versus Narrative Reports 446
    Elements of a Narrative Report 449
Summary 449

Appendix A: Detailed Solutions to Odd-Numbered End-of-Chapter Problems 451
Index 473

PART I The Appraisal Process and Real Estate Markets

CHAPTER 1

Real Estate Appraisal and the Appraisal Process

Introduction

An appraisal is an estimate of value. Many kinds of products and assets are regularly appraised, including art, jewelry, furniture, and real estate. With respect to real estate, a very descriptive definition of an appraisal is provided by a federal statute:[1]

> The term *appraisal* means a written statement independently and impartially prepared by a qualified appraiser setting forth an opinion of defined value of adequately described property as of a specific date, supported by the presentation and analysis of relevant market information.

While not all parts of the definition apply to all types of appraisals, there are key points worth emphasizing. A real estate appraisal (1) is an opinion (or estimate), (2) is impartial, and (3) is based on market evidence. It follows that the confidence we have in the credibility of an appraisal is a function of the training and experience of the appraiser, and of the quantity and quality of market evidence the appraiser is able to bring to the task. While the amount of available information cannot always be controlled, the better appraisers are those who make the best use of what is available. This book is intended to help appraisers do that.

Who Uses Estimates of Value?

Estimates of value are needed in a variety of circumstances. Buyers and sellers of property need opinions about value on which to base negotiations. Lenders peg mortgage loan amounts to the market value of the real estate

---

[1] Part of the "1987 Surface Transportation and Uniform Relocation Act."

that is being used for collateral. Appraisals also help lenders to differentiate properties on the basis of their relative risks. Much as auto insurers use driving records to price their products, investors in mortgages use appraisals to minimize the overpricing of loans on "safe" properties and the underpricing of loans on riskier properties. Governments compensate owners for property taken by condemnation based on appraisers' opinions of value. Local governments raise a significant portion of revenues through taxing real property, based on the properties' values. Insurance companies settle claims based on appraised values, and appraised values are often necessary in legal proceedings—for example, to settle estates or to divide property as a result of divorce.

Why Real Estate Appraisals Are Needed: Theory

It does not necessarily follow from the fact that estimates of value are needed for various purposes that appraisers are needed to make those estimates. Consider, for example, a trip to the supermarket, where transactions are routinely completed without the services of appraisers. Supermarkets run smoothly because buyers and sellers have a lot of information about what the items offered should sell for, that is, their market values. Competition among sellers is intense, and buyers, because they are experienced, are able to recognize "proper" price levels. Helping this process is the fact that the products offered are generally either identical or close substitutes. In this kind of environment, the services of appraisers are unnecessary.

Consider now the opposite extreme, the purchase of a rare (or even unique) item like a Rembrandt. It is said that such treasures are priceless. One interpretation of a priceless item is that it is very expensive. Another interpretation is that the item is literally "price-less." There are no past prices on which to base a current value estimate, and in such "no-market" cases, the appraiser can provide only the crudest estimate of the item's value.

The two market extremes just described are summarized in Figure 1–1. At the supermarket extreme are products for which so much information is freely available that an appraiser isn't needed. At the "Mona Lisa" extreme are products for which no market information is available, and the appraiser has nothing on which to anchor a value estimate.

All products can be placed somewhere on the continuum between supermarket goods at one end and art treasures at the other. In a market economy, most products fall closer to the supermarket end, and as a result, we observe most transactions occurring without the aid of an appraisal.

This is not the case in real estate markets, where appraisers are needed because their training and experience equips them to produce a credible value estimate when information is available but sparse, and where obtaining the necessary information would be too costly for the layman. Thus, while appraisers sometimes lament the scarcity of information and the costs of its

FIGURE 1–1

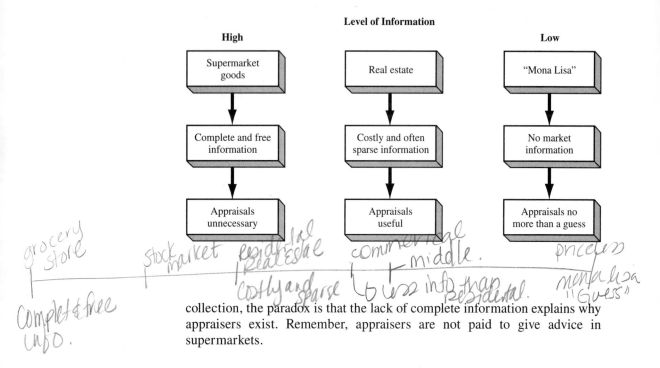

collection, the paradox is that the lack of complete information explains why appraisers exist. Remember, appraisers are not paid to give advice in supermarkets.

Why Real Estate Appraisals Are Needed: Evidence

There have been few attempts to empirically test the theoretical arguments for the existence of appraisal services. For single-family properties, while it is conceded that appraisers do a good job of estimating value, the relevant question is whether the layman would do just as good a job. Two studies conclude that they would not. The first study found that only 37 percent of the value estimates of homeowners and appraisers were within 10 percent of each other.[2] The second study found an average difference of 3–6 percent, with homeowners' estimates consistently higher than appraisers'.[3] A third study disagreed, however, finding little difference in the estimates of homeowners and appraisers.[4] Finally, in a comparison of appraised values and subsequent selling prices of houses, it was found that appraisers did a good

---

[2]Leslie Kish and John B. Lansing, "Response Errors in Estimating the Value of Houses," *American Statistical Association Journal,* September 1954, 520–38.

[3]Jon P. Nelson, *Economic Analysis of Transportation Noise Abatement* (Cambridge, MA: Ballinger), 1978.

[4]Philip K. Robins and Richard W. West, "Measurement Errors in the Estimation of Home Value," *JASA,* June 1977, 290–94.

job; that is, their estimates differed from the selling price by a very small amount, with no evidence of systematic under- or overestimation.[5]

There is mixed evidence concerning the reliability of appraisals of nonresidential properties. One study found that appraised values generally fell within 10 percent of actual selling prices.[6] An earlier study found no statistically significant differences between appraised values and subsequent selling prices of a sample of industrial and commercial properties.[7] More recently, however, there is evidence of significant appraisal "lag," then overreaction, to the office market collapse of the 1980s and early 1990s.[8]

Conclusions from these results must be drawn with caution. First, the evidence is very thin. Second, it is difficult to interpret some of the results. For example, one of the studies found little difference between the estimates of homeowners and appraisers. Does this mean that users of appraisal services for residential properties have been wasting their money for the better part of a century, and that no one has noticed? Probably not. A more likely interpretation is that while sellers may do quite well when estimating the value of a property they are very familiar with (like their own house), they will be less accurate when confronted with a different property, like a house they are considering purchasing, and would likely do quite poorly appraising a different kind of property, such as an investment property.

Note also that the use of average differences, whatever their magnitude, misses the important point that an appraisal fee is analogous to an insurance premium. Though only a small percentage of properties are damaged by fire or flood, this does not change the fact that when such an event occurs, insurance is generally necessary. So it is with appraisals. The stakes are high, and small percentage errors may translate into substantial dollar amounts.

Not surprisingly, satisfaction with appraisal services seems closely associated with market conditions. In a 1977 survey,[9] 77 percent of a sample of financial officers of Fortune 500 companies felt that an appraised value provided the best available estimate of market value, while only 15 percent felt that appraised values were not good estimates of market value. For decision-making purposes, 74 percent of the respondents felt that appraised values were superior to book values (depreciated historical costs). Contrast this very positive perception of appraisal quality in 1977 with the results of a 1992 survey, in which 70 percent of the users of appraisal services expressed the opinion that the quality and professionalism of appraisal reports

---

[5]Mark G. Dotzour, "Quantifying Estimation Bias in Residential Appraisal," *Journal of Real Estate Research,* Fall 1988, 1–11.

[6]R. Cole, D. Guilkey, and M. Miles, "Pension Fund Investment Managers' Unit Values Deserve Confidence," *Real Estate Review,* Spring 1987, 84–89.

[7]A. K. Zawati, *The Reliability of Appraisal Methods in Determining Current Asset Value: An Empirical Study,* unpublished dissertation, Louisiana State University, 1977.

[8]Pat Hendershott and Edward Kane, "U.S. Office Market Values during the Past Decade: How Distorted Have Appraisals Been? *Real Estate Economics,* Summer 1995.

[9]Zawati, *Reliability of Appraisal Methods.*

and services was less than desirable.[10] It is possible that the change in client attitudes between 1977 and 1992 was due to a perception that the absolute level of appraisal services had declined. However, it is more likely that the difference is associated with the market collapse of the late 1980s. The latter seems likely given the fact that appraisers have been heavily criticized for their perceived role in the market's problems.

As we move into the late 1990s, another factor has emerged that has the potential for enormous impact in the appraisal profession. Federal legislation and regulation have established property values that represent a "cutoff" point, below which a traditional appraisal will be unnecessary for certain uses, like establishing collateral value for home loans. As of late 1995, the *de minimus* level for residential properties was $250,000. The rationale is that in markets that are reasonably active, participants have sufficient knowledge to arrive at "fair" prices, therefore, the cost of a traditional appraisal is unjustified. This type of legislation is being intensely debated and it is as yet unclear where the *de minimus* level will settle. Further, many lenders continue to require appraisals for properties regardless of their value.

Estimating Value: An Introduction to the Appraisal Process and the Three Approaches

The answer to a client's questions about the value of real estate is found by following a sequence of analyses known as the appraisal process. While the specifics of each assignment will determine the exact process, the steps shown in Figure 1–2 are representative.

At this point you should not expect to understand what is done at each step of the appraisal process: that is what the rest of the book is about. At the same time, it is important to recognize that to proceed from the first step—Description of the Problem—to the final step—Writing the Appraisal Report—requires two kinds of knowledge and skills.

First, in order to estimate value, the appraiser must know what determines value. Without such knowledge, it is not possible to intelligently approach the task of collecting information about a property, or to use that information to estimate the property's value. Thus, the first part of this book is about value determination. Second, once the value-determining factors have been identified, this information must be processed into a value estimate. This is the topic of the second (and largest) part of the book. The value-estimating process is accomplished using techniques that fall into three appraisal approaches: (1) sales comparison, (2) cost, and (3) income. The remainder of the chapter briefly introduces these approaches.

---

[10]Robert P. White, "Assessing the Appraisal Community: A Customer Service Survey," *Real Estate Finance,* Spring 1992, 75–88.

FIGURE 1–2

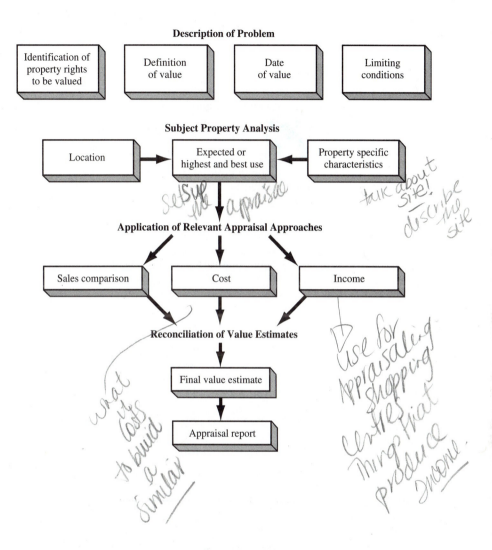

The Sales Comparison Approach

The supermarket was used as an example of the type of market where appraisal services are unnecessary. One reason is that the products offered are either identical or close substitutes, and in economics, the *one-price rule* states that equivalent goods should sell at equivalent prices. That rule works very well in the supermarket, where the value of an item is estimated by checking the prices of substitute items. The one-price rule also works in real estate markets,[11] and is put to use in the *sales comparison approach*.

The sales comparison approach involves two steps: (1) the collection of information about the prices (and value-determining characteristics) of properties that are comparable to the property being appraised, which is called the *subject property*, and (2) adjusting the prices of the comparable properties to account for differences between them and the subject.[12] Thus, the sales comparison approach looks like this:

$$\text{Value of subject} = \text{Prices of comparable properties} \pm \text{Adjustments for differences} \qquad (1)$$

In practice, the collection of information and the adjustment of prices is complicated by several factors. First, there are no perfect substitutes in real estate markets. Second, there is often only a small number of comparable sales to use as the basis for a value estimate.[13] Third, when there are a sufficient number of sales that qualify for use as the basis for estimating the value of the subject property, there is the problem of choosing which of those sales should be used as the basis for comparison. Fourth, there is often limited information as to the proper adjustments for differences between the comparables and the subject.

Notice the critical link between value determination and value estimation. That is, in order to intelligently select comparable sales and then adjust their prices for differences between them and the subject property, the appraiser must know what characteristics help determine value in the marketplace. Otherwise, it would not be known which properties are truly comparable to the subject, nor could price adjustments for differences be made with confidence.

The Cost Approach

A second way to approximate the market value of a property is based on its reproduction (or replacement) cost. The theoretical link between cost and value is straightforward. From the demand side, a buyer will not pay more for a product than it would cost to produce a substitute. This *principle of substitution* means that the price of an existing property should not exceed

---

[11]Though not perfectly. The appraisal implications of deviations from the one-price rule are discussed in Chapter 2.

[12]This introductory discussion of the sales comparison approach is limited to *direct* sales comparison, which uses a relatively small sample of transactional data. With larger samples, the sales comparison approach may rely on statistical inference, including econometric techniques like regression analysis. These variations of the sales comparison approach are discussed in detail later in the text.

[13]At the extreme, there may be no information on comparable sales. When that happens, the sales comparison approach cannot be used and the appraiser must default to the cost and/or the income approaches.

the cost (including normal profit) to purchase a comparable site and have comparable improvements made.

From the supply side, the cost of the site plus the costs of construction, including a normal profit to the developer, should equal the selling price, or market value. It is not that sellers of lots and builders of houses do not want higher prices, but simply that competition from other suppliers will drive prices down to a point where only normal profits can be made. This competitive discipline of prices also applies to sellers of existing houses.

The result is that for a "new" improvement, its cost to reproduce should approximate its market value. If the subject property's improvements are not new, as will often be the case, the cost to reproduce the improvements must be adjusted downward for any accrued depreciation. Thus, the cost approach looks like this:

Value = Cost to reproduce (or replace) the improvements as if new − (2)
Accrued depreciation on the improvements + Land value

In some cases, the cost approach is easy to apply and will produce a close approximation of market value. In other cases, the relationship between the results of the cost approach and actual market value will be tenuous. A detailed discussion of the conditions which favor the use of cost as a proxy for value is found in a later chapter. For now, it is sufficient to understand that the cost approach works well enough to be included as one of the three basic approaches to estimating value.

As is the case for the other appraisal approaches, there are several reasons why the effective use of the cost approach requires an understanding of what factors determine value. First, the appraiser must recognize those conditions under which cost is likely to produce a credible approximation of value. Second, when the cost approach is used, the land must be valued separately. In order to do that, it is necessary to understand the characteristics of land that determine its value. Third, because the cost to reproduce as if new must be adjusted to account for any loss in value due to depreciation, and the amount of the depreciation adjustment is often based on rates of depreciation extracted from sales of comparable properties, the determinants of value must again be known before comparable properties can be identified.

The Income Approach

The third appraisal approach is the income approach. The underlying assumption of the income approach is that the value of an income-producing property is a function of the flow of income it is *anticipated* to produce, just as the value of a firm is a function of the earnings it is anticipated to produce. The income approach processes the anticipated flow of income into a value estimate. This requires a forecast of income, which by its nature relies heavily on the judgment of the appraiser.

This does not imply that the sales comparison and cost approaches are not useful for valuing income properties. However, because income properties tend to trade less frequently and to be more heterogeneous than other property types, the available sample of comparable sales tends to be smaller, often eliminating the use of the sales comparison approach. You will also learn that the market for income properties has characteristics that may make the application of the cost approach relatively difficult. In this kind of situation, the income approach becomes the primary approach for estimating market value. The income approach is also widely used for assignments other than estimating market value, most importantly, for investment analysis. The income approach is:

$$\text{Value} = \text{Present value of anticipated income}$$

Familiarity with value-determining factors is as important when using the income approach as it is when using the sales comparison and cost approaches. Forecasts of variables such as rent and vacancy rates, and an estimate of the expected rate of return (the appropriate discount rate) cannot be made without an understanding of what market characteristics are associated with the level of these value-affecting variables.

The Three Approaches and the Final Value Estimate: Reconciliation

The value estimates produced by the sales comparison, cost, and income approaches generally will not produce identical value estimates for three reasons: (1) the "one-price rule" underlying the sales comparison approach does not work perfectly in imperfect real estate markets, (2) cost is often difficult to equate with value, and (3) the income approach requires forecasts of anticipated income, and no one can forecast precisely. Thus, the product of the three approaches is most likely to be a range of estimated values.

The *reconciliation* phase of the appraisal process is the point at which the appraiser considers the relative confidence he or she has in the estimates of value produced by the three approaches, and from that arrives at a final value estimate or range. That confidence is largely a function of the quality and quantity of data that were brought to the task. Reconciliation is a weighting process where the judgment of the appraiser is paramount.

Another Perspective on the Appraisal Process: A Mix of Results and Process

A different perspective on the continuum shown in Figure 1–1 between markets like supermarkets with nearly complete information, and markets for one-of-a-kind products with almost no information, is that at the supermarket end of the continuum, the *results* of market behavior—market prices—are readily observable. At the unique-product end of the continuum, there is neither market information nor prices to observe, and an estimate of value must rely on a *simulation of the process* by which prices theoretically would be established.

The fact that real estate markets fall between these informational extremes provides an important insight into the appraisal process. The appraiser's product—the value estimate—more often than not begins with the collection of data from past transactions, or *market results,* which are then adjusted to value the subject property based on the appraiser's understanding of the *process* by which values are determined. This mix of results and process is used to a varying degree in each of the three appraisal approaches. It most closely describes the sales comparison approach, but is also used to value the land (or site) and to extract rates of depreciation for us in the cost approach, and is the basis for forecasting rent, vacancy, and expense levels, and for selecting the proper capitalization or discount rate to be used in the income approach.

While "results" and "process" are partners in the appraisal process, they are not equal partners. The use of results is generally preferred. That is, when the market tells the appraiser what it thinks something is worth—through observable prices or such things as depreciation rates and rates of return—the appraiser should listen very carefully. The fact that real estate markets tend to provide such results grudgingly has already been used to explain the existence of appraisers, and is now seen to be equally useful as an explanation of why the simulation of the process of value determination is often a necessary part of the appraisal process. As in any simulation, a healthy dose of judgment is required, and it is here that the appraiser earns his or her keep.

Notice how the three approaches fit into this discussion. Earlier, it was pointed out that the appraisal of something like the Mona Lisa would be little more than a guess. You now see why. First, there are no sales of comparable substitutes to use in a sales comparison approach. Second, it cannot be reproduced or replaced, so the cost approach is not applicable. And third, it produces no stream of income for use in the income approach. Fortunately, this is not the case for real estate, and in almost every assignment, one or more of the three approaches will be applicable.

Summary

Appraisers are needed to estimate value in markets characterized by high search costs, scarce information, and heterogeneous, relatively expensive products. These characteristics are descriptive of most real estate markets.

Ideally, the appraiser anchors the value estimate on the observed results of market behavior, specifically, the prices commanded by properties identical to the subject. This ideal is almost never achieved, and the estimate of value is invariably the product of a blending of market results and a simulation of the value-determining process.

There are three approaches to estimating value: (1) sales comparison, based on the one-price rule, where V = Prices of comparable properties ± Adjustments for differences, (2) cost, based on the principle of substitution, where V = Cost to reproduce (or replace) the improvements as if new − Depreciation + Land value, and (3) income, based on the principle of anticipation, where V = Present value of anticipated income.

Due to the nature of real estate markets, the quality and quantity of data available, and the judgments required in the appraisal process, the value estimates produced by the three approaches cannot be expected to be equal. The purpose of the reconciliation phase of the appraisal process is to consider the relative merits of the estimates produced by the approaches used, and to come to a final opinion about value.

Questions and Problems

1. Suppose it was possible to purchase the Hope Diamond. Should you hire a diamond appraiser to estimate its value?
2. In what kinds of markets are appraisal services demanded? Where does real estate fit in?
3. What kinds of information are necessary to produce a credible value estimate?
4. What approaches are used to process information into a value estimate? Briefly describe them.
5. What is the reconciliation phase of the appraisal process?

Chapter 2
Price and Value in Real Estate Markets

Introduction

The first step in the appraisal process is to describe the task. The description will include such things as the date of the appraisal, a precise identification of the property rights being appraised, a listing of any limiting conditions and assumptions, and most important, a definition of the kind of value that is to be estimated. It is the definition of value that tends to create the most problems. One problem is that a property is likely to have several different values. As Bill Kinnard, a member of the Appraisal Institute and a past president of the American Real Estate and Urban Economics Association, puts it, before value can be defined the appraiser must answer the questions: "Value to whom? And for what?" Court decisions and contractual provisions may mean that the value on which an insurance claim is based will differ from the value estimated for the purpose of settling a condemnation case. Still a third value for the property may be its value to an individual investor, reflecting the investor's unique situation with respect to such things as taxes, investment objectives, and the need for liquidity. A fourth kind of value for a property, and the kind of value that most appraisal assignments request, is *market value*. Unlike most other kinds of values, market value is in theory a "same-for-all" number that the Random House Dictionary defines simply as what a property can be sold for on the open market.[1]

This is a straightforward definition, but in complex and imperfect real estate markets, most appraisers agree that a simple definition like what a property can be sold for on the open market isn't sufficient. But while appraisers seem to agree on what isn't sufficient, they don't agree on what is.

This is not surprising. Value, like truth and beauty, tends to be in the eye of the beholder, and the result of a search for the perfect value definition

---

[1] *Random House Dictionary of the English Language* (New York: Random House).

is likely to end in disappointment. This is especially so in the case of appraisal: Imperfect markets are unlikely to produce perfect estimates of value, which in turn are unlikely to generate universal agreement on how those estimates are best defined.

As a result, the definition of market value used by appraisers is best viewed as a *working definition;* perhaps not philosophically or theoretically pure, but one that meets current legal and regulatory requirements and is understood both by appraisers and users of appraisal services.

A Market Value Definition

A market value definition that is currently in wide use is as follows:[2]

> Market value is the most probable selling price which a specified interest in real property is likely to bring under all of the following conditions:
>
> 1. Consummation of a sale as of a specified date.
> 2. Open and competitive market for the property interest appraised.
> 3. Buyer and seller each acting prudently and knowledgeably.
> 4. Price not affected by undue stimulus.
> 5. Buyer and seller typically motivated.
> 6. Both parties acting in what they consider their best interests.
> 7. Adequate marketing efforts made and a reasonable time allowed for exposure in the open market.
> 8. Payment made in cash (US dollars) or in terms of financial arrangements comparable thereto.
> 9. Price represents the normal consideration for the property sold, unaffected by special or creative financing or sales concessions granted by anyone associated with the sale.

From a practical perspective, this definition has the advantage of being approved by the major professional appraisal associations, and most clients and appraisers are familiar with it. While this definition addresses explicitly many of the issues that result from estimating value in an imperfect market, certain parts raise questions of interpretation. They are the reference to the most probable selling price, the reference to "reasonable . . . exposure," and the assumption of a "competitive market."

Most Probable Price

The reference to the "most probable price" reflects the probabilistic nature of price setting. At the same time, "most probable" in a statistical sense is

---

[2]*The Appraisal News* (Appraisal Institute, Chicago), December 1993.

a reference to the single most likely outcome (the mode), as opposed to the "expected" price, which references the mean or average. This will become a more important distinction as the use of statistics and statistical models in appraisal increases.

As you will discover in a subsequent chapter, a more serious problem with a most probable price perspective is that it is not consistent with the highest and best use premise of market value, which holds that market value is the maximum (highest) price obtainable. Earlier definitions of market value routinely referenced not the most probable price, but the highest price, which was defined in terms of the land-value maximizing use, or highest and best use, of the land. As it became recognized that the highest possible price is not likely to be obtained in real estate markets, and that there is always uncertainty associated with making a value estimate, value definitions were changed to reference the most probable price. Medici was the first to suggest the use of "most probable selling price," though Ratcliff did the most to develop and popularize the idea.[3] However, the underlying highest and best use premise has not been changed in most of the educational programs of the appraisal associations, creating a conceptual inconsistency.

Reasonable Exposure

The key issue here is whether the exposure to the market is presumed to occur prior to or after the date of the appraisal. The Appraisal Foundation, which was established by the federal government to recommend standards for appraisers and appraisals, makes clear in its *Statement on Appraisal Standards Number 6*[4] that the exposure is assumed to have occurred prior to the appraisal.

"Exposure time," as it is used in the market value definition, differs from marketing time, as the latter is defined by the Appraisal Foundation. Marketing time is defined by the Foundation as the time it will take to market a property immediately after the effective date of the appraisal.[5]

Competitive Market

Historically, the definition's reference to a competitive market, and some of the accompanying wording (a "fair" sale, with buyer and seller acting "prudently and knowledgeably"), has been the focus of most of the discussion

---

[3]G. Medici, *Principles of Appraisal* (Ames: Iowa State University Press), 1953; R. Ratcliff, *Modern Real Estate Valuation, Theory and Application* (Madison: Democrat Press), 1965.

[4]*Appraisal Foundation,* 1992. The different views on this issue are discussed in A. Scruggs Love and James J. Mason, "Controversy in the Definition of Market Value," and James P. Ryan, "Market Value: A Refocus," *The Appraisal Journal,* October 1992.

[5]*Appraisal Foundation,* 1992, ibid.

and disagreement. The central problem is that real estate markets are not in fact *competitive,* as such markets are defined by economists. As the following discussion will reveal, this inconsistency can create problems for the appraiser.

Economists define competitive markets as those that tend to be in equilibrium. Prices in competitive markets clear the market so that there is neither unsatisfied demand nor excess supply. The equilibrium price is one that tends to be stable, because it is the "right" price. Thus, in competitive markets, prices can be trusted to represent "true" value.

An important characteristic of competitive markets is that they react quickly to new, value-affecting information. Another way of describing a market that reacts quickly to new information is that it is relatively efficient; that is, the market is an efficient pricing machine because it arrives quickly at a price that reflects true value. Relatively inefficient markets are those that react less rapidly. They *adapt* to new information over time. The difference is understood best by example.

Suppose Investment A in Figure 2–1 had been at equilibrium price A, at time t. Now suppose that new, price-affecting information was revealed at that time, moving the new equilibrium price to A_2. Perhaps Investment A is wheat futures on the commodity market and the new information was a weather forecast calling for an extended drought.

Notice that the price of wheat moved almost instantaneously from the old equilibrium price A to the new equilibrium price A_2. Recalling that *speed* of reaction is the measure of efficiency, Investment A is clearly trading in a very efficient market.

Compare this to Investment B in Figure 2–1, which had been at equilibrium price B at time t. When new price-affecting information was revealed at that time, the new equilibrium price moved to B_2. Perhaps B is the price of land in a city, and the new information was an announcement that a major employer will expand its plant capacity.

Notice that the price of B moved relatively slowly, settling at its new equilibrium in time $t+1$ after a period of adjustment. This is the characteristic of a less efficient market. Between time t and $t+1$, a number of market prices occurred. However, they tended to be unstable because they did not represent the equilibrium price.

Market Characteristics Associated with Relative Efficiency

The market for wheat futures was used in Figure 2–1 as an example of a relatively efficient market. Other markets that are relatively efficient are the markets for most household items, for automobiles, and for certain securities like those listed on the New York Stock Exchange. What do these markets have in common? First, there are numerous buyers and sellers, which provides liquidity and prevents a small number of buyers and sellers from controlling the price (as in a monopoly or oligopoly). Second,

Figure 2–1

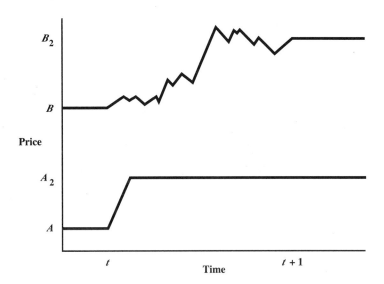

information in these markets is abundant and widely available at low cost; buyers and sellers know what is going on. Third, it is relatively easy and inexpensive to enter and exit the market. Fourth, the products tend to be homogeneous, making pricing easier. Fifth, these products are mobile, facilitating adjustments of supply to changes in demand. When new information enters a market with these characteristics, the environment is such that the market can move rapidly to the new equilibrium price.

Real Estate Markets

Just as the wheat futures market was purposely chosen as an example of a relatively efficient market, the land market was purposely chosen as an example of a relatively inefficient market.

Real estate markets, be they for land, houses, or commercial properties, do not fare as well on the checklist of characteristics associated with efficiency. The profile of a real estate market includes few buyers and sellers, a lack of full information, costly transactions, heterogeneous products, immobility, and a relatively slow reaction of supply. At the extreme, there may be almost no market activity for certain kinds of property over an extended time. What, for example, is the market for the Trump Tower?

This adds up to an expectation of relative inefficiency, an expectation that is only now being tested empirically. Research to date has produced mixed results, though there are indications real estate markets may prove to be more efficient than conventional wisdom has held.[6] Nevertheless, no one seriously suggests a level of efficiency comparable to that of stock markets.

In addition to the complications introduced by possible market disequilibrium, the appraiser is also likely to be faced with some degree of price dispersion even in markets that are in equilibrium. The reason is that there are differences among buyers and sellers in their costs to gather information.[7] For example, it is much less costly for a local homeowner wanting to move to a different house in the same community to gather and use market information than it is for an out-of-town buyer. For the out-of-towner each search trip is costly and it is rational for such a buyer to pay relatively more for a property if extending the search is likely to cost more than the expected savings from inspecting more properties, negotiating, and so forth.

Consistent with this logic, Norm Miller found that the larger the number of properties a buyer considered, the lower the price that was paid, and that nonlocal buyers of houses pay 5 percent more on average than do local buyers.[8]

Implications for the Market Value Definition

The fact that real estate markets are likely to be somewhat inefficient and to exhibit some degree of price dispersion even in equilibrium suggests the potential for differences between actual prices in the marketplace and the prices that would be produced if the market was competitive and in equilibrium. Given that the most widely used value definition references the price that would be produced in a competitive market, the appraiser's dilemma is clear: Does the appraiser estimate what the price *should be* assuming a competitive market, or what the price *will be* based on actual market behavior?

---

[6]See, for example, Jack Harris and Waldo Born, "Timing Real Estate Acquisitions," *Real Estate Review,* Summer 1986; Peter Linneman, "An Empirical Test of the Efficiency of the Housing Market," *Journal of Urban Economics,* September 1986; Norman Miller and Michael Sklacz, "A Note on Leading Indicators of Housing Market Price Trends," *The Journal of Real Estate Research,* Fall 1986; George Gau, "Efficient Real Estate Markets: Paradox or Paradigm?" *AREUEA Journal,* Summer 1987; William Rayburn, Michael Devaney and Richard Evans, "A Test of Weak-Form Efficiency in Residential Real Estate Returns," *AREUEA Journal,* Fall 1987. A review of the literature is found in Dean Gatzlaff and Dogan Tirtiroglu, "Real Estate Market Efficiency: Theory and Evidence," *Journal of Real Estate Literature,* July 1995. A comparison of the efficiency of public (securitized) and private real estate is found in Richard Barkham and David Geltner, "Price Discovery and American and British Property Markets," *Real Estate Economics,* Spring 1995.

[7]George J. Stigler, "The Economics of Information," *Journal of Political Economy,* June 1961.

[8]Norman G. Miller, *The Influence of Housing Market Transaction Phenomena on Residential Property Value,* unpublished dissertation, The Ohio State University, 1977.

Put differently, can the appraiser substitute his or her judgment for the judgment of the marketplace in cases when the appraiser suspects that market prices are wrong?

The accepted market value definition would imply the answer is yes, that the appraiser may be wiser than the market. But that is clearly not the position taken by the professional appraisal associations. The text of the Appraisal Institute, for example, states flatly that "In all cases, . . . market value is the price that is available in the marketplace."[9]

Not surprisingly, this contradiction is reflected in the perceptions of appraisers. When preparing this chapter, a survey of 50 professionally designated appraisers found that while a majority liked the accepted definition, they also rejected the idea that an appraiser should attempt to be wiser than the market.

It is not only appraisers who may be interpreting the accepted value definition differently. After the stock market crash of October 1987, the public inquiry focused on what went wrong with the *market,* and what steps should be taken to exert more control. Absent, and properly so, was the implication that brokers should have known that prices were too high and that the crash was coming.

Conversely, the crash of some real estate markets in the late 1980s was followed by a great deal of finger pointing, some of it at appraisers. The clear implication was that appraisers should somehow have foreseen the problem and that the value estimates should have reflected that insight. This has continued, with discussions in the early 1990s increasingly focused on a difference between short- and long-run values, with the former being the current market price and the latter the true long-run value. The clear implication is that appraisers should have been estimating "true long-run value" rather than current prices. While this is not to suggest the appraiser's market value definition was solely to blame, the confusion is understandable.

A Modified Definition

An acceptable working definition of market value must provide sufficient detail on the assumptions underlying the value estimate to minimize opportunities for misinterpretation by the appraiser and the client. While the currently accepted definition does a reasonable job of meeting these objectives, references to "the most probable price" and a "competitive market" create unnecessary conceptual and practical difficulties.

A definition that minimizes these difficulties is as follows:

> Market value is the expected selling price of the specified real property rights in an arm's-length transaction, as of the date of the appraisal, and assuming a reasonable exposure to the market.

---

[9]*The Appraisal of Real Estate,* 19–20.

The strengths of this modification are as follows:

- It explicitly recognizes the probabilistic nature of price setting in real estate markets, and properly refers to market value as the weighted average (the *expected* price) of a distribution of possible prices. The reference to expected price is preferred to most probable price because the latter suggests a single, most likely outcome (for example, the mode of prices of comparable sales) rather than the average outcome.[10]
- Reference to "the specified real property rights" separates the real property being valued from personal property, such as favorable financing, that may affect the total transaction price.
- The reference to "arm's-length transactions" precludes transactions under duress, forced sales, and so on. It reminds the appraiser and the client that market value is the product of market transactions.
- The definition is consistent with the behavior of most appraisers. As discussed, our observation is that whatever definition of value is quoted, most appraisers in fact provide an estimate of the expected selling price.
- It imposes no idealistic (and unrealistic) assumptions about market equilibrium. It also makes clear to the appraiser, the client, and the public that the appraiser reports and interprets the market, but does not *substitute* his or her judgment for that of the market. This is more than a philosophical point, as it is not clear that the typical appraiser is on average wiser than the market. Until there is evidence to the contrary, the appraiser who ignores the market does so at his or her risk.

Notice, however, that the fact the appraiser should not ignore the market does not necessarily mean the market value estimate will be different from an equilibrium value estimate. Certain markets will in fact be close to equilibrium, so that comparable sales will produce a market value estimate close to the equilibrium value. More importantly, because there is often insufficient data for comparable sales, other approaches—cost and income—must be used. In such cases the value estimate produced will be the appraiser's estimate of equilibrium value. This is because in such cases the only workable assumption is that the market will produce a correct price. Put differently, it isn't possible to estimate what an incorrect price might be, and therefore, the best estimate of the expected selling price is the appraiser's estimate of equilibrium value.

Before leaving this discussion, two points must be emphasized. First, the alternative market value definition recommended cannot now be used in most appraisal reports because regulations, clients, and the courts often require the currently accepted definition. Second, regardless of which definition is used, appraisers do in fact estimate expected prices, not "true" values, and this is the proper behavior.

---

[10]See P. Colwell, "A Statistically Oriented Definition of Market Value," *The Appraisal Journal,* January 1979.

Other Kinds of Value

While the estimation of market value dominates appraisal practice, estimates of other kinds of value are often requested and they need to be differentiated from market value.

The most common of these are: (1) investment value, (2) use value, (3) assessed value, and (4) insurable value.

Investment Value

The best way to describe investment value is with reference to market value. Recall that the assumption of the market value definition is that market value reflects the consensus opinion of buyers and sellers—the central tendency of a distribution of possible selling prices.

This distribution of possible market prices is composed of individual investment values. Thus, investment value is the value to a particular investor, using assumptions specific to that investor, while market value can be described as the point at which the individual investment values tend to cluster. Put differently, market value is a "same-for-all" number while investment value is investor-specific. This also leads to the important insight that different groups of investors may be responsible for determining the market values of different types of investments. For example, market prices for commercial properties may be determined primarily by large institutional investors, including foreign investors. For properties that offer tax shelter, prices are likely to be determined by investors in high marginal tax brackets. For raw land, prices are determined by those most interested in long-term gains.

Use-Value

While investment value is value to a specific investor, use value is value with reference to a specific use. As an example, the unique design of a McDonald's store helps attract traffic. Therefore, the building has a high value for the specific use as a McDonald's. Suppose though that a particular location did poorly and was abandoned as a franchise. In that case, the alternative uses of the empty building would likely justify a somewhat lower market value than the value with its originally intended use as a McDonald's.

A McDonald's store is an example of the kinds of property that tend to be built or altered for a specific, limited use, and which tend to sell infrequently. When they do sell, their uniqueness limits the pool of prospective buyers and in turn their value. Other examples of limited-use properties include churches, most service stations, and industrial plants built for a specific and perhaps unique manufacturing process. In cases when the potential market is in fact strictly limited to something close to the original intended use, the appraisal report should make this clear, and may even go so far as to identify the value estimate as a use value rather than a market value.

Assessed Value

Assessed value is the value of property for property tax purposes. While assessed values are intended to have some consistent relationship to market value, this is not always the case.

Insurable Value

Insurable value is that portion of an asset's value that is recognized under the provisions of an insurance policy. Generally, the value is based on the depreciated replacement or reproduction cost of a building subject to loss from hazards. The specific formulas used to calculate insurable value are determined by state laws.

Summary

A major part of describing the appraiser's task is to define the kind of value being estimated. In the case of market value, there is not a single definition that has been agreed on, though in practice only a small number of variations are commonly used. These definitions respond to the demands of clients and the courts and to assumptions about market behavior. Because these factors are in continual change, it is not surprising that the market value definition also changes over time.

Currently, the most widely used definitions reference selling price as the measure of value. In addition, the most popular variation is very explicit about the conditions under which the selling price is determined, specifically, in a market that is in equilibrium. The problem is that real estate markets, particularly nonresidential markets, tend not to be in equilibrium. For this reason, the following modified definition is recommended: Market value is the expected selling price of the specified real property rights in an arm's-length transaction, as of the date of the appraisal, and assuming a reasonable exposure to the market. This definition reflects the probabilistic nature of price setting in real estate markets, it imposes no idealistic (and unrealistic) assumptions about market equilibrium, it reminds the appraiser and the client that market value is the product of an arm's-length transaction, and the reference to real property value makes clear that it is only the real property (and not such things as favorable financing) that is being valued.

Questions and Problems

1. Why is market value difficult to define in an appraisal context?
2. What is investment value? How does it differ from market value?
3. Market value has been defined as the expected selling price of the specified real property rights in an arm's-length transaction as of the date of the appraisal, and assuming a reasonable exposure to the market. What are the strengths of this definition?
4. What is an efficient market?
5. What do theory and evidence suggest about the efficiency of real estate markets?
6. How does use value differ from market value? Give an example.

PART II Property Analysis: The Determinants of Value

CHAPTER 3

Property Analysis: Location

Introduction

> Rent is influenced by ". . . the general circumstances of the society or neighborhood."
>
> Adam Smith, *Wealth of Nations,* 1776–1784

Tell someone you've bought a new house, and the first question asked is, "Where is it?" The reason we think of real estate in terms of its location is that it can't move. A property cannot escape a poor location and it is difficult to avoid benefitting from a good one. There are a host of "quality of life" factors associated with a given residential location, and the income produced by a commercial property is closely associated with its location. Are public services available? Is the neighborhood reaching maturity or is it in decline? Are there problems with congestion? Pollution? And so on. Because property values are largely a hostage of their locations, a careful analysis of the subject property's location is an integral part of the appraisal process.

This chapter will help the appraiser analyze locational effects to determine what factors are likely to contribute to differences in property values. Because there are so many factors that contribute to locational quality, in practice appraisers generally take a "divide and conquer" approach, isolating individual factors and estimating how they may affect value. That is also how this chapter is arranged. We begin with a general discussion of the link between land values and the fundamental measure of location—accessibility—and how that link in large part determines the way land values and land uses are distributed in a community, and then move to a discussion of the locational factors that tend to affect the individual property.

Accessibility and Land Value

One of the enduring principles of land-value determination is that the more accessible a property, the higher its value. In 1903, Hurd stated the principle as follows:

> Since value depends on . . . rent, and rent on location, and location on convenience, and convenience on nearness, we may eliminate the intermediate steps and say that land value depends on nearness.[1]

Hurd's linking of value to accessibility (or nearness, or distance) can be rewritten like this:

$$\text{Land value} \rightarrow \text{Rent} \rightarrow \text{Location} \rightarrow \text{Accessibility (distance)}$$

and because each link depends on the next, can be simplified to:

$$\text{Land value} \rightarrow \text{Accessibility (distance)}$$

Graphically, the relationship between value and accessibility looks as shown in Figure 3–1:

The logic is straightforward: as distance from the center of the central business district (CBD) of a community increases, the cost of accessibility to the center increases, making land used for commercial purposes less profitable and thus less valuable. For example, suppose a site downtown (at distance zero) will produce annual rent of $100. If investors expect a 10 percent annual return, the site will have a market value of $\frac{\$100}{.10} = \$1,000$. Now suppose the site is in the suburbs, n miles from downtown, and that the annual rent it commands is only $80, reflecting the fact that the costs of accessibility are $20 per year (perhaps it is not as accessible to customers or employers). Given the 10 percent expected return, the site's value is

$$\frac{\$80}{.10} = \$800.\text{[2]}$$

The same kind of logic applies to residential land values. Households have budgets, and the amount that can be spent for land will depend on the amount that must be spent on accessibility costs to such things as the place of employment. The farther away, the higher the accessibility cost, and the lower the land's value for residential use. In addition, even if single-family households desire a downtown location, they cannot outbid commercial uses for those sites. Thus, the residential gradient is relatively low at distance

---

[1] Richard M. Hurd, *Principles of City Land Values* (New York: The Record and Guide), 1903. Hurd applied the ideas of Von Thunen in an urban setting. See Peter Hall, ed., *Von Thunen's Isolated State* (London: Pergamon Press), 1966.

[2] Alonso generalized and articulated the classic theory of rent and location in W. Alonso, *Location and Land Use* (Cambridge, MA: Harvard University Press), 1964.

FIGURE 3–1

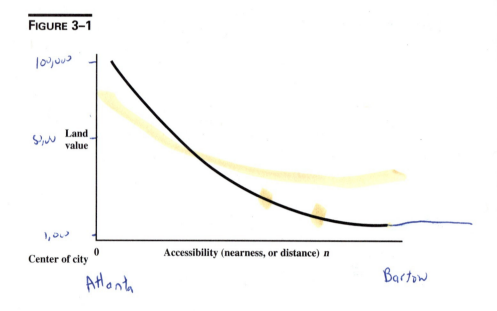

zero, but because it is flatter than the commercial gradient, it eventually becomes the dominant use.

What results from this accessibility driven model is the *land-value gradient* shown in Figure 3–1; as distance from the CBD increases, land value decreases. Though communities are more complex places than they were in Hurd's day, and exceptions to the "closer is more valuable" rule are easy to find, there remains a strong association between distance and land values. Consider the way most urban areas look. As distance from downtown increases, land becomes less intensively developed and buildings become more horizontal than vertical. The kinds of improvements also change, from mainly office, to multifamily and retail, to single-family residential, and finally to agricultural and unimproved land.[3]

Office buildings serve a market that values face-to-face conversation and prefer locations that will minimize total accessibility costs. On the other hand, retail land uses are often found in the suburbs because that is where they are accessible to their customers. Households, as noted, may also value accessibility, but tend to be outbid by commercial uses for the more central sites. In addition, households often value amenities such as good schools and accessibility to shopping. Thus, we find most households in the suburbs. Farmers have little reason to pay the accessibility premium to be close to

---

[3] A recent paper by Peter Colwell and Henry Munneke argues that while the land-value gradient exists, it is less steep than conventional wisdom suggests. See Colwell and Munneke, "The Structure of Urban Land Prices," forthcoming, *Journal of Urban Economics,* 1996.

downtown, because their incomes are largely unaffected by location, and like households they would be outbid for downtown sites by other types of uses.

Accessibility and Land Value: Empirical Evidence

Not only is the theoretical relationship between land value and distance confirmed by our casual observations of the way urban areas tend to look and to grow, more importantly, the value-distance relationship is supported by ample empirical evidence over an extended period of time. Knos'[4] early study (1962) of Topeka, Kansas, produced a land value pattern, shown in Figure 3–2, that is strikingly similar to the theoretical model. Kau and Sirmans[5] found declining (and flattening) bid rent curves in Chicago between 1836 and 1970. Harris' study (1992) of Austin, Texas, produced the same pattern,[6] as did Spinks,[7] who found that distance from downtown Austin accounted for between 27 percent and 54 percent of the variance in land prices, and Waddell et. al., who found a strong gradient in Dallas in 1990.[8] Foreign examples include studies of Ghana,[9] England,[10] Scotland,[11] and Japan.[12]

As would be expected, the same distance-to-value relationship is found when rent levels are compared. Table 3–1 shows office rent differentials between CBDs and suburbs in the United States from 1979 through 1993. The accessibility premium remains significant, though over time the differential appears to be narrowing. This narrowing began as transportation improve-

---

[4]Duane S. Knos, *Distribution of Land Values in Topeka, Kansas* (Lawrence, KS: Center for Research in Business, University of Kansas), May 1962.

[5]James Kau and C. F. Sirmans, "Urban Land Value Functions and the Price Elasticity of Demand for Housing," *Journal of Urban Economics,* February 1979.

[6]Matthew Harris, *Incentive Taxation,* September 1992, 1–2.

[7]James A. Spinks, "Von Thunen's Bid-Rent Curves: An Application to Austin," Professional Report, unpublished, University of Texas, August 1986.

[8]Paul Waddell, Brian J. L. Berry, and Irving Hoch, "Residential Property Values in a Multimodel Urban Area: New Evidence on the Implicit Price of Location," *Journal of Real Estate Finance and Economics,* September 1993.

[9]Paul K. Asabere, "The Determinants of Land Values in an African City: The Case of Accra, Ghana," *Land Economics,* August 1981.

[10]*Land Costs and Housing Development,* National Building Agency, London, 1968; also J. McQualin, "Residential Land Values, 1962–1965," *Chartered Surveys,* vol. 213, 1966.

[11]Peter F. Colwell and C. F. Sirmans, "Nonlinear Urban Land Prices," *Urban Geography,* vol. 1, 1980.

[12]Louis A. Rose, "Land Values and Housing Rents in Japan," *Journal of Economics,* March 1992.

FIGURE 3–2 Representation of the Structure of Urban Land Values

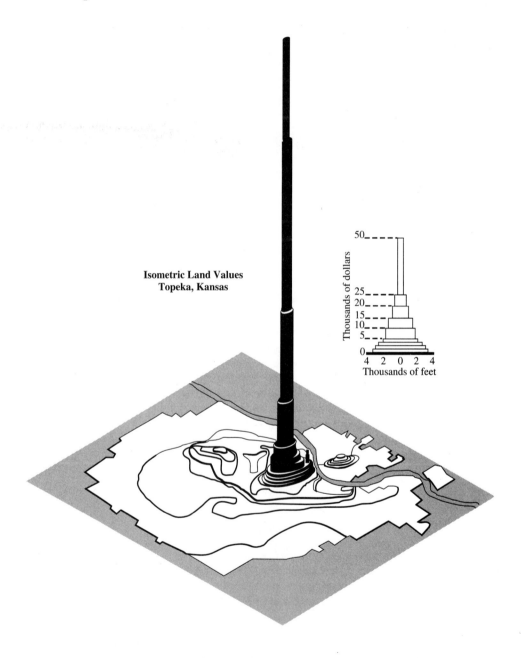

Source: Duane S. Knos, *Distribution of Land Values in Topeka, Kansas* (Lawrence, KS: Center for Research in Business, The University of Kansas) May 1962.

Table 3-1 U.S. Average Quoted Office Rental Rate Existing Class A Buildings ($ per square foot per year)

	CBD	Outside CBD	Difference
1979	$15.16	$11.56	23.7%
1980	17.95	13.00	27.6
1981	24.69	16.44	33.4
1982	23.56	17.57	25.4
1983	23.59	17.65	25.2
1984	24.46	19.83	18.9
1985	24.48	19.43	20.6
1986	24.14	17.94	25.7
1987	23.97	17.87	25.4
1988	24.02	19.57	18.5
1989	22.49	19.51	13.3
1990	24.41	19.11	21.7
1991	23.03	17.50	24.0
1992	20.88	18.04	13.6
1993	20.36	17.32	14.9

Source: Summarized from data supplied by ONCOR International, Houston, Texas.

ments began to dilute the accessibility advantage of the CBDs, and is likely to continue as telecommunications reduce the need to "be there."

Why Cities Grow in "Circles"

One common characteristic of cities is that unless they are prevented from doing so by geography, they tend to grow in circles. Some describe this in-to-out circular growth as producing cities that look like onion rings, with each ring dominated by a given type of development—intensive commercial as the most accessible, most valuable land in the center circle surrounded by declining land values and less intensive use as distance from the center increases.

This pattern of circular growth is not accidental. It follows from what we have learned about accessibility and its effects on land values and land-use patterns, and a lesson from geometry. Given an urban area of certain size, of all the possible geometric shapes that a city may take, the center of a circle is the single most accessible point. That is, given all of the locations possible, the total distance from each point to every other point is minimized from the point in the center of the circle. A circular urban shape, therefore, is optimal with respect to minimizing accessibility costs, and it is not surprising this is the shape taken by most cities.

The Land-Value Gradient and Transportation Improvements

While distance alone remains a powerful predictor of the distribution of urban land values, it is far from perfect. This is because modern transportation systems, notably rapid transit systems and highways, tend to distribute "accessibility" unevenly.

One result is that as a community's transportation system improves, its land-value gradient may flatten. This is most clearly understood by considering what the land-value gradient might look like in the presence of the ultimate transportation system, a "magic carpet" that reduces accessibility costs to zero. With such a system, the land-value gradient would be horizontal. Because accessibility between any two points would be costless, no location could claim a value premium due to an accessibility advantage. Though we will never achieve a magic carpet, we move *toward* it with improvements in transportation technology, and we would therefore expect a flattening of the gradient, as well as a spreading of the accessibility premium once monopolized by the center of the city. How much flattening has actually occurred is arguable and appears to be property-type specific. Table 3–1 suggests that for office properties in Houston, the gradient has not flattened very much. In Philadelphia, there is evidence of more flattening of the residential value gradient as the price of suburban properties reflects increased accessibility to the CBD offered by train and highway improvements.[13] Short-term market cycles may also affect the CBD-suburban relationship. The office market recovery of the early to mid-1990s has been uneven, with the suburbs leading the way. This has resulted in a large drop in the CBD premium for many cities. How long this will persist is not yet known.[14]

A second result of transportation improvements is that while downtown still commands the highest rents and land values, there is competition for accessibility around and along major arteries. Rather than a single economic nucleus at the center, urban areas are characterized by what MacKenzie[15] called *multiple nuclei*. As shown in Figure 3–3, in response to transportation improvements, the land-value gradient not only flattens but also becomes "lumpy" to correspond to the locations of the dispersed centers of economic activity. The lumps may represent suburban communities or "Edge Cities,"[16] or simply large shopping or commercial centers, such as those that tend to locate at major intersections, along expressways or perimeter highways, or at hubs near public transportation facilities.

It is important to recognize that a lumpy gradient does not contradict the negative relationship between value and distance. Instead it reflects the

---

[13]Richard Voith, "Changing Capitalization of CBD-Oriented Transportation Systems: Evidence from Philadelphia, 1970–1988," *Journal of Urban Economics,* May 1993.

[14]Bill Brueggeman, "The Impending Recovery in Ten Major Office Markets," *Real Estate Finance,* Spring 1995.

[15]D. M. MacKenzie, *The Metropolitan Country* (New York: McGraw Hill), 1933.

[16]Joel Garreau, *Edge City,* (New York: Anchor), 1991.

FIGURE 3–3

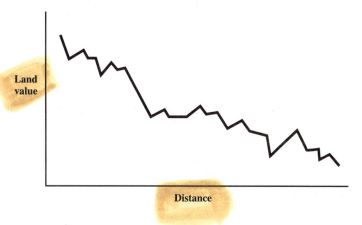

fact that distance to downtown is no longer the only consideration. Also important are the distances to other economic centers that have been encouraged by transportation improvements.

Transportation improvements may have yet another effect on land values. If an urban area is defined in terms of, say, a maximum commuting time, a transportation improvement effectively expands its boundaries because more distance can be covered at equal cost. For example, suppose a town has one north-south road and one east-west road, both paved for one mile in each direction from the center. If the town is defined in terms of the area within the paved roads, there are $\pi r^2 = 3.14$ square miles of available land.

Now assume that the radius of the paved roads is increased from one to two miles, doubling the distance to the effective boundaries of the town. This doubling of the radius quadruples the available land from 3.14 to 12.56 square miles, putting downward pressure on per-unit land costs. If the transportation improvement makes the area more attractive to households and firms, the resulting increased demand may offset the downward pressure of the increased supply. The net impact may be a flatter but higher value gradient, with total land value increased. On the other hand, if the transportation improvement has no significant effect on population and income, total land value may only be redistributed outward, but not changed. Given the complex interrelationships which determine land values in a growing urban area, it is not surprising that empirical evidence on the relationship between total land value and transportation improvements is thin and somewhat dated. In one study, Mike Goldberg[17] compared changes in land values in San Francisco (previously estimated by Paul Wendt)[18] and Vancouver,

---

[17]Michael A. Goldberg, "Transportation, Urban Land Values, and Rents: A Synthesis," *Land Economics,* May 1970, 153–62.

[18]Paul Wendt, "Economic Growth and Urban Land Values," *The Appraisal Journal,* July 1958, 427–43.

British Columbia, two cities similar except for their transportation systems. San Francisco had mass transit, Vancouver did not. Goldberg found that land values increased more rapidly in Vancouver, consistent with the theory that increases in land values are inversely related to transportation improvements.

As the 1990s unfold, it is interesting to speculate on how land use and land-value gradients will be further affected by information and communication technologies. Historically, technologies that reduce costs of accessibility and thus move us closer to the "magic carpet" have been forces that lead to decentralization and dispersal of economic activity. This is already beginning. Salomon Brothers, for example, has moved its branch office from Wall Street to Florida, and Citibank put its credit card business in South Dakota.

If communication networks do in fact turn out to be the trade routes of the 21st Century, then "being there" physically will be less important, and the value of location in the traditional sense will be greatly diminished. The result of this "virtual transportation" will be a weakening of the distance-value link, with "good" locations enjoying more fragile advantages.

Refining the Land Value Gradient: Other Sources of the Lumps

Transportation technology is not the only source of lumps in the land-value gradient. Other contributing factors are inertia, geography, government regulation, and social and cultural impacts.

Because buildings are durable, yesterday's decisions are not easily changed. This development inertia means that at any given moment, the best use of a site—which in theory should determine its value—is likely to not be its actual use. There is also the inertia created by long-term leases, with the potential conflict between the contracted use (and thus the property's rent and value) and what might be done with the land in the absence of the contract. This situation is so pervasive that in appraisal practice the valuation of leased properties is differentiated from the value of those that are not leased.

Geography also matters. Cities are not flat, featureless plains. Topography, soil composition, and the landscape affect land use and land value, whether the effect is on an individual site or an entire urban area. Most obviously, cities do not grow in perfect circles. The intersection of the three rivers of Pittsburgh explains both the existence and growth of the city and its noncircular development. The island of Manhattan is cigar-shaped, and Chicago follows the shores of Lake Michigan.

Market imperfections created by government regulation are another primary source of exceptions to the distance-value relationship. Zoning can influence land use and land value, as can property taxes. The land-value gradient for Atlanta shows a sharp valley a short distance from downtown corresponding to residential neighborhoods like Sherwood Forest, which have been "grandfathered" in by zoning restrictions.

Finally, we must recognize that cities are cultural and social as well as economic phenomena, and that this fact is reflected in property values. Appraisers call these phenomena *neighborhood effects*. Whereas the general accessibility of a property refers to its relationship to the community as a whole, the neighborhood of a property reflects its immediate surroundings.

Neighborhoods and Value

A neighborhood is often defined as a place—a geographically contiguous area with discrete boundaries. Boyce's[19] definition is typical: "[A neighborhood is] a portion of a larger community in which there is a homogeneous grouping of inhabitants, buildings, or business enterprises."

Some prefer the term *market setting* instead of *neighborhood,* because a property's value may be affected by factors from outside as well as inside a neighborhood's boundaries. Some examples of external factors are air pollution, the proximity of the labor force to an industrial neighborhood (or district), and the level of property taxes. Also, neighborhoods tend to blend together, and their nature may be closer to an overlay map than to a set of discrete boundaries.[20]

Actually, the terms *market setting* and *neighborhood* do not conflict. Market setting refers to the *source* of value-affecting factors, while neighborhood refers to the area that is more or less equally *affected* by a given market setting. With this in mind, richness can be added to the definition of a neighborhood: *A neighborhood is a geographically contiguous area that is affected by its market setting more or less equally.*

However we define a neighborhood, the common sense idea that a property's surroundings affect its attractiveness (and thus its value) is strongly supported by market behavior. Surveys of prospective new home buyers regularly find the neighborhood to be one of the top two or three selection factors.[21]

Components of "Neighborhood"

The bundle of characteristics which comprise the neighborhood can be separated into five categories: (1) special accessibility, (2) stability, (3) environmental and governmental influences, (4) demographics, and (5) the physical

---

[19]Byrl N. Boyce, *Real Estate Appraisal Terminology* (Cambridge, MA: Ballinger), 1981, 172.
[20]Thomas J. Walsh and Eric Stenejhem, "Neighborhood Influences on Residential Property Values," *Assessor's Journal,* April 1975.
[21]*Decisions for the 90s,* as quoted in *Keystone Builder* (Harrisburg, PA: Pennsylvania Builders Association), June 1987.

and functional characteristics of the neighborhood itself, sometimes called the neighborhood life cycle.

Special Accessibility (Proximity)

Whereas general accessibility is defined in terms of the costs of distance to all other urban uses, special accessibility, or *proximity,* refers only to those land uses that are of direct interest to the subject property. In some cases, special accessibility is more important than general accessibility in determining location decisions and property values for a specific land use. For example, certain users of space, like law firms, accounting firms, and the home offices of financial institutions, value face-to-face communication with clients and tend to cluster in central locations. This tendency helps to explain increasing land values in downtown areas even as their accessibility advantage has been eroded by transportation improvements.

Industrial properties may require accessibility to specific kinds of transportation, such as rail spurs or navigable water. They may also need access to skilled workers. In fact, if the primary market for the products of an industrial facility is outside the immediate urban area, accessibility to the urban area (with its accompanying costs like congestion and high property taxes) may actually be avoided.

While retailers offering specialized products may be concerned primarily with general accessibility—a more central location—so they can reach a market sufficiently large to produce a profit, mass merchandisers, like food stores, are likely to be more concerned with special accessibility—the potential market in a narrow geographical area. Households may think almost entirely in terms of special accessibility. It is common in many cities for much of the population to spend almost all their time in a relatively small portion of the metropolitan area, seldom visiting outside that area, and perhaps never going downtown.

For example, in one of the surveys referenced earlier, house buyers listed proximity to work, schools, shopping, and recreation as among the most important locational factors influencing the selection process.[22] Table 3–2 lists the results of a different survey of appraisers and Realtors® in the Chicago area showing that they believe the quality of other dwellings in the neighborhood has the most effect on property values.[23]

Table 3–2 suggests that the opinions of those closest to the market, appraisers and real estate agents, are consistent with what the evidence tells us about the determination of property values. This consistency is reassuring, as an appraiser's judgment should mirror market behavior as closely as possible.

---

[22]*The Homebuying and Selling Process* (Chicago: National Association of Realtors), 1986.

[23]Marvin Frankel, "The Effects of Airport Noise and Airport Activity on Residential Property Markets," *Illinois Business Review,* October 1988.

TABLE 3–2 Importance of Factors Affecting Residential Property Values (in rank order)

	Mean Score[a]	Percent of Respondents Indicating Small or Negligible Importance
1. Quality of other dwellings in neighborhood	1.23%	1.4%
2. Proximity to schools	1.78	11.4
3. Amount of property taxes	1.78	11.6
4. Proximity to shopping facilities	1.97	14.4
5. Access to main roads	1.97	18.8
6. Quality of municipal services	1.99	20.2
7. Trees, shrubs, and parks in neighborhood	2.00	21.7
8. Presence of moderate aircraft noise	2.06	23.1
9. Presence of moderate traffic noise	2.13	30.4
10. Proximity to medical services	2.55	52.2
11. Proximity to jobs at airport and in related activities	2.67	58.8
12. Access to the airport	2.85	69.5

[a]The scale is 1 (large), 2 (moderate), 3 (small), and 4 (negligible). Survey completed in 1988.

Guntermann and Colwell found a very significant association between the proximity to primary schools and residential values,[24] while accessibility to downtown was ranked as relatively unimportant. Walden also found a significant association between school quality and house values, and that the opportunity to choose a school (rather than have students assigned to a school) reduced the school proximity effect.[25] Proximity to recreation may also command a price premium. Smith found a strong inverse relationship between population density and distance to a coast or lake in 13 of 14 U.S. cities studied,[26] and a price premium of about 8 percent was found for homes proximate to golf courses.[27]

In general, as transportation systems improve, the importance of special accessibility increases relative to general accessibility. Again, this does not mean that the concept of special accessibility destroys the importance of general accessibility. Rather it adds to it, with the "lumps" in real-world land-value gradients reflecting the impacts of special accessibility.

[24]Karl L. Guntermann and Peter F. Colwell, "Property Values and Accessibility to Primary Schools," *The Real Estate Appraiser and Analyst,* Spring 1983.

[25]Michael Walden, "Magnet Schools and the Differential Impact of School Quality on Residential Property Values," *Journal of Real Estate Research,* Summer 1990.

[26]Bruce H. Smith, "The Effect of Ocean and Lake Coast Amenities on Cities," *Journal of Urban Economics,* January 1993.

[27]A. Quang Do and Gary Grudnitski, "Golf Courses and Residential House Prices: An Empirical Examination," *The Journal of Real Estate Finance and Economics,* May 1995.

Stability

Factors associated with neighborhood stability include the compatibility of land uses and the protection of that compatibility, generally through zoning, and the protection or insulation from externalities such as crime and congestion. This does not mean that stability is always associated with higher values. For example, a transition from residential to commercial uses may produce offsetting effects, with the value of properties which can be rezoned to commercial uses increasing and the value of properties unlikely to be rezoned declining. The exact pattern tends to be market-specific.

Li and Brown[28] found that in the Boston area, the least desirable location in terms of the sales price of houses was about 900 feet from major highways. Properties closer than that were valued more highly, likely in anticipation of the potential for conversion to commercial uses. Beyond 900 feet values also moved upward, apparently because that distance from the highway offered a sufficient buffer from noise and pollution. Other studies of Charlotte,[29] St. Louis,[30] and Boston[31] support the notion that nonresidential uses tend to adversely affect residential values, though this was not the conclusion reached in a study of Pittsburgh.[32]

The type of nonconforming use may also be important. In a study of New Haven,[33] residential prices were discounted by 2 percent within 200 yards of "light" commercial and low density apartments, and substantially more when the nonconforming use was industrial or public housing, a conclusion similar to that reached for Chicago by McMillen and McDonald.[34] In Dallas, high-rise office buildings were found to adversely affect residential property values within about 3/5 mile, to have positive effects on value from 3/5–1 1/2 miles, and no effect beyond 1 1/2 miles.[35]

---

[28]Mingche M. Li and James Brown, "Micro-Neighborhood Externalities and Hedonic Housing Prices," *Land Economics,* May 1980.

[29]G. Donald Jud, "The Effects of Zoning on Single-Family Residential Property Values," Charlotte, North Carolina, *Land Economics,* May 1980.

[30]J. F. Kain and J. M. Quigley, "Measuring the Value of Housing Quality," *Journal of the American Statistical Society,* 65, 1970.

[31]W. J. Stull, "Community Environment, Zoning and the Market Value of Single Family Houses," *Journal of Law and Economics,* 16, 1975.

[32]J. P. Crecine, O. A. Davis, and J. E. Jackson, "Urban Property Markets: Some Empirical Results and Their Implications for Municipal Zoning," *Journal of Law and Economics,* vol. 10, 1967; F. Reuter, "Externalities in Urban Property Markets: An Empirical Test of the Zoning Ordinances of Pittsburgh," *Journal of Law and Economics* 13, 1973.

[33]D. M. Grether and D. Mieszkowski, "The Effects of Nonresidential Land Uses on the Price of Adjacent Housing: Some Estimates of Proximity Effects," *Journal of Urban Economics,* July 1980.

[34]Daniel P. McMillen and John F. McDonald, "Could Zoning Have Increased Land Values in Chicago?" *Journal of Urban Economics,* March 1993.

[35]Thomas G. Thibodeau, "Estimating the Effect of High-Rise Office Buildings on Residential Property Values," *Land Economics,* November 1990, 402–9.

Cultural and social characteristics may also be associated with property values and their stability. The effect of a social or racial transition in a neighborhood remains a particularly difficult issue.[36] In general, while a neighborhood's relative stability *may* be significant, its effect on values cannot be taken for granted. Just the opposite is the case. It is because the effects of stability tend to be case-dependent that they must be carefully analyzed when estimating value. In an appraisal situation, the selection of market data must recognize this type of uncertainty by comparing similar situations or neighborhoods. This will control for social and cultural factors, whatever their impact may be.

Environmental and Governmental Influences

Environmental characteristics may also affect property values. Noise, pollution, and congestion are factors that often distinguish neighborhoods. For example, a 1992 study estimated that a 1 percent increase in air quality increased house prices by ½%.[37] Also important is the availability and quality of government services, including recreation and fire and police protection.

As in the case of neighborhood stability, environmental and governmental effects may not be uniform. The conventional wisdom that the availability of open space will have a positive influence on residential property values was confirmed in a study relating property values to their proximity to a park in Philadelphia,[38] but the results also showed that the value of properties that bordered directly on the park were adversely affected, likely due to the potential for noise, litter, and foot traffic.

Proximity to an airport is another example of a mixed-value impact. Certain land uses that service the airport or depend on airport services value

---

[36]See Micheal Devaney and William Rayburn, "Neighborhood Racial Transition and Housing Returns: A Portfolio Approach," *Journal of Real Estate Research,* Spring 1993. Portfolio returns from neighborhoods including racial transition were 10 percent lower. Race was also found to be a factor by Robin Duben and Chein-Hsing Sung, "Specification of Hedonic Regressions: Nonvested Tests on Measures of Neighborhood Quality," *Journal of Urban Economics,* January 1990. However, others find no effect of race. See Douglas Coate and James Vanderhoff, "Race of the Homeowners and Appreciation of Single-Family Homes in the United States," *Journal of Real Estate Finance and Economics,* November 1993. In 1995 the Appraisal Standards Board of the Appraisal Foundation issued an exposure draft (discussion paper) concerning the avoidance of racial discrimination in appraisals.

[37]Mark Thayer, Heide Albers, and Mortega Rahmatian, "The Benefits of Reducing Exposure to Waste Disposal Sites: A Hedonic Housing Value Approach," *Journal of Real Estate Research,* Summer 1992.

[38]Thomas R. Harner, Robert E. Coughlin, and Edward T. Horn, "The Effect of a Large Urban Park on Real Estate Values," *The Journal of the American Institute of Planners* 40, July 1974.

proximity highly, while the same proximity is considered undesirable by most households. Nelson[39] measured the effects of airport noise on residential property and concluded (based on 13 studies) that value discounts ranged from .4 to 1.1 percent per decibel of noise. More recent studies of Orange County, California,[40] and Chicago, Illinois,[41] however, concluded that overflights in residential areas had not had a significant adverse affect on property values. Noise from highways may also affect values, as Palmquist found in a study of three Washington State cities. Discounts ranged from .008 percent to .48 percent per decibel, with the biggest discounts in the highest-income neighborhood.[42]

An example of a potentially more serious environmental impact was the nuclear accident at Three Mile Island, Pennsylvania. Predictions of adverse effects on property values were not confirmed in the short run,[43] though the long-term effects have yet to be determined.

In the 1980s and 90s, environmental issues have come to the fore. Proximity to externalities such as overhead power lines, land fills, and hazardous waste sites may have significant effects, depending on other locational attributes and property type. Colwell found that residential lot prices abutting a power line suffered a 30 percent loss in value, while Hamilton, Schwann, and Carruthers found impacts averaging about 5 percent of total property value.[44] How these estimates may be affected by emerging concerns about the health hazards of electromagnetic fields is unknown. Nelson et. al., found a 12 percent adverse effect on properties that bordered a landfill, a 6 percent effect up to one mile away, and negligible effects beyond 2.5 miles.[45] Conversely, Bleich et. al., found no effects of proximity to "a well-designed" landfill.[46]

There is also the possibility that the effect of such things as contamination may linger beyond cleanup. Even after receiving a clean bill of

---

[39]Jon P. Nelson, "Airports and Property Values," *Journal of Transport Economics and Policy,* January 1980.

[40]Robert J. West, "Statistical Inference: An Aviation Easement Analysis," *Real Estate Issues,* Spring/Summer 1988.

[41]Marvin Frankel, "The Effects of Airport Noise and Airport Activity on Residential Property Markets," *ibid.*

[42]Raymond Palmquist, "Valuing Localized Externalities," *Journal of Urban Economics,* January 1992.

[43]Jon P. Nelson, "Three Mile Island and Residential Property Values: Empirical Analysis and Policy Implications," *Land Economics,* August 1981.

[44]Peter Colwell, "Power Lines and Land Value," *Journal of Real Estate Research,* Spring 1990; S. Hamilton, G. Schwann, and C. Carruthers, "Do Hydro Transmission Lines Affect Property Value?," Working Paper, University of British Columbia, 1994.

[45]A. C. Nelson, J. Genereux, and M. Genereux, "Price Effects of Landfills on House Values," *Land Economics,* November 1992.

[46]Donald Bleich, Chapman Findlay, and G. Michael Phillips, "An Evaluation of the Impact of a Well-Designed Landfill on Surrounding Property Values," *Appraisal Journal,* April 1991.

health, the stigma attached to affected properties may have significant value impacts.[47]

The *potential* risks associated with natural hazards may also be priced. Murdoch et. al., found that not only did the 1989 San Francisco earthquake have a residual impact on house values of about 2 percent, but that the potential for an earthquake was already reflected in prices by an average of 3.7 percent.[48]

What is striking about the existing evidence on environmental impacts, regardless of type, is the wide range of results. Perhaps even more so than most value-affecting factors, environmental impacts are market and even property-sensitive. As an example, the value impact of proximity to Superfund toxic waste sites in Houston changed markedly from 1976, when the impact was negligible, to 1985, when more information about the sites was available, and each mile farther from the site increased value by 33 percent.[49] Rich Peiser and Chris Taylor provide evidence that in certain situations, the market mechanism for contaminated properties ceases to function.[50]

Demographics

Sometimes lost in the attempt to measure the impacts of the host of factors included in a neighborhood's location and physical profile is the fact that an integral part of a neighborhood are the neighbors. It has been shown repeatedly that the demographics of a neighborhood (the characteristics of the population) can have a significant association with property values. Among the factors that appear to be most important are income and education levels, the average age of the residents, and their occupations.

This of course does not mean that things like higher incomes and education levels of a neighborhood's residents *cause* values to increase, but rather that those characteristics are likely to be proxies for such things as better maintenance within the neighborhood, and perhaps better public services, such as an above-average school system. In any case, the demographic profile of a neighborhood may help the appraiser make a better choice of sales for the sales comparison approach, and better estimates of rent and vacancy levels for the income approach. Even if the exact impact of demographics on value is unknown, matching the demographics will help control for any value impacts associated with the characteristics of individuals in the neighborhood.

---

[47] Peter Patchin, "Contaminated Properties—Stigma Revisited," *Appraisal Journal,* April 1991.

[48] James Murdoch, Harinder Singh, and Mark Thayer, "The Impact of Natural Hazards on Housing Values: The Loma Prieta Earthquake," *Journal of the American Real Estate and Urban Economics Association,* Summer 1993.

[49] J. E. Kohlhose, "The Impact of Toxic Waste Sites on Housing Values," *Journal of Urban Economics,* July 1991.

[50] Richard Peiser and Chris Taylor, "Does the Land Market Break Down for Contaminated Properties?", *Journal of Property Research,* Summer 1994.

Neighborhood Life Cycles

Neighborhoods, like individual properties, are subject to life cycles which affect the general level of property values within the neighborhood.[51] A typical pattern is for values to begin to increase as the neighborhood develops and matures, followed by a period of "stable" values, and finally by a period of declining values as the neighborhood ages.

The trick for the appraiser is to predict the turning points. The time period from development to decline will vary widely among neighborhoods depending on changes in accessibility, as well as social, cultural, and governmental factors. Also affecting the speed at which a neighborhood moves from phase to phase is its inherent quality, as reflected in the construction and design of improvements and subsequent levels of maintenance. Some neighborhoods remain in the "mature" phase for long periods, while others move rapidly from development to decline. This means that while a neighborhood's age is often a good indicator of where it stands in its life cycle, the association is far from perfect.

The location of the neighborhood relative to the growth pattern of the city is also important. Neighborhoods in growth corridors may be affected in two ways. If they are protected by zoning or deed restrictions, increasing demand may offset the effects of aging, with values remaining level or even rising. Conversely, it is more difficult to predict the future of a neighborhood which is in the path of growth, but which is not zoned or is inherently less stable. A transition to commercial use may be accompanied by increasing values, while a partial transition, such as strip zoning along a main corridor, may have differing impacts on properties, depending on their relative proximity to the mixed uses.

The Land-Value Gradient Revisited: Neighborhood Effects

When we introduced transportation improvements and imperfections such as zoning into the basic value-distance relationship, they produced lumps in the land-value gradient, but the basic idea that value declined as distance increased was not violated.

Allowing for neighborhood effects, however, may produce a value gradient that behaves differently: "Positive" neighborhood effects like privacy and freedom from congestion may dominate the negative impact of increased transportation costs, and the unit price of land may actually increase as distance increases. When combined with the existence of the multiple centers of economic activities that are found in most urban areas, these positive neighborhood effects provide a plausible explanation for positively

---

[51]See R. Andrews, *Urban Land Economics and Public Policy,* (New York: Free Press), 1971, for a thorough discussion of the analysis of location, including neighborhood life cycles.

sloping residential land-value gradients, such as that found in a study of Chicago.[52]

Non-single-family Neighborhoods: Districts

While neighborhood effects are generally discussed with reference to residential property, the immediate surroundings of apartment, industrial, and commercial properties are also likely to affect their values.[53] When referring to non-single-family uses, it is common practice to use the term *district* instead of *neighborhood*.

Apartment (Multifamily) Residential Districts

Factors that affect apartment districts are similar to those that affect single-family neighborhoods. Accessibility to work, shopping, and schools is important. The physical condition of the neighborhood, as well as the crime rate, pollution, and congestion must be considered, as they may also impact value.

As with single-family neighborhoods, the impact of the district surrounding an apartment must be judged with respect to the priorities of its residents. Increased living space appears to be more valuable in high-income neighborhoods, while proximity to public transportation and flexibility in lease terms are more important in low-income neighborhoods.[54] Similarly, proximity to a good school system may be of primary importance to an apartment district with characteristics that will attract young married tenants, but largely irrelevant in a district primarily attractive to singles or retirees. For university students, a high priority is proximity to campus. This is reflected in a very steep rent gradient from the center of campus outward.

Commercial Districts: The Central Business District and Shopping Centers

Commercial districts are there to serve customers. Thus, the most important factor is the accessibility of the district to customers, and the supply of commercial districts competing for those customers. Accessibility may be primarily by automobile, though public transportation is an important consideration for downtown districts.

---

[52]Berry, Brian J. L. and Robert J. Bednarz, "The Disbenefits of Neighborhood and Environment to Urban Property," *The Economics of Neighborhoods,* David Segal, ed., (New York, Academic Press), 1979.

[53]Detailed treatments of most property types is beyond the scope of this text. See the *Encyclopedia of Real Estate Appraising,* Edith J. Friedman, ed. (Englewood Cliffs: Prentice-Hall), 3rd ed., 1978.

[54]Andrea Heuson, "Physical, Locational, and Demographic Determinants of Apartment Rents," Working Paper, University of Miami, January 1989.

Future prospects for a commercial district will depend partly on the direction of growth of the community. From the mid-1950s to the mid-1970s, most central business districts lost business to the suburbs, because the federal highway program made the suburban districts relatively more accessible. The outward move has decelerated of late, traceable to the revitalization of downtown areas, and the trend toward smaller centers that are able to find sufficient space closer to downtown. This may again reverse itself in the near future, for as discussed earlier, information and communication technology is eroding the importance of "being there," and encouraging decentralization and dispersal of economic activities.

Various categories of shopping centers serve different markets and must be analyzed with those markets in mind. Regional and even "super-regional" centers are those with 400,000 to 1 million+ square feet and with 40 or more stores. Because they intend to serve a large market, regional centers should have a wide range of merchandise and price levels.

A community shopping center is smaller, with about 100,000 to 400,000 square feet. The primary market area tends to be residential neighborhoods within twenty minutes driving time. While community centers offer a wide range of products and prices, they tend to offer less high-priced merchandise than do regional centers.

A neighborhood shopping center is typically less than 100,000 square feet. Anchor tenants tend to be supermarkets and drug stores. Such centers appeal to a small market via special accessibility to a neighborhood or set of neighborhoods, and stress everyday items for which shoppers most value the convenience of location. As such, they are not seriously affected by regional centers, though a competing community center can be a problem. Easy access and sufficient parking are extremely important. Finally, "power" centers and discount malls, as well as "category killers" like Home Depot, began to emerge in the 1980s. These retailers offer large selections, often at discount prices.

In the future, traditional shopping centers may have to compete not only on price with discounters such as Wal-Mart, but also on the basis of convenience with catalogs and television merchandising. In response, shopping centers have begun to reposition themselves as "shopping experiences" which offer entertainment and restaurants as magnets.[55]

Industrial Districts

The most attractive and highest-valued industrial districts are those that are planned carefully with respect to the mix of industries and the services available to serve the occupants. Industrial districts often generate noise, traffic, and sometimes pollution, which can negatively affect their neighbors. It is

---

[55]The *Urban Land Institute,* Washington, DC, and the *International Council of Shopping Centers,* New York City, are excellent sources of information on retail trends and developments.

important that these externalities are sufficiently controlled to avoid future problems.

Perhaps most important to an industrial district is an accessible supply of labor. Transportation accessibility is critical, including specialized services such as rail spurs. Room for expansion is a positive factor. Current needs may change, and if added space is unavailable, occupants may be lost. Zoning is an important influence on future expansion. If zoning is specific with regard to such things as ground coverage and required parking, expansion may be restricted. If the current use is legally nonconforming, meaning it was grandfathered in when the zoning was changed, it is important to determine how this will affect future alterations or expansions of the facility.

Some kinds of industry, particularly heavy industry, may rely on secondary manufacturers for parts and services. Accessibility to these complementary facilities is a positive factor. Some manufacturing operations require a source of raw material, and easy access to these materials enhances the district's desirability. Finally, there is recent evidence that clearly differentiates between manufacturing and distribution facilities with respect to value-affecting characteristics.[56]

The Use of "Neighborhood" in Appraisal: Categorizing Neighborhoods

It is apparent that the elements that comprise the bundle of factors called "the neighborhood" can be difficult to identify, and even more difficult to quantify. In some cases, there is not sufficient empirical evidence to justify a firm conclusion about the impact of a certain factor(s) on value. Not only might the magnitude of the value impact be uncertain, but in some cases even the direction of impact will be unclear. How then can the appraiser reconcile the obvious impact of neighborhood on value, with the equally obvious fact that the impact of individual factors may resist measurement?

The answer is qualitative as much as it is quantitative. The appraiser attempts to avoid or minimize measurement problems by separating neighborhoods into categories corresponding to their overall value impact. By using data from properties in a comparable neighborhood category, the appraiser minimizes the burden of quantifying inherently subjective factors, such as stability, which may impact values but which tend to resist definitive conclusions.

Relative land values are one key to assigning neighborhood categories. This is because neighborhood, like general accessibility, is a function of location, and its impact on value will be reflected in land values. In practice then, by holding general accessibility and physical characteristics con-

---

[56]Roy Black, Robert Pittman, and John Warden, "Distance, Labor Market, and Property Type Variables in Industrial Hedonic Pricing Models," Working Paper, Georgia State University, 1995.

stant, the appraiser can conclude that similar land values suggest similar neighborhoods. That is, similar land values reflect similar locational attributes, including both general accessibility and neighborhood effects.

A practical problem in using relative land values as the measure of "location" is that in mature neighborhoods, land values may not be directly observable, because vacant sites are either unavailable or sell too infrequently to establish current market values. In this situation, locational effects can be extracted by comparing the selling prices of properties with comparable improvements. In such cases, any difference in price is attributable to land (or locational) value.

Neighborhoods and Appraisal Reports

More will be said about the relationship between location and value when the three appraisal approaches are discussed in detail. The discussions then will include coverage of standardized appraisal forms, which are used widely for residential appraisals, particularly those completed for lenders. At this point, however, it is useful to point out that the treatment of "neighborhood" on standardized appraisal forms is consistent with the discussion in this chapter.

Figure 3–4 is a portion of the *Uniform Residential Appraisal Report*, with the neighborhood portion highlighted. Various sections are concerned

FIGURE 3–4

X X
Property Description

UNIFORM RESIDENTIAL APPRAISAL REPORT **File No.**

SUBJECT

Property Address | City | State | Zip Code

Legal Description | County

Assessor's Parcel No. | Tax Year | R.E. Taxes $ | Special Assessments $

Borrower | Current Owner | Occupant ☐ Owner ☐ Tenant ☐ Vacant

Property rights appraised ☐ Fee Simple ☐ Leasehold | Project Type ☐ PUD ☐ Condominium (HUD/VA only) | HOA$ /Mo.

Neighborhood or Project Name | Map Reference | Census Tract

Sales Price $ | Date of Sale | Description and $ amount of loan charges/concessions to be paid by seller

Lender/Client | Address

Appraiser | Address

NEIGHBORHOOD

				Predominant occupancy	Single family housing	Present land use %	Land use change
Location	☐ Urban	☐ Suburban	☐ Rural		PRICE $ (000) / AGE (yrs)	One family	☐ Not likely ☐ Likely
Built up	☐ Over 75%	☐ 25-75%	☐ Under 25%	☐ Owner	Low	2-4 family	☐ In process
Growth rate	☐ Rapid	☐ Stable	☐ Slow	☐ Tenant	High	Multi-family	To:
Property values	☐ Increasing	☐ Stable	☐ Declining	☐ Vacant (0-5%)	Predominant	Commercial	
Demand/supply	☐ Shortage	☐ In balance	☐ Over supply	☐ Vacant (over 5%)		( )	
Marketing time	☐ Under 3 mos.	☐ 3-6 mos.	☐ Over 6 mos.				

Note: Race and the racial composition of the neighborhood are not appraisal factors.

Neighborhood boundaries and characteristics:

Factors that affect the marketability of the properties in the neighborhood (proximity to employment and amenities, employment stability, appeal to market, etc.):

Market conditions in the subject neighborhood (including support for the above conclusions related to the trend of property values, demand/supply, and marketing time -- such as data on competitive properties for sale in the neighborhood, description of the prevalence of sales and financing concessions, etc.):

with the growth prospects for the neighborhood, the current mix of land uses, the prospects for nonconforming uses in the future, the neighborhood in terms of value ranges, the neighborhood in terms of special accessibility, and its social, cultural, environmental, and governmental characteristics. The last section allows the appraiser to add commentary, or to provide an overall evaluation of the neighborhood.

Summary

The cliche that the three factors that determine real estate values are "location, location, and location" contains more than a kernel of truth. Because real estate is immobile its value is indeed a hostage of its location. The two categories of locational factors are accessibility and neighborhood.

With respect to accessibility, the covering principle is that, in general, "closer to the center of the city is more valuable." The linkage between value and distance looks like this:

Land value → Rent → Location → Distance

As urban areas grow and their transportation systems become more complex, the impacts of accessibility are more difficult to predict. In every case, the smoothly declining land-value gradient of the basic community gives way to a lumpier gradient that reflects the emerging multiple nuclei of economic activity.

The neighborhood is the second major category of location. Its effect on property value adds to, and sometimes even dominates, the basic value-distance relationship. The components of neighborhood are special accessibility (proximity), social factors that affect stability, environmental and governmental influences, demographics, and the life cycle of the neighborhood itself.

Analyzing locational effects can be a highly subjective task, because they are neither as identifiable nor as measurable as the physical and functional characteristics of the property itself. Moreover, neighborhood effects tend to be case-specific.

In practice, the appraiser attempts to minimize problems associated with neighborhood impacts by avoiding them. This is accomplished by utilizing data from properties in comparable locational categories; effectively, those locations which command similar land values. This categorization of location is reflected in appraisal reports, particularly those on standardized forms, which ask the appraiser to rate neighborhood characteristics from good to poor. From the preceding discussions, we can describe a good neighborhood as one with the following characteristics: adequate accessibility, sufficient public services, a minimum of negative externalities such as congestion, pollution, and crime, is in the developing or mature stage in its life cycle, and is stable and harmonious with regard to the current and prospective uses of its land. At the other extreme, a poor neighborhood will exhibit few if any of these favorable characteristics.

Questions and Problems

1. What is the basic set of causes and effects linking land value and distance?
2. Why do you think cities, particularly those with crude transportation systems, tend to grow in a circular form?
3. How do households fit into the accessibility model?
4. In practice, the relationship between value and distance is often lumpy. Why?
5. What is a neighborhood? What are the general categories or components of neighborhood effects?
6. On the *Uniform Residential Appraisal Report,* there is a note in the neighborhood section that states that "Race or racial composition of the neighborhood are not considered reliable appraisal factors." Comment.
7. What is a district?
8. "Being close to an airport has a negative effect on property value." Comment.
9. Given the large number of often interrelated factors that determine locational quality, how can appraisers confidently capture locational effects on value?
10. What effect might a transportation improvement have on land uses and land values?
11. An appraiser suggests that one way to categorize neighborhoods is by their ages. Comment.
12. "Residential lots closer to parks are worth more." Comment.
13. Some research has found upwardly sloping land-value gradients for portions of cities. Is there an explanation?

CHAPTER 4

Property-Specific Characteristics: The Site and the Improvements

Introduction

This chapter changes the focus from the impact of a property's location on its value to how the characteristics of the property itself affect its value. An evaluation of a property's physical and functional characteristics is necessary when identifying comparables for use in the sales comparison approach; for estimating reproduction (or replacement) cost, depreciation, and site value in the cost approach; and for estimating current rent and growth prospects for use in the income approach.

Though the discussion in this chapter will routinely reference physical and functional characteristics when discussing the determinants of value, it is the utility of the space that is actually valued by the market. Land, bricks, mortar, and a good floor plan have no inherent value. In practice, however, it is next to impossible to directly measure utility and then to convert that measure into an estimate of how it will affect value. Fortunately, because utility is generally associated with physical and functional characteristics, the appraiser is able to use those characteristics as a proxy. As a result, appraisers refer to value in terms of *x* dollars per square foot of living area, not in terms of *x* dollars per unit of utility.

Identifying the Physical Property: The Property Description

Before a property can be appraised, it must be described. The purpose of the property description is to provide, as precisely as possible, an identification of the physical property associated with the property rights being valued. There are several ways to legally describe a property, with the choice of method determined by the property's location, the information available, and sometimes, the requirements of the client.

- *Street Address:* This is a relatively imprecise description that is typically not considered a true legal description. Nonetheless, it has the advantages of being understandable, available, and inexpensive. The use of street addresses is most common in urban areas where official street numbering systems have been established.
- *Lot and Block Numbers:* This type of description is generally found in public records and refers to official maps, or plats, of developed areas like subdivisions. In urban areas where most land has been subdivided, lot and block numbers, along with a subdivision name, provide a precise property description. In more rural areas, however, the lot and block system is likely to apply only in a few scattered subdivisions.
- *Metes and Bounds:* This is a description using distances (metes) and compass directions (bounds) from permanent markers called monuments. These markers may be manmade or natural. A land survey is required. A metes and bounds description might read as follows:

> A tract of land situated in Pine Mill, Middle County, Pennsylvania, described as follows: Beginning at the intersection of the north line of Center Road and the West line of Johnson Road, then North from said point along the said sector of Johnson Road 400 feet, then South 60 West 185 feet more or less to the corner of the stone wall bordering the land of Jason and Janice Richards, formerly Ted and Irene Kirkpatrick, then South to Center Road, then East 167 feet, more or less to the place of beginning.

In the Colonial Era and in the early history of the United States, the so-called permanent markers were often large trees and stones that were not so permanent after all. The increased possibility of inaccuracy using such monuments (they may disappear or be moved or removed) means that their use today is generally confined to rural areas where there is no reasonable alternative.

- *Government (Rectangular) Survey:* This is a precise property description available in areas of the United States outside the original 13 states and Texas, West Virginia, Kentucky, and Tennessee. The land is divided into 36 square-mile (six-mile-square) townships, with each township identified by its position relative to a designated principal meridian (north-south) and base line (east-west). East-west rows of townships are called ranges, north-south rows are called tiers. Each township is divided into 36 sections, each one mile square, and these sections in turn can be divided into as small a rectangular area as desired. Sometimes reference to a government survey description is used to identify the general area of an irregularly shaped property, and then metes and bounds is used to describe the specific property within the area.

Non-Ownership Impacts on Property Value: Government Regulation and Private Contracts

The utility of a property is partly a function of how much of the complete bundle of property rights has been eroded by government regulation or private contracts. At one extreme, the bundle may be complete because there is no control over the use and disposal of the property by anyone other than the owner. This is the rare exception. More likely, there will be non-ownership interests or government rights in real property that affect its value. These interests may or may not involve actual possession of the property, and include zoning and deed restrictions, property taxes and assessments, and easements and encroachments. The existence of these non-ownership interests is discovered in two ways: (1) by physically inspecting the property, and (2) through a search of public records. When the public record is unclear or incomplete, interviews with those who may have an interest in the property may be required.

Zoning and Deed Restrictions

The legal uses of a property have a major impact on its value. Zoning regulations specify the uses allowed and may also specify allowable densities, building height and size, setbacks, required parking spaces, and sign restrictions. In some cases, the zoning code specifies the legal steps required to obtain variances, conditional uses, or rezoning. A variance is a use that typically differs from the zoning regulations in one or two details. For example, a building with a side setback of 15 feet rather than 20 feet. A conditional use is a special exception to the zoning code, such as permission to build a church in a residential zone. In addition, the zoning code may include specific or unique requirements that affect use, as in the case of flood plains or historic preservation districts. At the extreme, restrictions may be so complete that the zoning effectively precludes any use of the property. This is effectively a taking of the property with the same impact as condemnation, and courts are beginning to recognize this and allow compensation to the owner. Finally, a property may be a nonconforming use, which is a use that was permitted when the improvement was built, but which would not be allowed under current zoning. Thus, a nonconforming use is one that has been grandfathered in, and as such, there are likely to be restrictions on future changes to the improvements which could limit the value of the property.

The appraiser must also consider the effects of an imminent or probable change in zoning, particularly if such a change will affect the site's expected use. In such cases, the appraisal report must state the basis of the expected use conclusion, with the appraiser's judgment as to the probability of the change and its value impact should it occur.

Deed restrictions are like private zoning. They are commonly used in residential subdivisions where initial and subsequent marketing efforts may depend on the buyer's perception of future protection against "undesirable" neighbors. Common types of deed restrictions prohibit the building of such things as tool sheds, or require houses to be of a minimum size. Deed restrictions must of course stay within the bounds of law. In earlier days, restrictions on selling to certain racial or religious groups were relatively common, but these have been ruled to be unconstitutional and thus unenforceable.

Assessed Values and Property Taxes

The assessed value of a property and the accompanying level of property taxes are typically included in appraisal reports. While assessed values may provide reasonably good estimates of market value, in many jurisdictions this is not the case. Regardless, the absolute level of taxes may impact a property's potential use. For an investment property, taxes affect its expected income and thus its value.

Certain property tax laws are written to encourage or discourage certain market behaviors. For example, so-called "Clean and Green" laws may provide farmers tax relief as long as their land is kept in agricultural use, and differing tax rates on land and buildings may have the effect of stimulating or discouraging new development.

Easements and Encroachments

Easements are rights extended to non-owners for ingress and egress over a property for a specific purpose. Common examples are easements for access to a roadway or to make it easier for an abutting property owner to have access to his or her backyard. Utilities routinely acquire easements for such things as telephone poles and lines. Though appraisal reports often assume the property to be free and clear of easements, the appraiser remains responsible to report those that clearly impact value.

Encroachments are of two kinds: either the subject property's improvement extends into an abutting property or the improvements on an abutting property extend onto the subject property. Though appraisers are not expected to do surveys, and appraisal reports generally assume there are no encroachments, they must be reported if observed. Similarly, when a common wall or a driveway is shared by the subject property and an abutting property, it may affect future uses and utility and therefore it needs to be reported.

Leases

A lease is a contract that gives the lessee (tenant) possessory rights to a property for a specified time period. When a property is sold, the rights of the lessee(s) is typically not extinguished; therefore, the specifics of an existing lease can have a significant effect on the market value of the property.

Factors Associated with Site Value

After the initial task of properly describing the subject property and noting any non-ownership property rights, the appraiser is ready to inventory the characteristics of the site and buildings. Site and buildings will be discussed separately. This approach is not only easier for learning purposes, it also reflects the fact that at some point in most appraisals, separate value estimates are required for the site and the building.

Components of a Site

There are two components of a site: (1) the land, and (2) the improvements to the land, such as grading and removal of trees. These improvements *to* the land are distinguished from improvements *on* the land, which are the major buildings and minor improvements such as driveways, private sidewalks, fences, and landscaping. In addition, there may be off-site improvements that impact site value. Examples are the existence and quality of utility hookups, adjacent streets with curbs and gutters, and sewers.

The Size of a Site

The size of the site is generally expressed in whatever units are appropriate for the likely use of the land. Large tracts tend to be described in terms of acres, while smaller sites tend to be described in terms of square feet. For certain land uses, size is commonly referred to in terms of productive capacity. Ask a real estate broker the value of land that is zoned for apartments, and the answer will likely be framed in terms of the number of units allowed. For example, if the expected rate of return and current rent levels justify a land cost of $20,000 per unit, a land value of $160,000 may be associated with zoning that allows eight units. Similarly, a 50-acre parcel zoned for one house for each two acres will almost certainly have a lower value than if it were zoned for one house for each acre.

Like most factors associated with property value, the specific impact of a site's size will be a case-dependent function of the current or expected use of the site, market conditions, and its location. However, what we do know generally is that given some category of allowed land use, such as single-family residential, the size of a site is generally the characteristic that will have the most impact on its value. This commonsense "more is better" rule has been confirmed repeatedly in research on land values. What is not yet completely resolved is the question of whether the relationship between size and value is linear or nonlinear. Is a site twice as large twice as valuable? The answer to this kind of question is important to appraisers, because they must frequently compare sites of different sizes.

Theoretical arguments have been made on both sides. Those who argue that the size-value relationship is linear often do so by an appeal to arbitrage. That is, if larger parcels could be purchased at less per square foot than smaller parcels, investors would simply buy large parcels, divide them into smaller ones, and sell for an immediate profit.[1]

---

[1]For example, Edwin S. Mills, "The Value of Urban Land," *In the Quality of the Urban Environment,* H. S. Derloff, ed. (Baltimore: Resources for the Future), 1969. See

TABLE 4–1 **Marginal Prices for Lot Size (in Fractions of One Acre)**

Neighborhood	Lot Size		
	.20	.21–.50	.51–1.00
1	$ 1,801	$ 734	$ 373
2	10,160	4,102	2,065
3	15,323	6,483	3,382

Source: Robert L. Bland, "The Implicit Price of Housing Attributes: An Explication and Application of the Theory to Mass Appraisal Research," *Property Tax Journal*, March 1984.

However, those who argue for a nonlinear size-value relationship point out that there are costs involved in buying, dividing, and reselling, and that the difference in price between large and small parcels is largely offset by these costs.[2] In fact, given these costs, a price difference is necessary for subdividers to bring sites to market. Not surprisingly, the empirical evidence is mixed, but on balance seems to point to a nonlinear relationship, with value increasing at a decreasing rate with lot size.[3] Bland's[4] results are typical. He found a decreasing rate of price increase as lot size increased in three neighborhoods of varying household incomes in suburban Pittsburgh. As Table 4–1 indicates, this result held in all three neighborhoods.

An intuitive explanation for a nonlinear relationship between land value and size is that purchasers of land earn the same "wholesale" discount as purchasers of other products. On the other hand, this explanation may miss an important insight into land-value determination. That is, land value can be viewed as the sum of two components. The first component is fixed, and reflects the value of the right to improve the land. It is in a sense the value "to be there." It may also be thought of as the value of the option to de-

---

also F. H. Reuter, "Externalities in Urban Property Markets: An Empirical Test of the Zoning Ordinances of Pittsburgh," *Journal of Law and Economics,* 16, 313–49; S. M. Maser, W. H. Riker, and R. N. Rosett, "The Effects of Zoning and Externalities on the Price of Land: An Empirical Analysis of Monroe County, New York, *Journal of Law and Economics,* 20, 111–32.

[2] For example, Peter F. Colwell and C. F. Sirmans, "Nonlinear Urban Land Prices," *Urban Geography,* 1, 1980, 141–52.

[3] For example, see Paul K. Asabere and Peter F. Colwell, "The Relative Lot Size Hypothesis: An Empirical Note," *Urban Studies,* 22, 1985, 355–57; also Robert L. Bland, "The Implicit Price of Housing Attributes: An Explication and Application of the Theory to Mass Appraisal Research," *Property Tax Journal,* March 1984, 55–65; Tom J. Keith, "Applying Discounted Cash Flow Analyses to Land in Transition," *Appraisal Journal,* October 1991, 458–70.

[4] Bland, "Housing Attributes."

FIGURE 4–1 Sources of site value

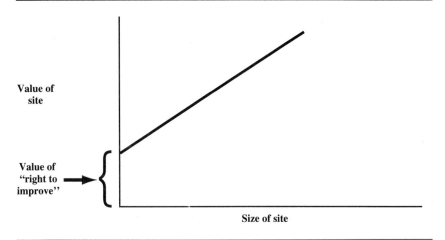

velop. The second component of land value is then a linear function of the size of the parcel. Researchers were able to measure the fixed-value component in a study of residential land values in Copenhagen, Denmark, and after controlling for the fixed-cost component, size was then found to be linearly associated with the remaining portion of value, as shown in Figure 4–1.[5] Given the fixed component of value, a nonlinear relationship between size and total value results, though the reason for it is somewhat different than is commonly thought. This may help explain why some studies have found a linear relationship and others a nonlinear relationship.

While none of this changes the basic idea that the relationship between total value and size is nonlinear, it does suggest that if the appraiser can estimate the fixed component of land value, the remaining (linear) component of value may be easier to estimate, even if observed transactions are on parcels of differing size.

The Shape of a Site

The market is likely to be interested not only in the size of a parcel of land, but also in its shape. The most important elements of shape are how the parcel is apportioned between frontage and depth, and whether the shape is regular or irregular. The appraiser should also take note of nonconformities. There may be valuation effects if a site is significantly bigger

---

[5]Anders Muller, "Separate Models for Computer Calculation of Land Values and Building Values for 1.3 Million Residential Properties in Denmark," *Property Tax Journal*, September 1988.

or smaller than is typical in the neighborhood, if the building-to-site ratio varies from the market norm, or if the frontage-to-depth ratio is atypical.

While it is generally agreed that frontage is more valuable than depth, the exact relationship seems to be a function of the type of property and what is typical for the market in which the property is located. Various rules of thumb that have been developed attempt to quantify the relationship between frontage and depth, but their accuracy is often suspect.

For example, Scheu and Colwell[6] used data on lots sold in New York City during the 1880s and found that some depth rules performed better than others. In a more recent study, the same authors found that depth rules generally understated the importance of frontage relative to depth in two central Illinois cities.[7] On balance, it appears that depth rules tend to be unreliable and should be used only if local experience suggests them to be applicable.

Another possibility that should be considered is that a site's value may be a function of its *relative* size; that is, how its size compares to the typical or average-sized site in the neighborhood. Asabere and Colwell[8] tested this aspect of "conformity" and found it to be significant. An example of their findings is that the value of a 10,000 square-foot lot in the study neighborhood would have been $11,788 if the average neighborhood lot size had also been 10,000 square feet. However, if the average neighborhood lot size had been 6,000 square feet, the sale price of a 10,000 square-foot lot would have been only $10,385. If the average lot size had been 12,000 square feet, the price of a 10,000 square-foot lot would have been $12,333.

This result is consistent with the hypothesis that the values of larger lots are reduced, while the values of smaller lots are increased, according to their size relative to the average lot size in the neighborhood. While these relationships may not apply in all markets, they should alert the appraiser to a potential size effect that bears watching.

Another interesting size-value relationship was uncovered by Li and Brown[9] in their study of a neighborhood 27 miles southwest of the Boston central business district. They found for smaller houses (defined as five rooms or less), lot size had a relatively small impact on value. As house size increased, however, the value difference among lots of different sizes also increased. This result supports the conventional wisdom that there are value-maximizing building-site ratios. Again, the exact nature of this relationship must be tested in a given market.

---

[6]Tim Scheu and Peter F. Colwell, "Site Valuation Rules," Working Paper, University of Illinois, 1987.

[7]Peter F. Colwell and Tim Scheu, "Optimal Lot Size and Configurations," *Journal of Urban Economics,* July 1989.

[8]Asabere and Colwell, "The Relative Lot Size Hypothesis."

[9]Mingche M. Li and H. James Brown, "Micro-Neighborhood Externalities and Hedonic Housing Prices," *Land Economics,* May 1980.

Corner Lots and Cul-de-Sacs

There are advantages and disadvantages to corner lots. An advantage is the added access provided by frontage on two sides. This can provide greater flexibility in building design and layout, and perhaps more privacy because on average there is one less neighbor than there is for inside lots. For commercial uses, particularly retail services, frontage and access on two sides may be valued quite highly.

On the negative side, at least for residential uses, corner lots mean added traffic, accompanying noise, and possibly air pollution. The costs of off-site improvements such as curbing, and periodic assessments for maintenance may be higher for corner lots, and tasks such as shoveling snow will be doubled. Finally, if the assessor assigns a relatively higher value to corner lots, the property tax burden will be higher.

Research results on the value impact of corner lots are mixed. In a study of Lubbock, Texas, Karl Guntermann found that corner lots on average sold at a small (2 percent) premium over comparable inside lots. However, in 10 of 15 census areas there was no significant corner lot influence, and there was a 3.5 percent average decline in the values of corner lots that abutted a heavy traffic artery.[10] Different conclusions were reached in a study of Edmonton, Canada,[11] where corner lots uniformly commanded a significant price premium.

Given the lack of an empirical consensus, and the commonsense observation that there are offsetting costs and benefits of corner lots, the appraiser should assume neither a positive nor a negative impact on value unless there is local market evidence to the contrary. It follows that tables providing rule of thumb value adjustments for corner lots should be viewed skeptically.

Sites on cul-de-sacs offer privacy and less traffic. Students in the author's appraisal classes have on several occasions measured the effect of cul-de-sac locations in State College, Pennsylvania. Their results show an average positive effect ranging from 2–6 percent, but with a wide variance. Asabere found a much larger 29 percent premium in Halifax, Nova Scotia.[12] As with corner lots, the appraiser must be aware of the possible influence of a cul-de-sac location and attempt to measure its effect in the local market.

---

[10] Karl L. Guntermann, "The Corner Influence on Value: Some Empirical Results," *The Real Estate Appraiser and Analyst,* September–October, 1979, 22–26; Karl L. Guntermann and Charles E. Wade, "Corner Influence and Assessment Value: Some Empirical Results," *Assessor's Journal,* December 1980, 173–79.

[11] See C. T. L. Janssen and D. G. MacLean, "Valuation of Single-Family Residences: Factors Considered by the Market and by Assessors," *Property Tax Journal,* December 1984, 239–53.

[12] Paul Asabere, "The Value of a Neighborhood Street with Reference to the Cul-de-Sac," *Journal of Real Estate Finance and Economics,* June 1990.

Plottage and Plattage

The relationship between the size of a site and its value was explained earlier in terms of two components: the fixed value of the right to improve and the value related to the size of the site. This approach also provides insight into why the unit values of sites may be affected by dividing larger sites into smaller sites (plattage), or by assembling smaller sites into larger sites (plottage). Plattage may allow the subdivider to capture the fixed "right to improve" value component two or more times rather than once, and plottage may produce a parcel that justifies the payment of the "right to improve" component, whereas the smaller sites from which it was assembled did not qualify.

The most common example of creating plattage value is when acreage is subdivided into residential lots. The most common example of creating plottage value is when parcels are assembled for a commercial development. For agricultural land, the economies of scale associated with such things as seeding and harvesting may also contribute to plottage value.

Topography, Contour, and Soil

The ideal residential lot is one which provides the best setting for the improvements, minimizes problems of drainage and erosion, is nicely landscaped, and is not so severely contoured as to eliminate recreation areas and make maintenance unreasonably difficult or expensive. For example, a desirable lot for a house with a basement would likely slope gently upward to the house, then slope gently downward. The upward slope from the street to the house enhances "curb appeal" by making the house look larger than it is. The downward slope allows a walkout basement door leading to the backyard. This kind of contour also minimizes drainage and erosion problems. Within this description of "the ideal lot" there is plenty of room for exceptions. A severely contoured lot, for example, may provide a view that offsets other problems. For commercial and industrial development, flat sites are even more valuable, as they typically lower the costs of development.

The quality of surface soil for residential sites is largely a function of the soil's ability to support the lawn and other landscaping. An important consideration in some areas is the water table, which is the depth below the surface at which water is found. While easily accessible water is typically a plus, if the table is too high it may create costly construction problems. For larger properties, the soil must be capable of supporting a building's weight. Below surface is important as well, because excessive bedrock is costly to excavate and fill may be required.

Excess Land

Excess land is the part of a site that is not necessary to support the existing or planned improvements. Excess land is sometimes found with oversized or double residential lots, and is likely to add to the property's value because it provides additional space and privacy. Of course, if excess land can be marketed it has value in addition to the value of the standard site and improvements.

An example occurred recently in the author's town of State College, Pennsylvania, and involved the purchase of a locally owned motel. Though the motel was a successful enterprise, some thought the asking price was excessive based on the expected income from the motel. However, the appraiser (and purchaser) recognized the value of the excess land, which at that time was idle. Their judgment was confirmed, as shortly thereafter the site supported a car rental agency and a bank in addition to the motel.

Government restrictions are critical when considering the value of excess land. While the physical ability to absorb additional improvements is a necessary condition, it is not sufficient. In order to be successfully marketed any prospective improvements must conform to zoning and other land use requirements.

The value of excess land that can be marketed is estimated separately, then added to the value of the property as if it were on a standard-sized site. If the excess cannot be marketed, perhaps because of zoning regulations or its shape or topography, a judgment must be made as to how much, if any, the excess contributes to the value "as is."

The "Micro-Neighborhood": A Property's Immediate Surroundings

The neighborhood in general has been identified as a major locational factor that affects property values, and particularly site values. No neighborhood is completely homogeneous, however, and it is the immediate surroundings of a subject property, the "micro-neighborhood," that is likely to have the greatest impact on value. Only rarely does even the most desirable neighborhood escape the occasional property that is less well-maintained or is of a nonconforming style. Conversely, some properties will be maintained and landscaped at above-average levels. In short, they are good neighbors.

The impact of the immediate neighborhood on a property's value was demonstrated in a study by Li and Brown.[13] In their sample neighborhood, the average difference in house price between those with lowest- versus the highest-rated surroundings was about 8 percent of value. This suggests a commonsense lesson for the appraiser: things closer impact value more than things farther away.

Environmental Laws and Regulations

The appraiser must be aware of the potential impact of environmental laws and regulations on property values. An enormous and growing volume of

---

[13]Mingche M. Li and H. James Brown, "Micro-Neighborhood Externalities and Hedonic Housing Prices," *Land Economics,* May 1980.

federal, state, and local legislation describes natural as well as man-made conditions that may negatively affect value. Familiar natural conditions include wetlands and wildlife habitats. Man-made conditions include such things as the presence of asbestos-containing materials, such as PCBs.

These kinds of conditions may affect a single property, or in the case of such things as wetlands, an entire neighborhood. The appraiser's responsibility with respect to identifying environmental problems and estimating their impact on value is discussed in the *Uniform Standards of Professional Appraisal Practice*. It requires that the appraiser either (1) have the expertise to evaluate the problem, or (2) disclose the lack of expertise and take the steps necessary to complete the assignment. Given the complexity of the environmental evaluation and the specialized nature of the task, as well as the potential exposure to liability in such cases, appraisers often acknowledge a lack of expertise and include a disclosure to that effect in the limiting conditions section of the appraisal.

The market has begun to recognize the specialized nature of the environmental problem, and transactional audits (or environmental property assessments) are increasingly required by buyers, sellers, and lenders prior to closing a sale. The audits are generally conducted by environmental consultants. Even in these cases there is no guarantee that a property is contamination free, as the costs involved in a completely thorough audit would generally be prohibitive.

Building Characteristics Associated with Value

The value of improvements typically contributes most of the total property value, with ratios of residential building-to-site values often in the 4/1 range. Commercial ratios show more variance, but tend also to be dominated by the building's value.

The categories of building characteristics that are likely to be significantly associated with its value are: (1) size, (2) building materials and their quality, (3) building design, (4) condition, and (5) compatibility and conformity with its surroundings.

The Size of the Building

Two of the conclusions drawn about the relationship of site size to site value also apply to the relationship between building size and building value. They are: (1) building size is the characteristic that tends to be most closely associated with its value, and (2) the relationship between building size and building value tends to be nonlinear, with value increasing at a decreasing rate as size increases. As in the case of site value, this means the appraiser must analyze the size-value relationships in local markets and use caution when comparing properties with buildings of different sizes.

Two practical questions that arise with respect to building size are the proper unit(s) of measurement and the proper way to take the measurement. The proper unit(s) of measurement is the unit(s) which tends to be used to describe the property in the marketplace. For residential properties it is generally square feet, broken down into the number of bedrooms, bathrooms, and so forth. For office properties, size is generally reported in terms of square feet of gross and net rentable areas. The gross rentable area includes common areas such as lobbies, hallways, bathrooms, mechanical rooms, and stairways. The net rentable area excludes the common areas. Apartments are measured in square feet as well as by reference to the type of unit: one-bedroom with one bath, two-bedroom with one bath, efficiencies, and so on. Industrial buildings are commonly measured on both a square-foot and cubic-foot basis. Specialty properties may have unique measures. Theaters, for example, are measured by the number of seats as well as by square feet.

Once the proper unit is determined, measuring must be done accurately. Local custom often dictates how the measurements are taken, and it is necessary that the appraiser be consistent. Typically, total living area is measured by multiplying the exterior dimensions of the foundation by the number of stories. Individual rooms, however, are measured based on their interior dimensions, as are attics and basements.

When cubic feet is the unit of measurement, there is an additional computational problem when ceilings are not flat. The consensus opinion is that the proper vertical measurement is from six inches below either the basement floor or the surface of the lowest finished floor to the top of the upper ceiling joists.

Inconsistent measurements are a bigger problem (and with larger value impacts) for commercial buildings. The author's discussions with appraisers in New Jersey, Miami, and Denver indicate that the basis for measurement is inconsistent among markets and even within markets. The industry standard for measuring office buildings is currently set by the Building Owners and Managers Association, which carefully defines rentable versus usable space. In some markets, however, those standards are not always followed.[14] Thus the appraiser must be familiar with local customs when comparing buildings, and be certain that measurements have been made on the same basis for both the subject property and any comparable sales used in the analysis.

Building Materials and Their Quality

Value is affected by the types and quality of building materials. Materials that are attractive, functional, and long-lasting tend to be valued most highly,

---

[14]See, for example, "The Incredible Shrinking Square Foot," *New York Times,* sec. 8, p. 1, August 5, 1984; also, Real Estate Board of New York, *1987 Diary and Manual,* January 1, 1987.

though the "pecking order" will vary among markets depending on such things as climate and availability. Studies in various parts of the country have found that brick and stone exteriors tend to command a premium over wood-frame and aluminum. Similarly, plaster interior walls are generally valued more highly than drywall. The same logic applies to the materials used for mechanical systems. There are quality differences among furnaces, piping, and wiring, as well as differences in the estimated lives of different roofing materials. All of these factors contribute to long-term utility and will affect value. Therefore, they need to be addressed in an appraisal report.

Design

The importance of design varies by property type. This section focuses on residential properties, the most extensively researched to date. The ideal house is one with a style and floor plan which maximizes value per unit of measurement. This tends to happen when functional utility is maximized while retaining aesthetic appeal. The problem for the appraiser is that no one knows with certainty what this ideal house looks like, and because tastes vary, different designs may command approximately equal prices. Moreover, different floor plans may be valued differently as a function of architectural style, as was found in a study of houses in suburban Philadelphia.[15]

An added problem is the fact that design preferences change, sometimes quickly. In the early 1970s, for example, cathedral ceilings were a desired feature in many markets. But when the cost of heating and cooling rose sharply with the energy crisis in the mid-70s, cathedral ceilings lost much of their appeal. When oil prices began dropping this was again reversed. This is a good example of the dynamics of real estate markets, where changing tastes continually alter market demand and property values.

Demographic patterns may also influence tastes in design. Smaller families, for example, may mean a desire for fewer but larger rooms. In the future, as telecommuting becomes more common, we are likely to find more work-oriented spaces built into new homes.

Despite the inherent difficulties in evaluating market tastes, there are guidelines to help the appraiser manage design in the appraisal process for residential properties. For example, Bloom and Harrison[16] suggested dividing the interior of a house into three zones: (1) the private/sleeping zone consisting of bedrooms, bathrooms, and dressing rooms, (2) the living/social zone consisting of the living room, dining room, recreation room, den, and enclosed porch, and (3) the working/service zone consisting of the kitchen, laundry room, pantry, and other work areas. The utility of a floor

---

[15] Kenneth M. Lusht, "The Use of Design Stratification in Mass Appraisal," *Assessor's Journal,* March 1976.

[16] George F. Bloom and Henry S. Harrison, *Appraising the Single-Family Residence* (Chicago: AIREA), 1978.

plan may be measured as a function of how well the three zones are separated by common areas like hallways, stairs, and entrances. The sleeping zone should be isolated from noise, and it should be possible to move from bedroom to bathroom without being seen from other areas of the house, including other bedrooms. A serious design deficiency that is found mainly in older houses is the placing of the single bathroom off the master bedroom, requiring others to go through the bedroom to gain access.

The work area should be in a position to control entrances and as much of the activity in the house as possible. Entrances should provide direct access to closets and a bathroom, and be isolated from the sleeping zone. Ideally, there should be interior access to the garage, and if there is a basement, there should be an outside exit. Beyond concerns about functional utility, certain room arrangements like bedrooms and living areas overlooking backyards and gardens may add to appeal.

Not to be overlooked is visual, or curb appeal, which is an aesthetic judgment based on first impressions. Such judgments can be made as the appraiser approaches the property, and should be based not on the appraiser's personal preference but rather on how it is felt the market will respond to the overall external appearance.

The visual appeal of commercial properties can also be an important factor in attracting tenants and determining rents. In one study, it was found that "good" new architecture commanded a rent premium, while "good" old architecture did not.[17] While these kinds of preferences will be market-specific and are unlikely to be as important as they are in residential markets, the appraiser should be aware they may affect relative values.

Proportion and Adequacy

The rooms in a house should complement each other. Thus, a four-bedroom house with only one bathroom in today's marketplace is likely to be penalized.[18] A second or even third bathroom would likely each contribute significantly to value. Beyond two or three, however, each additional bathroom would provide diminished added (or marginal) utility, and thus would not contribute as much to value. The relative size of rooms can also be important. For example, in some markets larger and more expensive kitchens are preferred,[19] and in many markets, living rooms have become smaller, with family rooms or combination kitchen-dens ("great rooms")

---

[17] Douglas E. Hough and Charles G. Kratz, "Can 'Good' Architecture Meet the Market Test?" *Journal of Urban Economics* 14, 1983.

[18] A survey of upper-income homebuyers showed that 78 percent of them listed the number of bathrooms as "very important." See *ERA National Real Estate Pool* (Opinion Research: St. Louis), 1987.

[19] Seventy-three percent of upper-income homebuyers listed a custom-designed kitchen as important. See *ERA National Real Estate Poll.*

substituting. The size of entrance stairs and hallways should meet typical standards.

Proportion may also refer to the balance among rooms. Thus, a bathroom that was remodeled at a cost of $15,000 will likely command much less than that in terms of added value if it is in a house that was otherwise worth only $60,000. Conversely, the same bathroom in a $100,000 house may be viewed as quite appropriate and be fully valued by the market.

The presence and condition of fixtures and appliances must be noted. Central air conditioning, the type of heating system, and the condition of plumbing and electrical systems will affect value.

Condition

The condition of a property's improvements will generally have a significant impact on its market value. The commonsense assumption is that the better the condition the greater the utility and the higher the value. The appraiser should note aging or obsolete parts of the structure or equipment. The condition of the furnace, water pipes, and roof are important. Are there cracks in walls, evidence of moisture in the basement, and do the windows work properly? On the plus side, has the furnace recently been replaced or the roof reshingled? In general, the appraiser is looking for conditions that add to or subtract from value, and while condition is usually associated with the physical structure, it can also include environmental conditions unique to the property. These may appear quite suddenly, as in the case of asbestos. The use of asbestos-containing materials had been an almost standard procedure over an extended period, with no measurable effect on property value. However, when the health hazards associated with these kinds of materials became known, it had a very adverse impact on the value of affected properties.[20] In extreme cases, the cost of curing the problem exceeded the value of the property.

The presence of radon gas is a more recent example. Only now are the potential health hazards being analyzed, and empirical work on the value impact of radon is as yet inconclusive.

The lesson for the appraiser is that the kinds of property conditions that affect value are varied, may change suddenly, and may differ from property to property.

Proxies for Condition: Age and Effective Age

The use of condition as a proxy for utility makes the appraiser's task easier but does not completely solve the problem, because (1) judging condition is difficult, with some conditions (such as faulty wiring) not easily observable, and (2) the cost of evaluating the condition of each component of an im-

---

[20]Jeffrey Fisher, George Lentz, and K. C. Maurice Tse, "Effects of Asbestos on Commercial Real Estate: A Survey of MAI Appraisers," *Appraisal Journal,* October 1993.

provement, as well as each piece of equipment, is prohibitive for most appraisal assignments.

Instead, appraisers often make judgments about the overall condition of the basic structure and its major components. As an aid to arriving at this bottom line, the age or the effective age of the structure is used as a guide to the overall percentage loss in value due to deteriorating condition. The age of a building refers to its physical (chronological) age. The effective age of a building is indicated by its condition and utility. If a building was originally constructed with quality materials and workmanship, and has been well maintained, its effective age is likely to be less than its actual age. Conversely, the effective age of a poorly maintained or cheaply constructed building may exceed its actual age. Computationally, effective age is the difference between a property's total economic life under normal conditions, and its remaining economic life. In practice, effective age is generally calculated as the property's total economic life times the percentage it has deteriorated. More will be said about the calculation and application of effective age estimates in the cost approach chapters. It is an important calculation, as effective age is often used as a proxy for condition, which in turn is a proxy for utility and therefore value. Thus, an estimate of effective age is a standard part of most appraisal reports and it is used directly in the estimate of accrued depreciation deduction in the cost approach.

Compatibility and Conformity

Brokers often caution prospective house buyers not to buy or build the best house on the block. This is an application of the principle of compatibility, which holds that there is a greater marketing risk for houses that are significantly different from their neighbors. In practice, deciding what is significantly different is difficult, and there is the question of whether compatibility is sufficient, or whether conformity is necessary.

For every example of a nonconforming house that is not penalized in the marketplace there seems to be an offsetting example of one that is. This difficulty is typical of real estate appraisal, in that the appraiser must attempt to judge (and ultimately quantify) factors which are inherently subjective, which tend to change over time, and which are characterized not by discrete conclusions ("it conforms," "it does not conform") but rather by a continuum from almost perfect conformity (row houses) to perhaps complete incompatibility (mixed uses).

Research into the effects of conformity is of little help, because it has generally addressed social nonconformity, such as racial transition and income levels, rather than structural nonconformity. However, conversations with designated appraisers in various cities produced some reasonably consistent viewpoints based on their experiences. These appraisers said they were most concerned about the clearly nonconforming structure in residential neighborhoods, such as the old frame house in a new brick or stone neighborhood, modern architecture in a traditional neighborhood, and the most costly structure in the neighborhood. They stressed, however, that even in these cases value impacts were not always predictable.

There was less agreement among the appraisers about the value impacts associated with nonconforming commercial buildings. While each of the appraisers could provide examples of a building that was successful partly because of its uniqueness (for example, the Seagram Building in New York), each of them also recalled examples where uniqueness apparently repelled tenants.

Other Property Types

The basic list of physical factors associated with a building's value is consistent among property types. Size, quality, and condition are always primary determinants of value.

However, the relative importance of individual factors may vary among different categories of property. For industrial buildings, value is strongly associated with such things as floor-load capacity, power, wiring, ceiling height, bay size, and in some markets, the sprinkler and toxic waste systems. For office buildings, recent emphasis is on energy efficiency, communication technology, and parking. Parking is also a critical component of the value of suburban shopping centers, along with the design of the center, including amenities such as open space. For hotels, safety and security features should be noted. If it is a resort hotel, the availability of on-site recreation is important. The size of guest rooms should be a function of clientele, with larger sizes generally associated with longer average stays. Facilities should conform to the targeted market; support space may or may not be needed for restaurants, lounges, and meeting rooms. If it is a motel, adequate automobile access is necessary.

The above is intended to provide a flavor of the wide variations in desirable and undesirable physical features among various nonresidential property types. A detailed discussion is available elsewhere.[21]

Summary

The characteristics of a property's site and improvements determine its utility, and thus are of major importance in determining its market value. Before a property's characteristics can be evaluated, however, the limits (boundaries) of the property must be properly described. There are several kinds of property descriptions, with the choice depending on data availability and

---

[21] For example, Miles, Malizia, Weiss, Berens, and Travis, *Real Estate Development: Principles and Process* (Washington: Urban Land Institute), 2nd ed., 1996.

applicability, the size and value of the property, and legal requirements or the client's wishes. The most commonly used descriptions are: (1) street address, (2) lot and block number, (3) metes and bounds, including the use of monuments, and (4) government survey in states in which it applies.

Various non-ownership rights may affect the value of property. Direct governmental regulation of land use includes zoning and building and health codes. Governments also determine the level of taxes and assessments. Private zoning through deed restrictions is also common, especially in residential areas. In addition, private agreements can establish non-ownership interests, including physical encumbrances such as easements and encroachments, financial encumbrances such as mortgage loans, and contractual encumbrances such as leases.

Having established the bundle of rights to be valued, attention is then turned to the characteristics of the bundle that are likely to affect its value. With respect to the site, theory and empirical evidence argue that its size and shape are generally the dominant value-affecting characteristics. The relationship between a site's size and its value may be linear or nonlinear, given the possibility of plottage or plattage value. Frontage is generally more valuable than depth, though the exact relationship tends to be market-specific.

There is limited evidence linking the per-unit value of sites to the size of the buildings on the site. Site value seems less sensitive to size when improved with smaller houses, and more sensitive to size when improved with larger houses. Other influences that should be investigated, but which may or may not impact value in a given market, are corner lots and cul-de-sac locations, and the site's topography, contour, and soil conditions. If the site is larger than typically needed to support its improvements, the excess land will add value if it is marketable. Finally, the property's immediate surroundings, its micro-neighborhood, will affect its value. This is a more intense neighborhood effect as it reflects the impact of what is closest to the property.

Moving to the building, the "bigger is more valuable" rule has been confirmed repeatedly in empirical studies which show that more often than not, the building's size is the variable that has the most to do with the property's value. Other important characteristics are the quality of the building, its floor plan, the kinds of equipment included, and the condition of the building and equipment.

Finally, there is the consideration of a building's compatibility and/or conformity with surrounding improvements, though there is conflicting empirical evidence as to its importance. As is always the case, the evaluation of the site and building must reflect the appraiser's sense of the market—what is in demand and what is not.

Questions and Problems

1. Distinguish between land and a site.
2. Discuss the general relationship between site size and site value.
3. Briefly describe four kinds of property descriptions.
4. What is the "micro-neighborhood" and why is it important?
5. What is excess land? How is it valued relative to the remaining part of the site?
6. How good are depth rules that relate frontage value to depth value?
7. What is the typical unit of measurement for houses? Office buildings? Warehouses?

8. How do gross and net rentable areas differ?
9. What is effective age? Why is age and/or effective age an important characteristic of a building?
10. How important is structural compatibility with surrounding improvements?
11. What are some of the most important characteristics associated with a building's value?

CHAPTER 5

Expected Use Analysis

Introduction

A cornerstone of value theory and appraisal practice is that a property's value is a function of its expected use. A site downtown is generally more valuable than a site in the country because it can be used more profitably. For the same reason, a lot zoned for single-family use may be less valuable than a lot zoned for commercial use. A location that justifies a 30-story office building is more valuable than one that can support only five stories, and so on. This is the basic idea that was used in an earlier chapter to explain how accessibility helped determine land uses and land values.

The practical impact of the link between property use and property value is that *before* an appraiser can estimate a property's value, he or she must make an assumption about the property's expected use. A survey of appraisers and appraisal clients confirms that both groups agree the analysis of a property's expected use is the focal point on which the valuation section of the appraisal is based.[1]

If the subject property is vacant land (or is assumed to be vacant), the appraisal is based on the property's expected use. If the subject property is already improved, a determination is made as to whether the value estimate should be based on an assumption that the current use will continue, or whether the improvements should be demolished and the site redeveloped.

This does not mean that for every property the appraiser must analyze every possible use to arrive at a value estimate. In a majority of cases (notably for most single-family properties), the expected use is either obvious or is legally determined by zoning or deed restrictions. In the balance of cases, however, the expected use of the land is not as obvious. One example

---

[1] Robert P. White, "Assessing the Appraisal Community: A Customer Service Survey," *Real Estate Finance,* Spring 1992.

is when the current use is single-family, but zoning allows a commercial use. Another is when a property is already commercially zoned, but a number of alternative uses are possible.

Criteria in Expected Use Analysis

The expected use of a property, whether vacant land or improved, must meet four criteria: (1) legally permissible, (2) physically possible, (3) financially feasible, and finally, (4) maximally productive. In general, the appraiser evaluates each potential use in the order listed—it makes no sense to evaluate financial feasibility until it is determined that the use is legally permissible and physically possible.

Legal constraints should shorten considerably the list of expected-use candidates. Legal constraints may be public or private. Zoning is the most pervasive legal constraint. If a zoning change that will affect value seems imminent, that change should be reflected in the analysis and this should be clearly stated in the appraisal report.

A property's value may also reflect the contribution of an "overimprovement," traceable to the fact the property is developed with a legally nonconforming use. When such an improvement is grandfathered in, it has the potential to contribute value for the time period over its legally defined economic life. In these cases, the appraiser must take care when applying the three approaches. For example, a property with a legally nonconforming use cannot be used as a comparable without proper adjustments to its selling price. Development costs, which influence the expected use analysis, are heavily influenced by environmental concerns and building codes. Private restrictions may be equally important. A property encumbered by a long-term lease or a deed covenant that disallows certain uses will likely have a different expected use, and thus a different value, than a physically identical property without such restrictions.

The second expected use criteria is that it be physically possible. Certain uses may be precluded by the physical characteristics of the site. For example, some improvements will be inappropriate when the threat of an earthquake is high. Basic considerations include such things as the ability of the ground to support the building, and the costs of grading and foundation construction.

The third expected use criteria is financial feasibility, which in turn leads to the fourth and final criteria, which is maximal productivity. Developers demand a fair return on their investments, and a use which does not promise such a return is eliminated. The expected use analysis then focuses on the remaining possibilities.

While there is agreement that the expected use must be legally permissible, physically possible, and financially feasible, opinions diverge on the proper interpretation of maximally productive. There are three main contenders.

- The *highest and best use* premise is a deterministic concept which holds that the expected use is the single, specific use that maximizes the value of the land. The highest and best use premise dominates appraisal practice.
- The *expected use* premise is that the expected use is a probablistic concept where market value reflects the expected value (a weighted average) of a representative set of feasible uses.
- The *most probable use* premise is also deterministic, and holds that expected use is the single, most probable use of the land. It differs from the highest and best use in that it does not assume the most probable use is necessarily the value-maximizing use.

The discussion that follows is divided into two parts—appraising land as if vacant and appraising a property already improved. For each part, the competing maximally productive criteria are discussed and compared.

Appraising Land as if Vacant

The Highest and Best Use Premise

We begin with the highest and best use premise of market value, because it has been dominant in the appraisal literature and in appraisal practice since Babcock's 1931 text.[2] The process of estimating land value under the highest and best use premise is the same as was used to illustrate how accessibility affects land value.

As a first step, the appraiser "scopes"[3] or "screens" the market to eliminate obviously unsuitable uses. This leaves a manageable number of feasible and competitive uses. Suppose scoping produces three potential uses for a vacant site. For these three potential uses, the development costs, expected incomes, expected rates of return, and resulting land values are shown in Table 5–1.

In this example, the highest and best use premise holds that competitive bidding would drive the market price to $500,000, and the site would be developed as a retail store. In terms of an appraisal, $500,000 would be the estimated market value.

---

[2]Frederick N. Babcock, *The Valuation of Real Estate* (New York: McGraw Hill), 1931.
[3]Thomas D. Pearson and Steve Fanning, "A Practical Method for Complying with R41c's Highest and Best Use Requirement," *The Appraisal Journal,* April 1987.

TABLE 5–1 **Calculation of Justified Land Values**

	Office	Retail	Service Station
Income	$ 295,000	$ 190,000	$ 20,000
Development cost	2,000,000	1,400,000	450,000
Expected return	12%	10%	10%
Income to improvements	240,000 (.12 × $2,000,000)	140,000	45,000
Residual income to land	55,000 ($295,000 − $240,000)	50,000	(25,000)
Land value	$ 458,333 ($55,000/.12)	$ 500,000	$(250,000)

When Comparables Are Available

A complete residual analysis as shown above is not always necessary. When the highest and best use is obvious, such as when zoning effectively determines the expected use, and there are sales of comparable properties, the prices obtained can be used to directly estimate the subject property's value. This will occur most often for single-family houses.

The Expected Use Premise

An alternative to the highest and best use premise is that value is based on the expected value of a representative set of feasible uses. It is a probabilistic approach that recognizes that obtaining *the* price at *the* highest and best use is extremely unlikely.

When Sufficient Comparables Are Available

Once scoping has identified a manageable set of feasible uses, it can be determined if prior transactions qualify as comparables. If the set of feasible uses for a comparable sale are in fact comparable to those for the subject property, the transaction price can be used in the direct sales comparison approach.

Notice here that there is an important practical advantage to the probabilistic perspective on expected use. Under the highest and best use premise, the highest and best use of a comparable sale must match the highest and best use of the subject or the comparable is not truly comparable.[4] This may put an unreasonable burden on the appraiser and effectively eliminates all potential comparables except those with identical highest and best uses. Except for residential appraisals (where zoning tends to determine land use), the probability of identifying such comparables is remote.

---

[4]Max Derbes, Jr., "Highest and Best Use—What Is It?" *The Appraisal Journal,* April 1981.

Chapter 5 Expected Use Analysis

On the other hand, the "expected value of a set of feasible uses" premise provides the appraiser with a more manageable basis for comparable selection. From this perspective the appraiser refers not to the highest and best use but rather to a set of feasible uses.

When Sufficient Comparables Are Not Available

If the set of feasible uses of the subject property cannot be matched to those of recent sales, a more fundamental land residual analysis must be undertaken. This requires that a land value be estimated for each of the feasible uses, just as they are under the highest and best use premise. This may involve discounting cash flows, or in cases where such detail is not economically justified, first-year income may be capitalized. In any event, a land value for each feasible use is estimated.

At this point, if highest and best use was the premise, the analysis would be finished. Market value would be the maximum value indicated, with the values for the other uses ignored. Notice then, that highest and best use is simply a special case of expected use. The expected value premise, however, recognizes there is some probability each of the feasible uses may capture the site. Those probabilities are used to weight the individual land values, and the result is the expected value of the site. This process does not rule out the possibility of a single expected use, or one that has an overwhelming probability of occurring. This use would simply be given a weighting of 100 percent or close to it.

An Example of Expected Use Analysis

Suppose the appraiser's preliminary scoping of the market has identified three competitive uses for a vacant site. They are: (1) an office building, (2) a small warehouse, and (3) a "flex-space" building, suitable for warehousing, light manufacturing, or offices, depending on the tenant's needs. The first step is to search for land sales that have a similar set of feasible uses. If they can be located, the appraiser will place primary reliance on the direct sales comparison approach, and a fundamental land residual analysis is unnecessary. Suppose, however, that is not the case.

The first step is to estimate a range of justified land values for each of the feasible uses, based on their distributions of incomes and accompanying risks. The appraiser then assigns probabilities to the various outcomes, based on past experience and the state of the market.

Using a variation of Vandell's[5] format, Table 5–2 shows example results for the three potential land uses. Note that unlike a traditional highest and

---

[5]Kerry D. Vandell, "Toward Analytically Precise Definitions of Market Value and Highest and Best Use," *The Appraisal Journal*, April 1982, 265.

TABLE 5–2 Expected Price Calculation

Potential Use	Overall Probability of Occurrence	Value Distribution of Overall Probability (000s)					Expected Land Value for Each Use	Probability of Use	Contribution to Expected Price
		$300	$400	$500	$600	$700			
1. Office	20%			10%	10%		$550,000*	× .2 =	$110,000
2. Warehouse	30	5	15	10			$416,667**	× .3 =	125,000
3. Flex-Space	50			15	15	20	$610,000***	× .5 =	305,000
								Expected Price	$540,000

*10%/20% ($500,000) + 10%/20% ($600,000) = $550,000.
**5%/30% ($300,000) + 15%/30% ($400,000) + 10%/30% ($500,000) = $416,667.
***15%/50% ($500,000) + 15%/50% ($600,000) + 20%/50% ($700,000) = $610,000.

best use analysis, the value estimate resulting from an expected use analysis is not tied to a single, specific land use. Rather, it is by definition a weighted average of the menu of possible uses. In an appraisal report, those uses would be discussed, including a presentation similar to Table 5–2. The appraiser could, however, state that the highest probability is for flex-space.

The expected selling price is $540,000, which is the weighted average of the land-residual values of the three uses.[6] The expected *use* is probabilistic. There is a 20 percent probability of office, a 30 percent probability of warehouse, and a 50 percent probability of flex-space. In contrast, the highest and best use criteria would produce an estimated value of $700,000, based on the 20 percent probability that the most optimistic flex-space user will actually make such a bid.

A similar probabilistic approach to estimating value, using decision-tree payoffs, has been suggested by Goodheim.[7] The analysis leading to the distribution of values can also recognize a succession of land uses—what Graaskamp[8] called a program of highest and best use—including such things as zoning changes.

No doubt it has occurred to you that estimating the value of a vacant site in this way is a highly subjective task, as are other types of land-use forecasts. That is why the appraiser should use this fundamental approach (whether it is based on highest and best use or a probabilistic concept) only when forced to by a lack of comparable sales.

---

[6] Once the logic of estimating the expected price is understood, the calculation can be simplified as follows: .05 ($300,000) + .15 ($400,000) + .35 ($500,000) + .25 ($600,000) + .20 ($700,000) = $540,000.

[7] Brian Goodheim, "The Decision-Tree Payoff: A Graphic Approach to Highest and Best Use," *The Appraisal Journal*, October 1982.

[8] James Graaskamp, "A Rational Approach to Feasibility Analysis," *The Appraisal Journal*, October 1972, 513–21.

In those circumstances, the use of a probabilistic approach, unlike a highest and best use approach, has the advantage of clearly and explicitly recognizing the uncertainties involved. Keep in mind also that this textbook example was selected to clearly differentiate highest and best use from a probabilistic alternative. In practice, "scoping" will often identify a highly likely expected (or most probable) use and the task of determining weightings will be minimized.

The Most Probable Use Premise

A third and increasingly popular expected use premise is that the expected use is the single, most probable use of the land. Like highest and best use, it is a deterministic concept, but unlike highest and best use, the most probable use is not necessarily the land value-maximizing use.

In practice, there will not be much difference between the value estimates produced by the expected use and most probable use approaches if the set of feasible uses produces values that are approximately normally distributed. However, if the distribution is not close to normal, the value estimated under the most probable use premise may differ considerably. In our example, under the most probable use premise, the most probable use is flex-space (50 percent versus 30 percent and 20 percent for the alternatives), with a resulting value estimate of $610,000 (the most probable price given the use as flex-space). This compares to value estimates of $700,000 under the highest and best use premise, and $540,000 under the expected value premise.

Appraising a Property Already Improved

A judgment as to expected use is also necessary when the subject property is currently improved. This is to determine whether its value should be estimated based on the assumption that the current improvements will remain, or whether value should be estimated based on the assumption that the current improvements will be demolished and replaced.

The rule is that when the value of the site as if vacant, less the costs of demolishing the existing improvements, exceeds the current value as is, a succession of use is justified and the market value estimate should reflect the higher "as if vacant" value.

Embedded in this rule is the important principle that it is the improvements which absorb the loss in value created by any gap between what they are, and what they *might be* if the site were vacant and available to be developed. Land value is unaffected. For an example of the application of this principle, refer back to Table 5–1. Suppose the site being valued was in fact improved as a service station (Column 3), and as shown the residual land value in that use was ($250,000). Is that really the value of the land? Of course not. It is something higher, as determined by its expected use as if vacant.

The service station is an example of a situation where the value of the land underlying an improvement, in this case $500,000, may exceed the value of the property as is. In such cases, it makes sense to demolish the existing structure(s) and replace it. A common application of this rule is when appraising a single-family home that is on a site zoned for (or which can be zoned for) commercial use. The "as is" value as a house is often less than if the land was vacant and available to be put to a commercial use.

Another way to state the rule is that succession is warranted, and therefore value is based on the land value as if vacant, only when the current improvements have zero or negative value. If the current improvements contribute positively to total value, even if only a small amount, it makes no sense to demolish them. For example, suppose the site analyzed in Table 5–2 was in fact already improved, say as a warehouse, and that it was producing $65,000 of annual income. Assuming an expected return of 10 percent, the value of the property would be $650,000. Clearly it would make no sense in that case to demolish the warehouse improvement worth $150,000 ($650,000 less $500,000).

However, if the same site was currently improved with a service station producing $20,000 of annual income, and it had a value of $20,000/.10 = $200,000, succession would be warranted, as the underlying land value of $500,000 would exceed the "as is" value of $200,000. In that case, the appraised market value of the land would be $500,000 less the costs of demolishing the service station.

Which Expected Use Premise Is Best?

Market value cannot be estimated until a judgment has been made about the property's expected use. The assumption that is generally made in practice is that the expected use is the land-value maximizing highest and best use. However, a growing number of practitioners and writers are questioning how compatible it is with what we believe today about how prices are actually determined in real estate markets. As Kerry Vandell points out, [most] real estate markets are not auctions "in which all bids are known and simultaneous, but . . . rather, a sequential bid process in which the seller does not have a clear perception of all [potential] bids."[9] The result of this bidding process is that at some point a decision is made to sell, even though there is the possibility of a higher bid. The sale is made because higher bids are perceived as unlikely to be received, and then only after further delay.

---

[9] Vandell, "Definitions of Market Value"; see also Richard Green and Kerry Vandell, "Optimal Asking Price and Bid Acceptance Strategies for Residential Sales," Working Paper, University of Wisconsin, 1995.

Thus, the highest possible bid will actually be received only a small percentage of the time, a conclusion that conflicts with the highest and best use assumption that the highest price will in fact be received. Max Derbes has gone further, pointing out that the highest bid is conceptually infinite and that alone is enough to disqualify such wording.[10]

Another way to arrive at a conclusion that market prices do not on average reflect the highest and best use is the observation that if prices did reflect highest and best uses, then the land would be put to that use and all net present values would be zero. Only markets in competitive equilibrium behave that way, and certainly real estate markets cannot generally be described that way. Because of these conceptual and practical difficulties, the expected value and most probable use assumptions are gaining popularity. These assumptions are also consistent with modern market-value definitions, which typically refer to either the expected or the most probable selling price.

Approaching expected use from a probabilistic perspective also has important practical advantages for the appraiser. First, when searching for comparables the appraiser is not forced to operate under the highly restrictive requirement that he or she must identify the highest and best use of the land as if vacant. Instead, a set of feasible uses is the standard. This makes the task of selecting comparable sales manageable. A set of feasible uses is matched up rather than a specific use. Second, when comparables of sufficient quantity and quality are not available and a more fundamental analysis is required, the expected use premise allows the appraiser to work from a set of feasible uses rather than attempting to speculate about the highest and best use.

Having pointed all of this out, however, it is also true that the highest and best use premise continues to dominate appraisal practice, is recommended by the Appraisal Institute, and is accepted most widely in courts of law. Until or unless this changes, the appraiser is well-advised to operate under the highest and best use premise. We follow that advice in the rest of this text.

Other Expected Use Issues

Interim Uses

An interim use is one which is currently the highest and best use of the site, but which is likely to be superseded by another use in a relatively short time.[11] Commonly cited examples are downtown parking lots and farmland on the fringe of development.

---

[10]Derbes, "Highest and Best Use."

[11]A good discussion is found in Mark Galleshaw, "Evaluating Interim Uses," *Appraisal Journal,* January 1994.

While a conclusion that the highest and best use of a property is likely to change in the foreseeable future may be useful information to a client, there is some question as to whether identifying the current use as an interim use has implications for the value estimate. Some writers conclude that it does, and provide rules to determine if the current improvements add value.

However, a careful evaluation suggests that these kinds of analyses may add unnecessary complexity. Because an interim use is defined as the current highest and best use, the analysis leading to the highest and best use conclusion must have concluded that the value in the current use, including any improvements, exceeds the value as if vacant or unused. Thus, the basic test of highest and best use applies equally to an interim use and we are back to where we started: Identifying an interim use provides information, but does not carry with it any valuation implications beyond those already captured in the highest and best use analysis.

Stating this differently, almost all uses can be described as interim uses, assuming that the improvements will eventually be replaced or renovated. From this perspective, all that separates properties "officially" designated as interim uses from all other properties is time; that is, whether a change in highest and best use is foreseeable. This categorization should not affect the value estimate.

Land, Improvements, and Consistent Use

Given that land is valued in its highest and best use as if vacant, it follows that the improvements must be valued under the same highest and best use assumption. For example, suppose a site is valued based on a highest and best use of multifamily, but that the current use is a single-family house. If the site value is $1 million for multifamily use and the property is valued at $200,000 as a single-family house, including $50,000 land plus $150,000 improvements, it would not be proper to value the property at $1,150,000. To do so would ignore the fact that the land is worth $1 million only as multifamily, not as single-family. The improvements have zero value in this case because they must be valued under the same use as was assumed when valuing the land as if vacant. In appraisal practice, this is called the consistent use requirement.

Mixed Uses

Some properties include more than one parcel of land or more than one kind of use. A tract may contain sites suitable for a planned community, including single-family, multifamily, retail, and recreation. In these cases, the value contributed by each use can be estimated separately, then added to arrive at total property value. The same applies to valuing air rights, surface rights, and subsurface (mineral) rights.

This brings up the question of whether the value of the sum of the parts equals the value of the whole. This question is discussed in depth in chapter 23. For now it is sufficient to answer, "sometimes." For example, the individual values of several small sites may be very low because they do not meet minimum size requirements and are therefore unsuitable for development. However, when assembled they become a site large enough to support a legally permissible use, and thus the value as assembled greatly exceeds the total of the individual values beforehand.

Further, if value can be added by dividing the whole (as in the case when subdivisions are developed), then the highest and best use is to divide. Thus, the adage that the parts cannot exceed the whole must be interpreted very carefully. If the assignment is to value the whole as is, it clearly applies. If, however, the assignment is to value the property (or properties) at its highest and best use, assembling or subdividing may in fact add value.

Excess Land

In some cases, there may be land in excess of what is necessary to support the highest and best use. For example, if zoning allows 16 residential units per acre, and a 32-unit apartment is situated on a four-acre tract, it is likely that the two acres of excess land can be developed or sold by the owners, and therefore adds value to the property.

When estimating the contribution of excess land, care should be taken to consider its impact on the value of the remaining property. Returning to the example of a 32-unit residential development, if the excess land is currently wooded and serves as an aesthetic buffer between the development and its neighbors, selling or developing the two acres may have an adverse impact on the rents and vacancies of the existing apartments, thus affecting their value. This must be reflected in the value estimate.

More Efficient Use, Renovation, and Additions

Three kinds of situations present potential conceptual and practical problems for the appraiser when estimating highest and best use and market value. They are (1) the possibility of a more efficient use of the existing improvements, (2) the possibility of profitable additions, and (3) the possibility of profitable renovations or remodeling. The issue in each case is whether the highest and best use conclusion, and in turn the value estimate, will be affected.

Clearly, a more efficient use of the existing improvement must be considered. An example is space that is currently (under)utilized for storage, but which can be leased. A second possibility is that profitable additions can be made. For example, if a 12-unit apartment is on a site zoned for 16 units, how is the value estimate affected by the possibility of additions?

The answer is that if the land value as if vacant is estimated for the entire site, then the value added by the excess land is already counted. If the land value is estimated for only the land necessary to support the units in place, the land available to support the additional four units is excess land, as discussed earlier. Its value is estimated separately and added to the value of the improved portion.

Finally, there is the question of how potentially profitable renovations or remodeling should be handled. It is best answered by example. Suppose land as if vacant has a value of $1 million, net of demolition costs, and that the value of the property as improved is $950,000. Given this information, the highest and best use is vacant land with a market value of $1 million. Now introduce an assumption that the existing improvements could be remodeled at a cost of $200,000, and that this would add $350,000 to the property's value. Thus, the seller could spend $200,000 and produce a value of $1,300,000 ($950,000 + $350,000), or $1,100,000 net of renovation costs. This is preferable to selling for $1 million.

In such cases, the appraiser may find it useful to report more than one value, depending on the definition(s) of the value(s) to be estimated. In a situation such as described above, the "as is" value is $1 million, while the value assuming that the renovations are to be considered is $1,100,000. In such situations the appraiser's best course is to report and explain the assumptions underlying the different value estimates.

Summary

A property's value is a function of its expected use. In practice, expected use is generally defined as that use which will support the highest land value. This land value maximizing use is called the highest and best use. Alternative definitions of expected use are that it is the weighted average of the values of the land under an array of possible uses, or that it is the values of the land under the most probable use, which may or may not be the highest and best use. The most probable use assumption has the advantage of being consistent with the prevailing market value definition, which references the most probable price. Regardless of the expected use definition, the use must be legally and physically possible, financially feasible, and maximally productive.

A determination of expected use requires an estimate of the value of the land as if vacant and the value of the property as is—including any improvements. If the value of the land as if vacant exceeds the value of the property as improved, properly adjusted for demolition costs, then a succession of use is justified, and the market value is the value of the land as if vacant less demolition costs. However, if the value of the property as is exceeds the value of the land as if vacant, then the expected use remains the current use.

The expected use premise is a probabilistic rather than a deterministic analysis. Thus, unlike highest and best use, expected use will produce an array of possibilities, with the estimate of market value being the sum of the weighted contributions to value of each possibility.

Other considerations in an expected use analysis are interim uses, the assumption of consistent use, mixed uses, excess land, and the possibilities of a more efficient use of the improvements as is, or that additions or renovations may have a net positive effect on value.

Questions and Problems

1. Why is a determination of the expected use of the subject property important?
2. What is the highest and best use of vacant land?
3. Discuss some weaknesses in using highest and best use as the underlying premise of market value.
4. What is scoping?
5. When is a succession of land use economically justified?
6. "If comparable sales are available, it is unnecessary to determine the highest and best use because the prices of the comparables will reflect the market's judgment in that regard." Do you agree?
7. Scoping has identified four uses of land with reasonable probabilities of coming to fruition. For each of the four uses, you have completed analyses based on optimistic, pessimistic, and most likely scenarios, and have assigned probabilities to each. Based on your results shown below, what is the expected price of the site? What is the most probable price?

8. If a given land use is certain or almost certain, how can the expected value of the set of feasible uses be identified and quantified?
9. The value of a site as if vacant is $150,000. It would support an improvement with an expected cost of $500,000. As is, the property is worth $185,000 including improvements. What is the estimated market value of the property? Why?
10. In many cases, a residual analysis is not necessary to estimate land value. Why?
11. *a.* Given the information below on two prospective land uses and their associated probabilities and values, what is the estimated market value based on expected use analysis? What is the expected use?

Use	Overall Probability %	Value Distribution of Overall Probability		
		$300,000	$320,000	$340,000
1	70	20%	30%	20%
2	30	—	15	15

b. Under the highest and best use premise, what is the estimated market value?

12. How does highest and best use differ from expected use and most probable use?

Use	Overall Probability (%)	Value Distribution of Overall Probability (000s)				
		$110	$120	$130	$140	$150
A	10	3%	5%	2%	—	—
B	10	2	3	4	1	—
C	20	—	2	7	8	3
D	60	—	20	15	15	10

PART III: Estimating Value: The Sales Comparison Approach

The first of the three appraisal approaches to be discussed is the sales comparison approach. Sales comparison is based on the intuitively appealing conclusion that the value of a property can be estimated based on the selling prices of similar properties. This conclusion is based on two assumptions.

1. Market price is acceptable evidence of market value.
2. Comparable bundles of property rights will sell for comparable prices. In the economics literature, this is often referred to as the law of one-price. In the appraisal literature, it is called the principle of substitution.

Neither of these assumptions works perfectly in any market, and certainly not in most real estate markets. Nevertheless, real estate markets function well enough, often enough, to justify the use of the sales comparison approach when there is sufficient sales data with which to work.

There are three variations of the sales comparison approach. They are: (1) direct sales comparison, (2) direct sales comparison using statistical inference, and (3) sales comparison using regression analysis.

Direct Sales Comparison
is the traditional variation and it continues to dominate appraisal practice. Its use requires only a small sample of comparable sales, there is a relatively high degree of appraiser judgment involved, and it produces a single point estimate of value.

Direct Sales Comparison Using Statistical Inference
is used less often. It requires a larger sample of comparable sales, and when properly used is a relatively more objective approach than is traditional direct sales comparison. A confidence interval around the point estimate of value can also be calculated.

Sales Comparison Using Regression Analysis
is also a statistically based technique, and it generally requires the largest sample of comparable sales. Regression is used to develop a value-estimating equation, or model, that can be used to appraise large numbers of properties. Regression can also be used to explain value as well as to estimate it, and like basic statistical inference it also produces confidence intervals around its estimates. Regression is used most often for mass appraisals, such as those necessary to make assessments for property tax purposes.

The three variations of the sales comparison approach are discussed in the following three chapters. The fourth chapter in this section discusses special considerations when valuing land and building sites.

Chapter 6
Direct Sales Comparison

Introduction

The direct sales comparison approach produces an estimate of the market value of the subject property based on the selling prices of similar properties. The approach is rooted in two fundamental assumptions: (1) that selling prices are a reliable indicator of market value, and (2) that equal (similar) properties should sell for equal (similar) prices. These are the same assumptions that are used when estimating the value of other investments. For example, for the price of a newspaper anyone can "appraise" a company whose stock is listed on an exchange. The market value of General Electric is what investors are paying for the company's publicly traded equity shares. The specific share that was last traded is irrelevant; its value is the value of all shares, because all shares are identical and identical products sell for identical prices.[1]

This process of estimating value by direct sales comparison is the same for real property. The market value of the subject property is the price at which the market participants are buying and selling similar properties. However, unlike securities markets where the homogeneous shares of a given firm are traded frequently, real property rights are generally heterogeneous[2] and tend to be traded infrequently.

This is both bad news and good news for the appraiser. The bad news is that heterogeneous products and infrequent trades make the task of

---

[1] If they didn't, arbitrage opportunities would exist. Smart investors would quickly take advantage of any price difference ("buy low and sell high"), and the difference would quickly disappear. In the real estate appraisal literature, the idea of equal prices for equal products is called the principle of substitution.

[2] Unless the property right has been "securitized," such as in a REIT. In that case, each share (or unit) in the property right is identical and sells for the same amount. This is like the stock market.

83

uncovering evidence of market value more difficult than for products like shares of common stock. We discussed the good news in an earlier chapter: These imperfections are the main reason appraisers exist. If real property rights and the markets in which they traded were like securities markets, the demand for the appraiser's services would be greatly diminished.[3]

In terms of using direct sales comparison as the basis for estimating value, one consequence of heterogeneous property and infrequent trading is that except in the rare case where the property being appraised has itself recently traded, what must generally be compared are not identical properties, but instead close substitutes. This means that adjustments must be made to the price of the comparable property to estimate the price of the subject. A second consequence of infrequent trading in markets with heterogeneous products is that the appraiser is often forced to work with a sample of comparable sales that is quite small.

The process of estimating value using direct sales comparison involves two steps: (1) finding transactions involving property right(s) comparable to those being appraised, including the matching of their respective highest and best uses, and (2) then adjusting the observed prices of the comparables for any differences from the subject to arrive at an estimate of value for the subject.

The discussion that follows is divided into single-family residential and income properties. This is not because the underlying concepts differ, but because the important determinants of comparability differ to such an extent that clarity and understanding are enhanced by separating the discussion into broad property types. We begin with houses.

Valuing Houses Using Direct Sales Comparison

The general strategy when using direct sales comparison is to minimize the number, the size, and the difficulty of necessary adjustments. Thus, it makes sense to select comparable sales based on a close matching of major value-affecting variables, then to adjust their sales prices for differences in the less important variables.

A second consideration in selecting and adjusting comparable sales is the trade-off between quantity and quality. The question of how many comparables are enough will be addressed in more detail later, but in general, the appraiser cannot be so selective as to have an insufficient sample of comparables, or so unselective that the comparables require so many or such large adjustments as to effectively make the "comparables" noncomparable.

---

[3] Investment bankers do employ analysts to ferret out "mispriced" securities; those selling too high or too low. Whether or not those analysts can beat the market is arguable, but in any case no one should confuse their personal estimates of what market value *should be* with what market value *is*.

Selecting Comparables

Suppose you are asked to appraise the fee simple interest in a residential property. Depending on the size of the market in which the house is located and how far back in time you go, there may have been dozens, hundreds, or even thousands of house sales from which to begin the comparable selection process.[4] Where do you begin looking, and at which potential comparables?

As discussed in earlier chapters, research results have confirmed that house prices are primarily a function of where a house is located, when it is sold, how big it is, and how old it is. Thus, the list of potential comparables should be trimmed by concentrating first on these major value-affecting variables.

Where Should You Look?

One of the first tasks is to limit the geographic area for the search. You do not search nationwide for residential comparables. This may seem obvious, but if we were discussing the relevant market for Toyotas, or gasoline, or even large warehouses, the market might well be regional or even national. For houses and for most relatively small properties, however, value theory and empirical evidence suggest that markets are more narrowly defined. This, together with the fact that residential and small-property markets tend to be relatively active, suggests it makes sense to try to confine the search area to a relatively small geographic area. For larger properties, the relevant search area tends to be larger, because these properties trade in a bigger market and tend not to trade frequently enough to provide sufficient comparables close to the subject.

Once the appropriate geographic area has been determined, the guiding principle again becomes closer is better. Comparables selected from the same neighborhood share the same locational attributes as the subject, and the necessity of making large locational adjustments is avoided.

What happens, however, when there are an insufficient number of comparables in the immediate neighborhood? Some writers suggest that in this circumstance, direct sales comparison may be unusable, in effect changing the "closer is better" rule to closer is necessary. That viewpoint defines location as a particular place. However, this may be unnecessarily restrictive because location is best described not only in terms of a place, but also in terms of the general market setting. Thus, there may be two or more equivalent locations in a community. If that is so, comparables can be selected

---

[4]Various agencies and institutions have developed guidelines with respect to comparable selection for appraisals in which they have an interest. An excellent summary of these guidelines is found in Donald Epley, "Guidelines on the Selection of Good Comparable Property for the Sales Comparison Analysis," *The Real Estate Appraiser and Analyst*, Spring 1988.

from equivalent but not necessarily geographically contiguous areas. While there is not much evidence as to the effect on appraisal accuracy of expanding the search area in such a way, research suggests there is no adverse effect. In addition, there is the advantage of allowing the use of direct sales comparison in cases where the immediate neighborhood yields insufficient comparables.[5] The point is, if sufficient comparables are available nearby, use them. If not, at least consider the wisdom of identifying equivalent locations and searching them. All of this assumes the appraiser's search area is at his or her discretion. This may not always be the case. Certain clients may require the use of a limited search area or require a persuasive justification for searching outside that area.

The Question of Time

After delineating the search area, which will trim the list of possible comparables substantially, the next question is, how far back in time should you go when searching for comparables? Again, the general principle is closer is better. If you can avoid time-related adjustments, do so. When a sufficient number of comparables that have sold recently are not available, however, there remains the question of how far back the appraiser should go. The answer is a case-dependent function of the volatility of the market.

Compare, for example, the city of Atlanta with the author's town of State College, Pennsylvania. Values are moving much faster in the former market than in the latter. Thus, while an appraiser in Atlanta may feel uncomfortable going back more than six months, an appraiser in State College may have no qualms using a year-old sale. It is a judgment call, with the decision based on whether or not there have been significant changes in the market during the interim.

In practice, appraisers seldom go back more than two years and an overwhelming percentage of comparable sales selected for use have sold within the past year. There is no reason to invite time-related adjustment problems if they can be avoided.

Physical Characteristics

Having chosen the search area(s) and the relevant time period for the selection of comparables, the appraiser next attempts to find properties that are physically similar to the subject. A reasonable strategy at this point is to attempt to match as closely as possible three physical characteristics: (1) the size and design of the house including, if possible, a matching of the number

---

[5]Kenneth M. Lusht and Frederick Pugh, "Appraising Houses: A Research Note on the Effects of Changing the Search Area for Comparable Sales," *The Real Estate Appraiser and Analyst,* Winter 1981.

FIGURE 6–1 Relationship between Size and Value

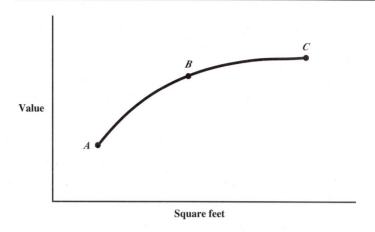

of bedrooms and bathrooms, (2) the size of the lot, and (3) the age of the house.

As far as the size of the house is concerned, recall that researchers have found a nonlinear relationship between square feet and value. That is, the marginal contribution of an added square foot tends to be smaller than the contribution of the previous foot, as in Figure 6–1.

Notice from Figure 6–1 that while the graph is curvilinear, small segments of it, like between points A and B, or points B and C, may be reasonably approximated by a straight line. So while it may be difficult to adjust for the difference between A square feet and C square feet because the line curves markedly between those points, an adjustment from A to B or B to C is easier. Casual evidence based on the experiences of appraisers and brokers suggests that in many markets, it is difficult to isolate a value impact of size differences of less than about 100 square feet unless a different number of rooms is involved.

Regarding lot size and value, the pattern of Figure 6–1 also holds (though if a fixed cost component of the "right to improve" can be isolated, the remaining value may be linearly related to size), and again the idea is to match up size and shape as closely as possible.

When the search area yields insufficient comparables which are the same size, you will be forced to make a bigger size adjustment, remembering the nonlinear size-value relationship for both living area and lot size. If there must be a trade-off between more comparable house size and more comparable lot size, the bias should be toward selecting the comparables closer in respect to house size, since house size generally contributes a larger percentage of total value.

Age

It is difficult to measure the effect of age on the value of real property. First, it is not really age itself that affects value, but rather that age is often associated with a loss of utility due to physical wearing out and out-of-favor characteristics (called functional obsolescence), and it is the loss of utility that is associated with a loss in value. Second, measuring a loss of utility is exceedingly difficult. Thus, age is an approximation for something that itself resists measurement.

Jack Corgel and Hal Smith[6] analyzed the age-value relationship in several markets and concluded that (1) different markets and even submarkets show different relationships, (2) the relationship is neither clearly linear nor nonlinear, and (3) it is effective age, which reflects the initial quality of construction and subsequent maintenance, and not chronological age, that best explains the age-value relationship. This makes sense, because we would expect the quality of construction and/or the level of maintenance of a property to be reflected in prices. It also implies that appraisers' estimates of effective age appear on average to be more reliable than the seemingly more objective measure of chronological age.

The preferred strategy is to select comparables within the narrowest possible range of ages around the age of the subject. In discussions with appraisers, they reported that the market generally has a difficult time pricing age differentials of less than five years. This suggests that for a subject property that is, say, effectively 18 years old, comparables with effective ages between 13–23 years may require relatively small adjustments to their prices. This, of course, may vary among markets.

Time on the Market

A key assumption in the market value definition is that the property will be exposed to the market for a reasonable length of time. Without this assumption, the value estimate is difficult to interpret since there is likely to be a relationship between the price obtained and the time on the market. For example, it is reasonable to speculate that a property that sold after only a few days on the market may have been underpriced, while a property that stayed on the market for a relatively long period may have been overpriced. The latter sells only when appreciation or inflation has time to correct the pricing error.

Thus, the appraiser should be suspicious of prices obtained in transactions that occurred either very quickly or very slowly. By eliminating potential comparable sales that had atypical times on the market, Norm Miller

---

[6]John B. Corgel and Halbert Smith, "The Concept and Estimation of Economic Life in the Residential Appraisal Process," *The Real Estate Appraiser and Analyst,* Winter 1982.

and Michael Sklarz[7] significantly improved the ability of a statistical model to predict the selling price of condominiums in Oahu, Hawaii. In their study, eliminating the 15 percent of the sample sales that had sold relatively slowly or quickly produced the best results. The general lesson for the appraiser is that extreme times on the market, like extremes of other potentially price-affecting variables, should be viewed with skepticism.

How Many Comparables Are Enough?

Real estate markets have characteristics that tend to be associated with inefficient pricing, which means that equivalent bundles of property rights may sell for different prices. Moreover, even if prices are efficient, the process of comparing nonidentical bundles of property rights introduces an element of subjectivity. Thus, while we may trust a single stock exchange transaction as representing current value, that may not be so for a single property transaction. The question then is, how many comparables are enough? There is no hard and fast rule, except that quantity is a function of quality. The higher the quality of the comparable sales, the fewer that are necessary.

A persistent rule of thumb, now institutionalized on many appraisal forms, is the use of three comparables. While no one is certain where the three-comparable rule of thumb came from (though some suggest it is because three fit nicely on 8″-wide forms), there is empirical support for that tradition. Two studies[8] found that appraisal accuracy, as measured by the difference between appraised value and market price, increased as the number of comparables went from one to three or four, but that very little increase in accuracy was achieved by using more than three or four comparables. A third study[9] used simulation to conclude that increasing the number of comparables beyond three or four did reduce the average error of the final value estimate, but that the error declined at a slower rate as the number of comparables increased. This should be comforting to the practitioner, and it also implies that housing markets may be more efficient than conventional wisdom suggests.

One of these studies[10] also investigated the trade-off between comparable quantity and quality. Comparables were chosen and subject properties valued using three alternative locational criteria: (1) restricting comparables to the immediate neighborhood, (2) restricting comparables to similar mar-

---

[7]Norman G. Miller and Michael A. Sklarz, "Multiple Regression Condominium Valuation with a Touch of Behavioral Theory," *The Appraisal Journal,* January 1987.

[8]Lusht and Pugh, "Appraising Houses."; Hans R. Isakson, "Arbitrage Pricing Theory, Adjustment Grid Methods, and the Market-Data Approach to Value," Working Paper, University of Texas at Arlington, 1985.

[9]Kerry D. Vandell, "Optimal Comparable Selection and Weighting in Real Property Valuation," *AREUEA Journal,* Summer 1991.

[10]Lusht and Pugh, "Appraising Houses."

TABLE 6–1 **Average Difference between Estimated Value and Actual Selling Price**

Number of Comparables	Source of Comparables		
	Immediate Neighborhood	Similar Neighborhood	Any Neighborhood
1	15.4%*	11.0%	19.4%
2	8.6	16.2	23.4
3	9.4	8.1	13.9
4	5.3	9.6	16.1
5	6.6	4.7	5.0
6	11.0	8.0	4.3
7	6.3	7.4	10.7

*A very basic computer-aided direct sales comparison approach was used to estimate the values. Thus, the percentage errors should be interpreted relatively, not absolutely.

Source: Kenneth Lusht and Frederick Pugh, "Appraising Houses: A Research Note on the Effects of Changing the Search Area for Comparable Sales," *The Real Estate Appraiser and Analyst*, Winter 1981.

ket settings, and (3) no restrictions, with the comparables selected from the entire community. Table 6–1 shows the results. As the locational criteria is relaxed (comparable quality is reduced), appraisal accuracy suffers and the number of comparables needed to reach a given level of accuracy increases. Notice though, that the biggest gains in accuracy occur up to three to five comparables (depending on the search area).

The Use of Asking ("List") Prices

Particularly when valuing vacant sites or single-family residential properties, it is common to have similar properties currently listed for sale. The question then arises whether the asking or "list" prices of these properties can be used as indicators of the value of the subject property. Hopefully, the adjusted prices of the actual sales and the listings will be consistent. If not, a judgment must be made as to the relative reliability of the transactions versus the listing prices. In general, while list prices can be used, actual transaction prices are strongly preferred.

In sum, while the question of how many comparables are enough is not completely settled, there is evidence to support the commonsense notion that the necessary quantity of comparables is negatively associated with the quality of the comparables, and that the housing market is efficient enough to lend support to the three-comparable rule of thumb. This is not to say that a larger sample would never be useful, especially when there is difficulty finding comparables which meet the basic size, location, timing, and age requirements. Balancing the benefits of a potential improvement in accuracy from gathering additional data against the costs of achieving that potential improvement is a judgment that is required in almost all appraisal assignments. Finally, list prices should not be used instead of transaction prices, but may be used when transactions are unavailable or to support the conclusions drawn from transactions.

Adjusting the Prices of the Comparables

Once a set of comparables has been selected the adjustment process begins. The idea is to begin with the transaction price of each comparable, then adjust it upward or downward to account for differences between the comparable property (and/or the conditions of sale of the comparable property) and the subject property. When making adjustments the subject property is the standard. This means that adjustments are always made from the comparable to the subject. For example, if a comparable property which sold for $100,000 had a garage valued at $7,500 that the subject did not have, the adjusted price of the comparable would be $100,000 − $7,500 = $92,500. This says that *if* the comparable had been like the subject, it would have sold for $92,500. Most of the time there will be several such adjustments to be made to the price of each comparable. When all of them have been made, the final adjusted price of the comparable is the estimated value of the subject property.

An Example

Assume the subject property is a brick ranch with 2,200 square feet of living area. It has 4 bedrooms and 2 baths, and is on a 23,000 square-foot lot. It is 15 years old, and has received average maintenance. It has central air conditioning and a 1-car garage.

From the population of sales that occurred within the past year, the four comparables in Table 6–2 have been selected on the basis of their similarity to the subject so far as location, living area and lot size, age, and condition. All were conventionally financed. Assume also that previous analysis has produced the following adjustments for certain property attributes of interest:

Square feet of living area: $30 per square foot
Bedrooms: $3,200 per bedroom
Bathrooms: $1,400 per full bath, $600 per half bath
Exterior (compared to brick):   Wood-frame   ($4,500)
                                        Aluminum siding ($4,000)
Air conditioning: $2,500
Garage (per car): $2,000
Design (compared to ranch):   Bi-level ($1,500)
Time since sale: 5% per year
Age of house: ($400) per year

TABLE 6-2 Data from Comparable Sales

Variable	Comparable Sale 1	Comparable Sale 2	Comparable Sale 3	Comparable Sale 4
Selling price:	$105,000	$115,000	$122,000	$100,000
Financing:	Conventional	Conventional	Conventional	Conventional
Date of sale:	6 months ago	9 months ago	10 days ago	1 year ago
Condition:	Similar	Similar	Similar	Similar
Location:	Similar	Similar	Similar	Similar
Age:	22 years	12 years	8 years	20 years
Design:	Ranch	Ranch	Bi-level	Ranch
Living area:	2,100 sq. ft.	2,350 sq. ft.	2,400 sq. ft.	2,000 sq. ft.
Bedrooms:	4	4	4	4
Baths:	2	2½	2½	1½
Construction:	Brick	Wood-frame	Brick	Brick
Air conditioning:	No	Yes	Yes	No
Garage:	1-car	1-car	2-car	1-car
Lot size:	Similar	Similar	Similar	Similar

Table 6-3 shows the completed adjustment grid. A conclusion that the value of the subject property is about $115,400 seems justified.

Weighting the Adjusted Prices

Using the average adjusted price of the comparables as the estimate of value (as done for the example above) implies the appraiser feels the comparables are of equal quality; that is, each is equally representative of the subject property. When that is not the case, the appraiser will weight the adjusted prices differently. Typical considerations in judging comparability are the number of adjustments necessary, the dollar amount of the adjustments, and the confidence the appraiser has in the adjustment amounts. If, based on these criteria, the appraiser of the example property above felt Sales #2 and #4 were relatively closer to the subject, or felt more confident with the adjustments made to those comparables as compared to the other two comparables, Sales #2 and #4 might be weighted more heavily. Using weights of .10, .40, .10, and .40 for comparables #1–4 respectively, the estimated value would be $116,248, say, $116,300. In an extreme case where an adjusted price is seriously out of line with the others, and the appraiser suspects there may be something that explains the divergence (such as a sale under duress), it may be ignored (given a weight of zero). However, it is not acceptable to throw out an "outlier" simply because it doesn't produce what the appraiser considers the "right" result. Four alternative weighting schemes that provide for systematic and reproducible methods of weighting are proposed by Cannaday et al.[11]

---

[11] Roger Cannaday, Peter Colwell, and Chunchi Wu, "Weighting Schemes for Adjustment Grid Methods of Appraisal," *Appraisal Review Journal,* Summer 1984.

TABLE 6-3 Sales Adjustment Grid

	Subject	Comparable Sales			
		1	2	3	4
Transaction price		$105,000	$115,000	$122,000	$100,000
Time	Current	+ 2,625*	+ 4,313	—	+ 5,000
Age	15	+ 2,800**	− 1,200	− 2,800	+ 2,000
Design	Ranch	—	—	+ 1,500	—
Living area	2,200	+ 3,000	− 4,500	− 6,000	+ 6,000
Bedrooms	4	—	—	—	—
Bathrooms	2	—	− 600	− 600	+ 600
Construction	Brick	—	+ 4,500	—	—
Air Cond.	Yes	+ 2,500	—	—	+ 2,500
Garage	1 car	—	—	− 2,000	—
Total adjustment		+ 10,925	+ 2,513	− 9,900	+ 16,100
Adjusted price of real property		$115,925	$117,513	$112,100	$116,100

*The time adjustments are based on the given assumption of 5 percent appreciation per year. Using Comparable #1 as an example, it sold 6 months ago, requiring a 2.5 percent upward adjustment to its selling price. $105,000 (.025) = $2,625. No time adjustment is made for Comparable #3 because it sold only 10 days ago.

**For example purposes, an adjustment for age was made to Comparable 1, though as discussed, ages within about five years will often require little or no adjustment.

Average adjusted price = $115,410, say $115,400
Range   = $112,100 – $117,513

Using Percentages Instead of Dollars for Adjustments

All of the adjustments in the grid shown in Table 6–2 were made on an *absolute* dollar basis. Differences between properties may also be described *relatively;* that is, on a percentage basis. For instance, one might say that there is a difference in the conditions of two properties that should produce a 10 percent difference in value. This difference is then translated into dollar terms. If a comparable property sold for $100,000, and its condition is such that it would lose 10 percent of its value if its condition was like the subject property, a $10,000 downward adjustment would be made to the price of the comparable.

When using percentages, they must be stated in terms of their effect on value, and not in terms of the difference in the specific characteristic. Returning to the example $100,000 property, suppose in addition to the 10 percent difference in value attributable to condition, there is also a 10 percent difference in value attributable to location. In this case, both adjustments would be $10,000. It would be misleading (and in most cases incorrect) to say that there is a 10 percent difference in condition, or a 10 percent difference in location, and to conclude that each difference is worth $10,000. A 10 percent difference in location may be worth more or less than a 10 percent difference in condition.

The Order of Adjustments

The order of the adjustments must follow a logical pattern. While there is more than one way to arrive at a correct result, an ordering procedure like the one recommended by the Appraisal Institute is a good model, not only because it is logical, but also because it often requires less number manipulation than other ordering schemes.

The Institute's recommended order is as follows: (1) property rights conveyed, (2) financing, (3) conditions of sale, (4) date of sale, and (5) all remaining locational, physical, and functional characteristics. After the first four adjustments are made (those through market conditions), the adjusted price becomes the base on which the remaining locational, physical, and functional characteristics are calculated.

Note that the first three adjustments reflect the situation *at the time the comparable property was sold.* For example, if a financing adjustment must be made, it must be made with reference to the financing conditions obtained at the time of the comparable sale, because those are the conditions which affected the transaction price. This means that any financing adjustments are made before any time adjustment, so that the time adjustment will be applied to the correct value base.

The date of sale adjustment, in turn, precedes the remaining adjustments because when the remaining adjustments are made on a percentage basis, the percentage refers to today's value, and the time adjustment estimates that value. After the time adjustment, the balance of adjustments can be made to the time-adjusted price in any order.

Sources of Adjustments

When the grid shown in Table 6–3 was presented, the adjustments for various characteristics were given: $2,500 for air conditioning, $400 per year of age, and so on. In practice, there are a number of ways to estimate adjustments. Four of the more commonly used are: (1) matched pairs, (2) regression analysis, (3) cost, and (4) survey.[12]

Matched Pairs

The matched pairs approach extracts the value of a particular characteristic by comparing the selling price of properties which are similar except for the

---

[12] An alternative list of adjustment methods is found in Roger Cannaday, "How Should You Estimate and Provide Market Support for Adjustments in Single-Family Appraisals?" *The Real Estate Appraiser and Analyst,* Winter 1989.

characteristic in question. For example, suppose houses A and B sold for $90,000 and $85,000, respectively. They are similar in all respects, except that A has a 2-car garage, while B has no garage. This observation suggests that the value of a two-car garage is $5,000.

While seldom will two properties differ with respect to only one characteristic, that is not always necessary to use the matched pairs technique. All that is required is that appropriate adjustments be made until only one difference remains. For example, suppose houses C and D sold for $97,000 and $85,000, respectively. They are similar except C has a 2-car garage and a pool, while D has neither. Prior analysis (either matched pairs and/or cost, and/or regression and/or survey) suggests the value of a 2-car garage to be $5,000. This brings the adjusted price of D to $90,000 (or the price of C to $92,000). Now there is only one difference between C and D, the value of the pool. Matching the pair at this point suggests the value of the pool to be $97,000 − $90,000 = $7,000. Given the heterogeneity of real property, and the potential for violations of the one-price rule, it is generally necessary to match several pairs before an adjustment factor can be estimated with reasonable confidence.

The Process of Matching Pairs

In practice, even a small number of comparables can produce what seems to be a sea of numbers to analyze. To deal with the task, the appraiser should develop a sequence of steps that will make the pair-matching process manageable and less prone to error. Below is a seven-step sequence that is relatively efficient, whether it is done by hand or with computer assistance.

- Step 1. Set up two grids, one for data only, the other for matching the pairs and making the necessary adjustments. The listing of variables on both grids should follow the recommended sequence for adjustments (property rights, financing, and so forth).
- Step 2. Cross out any variables for which there are no differences between the comparables and the subject.
- Step 3. Circle (or otherwise indicate) where adjustments must be made. That is, circle which variables differ from the subject. *These are the only adjustments that are to be made.* Differences between comparables do not require adjustments.
- Step 4. Make any adjustments that are given, or can be estimated from previous analysis, remembering that the only prices to be adjusted are those where the comparable differs from the subject. After this and all subsequent adjustments, calculate a new adjusted price for each comparable, and cross out the variable adjusted for.
- Step 5. Find a pair of comparables that match except for one of the remaining variables. The difference in their selling prices (adjusted to that point) is the adjustment for that variable. Make

this adjustment for all of the comparables that differ from the subject.

Step 6. Calculate the new adjusted price of each comparable and cross out the variable adjusted for.

Step 7. Repeat Steps 5–7 until all the necessary adjustments have been made. After all adjustments have been made, the adjusted price of each comparable is the estimated value of the subject property.

An Example

Suppose you have completed the data grid shown below.

		Comparables			
Variable	*Subject*	*1*	*2*	*3*	*4*
Sale price		$112,000	$120,000	$124,000	$120,000
Property rights	Fee Simple	Fee Simple	Fee Simple	Fee Simple	Fee Simple
Financing	Conventional	Conventional	Conventional	Conventional	Conventional
Sale date	2/93	2/93	2/93	2/93	2/92
Size (sq. ft.)	1,700	1,600	1,800	1,800	1,800
Age	16	20	20	18	20
Air conditioning	Yes	Yes	Yes	Yes	Yes
Condition	Good	Excellent	Good	Good	Excellent
Garage spaces	2	2	2	2	2

As part of Step 1, it is recommended that a second grid be used, leaving space to make adjustments.

Adjustment Grid

		Comparables			
Variable	*Subject*	*1*	*2*	*3*	*4*
Sale price		$112,000	$120,000	$124,000	$120,000
Property rights	Fee Simple				
Financing	Conventional				
Sale date	2/93	2/93	2/93	2/93	2/92
Adjusted price					
Size	1,700	1,600	1,800	1,800	1,800
Age	16	20	20	18	20
Air conditioning	Yes				
Condition	Good	Excellent	Good	Good	Excellent
Garage spaces	2				

Step 2 is to cross out (or remove) any variables for which all the comparables and the subject are the same. This is done on the Adjustment Grid above for Property rights, Financing, Air conditioning, and Garage spaces.

Chapter 6 Direct Sales Comparison

This leaves four variables that will need adjustments: Sale date, Size, Age, and Condition.

Step 3 is to circle those variables that differ from the subject. Using the data grid for reference, the circles have been entered on the adjustment grid as shown below.

Step 4 is to make any adjustments possible based on prior analysis. In this case, assume that prices have been rising at a 5 percent annual rate. The necessary adjustment to Comparable 4, which sold 12 months ago, is .05 × $120,000 = $6,000. New adjusted prices are then calculated, and the date of sale variable crossed out or removed.

		Comparables			
Variable	Subject	1	2	3	4
Sale price		$112,000	$120,000	$124,000	$120,000 2/92
Sale date					(+ 6,000)
Adjusted price		$112,000	$120,000	$124,000	$126,000
Size	1,700	(1,600)	(1,800)	(1,800)	(1,800)
Adjusted price		+ $7,000	− $7,000	− $7,000	− $7,000
		$119,000	$113,000	$117,000	$119,000
Age	16	(20)	(20)	(18)	(20)
Condition	Good	(Excellent)	Good	Good	(Excellent)

[Handwritten note in margin: inferior (+) / superior (−)]

Step 5 is to find a pair that matches, except for *one* of the *remaining* variables. Referring to the adjustment grid, Comparables 1 and 4 match except for size. There is a 200 square-foot difference between them, and a $14,000 difference in price. This gives an adjustment for size of $14,000/200 = $70 per square foot. This square-foot adjustment is made for each of the comparables circled. For example, Comparable 1 is 100 square feet smaller than the subject, requiring a $7,000 upward adjustment of its selling price, while Comparables #2–4 are 100 feet larger, requiring $7,000 downward adjustments.

Step 6 is to calculate new adjusted prices for all comparables, and to cross out the size variable. This is done on the grid below.

We now repeat Steps 5–7 as many times as necessary. In this case, adjustments are needed for Age and Condition. Comparables 2 and 3 are the same for Condition, but differ with respect to Age, requiring a $2,000 per year adjustment. Because the comparables are all older than the subject, the adjustments are all positive. This is shown below on the relevant portion of the grid.

		Comparables			
Variable	Subject	1	2	3	4
Adjusted price		$119,000	$113,000	$117,000	$119,000
Age		+ 8,000	+ 8,000	+ 4,000	+ 8,000
Adjusted price		$127,000	$121,000	$121,000	$127,000
Condition	Good	Excellent	Good	Good	Excellent
		− 6,000			− 6,000
		$121,000	$121,000	$121,000	$121,000

The age variable would now be crossed out, leaving only condition. Comparables #1 and #4 differ from Comparables #2 and #3, giving an adjustment of $6,000, and a final adjusted price of $121,000 for all four comparables. This adjusted price is the estimated value of the subject.

In Practice

The example above illustrates the matching pairs process. In the market, of course, there will never be these kinds of textbook-perfect matches where all of the comparables arrive at the same adjusted price. Also, a number of adjustments will probably have to be made not by a matching of the comparables in the grid, but rather from prior analysis or other methods such as cost.

It may also not be possible to find a pair that match exactly except for one variable, even under ideal circumstances. For example, repeat sales are often used by appraisers to estimate adjustments for price differences attributable to the date-of-sale; that is, the same house selling twice within a relatively short time period. However, even this apparently ideal matched pair differs in at least one other variable besides the date-of-sale; that is, the age of the house has also changed between sales. In some cases, the appraiser may decide that some differences are small enough to ignore. For example, a difference of a few months of age may have only a trivial impact on price.

The appraiser must also guard against double-counting. For example, suppose a comparable property had 200 more square feet and one more room than the subject. Adjusting for both size and the number of rooms would likely be double-counting. The decision in such cases must rely on the appraiser's experience and judgment.

Finally, regardless of the quality of available data, the final adjusted prices of the comparable can be expected to differ and the appraiser at that point must use judgment to arrive at a single number or a value range. This focuses on one of the weaknesses of the adjustment process. Because it relies heavily on judgment and is nonstatistical, there is no objective measure of the confidence the appraiser has (or should have) in the adjustments that are made.

Regression Analysis

Regression is a statistical tool that may be appropriate for use when a relatively large sample of transactions is available. It is covered in detail in Chapter 8. As you will learn, the coefficient of a value-affecting variable (like square feet) in a regression equation measures the impact of that variable on selling price. You will also learn that for various reasons, the coefficients may be subject to distortion and must be used with care.

Some analysts suggest that a "hybrid" sales comparison approach that combines the traditional matched pairs and regression analysis may produce better results than straightforward regression, particularly for relatively homogeneous properties.[13]

Cost

The depreciated cost to produce is one of the three basic appraisal approaches. The cost approach is covered in detail in subsequent chapters, so only enough description will be provided here to meet the present purpose. The cost approach can be used to value a structure as a whole, or the individual components of the structure. When making adjustments to sales prices using cost, it is the individual components of the structure that are important.

The rationale is straightforward: The value of a component should be approximately equal to what it would cost to have it added to the structure, less any accrued depreciation. The problem with using cost to estimate the value of individual components of a building is that the cost to produce each part of an improvement separately usually exceeds the cost to produce the component as part of the building in its entirety. Ask any homeowner who has added a room or a porch.

The potential seriousness of this problem for the appraiser is suggested by results from several different surveys. In 1986, *New Shelter* magazine asked appraisers and salespeople to estimate the value added by 20 different types of home improvement projects. The estimates were based on the assumption of a 25-year-old suburban ranch house with three bedrooms and one-and-a-half baths. Before the improvements, the house was assumed to have a value of $80,000, which at the time was mid-price.

Below are the estimated percentage increases in value, as a percentage of cost, for a sample of the improvements.

---

[13]Han-Bin Kang and Alan K. Reichert, "An Empirical Analysis of Hedonic Regression and Grid-Adjustment Techniques in Real Estate Appraisal," *AREUEA Journal,* Spring 1991. See also Joseph Lipscomb and J. Brian Gray, "An Empirical Investigation of Four Market-Derived Adjustment Methods," *Journal of Real Estate Research,* Spring 1990.

Interior facelift	107% (highest)
Basement conversion	98%
Standard bath remodel	71%
Landscaping	52%
Swimming pool	46%
Window and door replacement	43% (lowest)

A 1988 survey in *Remodeling Contractor* produced an equally wide range of results. For example, a fireplace was found to add 38 percent more value to a house than its cost to install. A full bath produced a 22 percent premium. At the other end of the spectrum, the value of a pool was only 33 percent of its cost to install. Similarly, a 1989 survey of real estate professionals in New York, published by Citibank, showed differences of up to 300 percent between remodeling costs and value added. The differences between the costs and values of various annuities will of course be market-specific. In Dallas, Texas, a property owner may be able to recover almost 100 percent of the cost of central air conditioning, while in Bangor, Maine, the percentage might approach zero.

Despite the potential gap between cost and value, cost may be the only available way to estimate the value of certain variables. How serious any resulting errors will be in terms of the estimate of total property value will depend on the size of the cost-value gap and the relative contribution to total value of the attribute. For example, if a garage has a "true" market value of $6,000, and the depreciated cost to reproduce is estimated to be $8,000, that 33 percent ($2,000/$6,000) error in estimating the garage's value translates into only a 2 percent error when valuing a house with a total value of $100,000.

Survey

Sometimes market participants can help the appraiser judge the value of a property characteristiccwhen direct market evidence is lacking. A simple survey of homeowners and/or those in the market for houses can provide ballpark estimates that may be as reliable as matched pairs, regression analysis, or cost. In effect, the appraiser sets up a hypothetical matched pair situation by asking how much extra a buyer would be willing to pay for the attribute in question.

Adjusting for Financing: The Cash Equivalency Model

When interest rates on mortgage loans rise to relatively high levels, as occurred in the late 1970s and early 1980s, there may be problems of affordability in housing markets and profitability in investment property markets.

These problems can be made less severe if the seller provides financing for the property at a below-institutional rate. Presuming the institutional rate to be the right rate given the risks involved, supplying a below-institutional rate means the seller/lender is accepting less return than the risk demands. In that situation, economic theory predicts that the seller will in turn demand compensation in the form of an increased transaction price. The resulting transaction price is therefore the sum of two values: the value of the real property plus the value of the favorable financing. Whenever an appraiser is using such a sale as a comparable, an adjustment must be made to the transaction price to remove the value of the premium paid by the seller. One way to estimate the necessary adjustment is by using the cash equivalency model.

The Cash Equivalency Model

When using the cash equivalency model, the value of the financing adjustment is measured as the present value of the difference between the mortgage payment on the favorably financed note and the mortgage payment that would have been required had the note been at the institutional interest rate.

The logic is straightforward. The present value of the favorable financing is what the seller is giving up by supplying the below market-value rate, and is therefore the amount we would expect to be added to the transaction price to compensate the seller. Subtracting this amount from the transaction price produces the value of the real property. This is the price the property would have sold for if the seller had not supplied favorable financing. That is, if the buyer had arranged standard institutional financing, and the seller had therefore received all cash from the buyer (thus the name cash equivalency).

To calculate the value of the difference between actual and institutional mortgage payments, we need two (related) skills not yet covered: (1) the calculation of the mortgage payment, given the loan amount and the terms of the loan, and (2) the discounting of the cash flows. Calculating the mortgage payment is covered in detail in Chapters 15 and 18, and discounting is covered in Chapter 16. In this chapter you will be given the necessary mathematical results.

Suppose a comparable sale occurred at a transaction price of $120,000, and was financed by the seller with a $90,000 note, amortized over 15 years at 9 percent interest. The market rate of interest at the time of the sale was 12 percent, and the assumption is that the price of $120,000 includes a premium traceable to the favorable interest rate. That premium must be subtracted from the $120,000 to arrive at the value of the real estate.

Using a calculator, we find:

Monthly mortgage payment at 12%:	$1,080.15
Monthly mortgage payment at 9%:	912.84
Difference:	$ 167.31

Thus, the seller is giving up $167.31 each month for 15 years. The second step is to calculate the present value of this difference at the market interest rate of 12 percent (1 percent per month).

The present value of $167.31 per month for 180 months (15 years × 12) is $13,941. The seller is giving up this amount by offering 9 percent financing, and we would expect that it would then be added to the transaction price. Therefore, the value of the real property is estimated to be:

$$V = \$120,000 - \$13,941$$
$$= \$106,059$$

An alternative way to estimate the value of the favorable financing is to discount the monthly debt service to be received ($912.84) at the monthly *market* interest rate (1 percent) for 180 months. This produces a mortgage value of $76,059, which when added to the equity of $120,000 − $90,000 = $30,000, produces the real property value of $106,059.

While the cash equivalency calculation is straightforward, most studies have found that the model does an uneven job of estimating the actual market value of the favorable financing.[14] The consensus is that the actual price of the favorable financing averages between 30–70 percent of the cash equivalency price.[15] In other words, the cash equivalency approach tends to overestimate the price of the favorable financing, which means that it underestimates the value of the real property.

There are a number of explanations for the divergence between the cash equivalency model and market experience. With reference to housing markets, one of the more plausible explanations is that buyers tend to prepay mortgage loans, and therefore they expect to receive only a portion of the savings they would receive if the loan were kept through maturity. From the seller's standpoint, there is some evidence of a negative association between time on the market and the offering of favorable financing, at least during periods of historically high interest rates.[16] Thus, the cost to the seller of accepting a below market interest rate is at least partially offset by a reduction in the opportunity cost associated with time on the market.

For income properties, there may be tax implications that offset some of the above. A higher price produces higher depreciation write-offs and

---

[14]See for example, Kenneth T. Rosen, "Creative Financing and House Prices: A Study of Capitalization Effects," *Housing Finance Review,* April 1984; G. Stacy Sirmans, C. F. Sirmans, and Stanley D. Smith, "The Effect of Assumptions Financing on Residential Property Values," *Federal Home Loan Bank Board Journal,* August 1983.

[15]One study of loan assumptions suggests that the percentage varies with the loan-to-value-ratio. See Mark Sunderman, Roger Cannaday, and Peter Colwell, "The Value of Mortgage Assumptions: An Empirical Test," *The Journal of Real Estate Research,* Summer 1990.

[16]E. J. Ferrerra and G. S. Sirmans, "Selling Price, Financing Premiums, and Days on the Market," Working Paper, Florida State University, 1989.

ultimately, lower capital gains. The empirical evidence is so thin, however, that any conclusions about behavior or motivation must be tentative.

When selecting comparables, the obvious suggestion (again!) is to avoid using non-institutionally financed properties. This choice, however, may not be available to the appraiser because of a lack of alternative comparables, leaving the problem of how to make the necessary adjustment for financing. Other approaches open to the appraiser are the same as for other value-affecting variables: matched pairs, regression, and survey. Regression is subject to the same limitations pointed out earlier. Surveys may produce reasonable results, though the subtleties of financing may be such that relatively uneducated opinions may produce unreliable results.[17] This leaves matched pairs. While conceptually sound, there is the difficulty that the terms of favorable financing tend to be case-dependent, and it is hard to find a sufficient sample of transactions from which to extract the values of the almost infinite variety of financing arrangements.

Where does this leave us? If avoidance is not possible, try to find comparables for which adjustments can be made on firmer ground. If that is not possible, then matched pairs is suggested. If that can't be done, an approximation of market value based on the cash equivalency approach is a last resort. When using the cash equivalency approach, keep in mind that historical evidence suggests better results are obtained if the likely prepayment period is considered. Mechanically, this means limiting the analysis to the expected holding period of the loan. Returning to the example of the $120,000 transaction financed with a $90,000, 9 percent loan for 15 years, if prepayment after 7 years is assumed, the present value of the debt service over the 7 years, plus the present value of the mortgage balance after 7 years is $78,723. When added to the downpayment of $30,000, the value of the real property is estimated to be $108,723.

Other Financing Issues

While the effects of favorable seller financing have received the most attention in the appraisal literature, the appraiser should be aware that other kinds of financing agreements may also affect transaction prices. For example, it has been found that the prices paid for houses are negatively associated with potential problems associated with mortgage contingency clauses. In one study, sellers were willing to accept less as the probability increased that buyers would be able to arrange the type of mortgage financing specified in the sales agreement.[18] In two other studies, it was found that

---

[17]Uneducated in the sense that when looking for a house, most buyers quickly become aware of the values of physical components, but are exposed to the subtleties of pricing nonmarket financing only when confronted with a specific negotiation.

[18]J. Shilling, C. F. Sirmans, G. Turnbull, and J. Benjamin, "Hedonic Prices and Contractual Contingencies," *Journal of Urban Economics,* July 1992.

sellers of row houses were willing to accept discounts of about 16 percent if the sales contract was not contingent on buyers being able to arrange for mortgage financing.[19]

These relatively recent findings are likely to reopen the question of the financing assumption incorporated in the most widely used market value definitions. Those definitions refer to . . . "cash or terms equivalent to cash . . . ," which is routinely interpreted to mean cash or typical terms of debt. Implicit in this interpretation is the assumption that the cash price will equal the price when the buyer obtains debt financing. Put differently, the definition is stated in terms of cash to the seller. The evidence, however, suggests that this is insufficient, as cash to the seller does not distinguish where the cash comes from. A decision will have to be made as to whether market value is to be defined in terms of an all equity sale or in terms of typical debt-equity ratios.

It is easy to think of other kinds of contractual arrangements which may also affect prices. One example would be a contract contingent on the buyer selling his or her current house. The appraiser must be aware of this possibility and carefully confirm that all sales being considered as comparables were transacted under typical contractual arrangements. When differences exist an appropriate adjustment must be made.

Is There a Business-Value Component?

An emerging issue with respect to allocating a transaction price is the extent to which the price may include business as well as real estate value. Traditionally, the adjusted selling prices of properties have been assumed to be totally attributable to real estate. This assumption is being challenged by some. Most attention has been focused on shopping centers, given that they are management-intensive and that rent is often partially or wholly a function of the (business) income of the tenants. If in fact part of a transaction price is properly attributable to business value, there are important tax implications such as allowable depreciation expense, the calculation of capital gains, and the assessment for property tax purposes. There would also be valuation issues relating to the differing risks of the income streams attributable to real estate versus business value.

Others do not accept the idea of a business-value component to real estate. They ascribe to the traditional notion that what some call business value is in reality simply an aspect of highest and best use and is therefore

---

[19]Paul K. Asabere, Forrest H. Huffman, and Seyed Mehdian, "The Price Effects of Cash versus Mortgage Transactions," *Journal of the American Real Estate and Urban Economics Association,* Spring 1992; Andrew Hansz and Kenneth Lusht, "Some Further Evidence on the Price of Mortgage Contingency Clauses," *Journal of Real Estate Research,* 1994.

properly reflected in land values. As of mid 1996, the issue was still largely unresolved, and with the exception of hotel properties it is not yet common in appraisal practice to allocate the transaction prices of run-of-the-mill properties into real estate and business components. Vernor and Rabianski[20] provide an excellent discussion of the issue.

Units of Comparison

To this point the direct sales comparison approach has been discussed in terms of adjusting the selling prices of comparable properties to estimate the value of the subject property. In other words, the unit of comparison has been the whole property.

There are two reasons the whole property is generally used as the unit of comparison for houses. First and most important, buyers and sellers tend to compare on the basis of the whole house and the appraiser attempts to mirror market behavior whenever possible. Second, housing markets are generally active enough to provide sufficient comparables that are similar in size to the subject.

When size differs enough to make a direct comparison difficult, the whole property may be broken into smaller units of comparison. For residential properties, the most commonly used unit of comparison (after the whole property) is the price per square foot of living area.[21]

Look back at Table 6–2. The four comparables have adjusted sales prices of $115,925, $117,513, $112,100, and $116,100, and living areas of 2,100, 2,350, 2,400, and 2,000 square feet, respectively. Their adjusted selling prices per square foot are:

Sale	Adjusted Price per Square Foot
1	$\frac{\$115,925}{2,100} = \$55.20$
2	$\frac{\$117,513}{2,350} = \$50.01$
3	$\frac{\$112,100}{2,400} = \$46.71$
4	$\frac{\$116,100}{2,000} = \$58.05$

---

[20]James Vernor and Joseph Rabianski, *Shopping Center Appraisal and Analysis*, Appraisal Institute, Chicago 1993.

[21]Other units which have been used (but seldom are) are the sales price per cubic foot, the sales price per room, and the sales price per square foot of site area covered.

The average adjusted price per square foot is $52.49, with a range of $46.71–$58.05. Using the average price per square foot of $52.49, a subject property of 2,200 square feet has a value of 2,200 × $52.49 = $115,478, or $115,500.

There is something of a catch-22 in using a unit of comparison like price per square foot as a solution for size differentials among comparables and/or among the comparables and the subject. Because the relationship between size and value tends to be nonlinear, it is not proper to apply a square foot price to a property that is significantly different in size from the comparable(s), yet a size difference is often the reason given for using such units of comparison. The point is that if nonlinearity is suspected, appropriate adjustments must be made. Keep in mind also that the conversion to the selected unit of comparison is generally made after the time adjustment. This gives a current unit value to which the remainder of adjustments are then made.

Income Properties

Recall that this chapter is divided into residential and income properties not because the theory of direct sales comparison differs by property type, but because the techniques and terminologies do. Because the theory remains intact, this part of the chapter is shorter. What is added is a discussion of guidelines for selecting comparables and examples of units of comparison that are routinely used in the valuation of income properties.

Selecting Comparables

Income properties are relatively heterogeneous and are infrequently sold. This often makes it difficult to find sales of properties that are similar enough to the subject to be used for direct sales comparison.

Offsetting this, the search area for income property comparables can often be larger than it is for residential properties. It is not uncommon to use comparables dispersed widely within a community and there are occasions when comparables from other communities are used. The key, just as it is for houses, is to identify the relevant market area. While the "closer is better" rule might still be a good one to follow when valuing a small apartment property, the appraiser may be justified in searching regionally or even nationally for the price of comparable properties when valuing a regional shopping mall or an industrial property.

Units of Comparison

For income properties, where the motivation for investment is future income, the units of comparison which tend to determine value are the units which generate that income. For example:

Chapter 6 Direct Sales Comparison

Type of Property	Commonly Used Units of Comparison
Apartments	Apartment units, number of rooms, square feet
Office space	Square feet
Retail space	Square feet
Warehouses	Square feet, cubic feet, loading docks
Factories	Square feet, cubic feet, machine unit
Theaters	Number of seats
Nursing homes, Hospitals	Number of beds

In addition to these physical units of comparison, a financial unit of comparison that is often used is the gross income multiplier (GIM), which is the relationship between gross income and selling price, and is similar to the price/earnings ratios often used in securities analysis. That is,

$$\frac{Price}{Gross\ Income} = GIM.$$

Many appraisers prefer to include the gross income multiplier in the direct sales comparison part of the appraisal report, though it is considered to be part of the income approach on the *Uniform Residential Report Form* for single-family residential properties.

Units of Comparison: An Office Building Example

You are appraising a 2-story office property with 37,000 square feet of gross area and 30,000 square feet of rentable area. Rent is $8.50 per foot of rentable area. You have judged the location to be good. There seems no threat of serious decline in either the community or the immediate area. The property is producing $255,000 of annual gross income (30,000 × $8.50). Three comparable sales are located, with the characteristics shown in Table 6–4.

TABLE 6–4 Characteristics of Comparable Sales

	Sale #1	Sale #2	Sale #3
Transaction price	$2,800,000	$1,700,000	$600,000
Financing	Conventional	Favorable	Conventional
Date of sale	18 months ago	7 months ago	30 months ago
Location	Similar	Similar	Similar
Gross income	$ 390,000	$ 210,000	$ 75,000
Number of floors	4	2	1
Rentable square feet	44,900	24,600	9,470
Gross square feet	56,000	32,000	13,500

TABLE 6–5 Adjustment Grid

	1	2	3
Transaction price	$2,800,000	$1,700,000	$600,000
Financing	—	− 125,000	—
	$2,800,000	$1,575,000	$600,000
Date of sale	315,000	68,906	112,500
Adjusted selling price of real property	$3,115,000	$1,643,906	$712,500
Adjusted price per rentable foot (average = $70.48)	$69.38	$66.83	$75.24
Adjusted price per gross foot (average = $53.26)	$55.63	$51.37	$52.78
Gross income	390,000	210,000	75,000
GIM (average = 7.56)	7.18	7.50	8.0

You have analyzed the favorable financing of Sale #2 and concluded that at the time of the sale, the selling price of $1,700,000 included $125,000 attributable to the below-market interest rate supplied by the seller. Also, office properties have been appreciating at 7.5 percent per year, and there is no reason to believe these properties were exceptions.

Table 6–5 shows the adjustment grid, with three units of comparison calculated.

Notice that the GIMs are calculated based on the finance-adjusted prices, but *before* the time adjustment. This is because it is assumed that if appreciation has occurred—at an annual rate of 7.5 percent in this example—it has affected both value and gross income. Adjusting both value and gross income by the same appreciation rate has no effect on the GIM, and it is easier to leave both alone. What cannot be done is to use a time-adjusted price with unadjusted gross income or vice versa.

This is not to say that GIMs don't change over time due to changes in the market. If you suspect that has occurred, however, the proper strategy is to look at income approach techniques (covered in succeeding chapters) other than the GIM to estimate value.

The use of GIMs is also limited in cases where the leases in place are written at below or above-market rents. Clearly this will affect the property's value, and again, it is not logical to calculate a GIM based on a property generating above-market rent to a subject property producing market or below-market rent. As is the case of time-related changes, the appraiser in this situation is generally better off to utilize a different income approach technique than to attempt to adjust the GIM.

Because nonmarket rents create problems, in practice GIMS are used mainly for appraising relatively small income-producing properties, especially multifamily, because such properties usually are not encumbered by long-term leases at nonmarket rents.

Returning to the example property, using the averages of the three units of comparison produces this set of value estimates:

GIM:	7.56 × $255,000	=	$1,927,800
Price per rentable foot:	$70.48 × 30,000	=	$2,144,400
Price per gross foot:	$53.26 × 37,000	=	$1,970,620

Further information is provided by the ranges of indicated values:

GIM:	7.18 ($255,000)	=	$1,830,900
	8.0 ($255,000)	=	$2,040,000
Price per rentable foot:	$66.83 (30,000)	=	$2,004,900
	$75.24 (30,000)	=	$2,257,200
Price per gross foot:	$51.37 (37,000)	=	$1,900,690
	$55.63 (37,000)	=	$2,058,310

Recall that when averages are used, the implicit assumption is that the comparables are equal, and are weighted equally. This is always a judgment call. Comparable #3, for example, is relatively small and it sold 2½ years ago. It produced a GIM and a price per rentable foot that are high compared to the other two comparables, but a price per gross foot that is similar. Should it be used? As in the case for houses, the covering principle is that if you have a sufficient number of comparables you feel more comfortable with, there is nothing wrong with ignoring an apparent outlier, assuming as in this case, there is evidence that the "comparable" may in fact be noncomparable.

Fortunately, including or rejecting an apparent outlier often won't make a big difference in the final result. If we discard Sale 3, the values based on the average of the units of comparison for Sales 1 and 2 are as follows:

GIM:	7.34 × $255,000	=	$1,871,700
Price per rentable foot:	$68.11 × 30,000	=	$2,043,300
Price per gross foot:	$53.50 × 37,000	=	$1,979,500

The results are similar. The biggest difference is in the value estimate based on rentable square feet, and it is only 4.7 percent.

There are other ways the appraiser may choose to weight the comparables. For example, if Sale 2 is across the street while Sale 1 is across town, and other things are about equal, you may choose to estimate value based on the units of comparison from Sale 2, with the evidence from Sale 1 (and perhaps Sale 3) relegated to a supporting role. Assuming all the comparables are weighted equally, a value estimate approaching $2 million seems justified.

Units of Comparison: An Apartment Example

Table 6–6 shows the relevant information, as well as the calculated units of comparison, from four comparables and a subject apartment property.

TABLE 6–6   Units of Comparison

	Subject	Comparable Sale			
		#1	#2	#3	#4
Transaction price		$3,400,000	$1,450,000	$1,700,000	$2,600,000
Financing†		− 200,000	Conventional	Conventional	Conventional
Time††		Current	+ 43,500	+ 68,000	+ 208,000
Time-adjusted selling price of real property		$3,200,000	$1,493,500	$1,768,000	$2,808,000
Units	130	160	70	95	112
Rooms	572	704	315	380	616
Rooms per unit	4.4	4.4	4.5	4.0	5.5
Gross income	$428,000	$ 525,000	$ 227,000	$ 293,000	$ 375,000
Gross income/Room/Month	$62.35	$62.14	$60.05	$64.25	$50.73
Price per room		$4,545	$4,741	$4,653	$4,558
Price per unit		$20,000	$21,336	$18,611	$25,071
GIM		6.10	6.39	5.80	6.93

†Sale #1 was financed by the seller at a favorable interest rate. You estimate that this added $200,000 to the transaction price.

††Apartment properties appreciated by 12 percent per year over the past 2 years. Comparable 2 sold Comparable 3 months ago, Comparable 3 sold 4 months ago, and Comparable 4 sold 8 months ago.

Sales 1, 2, and 3 produce relatively consistent levels for the indicated units of comparison. Sale 4 differs in gross income per room, and it also sold at a somewhat higher multiple of gross income. This may be a signal that it is not as comparable as the appraiser initially assumed, and further analysis of the property and sale are indicated.

Assuming Sale 4 is ignored, the units of comparison show the following:

	Range	Average
Price per room:	$ 4,545–$ 4,741	$ 4,646
Price per unit:	$18,611–$21,336	$19,982
GIM:	5.80–6.39	6.10

If equal weight is given to each of these three comparables, the estimated value of the subject property is:

	Value	Range
Per room (572 × $4,646):	$2,657,512	$2,599,740–2,711,852
Per unit (130 × $19,982):	2,597,660	2,419,430–2,773,680
GIM (6.10 × $428,000):	2,610,800	2,482,400–2,734,920

If there is no reason to choose a certain unit of comparison as more reliable, an estimated value around $2,600,000 seems appropriate.

Bracketing Prices to Estimate Value

There will be many times when the quantity or quality of the comparable sales data is insufficient to allow a traditional matched pairs analysis. In these cases, even though the magnitude of adjustments is unknown the appraiser may still be able to arrive at a reasonable value range based on the direction of adjustments.

An Example

A service station is being appraised. The grid below summarizes the information for those variables the appraiser believes have the most impact on value.

		Comparable		
Variable	Subject	1	2	3
Sale price		$340,000	$280,000	$400,000
Square feet (Bldg.)	1,200	1,300	1,100	1,700
No. of bays	2	2	2	2
Square feet (Site)	20,000	16,000	15,000	24,000
Corner	Yes	No	No	Yes
Traffic count	40,000	45,000	29,000	43,000
Age of building	9	15	13	9
No. of curb cuts	2	2	2	2

Five variables remain after deleting the Number of Bays and the Number of Curb Cuts because they are the same across all comparables and the subject. Assuming that prior analysis indicates a value of $60 per square feet of building area, the size-adjusted prices are $334,000, $286,000, and $370,000 for comparables 1–3, respectively. Our grid now looks like this:

		Comparable		
Variable	Subject	1	2	3
		$334,000	$286,000	$370,000
Square feet site	20,000	16,000(+)	15,000(+)	24,000(−)
Corner ?	Yes	No(+)	No(+)	Yes
Traffic count	40,000	45,000(−)	29,000(+)	43,000(−)
Age of building	9	15(+)	13(+)	9

Assuming that no other adjustments can be made from prior analysis, an inspection of the grid above shows that there are large differences among the remaining variables, and that there are no pairs that have only one difference. At this point, the appraiser can move to the price-bracketing procedure, judging each variable to require either a '+' or a '−' adjustment as shown next to the variable values above.

The '+'s and '−'s can be weighted if desired. For example, if the appraiser believes that a corner location is relatively more important than a few years of age, then the corner variable would be counted more heavily. An inspection of the grid above suggests that the value of the subject property is likely to be above $334,000 and below $370,000. Given the pattern of '+'s and '−'s in a particular situation and the relative importance of the variables, it may also be possible to be somewhat more precise; for example, that value is likely to fall toward the upper or lower end of the range.

Future Prospects and Comparability

When selecting comparable sales, one criterion that must be kept in mind is that the future prospects for the properties must be comparable. It is not sufficient that the comparables and the subject are currently producing similar rents in similar market settings. It is also necessary that they appear to have future prospects that are "similar." Remember, investors pay for *future benefits.* A common example is when an otherwise comparable property has a long-term lease in place at nonmarket rents. In such cases an adjustment is necessary to make it similar to the subject property. More will be said about this when we cover the income approach, but the basic idea will remain the same: The acid test of comparability is what the market expects to happen in the future.

Sources of Information

Unlike the stock market, where transaction prices are readily available and where audited corporate income and balance sheets are accessible, real property transactions tend toward private negotiations and a lack of standardized recordkeeping. Thus, the process of gathering data for a particular assignment often seems like fitting together the pieces of a jigsaw puzzle, and it is the appraiser's task to track down potential sources of information until he or she is satisfied with the quantity and quality of data that has been gathered.

There are many potential sources of data. They include public records, multiple listing books and other computerized sales and listing records, interviews with buyers, sellers, and lenders, sharing of data with brokers and other appraisers, and classified ads. In addition, there are data banks kept by professional appraisal associations and private firms.[22] As an appraisal business grows, a primary source of information will become the appraiser's own data generated during previous appraisals.

Supporting a Value Estimate: Other Indicators

Using Value Trends

Observers of real estate markets are often heard commenting on general market trends. For example, that house prices in a certain city increased by an average of 7 percent annually between 1991–94, or that hotel properties in a given region declined in value at an annual rate of 4 percent between 1989–93, or that nationally, office building values have remained level during the past two years. These kinds of facts about market trends have varying degrees of utility for the appraiser. While national trends probably will not mean much when appraising a house in Burlington, Vermont, the fact that prices in Burlington itself have increased by 32 percent during the past six years may be useful. Even more useful may be the fact that house prices in the subject property's neighborhood have increased 5 percent annually since the subject property last sold. The appraiser can use this kind of information about market trends to provide support for a value already estimated using the traditional approaches. In addition, market trends can be a primary source for time adjustments in the direct sales comparison approach.

For example, suppose that a subject house last sold 60 months ago for $79,000. You have appraised it for $89,750 using direct sales comparison.

---

[22] An extensive bibliography of data sources has been developed by the Pension Real Estate Association. It is found in C. F. Sirmans, *Data Sources for Real Estate Market Analysis,* (Storrs: CREUES), 1994.

TABLE 6–7 Value Changes for Neighborhood Properties

House	Date of Initial Sale (Months Ago)	Initial Price	Months between Initial Sale and Resale	Resale Price	Monthly Compound Value Change (%)
1	65 months	$54,500	36	$60,750	+.30
2	30 months	77,600	28	82,900	+.24
3	79 months	44,300	65	49,700	+.18
4	41 months	86,000	8	86,500	+.07
5	93 months	80,700	89	91,500	+.14
6	26 months	68,300	26	72,200	+.21
7	23 months	70,400	22	74,000	+.23
Average	51 months			Appraised	+.20
Subject	60 months	$79,000	60	value $89,750	+.21

You have also collected the information in Table 6–7, which shows the selling prices of houses located in the subject property's neighborhood that have sold at least twice during the past few years.

These houses had an average initial sale date of 51 months ago, similar to the 60 months for the subject. The average monthly rate of appreciation for the houses is +.20 percent. Applying this rate to the subject, its estimated value would be $79,000 $(1 + .002)^{60}$ = $89,062, which is close to the appraised value of $89,750.

The difference between trend analysis and direct sales comparison is that the properties used to establish the rate of value change are not necessarily comparable in the traditional sense. The market from which they are selected is defined primarily in terms of location (neighborhood), and not in terms of physical characteristics. The idea is that while value differences traceable to the individual characteristics of the properties will be captured in their relative selling prices, their rates of value change should be similar.

Put differently, trend analysis assumes that while differences in value exist, the ratios of values among properties remain reasonably constant. Whether or not this assumption is valid in a particular case is a decision the appraiser must make. Also, as is the case with any method that depends on extrapolation of the past, trend analysis tends to miss turning points, and the appraiser's knowledge of the market must serve to warn him or her if a turn has occurred. In such cases the results of "trending" will be less reliable.

Assessment Ratios

The tax assessor's records may also provide support for a value estimate. While the assessed value of a property is often not a true estimate of its market value because of time lags between assessments or because the assessment ratio is set at less than 1.00, there is sometimes a reasonably consistent ratio between assessed values and market values within a given market.

Suppose that five houses have recently sold, with the ratios of their assessed values to selling prices (at the time of sale) as follows:

Sale	Assessed Value	÷	Selling Price	=	Assessment/Price Ratio
1	$77,000		$ 88,500		.87
2	93,750		125,000		.75
3	96,700		132,500		.73
4	91,400		118,750		.77
5	99,400		140,000		.71
				Average	.77

If a subject property was assessed at $96,500, its estimated market value based on the average assessment to price ratio would be

$$\frac{\$96,500}{.77} = \$125,325.$$

Judgment is required when selecting the sales to include in an assessed value-selling price ratio analysis. In the example above, Sale 1 occurred at a price considerably below the other sales, and its assessed value was well below the assessed value of the subject. Notice also that the ratio for Sale 1—.87—is well above the others. The appraiser may decide in such a case to ignore this sale on the basis that it is not in the same market as the other sales and the subject, or because there is the suspicion that the assessor has not valued the property correctly.

As in the case of trend analysis, a necessary assumption when using assessment-price ratios is that the subject's ratio is similar to the sales from which the ratio is calculated. To the extent it differs, the result will be inexact.

Summary

The direct sales comparison approach is rooted in two simple but powerful principles: (1) market value is what the market says something is worth; specifically, its selling price, and (2) identical products should have identical prices—the one-price rule referred to as the principal of substitution. For real property, this principle must be restated, as similar products should have similar prices. Thus, by observing the prices of similar bundles of property rights, we can infer the price of the subject property.

This does not imply that direct sales comparison is always applicable. The key is the quantity and quality of available information.

When sufficient information is lacking, direct sales comparison cannot be used and the appraiser must default to either the cost and/or income approaches as the primary estimating approach.

The mechanics of direct sales comparison are straightforward: (1) information is gathered on sales of what appear to be comparable properties, (2) the selling prices of the selected unit(s) of comparison are adjusted for differences in characteristics between the comparable and the subject to arrive at an adjusted selling price, and (3) the value of the subject is estimated using the calculated values for the comparable properties, weighted based on the appraiser's judgment.

While the list of possible sources of information about market transactions seems quite long, in practice the tendency toward privacy in real property transactions can prove troublesome. Public records and direct interviews with market participants are widely used sources of information, while the appraiser's own files become a primary resource over time.

Closely related to direct sales comparison is the use of value trends. The rate of value change for properties in a given area is applied to the last selling price of the subject property to estimate its current value. This can be useful to support an already estimated value, but like any technique based on extrapolation, turning points will be missed. Value trends are also useful to estimate time adjustments.

Ratios of assessed values to sales prices can also be used to support a value estimate. The necessary assumption is that the ratio for the subject property is similar to that for the comparable sales that were used to extract the ratio.

Questions and Problems

1. What is the theoretical basis for the direct sales comparison approach?
2. You are reviewing an appraisal which in part includes the following sequence of adjustments to arrive at the adjusted price of a comparable sale:

Transaction price	$105,000
Time	+ 2,500
Time adjusted price	107,500
Financing (based on today's market interest rate)	− 3,200
Location	+ 3,000
Other adjustments	− 4,400
Adjusted selling price	$102,900

    Critique this adjustment process.
3. What general strategy would you follow when selecting the comparables to use when valuing an income property?
4. The adjustment for nonconventional financing is one of the more difficult for the appraiser. Why? How can the appraiser attempt to minimize the problem?
5. You are valuing an industrial property that includes some office space. It is located on one acre. Zoning will allow one-half acre to be sold or used for other improvements, and direct sales comparison indicates the value of this excess land to be $55,000. Shown below is information on the subject and three comparable sales. There are no other physical characteristics that require an adjustment.

Chapter 6   Direct Sales Comparison

	Subject	Comparables		
		#1	#2	#3
Transaction price		$350,000	$440,000	$400,000
Financing		Conventional	Conventional	Conventional
Date of sale		32 months ago	9 months ago	Current
Location	Average	Average	Average	Average
Land area	½ acre*	21,000 sq. ft.	20,000 sq. ft.	17,000 sq. ft.
Office space/ sq. ft.	1,600	1,400	1,650	2,200
Office space/† sq. ft. value	$12.50	$12.00	$13.50	$9.50
Industrial space/sq. ft.	13,000	12,500	15,600	15,000

*The excess half acre is valued separately.
†Based on prior analysis.

Industrial property has been appreciating at 4 percent per year. There is no excess land with any of the comparables and your experience in industrial markets suggests that small differences in land areas, such as those among the comparables, are generally ignored. Estimate the values of the industrial space and then the property in total.

6. You have valued a property for $98,500 using direct sales comparison. It is in a neighborhood where three other properties have sold twice during the past several years. The dates and prices of those sales are as follows:

a. Does your trend analysis support the value estimate?
b. What factors may explain the difference between the appraised value and the result of the trend analysis?
c. Which value (from direct sales comparison or trend analysis) is most credible? Why?

7. You have valued a house for $115,500 using direct sales comparison. Four other sales recently occurred in the same neighborhood, though not necessarily on properties you would have selected for direct sales comparison analysis. The assessed values and sales prices of these houses, as well as the assessed value for the subject property are as follows:

Property	First Sale (Months Ago)	Price	Resale (Months Ago)	Price
1	102	$ 47,000	4	$103,500
2	33	114,000	6	151,750
3	17	60,500	1	64,000
Subject	61	$ 71,000	—	$ 98,500

Sale	Assessed Value	Selling Price
1	$50,000	$122,600
2	51,300	135,200
3	54,300	118,600
4	34,600	102,000
Subject	40,500	

a. Appraise the subject using an assessed value/price ratio.
   b. How does this value relate to the $115,500 estimated "traditionally"?
8. Below is information on five comparables that are to be used to appraise a subject property as of October 1996. All of the comparables sold within a few weeks of the date of appraisal. Prior paired sales analysis indicates an upward adjustment of $2,000 for a storage building. Estimate the value of the subject.

	Subject	#1	#2	#3	#4	#5
Sales price	N/A	$134,800	$146,000	$136,600	$134,000	$156,000
Financing		Conventional	Conventional	Conventional	Conventional	Conventional
Sq. footage	1,711	1,661	1,684	1,607	1,436	1,810
Lot size	80 × 140	80 × 140	80 × 140	80 × 140	80 × 140	80 × 140
Location	Average	Average	Above Ave.	Above Ave.	Above Ave.	Above Ave.
Architecture	Ranch	Ranch	Ranch	Ranch	Ranch	Ranch
Garage	2-Attached	2-Attached	2-Attached	2-Attached	2-Attached	2-Attached
Bedrooms/bath	3-1	3-1	3-1½	3-1	3-1½	3-1½
Air cond.	Central	Central	Window	Central	Window	Central
Storage	Yes	No	No	No	No	No

CHAPTER 7

Sales Comparison with Basic Statistical Analysis

Introduction

The product of the traditional direct sales comparison approach is either a single-point estimate of value, or a more or less subjectively determined range into which the price is likely to fall. In most situations this is as much as the appraiser can provide, because the quantity and quality of the comparable data is not sufficient to justify a more rigorous analysis. This is slowly changing. Advances in computing technology and the ability to store and retrieve data means more and better information is becoming available to appraisers. With this comes an increase in the number of opportunities to provide a more systematic approach to making value estimates.

Statistical inference, or statistical estimating, produces not only a point estimate of value—the expected selling price—but also an accompanying interval (range) of values to which objectively determined probabilities can be assigned. Thus, the appraiser may state that the expected selling price is $100,000, and there is a 90 percent probability that the average value of houses comparable to the subject is between $96,000 and $104,000.

This chapter covers the basic tools of statistical inference as they are applied to estimate market value. Regression analysis, which is also a statistical estimating approach, is covered in the next chapter.

Populations and Samples

The essence of statistical estimating is to make inferences about a population based on information extracted from a sample drawn from that population. This is nothing new to the appraiser. Every subject property is part of a population of comparable properties. When using direct sales comparison, the value of the subject property is estimated based on a sample of properties (the comparable sales) drawn from the population of which the subject property is a member.

The difference between the traditional direct sales comparison approach and the use of statistical inference is that statistical inference is based on a set of estimating rules which provide a relatively objective measure of the reliability of the estimated value.

Describing a Population

Because the object of statistical inference is to make estimates about a population based on a sample from the population, the fundamentals of statistical inference are learned easiest by first discussing the characteristics of populations. Suppose an appraiser has identified 40 houses in a subdivision as being comparable enough to be considered in the same population. We begin by assuming that all 40 of the houses in the population have sold and that their *adjusted* selling prices, arranged in ascending order, are as shown in Table 7–1. Note that to arrive at the adjusted selling prices, most of the work needed for direct sales comparison would have to be done, but for a larger number of comparables. As is often the case, however, the result of the traditional adjustment process is a range of prices, as in Table 7–1. Statistical inference allows us to make objective probabilistic statements about

TABLE 7–1 Adjusted Prices of Comparables

House Number	Selling Price	House Number	Selling Price
1	$130,100	21	$136,000
2	130,400	22	136,000
3	131,500	23	136,400
4	132,200	24	136,500
5	132,500	25	136,700
6	133,100	26	136,700
7	133,300	27	137,000
8	133,400	28	137,200
9	133,500	29	137,400
10	133,600	30	138,200
11	134,700	31	138,400
12	134,800	32	138,400
13	134,800	33	138,600
14	134,900	34	139,200
15	135,000	35	139,300
16	135,100	36	139,900
17	135,200	37	139,900
18	135,600	38	140,700
19	135,600	39	140,800
20	136,000	40	141,400

the likely selling price based on the range and pattern of those adjusted prices. Also keep in mind that the appraiser need not start from scratch each time. A sample of adjusted prices from previous appraisals is often available in the appraiser's files.

Frequency Distributions: The Pattern of the Population Data

Arranging the population data in ascending order, as in Table 7–1, provides some insight into its pattern. For example, the range of prices from lowest to highest is obvious, and the array also provides a rough idea of the average price. Further insight into the pattern of the data can be gained by constructing a frequency distribution. One way to do this is to select class intervals (in this case, house price intervals), and to total the number of observations that fall into each interval. The selection of the proper size for the class intervals is a matter of judgment, though it is desirable that (1) all the intervals be of equal width, and (2) there are a sufficient number of intervals to provide useful insights. A common rule of thumb is that there be between 5 and 25 class intervals.

Assume that a class interval of $2,000 is used for the house sales. Beginning with $130,000, the first interval is $130,000–131,999, the second is $132,000–133,999, and so on. Outliers are lumped into catchall intervals of "below $130,000" and "above $141,999."

The result of separating the population of 40 house sales into the $2,000 class intervals is shown in Table 7–2.

Column 2 of Table 7–2 is the frequency distribution. Column 3 shows the relative frequency of each price interval, which is the ratio of the number of observations in each interval to the total number of 40 observations. For example, there are three sales in the $130,000–131,999 interval, producing its relative frequency of 3/40 or .075.

TABLE 7–2 Distribution by Class Intervals

1 Class Interval	2 Frequency Distribution	3 Relative Frequency
Under $130,000	0	0
130,000–131,999	3	.075
132,000–133,999	7	.175
134,000–135,999	9	.225
136,000–137,999	10	.250
138,000–139,999	8	.200
140,000–141,999	3	.075
Over $141,999	0	0
	40	1.00

FIGURE 7-1 Relative Frequency Distribution of House Prices

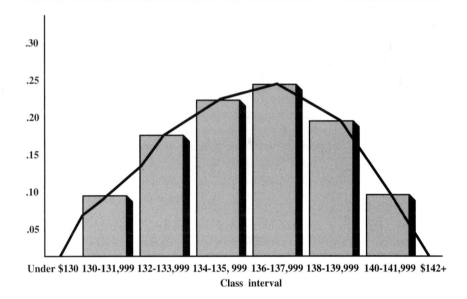

Graphing Relative Frequencies

More help in visualizing the pattern of house sales is provided by a *histogram*, or *bar graph*, of the relative frequencies. Figure 7-1 is a histogram of the data in Table 7-2.

It is common practice to smooth a bar graph into a *frequency curve* by connecting the midpoints of the bars, as is also shown in Figure 7-1.

Common Shapes of Frequency Curves

There are a number of shapes that a population's frequency curve may take. Statistical methodology has been developed for analyzing samples from populations with frequency curves of varying shapes. Some of the more common of these shapes are shown in Figure 7-2.

While there are statistical analyses that can be applied to all of the population shapes in Figure 7-2, most are very limited. The exception is the distribution on the bottom right, the normally distributed population. It is the familiar bell-shaped, symmetrical curve. The normal distribution is often called the "Boy Scout knife" of statistics, because it has mathematical properties that allow a relatively large number of useful probabilistic statements to be made about it.

FIGURE 7-2 Common Distributions

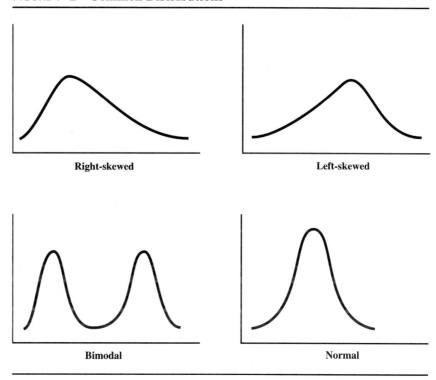

Fortunately, a large number of real world phenomenon form distributions that are approximately normal, including many appraisal applications. For example, we would expect the prices of comparable houses to be normally distributed, or close to it, with some prices higher than the average, an approximately equal number lower, but with most bunching up around the average. In fact, the assumption of a normally distributed population (though it is unstated) underlies the reference to the average or typical buyer in many market value definitions. Notice that the frequency distribution for the population of house sales shown in Figure 7-1 looks very much like a normal distribution. This fact will be put to good use later on.

Describing a Frequency Distribution

We have seen how a frequency distribution arranges population data into a visually meaningful pattern. Even more useful would be some summary information about the data. The most commonly used summary information about a distribution is its average. Statisticians call this a measure of central

FIGURE 7-3 Central Tendency and Dispersion

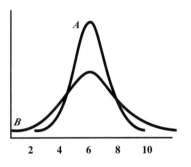

tendency; that is, the place in the frequency distribution where the individual members of the population tend to bunch up.

It is also useful to describe population data in terms of how the individual members of the population spread out, or are dispersed around the average. The importance of dispersion is clearly seen by comparing the frequency distributions shown in Figure 7-3.

The average of both distributions is the same. However, the dispersion around the average is much greater for population B than it is for population A. From this we see that the average is more representative of the individual members of population A than is the average of population B.

Thus, we need two summary measures to properly describe a frequency distribution: (1) the central tendency, or average, where the individual members bunch up, and (2) the dispersion, which indicates how much the individual members spread out around the average.

In an appraisal context the appraiser would feel more confident about the prospects for a selling price close to the average of the sample from population A than from population B above. Statistical analysis involving central tendency and dispersion allows the appraiser to calculate and communicate such differences.

Measures of Central Tendency

In statistics, the word *average* may refer to three different measures of central tendency: the mean, the median, and the mode. Most people use the word *average* to refer to the mean (M), which is simply the total value of all the members of the population, divided by the number of members.

$$M = \frac{\sum_{i=1}^{n} X_i}{N}$$

where

X is the value of an individual member, and
N is the number of members in the population

The mean price of the 40 houses listed in Table 7–1 is $136,000.

The median is a positional average. It is the midpoint of the distribution, the point above and below which 50 percent of the members of the population lie. The median house value of the population of 40 houses in Table 7–1 is between the 20th and 21st highest value. In this case, both the 20th and 21st highest values are $136,000, so the median is the same as the mean. If the 20th and 21st highest prices were different, the median would be the mean of the two prices.

The mode is the number that appears most frequently. In our population of house prices, $136,000 appears more frequently (three times) than any other price, so it is the mode. Thus, in this example, the mean, median, and mode are all $136,000.

Awhile back, a normal distribution was described as bell-shaped. We can now add more detail. A normal distribution is one that is symmetrical and has a single peak, and therefore has an equal mean, median, and mode. Our example population of house prices is normally distributed.[1]

In practice, the mean and the median are used much more frequently than the mode. When choosing between the mean and the median, the main consideration is how accurate a picture they provide of the phenomenon that is being described. As an example, suppose a population looked like this: 5, 6, 7, 8, 9, 10, 15, 20, 30, 50, and 70. The mean is 20.91, while the median is 10. If we take the differences between 20.91 and all of the individual members of the population, then square each difference and total them, that total will be less than the total of the squared differences from 10. On the other hand, if we sum the absolute differences without squaring them, the total will be closer to 10 than to 20.91.

The upshot of this is that the mean is a number that prefers to accept a lot of little errors rather than a few big ones. The median is a number that prefers a few big mistakes rather than a lot of little ones. Given this, the question becomes which is best in a given situation?

---

[1] Actually, the distribution of house prices is not quite symmetrical. However, it approximates a normal distribution closely enough that classical statistical analysis can be used. If exact normality was required, almost no distributions would qualify and classical statistical analysis would be relegated to the bookshelf. Therefore, references to normal distributions, including those in this text, refer to distributions that are at least approximately normal.

Realtors, for example, regularly report the average selling price of houses in a given market. They typically do so using the median, not the mean. This is because house prices are not normally distributed; they can't go below zero but can be infinitely high. The mean, because it avoids large errors, would fall toward the high end of the array of prices, and in doing so, could likely give a misleading impression of what was actually happening in the market. Look back at the example above and add a few zeros to each number. Now they might look like house prices. Notice there are only three "prices" above the mean of 20.91, while by definition, the median of 10 sits in the middle—five prices above, five below. Thus, it is felt that the median provides a more accurate picture of average house prices because it is not biased by a few outliers.

Measures of Dispersion

The mean, median, and mode tell us where the population members cluster. Recall, though, that it is equally important to provide information about how the individual members of the population are dispersed around the average. Are they closely bunched? Or rather spread out? For the population of house prices, we might say for example, that 19 out of the 40 houses, or 47.5 percent, sold for a price within $2,000 of the mean, and/or that the range of prices is $141,400 − $130,100 = $11,300. This kind of information is helpful, but we can do better. Because the population of house prices is normally distributed, more precise statements can be made about the dispersion of individual members around the mean.

A useful measure of dispersion is the standard deviation. To help with an understanding of what the standard deviation is and how it is calculated, an explanation of the average absolute deviation is a prerequisite.

The Average Absolute Deviation

To calculate the average absolute deviation of a population, the mean is subtracted from the values of each of the members of the population. The absolute differences (the signs are ignored) are then added, and the total is divided by the number of observations.

$$\text{Average absolute deviation} = \frac{\sum_{i=1}^{n} |X_i - M|}{N}$$

where

X_i = the value of the ith member of the population
M = population mean

Chapter 7 **Sales Comparison with Basic Statistical Analysis** **127**

N = number of observations in the population

$\sum_{i=1}^{n}$ = the sum of the $|X_i - M|$ values

The straight vertical lines surrounding $|X_i - M|$ tell us to use the absolute values (the difference expressed as a positive number). For example, if $X_i - M = -10$, the absolute value is 10.

Referring to the population of 40 house sales, the average absolute deviation calculation is shown in Table 7–3.

$$\text{Average absolute deviation} = \frac{\sum_{i=1}^{n} |X_i - M|}{N} = \$2,235$$

The average absolute deviation tells how far on average each member of the population falls from the mean. In the population of house prices, the average distance from the mean is $2,235. While this is a useful number that has some statistical properties, it is rarely used in practice. Instead, dispersion is generally measured based on the standard deviation.

TABLE 7–3 **Calculation of Average Absolute Deviation**

i	X_i	−	M	=	Absolute Deviation	i	X_i	−	M	=	Absolute Deviation
1	$130,100	−	136,000	=	5,900	21	$136,000	−	136,000	=	0
2	130,400	−	136,000	=	5,600	22	136,000	−	136,000	=	0
3	131,500	−	136,000	=	4,500	23	136,400	−	136,000	=	400
4	132,200	−	136,000	=	3,800	24	136,500	−	136,000	=	500
5	132,500	−	136,000	=	3,500	25	136,700	−	136,000	=	700
6	133,100	−	136,000	=	2,900	26	136,700	−	136,000	=	700
7	133,300	−	136,000	=	2,700	27	137,000	−	136,000	=	1,000
8	133,400	−	136,000	=	2,600	28	137,200	−	136,000	=	1,200
9	133,500	−	136,000	=	2,500	29	137,400	−	136,000	=	1,400
10	133,600	−	136,000	=	2,400	30	138,200	−	136,000	=	2,200
11	134,700	−	136,000	=	1,300	31	138,400	−	136,000	=	2,400
12	134,800	−	136,000	=	1,200	32	138,400	−	136,000	=	2,400
13	134,800	−	136,000	=	1,200	33	138,600	−	136,000	=	2,610
14	134,900	−	136,000	=	1,100	34	139,200	−	136,000	=	3,200
15	135,000	−	136,000	=	1,000	35	139,300	−	136,000	=	3,300
16	135,100	−	136,000	=	900	36	139,900	−	136,000	=	3,900
17	135,200	−	136,000	=	800	37	139,900	−	136,000	=	3,900
18	135,600	−	136,000	=	400	38	140,700	−	136,000	=	4,700
19	135,600	−	136,000	=	400	39	140,800	−	136,000	=	4,800
20	136,000	−	136,000	=	0	40	141,400	−	136,000	=	5,400

TABLE 7-4 Apartment Rental Data

Apartment	Rent	Mean Rent	$X_i - M$	$(X_i - M)^2$
1	$500	$500	0	0
2	500	500	0	0
3	505	500	5	25
4	500	500	0	0
5	495	500	−5	25
6	490	500	−10	100
7	510	500	10	100
8	500	500	0	0

$$\sum_{i=1}^{n}(X_i - M)^2 = 250$$

The Standard Deviation

The standard deviation is similar to the average deviation, except that it uses the average of the squared distances between the mean and each member, and the square root of that result is then taken.

In formula form, the standard deviation of a population, σ, is:

$$\sigma = \sqrt{\frac{\sum_{i=1}^{n}(X_i - M)^2}{N}}$$

To illustrate the calculation of the standard deviation, suppose we had rental data from a population of eight apartments, as shown in Table 7–4.

$$\sigma = \sqrt{\frac{\sum_{i=1}^{n}(X_i - M)^2}{N}}$$

$$= \sqrt{\frac{250}{8}}$$

$$= \$5.59$$

The standard deviation of the population of apartment rents is $5.59. Using a calculator, the standard deviation for the population of 40 house sales shown in Table 7–1 is $2,788.

Using the Mean and Standard Deviation

We now have two summary measures from the example population of 40 house prices: the mean of the population is $136,000, and the standard deviation of the population is $2,788. These summary measures are called population *parameters*.

Some useful probabilistic statements can be made based on the mean and standard deviation of a normally distributed population. For example, approximately 68 percent of the members of a population will fall within ± 1 standard deviation from the mean; approximately 95 percent of the members will fall within ± 2 standard deviations from the mean; approximately 99 percent of the members will fall within ± 3 standard deviations from the mean.

The probability of a sale price randomly selected from the population falling within a given range of prices can be calculated based on the number of standard deviations that it falls from the mean. Once the number of standard deviations (Z's) are calculated, the probability of occurrence can be found. The number of standard deviations from the mean (Z) is calculated as follows:

$$Z = \frac{|X - M|}{\sigma}$$

The associated probabilities are found in Table 7–5, which is a table of Z-values. The Z-table covers only half (.50) of the normal distribution, and provides the percentage of the area as measured from the mean.

For example, what is the probability of a sale in our population of houses falling above $133,000?

$$Z = \frac{|X - M|}{\sigma}$$
$$= \frac{\$133,000 - \$136,000}{\$2,788}$$
$$= 1.08$$

This tells us that a price of $133,000 is located 1.08 standard deviations from the mean. Referring to the Z-table, the probability of a sale falling 1.08 standard deviations from the mean is shown to be 35.99 percent.

Remember, however, that this is the percentage of the area between the mean and $133,000. The other 50 percent of the distribution is to the right of the mean so it is added to the 35.99 percent. Thus, there is an .8599 chance of a sale of $133,000 or above. Because we have the entire population in Table 7–1, we can check how close the Z-calculation came to the actual percentage of properties which sold for more than $133,000. In

TABLE 7-5 Areas Under the Normal Curve

Example:
If z = 1.96, then
.4750 of the area is
between 0 and 1.96

Z	0.00	0.01	0.02	0.03	0.04	0.05	0.06	0.07	0.08	0.09
0.0	0.0000	0.0040	0.0080	0.0120	0.0160	0.0199	0.0239	0.0279	0.0319	0.0359
0.1	0.0398	0.0438	0.0478	0.0517	0.0557	0.0596	0.0638	0.0675	0.0714	0.0753
0.2	0.0793	0.0832	0.0871	0.0910	0.0948	0.0987	0.1026	0.1064	0.1103	0.1141
0.3	0.1179	0.1217	0.1255	0.1293	0.1331	0.1368	0.1406	0.1443	0.1480	0.1517
0.4	0.1554	0.1591	0.1628	0.1664	0.1700	0.1736	0.1772	0.1808	0.1844	0.1879
0.5	0.1915	0.1950	0.1985	0.2019	0.2054	0.2088	0.2123	0.2157	0.2190	0.2224
0.6	0.2257	0.2291	0.2324	0.2357	0.2389	0.2422	0.2454	0.2486	0.2517	0.2549
0.7	0.2580	0.2611	0.2642	0.2673	0.2704	0.2734	0.2764	0.2794	0.2823	0.2852
0.8	0.2881	0.2910	0.2939	0.2967	0.2995	0.3023	0.3051	0.3078	0.3106	0.3133
0.9	0.3159	0.3186	0.3212	0.3238	0.3264	0.3289	0.3315	0.3340	0.3365	0.3389
1.0	0.3413	0.3438	0.3461	0.3485	0.3508	0.3531	0.3554	0.3577	0.3599	0.3621
1.1	0.3643	0.3665	0.3686	0.3708	0.3729	0.3749	0.3770	0.3790	0.3810	0.3830
1.2	0.3849	0.3879	0.3888	0.3907	0.3925	0.3944	0.3962	0.3980	0.3997	0.4015
1.3	0.4032	0.4049	0.4066	0.4082	0.4099	0.4115	0.4131	0.4147	0.4162	0.4177
1.4	0.4192	0.4207	0.4222	0.4236	0.4251	0.4265	0.4279	0.4292	0.4306	0.4319
1.5	0.4332	0.4345	0.4357	0.4370	0.4382	0.4394	0.4406	0.4418	0.4429	0.4441
1.6	0.4452	0.4463	0.4474	0.4484	0.4495	0.4505	0.4515	0.4525	0.4535	0.4545
1.7	0.4554	0.4564	0.4573	0.4582	0.4591	0.4599	0.4608	0.4616	0.4625	0.4633
1.8	0.4641	0.4649	0.4656	0.4664	0.4671	0.4678	0.4686	0.4693	0.4699	0.4706
1.9	0.4713	0.4719	0.4726	0.4732	0.4738	0.4744	0.4750	0.4758	0.4761	0.4767
2.0	0.4772	0.4778	0.4783	0.4788	0.4793	0.4798	0.4803	0.4808	0.4812	0.4817
2.1	0.4821	0.4826	0.4830	0.4834	0.4838	0.4842	0.4846	0.4850	0.4854	0.4857
2.2	0.4861	0.4864	0.4868	0.4871	0.4875	0.4878	0.4881	0.4884	0.4887	0.4890
2.3	0.4893	0.4896	0.4898	0.4901	0.4904	0.4906	0.4909	0.4911	0.4913	0.4916
2.4	0.4918	0.4920	0.4922	0.4925	0.4927	0.4929	0.4931	0.4932	0.4934	0.4936
2.5	0.4938	0.4940	0.4941	0.4943	0.4945	0.4946	0.4948	0.4949	0.4951	0.4952
2.6	0.4953	0.4955	0.4956	0.4957	0.4959	0.4960	0.4961	0.4962	0.4963	0.4964
2.7	0.4965	0.4966	0.4967	0.4968	0.4969	0.4970	0.4971	0.4972	0.4973	0.4974
2.8	0.4974	0.4975	0.4976	0.4977	0.4977	0.4978	0.4979	0.4979	0.4980	0.4981
2.9	0.4981	0.4982	0.4982	0.4983	0.4984	0.4984	0.4985	0.4985	0.4986	0.4986
3.0	0.4987	0.4987	0.4987	0.4988	0.4988	0.4989	0.4989	0.4989	0.4990	0.4990

Table 7–1, 35 of the 40 houses sold for more than $133,000. This is 87.5 percent, very close to the calculated percentage of 85.99 percent.

What is the probability that a house will sell for $137,000 or above?

$$Z = \frac{\$137,000 - \$136,000}{\$2,788}$$

$$= .3587$$

Chapter 7 Sales Comparison with Basic Statistical Analysis

In the Z-table, .36 standard deviations includes .1406 of the distribution. This is the area from the mean outward to $137,000, and in this example, we are interested in the tail of the distribution above $137,000. Thus, the probability of a sale of $137,000 or more is .50 − .1406 = .3594. Again, this comes close to the 35 percent or 14 houses in Table 7–1 which actually sold for $137,000 or above. There are 14, which is .35.

To summarize the use of the Z-table: (1) Z is the number of standard deviations a given number falls from the mean; based on Z, the probability of an occurrence can be obtained; (2) the Z-table includes only one-half of the normal distribution, and (3) the Z-table refers to the distance between the mean and the specified value. For areas in the tails of the distribution, the percentage must be subtracted from .50.

Using a Sample to Make Inferences about the Population Mean

In practice, an appraiser will almost never have the entire population from which to calculate its mean and standard deviation. Only a sample from the population is likely to be available, and based on the information extracted from that sample, inferences (or estimates) can be made about the population from which it was drawn.

A Sample of the House Sales

Suppose a subject property was one of the 40 houses in the population (Table 7–1) that we have been using as an example, and that in fact only 14 of the other houses in the population had actually sold. The prices of the houses in this sample of sold houses, arranged in ascending order, are shown in Table 7–6.

The mean of the sample ($\bar{X}$) is $136,093, and is calculated just like the mean of the population. However, the standard deviation of the sample, s, is calculated slightly differently than the standard deviation of the population. The formula is:

$$s = \sqrt{\frac{\sum_{i=1}^{n}(X_i - \bar{X})^2}{n-1}}$$

where

n is the size of the sample and
$\bar{X}$ is the mean of the sample.

The difference is that the denominator is $n - 1$ rather than n. The reason for using $n - 1$ instead of n is that statisticians have shown that the sample

TABLE 7-6 Selling Prices of Sample

House Number	
1	$130,100
6	133,100
7	133,300
12	134,800
16	135,100
17	135,200
18	135,600
20	136,000
23	136,400
24	136,500
28	137,200
37	139,900
38	140,700
40	141,400

$\bar{X} = \$136,093$

$s = \$3,060$

standard deviation will do a better job of estimating the population standard deviation if $n - 1$ rather than n is used. For our sample of 14 houses, the standard deviation is $3,060.

The mean and standard deviation are summary measures of the sample, and are called *statistics*. (Recall that the mean and standard deviation of the population are called *parameters*.)

Confidence Intervals with Small Samples

In most appraisal situations sample sizes will be small. If the sample size is less than 30, as is the case with our sample of 14 houses, the Z-table cannot be used. Instead, a t-table is used.[2] This is because when the sample size drops below about 30, the calculations become very sensitive to the size of the sample and the t-table is constructed to explicitly recognize this fact.

The number of t's is calculated and interpreted the same way as the number of Z's; both reference the number of standard deviations a particular number falls from the mean. However, because sample size must be explicitly considered when using the t-table, the structure of the t-table is different, and the precision of some of the resulting inferences will be af-

---

[2] Technically, the t-table should be used in all cases when working with statistics, regardless of sample size (because the population's standard deviation is not known). However, as sample size approaches about 30, the differences between the t and Z-tables become trivial.

TABLE 7–7 Student *t* Distribution

	Level of Significance for One-Tailed Test					
df	.10	.05	.025	.01	.005	.0005
1	3.078	6.314	12.706	31.821	63.657	636.619
2	1.886	2.920	4.303	6.965	9.925	31.599
3	1.638	2.353	3.182	4.541	5.841	12.924
4	1.533	2.132	2.776	3.747	4.604	8.610
5	1.476	2.015	2.571	3.365	4.032	6.869
6	1.440	1.943	2.447	3.143	3.707	5.959
7	1.415	1.895	2.365	2.998	3.499	5.408
8	1.397	1.860	2.306	2.896	3.355	5.041
9	1.383	1.833	2.262	2.821	3.250	4.781
10	1.372	1.812	2.228	2.764	3.169	4.587
11	1.363	1.796	2.201	2.718	3.106	4.437
12	1.356	1.782	2.179	2.681	3.055	4.318
13	1.350	1.771	2.160	2.650	3.012	4.221
14	1.345	1.761	2.145	2.624	2.977	4.140
15	1.341	1.753	2.131	2.602	2.947	4.073
16	1.337	1.746	2.120	2.583	2.921	4.015
17	1.333	1.740	2.110	2.567	2.898	3.965
18	1.330	1.734	2.101	2.552	2.878	3.922
19	1.328	1.729	2.093	2.539	2.861	3.883
20	1.325	1.725	2.086	2.528	2.845	3.850
21	1.323	1.721	2.080	2.518	2.831	3.819
22	1.321	1.717	2.074	2.508	2.819	3.792
23	1.319	1.714	2.069	2.500	2.807	3.768
24	1.318	1.711	2.064	2.492	2.797	3.745
25	1.316	1.708	2.060	2.485	2.787	3.725
26	1.316	1.706	2.056	2.479	2.779	3.707
27	1.314	1.703	2.052	2.473	2.771	3.690
28	1.313	1.701	2.048	2.467	2.763	3.674
29	1.311	1.699	2.045	2.462	2.756	3.659
30	1.310	1.697	2.042	2.457	2.750	3.646
40	1.303	1.684	2.021	2.423	2.704	3.551
60	1.296	1.671	2.000	2.390	2.660	3.460
120	1.289	1.658	1.980	2.358	2.617	3.373
∞	1.282	1.645	1.960	2.326	2.576	3.291

fected. However, these differences should not be allowed to obscure the fact that the Z- and *t*-tables are used for the same purpose, with sample size the only determinant of which table should be used.

Using the t-table

Table 7–7 is a *t*-table. First, note that the *t*-table shows only a few percentages and associated *t*-values (10, 5, 2.5, 1, .5, and .05 percent). Because there is a different result for each sample size (as opposed to the Z-table which considers all (relatively large) samples to be equivalent), a complete *t*-table would be too cumbersome. However, the percentages included are the ones most commonly used.

A second difference between the *t* and *Z*-tables is that with the *t*-table, you must consider sample size. More precisely, you must specify the degrees of freedom, which is defined as $n - 1$, the sample size minus 1.

A third difference between the *t* and *Z*-tables is that the *t*-table gives the probability that the population parameter being estimated is *not* within the specified confidence interval. Thus, if we are making an estimate at the 90 percent confidence interval, we look under the 10 percent column (100%–90%). Recall that the *Z* gives the probability that the parameter *is* within the interval.

To illustrate the use of the *t*-table, suppose we want to calculate a 95 percent confidence interval with a sample size of 14 (13 degrees of freedom). Wanting 95 percent confidence means we are willing to accept a 2.5 percent region outside the confidence interval on each side. Thus, we look at Table 7–7 under the .025 column and find 2.16. This *t*-value tells us that if we move 2.16 standard deviations to either side of the mean, the area outside these limits will include 5 percent of the distribution.

Given the mean of the sample of houses was $136,093, and the standard deviation was $3,060, what is the price range in which you can be 90 percent confident the price will fall?

$$\bar{X} \pm t(s)$$

$$\$136,093 \pm 1.771 (\$3.060)$$

$$\$130,674 - \$141,512$$

The Standard Error of the Mean

It is time to pause and reflect on what is likely to be the primary use of sample statistics in an appraisal context; that is, to infer, or estimate, the expected selling price of a subject property.

In our continuing example, the population includes 40 houses considered comparable to the subject. The sample of 14 sold houses in Table 7–6 is a subset of that population. That sample has a mean adjusted selling price of $136,093. In the traditional direct sales comparison approach, this mean price might be used as the expected selling price of the subject. However, statistical analysis can also provide information about the reliability of the estimated selling price. Remember, because a sample provides "incomplete" information about the population, the probability is close to zero that the mean of a sample will be exactly the same as the mean of the population from which the sample was drawn. (In our example, the true population mean was already calculated to be $136,000, while the mean of the sample is $136,093.).

Recognizing this, we would like to be able to provide a confidence interval around the mean of the sample, which we can then use to make a probabilistic statement about the mean of the population. To do this, we need another statistic called the *standard error of the mean*, $s_{\bar{X}}$. The formula is:

$$s_{\bar{X}} = \left(\frac{s}{\sqrt{n}}\right)\left(\sqrt{\frac{N-n}{N-1}}\right)$$

Notice that the standard error of the mean is simply the standard deviation of the sample divided by the square root of the sample size, multiplied by an adjustment term to reflect the size of the population and the size of the sample.[3]

The standard error of the mean for our sample of 14 houses is:

$$s_{\bar{X}} = \frac{\$3,060}{\sqrt{14}}\left(\sqrt{\frac{40-14}{40-1}}\right)$$

$$= \$817.82\,(.817)$$

$$= \$668\,(rounded)$$

We can calculate confidence intervals for the population mean from which our sample of 14 houses was drawn.

$$\bar{X} \pm t\,(s\bar{X})$$

$$\$136{,}093 \pm 2.16\,(\$668)$$

$$\$134{,}650 \text{ to } \$137{,}536$$

This interval ($134,650 to $137,536) is slightly larger than it would be if it had a large (30+) sample. This makes sense. As the sample size decreases the resulting statistics are less likely to closely approximate the population parameters.

Notice that the *t*-table dovetails into the *Z*-table. For a 95 percent confidence interval, the *Z*-table tells us to move 1.96 standard errors from the mean. That is the same number the *t*-table gives for a sample of 30+. Notice also that in this case, the 95 percent confidence interval does in fact include the actual population mean of $136,000.

Finally, if we look at the *t*-table for very small degrees of freedom, we see that the number of standard errors we must move to get a given confidence interval is extremely large. This in turn will produce a very wide range within which a price, or a mean price, may fall. Because the confidence intervals are so wide, they have very little utility. This illustrates the

---

[3]When the population is relatively large and the sample is relatively small, the adjustment term approaches 1.0 and can be ignored.

main obstacle to using statistical inference for many appraisal assignments; the sample size (degrees of freedom) is so small that not much is gained by the statistical exercise.

Using the Confidence Interval around the Mean

The interval within which we are 95 percent confident the mean value of the example population of houses falls has been calculated to be between $134,650 and $137,536. It is important to understand how this interval is properly interpreted with respect to estimating the value of a subject property.

Though it is often done, it is not correct to state that there is a 95 percent probability the subject house will sell for a price between $134,650 and $137,536. The correct statement is that there is a 95 percent probability that the *mean* (or expected) value of houses comparable to the subject is between $134,650 and $137,563.

The 90 percent confidence interval would be $136,093 $\pm$ (1.771)($668)=$134,910 to $137,276, which is slightly narrower than the interval at 95 percent confidence. Again, this makes sense; if you allow me to be less confident in my answer, I can be more exact.

Does the Population Have to Be Normally Distributed to Use Confidence Intervals around the Mean?

Throughout this chapter, statistical inference has been discussed with reference to a sample drawn from a normally distributed population. This presents a problem, because the appraiser will almost always be working with a sample and therefore will not know for certain the shape of the population. This is not unique to appraisers, of course. In most sampling situations the population distribution cannot be known with certainty. Fortunately, statistical inference can still be used in a large number of cases.

When the sample size is relatively large (30+), the central limit theorem comes to the rescue. It is perhaps the most important theorem in statistical inference. It states that the means of repeated samples from a non-normally distributed population will approach a normal distribution with a mean equal to the population mean. The practical effect of the central limit theorem is that classical statistical inference can be used to estimate the population mean, even when the population is not normally distributed.

With small samples (less than 30), however, the central limit theorem will not hold unless the population is in fact approximately normal. Sometimes previous experience or research will suggest that an assumption of normality is reasonable. When there is doubt, the appraiser may wish to test for normality using techniques that are beyond the scope of this text.

Summary

At the heart of the appraisal process is the making of inferences about (or estimates of) value based on information extracted from a sample. Traditionally, the result of this process has been a point estimate. Statistical inference provides objective measures of the reliability of the point estimate.

A normally distributed population can be described using two parameters, the mean (M) and the standard deviation (σ). Given M and σ, statements can be made about where in the distribution individual members of the population are likely to fall, based on their distance from M as measured by the number of standard deviations (Z) from the mean.

Appraisers seldom work with populations. Samples drawn from the population must suffice, and from the statistics calculated based on the sample, inferences can be made about the mean of the population. The statistics of interest are the mean of the sample ($\overline{X}$), the standard deviation of the sample, s, and the standard error of the mean ($s_{\overline{X}}$).

Confidence intervals are constructed around the sample mean using the estimated standard error and either the Z-value (for large samples) or t-value (for smaller samples). The result is a probability statement about where the true mean of the population is likely to fall.

When the sample size is relatively large (30+), the central limit theorem can be relied on so that even if the population from which the sample was drawn is not normally distributed, inferences can still be made about the population's mean. With smaller samples, however, such inferences can be safely drawn only if the population is normally distributed.

It is also possible to use statistics to provide an estimate of the range into which an individual member of the population is likely to fall. A Z-value is calculated using the mean and standard deviation of the sample. The corresponding percentage is then taken from the Z-table.

An example will be used to complete the summary. Suppose a sample of 31 house prices drawn from a large population has produced these statistics: $\overline{X} = \$108{,}540$, $s = \$3{,}741$, and $s_{\overline{X}} = \$672$. The 90 percent confidence interval around the mean is:

$$\$108{,}540 \pm 1.65\,(\$672) = \$107{,}431-\$109{,}649$$

If the houses in the sample were comparable to the subject, the appraiser could state with 90 percent confidence that the true mean value of houses comparable to the subject is between $107,431 and $109,649.

Probabilistic statements can be made about the range of prices into which the subject property should sell. With a sample size greater than 30, the Z-table is used. For samples less than 30, use the t-table. Given the mean and standard deviations of $108,540 and $3,741, respectively, and the sample size of 31, the probability of a price above $105,000 is:

$$Z = \frac{|X - \overline{X}|}{s}$$

$$= \frac{\$105{,}000 - \$108{,}540}{\$3{,}741}$$

$$= .95, \text{ which includes } .3289 \text{ of the distribution}$$

In this case, there is a $.3289 + .50 = .83$ probability of a selling price above $105,000.

Questions and Problems

1. What is another name for statistical inference?
2. What are the potential advantages of using statistical inference relative to traditional estimating procedures? What are the limitations of statistical inference?
3. What does a population parameter have to do with estimating the value of a single subject property?
4. What is the mean? Median? Mode? The standard deviation? The standard error of the mean?
5. Describe a normal frequency distribution. Why is it important?
6. You are estimating the ratios of expenses to income for comparable apartments and have gathered this sample from a large population: .41, .35, .38, .46, .48, .49, .34, .51, .46, .47, .47, and .49. What is the mean, standard deviation, and standard error of the mean?
7. Based on the information in Question 6, what is the 90 percent confidence interval around the estimated population mean? What does this confidence interval tell you?
8. From the sample of 10 house prices which follows, estimate the mean and standard error, assuming a large population so that no sample-size adjustment must be made. What is the 90 percent confidence interval in which the mean of the population of comparable properties is likely to fall? The sample is: $114,500, $121,700, $117,700, $118,000, $116,500, $122,600, $120,000, $119,250, $119,000, and $120,900.
9. Two appraisers are discussing statistical inference. One claims that no adjustments should be made to data prior to making inferences, as that would destroy the objectivity of the process. The other disagrees. Comment.
10. Confidence intervals around the estimated mean of a population cannot be calculated unless the population is normally distributed. Comment.

CHAPTER 8

Sales Comparison Using Regression Analysis

Introduction

In addition to traditional direct sales comparison and the use of basic statistical analysis, a third way that the sales comparison approach can be applied is with regression analysis. Regression analysis is used to predict the value of an unknown variable, like the selling price of a house, based on the value(s) of a known or measurable variable(s), like the size of the house, that the appraiser thinks the selling price will depend on. The prediction is based on a regression equation which measures the relationship between the variables. The equation is based on information from past transactions just as in traditional sales comparison. Once the regression equation is developed, it is then used to estimate the selling prices of subject properties.

Regression analysis has two strengths. First, it can be used to value a large number of properties quickly and economically, which helps explain its popularity with property tax assessors. Second, regression can be used to *explain* value as well as to estimate it. This is in contrast to basic statistical analysis, which produces a value estimate but cannot explain why the value is what it is. The ability of regression analysis to explain price means that it can be useful to estimate the prices of individual characteristics of properties, such as the price per square foot of living space or the difference in value between brick and vinyl siding. These estimates can then be used in traditional direct sales comparison.[1]

The limitations of regression analysis are that it requires much more data than does traditional direct sales comparison, and that it does not do a

---

[1] A discussion of the quantitative relationship between traditional sales comparison and regression analysis is found in Joseph Lipscomb and J. Brian Gray, "A Connection Between Paired Data Analysis and Regression Analysis for Estimating Sales Adjustments," *Journal of Real Estate Research* 10, no. 2, 1995.

good job of valuing unusual or unique properties. This helps explain why regression is used much more frequently for appraising houses than for appraising investment properties.

The term *regression* was first used in a statistical sense by Sir Francis Galton. In 1877, Galton studied the heights of children with tall parents and discovered that the children's heights tended to move back, or regress, toward the mean height of the population. Over time, the term *regression* has come to be used to describe any process in which a known variable(s), such as the living area of a house, is used to predict an unknown variable (the expected selling price of the house).

The known variable(s) in a regression analysis is called the independent variable, while the unknown variable is called the dependent variable. In the case of living area and selling price, the expected selling price depends on the size of the house. When only one independent variable (like living area) is used to explain a dependent variable (like the expected selling price), it is called simple regression. When two or more independent variables (for example the living area and the age of a house) are used to explain the dependent variable, it is called multiple regression.

Simple Regression

Suppose the subject property is a house and the information in Table 8–1 has been extracted from a sample of recent transactions involving reasonably comparable properties.

Experience suggests that one reason for the difference in prices is that the houses are different sizes. Regression analysis provides an answer to the question of what kind of mathematical relationship exists between size and selling price.

TABLE 8–1 Data from Comparable Sales

House	Selling Price	Living Area (square feet)
1	$75,500	1,258
2	93,300	1,637
3	77,500	1,313
4	65,500	1,023
5	81,100	1,352
6	77,400	1,269
7	82,000	1,365
8	85,000	1,393

A Scatter Diagram

One way to determine if the selling prices of the houses listed in Table 8–1 depend on their size is to construct a scatter diagram, as in Figure 8–1.

Visual inspection of Figure 8–1 indicates that there is a relationship between price and size, and what that relationship looks like. As has been done, we can "eyeball" a *regression line* through the scatter diagram to represent the general relationship between living area (the independent variable is always on the *X* axis) and selling price (the dependent variable is always on the *Y* axis).

There are two things to notice in Figure 8–1. First, the relationship between price and size is direct; that is, price increases as size increases. Second, the relationship is linear; it is well-described by the straight line.

A linear relationship between the independent and dependent variables is commonly assumed in practice and it will be used here to learn the basics of regression. Later, nonlinear relationships between variables will be discussed.

For linear relationships, the regression equation is:

$$\hat{Y} = a + bx \tag{1}$$

where

$\hat{Y}$ is the estimated value of the dependent variable
a is the *Y*-intercept (a constant)
b is the slope of the regression line
x is the value of the independent variable

FIGURE 8–1 Relationship between Selling Price and Living Area

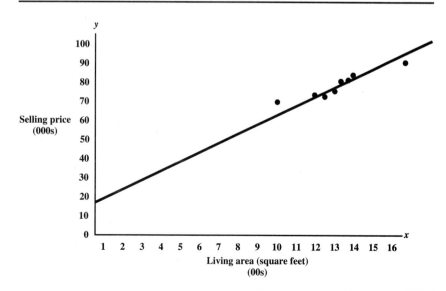

Notice that the value of the dependent variable (Y), in this case price, depends on the given value of the independent variable (x), in this case size. Thus, by using Equation (1) the estimated price of a house can be calculated based on the house's size. The constant, a, is called the Y-intercept because it is measured at the point where the regression line crosses the Y axis. The b is the slope of the regression line. It tells how much Y (price) will change for every unit change in x (square feet). From the visually drawn regression line in Figure 8–1, a looks to be between $16,000 and $20,000, with each square foot of house size adding another $40–50 to the selling price.

Obtaining Greater Precision: Calculating the Regression Line

A visually determined regression equation, as in Figure 8–1, provides a general idea about the relationship between the dependent and independent variables. In practice, we need a more precise estimate of the relationship. Statisticians have developed a number of alternative criteria for estimating the relationship, the most widely used of which is the least-squared error. Using least-squared error, the vertical differences between the regression line and the actual observations are squared, then summed, and the regression line selected is the one with the smallest sum of the squared errors. Because it squares the difference between the regression line and the actual value, least squares is a method that heavily penalizes large errors so that they can be avoided. Thus, the premise of the least-squared error criterion is that it is better to have several small errors than to have one large one. Recall that this was also a consideration in choosing between the mean and the median as the measure of central tendency.

The mathematics of finding the best regression line are manageable by hand only for a simple regression with relatively few observations. For a simple regression with a large sample, a programmable or preprogrammed calculator is necessary. For multiple regression, a computer is necessary.

The Regression Equation for Size and Selling Price

The data on selling price and size for the houses listed in Table 8–1 was fed into a computer, and the resulting regression equation was:

$$\hat{Y} = \$17{,}944.23 + \$46.54\,(x)$$

This tells us that the expected selling price is equal to $17,944.23 (the constant, a), plus $46.54 (the slope, b) for every square foot of size. In this example, our eyeball estimate of a constant of $16,000–20,000 and a square-foot price of $40–50 was pretty good.

The Standard Error of the Estimate

Though the regression line will be the best fit for the data, it will almost never be a perfect fit; that is, most of the points will not fall on the regression line exactly. Therefore, it is helpful to find out how good a fit it is. The standard error of the estimate, s_e, is a measure of reliability that is similar to the standard deviation. The standard error of the estimate measures the dispersion or "scatter" of the actual values in a sample around the regression line calculated from the sample. For the selling price/house size example, the computer calculated an s_e of $1,260.02.[2]

As with the standard deviation, the larger the standard error, the greater the variability of points around the regression line. Assuming the points are normally distributed, about 68 percent of the points will be found within $\pm 1\ s_e$ of the line, about 95 percent within $\pm 2\ s_e$, and about 99 percent within $\pm 3\ s_e$.

Making Inferences Using Regression

While a regression equation is useful to describe a sample, much more useful are the inferences that can be made about the population from which the sample was drawn. Put differently, the question to be answered is whether the regression equation is a reliable tool to *predict Y* for a given value of x.[3]

The standard error of the estimate is a statistic that allows us to make statements about the approximate interval around an estimated value ($\hat{Y}$), within which is found the actual value of Y. To illustrate, suppose that a subject property is a 1,200-square-foot house, and its value is to be estimated based on this regression equation developed above:

$$\hat{Y} = \$17{,}944.23 + \$46.54\ (x)$$

The expected selling price of the 1,200-square-foot house is $17,944.23 + $46.54 (1,200) = $73,792 (rounded). Now suppose you want to be approximately 80 percent confident that the price will fall within a given interval around the expected price of $73,792. To calculate the confidence interval, we need the standard error of the estimate, s_e, previously calculated to be $1,260 (rounded), and the *t*-table (because the sample size of eight on

---

[2] $s_e = \sqrt{\dfrac{\Sigma(Y - \hat{Y})^2}{n - 2}}$

[3] The population regression line is:

$$\hat{Y} = A + BX + e$$

where e is a random error. Because e is assumed to be random with an expected value of zero, it can be dropped and the sample regression line used to estimate the population regression line.

which the regression equation was based was less than 30).[4] There are six degrees of freedom (the sample size (n) less the number of variables, including the dependent variable). Because the t-table gives the probability of falling outside the prediction interval, the column of interest is $1.00 - .80 = .20$. At the intersection of the .20 column and six degrees of freedom, we find a t-value of 1.440. There is an 80 percent chance that the true value of the subject house will fall in the interval from 1.440 standard errors above the predicted price to 1.440 standard errors below. For the 1,200-square-foot house, the approximate 80 percent confidence interval is:

$$\hat{Y} \pm t\,(s_e)$$
$$= \$73{,}792 \pm (1.44)\,(\$1{,}260)$$
$$= \$71{,}978 \text{ to } \$75{,}606 \text{ (rounded)}$$

Thus, there is about an 80 percent probability that the selling price of a 1,200 square-foot house will be between $71,978 and $75,606.[5]

Correlation Analysis

Correlation analysis is used with regression analysis to measure the degree of association, or correlation, between the dependent and independent variables. The primary way to measure the degree of association is with the *coefficient of determination, r^2*.

Statistically, r^2 is defined as the amount of variation in the dependent variable that is explained by variation in the independent variable. With reference to the previous example of the regression of living area and selling price, the r^2 statistic tells us what proportion of the price differences are explained by the differences in the living areas of the houses. Because r^2 is a proportion, it must fall between 0 and 1. If there is absolutely no association between the dependent and independent variables, $r^2 = 0$. If the independent and dependent variables are perfectly associated, $r^2 = 1$, or 100 percent.

In practice, r^2 will almost never fall at either of the 0–1 extremes. If there is some *a priori* reason to have assumed a relationship between the dependent and independent variables, it is unlikely that zero correlation will be found. Conversely, real world relationships are generally too complex to hope to find a perfect correlation. Even in those rare cases when that situa-

---

[4] A t-table (and the related Z-table) is found in Chapter 7, with a discussion of its use.

[5] The prediction interval calculated using the standard error of the estimate is only a rough approximation. With a relatively large sample size the use of the standard error of the estimate will produce a close approximation of the true interval. With smaller samples the use of the standard error may introduce rather large errors. See the chapter apendix for a detailed discussion of this point.

tion exists, errors in measurement or in data collection will generally drop the r^2 below 1. Returning to the regression of selling price and size, an r^2 of 97.6 percent was calculated using a computer. This says that the differences in house size accounted for 97.6 percent of the differences in the selling prices of the sample of eight houses.

Making Inferences about the Slope (*b*) of the Regression Line

Just as the estimated dependent variable ($\hat{Y}$) has an associated standard error of the estimate that is used to calculate prediction intervals, the regression coefficient, *b*, which is the slope of the regression line, has an associated standard deviation. It is called the standard error of the coefficient, s_b. The standard error of the coefficient is used to test whether the independent variable is significantly associated with the dependent variable, and also to construct confidence intervals around *b*.

In the regression of selling price and size, the computer calculated an s_b of 2.79. Suppose we want to test with 90 percent certainty (that is, at a 10 percent significance level) whether size is actually associated with price. The null hypothesis, therefore, is that the true slope equals 0; that is, if size is not associated with price, we would expect $b = 0$, meaning that the number of square feet does not affect price.

What we hope to do in this case is to reject the null hypothesis and from that conclude that size and price are in fact associated. To test the null hypothesis with a small sample, we use the *t*-table. Under the .10 (1.00-.90) column at six degrees of freedom we find 1.943. This *t*-value is then compared to the calculated *t*-value for *b*, which is

$$t = \frac{b}{s_b}.$$

In the selling price-to-size regression, the calculated *t*-value is

$$\frac{46.54}{2.79} = 16.68.$$

When the calculated *t*-value is greater than the *t*-value from the table, the null hypothesis can be rejected. In this case, 16.68 > 1.943, and we can reject the null hypothesis of no relationship and conclude that size is in fact related to price. In other words, there would be less than a 10 percent chance of getting the results obtained if there was really no relationship. In fact, if you search the *t*-table at six degrees of freedom, you find that the calculated *t*-value of 16.68 exceeds all of the critical *t*-values. A conclusion that size is related to price is clearly justified. Thus, the appraiser could feel confident using $46.54 as the value of an added square foot when making adjustments to the sales price of comparables.

Confidence intervals can also be constructed for the true slope of the regression line. Suppose previous experience indicates that the selling price of a certain kind of house is $47 per square foot (plus the constant). However, the most recent regression (our example) suggests that the cost is $46.54 per square foot. Is this difference of $.46 per foot large enough to change our opinion about selling price? Or, given the inevitable difference between the sample and the true population, is the difference too small to merit a change of mind?

The null hypothesis is that the true slope equals $47, which we will test at the .10 level of significance. First, a confidence interval is constructed around the historical selling price using the t-table and the standard error of the coefficient.

$$b \pm t\,(s_b)$$

$$\$47 + 1.943\,(2.79)$$

$$\$41.58 \text{ to } \$52.42$$

This interval is then compared to the estimated b of $46.54. Because it falls within the .90 confidence interval, we cannot reject the null hypothesis and therefore we cannot conclude that the current construction cost is different from its historical level of $47. Instead, we conclude that the $.46 difference is attributable to the fact that the sample does not represent the population exactly. Intuitively, the $.46 is too small to conclude it represents a true change, given the uncertainties associated with the small sample.

Limitations and Pitfalls Using Regression and Correlation Analysis

It is easy to misuse regression analysis or to misinterpret the results. Some of the more common errors are to infer cause and effect, to use regression without a plausible theory, and to interpolate beyond the regression line.

Regression Measures Association, Not Cause and Effect

Regressions cannot determine cause and effect. For example, the average education of occupants in a neighborhood is regularly found to be significantly associated with the value of houses in the neighborhood. Clearly, the occupants' education levels do not cause the values of their houses to increase. Rather, upper-income families tend to live in higher priced housing. Thus, educational levels are associated with values, but do not cause them.

As another example, the racial mix of a neighborhood has sometimes been associated with house values. This result cannot be interpreted that the presence of minorities causes values to increase or decrease. It is equally if not more likely that the percentage of minorities in a neighborhood is itself associated with the income level of the neighborhood or the quality of the school system. Thus, the racial mix may serve as a proxy for the factors which are the true cause of value differences.

A Lack of Theory and Spurious Relationships

Some statistical relationship can be found between almost any two variables, regardless of whether or not they are in fact associated. Put differently, some level of r^2 will be achieved by accident. A classic example is the historical relationship between the performance of the stock market and (choose one) the length of women's skirts or the winner (AFC or NFC) of the Super Bowl.

The lesson is that the most important part of regression modeling is the choice of variables. There should be a solid reason for the inclusion (or exclusion) of each variable. This does not mean additions and deletions of variables cannot be made during the analysis. It does mean that without a reasonable theory of why the results are as they are, those results will lack some degree of persuasiveness regardless of the statistics supporting them.

Extrapolation and Trending

Suppose regression was used to measure the association between the selling prices and the GIMs of a sample of apartments, and that the range of GIMs in the sample was 5.0–7.5. It would not be proper to use the resulting regression equation to predict the selling price of apartments with GIMs that are outside that range (below 5.0 or larger than 7.5), because a different relationship may exist at those levels.

A similar caveat applies to trend lines. Few relationships remain stable over time. Because regressions are commonly used to predict, they should be rerun periodically with fresh data.

A Summary Example of Simple Regression

A sample of 27 transactions was used to develop a regression equation based on the association between gross income and selling price. The gross incomes in the sample of duplexes ranged between \$7,500 and \$10,850, and the resulting regression equation was:

$$\hat{Y} = a + b(x)$$
$$= \$4,281 + 6.04(x)$$

This tells us that the duplexes in the sample sold for \$4,281 plus \$6.04 for each dollar of gross income. If you are now appraising a duplex expected to produce $9,400 of gross income, this equation predicts that it will sell for $4,281 + 6.04 ($9,400) = $61,057.

Other statistics typically generated in a regression analysis are the standard error of the estimate (s_e), the standard error of the coefficient (s_b), and the coefficient of determination (r^2). For the example duplex regression, assume these statistics are:

$$s_e = \$2,990$$

$$s_b = 1.46$$

$$r^2 = .81$$

The standard error of the estimate is used to calculate an approximate confidence interval around an estimated value. If a 90 percent confidence interval is desired, the t-table tells us that with 25 degrees of freedom, this interval includes 1.708 standard errors to each side of the estimated value. For the example duplex valued at $61,057, the approximate 90 percent confidence interval is:

$$\text{Estimated value} \pm (t)(s_e) =$$

$$\$61,057 \pm (1.708)(\$2,990) =$$

$$\$55,950 \text{ to } \$66,164$$

The standard error of the coefficient, s_b, is used to test the significance of the association between the independent and dependent variable, and also to calculate a confidence interval around the coefficient. We hope to reject the null hypothesis that $b = 0$; that is, we hope to reject the hypothesis that gross income actually has no association with selling price.

The calculated t is

$$\frac{6.04}{1.46} = 4.14.$$

At the .05 significance level, the minimum t-value is 2.06, and the null hypothesis can be rejected. Selling price is apparently associated with gross income.

The 90 percent confidence intervals around the coefficient is:

$$\$6.04 \pm 1.708 \, (1.46)$$

$$\$3.55 \text{ to } \$8.53$$

There is a 90 percent probability that the true value of b (the actual GIM in the population) lies between $3.55–$8.53. Finally, the r^2 of .81 tells us that 81 percent of the differences in the selling prices in the sample are explained by differences in gross incomes.

There are limitations to the use of this regression equation. First, it measures association, not causation, between the variables. Assigning causality is the responsibility of the analyst, not the regression equation. Second, the equation can be used only to predict selling prices for properties producing gross incomes between $7,500 and $10,850, because that was the range in the sample. Finally, if gross income is to be used to predict selling prices in the future, the equation should be updated as frequently as possible to capture any changes over time in the relationship between gross income and selling price.

Multiple Regression

The basics of regression analysis have been discussed using simple regression—the relationship between one independent variable and the dependent variable.

In real estate markets, there are few situations when a dependent variable can be explained fully enough with a single independent variable. There are almost always several factors associated with the value of the dependent variable. Multiple regression is the name given to a regression analysis that uses more than one independent variable. The multiple regression equation looks like this:

$$\hat{Y} = a + b_1x_1 + b_2x_2 + \ldots b_nx_n$$

where

$x_1, \ldots x_n$ are the independent variables

The interpretation of a multiple regression equation is much the same as it is for a simple regression equation. The most common criterion for fitting the regression line remains the sum of the squared errors. Instead of one regression coefficient, however, there will be a coefficient for each independent variable, and each can be tested for significance. As independent variables are added, the complexity of the mathematics increases rapidly and a computer is necessary to estimate the regression line. Software for that purpose is widely available and is a standard part of most statistical packages.

A Multiple Regression Example

Mike Farrell[6] used multiple regression to explain the selling prices of a sample of 24 houses within a mile of downtown Barbary, Illinois.[7] The houses were single-story ranch style, 20–35 years old. The selling prices were between $57,000–68,500, with a mean price of $63,346.

---

[6]Michael D. Farrell, "Reporting Regression Results," *The Real Estate Appraiser and Analyst,* Summer 1984, 16–21.

[7]Most applications of regression analysis have been in residential markets due to data availability and relative homogeneity. For an application to valuing apartment properties, see Z. Sadevion, B. Smith, and C. Smith, "An Integrated Approach to the Evaluation of Commercial Real Estate," *Journal of Real Estate Research,* Spring 1994.

These are the dependent and independent variables that were used:

$\hat{Y}$ = estimated selling price
x_1 = the number of bedrooms
x_2 = the number of bathrooms
x_3 = garage size (0, 1, or 2-car)
x_4 = lot size (in square feet)

The resulting regression equation and accompanying statistics (with the standard errors of the coefficients in parenthesis below the coefficients) looked like this:

$$\hat{Y} = \$48{,}738.1 + \$1{,}224.44\, x_1 + \$3{,}892.52\, x_2 \quad\quad (2)$$

$$(546.12) \quad\quad (783.62)$$

$$+ \$1{,}358.643 + \$1.102394$$

$$(289.87) \quad (.360268)$$

Standard error of the estimate, s_e = $991.93

Coefficient of (multiple) determination, r^2 = .925

Interpretation and Analysis

Equation 2 tells us that the best estimate of the selling prices of the sample of houses is $48,738.10 + $1,224.44 for each bedroom + $3,892.52 for each bathroom + $1,358.64 for each car that can be parked in the garage and + $1.10239 for each square foot of lot size.

Suppose a subject property has 3 bedrooms, 1½ baths, no garage, on a 3,750 square-foot lot. Using the regression equation, the expected selling price of the house is:

$$\hat{Y} = \$48{,}738.10 + \$1{,}224.44\,(3) + \$3{,}892.52\,(1.5) + \$1{,}358.64\,(0)$$

$$+ \$1.10239\,(3{,}750)$$

$$= \$62{,}384.16$$

The standard error of the estimate (s_e) of $991.93 is used to construct an approximate confidence interval around the expected selling price of $62,384.16. From the *t*-table with 19 degrees of freedom, the .95 confidence interval is:

$$\$62{,}384.16 \pm 2.093\,(\$991.93)$$

$$\$60{,}308.05 \text{ to } \$64{,}460.27$$

There is a .95 probability that a house like the subject would sell for between $60,308 and $64,460.[8]

---

[8] Again, see the chapter appendix for a more precise way to estimate the confidence interval.

The r^2 of .925 tells us that the four independent variables explained .925 of the variation in the selling prices of the sample. Only .075 is explained by other (omitted) variables.

The Significance of the Independent Variables

As discussed earlier, regression is useful not only to explain the dependent variable, but to estimate the value of individual characteristics (the coefficients of the independent variables) for later use in making adjustments in traditional sales comparison.[9]

The significance of each of the coefficients of the independent variables is tested by comparing their calculated t-values $b/(s_b)$ with the necessary t-value from the table. At the .05 significance level, the necessary t-value is 2.093. The calculated t-values for the four independent variables were 2.24, 4.97, 4.66, and 3.06 respectively. All are significant at the .05 level and thus the coefficients can be used with confidence to make adjustments in the traditional sale comparison approach.

The Adjusted r^2

Because r^2 measures how much of the variation in the dependent variable is explained by the independent variables, adding independent variables to the equation will always increase r^2 (and will never reduce it). Therefore, it is possible to "force" a higher r^2 by adding independent variables even if the association between some of the independent variables and the dependent variable is weak. To correct for this possibility, it is sometimes suggested that a modified, or adjusted $r^2((\bar{r})^2)$ be calculated, which adjusts r^2 downward as a function of the number of independent variables used in the model.

$$\bar{r}^2 = 1 - (1 - r^2)\left(\frac{n-1}{n-k}\right)$$

$$= r^2\left(\frac{n-1}{n-k}\right)$$

where

k is the number of independent variables and
n is the sample size

With simple regression there won't be much difference between r^2 and $\bar{r}^2$, because only one independent variable is used. With multiple regression,

---

[9] See Roger Cannaday, "How Should You Estimate and Provide Market Support for Adjustments in Single-Family Appraisals," *The Real Estate Appraiser and Analyst,* Winter 1989. This study compares an estimate of the adjustment for differences in living area based on multiple regression to an estimate based on data from a cost manual.

especially with a small sample and a relatively large number of independent variables, there can be a large difference between r^2 and $\bar{r}^2$, and in such cases $\bar{r}^2$ is the preferred measure of association.[10]

Using Qualitative (Dummy) Variables

All of the examples to this point used independent variables that are quantifiable. Variables like lot size, number of bedrooms, distance from downtown, and so on, are expressed numerically. Some variables, however, are not easy to quantify. For example, a neighborhood is often put into a category such as excellent, average, or below average. Many other variables are of the yes–no type, such as whether or not there is air conditioning, a fireplace, or a swimming pool.

These kinds of variables are called *qualitative* variables, and they are entered into the regression analysis using a '1' or a '0' to indicate the presence or lack of presence of the variable. Suppose you wanted to measure the effect of neighborhood quality on apartment rent levels. Among the independent variables to be used is neighborhood quality, and each neighborhood is assigned to one of four categories: excellent, good, average, or poor.

Assume the complete list of independent variables used in the regression is as follows:

$\hat{Y}$ = monthly rent
x_1 = square feet
x_2 = number of rooms
x_3 = distance from downtown
x_4 = excellent neighborhood
x_5 = good neighborhood
x_6 = poor neighborhood

Notice that the variable "average neighborhood" has been omitted from the list. It is called the *default* variable, meaning that when the other three neighborhood categories for a particular property are entered as 0's, by default the property must be in an average neighborhood. Using a default variable saves a degree of freedom—a valuable saving when the sample size is small—and is necessary to properly estimate the variable coefficients and the intercept term.

Assume that a sample of 35 apartment rents produced the regression Equation (3), with accompanying statistics.

---

[10] Another common measure of association is the F-statistic, which is closely related to the adjusted r^2. A high adjusted r^2 generally produces a high F. The practical difference between them is that the F-statistic can be used to assign a significance level, while the adjusted r^2 cannot.

Chapter 8 Sales Comparison Using Regression Analysis

$$\hat{Y} = 81 + .30 \ (x_1) + 20.20 \ (x_2) - 6.10 \ (x_3) \quad (3)$$
$$\phantom{\hat{Y} = 81 + } (.24) (17.90) (1.45)$$
$$+ 45.21 \ (x_4) + 31.80 \ (x_5) - 38.40 \ (x_6)$$
$$ (12.26) (8.10) (6.60)$$

$r^2 = .786$

$s_e = 31.25$

The independent variables explain .786 of the variation in monthly rents. The distance variable is significant at the .05 level, and the neighborhood variables are all significant at the .01 level. (Notice that it is the absolute *t*-value that is important. A poor neighborhood has a negative coefficient, as we would expect, but the sign is ignored.)

Two surprising results are that the "square feet" and "number of rooms" variables are insignificant, even at the .20 level. This is counterintuitive given the theoretically strong relationship between apartment size and rent. The likely reasons for this will be discussed shortly.

Predicting Rent

Using regression Equation (3), what is the predicted monthly rent of an 840 square foot, 4-bedroom apartment, located 1.3 miles from downtown in a good neighborhood? What is the approximate 90 percent confidence interval around this estimate?

$$\hat{Y} = \$81 + \$.30 \ (840) + \$20.20 \ (4) - \$6.10 \ (1.3)$$
$$+ \$45.21 \ (0) + \$31.80 \ (1) - \$38.40 \ (0)$$
$$= \$437.67$$

The 90 percent confidence interval, with 28 degrees of freedom, is $437.67 ± (1.7) ($31.25) = $384.54 − $490.80.

Interpreting the Coefficients of Dummy Variables

The interpretation of the coefficients of dummy variables is always relative to the default variable. Referring to Equation (3), this means that the monthly rent for an apartment in an excellent neighborhood will be $45.21 more than the rent in an average neighborhood. Similarly, the monthly rent in a poor neighborhood will be $38.40 less than the rent in an average neighborhood. From this, it follows that the difference between the rents in excellent and poor neighborhoods is $45.21 + $38.40 = $83.61.

Improving Regression Results

At the end of the section on simple regression, three potential errors were discussed: They were (1) inferring causation between the independent and dependent variables, (2) finding spurious relationships, and (3) unwarranted extrapolation and trending. These errors are equally likely when using multiple regression. Other problems may be the result of multicollinearity, missing variables, or how the sample was stratified.[11]

Multicollinearity

While regression coefficients are intended to measure the association between the independent variables and the dependent variable, it is also possible that two or more of the independent variables are themselves associated. A common example is the association between the number of square feet and the number of rooms in a house, both of which are often used in regression equations designed to estimate house prices. The situation where two or more independent variables at least partly measure the same thing is called *multicollinearity,* and it has a generally negative effect on the utility of the regression equation.

Actually, the issue is not whether multicollinearity exists, because it almost always does in real estate applications, but rather how severe it is. Unfortunately there are no consistently reliable ways to test for the severity of multicollinearity, and the appraiser must rely on intuition, theory, prior experience, and indirect evidence to draw conclusions.

One symptom of multicollinearity is that parts of the regression results are counterintuitive. For example, one or more variables may turn out to be statistically insignificant, even if theory and prior experience suggest they should be significant. This is because the collinear variables are in effect "sharing" significance. Recall that in the previous apartment rent example, square feet and the number of rooms were both found to be insignificantly associated with rent. It is likely that these two variables were correlated; that is, they were measuring the same thing (size), and in the equation each got only part of the credit. Collinearity can also result in one or more of the signs of the variables being incorrect.

A *correlation matrix* can also indicate the presence of collinear relationships among independent variables. A correlation matrix shows the degree of association between each pair of independent variables. Those with high correlation coefficients are good candidates for collinearity. The correlation matrix is a standard output of most regression software.

---

[11] An excellent review of the issues relating to the use of multiple regression and the interpretation of the results is found in Jonathan Mark and Michael A. Goldberg, "Multiple Regression Analysis and Mass Assessment," *The Appraisal Journal,* January 1988.

Does Multicollinearity Matter?

The fact that multicollinearity can produce surprising results in a regression equation is not necessarily fatal to the utility of the regression equation. In fact, there is a continuing debate about how concerned the appraiser should be about multicollinearity.[12] In general, if the regression is to be used only to predict Y, the presence of multicollinearity is less damaging than if the primary concern is to test the significance and magnitude of the independent variables. When variables are added, coefficients are likely to become less precise (less significant), which in turn increases the confidence interval. At the same time, however, the estimate becomes more accurate in terms of the probability the true value will fall within the confidence interval.

One strategy to minimize multicollinearity is to omit independent variables which are likely to be associated with one or more of the other independent variables. For example, when developing an equation to predict house prices, either the number of bedrooms or the number of rooms would be included, but not both. The difficulty with this judgmental approach is that it is never certain which variables should be left in, and which omitted. Stepwise regression can be of help here. One variation of the stepwise procedure begins with all of the independent variables entered. They are then removed, one at a time, beginning with the independent variable that contributes least to the explanatory power of the equation, as measured by the r^2. Each time an independent variable is removed, of course, the magnitude and significance of the remaining independent variables is likely to change, and the r^2 will decline. How far the r^2 will decline will depend on how important the removed variable had been.

The optimal stopping point in the stepwise procedure is a matter of judgment, and will depend on the purpose of the regression. If the significance of individual coefficients is of primary importance, the decision rule might be to stop removing variables when the standard error of the regression coefficients is no longer reduced, and/or when the remaining variables are significant, at say, the .05 level.

If prediction is the primary purpose of the regression, it must be noted that the cost of eliminating variables (hopefully to stabilize the remaining coefficients) is a lower r^2. This may or may not be damaging. It is important to remember that the r^2 is a measure of how well the independent variables explain the dependent variable, based on the sample. It does not necessarily reflect how well the equation will predict. That is, a relatively high r^2 does not necessarily produce a relatively high predictive power,[13] and given a

---

[12] For a recent discussion based on U.K. markets, see N. A. Rowe, G. D. Garrod, and K. G. Willis, "Valuation of Urban Amenities Using an Hedonic Price Model", *Journal of Property Research,* Summer 1995.

[13] See, for example, George W. Gau and Dan Kohlhepp, "Multicollinearity and Reduced-Form Price Equations for Residential Markets: An Evaluation of Alternative Estimation Methods," *AREUEA Journal* 6, 1978.

choice, a smaller standard error of the estimate may be preferred to a higher r^2.[14]

Another consideration when using stepwise regression is that the benefits associated with reducing multicollinearity do not come without cost. The cost is that unless the variable removed is irrelevant (an irrelevant variable being one that has a true coefficient of zero, having absolutely no impact on the dependent variable), its removal will bias the results because the remaining coefficients will be affected. Thus, there is another trade-off between the bias that is introduced in the remaining coefficients and the (likely) reduction in their standard errors. Another way of saying this is that because the stepwise procedure substitutes a mechanical procedure for the analyst's judgment in the selection of variables, it tends to take relatively greater advantage of chance. This sometimes produces apparently significant associations between remaining variables that are in fact illusory.

Other Strategies to Reduce Multicollinearity: Principal Components and Ridge Regression

Two related and potentially useful strategies to reduce multicollinearity are principal components and ridge regression. Both are statistical methods designed to realign data to capture commonalities. With these techniques, data can be represented with fewer variables, hopefully reducing the opportunities for multicollinearity.

Various studies have compared principal components to ordinary regression. The results suggest that principal components is increasingly attractive as the sample size increases and/or with cases of serious multicollinearity. One weakness of principal components is that it is difficult to assign economic content to the new variables constructed by the model. Also, empirical evidence has yet to justify a conclusion that it is in general a superior approach for real estate applications.

The technique of ridge regression attacks the problem of multicollinearity by purposely biasing the estimates in order to increase the probability that individual regression coefficients will have the proper sign and be of the correct magnitude. Though the empirical evidence is mixed, a majority of studies have found that ridge regression does a better job of estimating coefficients and of predicting prices than does ordinary regression.[15] How-

---

[14] The *adjusted* r^2 and the standard error of the estimate, however, are closely related.

[15] For example, John E. Anderson, "A Comparison of the Predictive Ability of OLS and Ridge Coefficients on Property Valuation," *Assessors Journal,* December 1981, 187–93; Richard J. Curcio, R. Penny Marquette, and James R. Webb, "Improved Prediction of Real Estate Values Through the Use of Ridge Regression," *Property Tax Journal,* June 1984; Alan K. Reichert, James S. Moore, and Chien-Ching Cho, "Analyzing the Improved Stability of Appraisal Model Coefficients: An Application of Ridge Regression Techniques," *AREUEA Journal,* Spring 1984, 50–71. An exception is the results of Gau and Kohlhepp, who could not derive a stable model using ridge regression; "Alternative Estimation methods for Reduced Form Price Equations Under Conditions of Multicollinearity: A Comment," *AREUEA Journal,* Fall 1979, 437–41.

ever, some theoretical limitations have been identified,[16] and a practical limitation is that ridge regression is not yet widely available on software.

Missing Variables

While multicollinearity is a problem associated with too many (overlapping) independent variables, equally serious problems may result from the use of too few independent variables; that is, the omission of variables that are in fact significant.

Symptoms of Missing Variables

There are three symptoms of a missing independent variable(s): (1) a low r^2, (2) "surprising" coefficients for the variables that are in the equation, and (3) identifiable patterns in the regression residuals.

A Low r^2

Because the r^2 statistic is the percentage of variation in the dependent variable that is explained by the independent variables, a low r^2 may be the result of a missing variable(s). As an obvious example, if a regression was intended to explain house prices and there was no independent variable related to house size, the resulting r^2 would likely be relatively low.[17]

Surprising Coefficients

As in the case of multicollinearity, a missing variable can produce coefficients for other variables that are of unreasonable size, have the wrong signs, or which are statistically insignificant despite prior evidence that they should be found significant. The difference is that with multicollinearity, significance is improperly shared. When a variable is missing, its effect on value may be improperly attributed to a variable(s) that is in the equation. For example, suppose that two-car garages are found most often with larger houses, and one-car garages with smaller houses. If garage size is not included as an independent variable, its effects might well be improperly

---

[16] Alan K. Reichert and James S. Moore, "Using Latent Root Regression to Identify Nonpredictive Collinearity in Statistical Appraisal Models," *AREUEA Journal,* Spring 1986, 136–52.

[17] A low r^2 may also be the result of a narrow stratification of the dependent variable. This will be discussed shortly.

TABLE 8-2 Regression Residuals (000s)

Observation	Selling Price Actual (Y)	Selling Price Estimated (Y)	Residual
1	550	601.476	(51.476)
2	705	746.862	(41.862)
3	805	838.549	(33.549)
4	775.5	806.716	(31.216)
5	515	552.233	(37.233)
6	810	773.894	36.106
7	791.5	745.421	46.079
8	865	870.091	(5.091)
9	896.5	849.060	47.440
10	643.7	581.336	62.364

attributed to another independent variable that is also related to the living area of the house.

Regression Residuals

A good way to spot situations when a variable(s) is missing is to inspect the regression residuals. Regression residuals are the differences between the actual Y's in the sample, and the Y's that are estimated by the resulting regression equation. If the regression equation includes all of the important explanatory variables, the residuals should be random; some high and some low, but with no noticeable pattern. When the residuals are not random, it suggests that a variable may have been omitted.

For example, suppose a regression equation that used GIMs to explain the prices of apartment buildings produced the regression residuals shown in Table 8–2.

As seen in Table 8–2, the first five residuals are negative, while four of the last five are positive. Reviewing the data, large differences in age are noted between the first five and the last five buildings: The first five tend to be older buildings. Given this information, the age of the building is added as an independent variable, and the regression is rerun. The results are shown in Table 8–3.

The pattern in the residuals has disappeared. The under- and overestimates are now random, suggesting that the age variable indeed had been missing. Other supporting evidence for this conclusion would be a higher r^2, and whether or not the "age" variable was statistically significant.

TABLE 8-3 Regression Residuals (000s)

Observation	Selling Price Actual (Y)	Selling Price Estimated (Y)	Residual
1	550	538.016	11.984
2	705	723.627	(18.627)
3	805	815.345	(10.345)
4	775.5	752.218	23.282
5	515	491.199	23.801
6	810	822.267	(12.267)
7	791.5	776.043	15.457
8	865	880.986	(15.986)
9	898.5	903.221	(4.721)
10	643.7	643.690	.01

Inspecting the residuals is one of the most important parts of regression analysis, and one that is too often ignored. Most software includes a calculation of the regression residuals.

The Effects of Narrow Stratification

Suppose a sample of houses had all sold for approximately the same price, but that each of the houses differed from the others in at least one respect. In other words, different combinations of characteristics happened to produce approximately the same selling prices. If a regression were run seeking to explain the selling prices, would the r^2 be high or low? The answer is that the r^2 would be low, because there is almost no variation in the dependent variable for the independent variables to explain. Because there is no variation to explain—which is the purpose of regression analysis—a simple calculation of the mean and standard deviation of the sample of selling prices would provide about the same results as the regression so far as prediction is concerned.

This does not mean that a regression equation that results from a narrow stratification of the dependent variable has no utility. While it may not be up to the task of predicting the prices of most other houses, the equation may be very useful to measure the value impact of a specific independent variable(s). The fact that the selling prices were approximately the same does not mean the equation cannot produce significant coefficients for the independent variables.

Nonlinear Relationships[18]

Suppose an appraiser is attempting to determine the relationship between construction costs and the size of a structure. The construction costs (arranged in ascending order) for a sample of 15 houses are shown in Table 8–4.

A computer run has produced the regression statistics summarized in Table 8–5. The $\bar{r}^2$ of .88 tells us that size does an excellent job of estimating cost. The residuals are troubling, however, because they are not random. They begin with several negatives, then turn generally positive, and then negative again.

A scatter diagram of the data is shown in Figure 8–2. The solid line is the calculated linear regression line. The dotted line is a hypothetical regression line (using the "eyeball" method), which suggests that the relationship between size and cost is *curvilinear*. To this point, we have only fitted straight lines. To model a *curvilinear* relationship, we can mathematically transform the independent variable, size, into one that better reflects its curvilinear relationship to cost, or alternatively, enter the independent variable in a logarithmic term, which straightens out the curve.

TABLE 8–4 Construction Costs and Size for Sample Houses

Observation	Cost	Size (square feet)
1	$ 65,500	1,023
2	82,400	1,140
3	82,700	1,260
4	103,200	1,505
5	105,900	1,370
6	106,000	1,770
7	129,600	2,305
8	134,400	2,545
9	137,500	2,100
10	138,700	2,810
11	140,000	2,950
12	155,700	3,500
13	161,600	3,049
14	166,000	4,283
15	167,600	3,800

[18] A complete discussion of nonlinear relationships is beyond the scope of this text. A good introductory discussion is found in Pindyck and Rubinfeld, *Econometric Models and Economic Forecasts* (McGraw-Hill). The use of neural networks as an alternative to regression models is sometimes suggested when relationships are nonlinear. A comparison is found in E. Worzala, M. Lenk, and A. Silva, "An Exploration of Neural Networks and Its Application to Real Estate Valuation," *Journal of Real Estate Research*, Vol. 10, 2, 1995.

Chapter 8   Sales Comparison Using Regression Analysis

TABLE 8–5   Regression Results

Intercept = $54,609

Coefficient of size = $29.87

$\bar{r}^2 = .88$

$s_e = 11.250$

Observation	Residuals
1	(19,665)
2	(6,260)
3	(9,544)
4	3,638
5	10,370
6	(1,477)
7	6,143
8	3,774
9	20,166
10	159
11	(2,723)
12	(3,451)
13	15,920
14	(16,538)
15	(512)

FIGURE 8–2   Cost and Size "Eyeball" versus Linear Estimate

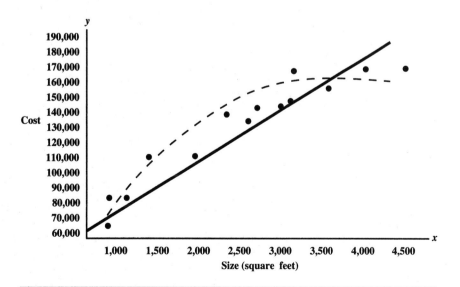

In this case, the natural logarithm of size was used, producing the following regression results.

$$\bar{r}^2 = .944$$

$$s_e = .7713$$

Observation	Residual
1	(8,683)
2	778
3	(5,798)
4	2,496
5	11,652
6	(5,847)
7	(390)
8	(2,395)
9	13,909
10	(4,900)
11	(6,940)
12	(2,985)
13	12,392
14	(6,555)
15	3,265

The transformation has produced better results, judging by the lack of a discernable pattern in the residuals. The relationship between construction cost and size is but one of many nonlinear relationships that may be of interest to the appraiser. The relationships between selling price and many of the more important price-affecting variables are also likely to be nonlinear. These variables include living area, lot area, and the number of bathrooms.[19] When developing regression equations, therefore, it is always important to consider transforming these kinds of variables.

Transformation of variables may not always be necessary. If the curve is slight and the sample is narrowly stratified with respect to the dependent variable so that only a small portion of the curve is included, that portion may be close enough to straight to be used without transformation.

Summary

Regression is a statistical model that measures the relationship among variables. It uses independent variables to explain a dependent variable. In appraisal, the resulting regression equation can be used to predict the selling price of properties and to determine whether or not

---

[19]For a readable and practical example, see David January, "Forecasting Lot Values Using Regression Analysis," *The Real Estate Appraiser and Analyst,* Fall 1989, 61–72.

certain variables are useful to explain or predict prices. Regression is widely used for mass appraisal, such as is necessary for property tax assessment purposes.

Among the most important statistics produced by a regression are the r^2 and $\bar{r}^2$, which measure the degree of association between the independent and dependent variables; the standard error of the estimate (or if available, the standard error of the forecast), which is used to calculate confidence intervals around the predictions made using the regression equation; and calculated t-values, which provide a measure of how confident we can be that the independent variables are in fact significantly associated with the dependent variable.

Because the regression model must work with the data given to it, the selection of the independent variables and the sample are of critical importance. Certain sample characteristics may be better if the equation is to be used for prediction, while a different sample may be better if the purpose is to test the magnitude and significance of individual variables. For example, a narrow stratification of the dependent variable may produce a low r^2 and limited applicability of the predicting equation, but it may do a good job of measuring the coefficients of the independent variables.

Regression analysis involves large doses of judgment in selecting the sample, choosing the variables, and deciding on any transformation of variables. This is a bit of a paradox. While proponents of statistical models point to the objectivity of the results, it is clear that the proper use of regression requires at least as much judgment as do the traditional appraisal approaches. Potential problem areas when using regression include inferring causation, a lack of theory, inappropriate extrapolation and trending, multicollinearity, and missing variables. Finally, an often overlooked part of regression analysis is a study of the regression residuals. The pattern of the residuals may indicate whether variables are missing or whether variables are better transformed from a linear to a curvilinear form.

Questions and Problems

1. What is regression analysis?
2. You are measuring the relationship between Y, annual office rent per square foot, and (1) x_1, the height of the office (the floor of the building on which it is located), and (2) x_2, how far (in feet) the building is located from a point considered the best downtown location. A sample of 24 leases produced this regression equation:

   $$\hat{Y} = \$32.14 - .71\ (x_1) - .003214\ (x_2)$$
   $$\qquad\qquad\quad (.36)\qquad\ (.000994)$$

   $s_e = 1.65$

   $\bar{r}^2 = .69$

   The standard errors of the coefficients are in parentheses below the coefficients.

   a. Which variables are significant at the .10 level?
   b. Calculate .90 confidence intervals around the coefficients of the independent variables.
   c. What is the predicted square-foot rent of an office on the fifth floor in a building one-half mile from the location reference point?
   d. Calculate the .95 confidence interval around the estimate made in c.
   e. What does the $\bar{r}^2$ tell you?

3. The three categories of neighborhood quality in a sample of houses were below average, average, and above average. The below average and above average categories were used in the regression, and

they produced coefficients of −$7,240 and +$3,860, respectively. Interpret these coefficients. Why was the average neighborhood not included as an independent variable?

4. What are the disadvantages and advantages of narrowly stratifying the dependent variable?

5. A regression has produced the following residuals:

Observation	Residual	Observation	Residual
1	15.245	9	−11.291
2	13.197	10	−9.357
3	12.048	11	−2.355
4	2.667	12	0.479
5	−1.457	13	3.866
6	−8.662	14	5.477
7	−9.332	15	7.991
8	−6.177	16	11.221

What does this pattern suggest?

6. What is correlation analysis used for?

7. An analyst interprets the simple regression equation below and concludes that a one-unit increase in the independent variable causes the dependent variable to increase by 4.3 units. Comment.
$$\hat{Y} = 12.72 + 4.3\,(x_1)$$

8. How are qualitative variables entered in a regression equation?

9. You are explaining house prices and have produced the following result:

$$\hat{Y} = \$8{,}780 + \$34.46\,(x_1)$$
$$+ \$18{,}806.67\,(x_2) - \$.07\,(x_3)$$
$$+ \$7{,}170.32\,(x_4) - \$8{,}999.46\,(x_5)$$
$$+ \$2{,}204.76\,(x_6)$$
$$r^2 = .82$$

where

x_1 = size of house (square feet)
x_2 = number of bathrooms
x_3 = size of lot (square feet)
x_4 = above average neighborhood
x_5 = below average neighborhood
x_6 = garage space (number of cars)

a. Predict the price of a house that is 2,200 square feet, has 2 bathrooms, is on a 32,000 square-foot lot, in an above average neighborhood, with a 1½ car garage.

b. The coefficient for bathrooms seems too high. What is a possible explanation?

c. Is there a way to check whether your explanation from b is correct?

d. The standard errors of the coefficients for house size and lot size were 22.05 and .05, respectively, suggesting neither to be highly significant. In addition, the sign for lot size is negative. Is there a possible explanation for these surprising results?

e. If you removed lot size from the regression, what impact do you think it would have on the results?

Appendix
A More Precise Confidence Interval[20]

In the chapter an approximate confidence interval was calculated as follows:

$$\hat{Y} \pm t\,(s_e) \quad (1)$$

Though widely used, the results of this approximation can differ substantially from the true confidence interval when the sample size is small. Because small samples are typical when working with real estate data the use of a more precise measure is suggested.

Using the simple regression example from the chapter, where the dependent variable was the selling price and the independent variable the living area of the house, we arrived at an expected selling price of $73,792 for a 1,200-square-foot house. We then calculated an 80 percent confidence interval of $71,978–75,606 using the standard error of $1,260 in Equation (1) above.

The problem is that this approach is likely to underestimate the true confidence interval because it reflects only one of two sources of uncertainty. The source of uncertainty that is reflected in the standard error of the estimate is the variation in prices that the regression model cannot explain. There is, however, a second source of uncertainty that is not captured. It flows from the fact that the estimates of the individual coefficients also have standard errors.

Thus, to properly measure the confidence interval around an estimated price, both the standard error of the estimate and the standard errors of the coefficients must be employed. To do so, we use a formula from statistics:

$$Var(mA + nB + pC) = m^2 * Var(A)$$
$$+ n^2 * Var(B) + p^2 * Var(C)$$
$$+ 2 * (mn * Cov(A,B) + mp * Cov(A,C)$$
$$+ np * COV(B,C))$$

where m, n, and p are known values, and A, B, and C are random variables. Remember that the variance is just the standard deviation squared. *Cov* stands for covariance, which is a statistic that captures how two variables move together. For convenience, we replace A with the random variable coefficient a, B with the random variable coefficient b, and C with the random variable, the residual. One way to write the model is

$$s_Y^2 = 1^2 * s_a^2 + 1200^2 * s_b^2 + 1^2 * s_e^2$$
$$+ 2 * (1 * 1200 * s_{ab}$$
$$+ 1 * 1 * s_{ae} + 1 * 1200 * s_{be})$$

where, s_{ab}, for example, is the estimate of the covariance between a and b. We have already calculated s_b and s_e, so it is easy to calculate their squares. As it happens, we need not worry about s_{ae} and s_{be}, because the residuals and coefficients are designed to have zero covariance. The reason for this is that if we can use the coefficient to help "explain" a residual, we are in a position to get a smaller residual and therefore reduce our uncertainty about the model.

Statistical packages will "spit out" the variances and covariances of coefficients in a manner that appears as follows for the example regression.

	a	b
a	9426478	−4590
b	−4590	7.73

The numbers on the diagonal (i.e., in cells *aa* and *bb*) are variances, the numbers elsewhere are covariances. Note that 7.73, the variance of b, is just 2.79 (the standard error of b) squared.

Now we may calculate the variance of our estimate. We find

---
[20] With slight editing, this discussion was provided by Richard Green.

$$s_{\hat{Y}}^2 = 1^2 * 9426478 + 1200^2 * 7.73 + 1^2 * 1260^2$$
$$+ 2 * 1200 * 1 * (-4560) = 3784779.$$

To get a confidence interval, we need a standard error. This is the square root of the estimate of the variance:

$$\sqrt{3784779} = 1945$$

Now we again turn to the *t*-table. Because the table gives the probability of falling outside an interval, the column of interest for getting an interval with 80 percent confidence is $1.00 - .80 = .20$. At the intersection of the .20 column and six degrees of freedom, we find a *t*-value of 1.44. There is an 80 percent chance that the true value of the subject house will fall in the interval from 1.44 standard errors above the predicted price to 1.44 standard errors below. For the 1,200 square-foot house, the 80 percent confidence interval is:

$$\$73792 \pm (1.44)(1945) = \$70992 - \$76592.$$

Note that roughly two-thirds of the uncertainty arises from the standard error of the estimate, and about one-third arises from the coefficient standard errors. As the size of the sample gets larger, a smaller percentage of the uncertainty will come from the coefficients. However, as variables are added to the model a larger percentage of the uncertainty will come from the coefficients.

The confidence interval as calculated above is $5,600, while the approximation using Equation (1) was calculated in the chapter to be $3,628. This is a substantial underestimate of about 35 percent.

CHAPTER 9
Special Considerations When Valuing Land and Sites

Introduction

This chapter discusses land and site valuation, which is an integral part of several appraisal topics. Land valuation has already been discussed in the chapters on accessibility and market value. Also, certain techniques for estimating land value presume an ability to use the income approach, which is covered later in the text. These techniques will be introduced here, with references to the appropriate chapters. Thus, this chapter has two purposes: to serve as a reference point for related discussions elsewhere in the text, and to discuss aspects of the appraisal process that are unique to the valuing of land.

A high percentage of appraisal assignments require the valuation of either land or a site. The most obvious situation is when the subject property is land that is unimproved. Even when a site is improved, the use of the cost approach requires that the site and improvements be valued separately. In all cases, the determination of highest and best use requires a judgment as to whether land value as if vacant would exceed value as improved. Other situations when land or a site are valued separately include valuation for property tax (state law may require separate valuations) or income tax purposes (depreciation cannot be applied to the land portion of the investment), to settle an insurance claim on a building, for condemnation, or when the site and improvements are to be sold or leased separately. The estimate of land or site value is increasingly important, as over time the land component has contributed an increasing percentage of total property value. Census Bureau Data indicates that in the late 1940s, land accounted for about 11 percent of the price of a single-family residence. By 1987, that percentage had risen to 25 percent, and by 1996, it is estimated to be about 30 percent. The average price of a lot has risen about 350 percent between the mid 70s and mid 90s, compared to an increase of 185 percent for the median price of a house and a 125 percent rise in the Consumer Price Index during the same period.

Finally, some clients routinely request a separate valuation of land. For example, Gibson's survey of real estate asset managers found that 29 percent of them always requested a separate valuation of land from their appraisers. Only 7 percent never requested a separate valuation.[1]

We begin by differentiating between land and site value, then proceed with a discussion of the determinants and mechanics of land and site valuation.

Site versus Land

There is a difference between a site and land. A site is land that is ready for building; grading, utilities, and access have been provided. Land is not yet ready for building. This is an important difference because the costs of preparing a site often exceed the cost of the raw land, and thus when using valuation techniques like direct sales comparison it is important not to mix site and land values.

So far as the appraisal *process* is concerned, however, the distinction between land and site is less important, because they are amenable to the same valuation techniques.

Highest and Best Use and Value

When valuing land or a site, the underlying assumption is that it will be put to its highest and best use as if vacant. The justification for this assumption is that if the property is currently under- or overdeveloped, the difference in total property value between "what is" and "what would be if vacant" is properly assigned to the value of the building. This has two implications: (1) the current improvement is irrelevant when estimating the site or land value, and (2) if the current improvements are not the current highest and best use (that is, they represent an under- or overdevelopment), it is the building that is assumed to suffer the loss in value, not the site.

The Determination and Estimation of Site and Land Values

To minimize redundancy from this point, we will refer only to valuing sites, recognizing the reference is to land as well as to sites except when it is indicated otherwise. The general categories of factors which determine the

---

[1]Robert Gibson, "Asset Managers' View of the Appraisal of Real Estate Assets," *Appraisal Journal,* January 1989.

value of sites are the same as those which determine the value of improved properties. They are (1) location, including its two components of accessibility and neighborhood, (2) the physical characteristics of the site, and (3) legal constraints such as zoning, height, setback and coverage restrictions, encumbrances, and deed restrictions. These general influences were discussed in Chapters 3, 4, and 6.

Methods of Estimating Site Value

Site value can be estimated using variations of four basic approaches: (1) direct sales comparison, (2) land residual, (3) allocation and assessment ratios, and (4) land rent capitalization. They are discussed in turn.

Direct Sales Comparison

As in the case of improved properties, sites can be valued using direct sales comparison when a sufficient number of comparable sales are available. The same general rule applies: In the selection of comparables, the appraiser should attempt to minimize differences between the comparables and the subject for the characteristics that are difficult to adjust for, especially if the necessary adjustments would be relatively large. Falling into this category more often than not are location and size. With respect to size, if it is an urban site, frontage (given adequate depth) may be the most important characteristic. If it is a suburban lot, square feet may be most important (assuming a reasonable frontage/depth relationship), and for unimproved rural land, the number of acres may be most important.

This leads naturally to the appropriate unit of comparison. It may be front feet, square feet, a standard lot, or an acre. By reducing price to the appropriate unit basis, physical differences in size and shape are more easily accounted for. Regardless of the unit of comparison, the appraiser must keep in mind the nonlinearity of land values. As size increases, per unit value tends to decrease.

Making Adjustments to Comparable Prices
The unit price of the comparables are adjusted to the price of the subject using the same order of adjustments learned earlier: (1) property rights conveyed, (2) financing, (3) conditions of sale, (4) market conditions (time), and (5) any remaining differences.

As discussed in the chapter on direct sales comparison, there are two ways adjustments can be reported: on a dollar basis and on a percentage basis. While the two methods should produce the same result, if you begin with percentages and then convert to dollars, remember that the percentages refer to their effect on value, not to the physical (or legal, etc.) difference between the comparable and the subject. That is, when comparing two sites, if the appraiser claims that there is a 10 percent difference attributable to their locations and a 10 percent difference attributable to their size, the dollar adjustment for both differences must be the same. Thus, what is really being said is that the location and landscaping differences both produce a 10 percent difference in value.

A Completed Adjustment Grid

When adjustment grids are used to estimate site value, they look the same and are based on the same logic as when they are used for improved properties. Table 9–1 is a completed adjustment grid for a residential site, based on information from four comparable sales plus adjustments the appraiser has made based on prior analyses. The unit of comparison is the site itself. Notice that where appropriate, both the percentage and dollar adjustments are reported. While this is redundant from a valuation standpoint, many appraisers include both because it provides additional information to the client.

TABLE 9–1 Completed Adjustment Grid

	Comparable Sale			
	1	2	3	4
Sales price	$21,500	$26,300	$27,900	$32,600
Financing adjustment	0	1,500	0	2,200
Financed adjusted sales price	$21,500	$24,800	$27,900	$30,400
Time adjustment (8% year)	(1 yr. ago, 8%) +1,720	(6 months, 4%) +992	(Current) 0	(18 months, 12%) +3,648
Time adjusted sales price	$23,220	$25,792	$27,900	$34,048
Other adjustments				
Location	0	0	−1,395 (−5%)	−5,107 (−15%)
Frontage	+2,322 (10%)	+2,579 (10%)	0	0
Depth	0	0	0	0
Landscaping	+1,161 (5%)	0	+1,395 (5%)	+1,702 (5%)
Adjusted sales price	$26,703	$28,371	$27,900	$30,643

The range of values is $26,703 to $30,643. The selection of the final estimate from this data is a matter of judgment, weighting the adjusted prices as seen fit. Using an equal weighting (the average) produces a value estimate of about $28,000. Given that Comparables #1 and #4 required three adjustments each, while Comparable #2 required only one adjustment and Comparable #3 required two, an argument could be made to weight #2 and #3 more heavily. In this case, the result (about $28,000) would be the same.

Plottage and Excess Land

Can the whole be greater than the sum of the parts? When dealing with assembling land, maybe so, and it is an important issue when using the sales comparison approach. Recall that plottage is the combining of two or more sites, resulting in a greater assembled value than the sum of the values of the individual sites. There are a number of situations which may produce plottage value. For example, zoning may have prevented the individual sites from being developed to a use as profitable as after assemblage. Or the shapes of the individual sites may not be conducive to an optimal use. While there is no a priori reason to conclude that bigger means more valuable per unit, the unit values of parcels that are too small, have odd shapes, or have insufficient room for such things as setback requirements will likely increase when assembled.

There is, of course, the possibility of an opposite outcome, that the value of the whole will be less than the sum of the values of the parts. This is sometimes referred to as plattage, which commonly occurs when land is subdivided for residential development.[2]

The possibility of plottage or plattage value is important when using direct sales comparison to value a subject parcel of land which differs significantly in size from a comparable. The question to be asked is whether the size difference is such that the properties are not really comparable.

It is also possible to have excess land. That is, land that exceeds the typical frontage or total size for the existing or proposed improvements. In such cases, the per-unit value of the excess may not equal the per-unit value for the standard size. The appraiser then must turn to the market to determine what value to assign the excess. Historically, certain clients like the Federal Housing Administration have required that the value of any excess land be ignored. In other cases, the potential use of the excess land will determine its contribution to the value of the entire property. At one extreme, the excess may have little value either because it is too small to be sold separately or its contribution is minimal to the utility of the property as

---

[2]Peter F. Colwell and C. F. Sirmans, "Area, Time, Centrality and the Value of Urban Land," *Land Economics,* November 1978.

is. If the excess can be sold, its existence and contribution to value is a special case of plattage value.

The Land Residual Approach

Basic variations of the land residual technique have already been used to illustrate how land values are determined in the marketplace, and Chapter 20 will provide a more detailed presentation of the land residual technique. We refer you to those discussions, with the reminder that the land residual technique is reliable as an indicator of market value only when the improvements or contemplated improvements are within the range of expected uses of the site as if vacant.

Allocation and Tax Assessment Ratios

A variation of the land residual technique is the practice of allocating total value to land and improvements on the basis of either the ratio of land to improvements for comparable properties, or by subtracting the building's cost from total value. For example, if a new, comparable house sold for $110,000, and the building's cost was $81,000, the value allocated to the site would be $110,000 - $81,000 = $29,000.

Another variation of allocation makes use of tax assessment ratios. If in a given area there is an improvement-to-site value ratio of 5:1 and the cost to construct a house is $75,000, it is inferred that the site value is $15,000. This approach must be used cautiously, given the inevitable distortion of assessed ratios of improvement-to-site values over time, and the possibility of differences in ratios among properties.

Finally, ratios of assessed value to selling prices may prove useful. This technique was covered in detail in Chapter 6. Briefly, the appraiser calculates the ratio of assessed values to selling prices, then uses that ratio to value the subject site. For example, if the average ratio of assessed values to market values for comparable sales is .40, and the assessed value of the subject site is $12,500, the estimate of market value is

$$\frac{\$12,500}{.40} = \$31,250.$$

The results of this kind of analysis should be accepted subject to the familiar caveats that the ratios may change over time, and because the assessments are not individually market extracted there may not be assessment equality among sites.

Capitalization of Land Rent

When data on ground leases is available, land can be valued by capitalizing annual rent. Suppose, for example, that ground leases on comparable sites required annual rent of $2.50 per square foot, and that the proper one-year rate of return (capitalization rate) for land of this type is 6.5 percent.[3] The value of a 13,000 square-foot property would be

$$\frac{\$32,500}{.065} = \$500,000.$$

Site Value When the Improvements Should Be Demolished

Suppose a site sold for $300,000. At the time of sale, the site was improved, but demolition was justified on the basis that the value of the site as if vacant, less demolition costs of $15,000, exceeded the value as improved.

If this sale is subsequently used as a comparable, the value of the site must be adjusted for demolition costs. The demolition costs are *added* to the transaction price to arrive at the value of the site. In this example, the value of the land is $300,000 + $15,000 = $315,000. The logic of adding demolition costs is straightforward. A buyer won't pay the same for a site that will require an expenditure for demolition as he or she would for a comparable but vacant site. If the example site had been vacant, therefore, a price of $315,000 would have been justified.

Sources of Data

While the sources of data on site and land values will vary from market to market, interviews with the parties to the transaction often produce the most reliable information. Public records may provide data about such things as the parties involved, the selling price, and encumbrances. Publications such as multi-list books also provide useful information, and government agencies like the Federal Housing Administration and Veterans Administration may also maintain records of transactions. An extensive bibliography of data sources has been developed by the Pension Real Estate Association.[4]

---

[3] Basic income capitalization techniques are discussed in Chapters 13 through 15.
[4] C. F. Sirmans, *Data Sources for Real Estate Market Analysis,* (Storrs, CREUES), 1994.

Summary

In addition to the valuation of vacant land or sites as the object of an appraisal, there are a number of circumstances that require a separation of building and site value. The most common is in the use of the cost approach. Others include tax assessment purposes, to settle insurance claims, to allocate condemnation proceeds, and when the land and improvements are to be transferred or financed separately.

There are several ways to estimate the market value of land or a site: (1) direct sales comparison, (2) the land residual technique, (3) the use of land/building allocations and assessment ratios, and (4) land rent capitalization.

When using direct sales comparison, the determinants of market value must be kept in mind. Accessibility, neighborhood, and physical characteristics such as size, shape, and topography are critical. The appropriate unit of comparison will depend on the location and potential use of the land. For example, front feet tend to be the criterion for commercial sites, while residential site values are quoted most often in terms of the size of the site (square feet, lots, or acres). Large size differentials between comparables and the subject property are a signal that there is potential for plottage value, plattage value, or excess land, and therefore, that the comparables may or may not be truly comparable.

The land residual technique assigns a land or site value based on the difference between total value and the value of the improvements. It is most reliable when the improvements are in the range suggested by the expected use of the land as if unimproved. Allocation techniques, including the use of ratios of site-to-improvement values must be used with extreme care, particularly in the case where ratios are taken from tax assessments because those ratios are not market extracted. Land rent can be capitalized when there is available data on rents and capitalization rates on comparable properties.

Finally, when valuing a site that was purchased and the improvements demolished, the value of the site is its purchase price plus the demolition costs.

Questions and Problems

1. Distinguish between land and site value.
2. A new building is built at a cost of $500,000. The value of the whole property is $700,000. Comparable sites are selling for $400,000.
   a. What is the value of the site?
   b. The value of the building?
3. Two contiguous parcels of commercially zoned urban land, A and B below, are for sale. They have the same number of square feet, and comparable topography. Which is likely to be more valuable? Why?
4. An appraiser is heard to say, "The topography of site A is 10 percent better than the landscaping of site B." Site A, the comparable, sold for $35,000, including landscaping value of $5,500. What adjustment should be made to the price of site A to make it equal to site B, the subject

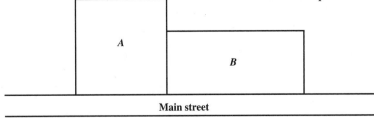

property, with reference to landscaping? Explain your answer.

5. You are valuing one of a remaining handful of lots in a subdivision. The last sale for $46,500 took place one year ago. However, two of the remaining lots are currently listed for sale, one for $53,000, the other for $55,500. What are some of the questions to be answered when valuing the subject lot?

PART IV

Estimating Value: The Cost Approach

The second of the three appraisal approaches is the cost approach. Like the sales comparison approach, the cost approach is based on the idea that comparable bundles of property rights will have the same values. In the sales comparison approach, the adjusted selling prices of comparable bundles of rights are used to estimate the expected selling price of the subject. In the cost approach, the adjusted cost to reproduce (or replace) the subject property is used to estimate its expected selling price.

The full cost approach model looks like this:

Market Value = Reproduction (or replacement) cost of the subject property's improvements as if new

− Accrued depreciation on the improvements

+ Land value.

Inspection of the cost approach model reveals that it estimates value by comparing the subject property with a new version of itself.

An important difference from the sales comparison approach is that the latter produces an expected selling price using direct evidence of value—transaction prices—while the cost approach produces an expected selling price using a proxy for value—the depreciated cost to reproduce (or replace) the subject. Thus, the cost approach works best for markets that are in equilibrium, for in those markets the cost to produce less depreciation equals market value.

This has obvious implications for the utility of the cost approach. In a previous chapter on price setting in real estate markets it was observed that real estate markets may not move as quickly to equilibrium as other markets. Thus, the cost approach works best in markets like single-family residential, where there are relatively large numbers of transactions and the chances of the market being in equilibrium are much greater than is the case in industrial, office, or commercial markets.

A second major factor in applying the cost approach is that making the estimate of depreciation can be quite difficult. The implication is that because newer buildings tend to have suffered relatively little depreciation, the cost approach generally works better for them than for older buildings.

Chapter 10

The Cost Approach: An Overview

Introduction

This chapter introduces the cost approach and the following two chapters provide details on how it is applied. The underlying assumption of the cost approach is that the cost to reproduce (or replace) a property, *as if it were new,* less any accrued depreciation, plus the land value, produces an acceptable estimate of market value.

> Market value = Reproduction (or replacement) cost of the subject property's improvements as if new
>
> − Accrued depreciation on the Improvements
>
> + Land value

The appraiser first estimates the value of the improvements as if they were to be built as of the date of the appraisal. Next, an estimate is made of any depreciation in value to the subject property compared to its cost new. The result of subtracting depreciation from cost new is an estimate of the current market value of the improvements. This is added to the value of the land to arrive at the estimate of the market value of the property.

It is helpful to think of the cost approach as a special case of sales comparison. Imagine two properties, say single-family houses, sitting side-by-side. They are identical as far as size, floor plan, building materials, and improvements to the site. However, one of the houses is 10 years old, the other is brand new. Suppose that the 10-year-old house is the subject property, and the identical (but new) house next door has just sold.

Using the identical house next door as a comparable, all that would have to be adjusted for would be any value effects associated with the ten-year difference in age. This is exactly what happens when using the cost approach, where the cost to duplicate a "new" subject property is estimated,

179

and then any value effects associated with the difference in age (accrued depreciation) between the new subject and the actual subject is subtracted from its cost new.

Conceptually then, the cost approach is the direct sales comparison approach, with all the variables held constant except the effects of depreciation. The subject is compared to a "new" duplicate of itself.

There is a strong intuitive appeal to the cost approach. On the demand side, potential buyers of a subject property have the alternative of purchasing an equivalent site and constructing equivalent improvements. Thus, a buyer will pay no more for an existing subject property than it would cost to reproduce the property. Cost also disciplines price on the supply side. While sellers would like to get the highest price possible, in competitive markets, the cost to produce—defined properly to include a normal profit—will effectively limit prices.

Limitations of the Cost Approach

There are some conceptual issues and mechanical limitations associated with the use of the cost approach. Most of them will be discussed in a succeeding chapter, but one, the estimation of depreciation, is of particular importance and merits mention here. Estimating the loss in value from depreciation is one of the appraiser's most challenging tasks. First, what is really being measured is the loss in value from a loss in utility, and utility is an elusive concept that tends to resist measurement. Second, market tastes and perceptions of utility may change rapidly. Third, because depreciation tends to be associated with the aging process, the problem of estimating depreciation becomes more acute for older properties. Fourth, because improvements tend to have long economic lives, it is often difficult to estimate losses in value from depreciation over relatively short time periods. Finally, older properties tend to be in older, built-up parts of town. In such areas, there may not be sufficient sales of vacant sites to use to estimate the value of the land.

Because of these limitations, the cost approach tends to work best for newer properties that on average will be less affected by a loss in value from depreciation and will be in less built-up areas that make it easier to estimate land value. The cost approach also tends to work better for houses than for other kinds of properties.

Other Uses of the Cost Approach

In addition to the cost approach being more applicable for newer properties and for houses, there are certain other circumstances that favor its use.

- Limited or No-Market Appraisals
  In some markets, often those in smaller communities or in slow markets, there may be too few transactions to justify a value

estimate based on direct sales comparison. This leaves the cost approach and/or the income approach.

- Property Insurance
  Most fire and casualty insurance policies specify the cost approach as the basis on which compensation for loss is to be calculated.
- New or Proposed Construction
  For new construction, most kinds of depreciation tend to be minimal, and from a mechanical standpoint, this makes the cost approach quite effective. However, as we observed in the late 1980s and early 1990s, there can be a misreading of the market by the industry, resulting in large amounts of built-in depreciation traceable to an oversupply.
- Investment Analysis
  Developers are interested in the relationship between the cost to develop and the estimated value of the project when completed. A positive gap between value and cost suggests an attractive opportunity, a negative gap the reverse.
- Special Purpose or Unique Properties
  There is often not a market for special purpose properties such as post offices and churches. In such cases the cost approach may be the only alternative available to the appraiser. The same is true of properties that are unique physically or functionally.

Steps in the Cost Approach

After inspecting the property and gathering the appropriate data, the application of the cost approach involves the following steps:

1. Estimate the reproduction (or replacement) cost of the main building(s) as of the date of the appraisal. This estimate includes direct (hard) costs, indirect (soft) costs, developer (entrepreneurial) profit, and any costs necessary to get the building to a normal occupancy level after construction.
2. Estimate the accrued depreciation on the main building(s) and deduct this amount from its reproduction (or replacement) cost.
3. Estimate the reproduction (or replacement) cost of other, secondary buildings and site improvements, and deduct accrued depreciation. Sometimes these kinds of improvements are valued directly; that is, already net of depreciation.
4. Estimate the land value assuming it is vacant and will be put to its highest and best use.
5. Add the estimated land value to the depreciated cost of the improvements to arrive at the estimate of the property's market value.

Reproduction or Replacement Cost?

To this point, each reference to cost has been accompanied by a choice between reproduction and replacement cost. While either can be used, there are differences in application and certain clients may request one or the other.

The accepted definitions of reproduction cost and replacement cost are as follows:[1]

> *Reproduction cost* is the estimated cost to construct, at current prices, as of the effective date of the appraisal, *an exact duplicate or replica* of the building being appraised, using the same materials, construction standards, design, layout, and quality of workmanship, and embodying all the deficiencies, superadequacies, and obsolescence of the subject building.
>
> *Replacement cost* is the estimated cost of construction, at current prices, as of the effective appraisal date, a building with *utility equivalent* to the building being appraised, using modern materials and current standards, design and layout.

Comparing these definitions indicates that the major difference between reproduction and replacement cost is that reproduction cost is defined in terms of the *physical structure,* while replacement cost is defined in terms of *utility.* This difference suggests certain relative strengths and weaknesses. The use of replacement cost, because it assumes current building standards and design, avoids the necessity to estimate depreciation that may have occurred in those areas. Another advantage of the use of replacement cost is that for older properties, estimating the current cost of an exact reproduction of materials and workmanship may be difficult. Finally, some argue that the use of replacement cost does a better job of simulating market behavior, because buyers and sellers tend to think in terms of utility rather than the physical structure.

These advantages of replacement cost over reproduction cost are offset by two factors. First, many clients, often in response to court decisions, will demand the use of reproduction cost. Second, the measurement of utility is difficult, and attempting to arrive at "equal" utility for two different structures (the subject property versus its replacement) may be difficult.

The result of these trade-offs is that in appraisal practice, many *kinds* of assignments—for condemnation purposes, for special purpose buildings, and for demonstration appraisal reports to gain professional designations—favor the use of reproduction cost. In addition, the *Uniform Residential Appraisal Report* required by most lenders requires the use of reproduction cost. Nonetheless, when they have a choice, many appraisers prefer replacement cost because it is a bit easier to apply and is less time-consuming to complete.

---

[1] *The Dictionary of Real Estate Appraisal,* 3rd ed., Appraisal Institute, Chicago, 1993.

Estimating Reproduction (or Replacement) Cost

$V =$ **Reproduction (or replacement) cost new** $-$ Accrued depreciation
$+$ Land value

There are three categories of reproduction (or replacement) cost (new): (1) direct costs, (2) indirect costs, and (3) developer's profit. Direct costs include the costs of labor, materials, and the contractor's profit. Indirect costs include professional fees, costs of feasibility studies, financing costs and taxes during construction, sales commissions, absorption expenses during the lease-up period, and leasing commissions.

In addition to these direct and indirect costs, a developer must be compensated for the entrepreneurial risks involved in bringing a property to market. The expected difference between market value when completed and the direct and indirect costs of development is the developer's profit. An estimate of that difference must be included as part of the cost estimate. It should not be confused with the contractor's profit, which is included in the direct labor and materials costs. If the developer is also the contractor, then he or she will be entitled to both sources of profit. In this situation, it is still proper conceptually to divide profit into two parts, both of which happen to flow to the same entity.

Estimating Accrued Depreciation

$V =$ Reproduction (or replacement) cost new $-$ **Accrued depreciation**
$+$ Land value

Accrued depreciation is defined as the difference between the cost to reproduce (or replace) the improvements to the subject property (new) on the date of the appraisal, and the market value of the improvements on the same date. There are three categories of accrued depreciation: (1) physical deterioration, (2) functional obsolescence, and (3) external obsolescence. Physical deterioration refers to the effects on value of "wear and tear." Examples are a leaky roof, loose boards, and peeling paint. Functional depreciation, or functional obsolescence, refers to the effects on value of out-of-date or out-of-favor characteristics of the property. Examples are a bathtub without a shower, separate hot and cold water spigots, or a poor floor plan.

Because items tend to both wear out and become functionally obsolete as they age, physical deterioration and functional obsolescence are often related. However, that isn't always the case. A new structure with no physical deterioration can suffer a loss of value from functional obsolescence. A bad floor plan is an example.

Unlike physical deterioration and functional obsolescence, external depreciation (or external obsolescence) comes from sources external to the subject property. There are two subcategories: (1) locational obsolescence, which is the effect on value of the subject property's neighborhood, and (2) economic obsolescence, which is the effect on value of economic conditions, both general (like a rise in interest rates), and specific (like an oversupply of a certain kind of property, pollution, or excessive noise). It is also possible for external obsolescence to be "positive." In markets where demand outpaces supply, market prices may exceed the cost to produce, requiring an upward adjustment for external obsolescence.

Estimating Land Value

V = Reproduction (or replacement) cost new − Accrued depreciation

+ Land value

A number of ways to estimate land value have been discussed in previous chapters. However land value is estimated, the important point is that it is assumed to be vacant and that it will be put to its highest and best use.

The complete cost approach model looks like this:

Value = Reproduction (or replacement) cost − Accrued depreciation + Land value

- Direct Costs
- Indirect Costs
- Developer's Profit

- Physical Deterioration
- Functional Obsolescence
- External Obsolescence

- Highest and Best Use As If Vacant

A Brief History of the Cost Approach

The cost approach has a checkered past. Prior to the 1930s, it was dominated in appraisal practice by the direct sales comparison approach, on the basis that sales comparison produces an estimate that is based on direct evidence of value, while the cost approach estimates value indirectly. This attitude changed with the collapse of real estate markets during the Depression. The collapse was blamed partly on the excesses of speculation, and in turn, on appraisals which reflected those excesses through heavy reliance on the sales comparison approach. As a result, the "bricks and mortar" cost approach gained social status, and was given an additional boost by the requirement of the newly founded Federal Housing Administration that the cost approach be included in appraisals for mortgage lending purposes. The cost approach was further strengthened by the FHA's emphasis on construction standards, which helped create and maintain the building cost service business.

The pendulum swung back again in the 1950s, when the cost approach began to lose ground in response to a changing investment environment that favored the use of the sales comparison and income approaches. At that time, the market began to view property value more in terms of financial (mortgage-equity) or contractual (leased fee-leasehold) components and less in terms of physical (land and building) components. The changed emphasis occurred mainly because financing became more sophisticated, with a trend toward higher loan-to-value ratios and more creative financing structures, and because the tax impacts of real estate investment, which were negligible prior to the 1950s, assumed a more important pricing role. The result was a movement toward an investment, rather than physical, perspective in real estate markets, with appraisal practice following.

The declining fortunes of the cost approach have continued to the present. Advances in computer technology have enhanced our ability to store, access, and analyze large amounts of market information, further favoring the use of the sales comparison and income approaches. Some now advocate making the cost approach optional for certain kinds of appraisals.[2]

Summary

It is helpful to view the cost approach as a special case of the direct sales comparison approach, where the subject property is compared to the cost to reproduce a new duplicate of itself. The estimate of accrued depreciation is the link between the cost of the new duplicate and the market value of the subject property.

The cost approach has strong intuitive appeal, because buyers should not be willing to pay more than the cost to produce a substitute, and in a competitive market, sellers should not be able to charge more than their costs.

The steps in the cost approach are as follows:

1. Reproduction (or replacement) cost new is estimated.
2. Accrued depreciation on the main improvement(s) is estimated and subtracted from its cost new.
3. The depreciated costs of any secondary structures and improvements to the site are estimated.
4. Land value is estimated, based on its highest and best use as if vacant.
5. Market value is the cost new less accrued depreciation plus land value.

Either reproduction or replacement cost new may be used. Reproduction cost assumes a building identical to the subject building. Replacement cost assumes a building with utility equivalent to the subject building, but constructed using modern technology and materials. The choice of reproduction or replacement cost new will depend on the specifics of the assignment and the requirements of the user(s) of the report.

Reproduction (or replacement) cost new includes three categories of costs: (1) direct

---

[2]See, for example, Mark Doutzour and Mark Freitag, "The Cost Approach in Residential Appraising: Make it Optional," *Appraisal Journal,* April 1995.

(hard) costs, (2) indirect (soft) costs, and (3) the developer's profit.

There are also three categories of depreciation: (1) physical deterioration, (2) functional obsolescence, and (3) external obsolescence. The source of physical deterioration and functional obsolescence is the subject property itself. The source of external obsolescence is outside the subject property and includes both locational and economic factors. The complete cost approach model looks like this:

Value = Reproduction (or replacement) cost − Accrued depreciation + Land value

- Direct Costs
- Indirect Costs
- Developer's Profit

- Physical Deterioration
- Functional Obsolescence
- External Obsolescence

- Highest and Best Use As If Vacant

Questions and Problems

1. What is the cost approach model?
2. Compare the cost approach to the sales comparison approach.
3. Provide three examples each of physical deterioration, functional obsolescence, and external obsolescence.
4. It is easier to apply the cost approach to new improvements than to old. Why?
5. What is the difference between reproduction and replacement cost? What are the strengths and weaknesses of each?
6. The cost approach was quite popular in the years between the Depression and the 1950s. It has since lost some of that popularity. Explain.
7. The estimate of reproduction (or replacement) cost includes an allowance for the developer's profit. Why?

Chapter 11 Estimating Building Costs

Introduction

In the previous chapter, the cost approach was introduced. Some important lessons from that chapter are as follows:

- The cost approach model is:

    Value = Reproduction (or replacement) cost new −

    Accrued depreciation + Land

- The difference between reproduction cost and replacement cost is that reproduction cost assumes a physical duplicate of the subject building, while replacement cost assumes utility equal to the subject building, but using modern materials and technology. Thus, replacement cost is estimated net of many kinds of functional obsolescence. Whether reproduction or replacement cost is used depends on the client's desires, legal requirements, the nature of the assignment, and the relative expenses involved.
- There are three categories of reproduction/replacement costs new: direct or hard costs, indirect or soft costs, and developer's profit. The estimate of direct costs includes material and labor. The estimate of indirect costs includes such things as feasibility studies and appraisals, insurance, taxes, architectural and engineering fees, surveys, title searches, demolition fees, short-term financing, and lease-up costs. The developer's profit is estimated separately, often as a percentage of direct and indirect costs, and added to the direct and indirect costs to arrive at the total cost. It is important to differentiate the developer's profit from the contractor's profit. The latter is part of the cost to construct and is included in a contractor's bid. The developer's profit is his or her entrepreneurial reward. If buildings could not be expected to be sold at a price higher than their direct and indirect costs to produce, there would be no incentive to develop them.

- There are three kinds of depreciation: physical deterioration (wear and tear), functional obsolescence (out-of-date or out-of-favor in the market), and external obsolescence (locational and economic). Because depreciation is difficult to measure and tends to be associated with a building's age, the cost approach tends to be more easily applied to new buildings rather than old.
- Land value is estimated based on its highest and best use as if vacant. Thus, the cost approach is most useful for estimating the market value of properties that are currently improved at or close to their expected use as if vacant. Also, it is sometimes difficult to value the land component of properties in older neighborhoods, as in those built-up areas, there tend to be few, if any, sales of vacant sites to use as comparables.
- The cost approach is relied on heavily to value properties for which the market is too thin to locate comparables for sales comparison and which do not generate a stream of income on which to base the income approach.

The topic of this chapter is the estimate of reproduction (or replacement) cost new. The topic of the following chapter is the estimate of accrued depreciation.

Sources of Cost Data

The two primary sources of building cost data are local building professionals and published cost services. These sources may vary in detail and accuracy. The specific appraisal problem will often dictate which source(s) is most appropriate.

Local contractors, builders, and professional cost estimators are primary sources of cost data, and tend to be quite reliable. When available, construction contracts for buildings similar to the subject are also a good source. Over time, an appraiser will build a file of updated cost estimates for various property types, which should be indexed with respect to the types and quality of construction. The file data should also include cost estimates for those building features that have significant impacts on value, such as building measurements, interior patterns, and equipment.

Benchmark structures are often used for common types of construction. For example, the cost to reproduce a standard two-story house becomes the base cost to which adjustments are made to reflect differences between it and a subject property. The greater the similarity between the benchmark and the subject, of course, the fewer the adjustments and the greater the accuracy of the resulting cost estimate. This is no different than the strategy for selecting comparable sales for use in the sales comparison approach.

In addition to these local and relatively direct sources of building cost data, there are a number of cost services that sell cost information based on both benchmark structures and more detailed segregated cost data for structural components and equipment. Among these companies are Marshall Valuation Services, Boeckh, F. W. Dodge, and R. S. Means. The *Kelley Blue Book* provides cost guidance for manufactured housing.

The cost manuals published by these companies generally include direct costs and some indirect costs such as legal fees, interest on construction loans, property taxes, and carrying charges. They do not generally include the cost of improvements to the site, such as storm drains, sewers, and any costs of demolition. Developer's profits are not generally included. Any of the costs that are omitted must be estimated separately.

An increasingly important consideration when choosing between locally generated cost estimates and those from a cost service are the policies of the major secondary mortgage market institutions. As part of the overall effort to standardize the criteria for acceptable loans, these institutions often require the cost estimate for their underlying collateral to be based directly on a cost service, or if it is not, to be consistent with the estimate that would be made based on those services. Many cost services now provide software for cost estimating, making them more attractive to the appraiser.

Cost Estimation

Regardless of the source of the appraiser's data, and regardless of whether it is reproduction or replacement cost that is being used, there are three basic methods of estimating building costs. In ascending order of detail, they are: (1) comparative unit, (2) unit-in-place (or segregated), and (3) quantity-survey. The method used will depend on the nature of the appraisal assignment and the relative importance of the cost approach in arriving at the final value estimate.

In practice, the comparative unit method is the most widely used method of cost estimation, followed by the unit-in-place. Detailed examples of the comparative unit and unit-in-place methods are provided in following sections. Quantity-survey is used only when the added expense of an extremely detailed cost estimate is justified. In these cases, the appraiser should consider consulting a professional cost estimator or architect, or at a minimum solicit bids from contractors. Because this will add to the expense of completing the appraisal, it should be discussed with the client prior to accepting the assignment. For the great majority of assignments, the cost approach can be completed without the service of a cost estimator. The *Uniform Residential Appraisal Report,* the most widely used form for residential appraisal assignments, requires the least-detailed cost estimating method—the comparative unit method—and very little detail about the estimate of accrued depreciation.

The Comparative Unit Method

The comparative unit method is based on the dollar cost per unit of area or volume. Generally, the larger the structure the smaller the unit costs, reflecting economies of scale for such things as heating and plumbing systems.

Therefore, when using the comparative unit method it is important to base the cost comparisons on structures of reasonably similar size.

Manuals published by cost services provide per-unit costs for benchmark buildings. These benchmarks are then matched to the subject property based on important cost-affecting features. The features that differentiate the benchmark building include the number of stories, the ground floor area, the type of exterior wall, and the "class of construction," which is based on factors like the basic shape of the building, the type of roof, the interior walls, and various types of equipment in the building. Because these services are used in different markets, local multipliers are provided which are used to adjust the base cost to reflect local market conditions. In addition, because costs will change more frequently than the basic manuals, a cost trend factor (current cost multiplier) is provided. Reliance on manuals to estimate reproduction (or replacement) cost dominates appraisal practice because their use is required by most major clients, including secondary mortgage market buyers.

Other sources of the cost estimate for the subject property are the costs to construct recently completed comparable buildings, using the selling price of the comparables (less land value) as a proxy for their costs. The net figure will include all costs, including developer's profit. This cost is then adjusted for differences between the comparable and the subject property, including any change in costs that have occurred between the date the comparable sold and the date of the appraisal. This adjusted cost is then converted into the appropriate unit cost, which for most assignments will be cost per square foot. The costs of comparable buildings can be obtained from surveys of builders and contracts for recently completed buildings.

Because the comparative unit method is both uncomplicated and sufficiently precise for the large majority of assignments, it is not surprising that it dominates appraisal practice. The comparative unit cost method is applied below to a house using an edited and updated example from the *Marshall Valuation Services Manual.*

General Description of the Subject Building

The subject building is a good quality, one and one-half story residence that has 2,987 square feet (1,696 square feet on the first floor and 1,291 square feet on the second floor). There is an attached, unfinished garage that has 496 square feet and a common wall of 18 feet. The covered front porch has 96 square feet.

There is a reinforced concrete foundation for both the residence and the garage. The first floor of the residence is a concrete slab, with a wood floor on the second floor. There is a concrete slab in the garage. The majority of the floor cover in the residence is carpet (approximately 80 percent). The kitchen and baths have a resilient floor finish and the entry has a terrazzo covering.

The predominant type of exterior wall finish is stucco. At the front elevation there is a small amount of wood shingle and wood siding used as wall ornamentation. The roof cover is wood shingle. The interior walls and ceiling have a painted plaster finish. At the rear elevation of the residence is a shed dormer which measures 43 feet across the face.

There are three baths in the house, which have a total of 12 plumbing fixtures and a plumbing rough-in for washer/dryer service. There is a single, two-story fireplace which opens to the living room. The warm and cooled air system is designed for a moderate climate. Wall and ceiling insulation are also designed for a moderate climate.

The overall quality of the built-in appliances is good, and they include a range and oven, range hood and fan, dishwasher, and garbage disposal.

Cost New of the Subject Property Using the Comparative Unit Method

Table 11–1 shows how the cost of the subject property is estimated based on square feet. Note the use of the current cost and local multipliers. They

TABLE 11–1 Residential Property–Comparative Unit Method

	Quantity	×	Cost per Unit	=	Cost
Basic Cost[†]	2,987		$37.25		$111,266
Adjustments to basic cost					
Concrete slab (1st floor)	1,696		(2.27)		(3,850)
80% carpet	2,987		2.60		7,766
Warm and cooled air	2,987		1.26		3,764
Plaster	2,987		1.13		3,375
Additional plumbing fixture	1		906		906
Range and oven w/hood	1		1,278		1,278
Dishwasher and disposal	1		858		858
Fireplace	1		2,310		2,310
Dormer	43		96		4,128
Adjusted basic cost					$131,801
Adjustments for other features					
Front porch					
(Slab and roof and ceiling)	96		12.05		1,157
Subtotal residence cost					$132,958
Garage	496		16.32		8,095
Minus common wall	18		(64.05)		(1,153)
Subtotal					$ 6,942
Subtotal of all building improvements					$139,900
Current cost multiplier (1.03) ×					
Local multiplier (1.09) × $139,900					
= Indicated cost new of:					$157,066

[†]Including builder's (and in this case developer's) profit.
Source: Marshall Valuation Service, One and One Half Story Example, edited and updated.

change periodically to reflect changes in building costs and the relationship of costs in the local market to the average level of costs.

If there had been other adjustments for things such as yard improvements and landscaping, they would have been added to the $157,066 total shown in Table 11–1.

Unit-in-Place (Segregated) Method

The unit-in-place, or segregated cost method, uses unit costs for various building components (or building units). Units are commonly stated in terms of lineal, area, and volume measures, with unit costs standardized in terms of structural components in place (installed). For example, roofing costs are often expressed in terms of square-foot units, while foundation costs are generally expressed in terms of dollars per linear foot or cubic yard of concrete. When all unit costs have been estimated, they are totaled to provide the direct costs of the total improvement.

Cost New of the Subject Property Using the Unit-in-Place Method

A cost of $157,066 was previously estimated for the example subject property using the comparative unit method.

Using the unit-in-place method, the cost of the same house is estimated in Table 11–2.

There is a slight difference between the cost estimates produced by comparative unit ($157,066) and unit-in-place ($154,618). This kind of difference is common and is traceable to the varying degrees of imprecision inherent in the process; it is difficult to make exact comparisons between the cost of, say, a square foot, and the costs of the various components that contribute to that square foot.

The unit-in-place method tends to be more accurate (and more time-consuming) than the comparative unit method. In practice, the dominance of the comparative unit method suggests that in most cases the increase in accuracy does not justify the added expense.

The Quantity-Survey Method

Quantity-survey is the conceptually ideal costing method because it is extremely detailed. To use quantity-survey, the appraiser must have complete familiarity with the current prices of materials, labor, and job conditions. Its use effectively duplicates the process a subcontractor goes through before submitting a bid to a contractor. A complete quantity-survey will require several hundred individual cost estimates with the finished report several pages long. For this reason a quantity-survey is seldom practical. It is used only when the client demands it, or for new structures when the cost approach will be relied upon heavily. In such cases, reliance on a professional cost estimator is suggested.

TABLE 11-2 Residential Property–Unit-in-Place Method

Unit-in-Place	Measurement Unit	Quality	Quantity	Unit Cost	Total[†]
Foundation (concrete)	Sq. ft.	2	1,696	$ 1.70	$ 2,883
Perimeter insulation		2	190	1.24	236
Floor structure					
(concrete slab	Sq. ft.	Average	1,696	2.32	3,935
wood joists)		Good	1,291	4.46	5,758
Floor cover					
(concrete/V.A.T./	Sq. ft.	Average/Good	2,987	2.72	8,125
terrazzo)		Very good			
Exterior wall					
(stucco–shingles)	Lineal feet	Good/Average	1	14,306	14,306
Gable wall					
(stucco & insulation)	Sq. ft.	Good/Average	416	5.00	2,080
Ceiling (plaster		Good/	2,987	1.27	3,793
and insulation)	Sq. ft.	Very good	1,696	.71	1,204
Roof (shingle)	Sq. ft.	Good	1,696	8.05	13,653
Roof dormers	Lineal ft.	Good	43	89.10	3,831
Interior construction					
(1–½ stories)	Sq. ft.	Good	2,987	10.74	32,080
Heating & cooling	Sq. ft.	2	2,987	2.56	7,647
Electrical	Sq. ft.	Good	2,987	3.28	9,797
Plumbing	Sq. ft.	Good	2,987	4.87	14,547
Fireplace	Each	Average	1	2,064	2,064
Built-in appliances					
(range/oven)	Each	Average/Good	1	1,362	1,362
Dishwasher, disposal	Each	Good	1	846	846
Stairways	Each	Very good	1	1,398	1,398
Porches (including					
roof)	Sq. ft.	Average/Good	96	10.36	995
Ceiling (porch)	Sq. ft.	Good	96	2.18	209
Garage					
Foundation	Lineal ft.	2	74	5.40	400
Exterior Wall	Lineal ft.	Good	74	40.54	3,000
Floor and Roof	Sq. ft.	Good	496	7.20	3,571
Subtotal of building improvements					$137,720
Current cost multiplier (1.03) × Local multiplier (1.09) × $137,720 = Cost new of:					$154,618

[†]Including indirect costs and developer's profit.
Source: Marshall Valuation Service, One and One-Half Story Example, edited and modified.

Estimating the Cost New of a Commercial Property

Though the cost approach is most widely used for valuing houses, it may also be applicable to other kinds of property. Because the dollar amounts tend to be larger and any errors more significant for commercial properties than for houses, the unit-in-place method is used relatively more frequently, although the comparative unit method still dominates.

Following is an edited and updated example of the comparative unit method applied to a mixed-use bank and office building from the *Marshall Valuation Service Cost Manual.*

General Description of the Subject Building

The subject building is a thirteen-story, Class B (reinforced concrete), bank and office building. There is no basement and the site is level with no unusual soil conditions.

There is a continuous concrete foundation around the perimeter, with grade beams included for support of the interior bearing walls. There are concrete footings under each of the columns. The entire building is heated and cooled by a zoned system utilizing ducts and diffusers. The building is located in a moderate climate.

There are four elevators capable of carrying 3,000 pounds at 500 feet per minute. The basic frame construction of the building is reinforced concrete columns and beams. The exterior wall is a combination of aluminum and glass and 12" poured-in-place concrete.

The interior walls are of drywall construction, with the exception of the main elevator and lobby entrance on the ground floor which has a wall cover of marble veneer. Recessed fluorescent lighting is used in the electrical system throughout.

Bank and Mezzanine

The first, or street floor, is occupied by a bank and contains a mezzanine floor across the rear of the building which is also occupied by the bank. The exterior wall has a good amount of serpentine veneer as wall ornamentation. The floor is a reinforced concrete slab on the ground, which has been waterproofed. Eighty percent of the first floor area is covered with carpet, and the remaining twenty percent in the entrance and elevator lobby area has terrazzo floor covering.

Offices

The second through the thirteenth floors are occupied as offices. Two restrooms on each floor contain a mosaic tile floor cover. Lavatory countertops and back splash are simulated marble. The office floor and roof are a concrete beam and slab system. Floor cover on upper-floor office areas is a combination of 30 percent vinyl asbestos tile and 70 percent carpet. Ceilings are all suspended with cane fiber coverings.

Penthouse

A penthouse on the roof contains the mechanical equipment for the elevators, heating and cooling system, and the hot water system, which is two

210-gallon tanks with circulating pumps. The penthouse has no heating, minimum electrical, and no plumbing, except that used for the mechanical equipment. The exterior wall is 8″ formed and poured concrete.

Quality

The materials and workmanship are of an average quality for both the bank and the mezzanine portions, and of good quality for the office areas.

Table 11–3 shows the estimate of costs for the office building using the comparative unit method.

Indirect Costs and Developer's Profit

To the cost new of $12,094,738 must be added indirect costs not included in that figure, as well as the developer's profit.[1] This is often done on a percentage basis. Assuming these costs total 20 percent of direct costs, the cost new of the subject property would be (1.2) × $12,094,738 = $14,513,686.

Improvements to the Site and Secondary Building Costs

The cost new of improvements *to* the site and of secondary buildings may be estimated just as the cost new of the primary building is estimated, with depreciation then deducted. If this is done, the appraiser can use the same sources of information used to estimate the cost of the primary building; that is, contractors, cost estimators, and cost services.

However, because improvements to the site and secondary buildings are generally a relatively minor component of total cost, it is common practice to estimate their individual costs net of any depreciation. Any resulting inaccuracies will not have a serious impact on total value, with over- and underestimates tending to offset. Of course, if certain "secondary" components are suspected to be an important part of total value they should be treated as such. For example, in the case of significant exterior landscaping, an appropriate cost estimator (like a landscaper) should be consulted. When possible it is best to use a matched pairs approach, rather than cost, to extract the value of this kind of improvement.

---

[1]The proper treatment of developers' (or entrepreneurial) profit is the subject of continuing controversy. While a line-item entry in the cost approach is widely used, arguments can be made that this is at least in part double-counting, as the site value, which is separately estimated, may reflect entrepreneurial profit. See Steve Kapplin, "Entrepreneurial Profit, Redux," *Appraisal Journal,* January 1992, 14–24; William Anglyn, "Analyzing "Unearned" Entrepreneurial Profit," *Appraisal Journal,* July 1992, 366–79.

TABLE 11-3 Estimating Cost New Using Comparative Unit Method
Square Foot Costs†

	Section I	Section II	Section III	Section IV
Occupancy	Bank	Bank Mezzanine	Office	
Building class and quality	Class B, Average Quality	Class B, Average Quality	Class B, Quality Good	Class Quality
Exterior wall	Conc.-Glass	Conc.-Glass	Conc.-Glass	
No. of stories & height per story	No. 1 Ht. 23'	No. ___ Ht. ___	No. 12 Ht. 11'	No. ___ Ht. ___
Average floor area	21,586 sq. ft.	6,825 sq. ft.	11,496 sq. ft.	
Average perimeter	681'			
Age and condition	Age ___ Cond. ___	Age ___ Cond. ___	Age ___ Cond. ___	Age ___ Cond. ___
Region: Western ___ Central X Eastern ___		Climate: Mild ___ Moderate ___ X Extreme ___		
Base square foot cost	$ 81.75	$ 39.54	$ 78.95	
Square Foot Refinements				
Heating, cooling, ventilation (warm and cooled air)	−4.10	—	−4.10	
Elevator deduction				
Miscellaneous				
Total	$ 77.65	$ 39.54	$ 74.85	
Height and Size Refinements				
Number of stories-multiplier	1.05	—	1.05	
Height per story-multiplier	1.253	—	.977	
Floor area-perimeter multiplier	.928	—	.949	
Combined height and size multiplier (1.05 × 1.253 × .928 = 1.221)	1.221	—	.974	
Final Calculations				
Refined square-foot cost	$ 94.81	$ 39.54	$ 72.90	
Current cost multiplier	1.00	1.00	1.00	
Local multiplier	.97	.97	.97	
Final sq. ft. cost ($94.81 × 1.00 × .97 = $91.97)	$ 91.97	$ 38.35	$ 70.71	
Area	21,586 sq. ft.	6,825 sq. ft.	137,952 sq. ft.	
21,586 × $91.97 =	$1,985,264	$261,739	$9,754,586	
Lump sums			93,149	
Cost new	$1,985,264	$261,739	$9,847,735	

Total direct cost new: $1,985,264 + $261,739 + $9,847,735 = $12,094,738
Plus 20% indirect costs = 2,418,948
Cost new = $14,513,686

Source: Marshall Valuation Service, One and One-Half Story Example, edited and modified for example purposes.

Cost Trending

In addition to extracting unit costs from the selling prices of comparables or from cost services, another way to approximate current costs is through the use of cost trend information that is part of the information included in the publications of most cost services. Information on cost trends is used to convert historical costs to current costs. Each time period (generally one month) is assigned an index number which reflects costs on that date compared to a base date, which is given a value of, say, 100. Thus, an index of 103.5 for a given month would mean that the cost in that month was 3.5 percent higher than it was on the base date. The relationship between indices is then used to update historical costs.

For example, assume a subject improvement cost $350,000 to construct in July 1992, and the appraisal date was July 1996. The index in July 1992 was 95.8. In July 1996, the index was 119.1. The estimated cost as of July 1996 was:

$$\frac{119.1}{95.8} (\$350{,}000) = \$435{,}125, \textit{say}, \$435{,}000.$$

This approach should look familiar, as it was used previously in the sales comparison approach. The same kind of caveat applies here as it did there. When using cost indexing the appraiser must confirm that the historical cost of the subject property was consistent with typical costs at that time. In general, the use of current costs is preferred to the use of historical costs trended to the present. Thus, the best use of a cost index is to support an estimate based on traditional cost estimating methods.

Summary

The steps in the cost approach are as follows:

    Value = Reproduction (or replacement) cost new

        − Accrued depreciation

        + Land

- Comparative Unit
- Unit-in-Place
- Quantity Survey

In practice, the comparative unit method is used most often and it is very dominant for residential appraisals. Apparently, the marketplace has judged that the potential increases in accuracy are not worth the added expenses of the unit-in-place method and quantity survey methods.

Cost data may be obtained locally from contractors' and appraisers' files, or from cost services that provide per-unit cost estimates. Published cost manuals include direct costs, and generally some indirect costs. Indirect costs that are omitted, as well as improvements to the site and the developer's profit, must be estimated and added separately.

In many cases, the cost of improvements to the site and the cost of secondary buildings are estimated on a net basis, rather than by estimating their costs new and then deducting depreciation. A more complicated procedure is not justified, given the relatively small dollar amounts involved and the lack of available data.

Information on cost trends may be useful to support a cost estimate produced by one of the three traditional methods. As in the case of price trends to support a value estimated using the sales comparison approach, cost trends update a known historical cost by applying the appropriate percentage increase.

Questions and Problems

1. Why is developer's profit included in the cost estimate?
2. The contractor's profit is already included in direct labor and material costs. Isn't it double-counting to add a developer's profit?
3. A building had a cost new of $171,000 two years ago. The cost index at that time was 96.4. Today the index is 101.6. Based on cost trends, what is the current cost to reproduce? Is this estimate believable?
4. Which costing method is used most often? Least often? Why?
5. Define the comparative unit, unit-in-place, and quantity survey methods of cost estimation.
6. The use of cost services is increasing. Why?
7. The current cost index is 105. When the subject property was built at a cost of $90,000, the index was 100. What is the current cost new?

Chapter 12

Estimating Depreciation

Value = Cost new − **Accrued depreciation** + Land value

Introduction

Because most improvements have suffered from the effects of depreciation (most but not all of which are associated with the passing of time), the estimate of cost *new* must be adjusted downward to arrive at an estimate of market value. Thus, for appraisal purposes, accrued depreciation is defined as the difference between the reproduction or replacement cost of an improvement as if new on the date of the appraisal, and the market value of the improvement on the same date. Accrued depreciation, then, is the link between cost new and market value. It is an estimate of how much less a buyer would pay, and a seller would accept, because the improvements have suffered the effects of depreciation. Notice again the similarity between the cost approach and direct sales comparison. The cost approach compares the subject property to a new version of itself, with the difference in values traceable to depreciation effects.

The appraiser's definition of accrued depreciation is different than the definition used by accountants. The accountant, in response to tax laws, defines accrued depreciation in terms of the difference between an improvement's *historical* cost and its current market value, while the appraiser defines accrued depreciation as the difference between an improvement's *current cost* (new) and its current market value. Thus, accrued depreciation in an appraisal context is a relative, not an absolute measure. It does not necessarily refer to an actual decline in value. Therefore, even if an improvement has increased in value over time (due either to fundamental market forces or inflation), it does not mean there is no accrued depreciation to estimate. Any absolute increase in value from appreciation will be reflected in the estimate of cost new and/or land value, and the accrued depreciation—the value difference between old and new—must still be estimated.

Recall that when using direct sales comparison, one of the most important criterion for choosing comparable sales is a similarity in age, to minimize the difficulties associated with estimating the effects of depreciation. When using the cost approach, however, estimating depreciation effects cannot be avoided because the comparison, by definition, is always between the subject property and a new reproduction of itself. It follows that as a property gets older it becomes increasingly difficult to make the estimate of accrued depreciation. For this reason, many appraisers are reluctant to use the cost approach if the subject property is older than some maximum age. While the age cutoff varies among appraisers and by the specifics of the assignment, twenty to thirty years is common.

The Cost Approach and Accrued Depreciation: Some Misconceptions

There are a number of misconceptions about the application of the cost approach, most of which can be traced to misunderstandings about the role of the accrued depreciation estimate. Three common misconceptions are that (1) the cost approach produces long-run equilibrium value, not market value, (2) the cost approach is *always* applicable (or at the other extreme, that the cost approach is *never* applicable), and (3) the cost approach is usable only when the current improvement is the same as the highest and best use of the land as if vacant. These misconceptions will be discussed in turn.

The Cost Approach Produces Long-Run Equilibrium Value, Not Market Value

The source of this misconception is a related truth, which is that the current cost to produce any product is equal to its current market value in long-run equilibrium. When a market is in long-run equilibrium, it means that supply and demand are in balance, and therefore, the market clearing price produces a return to suppliers that is at the appropriate level for the risks involved; no more or no less. Producers have no incentive to sell at a price below the market level because they are selling all of their products at the market price. At the same time, producers cannot raise their price due to competition. Thus, when a market is in a long-run equilibrium position the cost to produce (including a normal profit) must equal market value. Some jump from this fact to the conclusion that because real estate markets are seldom in a long-run equilibrium position, the results of the cost approach will only occasionally equal market value. But this is incorrect, because it improperly equates the cost to produce and the cost approach. The cost to produce is only part of the cost approach; specifically, the reproduction (or replacement) cost new. The estimate of accrued depreciation is the link between the cost to produce (reproduction or replacement cost new) and market value, regardless of whether or not the market is in equilibrium.

Of course, the closer the market is to an equilibrium position the easier it is to make the depreciation estimate. One of the main reasons the cost approach tends to work better for houses than for income properties is that housing markets tend to be closer to equilibrium than are income property markets, and therefore, certain elements of depreciation (to be discussed shortly) may not have to be estimated. This, however, is a mechanical, not a conceptual advantage.

The Cost Approach Is Always (or Never) Useful

Absolutes seldom apply to anything associated with real estate appraisal, and judgments about the utility of the cost approach are no exception. At one extreme, the idea that the cost approach is always useful can be traced to the post-Depression disillusionment with direct sales comparison and the associated idea that cost represents a long-run "anchor" on value that is less volatile than price. As a result, the cost approach became a required part of every appraisal until relatively recently. Today, the cost approach is often omitted when income properties are appraised. It is relegated to a relatively small portion of the *Uniform Residential Appraisal Report,* and if there are sales data of sufficient quantity and quality to use the sales comparison approach with confidence, it is often omitted.

There are also circumstances, generally associated with older structures, when the cost approach provides only weak support for the direct sales comparison or the income approach. For example, the cost approach is likely to be an inappropriate way to value a historic structure for the same reasons it is likely to be inappropriate for valuing antique furniture.

At the opposite extreme from the claim that the cost approach is always useful is the claim that the cost approach is never useful, because only by accident does cost equal value. However, as discussed above, while it is true that reproduction cost may not equal value, the cost approach bridges the gap between cost and value through the estimate of accrued depreciation. While the available data for any given assignment may not allow a precise estimate of accrued depreciation, that is a problem not unique to the cost approach.

Also in the "cost approach is never useful" camp are those who recognize that it is theoretically acceptable, but consider it redundant. The argument is that because the estimate of accrued depreciation must reflect the market's opinion, the proper source of data on which to base the depreciation estimate is the comparable sales. However, if comparable sales are available, they can be used to value the subject based on direct sales comparison, so the cost approach is redundant. There is some merit in this argument. Clearly, when comparables of acceptable quality and quantity are available to be used for direct sales comparison, extracting an accrued depreciation figure from the same set of comparables will produce a cost approach estimate that should be very close to the direct sales comparison estimate. Nevertheless, we should not lose sight of the fact that the main reason for the existence of the cost approach is that there are not always perfect comparables to use for direct sales comparison or to extract accrued depreciation. Moreover, the comparables that are selected for use in the direct sales comparison approach are often closely bunched with respect to age. That is not always the case when using the cost approach, and as we will find, major parts of the depreciation estimate are sometimes based on overall trends in the marketplace rather than on a specific matched-pairs approach.

Finally, some argue that the cost approach has simply outlived its usefulness for all but special purpose and condemnation properties because, among other reasons, market participants do not use the cost approach as a determinant of value.[1] This kind of argument, while certainly consistent with the eroding of the importance of the cost approach over time, is somewhat overstated. Because the cost approach is used in feasibility analysis to determine whether a project makes sense economically, it does indirectly discipline the market and thus market values. A comparison of costs and benefits is in fact what drives the market to equilibrium.

The conclusion is that while the cost approach may be redundant in some circumstances, and unusable in many others, these are not sufficient reasons to discard it entirely.

The Cost Approach Is Valid Only If the Current Improvements Are the Same as the Highest and Best Use As If Vacant

In the cost approach the estimate of land value is properly based on its value as if vacant, because the value of land is not affected by the improvements on it. This observation leads to the conclusion that if the subject property's improvement(s) is not the same as the highest and best use of the land as if vacant, then the cost approach will not produce accurate results because the land value estimate will be incorrect, given the existing improvements.

While this conclusion is correct in a theoretically perfect market where expected use and thus value are deterministic functions of the highest and best use, its weakness in practice is that it fails to recognize the probabilistic

---

[1]For example, Richard Marchitelli, "Rethinking the Cost Approach," *Appraisal Journal,* July 1992, 424–26.

nature of price setting in real estate markets. That is, there are likely to be various kinds (and sizes) of improvements for a given site that will provide an acceptable return to a developer. When the subject property's improvement falls into this acceptable range, the cost approach is likely to provide a reasonable if not theoretically exact estimate of market value. More importantly, in the remaining cases when the improvement is not in the acceptable range, the estimate of accrued depreciation can capture that fact, because as discussed, it is the unacceptable improvement that properly absorbs the adverse value impact. Finally, it should also be recognized that when the current improvement is outside the acceptable range, it will almost always involve a site with an income-producing highest and best use. In such cases, the appraiser will likely be relying more on the income approach than the cost approach. For houses, because the highest and best use is generally the current use (due to zoning), this issue is of less importance.

Categories of Accrued Depreciation

The three categories of accrued depreciation are (1) physical deterioration, (2) functional obsolescence, and (3) external obsolescence.

Physical Deterioration

Ask people what comes to mind when they think of depreciation and most will refer to physical deterioration, like peeling paint and loose boards. This is understandable, because buildings do wear out over time. Ordinary use, the elements, and disintegration reduce utility and cause values to decline. Physical deterioration proceeds at different rates for different buildings. The rate will depend on the original quality of construction and the subsequent maintenance of the structure. Thus, a relatively new but poorly constructed or undermaintained structure may suffer more physical deterioration than an older structure that was well-built and has been properly maintained.

Functional Obsolescence

The second category of depreciation is functional obsolescence. Functional obsolescence is the impairment of functional capacity or efficiency. Functional obsolescence "is reflected in the loss in value brought about by such factors as overcapacity, inadequacy, and changes in the [state of the] art that affect the property item itself or its relation with other items comprising a larger property."[2] Thus, functional obsolescence reflects the fact that a

---

[2]Byrl N. Boyce, *Real Estate Appraisal Terminology* (Cambridge, MA: Ballinger), 1981, 3.

structural component is outmoded or inefficient when judged by current market standards. An unappealing floor plan fits this description. So does a kitchen without sufficient space to add appliances (such as a dishwasher), ceilings that are too high (or too low), and bathtubs without showers.

Like physical deterioration, functional obsolescence tends to be related to the passage of time. In fact, the word *obsolete* would be defined by many as being out-of-date. However, there is not always a direct relationship between age and functional obsolescence. For example, a poor floor plan can be part of a new building. Also, new technology or new competition may create as much functional obsolescence as does the aging process. For example, "smart" buildings and energy efficient buildings have had negative effects on the value of relatively new but technologically inferior competition.

Finally, it must be kept in mind that tastes change in the market. A good example is the effect that the energy crises of the mid-1970s had on the value of houses with cathedral ceilings. As the price of heating oil quadrupled, cathedral ceilings quickly moved from being a desired amenity in many markets to becoming a negative pricing influence. When oil prices then started to move back toward their former levels, the functional obsolescence associated with high ceilings began to disappear. There is another lesson in this example: what is functionally obsolete in one market may not be in another. During the oil crisis, the value of houses with high ceilings in the South was unaffected, while the value of houses in the North declined.

External Obsolescence

The third category of depreciation is external obsolescence. External obsolescence is defined as a change in utility (and thus value) arising from market forces *outside the property*. Notice the difference from physical and functional depreciation, which arise from factors internal to the property. If you are appraising a recently developed property with no physical deterioration and no functional obsolescence, but which has a market value that is less than its cost to reproduce, the property by definition is suffering from the effects of depreciation, and in this case, the source of the depreciation must be external obsolescence.

There are two subcategories of external obsolescence: locational obsolescence and economic obsolescence. Locational obsolescence arises because of the fixed location of real estate. An example is the adverse effects of incompatible land uses in a neighborhood.

Economic obsolescence arises from market conditions. These conditions may affect properties in general, or be specific to a certain kind of property or even an individual property. An example of a condition that affects properties in general is the negative impact on values of increases in the interest rate on mortgages. An example of a condition more specific to a particular market or property is that the value of an office building is affected by the supply and demand for competitive space. This effect may be positive as well as negative. When demand rises faster than supply, market value may (temporarily) exceed cost, requiring a positive adjustment for external obsolescence.

In addition to the fact that external obsolescence arises from forces external to the property, external obsolescence differs from physical and functional depreciation in another important way. It is that the amount to be deducted from (or added to) reproduction cost new is only the pro rata share of the external obsolescence that can be allocated to the improvements. This is because external obsolescence also affects land values, and therefore, a pro rata share of the total impact of the obsolescence will be reflected in the estimate of land value. The amount of external obsolescence allocated to the improvements is generally calculated based on typical improvement/land ratios in the market. For example, if total economic obsolescence is estimated to be $10,000, and the improvement/land ratio in the neighborhood is 4/1, $8,000 would be subtracted from reproduction cost new to reflect economic obsolescence. The assumption is that the other $2,000 will be accounted for in the separate estimate of land value.

An Overall Perspective: Depreciation and Age

While depreciation is generally associated with the passage of time, the age-depreciation relationship is not likely to apply equally to physical depreciation, functional obsolescence, and external obsolescence. The closest association to age is generally found for physical deterioration, followed by functional obsolescence, then external obsolescence. Even for physical and functional obsolescence, the association between age and depreciation may be difficult to measure, as the rate of utility loss is often nonlinear. Think of a light bulb. It provides the same level of utility until it suddenly burns out. While depreciation has been occurring during the bulb's life, it is difficult to tell by observation where the bulb may be in its life cycle. Similarly, a roof begins to leak at a distinct time. Prior to that, the time-to-begin leaking is unknown. Using age as a proxy for utility does recognize, however, that as time passes, the time-to-the-roof-leaking is getting closer and thus it provides an approximation of actual depreciation. The association between external obsolescence and age tends to be especially weak because factors external to the subject property are not directly affected by the aging of the subject property's improvements.

Despite these limitations, the general relationship between age and accrued depreciation can be summarized as in Figure 12–1. Any accrued depreciation at age zero is traceable to external obsolescence, or less frequently, to built-in functional obsolescence. As the improvement ages, physical deterioration sets in, functional obsolescence tends to increase, and

FIGURE 12-1 Depreciation Over Time

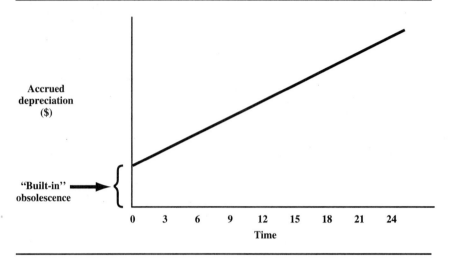

total accrued depreciation increases. In Figure 12-1, accrued depreciation is shown to be linearly associated with age. This pattern was chosen for illustrative purposes only. Research suggests that the association of depreciation and age tends to be market-specific, and in many cases it is not linear.

Regardless of the pattern of change, total accrued depreciation generally increases over time, making the estimating task more difficult as a building ages, and reinforcing the idea that the confidence the appraiser has in the result of the cost approach tends to be negatively associated with the age of the subject property's improvements. Cost services do provide tables that help with the estimation of physical depreciation.

Conclusions to This Point

The focus to this point has been on defining accrued depreciation and describing its role when estimating market value using the cost approach. The conclusions are as follows:

- Accrued depreciation is the link between the cost to reproduce the subject property as if it were new and the subject property's market value. Thus, accrued depreciation measures the loss or gain in value associated with the difference in utility between the subject property and a new reproduction of itself. This difference is often but not always associated with the aging process.

- The cost approach is analogous to direct sales comparison in the sense that the "comparable" (the reproduction cost new of the subject) is identical to the subject except for the effects of depreciation, which must be adjusted for.
- The three categories of accrued depreciation are physical deterioration, functional obsolescence, and external obsolescence.
- Accrued depreciation is associated with the aging process. The association is closest for physical deterioration, followed by functional obsolescence. The association of external obsolescence and age tends to be weak.
- Given the association between accrued depreciation and age, and the difficulties associated with estimating accrued depreciation, the results of the cost approach tend to be less reliable for older buildings than for newer.

Estimating Accrued Depreciation

In hindsight, the conclusions listed above are quite intuitive; buildings, like cars and clothes, tend to wear out and lose value over time. Getting from theory to practice, however, is a different story. Losses in value from perceived losses in utility are difficult to identify and even more difficult to quantify. The appraiser quickly discovers that the process of estimating accrued depreciation involves numerous judgment calls, blurred distinctions among categories of depreciation, data deficiencies, and the danger of double-counting.

There are two general methods for estimating accrued depreciation: (1) lump-sum age/life methods and (2) the breakdown method. These two methods differ markedly with respect to the degree of detail involved. When relatively less detail is necessary, accrued depreciation is often estimated in a lump sum based on an assumed overall relationship between age and depreciation. When relatively more detail is necessary, the breakdown method is used, because it requires separate estimates for each subcategory of depreciation. Thus, the breakdown method is analogous to the unit-in-place (or segregated) method of estimating the reproduction cost new.

Whether the lump-sum or the breakdown method is used will depend on the specifics of the appraisal assignment. Considerations include the kind of property being appraised, its age, the amount of any functional and external obsolescence, the available information, and the relative importance of the cost approach in arriving at the final estimate of market value. In practice, lump-sum estimates of accrued depreciation are used for most appraisals, and almost always when valuing houses. The breakdown method is used more frequently (though still in a minority of appraisals) for older houses and for investment properties. Appraisals sometimes include a mix of methods, with physical deterioration estimated in a lump sum, and functional and external obsolescence estimated using a breakdown method.

The balance of the chapter is devoted to discussions of the lump-sum and breakdown method.

Estimating Depreciation in a Lump Sum: Age/Life Methods

For most appraisal assignments, and particularly when functional obsolescence and external obsolescence are not significant, the extra cost of completing a detailed breakdown analysis is not justified. Instead, total accrued depreciation is estimated in a lump sum based on a ratio of the property's age to its economic life. Age/life methods put to practical use the basic idea illustrated in Figure 12.1, that accrued depreciation and age tend to be closely related. There are two commonly used age/life variations: (1) effective age/economic life, and (2) modified effective age/economic life.

The Effective Age/Economic Life Variation

To estimate total accrued depreciation using the effective age/economic life ratio, the ratio of a structure's effective age to its total economic life is applied to its reproduction (or replacement) cost new, as in Equation (1). This equation is based on the assumption that the relationship between depreciation and age is linear; that is, straight line depreciation.

$$\text{Accrued depreciation} = \frac{\text{Effective age}}{\text{Economic life}} \times \text{Cost new} \qquad (1)$$

Beginning with the denominator of the ratio in Equation (1), the total economic life of a structure is the period of time in years, beginning when the structure was new, over which the structure can be expected to contribute to the property's value. To estimate economic life, appraisers often use rules of thumb based either on past experience or on guidelines published by various sources such as building cost services and the IRS. The most common guidelines suggest that the total economic life of most properties will fall between 40–60 years. For houses, a 50–55-year assumption is frequently used.

A more formal approach to estimating economic life using data from comparable sales has been suggested by Don Epley.[3] Equation (2) is a simplified version of Epley's model.

$$EL = AA/[1 - (ASP/RCN)] \qquad (2)$$

---

[3] Don Epley, "The Concept and Market Extraction of Effective Age for Residential Properties," *Journal of Real Estate Research*, Spring 1990.

where

> EL = economic life
> ASP = adjusted selling price, which is the gross selling price adjusted for market conditions, financing and time, less site value and the value of the depreciated site improvements; this yields an estimate of the current value of the major improvement
> RCN = reproduction cost new
> AA = actual age of the property

Example: Assume the following data from a sale.

Selling price adjusted for market conditions, financing and time	$90,000
Site value	$20,000
RCN	$99,800
Depreciated site improvements	$ 4,500
ASP ($90,000 − $20,000 − $4,500)	$65,500
AA	15 years

Inserting this data into Equation (2) produces an estimate of economic life.

$$EL = 15/[1 - (65{,}500/99{,}800)]$$
$$= 43.64$$

The estimated economic life of this property is about 44 years. As in the case of any market-extracted data, a large enough sample of economic lives from comparables is needed to establish a likely range for a given type of property in a given market.

Moving to the numerator of the ratio in Equation (1), the effective age of a structure is the age indicated by its present condition or utility. A structure's effective age is often different from its physical age because effective age reflects initial construction quality, maintenance, and perhaps modernization or rehabilitation over time, while physical age reflects only the passage of time. Thus, a building completed 30 years ago has a physical age of 30, but it may have an effective age that is higher or lower. It follows that two buildings with different physical ages may have the same effective age and vice versa.

Thus, the denominator in the age/life ratio—the total economic life of the structure—remains the same over time, while the numerator changes to reflect the effective age of the structure. Therefore, the age/life ratio calculates the percentage of the current reproduction cost new that has been "used up." There is not yet a generally accepted methodology for estimating effective age. It remains a judgment the appraiser must make based on

TABLE 12-1 Effective Age/Economic Life Technique

Reproduction cost new		$245,000
Total economic life	55 years	
Effective age	20 years	
% accrued depreciation	20/55 = 36.4%	
Accrued depreciation	.364 × $245,000 =	89,180
Depreciated value of improvements		155,820
Plus land value		39,000
Estimated market value		$194,820

what is known or observed about the chronological age and the condition of the improvement.[4]

An Example

Table 12–1 is a summary example of the process of estimating accrued depreciation (and then market value) using the effective age/economic life ratio.

One weakness of estimating accrued depreciation in a lump sum is that it implies that all subcategories of physical, functional, and external obsolescence are related to age in the same way. While it may be argued that the estimate of effective age is a weighted average that reflects the various subcategories of depreciation, it must be realized that if that is truly the case, the appraiser has effectively used the breakdown method in order to arrive at the estimate of effective age.

Another weakness of this version of economic age/life method is that it assumes straight-line depreciation, while research indicates that the actual pattern of depreciation varies from market to market. Again, while it can be argued that the estimate of effective age should reflect the appropriate pattern of depreciation, the data manipulations required are such that the appraiser might be served equally well by using the breakdown method.

The significant advantage of the effective age/economic life method is its simplicity, and when valuing a property without serious functional or external obsolescence it is an appropriate and widely used method.

---

[4] Appraisers disagree as to whether the condition of the improvements is to be judged on an absolute scale, or relative to the surrounding neighborhood. Traditional thought favors the former, but others (see Don Epley, "The Concept and Market Extraction of Effective Age for Residential Properties") make a case for the latter.

TABLE 12-2 Modified Effective Age/Economic Life Technique

Reproduction cost new		$245,000
Physical and functional depreciation, curable		12,500
Adjusted cost		$232,500
Total economic life	55 years	
Effective age	17 years	
% Depreciation for incurable items (17/55) = 30.9%		
Incurable depreciation .309 × $232,500 =		$ 71,843
Depreciated value of improvements		160,657
Plus land value		39,000
Estimated market value		$199,657

Modified Effective Age/Economic Life

One particularly troubling aspect of the fact that the age/life method lumps all categories of depreciation together is that there is no separation between *curable* and *incurable* depreciation. Curable depreciation is depreciation that, if cured (repaired), will add an amount to the property's value that is equal to or greater than the cost to cure. The reasonable assumption in that case is that the item will be cured. Conversely, incurable depreciation is depreciation for which the cost to cure exceeds the value added by the cure. A common example of curable depreciation is a leaking roof. An example of incurable depreciation would be a poor floor plan. To correct it (in effect, extensively rebuilding the structure) would likely cost more than it would add to the value. The assumption is that these kinds of items will not be cured.

Note that the distinction between curable and incurable is one of economics, not physical possibility. A floor plan can be changed, but because the dollar costs of doing so exceed the dollar benefits it is considered incurable.

The problem for the appraiser using the age/life method is that the effective age of the structure is not directly affected by either the costs to cure or the impact of making the cures. The modified effective age/economic life technique attacks this problem by: (1) subtracting the costs to cure physical and functional depreciation from reproduction cost new, (2) adjusting the estimate of effective age to reflect the cured items, and (3) applying the (adjusted) effective age/economic life ratio to the adjusted cost. This process is shown in Table 12–2 for the same property used in Table 12–1.

In this example, there is about a $5,000 difference in the market values estimated by the effective age/economic life and modified effective age/economic life methods. This difference is traceable to the fact that the value added by curing the curable items of depreciation (as reflected in the resulting reduction in effective age) exceeded the costs to cure.

Except for the advantage of considering curable and incurable items separately, the modified effective age/economic life technique suffers the same conceptual weaknesses as the effective age/economic life technique; that is, it lumps physical, functional, and external depreciation together and it assumes a straight-line pattern of depreciation.

Using Age/Life Methods: Conclusions from Research

Many studies have measured the relationship between age and depreciation, usually in residential markets.[5] Two conclusions from those studies are of particular interest. First, the general relationship between age and depreciation varies from market to market. No single pattern has been found consistently, so the appraiser must determine a locally based relationship between age and depreciation.

Second, local depreciation patterns, regardless of their exact shapes, tend to be curvilinear[6] and may be irregular. Weicher and Hartzell, for example, found a relatively rapid rate of depreciation in years 1–10, a leveling during years 10–20, and a return to a higher rate beyond year 20.[7] This is not particularly good news for appraisers because the most commonly used age/life models assume straight-line depreciation.

Better news for the appraiser is that there is some evidence that the location of a property within a given market is not associated with its rate of depreciation. This suggests that depreciation rate indices can be based on data from a relatively wide geographical area.

There is also evidence (from a single study) that the use of effective age, even when based solely on appraisers' judgments,[8] is superior to the use of physical age when estimating accrued depreciation. This supports the idea that the relative difficulty of using effective age/life models compared to simpler physical age/life models is justified by the added accuracy which results.

---

[5]See, for example, Edward Sabella, "Determining the Relationship between a Property's Age and Its Market Value," *Assessor's Journal,* 8, 1974; John B. Corgel and Halbert C. Smith, "The Concept and Estimation of Economic Life in Residential Appraisal," *The Real Estate Appraiser and Analyst,* Winter 1982; and Roger E. Cannaday and Mark A. Sunderman, "Estimation of Depreciation for Single-Family Appraisals," *AREUEA Journal,* Summer 1986; Stephen Malpezzi, Larry Ozorne, and Thomas G. Thibodeau, "Microeconomic Estimates of Housing Depreciation," *Land Economics,* November 1987.

[6]Though not all. See Raymond B. Palmquist, "Hedonic Prices and Depreciation Indexes for Residential Property: A Comment," *Journal of Urban Economics* 6, 1979.

[7]John C. Weicher and David Hartzell, "Hedonic Analysis of Home Prices: Results for 59 Metropolitan Areas," *Research in Real Estate,* C. F. Sirmans ed., 2, 1982.

[8]Corgel and Smith, "The Concept and Estimation of Economic Life in the Residential Appraisal Process."

TABLE 12-3 Extraction of Annual Depreciation Rate

	Sale 1	Sale 2
Selling price	$130,000	$310,000
Land value	30,000	80,000
Value of improvements	100,000	230,000
Reproduction cost new of improvements	130,000	270,000
Accrued depreciation	$ 30,000	$ 40,000
% Accrued depreciation	30,000/130,000 = 23%	40,000/270,000 = 15%
Effective age[†]	18 years	12 years
% Annual Depreciation	.23/18 = 1.28%	.15/12 = 1.25%

[†]Physical age can be used if that is all that is available. Recall, however, that research results indicate that on average, the appraiser's estimate of effective age leads to a better estimate of accrued depreciation rates than does physical age.

In 1994, the author discussed the age/depreciation relationship with seven appraisers; two from central Pennsylvania, one from Florida, two from the Midwest, and two from urban areas in the Northeast. Though they differed on how they approached the task of estimating accrued depreciation, there was a surprising consistency in one important area. All seven reported that for houses with *physical* ages of 0–30 years, the value impact of total accrued depreciation ranged between .7 percent and 1.25 percent of reproduction cost per year.

This range of .7 percent to 1.25 percent per year of physical age is not suggested as a general rule, but rather as a benchmark that seems reasonably reliable. It is also consistent with the conclusions of many empirical studies.[9]

Estimating Age/Depreciation Relationships in Local Markets

While "rules of thumb" like .7 percent to 1.25 percent depreciation per year are useful starting points, the appraiser who makes regular use of age/life methods should develop a method to estimate the age/depreciation relationship for various property types in local markets. This is done by extracting data from sales, as shown in the example in Table 12–3.

Extracting depreciation rates in this manner should be done using as large a sample as possible to produce credible results for various age

---

[9]Frank C. Emerson, "Valuation of Residential Amenities: An Econometric Approach," *The Appraisal Journal,* April 1972; Michael G. Ferri, "An Application of Hedonic Indexing Methods to Monthly Changes in Housing Prices: 1965–1975," *AREUEA Journal* 5, 1977; Palmquist, "Hedonic Prices and Depreciation Indexes for Residential Property: A Comment."

intervals and for various property types and price ranges. The resulting tables of age/depreciation relationships can then be used to appraise other properties. These tables should be updated on a regular basis using recent sales data.

Developing a table of age/depreciation relationships involves the added effort of estimating reproduction costs and land values for transactions which may or may not have any immediate use except to help build the table. However, if the age/life method is used on a regular basis the effort should prove worthwhile. Note also that depreciation rates can be extracted on a regular basis as part of routine appraisal assignments. Suppose, for example, that you have used direct sales comparison to estimate a value of $120,000 for a property. The reproduction cost new and land value have been estimated to be $110,000 and $30,000, respectively. By inserting these figures into the cost approach model, you can solve for the implied amount of accrued depreciation.

$$\text{Value} = \text{Reproduction cost} - \text{Accrued depreciation} + \text{Land value}$$

$$\$120{,}000 = \$110{,}000 - \text{Accrued depreciation} + \$30{,}000$$

$$\text{Accrued depreciation} = \$20{,}000$$

Thus, accrued depreciation equals 18 percent (20,000/110,000) of reproduction cost. Assuming the improvements had an age of 15 years, the annual rate of depreciation has been $18\%/15 = 1.20$ percent.

Market Disequilibrium and the Depreciation Estimate: Economic Obsolescence

As discussed, one weakness of age/life methods is the implicit assumption that all categories of depreciation are associated with age in the same way. In practice, that isn't generally the case, especially for economic obsolescence resulting from a disequilibrium condition in the market.

Disequilibrium is an imbalance of supply and demand. The new but almost empty commercial buildings populating many markets beginning in the late 1980s were examples of the results of oversupply. Conversely, in the early 1980s the overheated housing markets in some Northeastern cities suggested an undersupply. In disequilibrium markets, the cost to produce will not equal market value, and thus for the cost approach to reasonably approximate market value economic conditions have to be reflected in the estimate of external obsolescence.

This presents a problem when using age/life methods, because while economic obsolescence can affect even new properties, new properties have an age of zero and therefore it is likely that age/life methods will improperly assign zero depreciation. The result can be serious estimation errors. Therefore, in markets that are in disequilibrium, a separate estimate of economic obsolescence should be made.

Disequilibrium and Depreciation on Residential Properties

An estimate of the effects of market disequilibrium on the value of a house can be made based on information from recent sales. The object is to determine the relationship of the selling price to the reproduction cost of the property's improvements, adjusted for accrued depreciation other than economic obsolescence. We will call this ratio the market conditions factor *(MCF)*.[10]

$$MCF = \frac{\text{Selling price of the improvement}}{\text{Reproduction (or replacement) cost less other accrued depreciation}} \quad (3)$$

The process of estimating an *MCF* is straightforward. For each sale, first subtract land value from the selling price to obtain the selling price of the improvements. This is the numerator in Equation (3). Cost new less accrued depreciation other than economic obsolescence is then estimated. This is the denominator in Equation (3).

Table 12–4 shows the calculation of an *MCF* for two sales.

This kind of calculation should be repeated for a sufficient sample of sales and be periodically updated to keep the *MCF* current. The use of the *MCF* is simple. The *MCF* is multiplied by the reproduction cost less depreciation to produce an adjusted figure, which is then added to land value to arrive at property value. Suppose a sample produced an average *MCF* of .95, and that the subject property has a reproduction cost new, less depreciation other than economic obsolescence, of $160,000. Land value is $30,000. The estimated value of the subject property is:

Value = (Reproduction cost less other depreciation × *MCF*) + Land value

= ($160,000 × .95) + $30,000

= $182,000

Notice that if the numerator in Equation (3) is larger than the denominator, the *MCF* is greater than one. This would result in a higher

---

[10]The *Boeck Building Cost Guide* calls the results of this kind of calculation an "economic condition factor." See *1988 Residential Building Cost Guide,* American Appraisal Association, p. 5. The Boeck manual analyzes economic conditions separately, then uses the results of the analysis to adjust the results of the cost approach. We treat economic condition here as an integral part of the accrued depreciation estimate. The semantic difference does not change the result.

TABLE 12–4 Calculation of Market Conditions Factor

	1	2
Selling price	$190,000	$172,500
Land value	60,000	47,000
Selling price of improvements	130,000	125,500
Reproduction cost	165,000	170,000
Less depreciation (other than economic obsolescence)	30,000	30,000
	$135,000	$140,000
	$130,000	$125,500
	$135,000	$140,000
MCF =	.963	.896

market value than reproduction cost, a situation of "negative" external obsolescence that occurs when there is an undersupply of properties.

Disequilibrium and Depreciation on Income Properties

The impact of disequilibrium conditions on income property values can be measured by using either a market conditions factor, or by capitalizing the lost (or excess) income attributable to the market imbalance.

An *MCF* for income properties is calculated the same as it is for residential properties. Its applicability for income properties, however, is likely to be limited due to insufficient sales information from which to extract a reliable *MCF*.

Capitalizing lost (or excess) income is therefore the most common way to estimate the effects of disequilibrium. The logic is straightforward. In long-run equilibrium, rents and vacancies are at typical levels, which produces normal returns to developers and investors. In disequilibrium, rents and/or vacancies are at atypical levels. It follows then, that the property's value will reflect the difference between the income that would be produced in equilibrium and that which will actually be produced, capitalized over the time period the disequilibrium condition is expected to persist.

For example, assume that the value of an office building would be $2,500,000 at normal vacancy and rent levels. This value can be estimated by capitalizing normal income, or by estimating reproduction cost less any physical or functional obsolescence, plus land. Suppose, however, that the building is in an overbuilt market and that the income produced is $60,000 per year less than it would be producing at normal levels. This condition is expected to persist for five years. At a 10 percent discount rate, the present value of the five years of "lost" income is about $227,500.[11] This is the value loss attributable to economic obsolescence, and the estimated value of the property would be $2,500,000 − $227,500 = $2,272,500.[12] In this simple example, the income loss was held level for the entire five-year period. In practice, any pattern of income loss can be discounted to a present value figure. As noted earlier, when demand exceeds supply, external obsolescence may be positive. Referring to the example above, if the expectation was for excess income of $60,000 per year for five years, the present value of $227,500 would be added to $2,500,000 to give a value of $2,727,500.

The Breakdown Method for Estimating Accrued Depreciation[13]

The breakdown method is very detailed, and its use in appraisal practice is typically limited to assignments involving large commercial properties. The major professional appraisal associations also may require demonstrated competence in applying the breakdown method in order to earn professional designations.

The breakdown method is analogous to the unit-in-place (segregated) method for estimating reproduction or replacement cost new. The appraiser identifies each source of depreciation, estimates its effect on value, then totals the individual estimates to arrive at total accrued depreciation. If replacement cost is used instead of reproduction costs, then certain types of functional obsolescence will not have to be estimated, because they will not be included in the estimate of replacement cost.

Applying the Breakdown Method

When using the breakdown method, the difficulties inherent in estimating depreciation are compounded because it is necessary to unbundle and separately evaluate structural components that tend to be interrelated and often interdependent. This means that there may not be a consistent relationship between the physical presence of depreciation and its impact on value. For example, consider a structure that suffers from functional obsolescence, say

---

[11]The mathematics of discounting are explained in Chapter 16. A similar approach and a more detailed example are found in MacKenzie S. Bottum, "Estimating Obsolescence in Supply-Saturated Office Markets," *The Appraisal Journal,* October 1988.

[12]If reproduction cost, less physical and functional obsolescence, plus land is used as the base figure, the value of the lost income must be prorated between buildings and land, and only the building's portion subtracted. The impact on land would have already been reflected in the original estimate of its value.

[13]Dick Stallings, MAI, SRA, was very helpful in developing this section of the chapter.

from a poor floor plan. If the structure is new and has no physical deterioration, the effect of the functional obsolescence on value would likely be substantial. Suppose, however, that the structure is old and near the end of its physical life. Given that physical deterioration in this case is approaching 100 percent, the presence of the functional obsolescence (the poor floor plan) would be largely irrelevant as far as its impact on market value. That is, if the structure is about ready for the wrecker's ball, its bad floor plan won't have much additional negative impact on value.

These kinds of interrelationships have led to some disagreements among writers and practitioners as to both the proper sequence that should be followed when estimating accrued depreciation, and the proper categorization of various types of depreciation. While it is important that the appraiser uses proper terminology and communicates correctly, what matters most is producing a credible estimate of depreciation, however the individual components are labeled.

There is also a more general issue concerning the utility of the breakdown method. If a strict cost/benefit analysis was applied to the trade-off between the effort required to learn and properly apply the breakdown method and the subsequent benefits it produces in appraisal practice, the result would suggest the breakdown method is not worth the learning effort. And as noted earlier, in appraisal practice the lump-sum methods do dominate. In fact, beyond the demonstration reports required to earn designation credits by the major professional associations, the breakdown method is infrequently seen. Whether this is due to an inability to make the necessary estimates or to the expense involved in doing so is debatable. Likely both factors contribute to its relative disuse.

Having pointed all of this out, however, the fact that the breakdown method isn't widely used does not mean it can be ignored by the appraiser. A major benefit of learning the breakdown method is the insight it provides into the sources and dynamics of depreciation. This insight is useful for several reasons: (1) it makes clear the limitations of the lump-sum estimating methods and suggests the kinds of situations in which those methods are most likely to err, (2) it may help the appraiser make wiser selections of comparables for use in the direct sales comparison approach, and to make more informed adjustments for depreciation-related differences, and (3) despite its infrequent use, rare is the appraiser who has never used the breakdown method or reviewed an appraisal in which it was used.

In order to use the breakdown method, the appraiser must go beyond categorizing depreciation as simply physical, functional, or external. More detail is needed, as shown in the list of depreciation categories in Table 12–5.

Many of the items and terms in Table 12–5 are familiar. Those that need additional explanation before proceeding are: (1) curable versus incurable depreciation, (2) short-lived versus long-lived items, and (3) defects, deficiencies, and superadequacies.

TABLE 12–5 Categories of Depreciation

1. Physical Depreciation
   a. Curable (sometimes called deferred maintenance)
   b. Incurable
      1. Short-lived items
      2. Long-lived items
2. Functional Obsolescence
   a. Curable
      1. Deficiencies
      2. Defects
      3. Superadequacies
   b. Incurable Functional Obsolescence
      1. Deficiencies
      2. Defects
      3. Superadequacies
3. External Obsolescence
   a. Locational
   b. Economic

Curable versus Incurable Depreciation

Curable and incurable depreciation were defined earlier and used in the modified lump-sum method. The distinction between curable and incurable depreciation is even more important when using the breakdown method because the measure of its effect on value depends on how it is categorized.

It is reasonable to assume that property owners will repair, or cure, an item of depreciation if as a result, the increase in the property's market value is equal to or greater than the cost of the cure. This is called *curable* depreciation. Conversely, if the costs to cure an item of depreciation exceed the resulting increase in the property's value, the assumption is that it won't be cured. This is called *incurable* depreciation. Notice two things. First, the test of whether an item of depreciation is curable or incurable is economic, not physical. It is not enough that something can be repaired. It must also make economic sense to do so. Second, as suggested by Table 12–5, the decision as to whether depreciation is curable or incurable must always be made for physical deterioration and functional obsolescence, but seldom for external obsolescence. It is generally assumed that external obsolescence is incurable, because it is outside the control of the owner of the subject property.

Short-Lived versus Long-Lived Items

If an item of depreciation is categorized as physical and is determined to be incurable, the appraiser must also determine whether the depreciation is affecting a short-lived or a long-lived item.

A short-lived item is one that is expected to have a remaining economic life that is shorter than the remaining economic life of the structure. A long-lived item is one that is expected to have a remaining economic life at least equal to that of the structure.

The reason for differentiating between short- and long-lived items has to do with the order in which the depreciation estimates are made. In practice, items of short-lived incurable deterioration are estimated first. This amount is then subtracted from the reproduction cost new to provide an adjusted amount on which to base the estimate of depreciation on long-lived items.

Deficiencies, Defects and Superadequacies

In Table 12–5, functional obsolescence is divided into three subcategories called deficiencies, defects, and superadequacies. A deficiency is a lack of a component or system, such as a lack of central air conditioning in a tropical climate. A defect is a component or system which is present but is inadequate by current market standards. An example is an outdated air-conditioning system. A superadequacy is something that represents excess capacity—too many or too much of a given structural component. An example is an oversized air conditioning system.[14]

The appraiser places each item of functional obsolescence into either the deficiency, defect, or superadequacy category, because their impacts on value may be measured differently.

An Estimating Sequence

There is not a universally accepted methodology or sequence for estimating total accrued depreciation via the breakdown method. The appraiser must do the best he or she can given the specifics of the assignment and the available information. Figure 12–2 is a representative sequence, but there are others in use that are equally acceptable. Notice that there is not a smooth ordering from one broad category of depreciation to another. Instead, appraisers often skip from subcategory to subcategory, again with the objective of completeness without double-counting.

An Example

The subject property is a 2,500-square-foot single-family house. It is 20 years old and typical for its neighborhood. The land value has been estimated to be $30,000. The depreciated value of the improvements to the

---

[14] Which raises the issue of whether a whole improvement can be superadequate; that is, an overimprovement. The answer is yes, though superadequacy is generally defined as too much of a particular component of the improvement. There is also the issue of whether overimprovements are functional or external obsolescence. Most writers place them in the former category, but a persuasive case can be made that they belong in the latter, and they are treated that way later in the chapter.

FIGURE 12–2 Estimating Accrued Depreciation: A Representative Sequence

Step

1. Field Inspection to Identify Sources of Depreciation

2. Physical and Functional Depreciation Are Placed into Curable versus Incurable Categories

3. The Value Impact of Physical Curable Depreciation Is Estimated

4.† The Value Impact of Functional Curable Depreciation Is Estimated

5. The Value Impact of Short-Lived Physical Incurable Depreciation Is Estimated

6. The Value Impact of Long-Lived Physical Incurable Depreciation Is Estimated

7.† The Value Impact of Functional Incurable Obsolesence Is Estimated

8. The Value Impact of External Obsolesence Is Estimated

9. The categories of depreciation estimated in Steps 3-8 are added to arrive at the estimate of Total Accrued Depreciation

†If Replacement cost new is used, many (but not necessarily all) items of functional obsolescence may be eliminated.

TABLE 12-6 Components of Reproduction Cost New

Direct Costs	Reproduction Cost
Excavation and site preparation	$ 1,500
Foundation	3,540
Concrete flat work	3,400
Framing	27,300
Exterior siding	11,500
Finished	14,000
Bath and plaster	4,700
Roofing	9,500
Finished flooring	4,500
Plumbing	17,500
Electrical	5,260
Heating	15,400
Insulation	1,600
Painting	3,200
Kitchen equipment	4,400
Carpeting	5,700
Total direct costs	$133,000
Indirect costs and profit (overhead, fees, permits and licensing, insurance, taxes, financing charge, selling and holding expenses, and profit)	$ 33,250 (25% of direct costs)
Reproduction cost new	$166,250

site has been estimated to be $15,000. The reproduction cost new of the house has been estimated to be $166,250, as broken down in Table 12-6.

The field inspection (Step 1 in Figure 12-2) revealed several items of physical and functional depreciation. They are placed into curable or incurable categories (Step 2), and their value impact is estimated as shown below.

Estimating the Effects of Physical Curable Depreciation (Step 3)

Measure: The measure of the value impact of curable deterioration is the *cost to cure.*

Item	(Assumed) Cost to Cure
Paint	$1,800
Replace front door	300
Total physical curable	$2,100

Logic: Because the cure will add an amount to value that is at least equal to the cost to cure, it is assumed that an owner will make the cure, and the impact on the current value is therefore the cost to make the cure.

Measuring the value impact of physical curable items such as painting and replacing a door is relatively straightforward. The task is more difficult in cases where there is partial wear. A common example is a roof that is partway through its physical life. Is it curable? Or as some appraisers argue, does it lose utility suddenly (like a lightbulb burning out) when it begins to leak? In such cases there is a choice, and the pro rata loss in value can be deducted as either curable or incurable physical deterioration. The final market value estimate will be the same, which underscores the importance of not getting needlessly bogged down in semantics.

Estimating the Effects of Functional Curable Depreciation (Step 4)

Assume that three items of curable functional obsolescence were identified during the field inspection. One is a deficiency, one is a defect, and one is a superadequacy.

The deficiency is a lack of insulation that would be required by current market standards. The defect is that the bathtubs in both bathrooms are too small and must be replaced. The superadequacy is an oversized heating system. These items will be discussed in turn.

The Deficiency

The lack of insulation required by current market standards is the deficiency.

Measure: The measure of the value impact of a deficiency is the *excess cost to cure*, which is defined as the cost to cure minus the reproduction cost new of the (deficient) item if it were included during construction on the date of the appraisal.

Assume that the cost to cure (the cost to add the necessary insulation) has been estimated to be $1,100. However, if the property had had the proper amount of insulation, its reproduction cost new would have been $2,100. Notice in Table 12–6 that the reproduction cost of the insulation, as is, is $1,600. This means that as part of new construction, the additional insulation would have cost only $500. "Retrofitting," however, will cost $1,100. Given these facts, the excess cost to cure the insulation is:

Cost to cure	$1,100
Reproduction cost during construction	− 500
Deficiency	$ 600

Logic: The logic of the "excess cost to cure" measure is understood best with reference to the example subject property, which has an estimated reproduction cost new of $166,250. From the facts above, we know that if the subject had had sufficient insulation, its reproduction cost would have been $166,750. We also know that the cost to cure is $1,100. Therefore, if this was the only item of depreciation, the subject property would be worth $166,750 − $1,100 = $165,650. The "measure" of curable functional obsolescence above (cost to cure − cost in new reproduction) is $600, and gets us to the proper value of $166,250 − $600 = $165,650.

The Defect

The bathtubs must be replaced.

Measure: The value impact of a defect is measured by the cost to cure *plus* any *undepreciated* reproduction cost (reproduction cost new less any depreciation already taken) remaining in the existing item.

Cost to cure	$700
Undepreciated cost of the existing bathtubs	+ 50
Defect	$750

Logic: The logic behind adding the undepreciated reproduction cost of the existing item to the cost to cure is that the reproduction cost new estimate includes the cost of the existing item which is to be removed.

Notice that it is the undepreciated reproduction cost of the existing item that is added. This is because it is possible that part of the reproduction cost new of the item has already been depreciated in the physical curable step. It is commonly found that functionally obsolete items are also physically deteriorated, and again, the appraiser must guard against double-counting.

In a case such as bathtubs to be replaced, it is unimportant whether the depreciation is labeled functional obsolescence, physical deterioration, or some combination of each, as long as the depreciation is recognized and measured.

The Superadequacy

The heating system is oversized.

Measure: The measure of the value impact of a curable superadequacy is the difference between the *undepreciated* reproduction cost new of the superadequate item, and the reproduction cost new for an item that is adequate.

Undepreciated reproduction cost for the oversized heating system	$15,400[†]
Reproduction cost new for an adequate heating system	− 11,300
Superadequacy	$ 4,100

[†]From Table 12–6

Logic: The market will not pay a premium for something that will not be used and may require additional operating expenses.

Again, the appraiser guards against double-counting by deducting from the reproduction cost new of the component any physical deterioration that had been previously charged. In this case, there was none. In practice, most functional obsolescence resulting from superadequacies will be incurable, because the cost to cure will exceed the value added by the cure. For example, a three-car garage in a given market may add no significant value to a house. However, it also costs very little to have it there and thus the cost to demolish it and make the resulting repairs to the house will likely exceed the cost to cure.

There are, however, instances where a superadequacy is justifiably placed in the curable category, and our example of the oversized heating system is a case in point. Unlike an oversized garage, a heating system may be curable because the present value of the added (wasted) heating and maintenance costs may exceed the cost to cure.

Estimating Incurable Depreciation

The impacts of all items of curable depreciation have now been estimated and we are through Step 4. Next comes the estimate of incurable depreciation, which is depreciation that would cost more to cure than it would add to value. In such cases, it does not make economic sense to make the cure, therefore, the impact of incurable depreciation is (in general) the amount by which its continued existence will reduce the market value of the property.

All three categories of depreciation—physical, functional, and external—may be incurable, and they will be discussed in turn.

Estimating the Impact of Physical Incurable Depreciation on Short-Lived Items (Step 5)

When estimating incurable physical depreciation, it is necessary to divide the items into short-lived and long-lived items. A short-lived item is one that is expected to have a remaining economic life that is shorter than the remaining economic life of the structure.

Measure: For short-lived items, the measure of the value impact of incurable physical depreciation is based on the ratio of the age of the item to

TABLE 12–7 Short-Lived Incurable Physical Depreciation

Item	Physical Age	÷	Physical Life Expectancy			×	Undepreciated Reproduction Cost[†]	=	Depreciation
Plumbing	20	÷	60	=	.33	×	$17,500	=	$ 5,775
Electrical	20	÷	60	=	.33	×	5,260	=	1,736
Roof	10	÷	20	=	.50	×	9,500	=	4,750
Carpet	5	÷	8	=	.625	×	5,700	=	3,563
Heating	20	÷	40	=	.50	×	11,300[††]	=	5,650
Total physical incurable, short-lived items									$21,474

[†]From Table 12–6, less any curable physical and functional depreciation already taken.
[††]$15,400 reproduction cost less $4,100 already taken as functional obsolescence (superadequacy).

its normal life expectancy, multiplied by the undepreciated reproduction cost of that item. The age used may be physical or effective. Using physical age, we have:

$$\frac{\text{Physical incurable}}{\text{depreciation}} = \frac{\text{Physical age}}{\text{Life expectancy}} \times \text{Undepreciated reproduction cost}$$

Physical life expectancies can be estimated by talking with subcontractors and dealers. For the example subject property, Table 12–7 shows the assumed estimated lives and the resulting calculations of physical incurable deterioration.

Effective age instead of physical age may be used as the basis for the estimation of short-lived, incurable physical depreciation. Physical age was used here for two reasons: (1) to illustrate how it is applied and (2) because appraisers often use physical age for items like heating and plumbing, on the basis that the effective age of such items may be difficult or impossible to estimate.

Estimating the Impact of Long-Lived Incurable Physical Deterioration (Step 6)

Long-lived items are those items with a remaining economic life equal to the remaining economic life of the basic structure. Because all items in a structure must be categorized as either long-lived or short-lived, and short-lived physical depreciation has already been estimated, by definition, everything else must be a long-lived item.

Given this fact, and because long-lived items have a remaining life expectancy equal to the structure and will thus all become "valueless" at the same time, the impact of physical depreciation on those items is generally measured on a lump-sum basis.

Measure: The value impact of incurable physical depreciation on long-lived items is measured as follows:

$$\text{Long-lived physical incurable} = \frac{\text{Effective age of structure after curable items have been cured}}{\text{Total economic life}} \times \text{Reproduction cost of incurable long-lived items} \quad (4)$$

A similar formula was previously used in the application of lump-sum methods. To review, the effective age of a structure is the age indicated by its condition and utility. The total economic life of a structure is the period of time over which a structure contributes to a property's value. Thus, the effective age of a structure may be equal to, longer than, or shorter than its actual or physical age, depending on the original quality of the construction, subsequent maintenance, and the effect of curing the appropriate items of depreciation.

Assume that the subject property (which has a physical age of 20 years) will have an effective age of only 5 years once all the curable items have been cured, and that the expected total economic life for a house of this kind is assumed to be 50 years. Given these assumptions, the first term on the right side of the equation for estimating long-lived physical incurable depreciation is 5/50 = .10.

Moving to the final term in Equation (4), the reproduction cost of incurable long-lived items is the reproduction cost of the entire structure, minus the reproduction costs of those physical curable and physical incurable short-lived items for which depreciation has already been estimated.

For the example subject property:

	Reproduction cost new	$166,250
Less	{Reproduction cost of items physical curable[†]	3,500
	{Reproduction cost of physical incurable, short-lived[††]	53,360
	Reproduction cost of incurable long-lived items	$109,390

[†]Painting ($3,200) + Front Door ($300) = $3,500
[††]Plumbing ($17,500) + Electrical ($5,260) + Roof ($9,500) + Carpet ($5,700) + Heating ($15,400) = $53,360.

It is the reproduction costs of the items that are subtracted, not the adjusted amount of depreciation previously taken. The reason for subtracting the reproduction costs of items for which the impact of physical depreciation has already been estimated is to avoid double-counting.

Based on the previous calculations, the value impact of physical incurable depreciation for long-lived items is estimated as follows:

Reproduction cost of long-lived curable items (from calculation above)	$109,390
Effective age ÷ Economic life (5/50)	× .10
Physical incurable depreciation for long-lived items	$ 10,939

Estimating the Impact of Functional Incurable Obsolescence (Step 7)

The bathrooms in the subject property are poorly located.

Measure: The value impact of an incurable defect like a poor floor plan can be estimated in two ways: (1) matched pairs analysis, or (2) capitalizing the rent loss due to the defect.

If the appraiser has comparables from which the negative impact of the poorly located bathrooms can be extracted, that is the best source of the estimate. Lacking data for a matched pairs analysis, a gross rent multiplier can be applied to estimate the value impact.

Assume the subject property's floor plan would result in monthly rent that is $20 less than it would be if "rearranged." Assuming a monthly gross rent multiplier of 120, the estimated value loss from this item of incurable functional obsolescence is: $120 \times \$20 = \$2,400$.

Estimating the Impact of Incurable External Obsolescence (Step 8)

External obsolescence is almost always incurable, though the reason is slightly different than the purely economic criterion that the cost to cure must exceed the value added by the cure. Instead, the reason that external obsolescence is generally considered incurable is because it is out of the direct control of the property owner and therefore it often cannot be cured.

In most cases, this logic will not contradict the rule based on the relationship of the cost to cure and the value added, because even if it were possible to make the cure, it generally would not be justified economically. There may be exceptions, however, and the appraiser must recognize that some items that are traditionally placed in the incurable category might in fact be ultimately cured, generally by others. For example, how much will a poorly maintained adjacent property affect the subject property's value? If the condition is permanent, the impact may be substantial. However, when a property changes hands, it is not uncommon for a change in maintenance to occur. It may also be possible for a property owner to cure a neighbor's property. Consider that physical depreciation on one property may contribute to external obsolescence on its neighbors. It is not uncommon for the neighbor(s) to pay for repairs on such properties, or even purchase and repair them in order to reduce or eliminate external obsolescence on their own property. This illustrates why it is so difficult to determine when external obsolescence exists, and if it does, to quantify its value impact.

Measure: As in the case of incurable functional obsolescence, matched pairs or capitalized rent loss are used to measure the effect of incurable external obsolescence.

Assume the subject property is located two doors from a corner site that is zoned for light commercial use. Matched pairs analysis indicates that the presence of such zoning adversely affects residential value by $5,000.

This, however, is not the final estimate because unlike physical and functional obsolescence, external obsolescence affects both land and buildings. Therefore, the separately estimated land value will capture some of the effects of the external obsolescence, and the total estimate of external obsolescence—$5,000 in this case—must be allocated between the land and buildings. If the typical building-to-land ratio in the subject property's neighborhood is 80 percent, the proper estimate of external obsolescence for the improvement would be:

$$\$5,000 \times .80 = \$4,000$$

Finally, it is assumed the example subject property is located in a market that is in equilibrium. Had that not been the case, the impact of disequilibrium would be estimated as described earlier, and would appear at this point in the appraisal.

Estimating Total Accrued Depreciation (Step 9)

All of the individual depreciation estimates are added together. For the example subject property, this is done in Table 12–8.

The Value Estimate

The value estimate using the breakdown method for estimating depreciation is:

Reproduction cost new	$166,250
Less accrued depreciation	46,363
Depreciated value of major improvement	$119,887
Plus assumed land value	30,000
Plus assumed value of depreciated improvements to the site	15,000
Fee simple value	$164,887

TABLE 12–8 Estimate of Total Accrued Depreciation

	Depreciation Estimate
Physical Depreciation	
Curable	$ 2,100
Incurable short-lived	21,474
Incurable long-lived	10,939
Functional obsolescence	
Curable	
Defect	750
Deficiency	600
Superadequacy	4,100
Incurable	
Defect	2,400
External obsolescence	
Incurable (building portion)	$ 4,000
Total accrued depreciation	$46,363

Summary

Accrued depreciation is the difference between the reproduction (or replacement) cost of an improvement on the date of the appraisal and the market value of the improvement on the same date. Thus, accrued depreciation is the conceptual and mechanical link between reproduction (or replacement) cost new and market value. The three categories of accrued depreciation are physical deterioration, functional obsolescence, and external obsolescence.

The two general methods used to estimate accrued depreciation are the lump-sum (or age/life) method and the breakdown method. The lump-sum method relies on general relationships between depreciation and age and is most useful when there are not significant amounts of functional and external obsolescence. The breakdown method treats items of depreciation separately and is analogous to the unit-in-place method of estimating cost new. Lump-sum methods dominate appraisal practice because functional and external obsolescence are often not significant factors, and because the added expense of estimating individual items of depreciation tends to exceed the benefit of greater accuracy.

Items of depreciation are identified during the field inspection and from the appraiser's knowledge of general market conditions. Their impacts on value are then estimated, with care taken to measure the impact of all items of depreciation but to avoid double-counting. This can be accomplished by a well thought-out estimating sequence, with adjustments made for items of depreciation previously taken.

The lump-sum methods for estimating accrued depreciation multiply the cost new of the improvement by the ratio of the improvement's effective age to its estimated total economic life. The appraiser can develop benchmarks for annual rates of depreciation by extracting those rates from sales data. The appropriate rate is then multiplied by a property's effective (or physical) age to provide a percentage estimate of total depreciation.

When using the breakdown method, depreciation must be categorized as either curable or incurable, with the test of curability being economic—whether the cost to cure an item of depreciation is equaled or exceeded by the value added to the property. In addition, items of incurable physical deterioration must be further divided into short-lived and long-lived categories, depending on whether the remaining useful lives will be shorter than, or equal to, the remaining useful life of the structure as a whole.

One component of depreciation that is sometimes misunderstood is the economic obsolescence that results from a market that is in disequilibrium. For houses, a market condition factor, which is the ratio of selling price to reproduction cost less other categories of depreciation, can be extracted from comparable sales and then applied to the reproduction cost less other depreciation of a subject property. A market condition factor can also be calculated and used to value investment properties, although there may be a lack of sufficient sales from which to extract a reliable factor. In such cases, the loss (or excess) of income from the over (under) supply can be capitalized into a value loss (gain) which is then subtracted (added) from reproduction cost less any depreciation already taken.

Questions and Problems

1. Define accrued depreciation.
2. Describe the three main categories of depreciation.
3. What is a deficiency? Defect? Superadequacy?
4. "The cost approach does not work in places where there is overbuilding." Comment.
5. What are the two subcategories of external obsolescence?
6. Differentiate between physical and effective age.
7. Extract an annual rate of depreciation from the sales below:

	1	2
Selling price	$94,000	$131,000
Land value	18,500	25,000
Reproduction cost new	90,000	123,500
Effective age	13 years	15 years

8. "The cost approach works best for new improvements because there is no depreciation to estimate." Comment.
9. Graph (and explain) a likely pattern of accrued depreciation over time.
10. External obsolescence for a property has been estimated to be $7,500. This amount should be subtracted from reproduction cost as part of the appraisal process. Comment.
11. Reproduction cost has been estimated to be $115,000 for a property with a 60-year total economic life. Its effective age is 12 years. Land value is $24,000. What is the estimated market value using the cost approach, assuming no external or functional obsolescence?

PART V

Estimating Value: The Income Approach

The rationale of the income approach is straightforward: The value of a property is a function of the income it is expected to produce. The income approach processes the expected income into a value estimate.

There are many analytic techniques, or models, under the income approach umbrella. These models can be divided into two categories: (1) ratio models and (2) discounted cash flow models. Ratio models estimate value based on the ratio between a single year of income and value. Ideally, these ratios are extracted from comparable sales, then applied to the expected income of the subject property to estimate its value. An example of this type of model is the Gross Income Multiplier *(GIM),* which was introduced in the chapter on the direct sales comparison approach. In effect, the *GIM* is a unit of comparison, and many appraisers place them in the direct sales comparison approach. Because the units of comparison involve a measure of income, we have chosen to include a detailed discussion of them in the income approach section.

The other category of income approach model is the discounted cash flow model. It differs from ratio models in three ways: (1) it requires explicit forecasts of the income from the entire assumed holding period, rather than just a single year, (2) there is a much greater analytic burden on the appraiser, because forecasts of future cash flows are not extractable from past sales, and (3) the discounted cash flow model requires the appraiser to estimate the discount rate for the projected holding period, while ratio models are based on a single year's return (or ratio).

The following 12 chapters cover the income approach. They are divided into three sections. Section A deals with direct capitalization models, beginning with the estimation of income, Section B covers discounted cash flow models. Section C discusses relationships among income approach models, other conceptual issues, and investment analysis.

SECTION A: DIRECT CAPITALIZATION

CHAPTER 13

Estimating a Property's Productivity: Net Operating Income

Introduction

The income approach is based on the premise that a property's value is a function of the income it is expected to produce. Thus, regardless of which income approach model is to be used, the first major step is to make the income estimate. The income of interest in most cases is net operating income *(NOI)*, which is the bottom line measure of a property's productivity. *NOI* is shared by the mortgage lender, the Internal Revenue Service, and the equity investor. Because *NOI* represents the size of the productivity pie, it is typically the income that is processed into a value estimate. Thus, for most income approach models, an estimate of *NOI* is necessary. The exception is the gross income multiplier model, which requires an estimate of gross income only.

Estimating Net Operating Income

When appraising income property, the estimate of net operating income *(NOI)* is made on an annual basis, using a standard format that looks like this:

NOI Statement

Potential gross income

− Vacancy allowance

+ Other income

= Effective gross income

− Operating expenses

= Net operating income

Each of the entries on the *NOI* statement will be discussed in turn.

Potential Gross Income

higher cap rate lower the value

Potential gross income
− Vacancy allowance
+ Other income
= Effective gross income
− Operating expenses
= Net operating income

Potential gross income *(PGI)* is the amount of rent the property will produce if it is 100 percent occupied for the entire year and all occupants pay their rent. The term *potential gross income* is very descriptive, as it refers to the maximum, or potential, gross income the property can produce. For example, if an apartment building has 24 units, with market rent at $500 per unit per month, the annual *PGI* would be 24 × $500 × 12 = $144,000. There are three sources of information to help the appraiser estimate potential gross income: (1) competitive properties, (2) the subject property, and (3) published survey results.

Estimating Potential Gross Income From Competitive Properties

The process of extracting rents from competitive properties is the same as the process used to make adjustments to the selling prices of comparables in the direct sales comparison approach. Suppose you are appraising a small office building, the ABC building, and have collected the information on competitive properties shown in Table 13–1.

TABLE 13–1 Data on Competitive Properties

	Subject	Competitive Properties						
	ABC Building	1	2	3	4	5	6	7
Net leasable (square feet)	16,000	17,000	22,500	20,500	30,000	37,000	27,000	30,500
Age	4 years	5	6	5	5	8	6	5
Location (relative to subject)	—	Inferior	Similar	Similar	Superior	Similar	Inferior	Similar
Vacancy	4%	6%	5%	4%	6%	5%	3%	4%
Gross rent (average, per square foot)	$10.00	$7.80	$8.50	$8.90	$9.25	$7.30	$6.50	$7.85

FIGURE 13–1 Rent and Size

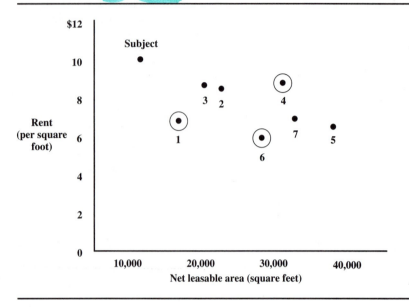

Inspection of Table 13–1 shows a range of rents from properties that differ with respect to age, size, and location. Your experience as an appraiser suggests that in this market, age differentials of five years or less have little effect on rents. This leaves the size and location as possible explanations for the rent differentials. One way to begin the analysis is by attempting to find a relationship between size and rent per square foot. In Figure 13–1, rent and size are plotted for the comparables and the subject. Comparables 1, 4, and 6 differ locationally, and are circled.

The picture is now clearer. Apparently the size of the building influences rent per square foot in this market; as size increases, rent per square foot declines. From this perspective, the current rent of $10 per foot for the ABC building seems reasonable when compared to Properties 2, 3, 5, and 7. Figure 13–1 also supports the predicted effect of locational differences. Properties 1 and 6 are in inferior locations, and they produce lower rents. Property 4 is in a superior location, and it produces higher rents. These locational effects are consistent with the rents shown in Table 13–1.

The inferior location of Property 1 decreases rent by about $2 per square foot, while the inferior location of Property 6 (comparing it to Property 7) appears to be worth about $1.35 per foot. The superior location of Property 4 is worth about $1.40 per foot when compared to Property 7. Based on this analysis, $10 per foot is a reasonable estimate of the market rent for the subject property,[1] and the potential gross income is forecast to be $10 × 16,000 = $160,000. This forecast would be adjusted upward if rents were expected to increase in the forthcoming year due to inflation or escalation clauses in the current leases.

Published and Private Surveys

In addition to using data from competitive properties, other sources of information about market rent levels are published reports such as the annual income/expense analyses for apartments, office buildings, condominiums, co-ops, and planned unit developments published by the Institute of Real Estate Management (IREM). These reports contain detailed breakdowns of income and expense data based on surveys which include thousands of properties. The data is segregated by geographical area, with many metropolitan areas listed separately.

Many appraisers also survey local property managers to assist in estimating proper rent levels. Surveying tenants to find out how much they would pay for various amenities can also be helpful.[2]

Using the Subject Property As Its Own Comparable

When estimating potential gross income it is a mistake to ignore the subject property. It is part of the market and is the best comparable you will find. Try to obtain the past operating statements for the subject property, which should include the current and past rent rolls. Owner-supplied statements are not always as accurate as you would like and it is better if the operating statements have been audited. Past rent levels can be verified by checking with the tenants listed on the rent rolls. If there are long-term leases they may be recorded in the courthouse. A history of rents produced by the subject that are consistent with what you have extracted from the current market is the strongest evidence that those rents have been (and currently are) at the market level. This does not mean that historical rents must equal current rents. If market rent levels have been rising or falling, you would expect to find the same pattern for the subject.

In short, the proper mind-set when estimating potential gross income is to presume the current rents for the subject property are correct unless they can be shown to be incorrect.

---

[1] With a sufficient number of comparables, regression analysis can be used to estimate rents. An example based on the ABC building is shown in the chapter Appendix. Regression analysis is discussed in detail in Chapter 8.

[2] See Charles A. Smith and Mark Kroll, "Improving Estimates of Potential Gross Income in Multifamily Properties through Market Research," *The Appraisal Journal*, January 1988.

Units of Comparison

The appropriate unit on which to base the potential gross income estimate should be a function of the way in which the property is typically rented. That is, the estimate of potential gross income should be based on the unit that renters (and investors) tend to pay for. This is the same logic that underlies the application of the sales comparison approach. Some units of comparison, like square feet for office properties, are more obvious than others. Commonly used units of comparison for various property types are as follows:

1. Offices: square feet or office units
2. Apartments: square feet of livable area, apartment units, rooms
3. Factories and warehouses: square feet, cubic feet, loading docks
4. Hospitals and nursing homes: beds, square feet
5. Theaters: seats, square feet

Mixed Uses and Mixed Sizes

Many properties contain mixed uses, such as a mix of office and warehouse space or retail and office space. In such cases, the appraiser is dealing with more than one rental market and a separate estimate of potential gross income should be made for each use.

Sometimes there is a single use but different sizes. An apartment building with two- and three-bedroom units is an example. Because the square-foot rents may or may not be the same for different size units, a potential gross income estimate should be made for each.

The Search Area for Comparable Rents

In the discussion of where to search for comparable sales to use for appraising houses, it was pointed out that limiting the search area to the subject property's neighborhood may be too restrictive, because usable sales can often be found in comparable market settings, whether or not they are geographically contiguous. This is also true for investment properties, because rejecting data that is not from geographically close properties often leaves the appraiser with little or nothing to work with. It is sometimes necessary to gather whatever data is available, and then adjust the rents for any significant differences between the comparable property and the subject. It is also the case that the market for some kinds of investment properties, for example warehouses, may be regional or even national, and the search for comparables should recognize this fact. As data processing technology develops, and if the trend toward securitizing real property interests continues, it is reasonable to expect an expansion of market areas for other kinds of commercial properties.

This is not to suggest that the appraiser should ignore the property next door; the "closer is better" rule is still valid. What is being suggested is that it may be necessary to expand the search beyond the immediate geographic area and that modern tools of analysis increasingly allow reasonable comparisons to be made in such cases.

Quoted versus Effective Rent

When estimating gross rent, it must be recognized that quoted (or "face") rents often obscure the fact that in order to attract tenants, free rent and generous tenant build-out allowances may be offered. These types of giveaways are used when the vacancy rate rises, and they can have a significant impact on the effective rent that is the basis for the estimate of potential gross income.

As an example, in 1994 the asking rent for central business district (CBD) office space in Pittsburgh was in the $25–$30 per square foot range. After negotiation and concessions the true market rent was closer to $20. Differences of this magnitude are of obvious importance. Getting accurate information is often difficult, and typically requires interviews with landlords and tenants, and a careful reading of lease agreements. This applies to the rents for comparable properties as well as the subject property.

The Vacancy Allowance

Potential gross income

− **Vacancy allowance**

+ Other income

= Effective gross income

− Operating expenses

= Net operating income

Only in certain cases (such as a single-tenant property) will an appraiser feel comfortable assuming that the potential gross income will actually be collected. In most cases, a portion of the potential gross will be lost through (1) vacant space and (2) rent loss from delinquent tenants. These two elements are included in the vacancy allowance.

As in the case of potential gross income, the vacancy allowance is best estimated with reference to competitive properties. Look back at the vacancy rates for the comparable office buildings listed in Table 13–1. They average 4.7 percent, with the subject property currently at 4 percent. Unless you have reason to suspect that the average is not representative of the subject, it is as good an estimate as any, and we will assume a reasonable vacancy allowance for the ABC office building is 4.7 percent. Multiplying this rate by the previous estimate of the potential gross income (in this case, $160,000) gives a vacancy allowance of .047 × $160,000 = $7,520.

Estimating the Vacancy Allowance for Mixed Use Properties

Suppose you are appraising an apartment with 30 2-bedroom (800 square feet) and 30 3-bedroom (1,200 square feet) units. Average competitive rents are $250 and $350 for 2-bedroom and 3-bedroom units, respectively. The vacancy rate is 3 percent for 2-bedroom units and 5.5 percent for 3-bedroom units.

This information might be presented on the *NOI* statement as follows:

Potential Gross Income			
2 Bedroom	30 × $250 × 12	$ 90,000	
3 Bedroom	30 × $350 × 12	126,000	$216,000
Vacancy Allowance			
2 Bedroom	.03 × $90,000	$ 2,700	
3 Bedroom	.055 × $126,000	6,930	$ 9,630

Other Income

> Potential gross income
> − Vacancy allowance
> + **Other income**
> = Effective gross income
> − Operating expenses
> = Net operating income

Earlier, potential gross income was defined as the rent that would be produced with 100 percent occupancy. This refers to the primary source of income from the property, which is the leasing of space. However, properties often produce income in addition to that produced by renting space. Two common examples are the income from parking stalls and the income from vending and laundry machines.

This kind of other income is included in the estimate of effective gross income. However, a decision must be made as to how it is affected by the vacancy allowance. Some appraisers add it to potential gross income, then apply the vacancy allowance to the total amount. The logic is that other income is likely to change as the occupancy rate changes. If this is done, the entry is, effectively, "potential other income." Other appraisers prefer to apply the vacancy allowance to potential gross income only, then add other income on a net basis. The argument for this approach is that the relationship between the income from renting space and the income from secondary sources is often difficult to quantify. For example, if parking spaces are rented to the general public, the income produced will not be closely associated with the vacancy rate of the property. In such cases, the net amount of other income is estimated, and the vacancy allowance is not applied.

The same is true for vending machines, for which estimating the potential gross income is impossible. It makes more sense to simply add an estimate for this type of other income after applying the vacancy allowance to rental income. Furthermore, it may be equally impractical to attempt to assign other income (and apply appropriate vacancy rates) to the various mixed-use components of properties. It is more trouble than it is worth to separate a soda machine's potential income between two- and three-bedroom apartments.

Returning to the ABC office building, assume that other income is estimated to be $6,500 and that it is estimated on a net basis. The calculation of effective gross income would look like this:

Potential gross income	$160,000
− Vacancy allowance (.047)	7,520
	152,480
+ Other income	6,500
= Effective gross income	$158,980

How Much Other Income Should Be Counted?

Another issue when estimating other income is to decide how much of it should be counted. The author lives in State College, Pennsylvania, a town of approximately 90,000 people, including 40,000 university students. Many students live in off-campus apartments and rooming houses, some of which have laundry facilities. It is common for these machines to generate income not only from the tenants of the property, but also from tenants from nearby properties with no laundry machines.

A question arises as to the disposition of this type of income when estimating *NOI*. If all of it is counted in the estimate of other income, the property rights being appraised will effectively include a laundromat business. In such cases, it makes sense to include in the estimate of other income only that portion of the total that can be reasonably attributed to the tenants of the property. If desired, a separate valuation of the remaining (nontenantgenerated) income can be used as the basis for negotiating the price of the laundromat business, and the real estate appraiser may or may not be involved in that part of the valuation. When this kind of situation arises, it should be discussed with the client. In every instance, the assumptions the appraiser makes concerning other income should be clearly stated in the appraisal report.

Operating Expenses

Potential gross income
− Vacancy allowance
+ Other income
= Effective gross income
− **Operating expenses**
= Net operating income

Operating expenses are expenses which relate to the operation of the property. They are subtracted from effective gross income to arrive at the estimate of net operating income.

There is a long list of commonly encountered operating expenses, and it is useful for analysis and common for reporting purposes to separate them into four categories: (1) fixed expenses, (2) variable expenses, (3) maintenance and repair, and (4) reserve for replacement.

Fixed Operating Expenses

Fixed operating expenses are those, which for a given year, are relatively predictable, tend to be independent of the occupancy level, and tend not to be subject to budgetary control. The standard examples of fixed expenses are property taxes and insurance.

Notice that their description as fixed does not mean these expenses remain at the same level over time. Insurance premiums and property taxes do change. Fixed is a function of the period of analysis, and in any given year insurance premiums and property taxes do tend to be fixed.

The insurance premiums for such things as workmen's compensation, liability, fire and extended coverage, and perhaps such things as water and boiler damage, may be estimated with reference to past premiums, and quotes for future premiums can be obtained. Making the property tax estimate may be trickier because property taxes are based on the property's market value, and it is market value that is being estimated. However, unless the appraisal is for the purpose of property tax assessment, this isn't a real problem. The property owner is currently paying some amount of property tax, and the most reasonable estimate of future property tax is generally that which is now being paid, adjusted by whatever change is expected in the forthcoming year.[3]

Variable Expenses

Variable expenses are those that are relatively less predictable than are fixed expenses, tend to be affected by the occupancy level, and are more subject to budgetary control.[4] Some variable expenses, like the management fee, are common to almost all properties, while others, like snow removal, will be applicable only in certain markets. The level of other variable expenses will depend on the particulars of the lease agreement. Specifically, which operating expenses the tenant must pay and which the owner must pay. The variable operating expenses that are typically encountered are discussed below.

- Management Fees. Fees for management services are generally based on a percentage of rents collected. The exact percentage varies by property type and size, but 3–6 percent of rents is a common range. All properties must be managed, whether it is by the owner or by a professional manager. An entry for the management fee is necessary regardless of who manages the property, unless the tenant is responsible. If the owner of the property also does the managing, the entry for the management fees reflects the owner's compensation for performing the management duties.

- Utilities. This entry includes electricity, water, sewer, and heating fuel. Again, the entry for utilities will depend on what the tenant and owner are responsible for. Owners of office buildings often pay all utilities. For warehouses, tenants tend to pay, while for apartments, the owners and tenants often each pay a share. While apartment units may be individually metered, the owner may still be responsible for the utilities used in common areas. Again, tenant leases are the source of information as to who pays what. Once that is established, the estimate is made based on actual past expenditures and what can be learned from utility companies.

- General Payroll. This entry includes those wages, salaries, and benefits to employees that are not included in other expense categories. Examples are the wages of janitorial and security personnel, and doormen. Items like Social Security may be included on the general payroll entry, though a separate expense entry is sometimes made.

- Other Variable Expenses. Other commonly encountered variable expenses are for trash and snow removal, exterminating, grounds maintenance and landscaping, legal and professional fees, and advertising and promotion.

---

[3] The handling of valuation for tax assessment purposes is discussed in Chapter 14.

[4] The allocation of expenses to the fixed and variable categories is somewhat arbitrary, because many expenses are hybrids that have both fixed and variable elements. The allocation in these cases is somewhat subjective, and is often based on traditional practice.

Maintenance and Repair

Maintenance and repair is the third major operating expense category. It is generally estimated separately because maintenance and repair can be a major expense item by itself, and because it doesn't fit very well into either the fixed or variable expense categories. It is truly a hybrid. The expense of things like roof repairs and exterior painting tends to be fixed because they must be done regardless of the occupancy rate. On the other hand, the expense of such things as the maintenance of elevators may be more closely tied to usage and thus is closer to the variable expense category.

Other expenses which may be included in the maintenance and repair category are interior painting and wall cleaning and papering, though some appraisers choose to include these items in a separate account called decorating. When estimating maintenance and repairs, particular care must be taken to avoid double-counting. For example, the general payroll account may include the salary of a laborer whose duties include making minor repairs. In this case, the maintenance and repairs account should not include that salary.

Because future outlays for maintenance and repair tend to be "lumpy," and by nature difficult to predict, it is common practice to use a percentage of effective gross income as the estimate of maintenance and repair. One study of appraisal practice[5] showed that on average, appraisers used 5 percent of effective gross income as the estimate of maintenance and repair, with a very small variance around that figure.

Reserve for Replacements

Certain parts of a building, like the roof and the escalators and elevators, as well as personal property like carpeting, drapes, and appliances, may need renovation or replacement periodically. These kinds of major investments are not reflected in the maintenance and repair entry in estimating operating expenses. Rather, they are capital expenditures which generally require a relatively large investment and tend to be lumpy as far as their timing.

These lumpy outflows may present a problem when estimating *NOI*. For example, if *NOI* is expected to be $100,000 annually, except in year 5, when $50,000 is expected to be invested to replace worn-out items, this one-time outlay will affect market value even though it doesn't occur each year. Whether this presents a valuation problem depends on the income approach model being used. When using a discounted cash flow model, which explicitly considers each year of income during the expected holding period, lumpy expenses are not a problem because they can be included in the year they are expected to be incurred. However, for ratio models, which use only a single year of income, a way must be found to incorporate this lumpy outflow.

---

[5]Kenneth M. Lusht, "The Behavior of Appraisers in Valuing Income Properties: A Status Report," *The Real Estate Appraiser and Analyst,* July–August 1979.

The solution is to smooth the lumps by prorating them on an annual basis. If $10,000 is the expected average annual expenditure on replacement items ($50,000 each 5 years), the annual *NOI* would be $100,000 − $10,000 = $90,000. The $10,000 would be shown as an operating expense entry called *reserve for replacements,* which increases operating expense (and decreases *NOI*) by that amount. There are actually several ways to estimate the reserve account. They differ with respect to the assumption made concerning whether or not a sinking fund will be established to pay for future expenditures. A sinking fund is a savings account into which periodic payments are made. Because the payments earn interest, the annual amount set aside in the reserve account is smaller than the amount calculated by simply dividing the future outlay by the number of years before replacement, as above.[6] The sinking fund assumption is not widely used in practice.

The rule for deciding which structural components, equipment, and personal property are to be included in a reserve account is straightforward: include those items which are expected to have a measurably shorter useful life than the useful life of the basic structure. Because items with useful lives equal to or exceeding the life of the structure won't have to be replaced, no reserve entry is required. Once the items subject to replacement have been identified, their costs are prorated over their estimated useful lives. This becomes the annual reserve for replacement amounts.

The Complete *NOI* Statement for the ABC Building

Returning one again to the ABC building, and assuming the total of all operating expenses would be $63,500, the *NOI* statement would look like this:

Potential gross income	$160,000
Vacancy allowance	7,520
Other income	6,500
Effective gross income	158,980
Operating expenses	63,500
Net operating income	$ 95,480

A More-Detailed Example

Table 13–2 shows an actual net operating income statement for a 30-unit (25,800 rentable square feet) apartment property in central Pennsylvania. As is common practice, the entries are made both in total and on a per-unit (square foot, in this case) basis.

---

[6]The mathematics of sinking funds are covered later in Chapter 21.

TABLE 13-2 NOI Statement

	Total	Per Square Foot
Potential gross income		
30 units × $450 × 12	$162,000	$6.28
Vacancy allowance (.0625)	10,125	.39
Net rent collected	$151,875	5.89
Other income		
Vending machines	$ 85	
Laundry machines	2,090	.08
Parking	2,865	.11
Total other income	$ 5,040	0.20
Effective gross income	$156,915	6.08
Operating expenses		
Fixed:		
Insurance	$ 3,910	.15
Real estate taxes	11,240	.44
Variable:		
Management fee	8,350	.32
Electricity	12,620	.49
Heat/Gas, Oil	8,310	.32
Water and sewer	4,275	.17
Trash removal	1,620	.06
Exterminating	550	.02
Ground and landscaping	50	
Cable (television)	1,150	.04
Snow removal	245	.01
Legal and professional fees	520	.02
General payroll	9,500	.37
Maintenance and repair:	6,200	.24
Cleaning and decorating	3,600	.14
Reserves for replacement	6,000	.23
Total operating expenses	$ 78,140	$3.03
Net operating income	$ 78,775	$3.05

The Operating Expense Ratio

The operating expense ratio *(OER)* is a number that is useful to judge whether estimated operating expenses are in line with the market. The *OER* is defined as

$$OER = \frac{\text{Operating expenses}}{\text{Gross income}}.$$

The *OER* for the *NOI* statement shown in Table 13–2 is

$$\frac{\$78,140}{\$156,915} = .498,$$

using effective gross income in the denominator. The *OER* can also be calculated using potential rather than effective gross income in the denominator. The choice is sometimes dictated by the client, other times by local custom. Whichever variation is used, the key is to be consistent. An *OER* based on effective gross income can't be compared to an *OER* based on potential gross income.

The *OER* is useful because it focuses on the forest rather than the trees. With few exceptions, individual operating expenses will not be estimated exactly. Some will be too high, others too low. These errors tend to offset, however, and the total, represented by the *OER*, should be reasonably close to the market average. When the estimated *OER* is not consistent with the market it is a signal to recheck your numbers. While the subject property may indeed be atypical, it is also possible that certain operating expenses have been misestimated.

Two Expenses That Are Not Operating Expenses: Depreciation and Interest

Net operating income measures the property's operating productivity. *NOI* is neither earnings in an accounting sense nor is it taxable income. Thus, absent from the net operating income statement are depreciation expense and the interest paid on mortgage debt, because these expenses have nothing to do with the operation of the property.

If, in the course of an appraisal, a statement of accounting (or taxable) income is obtained, it can be converted to an *NOI* statement by removing depreciation and interest expense. If you are concerned that ignoring things like depreciation and interest expense is ignoring things important to investors, you are right. The impact on market value, if any, of how *NOI* is split among equity investors, lenders, and the tax collector will be covered in due time. First things first, however, and the concern at this point is to define and estimate *NOI*.

It is also possible that an owner's statement will overstate certain operating expenses. This may occur when the statement is also used by the owner for tax purposes. Furthermore, the owner's statement may also include expenses which the owner incurs in the current business use of the property, but which are not directly related to the operation of the property itself. Examples would be the salary of a store manager or the expenses of advertising a business or entertaining clientele. This kind of expense must be removed from the operating statement before it can be used to value the property.

Using the Seller's Records

When using the current owner's (seller's) *NOI* statement, the appraiser should be on the lookout for distortions. Few owners are accountants or appraisers, and they cannot be expected to provide statements that reflect a high level of expertise in those areas. While some comfort is gained if the statements have been audited, auditing does not guarantee that the entries are at market levels. Experience shows that certain kinds of entries on owners' *NOI* statements are more susceptible to distortion than others, and that these entries tend to be underestimated. They are listed below in the order in which they generally appear on the *NOI* statement.

- Rent and Vacancy Levels. When the vacancy rate is relatively high, inducements may be offered to prospective new tenants. These inducements come in many forms, a common type being free rent for some period of time. The owner's statement may not reflect this, showing only the current monthly rent level. The appraiser's best defenses are a careful reading of leases and, if necessary, interviews with tenants. Also useful is a representation by the owner that there are no nonlease agreements with tenants.

At the extreme, tenants may be given extraordinarily favorable terms, even zero rent, in order to raise the occupancy level just prior to selling a property. In addition to the basic step of obtaining a claim by the owner that this hasn't been done, tenants may be asked to sign estoppel statements which confirm their continuing obligation under the terms of their written lease agreements.

- The Management Fee. Some owners, especially of smaller properties, do their own managing. Because no cash outlay occurs for the management function, sometimes no entry for a management fee is made on the owner's *NOI* statement. When estimating market value, an estimate of the management fee is necessary whether or not the current (or future) owner performs the management function or retains a professional manager.

- Property Taxes. If the current level of tax is unrealistically low, taxes may be increased when a sale occurs or when there is a reassessment.

- Expensing versus Capitalizing. The maintenance and repair entry in the operating expense statement reflects expenditures for day-to-day operations. Conversely, capital expenditures are expenditures for major improvements to the property. For income-tax purposes, capital expenditures are not expensed in the year they are made, but instead are depreciated over time, just like the original cost of the improvements. For appraisal purposes, when using ratio models, future capital expenditures like the replacement of a roof will be prorated and appear in the reserve for replacement account. When using a discounted cash flow model, the expenditures will be entered in the year they are expected to occur.

If capital expenditures appear improperly as part of operating expenses, or if operating expenses are improperly omitted, the *NOI* estimate will be incorrect. At best, this conveys misleading information. At worst, it can lead to an incorrect value estimate.

- Deferred Maintenance. Deferred maintenance is a failure to properly maintain and repair a property. It results in a currently lower repair and maintenance expense entry, and therefore a currently higher *NOI*. Owners may not properly maintain items like driveways and landscaping, or may paint less frequently than they should. Reasons for deferred maintenance are a lack of necessary cash or an attempt to produce an artificially high *NOI* prior to sale. In the long run, of course, chronic deferred maintenance will show up in lower rent levels and higher vacancy.

Market or Actual Net Operating Income?

The process of estimating *NOI* has been discussed with reference to market levels of the various entries. In practice, a property's actual income often differs from market levels because of existing leases. When the rent specified in a lease (particularly if it is a long-term lease) is not equal to the "going" market rent, the value of the property will differ from that of a property with rents and income at market level. To be more concrete, if two identical buildings sit side by side, and one is leased for 10 years at $15 per square foot, while the other is leased for 10 years at $22 per square foot, the latter will obviously be worth more in the marketplace.

The appraisal assignment will determine whether it is market income, actual income, or a combination of both that is required. If the assignment is to value the unencumbered fee simple, the assumption is that rents will be at market level. This occurs most often for properties that are leased short-term (for example, apartments) or for properties that are not yet developed, because the assumption is that the rent will be adjusted to the market level relatively quickly.

When a subject property is encumbered by long-term leases, the assignment often calls for an estimate of the *lessor's interest* (called the *leased fee*). In these cases, estimates of both actual and market income are generally needed, because while all current rents may not be at market levels, those that are not will likely move to market levels only when the individual leases expire. Appraising leased fee interests is the subject of Chapter 19. Regardless of whether it is actual or market income that is to be estimated for a given year, the format for estimating net operating income is the same.

Estimating Multiyear Income

When using a discounted cash flow model, income must be forecast for each year of the assumed holding period. As noted earlier, when a property is currently encumbered by long-term leases, and the value of the lessor's interest is to be estimated, this process may be complicated by the fact that some (or all) of the leases require rent that is not at current market levels, and that some (or all) of the leases will expire during the assumed holding period. In these cases, the first steps when forecasting income are to carefully read and analyze individual leases, and to make assumptions about the likely renewal of leases.

This section begins with a description of common lease clauses, and follows with a sample multiple-year income forecast for an office property.

Lease Analysis

A lease is a written document by which the rights of use and occupancy of land and/or structures are transferred by the owner to another person or entity for a specified period of time in return for a specified rental. The parties to a lease are the lessor (landlord) and the lessee (tenant).

The appraiser must analyze leases of the subject property (or have it done by an expert) to help determine the level of income as well as the risk involved in the lessor's position. In addition, leases of competitive properties must be analyzed to determine the true market level of rents.

There are several categories of leases that are differentiated by clauses which set out the rights and responsibilities of the lessor and lessee. Perhaps the most important clause is the one which specifies how rents are determined, and leases are often categorized based on that clause. The most common rent arrangements are: (1) flat rental, (2) periodic revaluation, (3) indexed, (4) graduated rental, and (5) percentage.

Flat Rental

A flat rental lease agreement calls for a given (unchanging) level of rent throughout the lease period. Flat rentals were once common, but because lessors generally want protection against inflation, flat rentals are used less often today. When they are used they tend to be relatively short-term.

Periodic Revaluation

Rentals under some leases are tied to the value of the property, with rent specified to be a certain percentage of value. The lease will state how often the property is to be revalued and how the new rent level is to be determined.

Indexed

An indexed lease is one in which the rent is tied to a specific index, such as the consumer price index. The lease may call for rent to change by the same percentage as the change in the index, or by some portion of that percentage. Because indexing provides inflation protection for the lessor, it is often part of long-term leases.

Graduated Rental

A graduated-rental or "step-up" lease specifies that rent will increase periodically according to an agreed upon formula. The size of the increases can be stated as dollar amounts or on a percentage basis, with the dollar amount or percentage remaining the same or changing over time. The object is to tie rents to value or to the inflation rate, but unlike periodic revaluation and indexed leases, there is not a direct relationship. Before inflation became an issue, step-down leases, where rent decreases over time to correspond to decreasing value, were also used. A famous step-down example is the master lease for the Empire State Building, which was written in the early 1960s.

Percentage Leases

Under a percentage lease, some (or all) of the rent is tied to the productivity of the leased space. Percentage leases are used most often for retail space, with rent calculated as a percentage of sales. Many percentage leases are hybrids that require a base rent, which may itself be indexed, plus a percentage of sales. Often percentage rent is paid only on sales over and above some minimum, which is why this variety is also called an overage lease.

Other Important Lease Clauses

While the rental clause is of primary importance when estimating future income, other potentially important clauses are as follows.

Division of Expenses

A critical clause is one that specifies how operating expenses are to be divided between the lessor and the lessee. Many leases, especially those involving a small number of long-term tenants (like many industrial properties), require the tenants to pay a large portion of operating expenses. These kinds of leases are sometimes called *net leases*. The estimates of both potential gross income and operating expenses will be affected. For example, if property A is leased at $14 per square foot, but the tenant is responsible for paying all of the $7 per square foot operating expenses, the *NOI* will be the same as it is for property B, that is leased at $21 per square foot, but the landlord pays all expenses.

Escape Clause

An escape clause allows cancellation of a lease, typically for such things as a condemnation of the property or a casualty loss. Alternatively, in the event of a casualty, the lease may specify a reduction in rent during the period of time the premises are put back in operational condition.

Renewal and Purchase Options

A lease may give the lessee a renewal option after the initial term. There may be one or several renewal options, which generally specify how rents will change. It is thought that a renewal option favors the lessee, because it obligates the lessor but not the lessee. However, because the renewal option is valuable, it is likely that the contract rent paid by the lessee will be higher than in cases where the lessee is not given an option.

A purchase option gives the lessee an option to purchase the property at a specified time, either when the lease expires or at some point while the lease is still in effect. Purchase options, like lease options, are generally considered favorable to the lessee, and this fact also may be reflected in a higher contract rent than the same lease without the purchase option.

Tenant Improvements

Leases on commercial properties should specify who is responsible for property improvements. For example, when a tenant moves in, the landlord will often provide funds to "personalize" or "build out" the tenant's space. The amount of that expenditure may have an impact on the contract rent.

An Example of a Multiyear Income Forecast

You are estimating the income that will be produced by a 15-year-old, 318,500 net rentable square-foot office building. There are 305,000 square feet currently rented, which gives a vacancy rate of 4.2 percent. Table 13–3 shows the lease terms, lease expiration dates, and the current contract rent paid by the property's 15 tenants.[7] All current leases call for flat rentals.

The market rent for competitive space is estimated to be $11.75 for the coming year (beginning of Year 1). All new leases will include rents that graduate at a 3 percent annual rate, which is typical in the market. Twenty-five parking stalls each rent for $22 per month. They have been 100 percent rented for several years. The operating expense ratio has been between 35–40 percent for the past four years, with a vacancy allowance between 2–7 percent.

---

[7]A good example of the use of lease expiration information is found in Peter F. Korpacz and Mark I. Roth, "Changing Emphasis on Appraisal Techniques: The Transition to Discounted Cash Flow," *The Appraisal Journal,* January 1983. A detailed analysis of lease expiration as the basis for forecasting demand is found in Terry V. Grissom and James C. Kuhle, "The Space Time Segmentation Technique (ST^2): A New Approach to Market Analysis," *Real Estate Issues,* Fall/Winter 1983.

TABLE 13-3 Lease Data by Year

(1) Beginning of Year	(2) No. of Expiring Leases	(3) Area (sq. ft.)	(4) % of Rented Space (Col. 3 ÷ 305,000)	(5) Current Rent	(6) Weighted Rent (Col. 4 × Col. 5/100) (rounded)
1	0	0			
2	3	64,300	21.1	$ 8.65	1.83
3	3	49,756	16.3	9.05	1.48
4	1	29,080	9.5	10.15	.96
5	4	88,440	29.0	10.20	2.96
6	2	41,665	13.7	10.25	1.40
7–10	0	0		0	
11	1	12,140	4.0	10.75	.43
12–20	0	0		0	
21	1	19,619	6.4	11.15	.71
Totals	15	305,000	100.0		$9.77

Forecasting the Future Income from the Property

Because our crystal balls tend to be cloudy, no one forecasts consistently well. However, it is important to realize that market value, and thus the appraised value, is based on the *expectations* of the market and not on what actually occurs. Therefore, if the appraiser can incorporate into his or her forecasts the expectations of market participants, the value estimate will be reasonable regardless of what actually occurs in the future. There are four basic forecasting strategies: (1) assume that past trends will continue and extrapolate those trends into the future, (2) survey those active in the market, such as investors, brokers, lenders, and other appraisers to determine their expectations, (3) use fundamental market analysis to forecast future changes in supply and demand, and thus income levels, and (4) assume no change; that is, what is happening now will continue.

We can quickly eliminate the no-change approach. This is not because an assumption of no change is always wrong, but rather because it lacks economic content. It makes no sense to do a discounted cash flow analysis if the reason for doing it—to explicitly consider the future—is gutted by a failure to make an effort to forecast change. Moreover, if no change is the assumption, whether justified or not, we shall find in succeeding chapters that there are much easier ways to estimate market value than the use of discounted cash flows.

Once the assumption of no change is eliminated, the appraiser's forecast of cash flows will result from some combination of the other three possibilities: the extrapolation of past trends, attempts to survey the expectations of

TABLE 13-4 Expectations of Recent Buyers of Competitive Properties

Buyer	% Change in Sq. Ft. Rent			% Change in OE*			Vacancy Rate		
	Yr. 1–5	6–10	11+	Yr. 1–5	6–10	11+	1–5	6–10	11+
1	4.0	3.0	1.5	5.5	5.0	3.0	5.0	4.0	4.5
2	3.0	2.5	2.0	6.0	5.5	2.5	4.0	3.5	4.0
3	4.0	3.5	2.0	4.5	4.0	1.5	4.5	4.5	4.0
4	6.0	4.0	1.5	5.0	3.5	1.0	6.0	5.5	5.0
5	4.5	2.5	1.0	5.0	3.5	2.0	6.0	5.0	5.0
Average	4.3	3.1	1.6	5.2	4.3	2.0	5.1	4.5	4.5

Expectations of a Sample of Brokers (B), Appraisers (A), and Lenders (L)

Expert	% Change in Sq. Ft. Rent			% Change in OE			Vacancy Rate		
	Yr. 1–5	6–10	11+	Yr. 1–5	6–10	11+	1–5	6–10	11+
1 (B)	5.0	4.5	2.5	4.5	4.5	3.0	5.0	4.5	5.0
2 (B)	5.5	4.0	2.0	5.5	4.0	3.0	5.0	5.0	5.0
3 (A)	4.5	3.5	2.0	6.0	4.5	2.5	5.5	5.0	5.0
4 (A)	4.0	3.0	1.5	6.5	4.0	3.0	4.5	4.5	4.5
5 (L)	5.0	2.5	1.0	6.0	5.5	4.0	4.0	4.0	4.0
6 (L)	4.5	2.0	-0-	5.5	3.5	3.5	3.5	3.5	4.5
7 (A)	4.5	5.0	4.0	6.0	4.0	4.0	5.5	5.0	5.0
Average	4.7	3.5	1.9	5.7	4.3	3.3	4.7	4.5	4.7

*Except for management fees, leasing fees, property taxes and insurance, and maintenance and repair.

those who make the market, and fundamental market analysis.[8] The appraiser will also be helped by the current rent roll of the property.

Table 13–4 shows the results of a survey of the market expectations of recent purchasers of similar properties, as well as local brokers, appraisers, and lenders. The results are divided into three time periods: Years 1–5, Years 6–10, and Year 11 and beyond. The choice of time periods is case-dependent. In this situation, a majority of those surveyed forecasted a pattern of increasing rents and operating expenses for five years, followed by a lesser increase through the projected 10-year holding period, and a further leveling in the years beyond the holding period.

Table 13–5 summarizes the trends in the operating history of the subject property over the past five years.

---

[8] A detailed discussion of forecasting techniques is beyond the scope of this text. Two good references are John M. Clapp, *Handbook for Real Estate Market Analysis* (Englewood Cliffs: Prentice-Hall), 1987; John M. Clapp and Stephen D. Messner, ed., *Real Estate Market Analysis: Methods and Applications* (New York: Praeger), 1988.

TABLE 13–5 Subject Property Trends during Past Five Years

Years Ago	% Change in Sq. Ft. Rent	% Change in OE	Vacancy Rate
5	0.4	4.6	3.9
4	3.1	4.8	2.9
3	4.2	3.9	4.5
2	4.7	5.1	4.2
1 (Current year)	5.0	5.2	4.2
Average	3.5	4.7	3.9

The Rent Forecast

Table 13–6 shows the forecast of rents over the assumed 10-year holding period. Rents are estimated at $11.75 per square foot the first year, and it is expected they will increase by 4.5 percent per year for Years 2–5, then by 3 percent per year in Years 6–10. As the present leases expire, the market rent at that time will be used to estimate potential gross income.

In order to complete the 10-year income forecast, the appraiser has also made the following assumptions based on his or her market analysis:

- Parking income will increase by 10 percent per year, beginning in Year 2.
- The vacancy allowance will be 5 percent of effective gross income.
- Property taxes and insurance will increase by ½ percent per year through Year 3. In year 4, an expected reassessment will produce a 30 percent increase in this entry, followed by the normal increase of ½ percent per year through Year 10.
- The management fee will remain at 4 percent of effective gross income.
- Leasing fees will be 15 percent of first-year rents.
- Maintenance and repair will be 6 percent of effective gross income through Year 5, then will be 7 percent.
- Other operating expenses will increase by 5.5 percent in Years 1–5, and 4.5 percent in Years 6–10.
- Personal property will be replaced at the end of Year 6 at an estimated cost of $450,000.

The 10-Year Forecast

Based on these assumptions and the information given earlier, the 10-year forecast of *NOI* is shown in Table 13–7.

TABLE 13–6 Forecasted Market Rent Schedule
Years 1–5 Reflect 4.5% annual increase (from survey)
Years 6–10 Reflect 3% annual increase (from survey)

	1	2	3	4	5 (Base Year)	6	7	8	9	10
	11.75	12.28	12.83	13.41	14.01	14.43	14.86	15.31	15.77	16.24
3		12.65*	—	—	—					
4		13.03	13.21	—	—					
5		13.42	13.61	13.81	—					
6		13.82	14.02	14.23	14.43	—				
7		14.23	14.44	14.65	14.86	14.86	No Lease Expirations, Years 7–10			
8		14.66	14.87	15.09	15.31	15.31				
9		15.10	15.32	15.55	15.77	15.77				
10		15.55	15.78	16.01	16.24	16.24				

*All succeeding years reflect the 3 percent lease escalation clause.

Inflation Expectations and Income Forecasts

The high rates of inflation during the late 1970s and early 1980s focused attention on the important question of whether it is nominal growth, real growth, or both, that should be reflected in forecasts of *NOI* and the future selling price. Nominal growth is the absolute increase in the number of dollars to be received each year, regardless of their purchasing power. That is, if income grows at 5 percent, and the inflation rate is 5 percent, the investor is experiencing a 5 percent nominal growth rate, even though the investor is no better off in terms of what can be purchased. Conversely, real growth is measured in terms of what can be purchased. It is the portion of nominal growth that exceeds what is eaten up by inflation. Thus, real growth is a number which tells the investor how much better off he or she will be in terms of purchasing power. With a 5 percent inflation rate, income growing at a nominal rate of 5 percent is producing a zero real rate of growth.

The answer to the question of whether forecasts of income and future selling price should be in terms of nominal or real dollars is that it depends on whether the appraiser uses a discount rate that is nominal or real. A nominal discount rate is one which reflects inflation expectations. A real discount rate does not reflect inflation expectations. The rule is that when a nominal discount rate is used, nominal income flows must also be used. When a real discount rate is used, real income flows must be used. Why this is so is best understood by example.

Suppose the expected inflation rate is zero, and the expected rate of return, with zero inflation, is 10 percent. This is the real rate of return. We will call this rate y_r. Under these conditions, the present value of an

TABLE 13-7 Net Operating Income

Year	1	2	3	4	5	6	7	8	9	10
Effective gross income	$2,980,350*	$3,183,102	$3,394,700	$3,532,320	$3,926,320	$4,312,334	$4,312,334	$4,432,280	$4,555,907	$4,683,332
Operating expenses										
Property taxes & insurance	350,000	351,750	353,509	459,562	461,859	464,168	466,489	468,822	471,166	473,522
Management 4% of EGI	119,214	127,324	135,788	141,313	157,053	167,838	172,493	177,291	182,236	187,333
Leasing fees 15% of 1st yr. rent	-0-	112,519**	90,967	55,569	176,564	85,675	-0-	-0-	-0-	-0-
General payroll	77,500	81,763	86,259	91,004	96,009	100,329	104,844	109,562	114,492	119,644
Electricity	190,000	200,450	211,475	223,106	235,377	245,969	257,037	268,604	280,691	293,322
Water, sewer	14,000	14,770	15,582	16,439	17,344	18,124	18,940	19,792	20,683	21,613
Heat, air conditioning	105,000	110,775	116,868	123,295	130,077	135,930	142,047	148,439	155,119	162,099
Administrative	76,000	80,180	84,590	89,242	94,151	98,387	102,815	107,442	112,277	117,329
Cleaning	11,000	11,605	12,243	12,917	13,627	13,627	14,881	15,551	16,251	16,982
Maintenance & repair	178,821	190,986	203,682	211,969	235,609	293,717	301,863	310,260	318,913	327,833
Total operating expense	1,121,535	1,282,122	1,310,963	1,424,416	1,617,670	1,624,377	1,581,409	1,625,763	1,671,828	1,719,677
Net operating income	$1,858,815	$1,900,980	$2,083,737	$2,108,403	$2,308,650	$2,687,957	$2,730,925	$2,806,517	$2,884,079	$2,963,655

*Rounded for simplicity.

**64,300 square feet will become available in Year 2. Of this, 5 percent will remain vacant, leaving 64,300 (.95) ($12.28) = $750,124 in first-year rent. At a 15 percent leasing fee, this equals .15 × $750,124 = $112,519. This approach also applies to the leasing fees for Years 2–6.

investment producing $1,100 in one year is

$$V = \frac{\$1,100}{(1 + .1)} = 1,000.$$

Now change the expected inflation rate, call it b, from 0 to 5 percent. In nominal terms, the expected rate of return, y_0, becomes

$$y_0 = (1 + y_r)(1 + b) - 1 = (1 + .10)(1 + .05) - 1 = .1550.$$

Suppose now that the investment is a perfect inflation hedge, in the sense that its income changes exactly with the inflation rate. Therefore, instead of producing $1,100 in one year, the investment is now expected to produce $1,100 (1.05) = $1,155. The present value of the investment is still

$$V = \frac{\$1,155}{1 + .155} = \$1,000.$$

With an expected inflation rate of, say, .03, the nominal discount rate is $(1 + .10)(1.03) - 1 = .133$, the expected cash flow is $1,100 (1.03) = $1,133, and the present value is still

$$\frac{\$1,133}{1 + .133} = \$1,000.$$

Does it make sense that present values don't change with the expected rate of inflation? Yes, because regardless of the rate of expected inflation, with a perfect inflation hedge the investor is no better or worse off in terms of purchasing power.

It follows that if you do not use nominal income with nominal discount rates, you get wrong answers. Using the preceding example, if, with an expected inflation rate of 5 percent, the expected increase in income of 5 percent per year was ignored because it does not represent a real increase in the investor's wealth, the estimated present value would have been

$$\frac{\$1,000}{1 + .155} = \$866.$$

Someone paying $866 would have ended up with a nominal return of

$$\frac{\$1,100 - \$866}{\$866} = 27\%.$$

Subtracting the 5 percent loss of purchasing power due to inflation, this represents a real return of 22 percent, which is more than twice the real rate of 10 percent that investors demand.

Consider now an investment that is not expected to keep up with inflation; it will produce only $1,000 in income, regardless of the inflation rate. With an expected inflation rate of 5 percent, the value of this investment is

$$V = \frac{\$1,000}{1 + .155} = \$866.$$

The resulting nominal return,

$$\frac{\$1,000 - \$866}{\$866} = 15.5\%,$$

is what investors expect.

Conversely, the value of those investments expected to outperform inflation is driven upward. Expected income of $1,200 would have a value of

$$\frac{\$1,200}{1.155} = \$1,039.$$

Again, this promises only the expected .155 return

$$\left(\frac{\$1,200 - \$1,039}{\$1,039}\right)$$

to the investor.

You also get the right answer using *real* income and *real* discount rates. If the nominal market discount rate is 15.5 percent, and the expected inflation rate, b, is 5 percent, you can work backward to find the underlying real rate of return. The formula is

$$Y_r = \frac{1 + Y_o}{1 + b} - 1 = \frac{1.155}{1.05} - 1 = .10.$$

Because we are now working with real returns, we must also work with real cash flows. Therefore, the expected cash flow is estimated to be the original $1,100, and present value is

$$\frac{\$1,100}{1 + .1} = \$1,000.$$

To repeat the inflation rule: Be consistent. When using a nominal discount rate, use nominal income flows. When using a real discount rate, use real income flows. In practice, expected rates of return (discount rates) are almost always quoted in nominal terms, and therefore the appraiser should estimate income and value in nominal terms. Put differently, when using nominal discount rates, don't worry about whether expected changes in income and value are real or nominal—their absolute amounts are all that matter.

Adjusting Rents for Market Disequilibrium

There is one last situation to consider when estimating future rents. When a property is earning market rents, but those rents are above or below historical levels as a result of market disequilibrium—an under- or oversupply of space—it is a mistake to assume that the imbalance will persist indefinitely. In the case of historically high rents, other developers will notice the excess returns being earned by current investors, add to the supply, and drive rents to their proper level. In terms of forecasting future cash flows, this means that the future flows must reflect whatever move toward equilibrium rents you feel is likely. In some cases, for example when new units are being developed, rent may move quickly (within 1–3 years) to its equilibrium level. In other cases, particularly in rapidly growing areas, high rents may persist longer.

Estimating Sales Proceeds at the End of the Holding Period

When using a discounted cash flow model, the appraiser needs an estimate of the proceeds of sale after the assumed holding period in addition to the estimates of annual *NOI*. Because the process of estimating sale proceeds relies on skills associated with the use of ratio and discounted cash flow models, it will be discussed after those models are presented in subsequent chapters.

Summary

The income approach is based on the premise that the value of a property is related to the net operating income it is anticipated to produce. Net operating income is the measure of a property's productivity, and is the pie that is divided among the equity investor, the lender, and the IRS. *NOI* is generally calculated annually, like this:

$$\begin{array}{l} \text{Potential gross income} \\ - \text{ Vacancy allowance} \\ + \text{ Other income} \\ \hline = \text{Effective gross income} \\ - \text{ Operating expenses} \\ \hline \text{Net operating income} \end{array}$$

Sources of market data for the *NOI* statement entries are the history of the subject property itself, the experience of competitive properties, the opinions of investors and market experts, and published surveys. When using an owner-supplied income statement, the appraiser may have to distinguish between accounting income and net operating income. Accounting income is taxable income. It includes nonoperating expenses like interest and depreciation. If these are mixed in with the operating expenses, they must be removed to find *NOI*. The appraiser's second concern with the use of owner-supplied statements is the possible distortion of certain entries. Things to watch for are hidden rent concessions, short-term tenants (perhaps paying little or no rent), deferred maintenance, capital improvements being expensed, and an underestimation of management fees. Audited statements are preferred. Market analysis, a careful reading of leases, and tenant interviews are ways of determining the credibility of reported rents, vacancies, and expenses.

Depending on the appraisal assignment, and in turn the specific valuation model(s) to be used, either a single or multiyear forecast of *NOI* is required. Ratio models use a single-year estimate of income, while discounted cash flow models use a multiyear estimate.

The specifics of the assignment will help determine whether it is market income, actual income, or a combination of both, that must be estimated. Regardless of the assignment, a careful reading and analysis of lease clauses is necessary to determine the proper level of contract and market rents.

Conceptually, forecasts of income and estimates of discount rates may be made in either real or nominal terms. In practice, the use of nominal rates and forecasts dominates. Nominal forecasts include the effects of expected inflation, real forecasts do not. If a nominal discount rate is used, income must be forecasted in nominal terms. If a real discount rate is used, income must be forecasted in real terms.

Questions and Problems

1. The property being appraised is an apartment with 22 2-bedroom units and 15, 3-bedroom units. Rent is $275 per month for the 2-bedroom and $325 per month for the 3-bedroom units. The vacancy allowance is 4 percent for the 3-bedroom units and 6 percent for the 2-bedroom. Fixed operating expenses are $15,500. Variable operating expenses are 35 percent of effective gross income. Income from laundry machines is $60 per month. Parking stalls rent for $7.50 per month, and on average, 1.3 stalls are rented for each apartment unit occupied. The mortgage payment is $35,000 per year, and the allowable depreciation expense is $33,600. Calculate first year NOI.

2. Why is *NOI* an important number?

3. *a.* What is the role of the *actual* rents and vacancies of the subject property when estimating *market* rent and vacancies?
   b. You are appraising a property, and arrive at an operating expense ratio (*OER*) that differs markedly from the *OER*s of what appear to be competitive properties. What do you do?

4. What units of comparison are commonly used for estimating the rent of the following kinds of properties?
   a. Theaters
   b. Nursing homes
   c. Warehouses
   d. Office buildings
   e. Shopping centers
   f. Apartments

5. What is a variable operating expense? A fixed expense?

6. One approach sometimes used to estimate future income is to rely on the opinion of those knowledgeable in the market, such as appraisers, brokers, and lenders. Is this legitimate? Why or why not?

7. What is the major difference between forecasting effective gross income for an apartment versus an office building?

8. If investors value real estate on the basis of expected future income, why does current income matter?

9. What are four basic approaches to estimating future income?

10. When forecasting income, it is an appraiser's policy not to include increases due simply to inflation. Comment.

11. A 7-tenant property has 54,000 square feet of rentable area, of which 52,200 square feet is currently rented according to this rent and lease expiration schedule:

Beginning of Year	No. of Expiring Leases	Area (sq. ft.)	First-Year Rent
1	0	0	—
2	2	12,500	9.50
3	4	31,000	9.80
4	0	0	—
5	1	8,700	10.00

Normal vacancy is 5 percent, and first year market rent is $10.20, which is expected to increase by 4 percent per year. The rent on existing leases graduates at a rate of 2 percent per year. Forecast effective gross income over the next five years.

APPENDIX
ESTIMATING POTENTIAL GROSS INCOME USING REGRESSION ANALYSIS*

When a sufficient number of observations are available, the appraiser may be able to use regression analysis to make rent estimates.

Assume that you are appraising the ABC office property used as an example in the chapter, but that instead of only seven observations of competitive office rents, you are in a larger market and are able to gather the sample shown in Table 13–8 (Comparables #1–7 are the same as those in Table 13–1). In the regression, the qualitative location variable is entered in dummy form (0,1). Recall that when dummy variables are used, one of the possibilities, in this case a similar location, is left out of the equation because it serves as the standard by which the other possibilities (superior and inferior) are valued.

You have chosen to use five independent variables to estimate rent, as shown in Equation (1).

$$Y = a + b_1 x_1 + b_2 x_2 + b_3 x_3 + b_4 x_4 + b_5 x_5 \quad (1)$$

where

Y = Rent per square foot
x_1 = Net leasable square feet (in thousands)

---
*Regression analysis is the topic of Chapter 8.

TABLE 13–8 Data on Comparable Properties

				Independent Variables		
Property	Rent (sq. ft.)	Net Leasable Area (sq. ft.)	Age	Location Superior, (0,1)	Inferior	Vacancy Rate
Subject	$10.00	16,000	4	0	0	.04
Comparable Property #1	7.80	17,000	5	0	1	.06
#2	8.50	22,500	6	0	0	.05
#3	8.90	20,500	5	0	0	.04
#4	9.25	30,000	4	1	0	.06
#5	7.30	37,000	8	0	0	.05
#6	6.50	27,000	6	0	1	.03
#7	7.85	30,500	5	0	0	.04
#8	10.35	17,500	3	0	0	.06
#9	7.50	33,000	9	1	0	.04
#10	6.40	41,000	7	0	0	.05
#11	6.00	39,500	10	0	1	.06
#12	11.25	15,500	5	0	0	.03
#13	6.75	20,000	12	0	0	.06
#14	9.75	22,500	6	1	0	.03
#15	8.00	27,000	13	1	0	.04
#16	10.75	18,000	2	0	1	.05
#17	9.30	17,500	4	0	0	.04
#18	8.15	22,000	9	0	0	.08

x_2 = Age
x_3 = Superior location
x_4 = Inferior location
x_5 = Vacancy rate

The resulting regression (including the data from the subject property) with standard errors in parentheses, is:

$$Y = 12.8 - .101X_1 - .26921X_2$$
$$\quad\quad (.02621) \quad (.07462)$$
$$+ .9464X_3 - .7895X_4 - 1.52X_5$$
$$(.5111) \quad\; (.4781) \quad\; (15.41)$$

Using the regression to estimate the subject property's rent, we have:

$$Y = 12.8 - .101(16) - .26921(4)$$
$$+ .9464(0) - .7895(0) - 1.52(.04)$$
$$= \$10.05.$$

This is very close to the current rent of $10, and is consistent with the relationship between size and rent plotted in Figure 13–1 that was based on the smaller sample of seven comparables.

How far you can go with regression analysis to estimate rent depends on the quantity and quality of your data. Brennan, Cannaday, and Colwell[9] estimated office rents in downtown Chicago using not only traditional variables like the location of the property, but also variables specific to individual office units within buildings, such as escalation clauses in their leases, and the position of the office space within the building. Their best equation produced an r^2 of .928. Variables relating to building size, the vertical location of the office space, and certain lease clauses were significant, as was accessibility (distance) to the most valuable downtown location.

---

[9]Brennan, Thomas P., Roger E. Cannaday, and Peter F. Colwell, "Office Rent in the Chicago CBD," *AREUEA Journal*, Fall 1984.

CHAPTER 14

Estimating Value Using Ratio Models: Gross Income Multipliers and Overall Capitalization Rates

Introduction

The income approach can be divided into two kinds of models: (1) ratio models, which are based heavily on data extracted from sales of comparable properties, and (2) discounted cash flow models, which are based on explicit forecasts of the expected cash flows from a property. This chapter is devoted to two commonly used ratio models, the gross income multiplier *(GIM)* and the directly extracted overall capitalization rate *(OAR)*.

To use these models, sales of comparable properties are identified, *GIM*s or *OAR*s are extracted from the comparables, and they are then used to estimate the value of the subject property. This is very similar to the process used in the direct sales comparison approach, and Paul Wendt summarized it nicely by observing that gross income multipliers are the meeting place of the market comparison and income approaches.[1] Though *GIM*s are part of the income approach on the *Uniform Residential Appraisal Report* (URAR), some appraisers include them (and some the overall capitalization rate) as part of the direct sales comparison approach. The decision to include these techniques as part of the income approach is based on the fact that the units of comparison for income properties are income based, and for learning purposes it was better to delay coverage of the techniques until after the *NOI* statement had been covered.

---

[1] Paul Wendt, *Real Estate Appraisal: Review and Outlook* (Athens GA: University of Georgia Press, 1974).

The Gross Income Multiplier (GIM)

The *GIM* measures the relationship between a property's gross income and its selling price. For example, a property forecasted to produce $50,000 of gross income, and which sells for $400,000, is said to have sold at a *GIM* of

$$\frac{\$400,000}{\$50,000} = 8.00.$$

That is, the property sold for eight times gross income.

Sometimes the term *gross rent multiplier* is used. Technically, the *GIM* refers to all income, while the *GRM* refers to rent only. In practice, however, some appraisers use the term *GRM* when referring to monthly rent, and the *GIM* when referring to annual rent. Other appraisers use the terms *GRM* and *GIM* interchangeably. To avoid confusion, it is important that the *GIM* be precisely defined in reports.

The Mechanics of Using the GIM

A subject property is valued by multiplying its expected gross income by the *GIM* extracted from comparable sales. Suppose you are valuing a property expected to produce $60,000 of gross income, and comparable sales have produced the data shown in Table 14–1.

One way to estimate the value of the subject property would be to multiply its gross income of $60,000 by the average *GIM* of 5.76, giving a value estimate of 5.76 × $60,000 = $345,600. Or, the *GIM*s may be weighted on the basis of how comparable the properties are to the subject. For example, the *GIM* from Comparable #5 is much lower than the others. If you suspect the data from the sale may be inaccurate or that the sale itself is not truly comparable for example, because the property was on the market an extremely short time you may choose to give it less weight or even to ignore it (give it a weight of zero). If it is ignored, the four remaining comparables

TABLE 14–1   Data Extracted from Comparable Sales

Sale	Expected Gross Income	Selling Price	GIM
1	$65,500	$395,000	6.03
2	55,000	340,000	6.18
3	72,000	425,000	5.90
4	44,500	256,000	5.75
5	90,000	445,000	4.94
			Average 5.76

produce an average *GIM* of 5.97, and the value estimate would be 5.97 × $60,000 = $358,200. The results of the other appraisal approaches can be helpful in deciding what weight should be given to an "outlier." If other approaches produce value estimates consistent with the *GIM*, including the outlier, that is evidence in favor of its inclusion.

The Logic of GIMs

The *GIM* is sometimes criticized as being too crude to produce credible value estimates. That criticism is unfair. Gross income is an acceptable unit of comparison if the comparables and the subject property are reasonably similar as far as their other value-affecting characteristics. Specifically, the comparables and the subject must have similar operating expense ratios, prospects for future income and value change, and risk. That is a big "if," and the appraiser will often decide that the differences among a group of properties are so large that the use of a *GIM* is not appropriate.

The lesson is that close comparability is a necessary condition for the use of *GIM*s. This was strikingly illustrated in a 1992 study with respect to differences in gross rent multipliers for single-family housing among metropolitan areas. Phillip Kolbe found that *GRM*s varied widely among cities, from a low of 91.87 times monthly rent in Miami, to 191.24 times monthly rent in San Francisco.[2]

When *GIM*s are used properly, there is evidence over an extended time period that they do a good job of predicting value. Shenkel[3] (1969) found that the *GIM* accounted for most of the variance in the selling prices of small- to medium-sized apartments in several regions of the country. Ratcliff[4] (1971) found that on a sample of small- and medium-sized properties, a majority of the differences between *GIM*-derived value estimates and subsequent selling prices fell in the 4–8 percent range. Kang and Reichert[5] (1988), in a more recent study of apartment sales in the Los Angeles area, showed that gross income was as closely associated with selling price as was net operating income, and Bernes and Mitchell (1990) found that *GIM*s did an exceptional job of predicting the selling prices of relatively large apartment complexes in Atlanta.[6]

---

[2]Phillip Kolbe, "Real Estate Markets Are Local," *The Real Estate Appraiser,* August 1992, 42–46.

[3]William M. Shenkel, "Cash Flow Analysis and Multiple Regression Techniques," *Journal of Property Management,* November–December 1969.

[4]Richard U. Ratcliff, "Don't Underrate the Gross Income Multiplier," *Appraisal Journal,* April 1971.

[5]Han-Bin-Kang and Alan K. Reichert, "Statistical Models for Appraising Income Properties: The Case of Apartment Buildings," *The Real Estate Appraiser and Analyst,* Summer 1988.

[6]Gary L. Bernes and Phillip S. Mitchell, "Validation of Basic Valuation Models: Multi-Family Housing Example," *Real Estate Issues,* Spring 1992.

TABLE 14–2 Use of the *GIM* by Property Size

	4–8 Units	9–24 Units	25–49 Units	50+ Units
Percent of Appraisals	$47\% \left(\dfrac{45}{96}\right)$	$44\% \left(\dfrac{59}{134}\right)$	$32\% \left(\dfrac{70}{218}\right)$	$24\% \left(\dfrac{46}{192}\right)$

Given the evidence that *GIM*s can produce reliable estimations of value, it is not surprising that appraisers make liberal use of them for appraising multifamily properties. In the most recent available study, the author[7] found that *GIM*s were used, often in conjunction with one or two other income approach models, in 34 percent of a sample of 640 appraisals.

Table 14–2 shows the results by property size. The figures support the conventional wisdom that the size of a property is a major determinant of whether a *GIM* is used. The negative relationship between the size of the property and the use of *GIM*s is sometimes explained on the basis that investors in smaller properties tend to buy and sell on the basis of *GIM*s. While that is certainly a contributing factor, there is another important explanation. Because smaller properties are more numerous, sell more frequently, and are more homogeneous than larger properties, there is more available data on truly comparable sales—the necessary condition to use *GIM*s—for smaller properties.

How Many Comparables Are Enough?

An important question is the number of comparables needed to produce a reliable *GIM*. This is the same as asking how many sales are needed in the direct sales comparison approach and again the answer is case-dependent. If markets were perfectly efficient, one comparable would be enough, assuming it was truly comparable in all respects. As efficiency declines a larger number of comparables are preferred. Recall that empirical evidence on the effect of the number of comparables on the ability to predict selling price has generally found merit in the "three-comparable" rule of thumb. However, those studies were based on house sales and the results may or may not hold for income-producing properties. What sample size comes down to is the appraiser's judgment as to the reliability of the sales information, the comparability of the sale(s) to the subject, and the relative efficiency of the market. As quality, comparability, and efficiency increase, sample size can decrease, and vice versa.

---

[7]Kenneth M. Lusht, "The Behavior of Appraisers in Valuing Income Property: A Status Report," *The Real Estate Appraiser and Analyst,* July–August 1979.

Property Size

One element of comparability which deserves special attention is property size. The issue is whether relatively larger properties have *GIM*s that are different than smaller properties. While there isn't sufficient empirical evidence to support a definitive answer, it is the opinion of many practicing appraisers that there tends to be a relationship between property size and the level of the *GIM*. Probably the best strategy is to avoid a potential problem by restricting comparables to those that are reasonably similar to the subject property with respect to size, unless you have gathered evidence as to the proper size/*GIM* relationship in your market.

Potential versus Effective Gross Income

There is not a rule concerning whether it is potential or effective gross income that should be used in a *GIM* analysis, though certain "form" appraisals, or clients, may require the use of one or the other. In any case, the important thing is to be consistent. A *GIM* based on potential gross income extracted from comparable sales cannot be applied to the effective gross income of the subject property, or vice versa.

GIMs and Inflation

The effect of inflation on *GIM*s is sometimes misunderstood. Look back at Table 14–1. There are no dates of sale indicated for the comparables. Would it have affected the *GIM* calculation had that information been included? Probably not. It is sometimes thought that gross income must be adjusted to account for any inflation between the date of the comparable sale and the date of the appraisal. But that would ignore the fundamental relationship between income and value; that is, if income has changed over time in response to inflation, it is likely that value has also changed and the result is a wash. For example, if one year ago a property producing \$100,000 of gross income sold for \$500,000, and since then both income and value have increased by 5 percent, the *GIM* remains at $5.00 \left(\dfrac{\$500,000}{\$100,000} = \dfrac{\$525,000}{\$105,000} = 5.00 \right)$.

Real Changes in the GIM

While inflation alone is unlikely to affect *GIM*s, other factors may. For example, *GIM*s could change in response to a change in general inflation *expectations* (historically, *GIM*s have tended to increase as inflation expectations increased), a change in income tax law, or to fundamental changes in supply and demand. If these kinds of changes have occurred, it is possible to adjust *GIM*s extracted from sales that occurred prior to the change(s). In practice, however, there is not much to be gained from such an exercise. First, where would the adjustments come from? The only source of what *GIM*s are now (and therefore what the adjustment to the "real" *GIM* should be) are *GIM*s extracted from more current comparables. But if you have those, why bother with the old ones? Second, once you begin tinkering with a *GIM,* you are admitting that the comparable from which it was extracted isn't really comparable any more. When that is the case, there are other valuation techniques at your disposal. In sum, if you suspect that the market *GIM* has changed and all you have is the old one, use it only as a rough guide to value.

Applying the GIM Consistently

There is another timing issue with respect to the use of *GIM*s. It is whether they should be based on the relationship of *current* (past year) gross income and selling price, or on expected *first-year* income and selling prices. Because investors determine value based on expectations, the use of expected first-year income is preferred. In practice, because it tends to be more difficult to estimate first-year income compared to current income, the latter is sometimes used. As in the case of potential or effective income, the rule is to be consistent. Make certain the same income base is used for all of the comparables and the subject. This may require an income adjustment. If one *GIM* is based on current income and all the others on first-year income, adjust the income of the outlier to a first-year basis.

The Effect of Financing on GIMs

Finally, there is the question of financing. Because nonmarket financing can affect transaction prices, it is necessary that such prices be adjusted to remove any distortion traceable to nonmarket financing *prior to* the calculation of the *GIM*. This can be difficult, given (1) the tendency toward complex financing arrangements for income properties, and (2) the fact we don't as yet have a generally applicable rule on how to adjust for nonmarket financing. Again, the best strategy is avoidance. Try not to use comparables which were financed with nonmarket terms unless you are confident of the proper adjustment in your market. Lacking that confidence, the *GIM* loses some of its credibility.

Moving from *GIM*s to Overall Capitalization Rates (R_0s): The Operating Expense Ratio

In order to use a *GIM* with confidence, it must be extracted from sales that are closely comparable to the subject property. One important element of comparability is the operating expense ratio *(OER)*. Recall that the *OER* is the ratio of operating expenses to gross income. For example, if a property is expected to produce $50,000 of gross income, and $22,000 of that will be spent on operating expenses, the OER is $22,000/$50,000 = .44. This means that out of every dollar of gross income generated, $.44 will be spent on operating expenses. The OER can be measured using either potential or effective gross income. If potential gross income is being used, the OER includes the vacancy rate. If effective gross income is being used, the vacancy rate is already reflected in the effective gross income, so it is not explicitly included in the OER.

Suppose now that the OER from a property that has sold is different than the OER for the subject property. In such a case, it is reasonable to assume that other things equal, the property with the higher OER will be worth less than the property with the lower OER because there will be fewer dollars left (a lower NOI) for the investor after paying operating expenses. This observation provides the link between GIMs and the second ratio model we are now ready to discuss, the directly extracted overall capitalization rate.

Referring to the example above, a .44 OER was calculated. After spending $.44 for operating expenses out of every dollar of effective gross income, $.56 of NOI would be left for the investor. Now suppose another property was for sale, and that it had exactly the same gross income of $50,000, but its expected OER was .55. This means that the investor would be left with only $.45 out of every dollar of gross income. Other things being equal, this property would be worth less.

To continue the example, suppose that the property with a .44 OER had sold for $300,000, or at a GIM = $300,000/$50,000 = 6.0. Could this GIM be applied to the subject property with an OER of .55 in order to estimate its value? No, because that would imply equal NOIs for both properties, which is not the case. This also helps to explain another characteristic of GIMs. Not only are they used relatively more frequently for smaller properties, but also for apartments rather than other property types. This is because apartment properties in a given market tend to be more consistent than other kinds of properties with respect to operating expense ratios.

Appraisers faced with differing expense ratios must use a ratio model that takes operating expenses explicitly into consideration. That model is one that uses the overall capitalization rate.

The Overall Capitalization Rate

The overall capitalization rate (the OAR, or simply R_0), is the ratio of net operating income to selling price:

$$R_0 = \frac{NOI}{\text{Selling price (or value)}} \quad (1)$$

TABLE 14–3 Rates and Ratios from Comparable Sales

	Gross Income	Selling Price	GIM	OER	NOI	OAR (R_0)
1	$65,500	$395,000	6.03	.35	$42,575	.108
2	55,000	340,000	6.18	.33	36,850	.108
3	72,000	425,000	5.90	.35	46,800	.110
4	44,500	256,000	5.75	.32	30,260	.118
5	90,000	444,000	4.94	.49	45,900	.103
						Average .109

Rearranging Equation (1) gives the value model

$$V = \frac{NOI}{R_0}.$$

This model uses *NOI* rather than gross income as the measure of productivity, and thus directly reflects the level of operating expenses. Table 14–3 shows the *GIM*s, *OER*s, *NOI*s, and R_0s for the five comparable sales used previously to value a property based on the *GIM* (see Table 14–1). Recall that the property's value was estimated to be $358,200, based on its gross income of $60,000 and the average *GIM* of 5.97 from Comparables #1–4.

To value the same example property using the R_0, we need an estimate of *NOI*. Assuming that the subject property's operating expense ratio is .37, the *NOI* is $60,000 − 0.37 ($60,000) = $37,800. Using the average R_0 of .109 from the five comparable sales, the estimated value is:

$$V = \frac{NOI}{R_0}$$

$$= \frac{\$37,800}{.109}$$

$$= \$346,789$$

Now look at the *OER* from Comparable #5. It is .49, which is much higher than the other four. This explains why the *GIM* is lower for Comparable #5, and is a sufficient reason to ignore that comparable as we did when using the *GIM*. In fact, one reason that the value estimated using the *GIM* ($358,200) is quite close to the estimate using the R_0 ($346,789) is that we did ignore Comparable #5 when calculating the *GIM*.

The fact that the link between *GIM*s and R_0s is the operating expense ratio can be shown in mathematical form as follows:

$$R_0 = \frac{1 - OER}{GIM}$$

Using Comparable #3 to illustrate,

$$R_0 = \frac{1 - .35}{5.9} = .11$$

In sum, when the *OER*s among comparable sales and the subject property differ significantly, the appraiser must move from using *GIM*s to using R_0s, because the R_0, unlike the *GIM*, explicitly reflects the impact of operating expenses on a property's value through the use of *NOI*.

R_0s and Price/Earnings Ratios

The reciprocal of the R_0 is the net operating income multiplier (*NIM*). The R_0 of .109 that was extracted from five comparable sales to value the example subject property is equivalent to a *NIM* of

$$\frac{1}{.109} = 9.17.$$

Using this multiplier, the example subject property with *NOI* of $37,800 would be valued as $37,800 × 9.17 = $346,626. The result is of course the same (allowing for rounding), and in general, it makes no difference whether *NOI* is divided by the capitalization rate or multiplied by the multiplier.[8]

It was once common practice for appraisers to use *NIM*s rather than R_0s. But now R_0s are used almost exclusively. This change began in earnest in the 1950s, likely because most real estate investors think in terms of rates (or return, etc.) rather than multiples. This is not the case in securities markets, however, where analysts talk in terms of price/earnings (*P/E*) multiples and not capitalization rates. Thus, General Motors is said to sell for, say, 8 times earnings, rather than at a capitalization rate of 1/8 = .125.

Why R_0s Differ among Properties

Suppose two properties sell, one at an overall capitalization rate of .10 and the other at an overall rate of .15. Thus, the first property is 50 percent more expensive per dollar of expected first-year income than a property that sells at a capitalization rate of .15. This difference is logically traceable to those

---

[8] The *GIM* can also be converted to a capitalization rate by taking its reciprocal. For example, a *GIM* of 6.03 is equivalent to a capitalization rate of $\frac{1}{6.03}$ = .166. For a property producing $65,500 of gross income, like Comparable #1 in Table 14–3, value is

$$V = \frac{\$65,500}{.166} = \$395,000 \text{ (rounded)}.$$

things which affect value; first-year income, income growth, and risk associated with the income stream. This being the case, the R_0 must implicitly reflect investor expectations: It will be positively associated with expected growth rates and negatively associated with the expected return. Put differently, given equal risk, an investor will be willing to pay more per dollar of first-year income for one property than for another only if there is an expectation that the former property's future prospects are relatively better. For the properties that sold at cap rates of .10 and .15, the first must have significantly better future prospects than the second.

The relationship between cap rates and future income was investigated by Sirmans, Sirmans, and Beasley,[9] who analyzed variations in the net operating incomes and selling prices of apartment complexes in the Chicago area. Their results showed that while variations in current income explained a large percentage of variations in selling price, the overall capitalization rate was also sensitive to location and size. Presumably, these variables carry with them implications for future income productivity.

Thus, the necessary condition for the use of market-extracted R_0s is that there is a high degree of comparability between the properties from which the R_0 was extracted and the subject property, as far as future income expectations and risk. Like *GIM*s, the price of any nonmarket financing of comparables must be adjusted out of the transaction prices of the comparables before calculating the R_0.

Directly Extracted R_0s Are Widely Used

For multifamily rental properties, appraisers use directly extracted R_0s only slightly less than they use *GIM*s (R_0s were used in about 29 percent of my 1979 sample of 640 appraisals, versus 34 percent for *GIM*s), and like *GIM*s their use is negatively associated with property size.

Also, while *GIM*s tend to be used most frequently for multifamily properties, R_0s tend to be used in the valuation of all types of properties. As far as the future use of *GIM*s and directly extracted R_0s, advances in computer technology and data storage at reasonable cost argues for more access to data and a greater chance of finding comparables. Other things being equal, this should increase the use of R_0s (and *GIM*s). On the other hand, transactions are becoming more complex, which makes it more difficult to unbundle them (for example, to remove financing effects) or to rebundle them (as in the case of limited partnerships), to make any necessary adjustments. The future of *GIM*s and R_0s would therefore appear to rest on a tug-of-war be-

---

[9]C. F. Sirmans, G. Stacy Sirmans, and Ben T. Beasley, "Income Property Valuation and the Use of Market Extracted Overall Capitalization Rates," *The Real Estate Appraiser and Analyst,* Summer 1986, pp. 64–68.

A Special Problem with Property Taxes

Estimating the level of property taxes is a problem when appraising a not-yet-developed property or when doing tax assessment or appeal work, because property taxes are a function of the value that is being estimated. The solution to this chicken-and-egg problem is to ignore property taxes in the valuation.

For example, assume that the *NOI* of Comparable #1 in Table 14–3 reflects $7,500 in property tax. Ignoring that tax, *NOI* would be $42,575 + $7,500 = $50,075, and the R_0 would be

$$\frac{\$50,075}{\$395,000} = .127.$$

Property taxes could be similarly deleted for all the comparables, resulting in an average R_0 without property taxes. Assuming the average R_0 without taxes is .127, and that without property taxes, the subject property has *NOI* of $44,000 (as compared to $37,800), its value would be:

$$V = \frac{NOI_{\text{without Tax}}}{R_{\text{without Tax}}}$$

$$= \frac{\$44,000}{.127}$$

$$= \$346,457$$

This is the same valuation (allowing for rounding) as before.

Reserve for Replacements

While an entry for reserves is appropriate when capitalizing a single year's *NOI* (and is required by some clients, notably government agencies), such an entry is not always made. The reasons are unclear, though some appraisers feel that because most investors—particularly in the market for relatively small properties—do not think in terms of replacement costs, for the appraiser to do so would not be consistent with market behavior. Therefore, when extracting R_0s from comparable sales, check whether a reserve for replacements account was part of the operating statement of the comparable. You cannot apply an R_0 from a comparable(s) that does not reflect reserves, to an *NOI* that does, or vice versa.

Summary

One of the fundamental principles of appraisal practice is to listen to what the market is saying. The best market evidence comes from the sale of comparable properties, and within the income approach there are techniques that make heavy use of data from comparable sales. They are the *GIM* and the directly extracted *OAR*, or its reciprocal the net income multiplier.

The *GIM* is the ratio of sales price to gross income, where either potential or effective gross income can be used. Gross income, of course, is only the tip of the cash-flow iceberg. Those value affecting factors that are not explicitly reflected in the *GIM*—operating expenses, tax impacts, and future changes in income and value—are implied. In practice, this means that as far as the implied factors are concerned, there must be a high degree of comparability between the sales from which the *GIM* was extracted and the subject. Further, there is always the assumption of typical financing, which means sales that are not typically financed either cannot be used as comparables, or the effect of the nonmarket terms must first be removed from their transaction prices.

When there is a difference in the operating expense ratios between otherwise comparable properties, the appraiser should use a market-extracted measure which, unlike *GIM*s, explicitly picks up differences in expense ratios. That measure is the overall capitalization rate (*OAR*, or R_0), which is *NOI*/Selling Price. The reciprocal of R_0, (Selling Price/*NOI*) is the net operating income multiplier (*NIM*), a price/earnings ratio that produces the same value estimate as the R_0.

Implicit in the use of a directly extracted R_0 is comparability between the sales from which the R_0 is extracted and the subject property to which it is applied, with respect to future income and value change prospects.

Questions and Problems

1. React to this comment by an appraiser: "I don't use *GIM*s because they don't explicitly consider the price-determining benefits of real estate investment, like before-tax cash flow, tax shelter, and value change."
2. Aren't *GIM*s and R_0s really units of comparison? And if so, why aren't they included in the direct sales comparison approach?
3. *a.* What is the average *GIM* from the following sales data?

Sale	Gross Income	Transaction Price
1	$105,500	$ 740,000
2	121,700	835,000
3	118,000	830,000
4	170,300	1,445,000

  b. What might account for the large difference between the average *GIM* for Sales #1–3, and the *GIM* for Sale #4?

c. Suppose you rechecked the data from Sale #4, and were convinced it was accurate and that the property was comparable to the others. What use could you then make of the *GIM* from Sale #4?

4. a. Extract R_O from the following sales data (which we first used in Question 2 to extract *GIMs*):

Sale	Gross Income	Transaction Price	OER (including vacancy)
1	$105,500	$ 740,000	.35
2	121,700	835,000	.34
3	118,000	830,000	.32
4	170,300	1,445,000	.20

b. Now how do you view Sale #4?

5. What are reserves for replacements? What are they used for?

6. What is an overall capitalization rate? A price/earnings ratio?

7. What is the relationship between *GIMs* and R_Os?

8. Two properties sold at R_Os of .098 and .121, respectively. What might explain the difference? What implications are there for the appraiser?

CHAPTER 15

Estimating the Overall Capitalization Rate Using a Weighted Average of First-Year Returns to Debt and Equity: The Band of Investment Approach

Introduction

The previous chapter showed how the overall capitalization rate can be extracted directly from comparable sales. This chapter presents a second way to estimate the overall rate, which is by weighting the expected first-year cash returns to the lender and the equity investor.

The rationale for this weighting approach is straightforward. Most real estate is purchased using both debt and equity, and therefore, two "slices" must come out of the *NOI* "productivity pie." The first slice is the mortgage payment (debt service or *DS*). It provides a return to the lender. The second slice is the residual income, called before tax cash flow (*BTCF*), which provides a return to the equity investor. It follows that the overall capitalization rate, R_0, which is used to capitalize *NOI*, must be a weighted average of the returns to the lender (R_m) and the equity investor (R_e).

Use of the weighted average of the returns to the lender and the equity investor to estimate R_0 dates back to at least 1944 in the appraisal literature,[1] and it is traditionally referred to as the band of investment model. It is a model that is widely used by appraisers, for reasons which will be discussed shortly.

---

[1] S. Edwin Kazdin, "Capitalization Under Present Market Conditions," *The Appraisal Journal*, October 1944. In the finance literature, similar models are called the weighted average cost of capital.

The Band of Investment Model

The band of investment model looks like this:[2]

$$V = \frac{NOI}{R_0} \quad (1)$$

where

$$R_0 = (m)(R_m) + (1 - m)(R_e)$$

and

m is the percentage of funds provided by the mortgage lender (the mortgage loan-to-value ratio)

$(1 - m)$ is the percentage of funds provided by the equity investor (the down payment)

R_m is the one year cash return to the lender, calculated as $\frac{\text{Debt Service}}{\text{Loan Amount}}$.

R_e is the one year cash return (called the *equity capitalization rate*) to the equity investor, which is calculated as $R_e = \frac{BTCF}{\text{Cash invested}}$.[3]

An Example

Suppose equity investors expect a 10 percent equity capitalization rate and lenders expect a 12 percent cash return. Assume also that lenders typically provide 75 percent of the funds for purchase and equity investors provide the remaining 25 percent.

$$R_0 = (.75 \times .12) + (.25 \times .10)$$
$$= .09 + .025$$
$$R_0 = .115$$

If a subject property is expected to produce $100,000 of *NOI*,

$$V_0 = \frac{NOI}{R_0}$$
$$= \frac{\$100,000}{.115}$$
$$= \$869,565, \text{ say, } \$870,000$$

---

[2] An alternative model based on the debt service coverage ratio is found in the chapter Appendix.
[3] The equity capitalization is sometimes referred to as the equity dividend rate.

The value estimate of $870,000 means that if $870,000 is paid for the property, and it is financed with 75 percent debt and 25 percent equity, the expected cash returns to the lender and the equity investor will be 12 percent and 10 percent, respectively. The "proof" is as follows:

Lender's Position

Investment (loan) amount $= .75 \times \$870,000 = \$652,500$

Annual cash return (debt service) $= .12 \times \$652,500 = \$78,300$

Equity Position

Investment amount $= .25 \times \$870,000 = \$217,500$

Cash return (Before-tax cash flow) $= NOI -$ Debt Service

$= \$100,000 - \$78,300$

$= \$21,700$

$$\text{Equity capitalization rate } (R_e) = \frac{\text{Before tax cash flow}}{\text{Equity investment}}$$

$$= \frac{\$21,700}{\$217,500}$$

$$= .10 \text{ (rounded)}$$

This example shows the logic of the band of investment model (and, in fact, all income approach models): The estimated value will produce exactly the expected returns to the lender and the equity investor, no more or no less. This makes sense, as the motivation for investing is to generate an expected rate of return. In the example above, the expected return to the equity investor is 10 percent and the expected return to the lender is 12 percent. The estimated value of $870,000 produces those returns.

The Relationship of R_m and R_e

The band of investment model was introduced above by using an example in which R_m, the cash return to the lender, was assumed to be 12 percent, while R_e, the equity capitalization rate, was assumed to be 10 percent. The fact that the return to the lender was higher than the return to the equity investor in this example (and quite often in actual appraisal applications), may raise a question, because higher risk should be associated with higher returns. Why then isn't the expected return to equity higher than the expected return to the lender? The answer lies in recognizing that R_m and R_e are expected *one*-year returns (in practice, generally the first year), and don't directly reflect future returns. Often the equity capitalization rate will increase over time, and the equity investor may also have a gain when the property is sold. Therefore, the expected equity *yield* (which includes all anticipated cash flows) should in fact exceed the interest rate on debt, but that is not necessarily so for the first-year equity capitalization rate. More will be said about the relationship between equity capitalization and equity yield rates after the discounted cash flow model has been introduced. For now, it is important to understand that there is no conflict between the common situation where R_m exceeds R_e, and what is the accepted theory concerning the relationship between risk and return.

More about the Rate of Return to the Lender (R_m)

In the example above, the 12 percent cash return to the lender was given. This rate of return, R_m, is called the *loan constant* or the *mortgage constant,* and it includes both the interest rate and the periodic repayment of the principal of the loan, called amortization.

Because most real estate transactions involve the use of debt, it is important that the appraiser understand the fundamentals of mortgage loan arithmetic. The loan constant is the percentage of a loan which must be paid periodically in order for the interest to be paid and the loan to be fully amortized over the term of the loan. The formula for the loan constant is:

$$R_m = \frac{Y_m}{1 - \frac{1}{(1 + Y_m)^n}}$$

where Y_m is the interest rate (the yield on the mortgage loan) and n is the number of periods over which the loan is to be amortized.

To illustrate the calculation of the loan constant, assume a 3-year loan for $1,000 at 10 percent interest, with payments made annually at the end of the year.

$$R_m = \frac{.10}{1 - \frac{1}{(1 + .10)^3}}$$

$$= .40211$$

This means that .40211 of the loan must be paid each year. For a loan of, say, $1,000, the required mortgage payment, or debt service, would be .40211 × $1,000 = $402.11. To demonstrate how amortization works and to show that the loan constant of .40211 is correct, the amortization schedule would look like this:

Year	1	2	3
Debt service	$402.11	$402.11	$402.11
−Interest (.10)	100.00	69.79*	36.56
Amortization	302.11	332.32	365.55
Mortgage balance	697.89	365.57	-0- (allowing for rounding)

*The interest rate is applied to the outstanding mortgage balance.

In practice, mortgage loans are almost always paid monthly, not yearly. The loan constant formula remains the same, but is based on monthly interest and monthly payment periods. A $1,000, 3-year, 10 percent loan, amortized monthly, would require a monthly constant of:

$$R_m = \frac{\frac{.10}{12}}{1 - \frac{1}{\left(1 + \frac{.10}{12}\right)^{36}}}$$

$$= .03227$$

The monthly debt service on the $1,000 loan would be $.03227 \times \$1,000 = \$32.27$.

Allowing for some rounding, total debt service for the year would be $\$32.27 \times 12 = \$387.24$, which is lower than the $402.11 if the loan was amortized annually. This makes sense. Because the loan is being paid monthly instead of yearly, amortization occurs more quickly and this reduces the amount of interest paid. As a result, the total payment to the lender is lower. Loan constants can be found using a calculator and are also available in tables.

The Band of Investment Is an Equity Residual Model

One way to describe the band of investment model is that it is an *equity residual* model. Notice that the value of the equity portion is effectively determined by capitalizing (at R_e) the *residual before-tax cash flow* that is left for the equity investor after the lender has been paid the required debt service. In the previous example, before-tax cash flow (*BTCF*) was $100,000 − $78,300 = $21,700, which when capitalized at .10 produces the equity value of $217,000 (rounded).

From a different perspective, the value produced by the band of investment model is the sum of the values of the debt and equity positions:

$$V = V_m + V_e$$

where

V_m = the mortgage value
V_e = the equity value

Again from the previous example,

$$V = V_m + V_e$$

$$= \frac{DS}{R_m} + \frac{BTCF}{R_e}$$

$$= \frac{\$78{,}300}{.12} + \frac{\$21{,}700}{.10}$$

$$= \$652{,}500 + \$217{,}000, \text{ say}$$

$$= \$870{,}000 \text{ (rounded)}$$

While the exercise above is a good way to help the appraiser understand the logic of the band of investment model, in most cases, value cannot be estimated directly using the $V_0 = V_m + V_e$ approach, because the appraiser will know neither the amount of debt service nor the cash returns to equity. Those numbers are the *result* of the value estimate. Instead, the basic band of investment model is used, because the only inputs necessary are the expected rates of return and the loan-to-value ratio.

Estimating R_m and R_e for Use in the Band of Investment Model

The three variables in the band of investment model are the loan-to-value ratio (m), the loan constant (R_m), and the equity capitalization rate (R_e). The first two variables (m and R_m) are relatively easy to estimate, because current loan terms are available from lenders. Estimating the equity capitalization rate is more difficult because equity investors, unlike lenders, do not publish their current expected rates of return. Thus, the equity capitalization rate is best extracted from comparable sales. For example, assume you are valuing a property that is comparable to properties with the sales, income, and financing data shown in Table 15–1. The final column of Table 15–1 shows the calculated equity capitalization rates from the comparable sales.

Suppose now that a subject property is expected to produce \$37,800 of NOI, and that you are using the band of investment model with m, R_m, and R_e based on the averages from the comparable sales listed in Table 15–1.

$$V = \frac{NOI}{R_0}$$

$$= \frac{NOI}{(m)(R_m) + (1 - m)(R_e)}$$

$$= \frac{\$37{,}800}{(.69)(.1460) + (.31)(.029)}$$

$$= \frac{\$37{,}800}{.1097}$$

$$= \$344{,}576$$

TABLE 15-1 Equity Capitalization Rates from Comparable Sales

Comparable	Selling Price	NOI	m	Terms	R_m	DS	BTCF	R_e
1	$395,000	$42,575	.70	.135, 24 years	.1406	$38,876	$3,699	.031*
2	$340,000	$36,850	.67	.140, 25 years	.1445	$32,917	$3,933	.035
3	$425,000	$46,800	.72	.1425, 23 years	.1482	$45,349	$1,451	.012
4	$256,000	$30,260	.70	.1375, 20 years	.1470	$26,342	$3,918	.051
5	$445,000	$45,900	.65	.145, 24 years	.1497	$43,301	$2,599	.017
	Averages		.69	.140, 23.2 yrs.	.1460			.029

*For example, the R_e for Comparable #1 is calculated as

$$\frac{BTCF}{\text{Cash Invested}} = \frac{\$3,699}{(1-.70)(\$395,000)} = .031.$$

"Proof"

Loan amount = .69 ($344,576) = $237,757

Debt service = $237,757 (.146) = $34,713

Equity amount = .31 ($344,576) = $106,819

BTCF = NOI − Debt service

= $37,800 − $34,713

= $3,087

$$R_e = \frac{\$3,087}{\$106,819}$$

= .029

The estimated value will produce the correct expected equity capitalization rate.

The Reliability of the Band of Investment Model

In the last chapter we used both a *GIM* and a directly extracted R_0 to estimate the value of an example property that was expected to produce *NOI* of $37,800. We have now valued the same property using an R_0 calculated by weighting the cash returns to debt and equity, and in doing so, are reminded that the band of investment model is nothing more than a disaggregation of R_0 into its debt and equity components.

This being the case, the same caveat applies to the use of the band of investment model as does to directly extracted R_0s. The comparables from which the variables are extracted must be comparable to the subject property as far as future income expectations are concerned. If that assumption cannot be made with reasonable confidence, the resulting value estimate will lose credibility.

Multiple Mortgages

The band of investment model can be used with more than one mortgage. With a first and second mortgage, it would look like this:

$$R_0 = (m)_1 (R_{m_1}) + (m_2) (R_{m_2}) + ((1 - (m_1 + m_2)) (R_e)$$

where the subscripts 1 and 2 refer to the first and second mortgages.

An Example

Suppose 70 percent first-mortgage money is available at 14.5 percent, amortized over 20 years, and 20 percent second-mortgage money is available at 11 percent, interest-only. Equity investors expect an equity capitalization rate of 8 percent.

$$R_0 = .70 (.1536) + .20 (.11) + .10 (.08)$$
$$= .1375$$

If NOI is expected to be $100,000,

$$V = \frac{\$100,000}{.1375} = \$727,273$$

As it must, this value estimate produces the expected 8 percent equity capitalization rate.

```
Debt service on first mortgage  = $727,273 × .70 × .1536  = $78,196
Debt service on second mortgage = $727,273 × .20 × .11    = $16,000
                                          Total debt service = $94,196
Equity invested: .10 × $727,273 = $72,727
```

$$NOI \ \$100,000$$
$$- DS \ \$ \ 94,196$$
$$BTCF \ \$ \ \ 5,804$$

$$R_e = \frac{\$5,804}{\$72,727} = .08$$

Financing and Value

It is important to understand that while finance-explicit models like the band of investment do a good job of describing price-setting behavior, they do not imply that a property's market value is affected by how it is financed. In practice, this means that when estimating market value, *typical* financing terms must be used in the model. Thus, at any given time, the variables in the model—the loan-to-value ratio, the loan constant, and the equity capitalization rate—are "fixed" by the market. This has important appraisal implications. First, when choosing comparable sales from which to extract the equity dividend rate, it is necessary that the sales were typically financed. Second, when multiple mortgages are involved, the resulting estimate will be a market-value estimate only if multiple mortgages with comparable terms are typical in the market. If they are not, investment value, not market value, will have been estimated. The same is true when there are existing mortgages that can be assumed by a new owner.

How Useful Is the Band of Investment Model?

The band of investment model is popular with appraisers. In a 1977 study,[4] it was used in 24 percent of a sample of 640 appraisals. While there have been no published studies on usage since then, the author's casual contacts suggest it continues to be widely used. Despite this popularity, however, there are some who question its utility for valuation purposes. Their argument is that the model is largely redundant.

For example, look back at the information from the comparable sales summarized in Table 15–1. Earlier, the financing terms and the equity capitalization rates were extracted from those sales and used to value an example property. Notice, however, that if the appraiser has the data necessary to directly extract the financing terms and the equity capitalization rate from comparable sales, he or she also has the data necessary to extract R_0 directly, and vice versa. For example, the R_0 for Comparable #1 in Table 15–1 is

$$\frac{NOI}{\text{Selling Price}} = \frac{\$42,575}{\$395,000} = .108,$$

which is the same result we get by weighting R_m and R_e.

In this kind of situation the band of investment model is in fact redundant. However, the model can be useful when there is not comparable data

---

[4] Kenneth M. Lusht, "The Behavior of Appraisers In Valuing Income Properties: A Status Report," *The Real Estate Appraiser and Analyst,* July–August 1979.

TABLE 15–2 Errors in R_0 from Misestimating R_e

Estimated R_e	Estimated R_0	Resulting Error (rounded)
.05	.1244	$\left(\dfrac{.1369 - .1244}{.1369}\right) = .091$
.075	.1307	.046
.10	.1369	-0-
.125	.1432	.046
.15	.1494	.091

of sufficient quantity and quality to directly extract the R_0. For example, when typical financing terms have changed, it may be necessary to use judgment to estimate the R_0, and this is when the band of investment model can be a big help. Because the expected cash return to the lender (the loan constant) is readily available, and because the lender historically contributes a majority of the total funds, the loan constant dominates R_0, and any "errors" made when estimating the equity capitalization rate will do relatively little damage to the final value estimate.[5]

For example, assume that the typical loan-to-value ratio is 75 percent, at 14 percent interest, amortized over 20 years. Assume also that the "true" equity capitalization rate is 10 percent, giving a "true" R_0 of (.75) (.1492) + .25 (.10) = .1369. This true R_0 is not known to the appraiser, and must be estimated. Table 15–2 shows a sample of the errors in the estimates of R_0 that result from using equity capitalization rates which vary from the true rate of 10 percent.

At the extreme, an error of 50 percent when estimating R_e (in this case, using 5 percent or 15 percent instead of 10 percent) produces an error of only about 9 percent in the R_0, and thus in the resulting value estimate.

We find then, that the use of a directly extracted R_0 will indeed give the same results as the band of investment model, *assuming* the needed variables can be extracted from the same set of comparable sales. However, when a lack of sufficient comparables precludes the use of a directly extracted R_0, a reasonable estimate of R_0 can be obtained using the band of investment model, because the relatively certain loan constant dominates R_0.

---

[5] See Lloyd D. Hanford, "The Capitalization Process Revisited," *The Appraisal Journal*, July 1976.

Summary

When R_0 cannot be directly extracted because of a lack of sufficient comparable sales, or when it is useful to make the annual cash rates of return to lenders and equity investors explicit, R_0 can be estimated by weighting the expected one-year returns to lenders and equity investors. This band of investment model is

$$V = \frac{NOI}{R_0}$$

where

$$R_0 = (m)(R_m) + (1 - m)(R_e).$$

When the same comparables are used both to directly extract an R_0, and to extract the inputs to the band of investment model, the value estimates will be the same. Frequently, however, there will not be sufficient data from comparable sales from which to directly extract R_0. In those cases, the appraiser must use the band of investment model. Because lenders historically have contributed a larger portion of value than the equity investors, and because current terms of debt are readily available, a major portion of the overall rate is "predetermined." Errors in estimating the return to the minority investor—equity—will not have a serious impact on the accuracy of the estimated R_0, nor, in turn, on the value estimate.

When using the band of investment for market valuation, typical financing terms must be used. The use of nontypical terms in the model may produce an estimate of investment value, but not market value.

Questions and Problems

1. a. Where do the inputs for the band of investment model come from?
   b. Given your answer to (a.) above, what does this imply about the utility of the band of investment model for market valuation? When is the band of investment model *most* useful?

2. You are reviewing an appraisal which estimated value using this model:

   $$V = \frac{NOI}{(m_1)(R_{m_1}) + (m_2)(R_{m_2}) + ((1 - (m_1 + m_2))(R_e)}$$

   What question would you have?

3. An appraiser used $R_m = .135$ and $R_e = .08$ in the band of investment model. A reader of the appraisal was heard to say: "This can't be correct. Equity investors take more risk than lenders, and their expected returns must therefore be higher than lenders'." React to this statement.

4. Given the information below, estimate the value of the property and show that your estimate is correct.

   NOI: $150,000
   Y_m: 10.5%, 18-year amortization with monthly payments
   m: .70
   R_e: 9%

5. The band of investment model is often described as an equity residual model. Explain.

*6. Given the information below, estimate the value of the property.

   NOI: $150,000
   Y_m: 10.5%, 18-year amortization, monthly payments
   DSCR: 1.3
   R_e: 9%

*7. Under what market conditions is it likely that the DSCR will become the primary constraint on loan amounts?

8. What is the monthly loan constant on a 11.50-percent loan for 30 years, amortized monthly?

9. a. What is the annual loan constant on a 12 percent loan for 22 years, amortized monthly?
   b. What is the constant if it is amortized yearly?
   c. Why is the yearly payment higher than the sum of the 12 monthly payments?

---

*Questions 6 and 7 are based on material in the chapter appendix.

Appendix
An Alternative Band of Investment Model Based on the Debt Service Coverage Ratio

In the traditional band of investment model, the mortgage amount is based on the loan-to-value ratio. The rationale is that lenders (and sometimes equity investors) control risk by constraining the amount of debt to some percentage of the property's value. In case of default and foreclosure, this provides a value "cushion" before the lender's principal is at risk.

This value cushion is extremely important, but it is not all that concerns lenders. Also important is the borrower's *ability to pay the debt service* out of the expected income from the property. One measure of ability to pay is the debt service coverage ratio (*DSCR*), which is:[6]

$$DSCR = \frac{NOI}{\text{Debt Service}} \quad (1)$$

Thus, the *DSCR* provides a measure of another kind of cushion, which is the relationship between the expected *NOI* and the required debt service (*DS*). In practice, the *DSCR* is often used instead of the loan-to-value ratio as the primary constraint on the loan amount.

Rearranging the *DSCR* Equation (1) shows that the maximum allowable debt service is:

$$DS = \frac{NOI}{DSCR} \quad (2)$$

For example, with expected *NOI* of $35,000 and a minimum coverage ratio of 1.2, the maximum debt service is:

$$DS_{max} = \frac{\$35,000}{1.2}$$
$$= \$29,167$$

Assuming a .12 loan constant (R_m), the maximum loan amount is:

---
[6]Additional discussion of the DSCR is found in Chapter 18.

$$V_m = \frac{DS}{R_m} \quad (3)$$
$$= \frac{\$29,167}{.12}$$
$$= \$243,058$$

This loan will require $29,167 of debt service, which will meet the constraint of a 1.2 *DSCR*. The two steps to estimate the loan amount can be combined as shown in Equation (4):

$$V_m = \frac{NOI}{(DSCR)(R_m)} \quad (4)$$
$$= \frac{\$35,000}{(1.2)(.12)}$$
$$= \$243,056$$

When "market" *DSCR*s can be estimated, the appraiser can use a *DSCR*-based band of investment model to estimate market value:

$$V = V_m + V_e \quad (5)$$
$$= \frac{NOI}{(DSCR)(R_m)} + \frac{\text{Before tax cash flow}}{R_e}$$

An Example

Above, we calculated the maximum loan amount (V_m) for a property expected to produce *NOI* of $35,000, if lenders expect a *DSCR* of 1.2 and an R_m of .12. To estimate the value of this property using Equation (5), the remaining variable needed is expected equity capitalization rate. Assume it is .09.

$$V = V_m + V_e$$
$$V_m = \frac{\$35,000}{(1.2)(.12)}$$
$$= \$243,056$$

Debt Service = $243,056 (.12)

$$= \$29{,}167$$

$$BTCF = NOI - DS$$

$$= \$35{,}000 - \$29{,}167$$

$$= \$5{,}833$$

$$V_e = \frac{BTCF}{R_e}$$

$$= \frac{\$5{,}833}{.09}$$

$$= \$64{,}811$$

$$V = V_m + V_e$$

$$= \$243{,}056 + \$64{,}811$$

$$= \$307{,}867$$

This value estimate implies a loan-to-value ratio of

$$\frac{\$243{,}056}{\$307{,}867} = 79\%.$$

Note that the main difference between this model and the loan-to-value based band of investment model is that in this model it is the *DSCR*, not the loan-to-value ratio, which determines the loan amount. The loan-to-value ratio is a result, not a determinant, of the value estimate. Conversely, in the traditional band of investment model, the loan-to-value ratio determines the loan amount, and the *DSCR* is a result.

There *is* a model that seems to offer the best of both worlds; it uses *both* the *DSCR* and the loan-to-value ratio, as shown in Equation (6).

$$V = \frac{NOI}{(DSCR)\,(R_m)\,(m)}$$

Unfortunately, there may be less here than meets the eye, because in this model the loan-to-value ratio has no impact on the loan amount; it will be the same regardless of the loan-to-value ratio used. To show this, assume that for a subject property, the expected *NOI* is $50,000, the *DSCR* is 1.3, the loan constant is .11, and the loan-to-value ratio is .70:

$$V = \frac{\$50{,}000}{(1.3)\,(.11)\,(.70)}$$

$$= \$500{,}000 \text{ (rounded)}$$

The loan amount is $500,000 × .70 = $350,000. Now, change the loan-to-value ratio to .80.

$$V = \frac{\$50{,}000}{(1.3)\,(.11)\,(.80)}$$

$$= \$437{,}000 \text{ (rounded)}$$

The loan amount is still $437,000 × .80 = $350,000; the same as it was for a .70 loan. The lesson for the appraiser is that in this variation of the model, the loan-to-value ratio affects the equity amount, not the loan amount, which is very different than the traditional role of the loan-to-value ratio.

Which Band of Investment Variation Is Best?

As in most cases when the appraiser has a different choice among valuation models, the choice will depend on market circumstances; that is, which model(s) tends to best simulate the current behavior of market participants.

The use of the *DSCR* in place of the loan-to-value ratio in the band of investment model becomes relatively more popular with lenders during periods of inflation, when high future income expectations contribute heavily to present value, as shown for investment A in Figure 15–1.

This is contrasted to investment B, which has a stable expected income stream. Assuming for example purposes that the market values of investments A and B are the same, applying a given loan-to-value ratio to each will produce equal loans, and therefore, equal amounts of debt service. However, the *DSCR* for A will be lower than for B in the critical early years.

In such circumstances, lenders may rely more heavily on the *DSCR* as the primary constraint on debt. When that is the case, and when market levels of the *DSCR* and the equity capitalization rate can be estimated, market value can be estimated using the *DSCR*-based model.

FIGURE 15-1 Income Patterns over Time

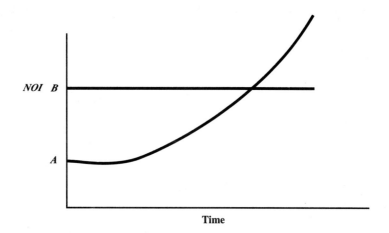

SECTION B: DISCOUNTED CASH FLOW MODELS

CHAPTER 16
Discounting and Present Values

Introduction

The last few chapters have been devoted to direct capitalization—the category of income approach models that use rates and ratios to process a single year's income into a value estimate. We move now to discounted cash flow models, which base the value estimate on explicit forecasts of income over the entire holding period.

The Popularity of Discounted Cash Flow Models

In a study completed in 1978,[1] discounted cash flow models were included in 48 percent of the sample of 640 appraisals. Though no recent studies have been published, the author surveyed 41 appraisers in 1993. Their responses suggest that discounted cash flow models now appear in about 30–40% of income property appraisals. Comparing these percentages to the 23 percent found by Ratcliff in 1968,[2] it appears that the use of discounted cash flow models has increased over the past several decades.

The popularity of discounted cash flow models is not surprising. Because models based on market-extracted rates and ratios rely heavily on data from comparable sales, there must be a high degree of comparability among the comparable sales and the subject. Given the heterogeneous nature of income properties and the increasing complexity of many transactions, there is often a lack of comparable sales data, and the use of discounted cash flow models becomes a necessity. These models are also useful for investment analysis purposes.

---

[1] Kenneth M. Lusht, "Appraiser Behavior in Valuing Income Properties: A Status Report." *The Real Estate Appraiser and Analyst,* July 1979.

[2] Richard U. Ratcliff, "Capitalized Income is Not Market Value," *Appraisal Journal,* January 1968.

The Concept of Present Value

Discounted cash flow models discount the expected *future income* from a property to estimate the property's *present (market) value*. Put differently, the present value of a property is the amount investors are willing to pay for it today (in the present), in expectation of receiving a given amount in the future. The key to understanding present value is that it is always less than the amount of the expected future cash flow because a dollar received in the future is worth less than a dollar received today. The logic of this "faster-is-better" rule is straightforward: A dollar received today can either be put to work earning more dollars, or, if the individual chooses, spent on consumer goods. If some amount of money is expected, say, $100,000, to be received one year from today, the faster-is-better rule tells us that the present value of that future receipt must be less than $100,000. The question is, how much less? Mathematically, the answer depends on the *discount factor*. The discount factor, when multiplied by the expected future cash flow, or future value (*FV*), gives the present value (*PV*).

$$\text{Present value } (PV) = \text{Discount factor} \times \text{Future value } (FV) \quad (1)$$

Because some portion of the expected future cash flow (or future value) must be discounted (removed) to find its present value, the discount factor must always be less than one. If it were more than one, the present value would be more than the future value, a result which violates our commonsense rule that faster is better.

We are now ready to answer the question of *how much* the discount should be. In terms of Equation (1), the question is, how large should the discount factor be? The answer depends on two variables. The first is the rate of return (or discount rate) used to calculate the discount factor. This rate of return, *Y*, expresses in annual percentage terms how much investors demand as compensation for waiting for their money. The higher the rate, the lower the discount factor.

The second variable that determines the size of the discount factor is the length of time the investor must wait for the expected cash flow. The longer the wait, the lower the discount factor. Mechanically, the discount factor is found by taking the reciprocal of one plus the rate of return, *Y*, raised to a power, *t*, which reflects how long the investor must wait to receive the expected cash flow, as shown in Equation (2).

$$\text{Discount factor} = \frac{1}{(1 + Y)^t} \quad (2)$$

Suppose a property to be valued, say a duplex, is expected to have a future value of $100,000 one year from today and that *Y* is 10 percent per year.

$$PV = \text{Discount factor} \times FV$$

$$= \frac{1}{(1 + .10)^1} \times \$100,000$$

$$= .9091 \times \$100,000$$

$$= \$90,910$$

This means that if we invest $90,910 in the duplex today, and receive $100,000 a year from today, we will have made exactly the expected 10 percent rate of return on our investment ($90,910 × 1.1 = $100,000).

The discount factor—in this example .9091—tells us what percent of *each* dollar to be received can be invested today to make the expected rate of return. Thus, the discount factor is the present value of *each* dollar to be received. In the example above, the .9091 discount factor means that if just under $.91 is invested today, and $1.00 is received a year from today, a 10 percent return will be earned on the $.91 investment. If we expect to receive $100,000 in a year, and the present value of each of the dollars is .9091, then the present value of all of the dollars must be .9091 × $100,000 $90,910. Again, the return is

$$\frac{\$9,090}{\$90,910} = .10.$$

The $9,090 is the difference between the $100,000 we expect to receive and the $90,910 we will pay.

Present Value is Market Value

The present value of the expected income for a property is an estimate of the property's market value. Because estimating market value is what this book is about, we need to understand why present value is assumed to be equal to market value. Recall that in the last example, the present value of $90,910 for a duplex was based on a $100,000 payoff in one year, assuming a discount rate of 10 percent. That discount rate represents the rate of return investors expect on the kind of investment being valued—it is the market rate.

Now suppose that the owner of the example duplex asked a price of $95,000. Would you buy it at that price? No, because if you did, the return you would receive would only be 5.3 percent

$$\left(\frac{\$5,000}{\$95,000} = 5.3\% \right)$$

rather than the required 10 percent[3]. Now suppose you offered the seller

---

[3] Remember, you would still receive $100,000 in one year regardless of what you had paid for the property.

$85,000. Is the seller likely to accept? No, because there is no reason to expect a seller to take less than the price which will produce the market return for the buyer. Thus, at the 10 percent expected market return, $90,910 is the only price that will make *both* the seller and the buyer happy. It is, therefore, not only the duplex's present value, but also its market value.

Risk and the Expected Rate of Return

For some investments, estimating the discount rate is relatively easy. The current expected return on treasury bills and AAA corporate bonds can be found by looking in a newspaper. It is not that way for real estate. Discount rates are not listed in newspapers and they are not etched on the cornerstones of buildings. In this section, we will introduce the topic of where discount rates come from. In a subsequent chapter, the topic is covered in greater detail.

Returning to the duplex example, if our investment opportunities are expanded to include not only the duplex, but also a government bond and a gold mine, and the expected payoff to each is $100,000 in one year, how much would you be willing to pay for each? Would it be the same as the $90,910 you were willing to pay for the duplex? Or would the present values of these other investments be more or less? Put differently, if in fact the asking price of each was $90,910, which would be the most attractive investment? The answer, of course, is the government bond, and the most important reason is that it carries less risk. While $100,000 is the expected cash flow from all of them, it is certain to be received only in the case of the government bond. It is not certain in the cases of the duplex and the gold mine. Risk means we are not sure what will happen. Most investors dislike risk, and require added compensation to accept it. What that means in terms of valuing risky investments is that the present value of an investment is negatively related to the uncertainty that the expected cash flows will actually be received. The greater the uncertainty, the lower the present value per dollar of expected cash flow.

Another way to state this important idea is in terms of the expected (or required) rate of return (the discount rate) used to calculate present value. The higher the risk, the higher the expected return. What would the expected return be on the government bond? Because it is considered a riskless asset,[4] investors will demand no risk premium on top of the "risk-free" rate of return. Assuming the risk-free rate is 8 percent, the market value of

---

[4] Actually, it is not completely risk free because there are some purchasing power (inflation) and political risks in the bond. For purposes of simplicity, we are ignoring those kinds of risks.

the bond is

$$\frac{1}{1 + .08} \times \$100{,}000 = .9259 \times \$100{,}000 = \$92{,}590.$$

An investor paying this amount will receive an 8 percent return

$$\left(\frac{\$7{,}407}{\$92{,}590} = 8\%\right).$$

Notice that because government bonds are considered risk free, all that is being compensated for is the time the investor must wait for the payoff, plus inflation expectations. Now consider the gold mine. It is riskier than the bond and almost certainly riskier than the duplex. Say the market evaluates the risk as requiring an expected return of 15 percent. The market value of the expected $100,000 is

$$\frac{1}{1 + .15} \times \$100{,}000 = .8696 \times \$100{,}000 = \$86{,}960,$$

producing a 15 percent return on investment

$$\left(\frac{\$13{,}043}{\$86{,}960} = 15\%\right).$$

It is clear that the duplex, the government bond, and the gold mine will not be priced equally, because equal prices would produce equal expected returns for investments with different risks. This is a violation of the basic notion that investors demand compensation for assuming risk. What would happen if the asking price for the three investments was the same? Sharp investors would demand only the underpriced bond, quickly driving its price up to its proper level of $92,590. Meanwhile, the lack of demand for the overpriced gold mine would drive its price downward, to its proper level of $86,960. The duplex, priced to yield a return appropriate to its risk level, would sell at its asking price of $90,910.

Notice how discount rates (and the resulting discount factors) reflect risk-return relationships. For the bond, duplex, and gold mine, the discount factors are .9259, .9091, and .8696, respectively. As the risk of not receiving what we expect to receive increases, the amount we are willing to pay to receive the expected amount decreases. This is reflected on a per-dollar basis in discount factors. As risk (and the expected return) increases, the discount factor decreases.

While the notion that risk is reflected by a higher expected return is intuitively appealing, the trick is to quantify the differences. Exactly how much should be added to the rate for bonds to provide proper compensation for investing in the duplex? Or the gold mine? In practice, as suggested earlier, this is an extremely difficult question, and one for which there isn't a completely satisfactory answer. Quantifying the risk premium is the topic of Chapter 22.

Time and the Discount Factor

We have been working with an example duplex expected to produce $100,000 after a one-year holding period. With an expected return of 10 percent, it was valued at $90,910. Because the calculations from this point on will get a bit more complicated, it will help to look at the expected cash flows as we work with them. For the one-year duplex investment, the cash flows look like this:

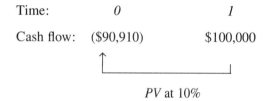

Time 0 is the present—the date of the investment. Discounting the $100,000 at a 10 percent rate of return produces a present value of $90,910. The parentheses around the $90,910 means it is a cash outflow; in this case, the amount invested.

Now consider a different investment, say vacant land, which we expect to hold for two years, then sell for a price which also will produce $100,000 in cash. For the time being don't worry about holding costs (like the property tax). Later on there will be plenty of opportunities to fit such things into the present-value calculations. The expected cash flow from the investment in the land looks like this:

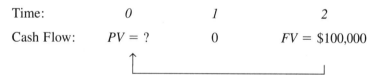

The assignment is to estimate the present value of this cash flow, or equivalently, to find the answer to the question of how much investors are willing to invest today to receive $100,000 two years from today. To do that, we need to know the rate of return investors expect on this type of investment. Say it's 10 percent, just like the duplex. Thus, the amount of the expected cash flow and the discount rate are the same for the land as for the duplex. The difference is that the investor must wait two years instead of one year for the $100,000 payoff, and the "sooner is better" rule tells us that the present value of the land will be less than $90,910. To find out how much less, we again apply the discount factor, given the two-year wait for the cash flow:

$$PV = \frac{1}{(1 + .10)^2} \times CF_2$$

$$= \frac{1}{1.21} \times \$100,000$$

$$= .8264 \times \$100,000$$

$$= \$82,640$$

The present value estimate supports our common sense. If time has value, investors will pay less the longer they must wait to receive money. The discount factor of .8264 is the present value of receiving $1 two years from today. Multiplying the discount factor by the expected cash flow, we arrive at the present value of $82,640. If we invest $82,640 today, and receive $100,000 two years from today, we will have earned a 10 percent annual return on the $82,640.

To reinforce the idea that present value is a function of the timing of expected cash flows, let's look at one more calculation. What are the present values of cash flows A and B, below, if each is discounted at a 10 percent rate?

Time:	0	1	2	3
	PV_A = ?	$100,000	0	0
	PV_B = ?	0	0	$115,000

We've already calculated the present value of A—it is $90,910. The present value of B is

$$\frac{1}{(1 + .10)^3} \times \$115,000 = \$86,401.$$

Notice that receiving $115,000 three years from today is less attractive than receiving $100,000 one year from today, given a 10 percent discount rate. This reinforces the important lesson that value depends not only on *how much* is expected, but also on *when* it is expected. Discounting reflects the "when."

Compound Interest and Simple Interest

When interest is compounded, it means the investor earns interest on not only the original investment, but also on the interest earned in previous years. If $1 is invested at 10 percent compounded, it will earn .10 × $1 =

$.10 the first year. In the second year, the investment becomes the initial $1, plus the $.10 previously earned, and the interest earned in the second year will be .10 × $1.10 = $.11. In the third year, the interest earned will be .10 × $1.21 = $.121, and so forth.

Earlier, we valued a $100,000 payoff in two years at $82,640, given a discount rate of 10 percent. We can now show that that value estimate was correct. If $82,640 is invested at 10 percent in time *0*, it will earn .10 × $82,640 = $8,264 the first year. In the second year, the effective investment becomes $90,904 ($82,640 + $8,264). It earns .10 × $90,904 = $9,090 in the second year, and the wealth of the investor after the second year is $90,904 + $9,090 = $100,000 (rounding). We see then that $82,640 is the present value of receiving $100,000 in two years.

Actually, this exercise has done more than prove the present-value calculation was correct. It demonstrates the more general truth that present values, and therefore all discounted cash flow value models, are based on the idea of compound interest. In effect, the process of discounting is the reverse of compounding. *Compounding adds value, while discounting subtracts value.*

This is seen by looking at the equation for finding how much we will have accumulated some time in the future at a given compound interest rate, *Y*. The equation for future value is

$$FV = (1 + Y)^t \times PV$$

where again t is the number of years[5] the investment will be held. The $(1 + Y)^t$ term is called the compound interest factor. For the 2-year investment of $82,640 at 10 percent, $FV = (1 + .10)^2 \times \$82,640 = 1.210 \times \$82,640$ $100,000 (rounded).

The *compound interest factor* is the amount $1 will grow to in t years at Y interest, compounded. In this case, if $1 is invested, it will grow to $1.21 in two years. The compound interest factor is 1.21. If $82,640 is invested, it will grow to 1.21 × $82,640, which equals approximately $100,000. Not only is the concept of compound interest the foundation of present-value calculations, but we will find it is also useful when we do things like forecasting future cash flows and sale proceeds.

There is another kind of interest, called simple interest, which is computed on the basis of the original investment only, instead of on the original investment plus previously earned interest. If $1 is invested at 10 percent simple interest, it earns $.10 interest not only in the first year, but $.10 for every year it is invested. The applications of simple interest are limited, particularly for real estate valuation and investment analysis. Only in the first period (before compounding begins) is the interest earned the same

---

[5]Compounding periods are often less than a year. The compounding equation can handle that. Simply divide *y*, and multiply *t*, by the number of time periods in a year. For example, for a *y* of .10, with monthly compounding for 2 years, $FV = (1 + .10/12)^{(12 \times 2)} \times PV$.

whether it is simple or compounded. That is why in the last chapter we were able to show that the present value of the one-year duplex investment was correct without reference to compounding.

Valuing More Than One Cash Flow

We now know how to find the present value of a single cash flow, regardless of when in the future it is expected to be received. However, the real estate appraiser will seldom encounter an investment expected to produce only a single future cash flow. Real estate investments typically require an initial investment, then produce a series of annual cash flows plus the cash proceeds when the property is sold.

Consider an investment with an expected return of 10 percent, and expected cash flows of $100,000 each year for two years, like this:

Time:	0	1	2
Cash flow:	PV = ?	$100,000	$100,000

Before introducing a formal model to value these cash flows, is it possible to value the property intuitively, based on what we've already done? Recall the duplex that was valued at $90,910, and the land that was valued at $82,640. Both values were based on a discount rate of 10 percent, and they had expected cash flows that looked like this:

	Duplex		Land		
Year	0	1	0	1	2
Cash flow	($90,910)	$100,000	($82,640)	0	$100,000
	PV at 10%		PV at 10%		

Because we agreed that, given an expected rate of return of 10 percent, an investor would be justified paying $90,910 to receive $100,000 in one year, and $82,640 to receive $100,000 in two years, you may be tempted to conclude that an investor would be justified paying $90,910 + $82,640 = $173,550 for an investment expected to return $100,000 each year for two years. If so, you are exactly right. We can add present values, so that

$$PV = PV \text{ of Cash Flow}_1 + PV \text{ of Cash Flow}_2 + \ldots + PV \text{ of Cash Flow}_n$$

where n is the final year of the investment.

Had we not been able to easily calculate the present value of the example investment from what we had done before, we would have calculated it as follows:

$$PV = \frac{1}{(1 + .1)^1} \times \$100,000 + \frac{1}{(1 + .1)^2} \times \$100,000$$

$$= (.9091 \times \$100,000) + (.8264 \times \$100,000)$$

$$= \$173,550$$

One way to demonstrate that a $173,550 investment will in fact produce the expected rate of return of 10 percent, is through compounding. If $173,550 is invested at 10 percent, compounded for two years, it will grow to:

$$FV = (1 + .10)^2 \times \$173,550$$

$$= \$209,996, \text{ say, } \$210,000$$

How much wealth will we have if we invest the $173,550 in the real estate investment? After the first year, we expect to receive $100,000, which may be reinvested at 10 percent. If it is, it will remain invested until the end of year two, at which time the investment is finished. So the first year's cash flow of $100,000 will have a value of $110,000 at the end of two years. The second year's cash flow of $100,000 will be received at the end of the investment, and will not be available to compound. Thus, our total wealth after two years will be $210,000, the same as investing the $173,550 at time zero at 10 percent compound interest. The present value calculation is correct.

Another Example

An apartment is expected to produce a cash flow of $5,000 the first year. This annual cash flow is expected to increase at a compound rate of 5 percent each year through a 5-year holding period. When the property is sold, the cash proceeds are expected to be $127,629. Thus, the expected cash flows look like this:

Year:	0	1	2	3	4	5
Cash Flow:	PV = ?	$5,000	$5,250	$5,513	$5,788	$ 6,078
						127,629
						$133,707

At a 10 percent discount rate, the apartment is valued by adding the present values of each of the yearly cash flows.

$$PV = \frac{1}{(1+.1)} \times \$5{,}000 + \frac{1}{(1+.1)^2} \times \$5{,}250 + \frac{1}{(1+.1)^3} \times \$5{,}513 +$$
$$\frac{1}{(1+.1)^4} \times \$5{,}788 + \frac{1}{(1+.1)^5} \times \$133{,}707$$
$$= (.9091 \times \$5{,}000) + (.8264 \times \$5{,}250) + (.7513 \times \$5{,}513) +$$
$$(.6830 \times \$5{,}788) + (.6209 \times \$133{,}707)$$
$$= \$100{,}000$$

Notice that because both the final year's cash flow and the proceeds of sale are to be received in the same time period, they can be combined before applying the discount factor for that year.

Lenders, Loans, and Discounting

Lenders are also investors. Their investment is the loan amount, and their expected cash flows are the payments of debt service on the loan. Therefore, the present value of debt service, when discounted at the interest rate on the mortgage, is the present value of the loan. This is true regardless of the specific pattern of debt service payments. For example, a fully amortizing 20-year loan of $100,000 at a 15 percent interest rate requires debt service of $15,976.14 per year (assuming for simplicity that payments are made annually rather than monthly).

Rounding to the nearest dollar, the lender's expected cash flows look like this:

Year	0	1	2	3	....	20
	PV = ?	$15,976	$15,976	$15,976	....	$15,976

When discounted at 15 percent, the present value of the stream of debt service is $100,000, which of course is the loan amount. This shows the logic of the loan constant. It produces a debt service which exactly repays the original loan, plus interest, over the life of the loan.

If this was an interest-only note, which would require debt service of $15,000 at the end of each year, plus a balloon payment of $100,000 at the end of the 20th year, the lender's expected cash flows would look like this:

Year	0	1	2	3	....	20
	PV = ?	$15,000	$15,000	$15,000	....	$ 15,000
						100,000
						$115,000

Discounted at 15 percent, the present value is still $100,000. The cash flows to the lender have simply been rearranged; the lender receives slightly less each year, but then receives a larger check at the end.

Two Shortcuts

No matter what the pattern of the expected cash flows from an investment looks like, present value can always be calculated as we have been doing—by discounting each of the cash flows separately, then adding them up. Under certain conditions, however, present value can be calculated using shortcuts. They produce the same answer, but may make the job of getting the answer a little easier.

Shortcut One: When Annual Cash Flows Are Level

Suppose you are valuing a leased property which is expected to produce cash flows of $10,000 per year. The lease expires 10 years from today. At that time, it is expected that the tenant will exercise an option to buy the property for $150,000. The expected cash flows look like this:

0	1	$\longrightarrow$	10
PV = ?	$10,000	$\longrightarrow$	$10,000 + $150,000

The characteristic of these cash flows that allows the use of a shortcut to value the property is that the cash flows don't change. This kind of pattern is called a *level annuity*. As always, the 10 years of level cash flows could be valued by discounting each of them separately and adding them. Assuming a .10 discount rate, the factors for years 1–10 are .9091, .8264, .7513, .6830, .6209, .5645, .5132, .4665, .4241, and .3855. Applying these factors to each year's cash flow produces a present value of $61,450. But there is an easier way. The present value of an annuity can be found using this formula:

$$PV = \frac{1 - \frac{1}{(1+Y)^n}}{Y} \text{(Annual cash flow)}$$

where n is the number of periods the cash flow will be received.

The value of the cash flow stream above is:

$$PV = \left(\frac{1 - \frac{1}{(1+.10)^{10}}}{.10}\right)(\$10{,}000)$$

$$= \left(\frac{1 - .3855}{.10}\right)(\$10{,}000)$$

$$= (6.145)(\$10{,}000)$$

$$= \$61{,}450$$

The 6.145 is the discount factor for an annuity. It is the present value of receiving $1 *each* year for *n* years. In this example, an investment of about $6.15, followed by the receipt of $1 each year for 10 years, will produce a 10 percent return on the $6.15 investment. Now go back and add up the individual discount factors for each year, that is, .9091 + .8264, etc. You will get 6.145. That makes sense. Each of the yearly factors tell us how much we can invest today to receive $1 in a given future year and make 10 percent on that investment. Since we are receiving $1 *each* year for 10 years, we are willing to invest the total of the individual year's factors. The annuity formula does that for you.

The valuation of the leased property isn't finished, however. The annuity formula can be used to value only the stream of level annual cash flows. That doesn't include the sale proceeds of $150,000. Its present value is found just as before:

$$PV = \$150{,}000 \, \frac{1}{(1+.10)^{10}}$$

$$= \$150{,}000 \, (.3855)$$

$$= \$57{,}825$$

The value of the property is $61,450 + $57,825 = $119,275.

Shortcut Two: Perpetuities

A perpetuity is something that is assumed to last forever. Whether it is level or changing, a perpetuity is a cash flow that continues indefinitely rather than stopping after *n* years. An expectation of level cash flows into perpetuity from a real estate investment is not something that is encountered very often. However, there are situations that come close enough so that the assumption of a level perpetuity will produce a credible value estimate. This is important because level perpetuities are easy to value. The value of a level perpetuity is:

$$V = \frac{CF_1}{Y}$$

For example, the value of a $10,000 perpetuity at a discount rate of 10 percent is

$$\frac{\$10,000}{.10} = \$100,000.$$

It is the same answer you would get by adding the individual present values of an infinite series of $10,000 cash flows.[6]

The present value of a perpetuity that will change (grow or decline) at the same rate each period is:

$$V = \frac{CF_1}{Y - g}$$

where g is the rate of growth of the perpetuity.

To illustrate, if a $10,000 beginning perpetuity (that is, $10,000 in year 1) is expected to grow at a rate of 5 percent per year, its value is

$$V = \frac{\$10,000}{.10 - .05}$$

$$= \$200,000$$

This is the same result you would get by discounting at 10 percent a perpetual cash flow stream beginning in year 1 at $10,000 and increasing by 5 percent each year. The only restriction on the use of the changing perpetuity formula is that the discount rate, Y, must be greater than the rate of change, g.

At this point, you may be questioning the utility of the perpetuity model, given that real estate improvements eventually become obsolete and the expectation of perpetual cash flows therefore seems questionable. True, but in practice, the fact that improvements eventually wear out economically may not be *quantitatively* serious.

For example, assume an annual cash flow of $100,000 from a 40-year lease. The discount rate is 13 percent. A 40-year annuity is valued at 7.6343 × $10,000 = $76,343. Now, instead of 40 years of $10,000 cash, assume a perpetuity of $10,000. At a discount rate of 13 percent, its value is

---

[6]The logic is straightforward. For an investment of $100,000, an annual return of 10 percent will produce $10,000 of cash flow forever. Therefore, the value of receiving an annual cash flow of $10,000 at an expected return of 10 percent must be $100,000, or $10,000/.10.

$$\frac{\$10,000}{.13} = \$76,923.$$

The difference is trivial, because at a 13 percent discount rate, the present values of cash flows to be received beyond 30 or 40 years are close to zero. This can be seen by calculating discount factors that far in the future and seeing how small they become.

The Discounted Cash Flow Model

The present value calculation is based on the fact that there are three variables that affect value: (1) *how much* cash is expected, (2) *when* is it expected, and (3) *how certain* it is that the cash flow will be what it is expected to be (the risk). "How much" and "when" are reflected in the estimated cash flows. The degree of certainty is reflected in the expected rate of return used to discount the expected cash flows.

Mechanically, we've represented these variables like this:

$$PV = PV \text{ of } CF_1 + PV \text{ of } CF_2 + \ldots + PV \text{ of } CF_n, \qquad (1)$$

or equivalently like this

$$= \frac{1}{(1+Y)^1} \times CF_1 + \frac{1}{(1+Y)^2} \times CF_2 + \ldots + \frac{1}{(1+Y)^n} \times CF_n \qquad (2)$$

Algebraically, the present value model is expressed like this:

$$PV = \sum_{t=1}^{n} \frac{CF_t}{(1+Y)^t}$$

The summation sign, Σ, tells us to add all the individual present values from year 1 to the end of the investment holding period, year n. The term

$$\frac{CF_t}{(1+Y)^t}$$

is the same as

$$\frac{1}{(1+Y)^t} \times CF_t,$$

because dividing by a number gives the same answer as multiplying by the reciprocal of the number. For example, the present value of a cash flow of $1,000 to be received in two years at a discount rate of 10 percent is

$$\frac{1}{(1+.1)^2} \times \$1,000 = \$826, \text{ or } \frac{\$1,000}{(1+.1)^2} = \$826.$$

Adding Detail to the Model

When valuing real estate investments it is common practice to distinguish between the annual cash flows from the operation of the property and the cash expected to be received at the end of the projected holding period. This "fine tuning" of the model doesn't change the value estimate, but it does provide more detailed information as to where the value estimate comes from.

For investments with projected finite holding periods, like real estate, the basic value model appears in this form:

$$V = \sum_{t=1}^{n} \frac{CF_t}{(1+Y)^t} + \frac{\text{Proceeds of sale}_n}{(1+Y)^n}$$

For example, given a discount rate of 12 percent, a property expected to produce cash flows of $5,000 per year for 10 years, plus $60,000 in sale proceeds when the property is sold after 10 years, would be modeled like this:

$$V = \sum_{t=1}^{n} \frac{\$5,000}{(1+.12)^t} + \frac{\$60,000}{(1+.12)^{10}}$$

Whether calculated by hand or with a calculator or computer, the present value of the cash flows and sale proceeds is $47,565.[7] That is the sum of the present values of each of the expected cash flows.

The Internal Rate of Return and Net Present Value

We know that the present value of an investment is the price that, given the expected cash flows, will produce the expected rate of return (the discount rate). Put differently, given the cash flows and the expected rate, value can be estimated.

Suppose the problem is reversed. If an investor paid a given price in expectation of receiving a given set of cash flows, what rate of return would be expected? In this case, the price and the expected cash flows are given and the problem is to solve for the expected rate of return. That rate of return is called the internal rate of return (*IRR*). The *IRR* is the discount rate that makes the present value of the cash flows equal to the price of the investment.

To illustrate, given an expected return of 17 percent, the present value of the cash flows below is $234,973:

---

[7]Or within a few dollars of $47,565, depending on how many decimal places you carry throughout the calculations. These slight rounding differences will occur with any problem you solve and can be ignored.

Year	0	1	2	3	4	5
Cash Flow	PV = ?	$22,000	$23,000	$24,000	$25,000	$375,000

If an appraiser was estimating the *value* of the property at a 17 percent discount rate, $234,973 would be the answer. Suppose, however, that the actual *asking price* for the property is only $200,000. At a 17 percent discount rate, the difference between the present value of the cash flows and the asking price is +$34,973. This difference is called the *net present value* (*NPV*) of the investment.

$$NPV = PV - \text{Actual investment, or}$$

$$NPV = PV \text{ of Cash inflows} - PV \text{ of Cash outflows}$$

Now if an investor could pay $234,973 and receive an expected return of 17 percent, but can acquire the property for only $200,000, it is clear that the investor will receive an expected return higher than 17 percent. Whenever *NPV* is positive, the expected return is higher than the discount rate. Conversely, when *NPV* is negative (*PV* < Investment), the expected return is lower than the discount rate. From this, it follows that when *NPV* is zero (*PV* = Investment), the expected return *is* the discount rate. This rate is called the internal rate of return (*IRR*). From an appraisal standpoint, the discount rate used to estimate the value of a property is the expected IRR on that investment.

Finding the *IRR* is a matter of trial and error: Different discount rates are tried until the right one is found (or until you get close enough). For example, suppose an investment of $500,000 is expected to produce cash flows of $40,000 per year for 7 years, plus $600,000 of sale proceeds at the end of the holding period. Given that the equity capitalization rate is 8 percent each year, and that there is some appreciation, try 9 percent. The *NPV* at 9 percent is +$29,539, meaning that the *IRR* is higher than 9 percent. At 11 percent, *NPV* is ($22,517). Because *NPV* equals zero is between a positive and a negative *NPV*, we know that the *IRR* is between 9 percent and 11 percent. By interpolating we can get reasonably close. Of the $52,056 difference between the *NPV*s, 43 percent ($22,517/$52,056) is accounted for by the calculation at 11 percent. Thus, if we move 43 percent of the distance from 11 percent to 9 percent we will have an approximation of the *IRR*. The approximate *IRR* is .11 − [.43 (.11 − .09)] = 10.14%, which in this case is very close to the "true" *IRR* of 10.10 percent. Financial calculators and computers also use the trial and error method to find the *IRR*, which is why it seems to take such a long time for the calculation.[8]

---

[8] There are a number of conceptual issues relating to the use of the *IRR*. Good discussions can be found in most corporate finance or investment texts.

Summary

The present-value calculation is based on three principles: (1) receiving money sooner is better than receiving money later, so investors, even in risk-free investments like government bonds, demand compensation for waiting for the return on their investment; (2) the amount of compensation above the risk-free rate that investors demand for waiting for their expected returns is based on the risk that the payoff will be more or less than the amount expected; and (3) the level of risk is in turn reflected in a risk premium which is added to the risk-free rate to find the investor's expected rate of return, or discount rate, on the investment: the greater the risk, the higher the discount rate.

Mathematically, present value is calculated by multiplying the discount factor, which is the reciprocal of one plus the discount rate, Y, raised to a power, t, which reflects the waiting period, times the expected cash flow, or future value *(FV)*.

$$PV = \frac{1}{(1+Y)^t} \times FV$$

There are some characteristics of discount factors which help us to understand present value. Discount factors must always be less than one. If they were more than one, that would mean dollars received later are worth more than dollars received sooner. It is also useful to think of a discount factor as the present worth of one dollar, or equivalently, what percent (how many cents) of a dollar an investor is willing to invest today to receive a dollar in the future. Each dollar that is expected to be received is worth the discount factor today. The more uncertain you are about receiving exactly the dollar, the less you are willing to pay, and therefore, the higher the discount rate. Finally, when you expect to receive more (or less) than one dollar, all that needs to be done to find present value is to multiply the discount factor times the number of dollars expected.

A fundamental relationship that is very important for the appraiser is that when the discount rate reflects the market's return expectation, the estimated present value is the estimated market value. Buyers who hope for a higher than market rate of return and offer less than the present (market) value for a property will be disappointed. Most sellers know the going market price and won't accept less. Sellers hoping for a higher than market return and who ask more than market value for their property will also be disappointed. Buyers are just as smart and are not likely to pay too much.

We also learned that present values can be added. This means that the present value of each of the cash flows from an investment can be calculated separately, then added to find the present value of the investment. This value additivity principle will be used in several of the income approach techniques to be developed in following chapters.

The present-value calculation is based on the idea of compound interest. Discounting is like compounding in reverse. When compounding, interest is added. When discounting, interest is removed.

The present-value model looks like this,

$$V = \sum_{t=1}^{n} \frac{CF_t}{(1+Y)^t} + \frac{\text{Proceeds of sale}_n}{(1+Y)^n}$$

and it can be used to estimate the value of any stream of expected cash flows and proceeds of sale. However, there are certain patterns of expected cash flows which can be valued using techniques that are quicker than valuing each cash flow individually and adding them up. Level annuities are valued by multiplying an annual cash flow by the appropriate annuity factor, found like this:

$$V = \frac{1 - \frac{1}{(1+Y)^n}}{Y} \text{ (Annual cash flow)}.$$

Level perpetuities are valued by capitalizing the first year's cash flow by the discount rate like this:

$$V = \frac{CF_1}{Y}.$$

Changing perpetuities are valued the same way, except the capitalization rate is adjusted by the annual rate of change in the cash flows, like this:

$$V = \frac{CF_1}{Y - g}.$$

We also learned that the *IRR* is the discount rate at which *NPV* is zero. When estimating present value, the appraiser chooses the discount rate, and by definition, the resulting *NPV* is zero. When the actual investment is different than market value, it may be of interest to know the *IRR*, which is the actual expected rate of return. The *IRR* is found by trial and error, whether a calculator or computer does it or you do it by hand.

Questions and Problems

1. What is the relationship between risk and expected return?
2. *a.* What is the formula for the discount factor?
   b. What is the relationship between the discount factor and risk?
   c. What does the discount factor tell us?
3. Each of the three investments listed below will produce an expected cash flow of $1 million one year from today. The expected return on the government bond is 8 percent. Using your own estimates of the proper expected rates of return for the other two investments, calculate the present value of each.
   a. A government bond
   b. A lease on land which may produce oil
   c. An apartment house
4. Why is your answer to 3 *a.* higher than 3 *b.* or 3 *c.*, and why is 3 *c.* higher than 3 *b.*?
5. Can the expected yield, *Y*, be negative? Why or why not?
6. *a.* What is the discount rate?
   b. What symbol are we using for the discount rate?
7. What is the present value of an expected $325,000 in one year,
   a. If the expected rate of return is 10 percent?
   b. If the expected rate of return is 12 percent?
   c. If the expected rate of return is 14 percent?
8. Why do we discount the expected cash flows from an investment, even when there is no risk involved?
9. *a.* What discount (or present value) factor is applied to an expected cash flow to be received in 7 years if the expected rate of return is 13 percent?
   b. What does this discount factor mean?
10. *a.* Prove your answer to Question 9 *a.* is correct.
    b. What does the compound interest factor mean?
11. Set up and describe the basic discounted cash flow value model.
12. An investment is expected to produce $31,500 each year for 30 years, then be sold for $200,000. What is its value at a discount rate of 15 percent?

13. *a.* Suppose a perpetuity will produce $31,500 each year. Value it at a 15 percent discount rate.
    b. What is the relationship between a long-term annuity and a perpetuity? Why?
14. How does the *IRR* relate to net present value?
15. The expected cash flows from a project are:

0	1	2	3
($390,000)	$18,000	21,000	24,000
4	5	6	7
27,000	30,000	33,000	500,000

   What is the *IRR*?
16. You paid $17,500 for a vacant lot. If it increases in value at the rate of 6 percent per year, how much will it be worth in 5 years?
17. *a.* What is the difference between compound interest and simple interest?
    b. How wealthy would you be after 50 years if you invested $500 today at 12 percent simple interest? At 12 percent compound interest?
18. *a.* An investment produces the cash flows below, plus sale proceeds of $150,000 at the end of year 6. What is its present value at a discount rate of 14.5 percent?

0	1	2	3
?	$10,500	11,000	12,000
4	5	6	
12,500	14,000	15,000	

19. An investment is expected to produce a positive net present value. The internal rate of return in this case will be higher than the discount rate used to calculate the net present value. Explain.

CHAPTER 17

Completing the Basic Discounted Cash Flow Model: Estimating Future Value (Reversion)

Introduction

Though real estate is sometimes developed and held for its entire economic life, most investors have a much shorter investment horizon. The appraiser simulates this behavior by assuming a finite holding period, at the end of which it is assumed the property will be sold. The model presented in the last chapter reflects the fact that a property's present value can be separated into the value of the estimated *NOI* (or cash flow) it will produce while it is owned, plus the value of the estimated proceeds when it is sold, as shown in Equation (1).

$$V = \sum_{t=1}^{n} \frac{NOI_t}{(1+Y_o)^t} + \frac{\text{Proceeds of sale}}{(1+Y_o)^n} \quad (1)$$

Notice that Y_o is now being using as the discount rate. The subscript o indicates that it is the overall discount rate applicable to the entire property. Also, when working with the value model in the last chapter, the proceeds of sale were always given. In this chapter, we first learn how sale proceeds are estimated in practice, then use that information to complete the discounted cash flow model.

An Example Property

Because the logic and mechanics of estimating a future selling price are closely tied to the estimates of annual *NOI*, we begin with a forecast of income for an example property.

Market analysis has produced the following estimates for a 23-unit apartment:

Chapter 17 Completing the Basic Discounted Cash Flow Model

TABLE 17-1 *NOI* Forecast

Income	1	2	3	4	5
PGI (23 × $350 × 12)	$96,600	$99,498	$102,483	$105,557	$108,724
Vacancy (.05)	4,830	4,975	5,124	5,278	5,436
EGI	91,770	94,523	97,359	100,279	103,288
Operating Expenses (.35)	32,120	33,083	34,076	35,098	36,151
NOI	59,650	61,440	63,283	65,181	67,137

Rent, first year	$350 per month
Growth in rent:	3% per year
Vacancy allowance:	5%
Operating expenses:	35% of Effective gross income
Holding period:	5 years

Table 17-1 is the forecast of *NOI* that results from the above assumptions.

Estimating the Proceeds of Sale (The Reversion)

The proceeds of sale (the "reversion") at the end of the holding period are the expected selling price less the costs of sale. Making the estimate of the selling price can be challenging—so much so that it has sometimes been observed that if appraisers could really estimate a sale price several years in the future, there would be no problem estimating the sale price today, which of course is the objective of the appraisal.

Others suggest that attempting to estimate a future selling price is largely an exercise in futility, given the degree of uncertainty involved. While there may be some truth in these observations, they go too far. In this chapter, we develop some conceptually sound ways to estimate a future selling price based on the relationship between that selling price and the income the appraiser has already forecast.

Future Selling Price: Theory

The idea is simple: The selling price at any time in the future will be the market value of the property at that time, and as is always the case, the market value at that time will be a function of the expected *future* income from the property. Therefore, the expected selling price n years in the future will be the present value of the expected income beginning in year $n + 1$.

Estimating Future Selling Price: Practice

The application of the theory is not as simple. The farther into the future we attempt to forecast, the less reliable the forecasts become. Forecasting 5 or 10 years is difficult. Beyond that, it is truly heroic. Remember, however, that it is equally difficult for the market, and it is the market's expectations the appraiser is trying to simulate.

There are two widely used ways to estimate a future selling price: (1) capitalize the forecasted *NOI* for year $n + 1$; or (2) assume the future selling price is some function of present value, based on an expected percentage change in value over the holding period.

Capitalizing NOI_{n+1}

The most commonly used way to estimate the future selling price is by capitalizing the expected *NOI* in year $n + 1$ by what is commonly called the "going-out" cap rate. Income from year $n + 1$ is used because year $n + 1$ will be the *first* year of ownership for the buyer of the property at that time. Looking back at Table 17–1, and assuming the forecasted 3 percent annual increase in *NOI* through year 5 will continue through year 6, the expected *NOI* in year 6 will be $67,137 \times 1.03 = \$69,151$. If the capitalization rate for apartment properties in year $n + 1$ is expected to be, say, 12 percent, the expected selling price at the end of the five-year holding period would be $\$69,151/.12 = \$576,258$. Assuming 5 percent costs of sale, the net selling price would be $.95 (\$576,258) = \$547,445$.

While the use of a capitalization rate to estimate a future selling price is theoretically sound, some would argue that if an appraiser can make a reasonable forecast of the capitalization rate for year $n + 1$, then the appraiser could make an even better estimate of the current capitalization rate, and apply it to first-year *NOI* to estimate market value directly. In other words, why bother with a discounted cash flow model in such circumstances? The answer is that if the only objective is to arrive at *the number* (an estimate of market value), then capitalizing first-year income may in fact be sufficient. If, however, the objective is to describe where the number came from, explicitly forecasting cash flows and income is a useful exercise.

Estimating the Future Value Based on the Present Value

Suppose you are appraising the apartment shown in Table 17–1, and decide to ask investors what they expected the selling price would be after the five-year holding period. Likely, they would respond in percentage terms, for example, that value will increase at a rate of 2 percent per year over the next five years. In other words, *whatever* value is today, they think it will increase by 2 percent per year. If investors think about future value in this way, it is reasonable for the appraiser to think about it the same way; that is, by stating the future selling price in terms of current value.

This, however, produces a catch-22; the appraiser is trying to estimate a future value (selling price) of a property based on its relationship to its current value, but it is its current value the appraiser is attempting to estimate. The solution is simple. Two things are known: (1) there is a present (though as yet unestimated) market value, and (2) the expected future value (expected selling price) can be expressed in terms of that present value. That is, $SP_n = (1 + g_v)^n (V)$, where g_v is the assumed annual growth rate in property value, and n is the projected holding period. For example, if the value of the apartment in Table 17–1 is expected to increase at a 1 percent annual rate over the five-year holding period, the selling price after the fifth year would be:

$$SP_n = (1 + .01)^5 (V)$$

$$SP_n = (1.1041) (V)$$

Deducting 5 percent for costs of sale, the net selling price would be .95 (1.1041) (V) = 1.0489 (V). If no change in value is expected, the future selling price would be the same as the current value, and the expected selling price would be 1.0 (V). A property expected to lose value at a simple rate of 2 percent per year would be worth .90 (V) after five years. If the decline (or increase) in value is expected to vary each year, say, at 5 percent, 4 percent, 3 percent, 2 percent, and 1 percent for a 5-year holding period, $SP_n = (1 - .05) (1 - .04) (1 - .03) (1 - .02) (1 - .01) (V) = .8583 (V)$.

Estimating Value Using the Discounted Cash Flow Model

The value of the example apartment can now be estimated based on the forecasts of NOI (from Table 17–1), and the estimates of the future selling price made above using the two different approaches. To summarize, the income and selling price estimates are as follows:

Year	1	2	3	4	5
NOI	$59,650	$61,440	$63,283	$65,181	$67,137

Net selling price after year 5:

Based on capitalizing NOI_{n+1}: $547,445

Based on a 2 percent annual rate of value change and 5 percent costs of sale: $NSP = 1.0489 (V)$

Value based on capitalizing income in Year $n + 1$

$$V = \sum_{t=1}^{n} \frac{NOI_t}{(1 + Y_o)^t} + \frac{Proceeds\ of\ Sale_n}{(1 + Y_o)^n}$$

Assuming Y_o is 13 percent, the present value of the *NOI* is $221,178. The present value of the $547,445 of sale proceeds is $297,131, and the apartment value is:

$$V_0 = PV_{NOI} + PV_{NSP}$$
$$= \$221{,}178 + \$297{,}131$$
$$= \$518{,}309$$

Estimating Value Assuming a 2 percent Rate of Value Change

$$V = PV_{NOI} + PV_{NSP}$$
$$= \$221{,}18 + 1.0489 \, (V) \, (P.V. \text{ factor at } .13)$$
$$= \$221{,}178 + 1.0489 \, (V) \, (.5428)$$
$$V = \$221{,}178 + .5693 \, (V)$$
$$.4307 \, (V) = \$221{,}178$$
$$V = \frac{\$221{,}178}{.4307}$$
$$V = \$513{,}531, \text{ say, } \$500{,}000$$

The slight difference in value estimates can be expected given the forecasting involved and is well within an acceptable range.

Note that when estimating the future selling price using a rate of value change, the expected *dollar amount* of the future price can be estimated only after its present value has been estimated. In this case, the expected selling price is

$$SP_n = (1.1041) \, (\$513{,}531)$$
$$= \$566{,}990$$

An Example with Declining NOI

The *NOI*s below have been forecasted over a holding period of seven years.

Year	1	2	3	4	5	6	7
NOI	$20,000	19,500	19,000	18,500	18,000	17,500	17,000

Assume also that property value will decline by 3 percent per year, the discount rate is 13 percent, and that costs of sale (*CS*) will be 6 percent.

Chapter 17 Completing the Basic Discounted Cash Flow Model

$$V = \sum_{t=1}^{n} \frac{NOI_t}{(1 + Y_o)^t} + \frac{(1 - CS)(1 + g_v)^n V}{(1 + Y_o)^n}$$

$$V = \$82,886 + \frac{(1 - .06)(1 - .03)^7 (V)}{(1 + .13)^7}$$

$$V = \$82,886 + .94(.8080)(V)(.4251)$$

$$V = \$82,886 + .3229(V)$$

$$.6771(V) = \$82,886$$

$$V = \$122,413$$

Is the Value Estimate Correct?

A fundamental principle of income property valuation is that if the estimated value is paid, the investor should expect to receive the assumed rate of return (in this case, the discount rate). In the example immediately above, if $122,413 is paid and value declines by 3 percent per year, the selling price in seven years will be $(.97)^7(\$122,413) = \$98,910$. Subtracting the 6 percent costs of sale, the net selling price $= .94(\$98,910) = \$92,975$. The complete cash flow forecast, given a purchase price of $122,413, looks like this:

Year	0	1	2	3	4	5	6	7
CF	($122,413)	20,000	19,500	9,000	18,500	18,000	17,500	17,000
							NSP	92,975
								$109,975

If the value estimate is correct, the present value of these expected cash flows must be $122,413 when discounted at 13 percent.[1] Allowing for a few dollars of rounding, it is.

The Relationship of Income Change and Value Change

It is important to understand the relationship between the forecasted income during the holding period and the assumed selling price at the end of the holding period. A key insight is that *when the rate of change in value is set equal to the rate of change in income,* the resulting value estimate is the same as it would be if the forecast had been for a perpetual stream of income growing at the same rate that was assumed during the holding period.

---

[1] Stated differently, the *IRR* is 13 percent.

Let's make this more concrete. Assume a property is expected to produce $10,000 of *NOI* the first year, increasing by 5 percent per year for the next two years. Value is also expected to increase by 5 percent per year. The discount rate is 15 percent.

Discounting *NOI* of $10,000, $10,500, and $11,025 at 15 percent gives $23,884, and the property's value is estimated as follows:

$$V = \$23,884 + (1 + .05)^3 \, V \,(.6575)$$
$$= \$100,000$$

Now value the same income stream assuming a perpetuity growing at 5 percent per year:

$$V = \frac{NOI_1}{Y_o - g}$$
$$= \frac{\$10,000}{.15 - .05}$$
$$= \$100,000$$

The value estimate is the same. To repeat, when the assumed rates of change in value and income are the same, the resulting value estimate is the same as it would be if it is assumed the income stream will increase at that rate in perpetuity.[2]

It follows then, that: (1) when the forecasted rate of value change *exceeds* the forecasted rate of income growth during the holding period, an accelerating rate of growth of income at some time beyond the holding period is implied, and (2) when the forecasted rate of value change is less than the forecasted rate of income change during the holding period, a declining rate of growth of income at some time beyond the holding period is implied.[3]

The same logic applies when estimating the selling price by capitalizing expected *NOI* in year $n + 1$. That is, given some rate of income growth, if the capitalization rate applied to NOI_{n+1} is the same as the current capitalization rate, the valuation result is the same as if a perpetuity had been assumed.

---

[2]This does not imply that the assumption of a perpetuity is necessarily wrong. Consider the tradeoff between increases in land value and decreases in building value. If at time 0, 75 percent of property value is traceable to the building, and 25 percent to the land, and if the value of the building is expected to decline at a simple rate of 2 percent per year, while land value is expected to increase at a simple rate of 6 percent per year, total property value would remain unchanged. Thus, in come cases, the assumption of a value increase into perpetuity may be defensible.

[3]The chapter Appendix develops a model which replaces the estimate of sale proceeds with an explicit forecast of income beyond the holding period.

This can be shown by returning to the example immediately above, where *NOI*s of $10,000, $10,500, and $11,025, combined with a 5 percent annual increase in property value, produced a present value of $100,000 when discounted at 15 percent. The resulting first-year capitalization rate for the property is

$$\frac{\$10,000}{\$100,000} = .10.$$

If *NOI* for year 4 is forecasted to be $11,025 (1.05) = $11,576, and this is also capitalized at .10, the estimated selling price after year 3 is $115,760. Discounting the three years of *NOI* and selling price at 15 percent again produces a present value of $100,000.

It follows then, that if the capitalization rate applied to NOI_{n+1} exceeds the current rate, a declining income stream some time beyond year $n + 1$ is being assumed. If the rate applied to NOI_{n+1} is lower than the current rate, then an increasing income stream some time beyond year $n + 1$ is being assumed.

There are, of course, an infinite number of income patterns between years $n + 1 \to \infty$ that will produce the same value at the end of year n. Nevertheless, the relationship between the given rates of income and value change during the holding period implies that beyond year n, income will eventually rise, fall, or remain level.

Perhaps the most important lesson from all of this is the fact that the typical assumption of a finite holding does not relieve the appraiser of the burden of forecasting income beyond the holding period. That forecast is simply embedded in the estimate of the proceeds of sale.

Summary

Market value can be estimated by discounting *NOI* and the (net) proceeds of sale. The value model is:

$V = PV$ of $NOI + PV$ of Proceeds of sale

$$V = \sum_{t=1}^{n} \frac{NOI_t}{(1 + Y_o)^t} + \frac{\text{Proceeds of sale}}{(1 + Y_o)^n}$$

There are two widely used ways to estimate the proceeds of sale: (1) capitalizing *NOI* for year $n + 1$, and, (2) basing the forecasted selling price (future value) on the present value, and expressing the relationship in terms of an annual percentage change in value: $SP = (1 + g_v)^n V$.

Whichever way the future selling price is estimated, the key relationship is that the future selling price will be the discounted value of income beginning then; that is, the present value of income beginning in year $n + 1$. The practical impact is that if over the holding period, the same rates of change are assumed for income and value, or the same capitalization rate is used for year $n + 1$ that applies to year 1, then the resulting value estimate will be the same as if a perpetual income stream was assumed. While the assumption of perpetuity may or may not be appropriate for a given appraisal, it should be recognized as such.

Questions and Problems

1. What are two ways to estimate a future selling price?

2. Assume the information below for a subject property:

	Year				
	1	2	3	4	5
NOI	$20,000	21,200	22,472	23,820	25,250

   R_o for year $n + 1 = .10$
   $Y_o = .15$
   $g_I = 6\%$
   $g_V = 5\%$
   Costs of sale $= 0\%$
   Estimate the selling price after year 5 using two different methods.

3. A property is leased for 12 years.
   a. Estimate its value if it is expected to produce $15,000 of NOI each year, then sell for 50 percent more than its current value when the lease expires. Investors expect a return of 15 percent on properties of this risk class.
   b. What are you estimating the property will sell for after 12 years?
   c. Value the property under the assumptions above, except that rent will increase to $18,000 annually after year five.

4. a. Value a 60-year lease producing $75,000 per year, given a discount rate of 8 percent.
   b. How close would you have come if you had assumed the property was leased in perpetuity?

5. A small shopping center is expected to produce net operating income of $22,880 in year 1. You expect NOI to increase by 4 percent per year over an expected holding period of seven years. Property value is expected to increase by 3 percent per year. The discount rate is 12 percent. Assume there will be no costs of sale.
   a. Set up the model (using symbols, not numbers) you would use to value the shopping center.
   b. Estimate the value of the shopping center.
   c. Assume that you expect the property's value to increase by 4 percent per year rather than 3 percent. Reestimate the value of the shopping center.

6. You have forecasted the NOIs below. The capitalization rate in year 6 is expected to be 10 percent, with NOI in year 6 of $130,000. The discount rate is .1125. Estimate the property's value, assuming zero costs of sale.

	Year				
	1	2	3	4	5
NOI	$105,000	$111,000	$115,000	$120,000	$125,000

7. In reviewing an appraisal, you notice two assumptions: (1) that NOI will remain level, and (2) that the property will sell for 40 percent more than its current value in six years. What is your initial reaction to these assumptions?

APPENDIX
REPLACING THE ESTIMATE OF FUTURE SELLING PRICE WITH AN EXPLICIT FORECAST OF INCOME BEGINNING IN YEAR $N+1$

While assuming a finite holding period truncates the time over which explicit forecasts of income are required, the burden of forecasting beyond the holding period is not avoided, but rather is implied in the estimate of the future selling price. As long as the relationship between the rates of change in forecasted income and the future selling price are understood, this presents no theoretical problem. However, it may be *mechanically* difficult to estimate the property's rate of value growth, especially when the growth rate of income is expected to change. In such cases, the estimate of value growth must in theory be a weighted average of the current and future rates of growth. Estimating the weighted average may prove cumbersome, and thus, when the growth rate is expected to change, it may be easier to replace the estimate of future selling price with an explicit forecast of income beyond the holding period. This can be done using a two-period model, in which period one is the period income is expected to grow at rate g_1, and period two is the period income is expected to grow at rate g_2.

In the two-period model, the estimate of a future selling price is replaced by an estimate of the value of income beyond a selected year, which is the year the rate of income growth is expected to change:

$$V_{n+1} = \frac{NOI_{n+1}}{Y_o - g_2} \qquad (1)$$

where V_{n+1} is the value of income beyond year n, the year the rate of income growth is expected to change.

g_2 is the expected rate of income growth beginning in year $n+1$.

The numerator in Equation (1) is now stated in terms of income in the first period, giving:

$$V_{n+1} = \frac{NOI_1 (1 + g_1)^{n-1} (1 + g_2)}{Y_o - g_2} \qquad (2)$$

The value model is completed by adding the discount factor $(1 + Y_o)$ to the denominator of Equation (2), and adding the present value of NOI through year n. Assuming $n = 5$,

$$V = \sum_{t=1}^{n} \frac{NOI_t}{(1 + Y_o)^t}$$
$$+ \frac{NOI_1 (1 + g_1)^{n-1} (1 + g_2)}{(1 + Y_o)^n (Y_o - g_2)} \qquad (3)$$

An Example

A property is expected to produce $10,000 of *NOI* the first year. *NOI* is expected to grow at a rate of 6 percent through year 7, then at a rate of 2 percent beyond year 7. The discount rate is 13 percent.

$$V = \sum_{t=1}^{n} \frac{NOI_t}{(1 + Y_o)^t}$$
$$+ \frac{\$10,000 (1 + .06)^6 (1 + .02)}{(1 + .13)^7 (.13 - .02)}$$
$$= \$51,552 + \$55,910$$
$$= \$107,463$$

Estimating Future Value (Reversion). The two-period model explicitly reflects the income growth rate "turning point" where it is expected to occur, rather than forcing the estimate of a weighted growth rate over an assumed holding period. It does not, however, directly produce an estimate of the expected proceeds of sale. If a sale is expected sometime *after* the first period ends, the proceeds could be estimated using Equation (4) below. For the example immediately above, the selling price after, say, eight years, would be:

$$\frac{\text{Selling}}{\text{Price}_8} = \frac{NOI_1 (1 + g_1)^{n-1} (1 + g_2)^{b+1}}{Y_o - g_2} \quad (4)$$

where b is the number of years the property will be held beyond period one.

$$= \frac{\$10,000 (1 + .06)^{7-1} (1 + .02)^2}{.13 - .02}$$

$$\frac{\text{Selling}}{\text{Price}_8} = \$134,166$$

If the sale is expected to occur *during* period one, the calculation requires explicit discounting of the expected cash flows remaining in period one, plus the present value of the perpetuity beginning in period two.

For example, the estimated selling price after a holding period of five years would be:

Year	1	2	3	4	5	6	7	8
NOI	$10,000	10,600	11,236	11,910	12,625	13,382	14,185	14,469

$$\frac{\text{Selling}}{\text{price}_5} = \frac{\$13,382}{(1 + Y_o)^1} + \frac{\$14,185}{(1 + Y_o)^2}$$

$$+ \left[\frac{NOI_1 (1 + g_1)^{n-1} (1 + g_2)}{Y_o - g_2} \right] \left(\frac{1}{(1 + Y_o)^2} \right)$$

$$= \$11,842 + 11,109$$

$$+ \left[\frac{\$10,000 (1 + .06)^{7-1} (1 + .02)}{.13 - .02} \right] \left(\frac{1}{(1 + .13)^2} \right)$$

$$= \$22,951 + 103,012$$

$$= \$125,963$$

Summary

The use of traditional discounted cash flow models creates the problem of estimating the future selling price, which is especially difficult when the rate of income growth is expected to change during or after the holding period. A two-period model makes explicit the expected change in the income growth rather than forcing an estimate of value change over an assumed holding period. If desired, the expected reversion at any time can be estimated using variations of the model.

CHAPTER 18
Finance and Tax Explicit Discounted Cash Flow Value Models

Introduction

To summarize from previous income approach chapters, the value of income properties is a function of how much income is expected, when it is expected, and how certain (the risk) it is to be received. When using a discounted cash flow model, "how much" is reflected in the appraiser's estimates of net operating income during the holding period and the net selling price (or reversion) at the end of the holding period. "How certain" is reflected in the rate used to discount the estimated income and reversion. The discounting process itself takes care of the "when" by assigning a present value to income as a function of when it is expected to be received. There are three kinds of discounted cash flow models that are commonly used to appraise income properties.

1. The most direct approach is to discount net operating income (*NOI*), and net selling price (*NSP*), which are the before-tax measures of property productivity. This kind of model was developed in the last chapter.
2. The second kind of discounted cash flow model is the *finance-explicit* model. Commonly called the *mortgage-equity* model, it divides the before-tax measures of property productivity (*NOI* and *NSP*) into the portions flowing to the lender and equity investors, values each portion separately, and then adds them together to arrive at the property's value. The mortgage-equity model explicitly considers not only how much income a property is expected to produce, but also who gets it.
3. The third kind of discounted cash flow model is *tax-explicit*. Like finance-explicit models, tax-explicit models value the lender and equity investor's cash flows separately and add them to arrive at the

value estimate. The difference is that the cash flow to equity is valued on an after-tax rather than a before-tax basis.

While the three kinds of models differ in their mechanics, they are simply different routes to (hopefully) arrive at the same value estimate—certainly the market value estimate should not vary simply on the basis of the kind of value model that was used. This will be demonstrated shortly by using each of the three models to value the same example property.

The emphasis in this chapter will be on the underlying logic and mechanics of the models. Succeeding chapters discuss the relative strengths and weaknesses of the models, the relationships among the different discount rates used in the models, and some valuation shortcuts that can be used in certain circumstances.

Model 1: Discounting Net Operating Income and the Net Selling Price

This kind of model was developed in the last chapter, using as an example a 23-unit apartment. The same property will be used in this chapter, so we begin by reviewing the underlying assumptions shown in Table 18–1.

Also needed is an estimate of the selling price at the end of the holding period, which can be estimated by capitalizing NOI_{n+1}, or by assuming a rate of value change beginning in year 1.

Assuming as we did before that the property will increase in value at a rate of 2 percent per year, that the proper discount rate is 13 percent, and that costs of sale at reversion will be 5 percent, the value estimate is:

TABLE 18–1 Data for Subject Property

Monthly rent, first year	$350
Growth in rent	3% per year
Vacancy allowance	5%
Operating expenses	35% of Effective gross income
Holding period	5 years

The forecast of *NOI* that results from the above assumptions is as follows:

Income	1	2	3	4	5
PGI (23 × $350 × 12)	$96,600	$99,498	$102,483	$105,557	$108,724
Vacancy (.05)	4,830	4,975	5,124	5,278	5,436
EGI	91,770	94,523	97,359	100,279	103,288
Operating Expenses (.35)	32,120	33,083	34,076	35,098	36,151
NOI	$59,650	$61,440	$ 63,283	$ 65,181	$ 67,137

$$V = V_{NOI} + V_{NSP}$$

$$= \sum_{t=1}^{n} \frac{NOI_t}{(1 + Y_o)^t} + \frac{NSP_n}{(1 + Y_o)^n}$$

$$= \$221{,}178 + (.95)(1 + .02)^5 (V)(.5428)$$

$$= \$221{,}178 + .5693 (V)$$

$$.4307 (V) = \$221{,}178$$

$$V = \$513{,}531 \text{ (rounded)}$$

As is the case for all income approach models, the proof of the pudding is whether the estimated value will produce the expected rate of return (the discount rate). In this case, if the $513,531 estimate is correct, the resulting IRR should be 13 percent, and it is.

Model 2: Finance-Explicit (Mortgage-Equity) Models

While discounting net operating income and net selling price is a conceptually sound approach, appraisers often use a model that is more detailed; specifically, one that is *finance-explicit*. Finance-explicit models are concerned not only with the amount of property productivity, but also with who gets it. Thus, finance-explicit models divide each of the productivity pies—*NOI* and *NSP*—into two slices. One slice of each pie goes to the lender (annual debt service (*ADS*) out of *NOI*, and the mortgage balance (*MB*) out of the net selling price), and the residual slices go to the equity investor (before-tax cash flow (*BTCF*) out of *NOI*, and before-tax equity reversion (*BTER*) out of the net selling price). These slices are valued separately, then added:

$$V = V_{\text{mortgage}} + V_{\text{equity}}$$

One reason for the popularity of finance-explicit models is that they simulate the thinking of equity investors, who are concerned with not only the property's productivity and the rate of return on the total investment, but also with how much of that productivity they will get to keep and how that translates into a rate of return to the equity position.

Keeping in mind that alternative models are in theory simply different routes to the same value estimate, the equivalency of the finance-explicit model and the model based on property productivity is shown as follows:

$$V = V_{NOI} + V_{NSP}$$

$$= V_{(ADS + BTCF)} + V_{(\text{Mortgage Balance} + BTER)}$$

Rearranging to group the cash flows according to whether they flow to the lender or to the equity investor produces:

$$V = \underbrace{V_{(ADS + \text{Mortgage Balance})}}_{V_m} + \underbrace{V_{(BTCF + BTER)}}_{V_e} \quad (1)$$

Thus, we arrive at the finance-explicit, or mortgage-equity model, where property value is divided into two financial components: the lender's position, which is the value of the mortgage, V_m, and the value of the equity investor's position, V_e.

In algebraic form, the finance-explicit model looks like this:

$$V = V_m + \overbrace{V_e}^{} \quad (2)$$

$$= m(V) + \sum_{t=1}^{n} \frac{BTCF_t}{(1+Y_e)^t} + \frac{BTER_n}{(1+Y_e)^n}$$

$$= m(V) + \sum_{t=1}^{n} \frac{\overbrace{NOI_t}^{1} - \overbrace{DS_t}^{2}}{(1+Y_e)^t} + \frac{\overbrace{NSP_n}^{3} - \overbrace{MB_n}^{4}}{(1+Y_e)^n}$$

where

m is the loan-to-value ratio[1]
$BTCF$ is Before-tax cash flow = NOI − Annual debt service (ADS)
$BTER$ is Before-tax equity reversion = NSP − Mortgage balance (MB)
Y_e is the expected yield to the equity investor

Estimating value using the mortgage-equity model is accomplished in the numbered steps above Equation 2: (1) V_m is estimated, (2) the present value of NOI is estimated, (3) the present value of ADS is estimated, (4) the present value of the $BTER$ is estimated, and finally, (5) V_m and V_e are added to produce V.

Computer software for estimating value using a finance-explicit model is widely available, and some typical output will be shown shortly. A computer is not necessary, however. A calculator is sufficient, and learning how to estimate value without a computer has the advantage of exposing the appraiser to the underlying logic of the model, making it easier to understand and to explain to others. Therefore, that is how we will begin.

Valuing the Apartment (Again) Using the Finance-Explicit Model

An apartment property was valued earlier at about $500,000 by discounting net operating income and the net selling price. The assumptions and result-

---

[1] The chapter Appendix discusses the use of the debt service coverage ratio as an alternative to the loan-to-value ratio as the measure of debt.

ing income forecasts were shown in Table 18–1. The same property will now be valued using the finance-explicit model.

We assume as before that the property's value will increase at a rate of 2 percent per year and that costs of sale will be 5 percent. Other assumptions needed to use the finance-explicit model are as follows:

Debt: 80% loan-to-value ratio, Y_m (the interest rate, or yield on the loan) is 12%, 15-year amortization, monthly payments

Equity yield (Y_e): 15.00% (The equity yield rate (Y_e) exceeds the property yield rate (Y_o) because using debt adds financial risk)

Step 1: Estimate V_m. The dollar value of the mortgage loan is unknown, because it is a function of the value we are estimating. However, the amount of the loan can be expressed in terms of V and the given loan-to-value ratio.

$$V_m = .80\ (V)$$

Step 2: Estimate the present value of NOI.
From Table 18–1, the estimated NOIs are:

Year	1	2	3	4	5
NOI	$59,650	$61,440	$63,283	$65,181	$67,137

The present value of this stream of NOI, discounted at 15.00 percent, is:

$$PV\ of\ NOI = \$210{,}583$$

Step 3: Estimate the present value of annual debt service, which is the present value of net operating income minus the present value of annual debt service. The present value of net operating income was estimated in Step 2. The present value of annual debt service, however, cannot be estimated in terms of dollars, again because debt service is a function of the mortgage amount (V_m), which is a function of value. However, as we did for the value of the mortgage amount (V_m), we can express the present value of annual debt service (ADS) in terms of value. By definition, $ADS = (m)\ (V)\ (R_m)$ where R_m is the loan (or mortgage constant). R_m is the percentage of the original loan amount that is paid to the lender each time period and includes both interest and principal. The loan constant is calculated as follows:

$$R_m = \frac{i}{1 - \frac{1}{(1+i)^n}}$$

where i is the interest rate and n is the number of periods over which the loan will be amortized. Using the 12 percent, 15-year example loan, and assuming monthly payments, the monthly loan constant is:

$$R_m = \frac{.01}{1 - \frac{1}{(1 + .01)^{180}}} = .012002.$$

This produces an annual mortgage constant of $.012002 \times 12 = .1440$.

$$PV \text{ of } ADS = [(m)(V)(R_m)] (PV \text{ of annuity at } Y_e)$$

For the apartment property:

$$PV \text{ of } ADS = [(.80)(V)(.1440)](3.353)$$

$$PV \text{ of } ADS = .3863 (V)$$

Step 4: Estimate the present value of before-tax equity reversion. Again, there is the problem that the future selling price is a function of current value. Therefore, just as we did for V_m and ADS, we enter before-tax equity reversion ($BTER$) algebraically in terms of value.

$$PV \text{ of } BTER = [(NSP - MB)] (PV \text{ factor})$$

$$NSP = (1 - \text{Percent cost of sale})(V)(1 + g_v)^n$$

$$= (1 - .05)(V)(1 + .02)^5$$

$$= (.95)(V)(1.1041)$$

$$= 1.0489 (V)$$

The mortgage balance (MB) can be read from an amortization schedule or calculated on a computer or calculator.

A formula for finding the percentage of a loan outstanding after a given year, b, is:

$$b = \frac{R_{m_{\text{original term}}}}{R_{m_{\text{remaining term}}}}$$

$$= \frac{.1440 \ (15 \text{ years})}{.1722 \ (10 \text{ years } remaining)}$$

$$MB = b (V_m)$$

$$= .8362 (.80)(V)$$

$$PV \text{ of } BTER = [(.95)(V)(1.1041) - (.8362)(.80)(V)](.4972)$$

$$PV \text{ of } BTER = .1889 (V)$$

Step 5: Add $V_m + V_e$ to estimate value.

$$V = V_m + V_e$$

$$= \overset{1}{m(V)} + \overset{2}{(PV \text{ of } NOI)} - \overset{3}{(PV \text{ of } ADS)} + \overset{4}{(PV \text{ of BTER})}$$

$$V_m + V_e = .80(V) + \$210{,}583 - .3863\,(V) + .1889\,(V)$$

$$V = .6026\,(V) + \$210{,}583$$

$$.3974\,(V) = \$210{,}583$$

$$V = \$529{,}902$$

This is close to the same estimate produced by discounting *NOI* and *NSP*, and well within an acceptable range given the forecasting involved. Remember that using a finance-explicit model adds detail—it shouldn't change the value estimate.

Another Example

Suppose a property is expected to produce \$101,745 of *NOI* in year 1, and that *NOI* is expected to increase by 5 percent per year over a five-year projected holding period. Typical financing is 67 percent debt, at 14 percent interest amortized monthly over 29 years ($R_m = .1425$). Property value is expected to increase by 5 percent per year. Assume there will be no costs of sale. Equity investors expect a 20 percent return.

Step 1: Estimate V_m.

$$V_m = .67\,(V)$$

Step 2: Estimate the *PV* of *NOI*.

Year	1	2	3	4	5
NOI	$101,745	$106,832	$112,174	$117,783	$123,672

$$PV \text{ at } .20 = \$330{,}394$$

Step 3: Estimate the present value of *ADS*. This must be stated in terms of *V*.

$$PV \text{ of } ADS = [(m)(V)(R_m)] (PV \text{ factor for an annuity at } 20\%)^2$$
$$= [(.67)(V)(.1425)](2.991)$$
$$PV \text{ of } ADS = .2856 (V)$$

Step 4: Estimate the present value of BTER. $BTER = NSP - MB$, and both NSP and MB must be stated in terms of V.

$$NSP = V(1 + g_v)^n$$
$$= V(1 + .05)^5$$
$$= 1.2763 (V)$$
$$BTER = NSP - MB$$
$$= 1.2763 (V) - b(.67)(V)$$
$$= 1.2763 (V) - (.9819)(.67)(V)$$
$$= .6184 V$$
$$PV \text{ of } BTER = (.6184 (V))(.4019)$$
$$PV \text{ of } BTER^3 = .2485 (V)$$

Step 5: Add V_m and V_e to estimate the value.

$$V = V_m + V_e$$
$$= m(V) + (PV \, NOI) - (PV \, ADS) + (PV \, BTER)$$
$$V = .67(V) + \$330{,}394 - .2856(V) + .2485(V)$$
$$V = .6329(V) + \$330{,}394$$
$$.3671(V) = \$330{,}394$$
$$V = \$900{,}011$$

The Utility of the Finance-Explicit Model

The finance-explicit model presented here is usable regardless of the expected pattern of cash flows. While there are other variations of finance-explicit models in use, they are of limited applicability because they can

---

[2] The PV factor for an annuity is the present value of $1 per period. In this example, $2.991 is the PV of $1 each year for 5 years discounted at 20 percent.

[3] Alternatively, the NSP could be estimated by capitalizing the estimated NOI in year 6 by the assumed overall rate at that time. If $NOI = \$123{,}672 (1 + .05) = \$129{,}856$, and the "going-out" rate is assumed to be .113, the $NSP = \dfrac{\$129{,}856}{.113} = \$1{,}149{,}168$. The PV of BTER would be $[\$1{,}149{,}168 - (.9819)(.67)(V)](.4019) = \$461{,}851 - .2644(V)$.

manipulate only level income streams or streams that will change at the same rate or dollar amount over the projected holding period. Further, a different variation is needed for each kind of income pattern. These models were necessary prior to calculator and computer technology but are now technologically obsolete. Because they are still used by some, however, they are covered in detail in Chapter 20.

Constructing the Resulting Cash Flows

One benefit of discounted cash flow modeling is that it forces explicit consideration of cash flows, which helps the user of the appraisal to plan on cash flow needs. Also, the cash flows provide a check on the internal accuracy of the value estimate itself, because they should produce an *IRR* equal to the expected equity yield rate used in the value model.

For the example property immediately above, the value estimate of $900,011 produces these cash flows:

$$V_m = \$900,011 \,(.67) = \$603,007$$

$$ADS = \$603,007 \,(.1425) = \$85,928$$

$$V_e = \$900,011 \,(.33) = \$297,004$$

Given the *NOI* forecasts, the resulting *BTCF*s are as follows:

	1	2	3	4	5
NOI	$101,745	$106,832	$112,174	$117,783	$123,672
− ADS	85,928	85,928	85,928	85,928	85,928
= BTCF	$ 15,817	$ 20,904	$ 26,246	$ 31,855	$ 37,744

The estimated selling price at the end of the holding period is:

$$\$900,011 \,(1.2763) = \$1,148,684$$

From this selling price, the mortgage balance is subtracted to find BTER. The mortgage balance is $603,007 (.9819) = $592,093. BTER = $1,148,684 − $592,093 = $556,591.

In sum, we have an investment which is expected to produce the following before-tax cash flows and sale proceeds to equity, assuming the estimated value of $900,011 is paid:

0	1	2	3	4	5
($297,004)	$15,817	$20,904	$26,246	$31,855	$37,744
					+ $556,591

Calculating the *IRR* finds it to be 20 percent, which was the expected Y_e used in the model. The value estimate is correct.

A Computer Solution

The increasing accessibility of computers has made the application of finance-explicit models much easier. Available software generally estimates value in one of two ways: (1) algebraically, just as we have done, or (2) by using an iterative approach, beginning with an assumed value, and testing whether it will produce the expected yield to equity. Through trial and error

TABLE 18–2 Cash Flow Analysis
Summary of Input Assumptions

Basic Inputs

Equity yield rate	0.15000	Net operating income	$59,650
Holding period	5	Annual change	0.03000
Annual change in value	0.02000	Selling cost	0.05000

Loan Inputs

Loan number	1
Interest rate	0.12000
Loan term	15.00000
Payments per year	12
Points	0.00000
Loan constraints	0.80000

Annual Inputs

	Year 1	Year 2	Year 3	Year 4	Year 5
NOI	$59,650	$61,440	$63,283	$65,181	$67,137

Cash Flow Analysis
by Martin & Associates
Value Solution Summary

Value	529,813
Before-tax yield	0.15000
Overall rate	0.11259
Mortgage constant	0.14402
Mortgage value	423,851
Equity value	105,963
Equity plus points	105,963

TABLE 18–2 Cash Flow Analysis *(Concluded)*

Annual Cash Flow Summary

	Year 1	Year 2	Year 3	Year 4	Year 5
NOI	$59,650	$61,440	$63,283	$65,181	$67,137
Debt service #1	−61,043	−61,043	−61,043	−61,043	−61,043
Cash flow (BT)	−$1,393	$397	$2,240	$4,138	$6,094

Reversion Cash Flow

Resale price	584,956
Selling cost	−29,248
Loan balance #1	−354,561
Before-tax proceeds	201,148

Equity Cash Flow Summary

Year	Cash Flow	PV Factor	Present Value	Debt Coverage Ratio	Equity Dividend
0	−105,963				
1	−1,393	0.86957	−1,211	0.97718	−0.01315
2	397	0.75614	300	1.00650	0.00375
3	2,240	0.65752	1,473	1.03669	0.02114
4	4,138	0.57175	2,366	1.06779	0.03905
5	207,242	0.49718	103,036	1.09982	0.05751
		Total	105,963		

the correct value is zeroed in on, much like an *IRR* is found. Most software also provides the cash flows and reversion proceeds which result from the value estimate.

Table 18–2 is a computer-generated[4] summary of the input assumptions and the resulting valuation output for the 23-unit apartment we valued earlier by hand. The result of course is the same.

---

[4] The software was provided by Bob Martin, MAI, through the *Valu-Soft* Company in Winston-Salem, NC. Texas A&M University publishes *The Real Estate Applications Software Directory,* a directory of real estate software comparing languages, operating systems, and hardware requirements. Texas A&M Real Estate Center, College Station, Texas.

Income Participation and Interest Only and Variable Rate Loans

Mortgage loan agreements may call for lender compensation in addition to the basic interest rate. For example, a loan contract may entitle the lender to a portion of income or a portion of the future selling price. These kinds of provisions are easily fit into a discounted cash flow model by adjusting the *BTCF* or the *BTER* to reflect the lender's participation.

The handling of interest-only loans is also straightforward. First, annual debt service is all-interest. Second, with interest only and partially amortizing loans, there is a balloon provision. Balloons are handled just like a mortgage balance, though with short-term loans, which mature before the end of the projected holding period, some assumption must be made about refinancing beyond the balloon.

Variable rate mortgages may also be used, though lenders on investment properties currently tend to prefer a combination of shorter maturities and/or income participation rather than a variable interest rate. If a variable interest rate is involved, the most defensible assumption is that the interest rate will move in response to the *changes* in the inflation rate you assumed when forecasting income. One misconception about variable-rate loans is that the interest rate changes in response to the rate of inflation; for example, if the inflation rate remains at, 5 percent per year, the interest rate will increase by 5 percent per year. This is incorrect. What matters are *changes* in the rate of inflation, not the absolute level.

Property Taxes

When estimating the value of a not-yet-completed development, or when doing tax assessment work, the property tax entry on the income statement may present a problem, because like the future selling price, property taxes are a function of the value being estimated.

The solution is the same one that was used to estimate the selling price at the end of the holding period. While the actual dollars of property tax will not be known until value is estimated, the appraiser can use the property tax *rate,* which, like the future sales price, can be quoted in terms of the property's present value.

An Example: The Apartment Property

When valuing the 23-unit apartment earlier in the chapter, the amount of property tax was not specified. Assume now that the effective property tax rate is 1.5 percent of market value. Using $500,000 as the value, the property tax is .015 × $500,000 = $7,500 of tax. While this dollar amount will not be known until after the fact, the property can be valued with the knowledge that the tax will be 1.5 percent of value, like this:

$$V = PV\ NOI\ \text{(without the tax)} - PV\ \text{tax} + PV\ NSP$$

NOI without property taxes would be $7,500 per year higher than estimated earlier, and the value of the property tax would be:

$$.015\ (V)\ (3.517) = .0528\ (V),$$

where 3.517 is the annuity factor for five years at the 13 percent discount rate.

$$V = \$247{,}558 - .0528\ (V) + .5693\ (V)$$
$$V = \$512{,}012$$

The Relationship Between Equity Yield (Y_e) and Equity Capitalization (R_e) Rates

Finance-explicit models discount the cash flow to equity at Y_e, which is the equity yield rate over the projected holding period. Recall that the band of investment model, which is also a finance-explicit model, is based on the *first year* expected return to equity, R_e. If we accept the fact that investors are ultimately interested in equity yield, because it reflects all expected benefits, it is clear that the first-year return used in the band of investment model must imply something about future prospects; specifically, the market's expectations about future cash flows and value. Therefore a "low" current equity capitalization rate suggests that equity investors are counting on future increases in income and property value to produce the expected yield. This explains why in certain situations, appraisers may observe what seems to be equity capitalization rates that appear "too low."[5]

Put differently, *given* some expected yield rate, the higher the expected rate of increase in cash flows and equity value, the lower the current equity capitalization rate will be, and vice versa. For example, consider these expected before-tax cash flows from properties A, B, and C:

---

[5] Sometimes even negative. Negative capitalization rates come from negative expected cash flows and are processed just as positive capitalization rates. Suppose an R_e of $-.05$ was expected, with typical debt financing of 75 percent at a constant of .15. Using the band of investment model, the OAR would be $(.75)(.15) + .25(-.05) = .10$. If NOI were $1, value would be $10. Debt would be $7.50, and debt service .15 ($7.50) = $1.125. Before-tax cash flow would be $-.125, and $R_e = \dfrac{\$-.125}{\$2.50} = -.05$.

	0	1	2	3	4	5		Equity Reversion
A	($10,000)	$ 500	$ 700	$ 900	$1,100	$1,300	+	$10,842
B	(10,000)	1,200	1,100	1,000	900	800	+	9,884
C	(10,000)	1,000	1,000	1,000	1,000	1,000	+	10,000

The equity yield, Y_e (the *IRR* to equity) is 10 percent for each property. However, the R_es are 5 percent, 12 percent, and 10 percent for properties A, B, and C, respectively. Notice that if neither the cash flows nor the value of equity is expected to change, as is the case for property C, then $R_e = Y_e$; that if cash flow and equity value are expected to increase, then $R_e < Y_e$, as is the case for A; and that if cash flow and equity value are expected to decrease, then $R_e > Y_e$, as is the case for B.

Given these basic relationships between R_e and Y_e, it is not surprising that during periods like the late 1970s, when appreciation expectations were at historically high levels, first year equity capitalization rates were at historically low levels.

The Relationship between the Overall Capitalization Rate (R_o) and the Overall Discount Rate (Y_o)

The relationship between R_o, which is the return based on first-year net operating income, and Y_o, which is the yield (based on *NOI* and *NSP*) over the entire holding period, mirrors the relationship between R_e and Y_e. If the market's expectation is for future increases in income and property value, R_o is likely to be relatively low compared to Y_o. When expectations are for stable income and value, R_o and Y_o will converge. In a declining market, R_o will likely exceed Y_o.

Like R_o, which is the weighted average of the first-year cash returns to the equity investor (R_e) and the lender (R_m), Y_o the rate used to discount *NOI* and *NSP*, is a weighted average of the yields to the equity investor (Y_e) and the lender (Y_m), who share *NOI* and *NSP*.[6]

Model 3: Tax-Explicit Models

Both models discussed to this point discount before-tax cash flows to estimate value, and in appraisal practice, the overwhelming percentage of valuations are made on a before-tax basis. Nonetheless, taxes do affect property values and they are very important to investors. This does not mean before-

---

[6]Though not a simple weighting as in the band of investment, because over time, the loan-to-value ratio changes as the loan is amortized and/or the property's value changes.

tax models are incorrect, but rather that any tax impact on value is implied in the before-tax discount rate. The alternative is to reflect tax impacts explicitly in the estimated cash flows and to use an after-tax discount rate. Encouraged by advances in computing technology and a more sophisticated investment environment, a relatively small but increasing number of appraisers and clients are using an after-tax approach.

The After-Tax Model

Value can be estimated on an after-tax basis algebraically, using an extension of the before-tax finance-explicit model. The difference is that while the before-tax model divides *NOI* and *NSP* between the lender and equity investor, the after-tax model divides it between the lender, the tax collector, and the equity investor.

As before, the pieces of the pie flowing to the lender (*ADS* and the *MB*) and the equity investor (after-tax cash flow and after-tax equity reversion) are valued separately, then added to estimate the value of the fee simple.

$$V = \underbrace{PV \text{ of } ADS + PV \text{ of } MB}_{V_m} + \underbrace{PV \text{ of } ATCF + PV \text{ of } ATER}_{V_e}$$

Notice that the IRS' share (taxes) is not valued explicitly. Value models are concerned with the behavior of those who set prices—lenders and equity investors. The impact of taxes on value, whatever it is, will be reflected in the expected after-tax cash flows and the expected return to equity.

Also, only the cash flows to the equity investor are valued on an after-tax basis. The lender's cash flows are still valued on a before-tax basis. The reason is that mortgage interest rates are quoted on a before-tax basis, and there is no need to be any more detailed in specifying the value of debt.

Thus, the after-tax discounted cash flow model, in its most basic form, looks like this:

$$V = V_m + V_e$$

$$= V_m + \sum_{t=1}^{n} \frac{ATCF_t}{(1 + Y_a)^t} + \frac{ATER_n}{(1 + Y_a)^n}$$

where Y_a is the expected after-tax yield to equity.

Detailed after-tax discounted cash flow models have been developed by Wendt and Cerf;[7] Fisher;[8] Randle, Swensen, and Carman;[9] and Sirmans and Newsome.[10] Most are procedurally similar, and are a straightforward extension of the finance-explicit model, as follows:

---

[7] Paul F. Wendt and Alan R. Cerf, *Real Estate Investment Analysis and Taxation,* (New York: McGraw Hill), 1969.

[8] Jeffrey D. Fisher, "Ellwood After Tax—New Dimensions," *The Appraisal Journal,* July 1977.

[9] Paul A. Randle, Philip R. Swensen, and Kenneth Carman, "A Generalized Model For

$$V = V_m + V_e \qquad (2)$$

$$= m(V) + \sum_{t=1}^{n} \frac{NOI_t - ADS_t - Tax(O)_t}{(1+Y_a)^t} + \frac{NSP_n - MB_n - Tax(S)_n}{(1+Y_a)^n}$$

where

Tax (O) is the tax on income from annual operations, and
Tax (S) are the taxes due as a result of the future sale.

Most parts of the model are familiar. In fact, the only differences between the before- and after-tax models are Tax (O) and Tax (S), and the use of Y_a instead of Y_e. While the tax-explicit model can be solved by hand just as the finance-explicit model,[11] it is much more complex, and in practice, a computer is almost always used.

Valuing the Apartment (Again!)

Twice previously, the value of a 23-unit apartment has been estimated to be about $500,000. One estimate was made by discounting NOI and NSP, the other using a finance-explicit model. The apartment will now be valued using the tax-explicit model.

The data used to this point are as follows:

	Monthly rent	$350
	Growth in rent	3% per year
	Vacancy allowance	5%
Used for	Operating expenses	35% of effective gross income
discounting	Forecasted growth in	
NOI and NSP	property value (g_v)	2% per year
	Holding period	5 years
	Costs of sale	5%
	Y_o	13%
Additional	Debt	80% loan to value, 12% interest,
data used		15-year amortization, monthly payments
for finance-	Y_e	15%
explicit	Costs of sale	5%
model		

To value on an after-tax basis, we need additional assumptions about expected tax impacts. Assume that the improvements will be depreciated

---

Valuation of Income Real Estate," presented at Eastern Finance Association Meetings, New York, NY, 1983.

[10]C. F. Sirmans and Bobby Newsome, "After-Tax Mortgage Equity Valuation," *The Appraisal Journal,* April 1984.

[11]See Sirmans and Newsome, "After-Tax Mortgage Equity Valuation."

using straight-line depreciation over 27.5 years, that Y_a the after-tax yield to equity is 11 percent, and that the applicable tax rate for the income and capital gains is 28 percent. There is also $20,000 of personal property (such as appliances and drapes) which will be depreciated over 5 years using straight-line depreciation.[12]

The resulting valuation output[13] is shown in Table 18–3:

TABLE 18–3 Cash Flow Analysis
Summary of Input Assumptions

Basic Inputs

Equity yield rate	0.11000	Net operating income	$59,650
Holding period	5	Annual change in NOI	0.030000
Annual change in value	0.02000		
Selling cost	0.05000		

Tax Inputs

Tax rate	0.28000	Taxes at resale	0.28000
Depreciation method	SL	Building ratio	0.66000
Cost recovery period	27.5	FF&E value	$20,000

Loan Inputs

Loan number	1
Interest rate	0.12000
Loan term	15
Payments per year	12
Points	0.00000
Loan constraints	0.80000

Annual Inputs

	Year 1	Year 2	Year 3	Year 4	Year 5
NOI	$59,650	$61,440	$63,283	$65,181	$67,137

Cash Flow Analysis

Value Solution Summary

Value	$541,104
After-tax yield	0.11000
Overall rate	0.11024
Mortgage constant	0.14402
Mortgage value	432,883
Building value	357,129
Equity value	108,221
Equity plus points	108,221

---

[12] Tax details are incorporated into most valuation software. Straight-line depreciation means the cost of the asset is expensed in equal annual amounts over a period of time determined legislatively.

[13] *Valu-Soft*, Bob Martin, MAI.

TABLE 18–3 Cash Flow Analysis *(Concluded)*

Annual Cash Flow Summary

	Year 1	Year 2	Year 3	Year 4	Year 5
NOI	$59,650	$61,440	$63,283	$65,181	$67,137
Debt service	−62,344	−62,344	−62,344	−62,344	−62,344
Cash flow (*BT*)	−$2,694	−$904	$939	$2,837	$4,793
NOI	$59,650	$61,440	$63,283	$65,181	$67,137
Interest	−51,355	−49,961	−48,390	−46,621	−44,627
Depreciation	−12,986	−12,986	−12,986	−12,986	−12,986
PP depreciation	−2,858	−4,898	−3,498	−2,498	−1,786
Taxable income	−7,549	−6,406	−1,592	3,076	7,737
Taxes	−2,114	−1,794	−446	861	2,166
Cash flow (*AT*)	−$580	$890	$1,385	$1,976	$2,627

Reversion Cash Flow

Resale price	597,422	Resale price	597,422
Selling cost	−29,871	Selling cost	−29,871
Loan balance	−362,117	Adjusted basis—FF&E	−4,462
Before-tax proceeds	205,434	Adjusted basis	−456,172
Taxes	−29,937	Taxable gain	106,918
After-tax proceeds	175,497	Taxes at resale	29,937

Equity Cash Flow Summary

Year	Cash Flow	PV Factor	Present Value	Debt Coverage Ratio	Equity Dividend
0	−98,868				
1	1,272	0.90090	1,146	0.99344	−0.00399
2	2,778	0.81162	2,255	1.02324	0.01412
3	3,310	0.73119	2,420	1.05394	0.03276
4	3,937	0.65873	2,593	1.08555	0.05196
5	152,422	0.59345	90,455	1.11812	0.07174
		Total	98,869		

The value estimate of $541,104 compares to the estimates of $513,531 and $529,902 produced by the basic model and finance-explicit model, respectively. This 5 percent range between the highest and lowest estimates is quite reasonable, given the difficulties in forecasting income and selecting discount rates. Once again, alternative models may add richness and detail, but they don't change the value.

Choosing Which Model to Use

We have discussed three sets of cash flows that can be discounted to estimate value: *NOI* and *NSP*, *BTCF* and *BTER* (finance-explicit), and *ATCF* and

ATER (tax-explicit). This brings up the question of how the appraiser decides which set of cash flows to use. Because a basic consideration in the choice is whether it is market value or investment value that is being estimated, the discussion below is divided that way.

When Estimating Market Value

The cash flows from an apartment property have been used as a continuing example to learn the mechanics of discounted cash flow valuation. Recall that regardless of which set of cash flows was discounted, the market value of the property was estimated to be approximately $500,000. That outcome was not a coincidence. Market value is market value, whatever the mathematical manipulations we go through to make the estimate. It is another illustration of the value additivity rule; no matter how we slice the cash flows, their present value is not changed—market value is a single, "same-for-all" number.

This raises the question of *why* it is useful to learn to estimate market value based on three sets of cash flows if they all give the same answer. The reason is that despite their theoretical equivalence, in practice, there is disagreement about whether the use of one set of cash flows is preferable to another for reasons such as the informational content of the models or the client's wishes. Pro and con arguments for each of the alternatives are set out below, followed by a survey of evidence about what market participants and appraisers seem to prefer.

Discounting NOI *and* NSP

In one camp are practitioners and academics who argue that the only cash flows that matter are those which reflect the property's productivity (*NOI* and *NSP*). Their argument is straightforward: *NOI* and *NSP* represent the size of the economic pie, and the value of the property is not affected by how the pie is sliced among lenders, equity investors, and the IRS. Therefore, there is no need to waste time with more detailed manipulations of cash flows which will have no effect on the resulting value estimate. Conceptually, this position is difficult to attack. It is based solidly on the value-additivity rule, which we take very seriously.

Discounting BTCF *and* BTER *(Finance-Explicit)*

Over time, the "*NOI–NSP* position" has lost some adherents. The main reason is that there is more to an appraisal than the "answer." Because equity investors are interested in their share of cash flow, many appraisers prefer a finance-explicit model, which more closely simulates investor thinking. This is the same kind of rationale used to argue for explicit forecasting of cash flows, even though the resulting value estimate is unaffected. Many clients want to know not only how much, but from where.

A second reason some appraisers prefer finance-explicit models is that given historically high loan-to-value ratios, the value estimate tends to be dominated by the interest rate on debt, which, compared to the expected return to equity, is relatively easy to estimate. As demonstrated previously, any errors in estimating the expected return to equity will therefore have a relatively minor impact on the value estimate.

Most of those who prefer finance-explicit models stop short of preferring an after-tax valuation. Their reasons are practical rather than conceptual. They point out that expected returns on competitive investments are almost always quoted on a before-tax basis, and it is therefore easier to gather market-based information on expected before-tax rather than after-tax returns. Furthermore, marginal tax rates and depreciation methods used tend to be investor-specific, and it is therefore difficult to estimate the typical levels of each for use in an after-tax model.

Discounting ATCF and ATER (Tax-Explicit)

There is a small (but increasing) minority who agree with those who prefer finance-explicit models but don't think they go far enough. They point out that income tax payments (or tax savings) are made in real dollars, and in fact are no different than, say, payments for operating expenses. Moreover, there is no more reason to assume equity investors ignore the cash flows due to income tax law than there is to assume they ignore cash flow due to things like property tax law. It follows that equity investors base value on expected after-tax cash flows, rather than before-tax cash flows, and that investor-simulating appraisal models should do the same.

After-tax adherents also point out that while it is true that competitive before-tax returns are more available than after-tax returns, most real estate investors think in terms of after-tax returns. Therefore, surveys of investors should produce usable after-tax expectations. Further, given whatever tax rules are in effect, it is not difficult to estimate the going relationship between before- and after-tax rates and depreciation methods. And finally, an error of a few percentage points in the estimated income tax rate will be empirically trivial for valuation purposes. As for depreciation methods, a blizzard of literature appears before and after each tax rule change, suggesting optimal strategies for all but the truly exceptional case.

What Investors Tell Us

It would appear that the debate over whether it is property productivity, before-tax cash flows, or after-tax cash flows that should be discounted to estimate market value could be settled empirically. Simply find out what investors discount and discount whatever they do. Studies like that have been done. The problem is that the results over time have tended to reflect the debate—they are inconclusive. All three viewpoints are reported, in addition to a fourth category of investors who do not use discounted cash flow models at all.

Robert Wiley (1976)[14] surveyed a group of 158 real estate equity investors—life insurance companies, REITs, and investment companies. He found a lack of uniformity in the types of analytical return techniques used, and that most used more than one return measure. A little over a third of the respondents used *NOI* to measure return, while almost 60 percent used before-tax cash flows, including 32 percent that used a before-tax discounted cash flow model. Over half of the investors (54 percent) used some form of after-tax analysis, including 22 percent that used an after-tax discounted cash flow model.

Edward Farragher (1981)[15] surveyed 354 real estate firms, including insurance companies, investment trusts, pension fund advisors, syndicators, and publicly and privately owned real estate development firms. As in the Wiley study, many respondents indicated they used more than one evaluation technique. It appears, however, that the respondents relied heavily on discounted cash flow models (about two-thirds used them), and seemed to be equally divided as to reliance on before- and after-tax analysis, though the reported percentages suggest a majority of respondents used both.

Page (1983)[16] found that 57 percent of a sample of institutional real estate investors used a before-tax, and 70 percent used an after-tax discounted cash flow approach. Again, a large proportion used both. It also appears that over time, after-tax analysis is increasing in popularity.

More recently, Marc Louargand (1992)[17] surveyed 426 pension fund portfolio managers and sponsors. Sixty-nine percent used discounted cash flows in their investment analysis, up from the 65 percent found by Webb[18] eight years earlier.

Regardless of its methodological soundness, published survey data of this nature must be used with caution. Studies to date have largely measured the opinion of large, institutional investors. These opinions may or may not be representative of all investors.

---

[14] Robert J., Wiley, "Real Estate Investment Analysis: An Empirical Study," *Appraisal Journal,* October 1976, 586–92.

[15] Edward J., Farragher, "Investment Decision-Making Practices of Equity Investors in Real Estate," *The Real Estate Appraiser and Analyst,* Summer 1981, 36–41.

[16] Dan Page, "Criterion for Investment Decision Making: An Empirical Study," *The Appraisal Journal,* October 1983.

[17] Marc Louargand, "A Survey of Pension Fund Real Estate Portfolio Risk Management Practices," *Journal of Real Estate Research,* Fall 1992.

[18] Jim Webb, "Real Estate Investment Acquisition Rules for Life Insurance Companies and Pension Funds," *AREUEA Journal,* 12:4, 1984.

What Appraisers Use

As far as appraisers are concerned, the picture is less clear. The author's 1977 sample of 640 investment property appraisals completed between 1975–1977 showed that 48 percent of them contained a discounted cash flow value model. In *every* case, the model used was finance-explicit, but not tax-explicit. At that time, the finance-explicit party apparently included almost everyone. However, more recent casual evidence suggests a trend away from finance- and tax-explicit models, due to the drying up of debt financing after the collapse of markets in the late 1980s, and the 1986 Tax Act, which reduced the tax incentives for investment.

A Comment

If a discounted cash flow model is being used as the primary approach to estimating market value, it is *conceptually* difficult to justify the use of a model that is incomplete as far as explicit consideration of value-affecting variables. Certainly taxes are one such variable. On the other hand, the practitioner's concern with getting the job done cannot be ignored. After-tax analysis is a bit more subjective; after-tax returns on competitive investments are not as observable as before-tax returns, and many large institutional investors are relatively uninterested in tax impacts. Moreover, empirical work on risks and returns to real estate (as well as other investments) tend to be on a before-tax basis, whether or not they are finance-explicit. Until more and better market data on tax impacts become available, it is likely that appraisal practice will continue to be dominated by before-tax analysis.

Estimating Investment Value

If investment value is the objective, the use of after-tax cash flows is preferred for all of the reasons discussed above. This does not imply that all investors are equally concerned with tax impacts. But even at the extreme, say for a nontax-paying investor like a pension fund that is considering an all-equity investment, the $ATCF = NOI - ADS -$ Tax model simply collapses to $ATCF = NOI$, as both debt service and taxes are zero. If a nontax-paying investor is using debt, $ATCF = NOI - ADS = BTCF$.

The preference for after-tax investment analysis also does not imply that there will never be a use for before-tax models. For example, a tax-paying investor may desire both a before- and after-tax calculation of the *IRR*, to provide insight into the relative contributions of before-tax cash flows and tax shelter to the *IRR*.

Summary

Discounted cash flow models come in three varieties: (1) those that discount measures of property productivity directly, without regard to their disposition, (2) finance-explicit models, which value the lender and equity positions separately on a before-tax basis, then add them to estimate the value of the property, and (3) tax-explicit models, which value the lender and equity positions separately, the latter on an after-tax basis, then add them. The models look like this:

Discounting Property Productivity

$$V = V_{NOI} + V_{NSP}$$
$$= \sum_{t=1}^{n} \frac{NOI_t}{(1 + Y_o)^t} + \frac{NSP_n}{(1 + Y_o)^n}$$

Finance-Explicit

$$V = V_m + V_e$$
$$= V_m + \sum_{t=1}^{n} \frac{BTCF_t}{(1 + Y_e)^t} + \frac{BTER_n}{(1 + Y_e)^n}$$

Tax-Explicit

$$V = V_m + \sum_{t=1}^{n} \frac{ATCF_t}{(1 + Y_a)^t} + \frac{ATER_n}{(1 + Y_a)^t}$$

Estimating value by discounting *NOI* and *NSP* is easy with a calculator. The finance-explicit model can also be solved with a calculator, but a computer saves time and reduces the chance for error. The complexity of the after-tax model strongly suggests the use of a computer. These models can accommodate various assumptions about lender compensation and loan repayment arrangements. It is critical to understand that the finance-explicit and tax-explicit variations of the discounted cash flow model should not produce estimates of market value that are different than the estimate produced by discounting net operating income and net selling price. They are simply more detailed as to the division of income and sale proceeds.

When choosing which set of cash flows to discount, there are both conceptual and mechanical considerations. For estimating market value, there is no conceptual difference, as all sets of cash flows should produce the same number. Current practice (as of 1996) leans toward a preference for discounting *NOI*, followed by finance-explicit models, with after-tax models a distant third. As compared to discounting *NOI* and *NSP*, finance-explicit models have the advantage that the overall discount rate is weighted heavily toward the return to the lender, and the lender's return (the interest rate) is relatively easy to estimate. Any errors made when estimating the return to equity will therefore have a relatively small impact on the value estimate.

Another consideration is the informational content of valuation reports. Most users of appraisal services are interested not only in the number, but also in where it came from. The more explicit the model, the more information provided.

Where does this leave us? For market valuation, the conceptual preference is for after-tax market valuation, but given data problems, it is understandable why it is not yet widely used. When and if more after-tax data is generated, a stronger stand may be justified. For investment valuation, after-tax cash flow should be the primary basis for analysis. It is imperative the appraiser be completely familiar with the underlying concepts and mechanics of discounting all three sets of cash flows, because it is likely all of them will be confronted at one time or another.

Questions and Problems

1. What is the difference(s) between a value model based directly on property productivity and a finance-explicit (mortgage-equity) model?
2. What is the relationship between the equity yield (Y_e) and the equity dividend (R_e) rate?
3. What are the relationships among Y_o, Y_m, and Y_e?
4. What is the relationship between R_o and Y_o?
5. A property is expected to produce $70,000 of first-year NOI, increasing at 3 percent per year over a six-year holding period. The discount rate, Y_o, is 12 percent. To estimate reversion, the going-out cap rate to be applied to year 7 NOI is 10 percent. Costs of sale at reversion will be 4 percent. Estimate the value of the property.
6. Briefly summarize the arguments of the proponents of
   a. nonfinance, nontax-explicit market value models
   b. finance-explicit, nontax-explicit market value models
   c. finance and tax-explicit market value models.
7. What models do investors prefer?
8. What models do appraisers prefer?
9. The financing of property typically includes a high percentage of debt. What are the implications for estimating value?
10. "After-tax models are unreliable for estimating market value because investors' tax brackets are too widely dispersed." Comment.
11. You are appraising an apartment with estimated first-year NOI of $108,000. You forecast an 8 percent annual increase in NOI, as well as an 8 percent annual increase in property value. A 10-year holding period is projected. The interest rate on the mortgage loan is 15 percent, amortized over 20 years with monthly payments. A 75 percent loan-to-value ratio is assumed. Equity investors expect a 17 percent return on this kind of investment.
    a. Estimate the value of the apartment.
    b. What is V_m? V_e?
12. An office property with 50,000 square feet of rentable space is expected to rent for $30 per square foot in the coming year. Rent is expected to decline by 3 percent per year over a projected holding period of seven years. Vacancy will be at 6 percent, and the operating expense ratio (based on effective gross income) will be at 38 percent. The property is expected to lose value at the rate of 2 percent per year. It will be financed using 70 percent debt at an interest rate of 13 percent, amortized over 15 years with monthly payments. Equity investors expect an 18 percent before tax yield.
    a. Value the property.
    b. Construct the resulting cash flows and demonstrate that your value estimate is correct.
13. (This question is from the material in the Appendix.)
    a. Compare the theoretical basis of the use of loan to value ratios versus DSCRs to estimate V_m.
    b. What is the DSCR, based on expected first-year NOI, for the apartment presented in Question 11?
    c. Why is the DSCR relatively low? What is the relationship between the DSCR and the rates of anticipated growth of income and value?
    d. Reestimate the value of the apartment described in Question 11 this time

based on an assumption that the constraint on debt is a *DSCR* of 1.3, calculating the *DSCR* as a function of *current NOI*. Current *NOI* is the *NOI* for the year prior to year 1 of the holding period.

e. Prove your value estimate for *d* is correct.

14. In the tax-explicit model, V_m is on a before-tax basis, and the tax collection share is not explicitly valued. Explain.

Appendix
Using the Debt Service Coverage Ratio to Estimate V_m

The finance-explicit model developed in this chapter estimates the loan amount (V_m) as a percentage (the loan-to-value ratio) of value.[1] The theory is that debt capacity is properly based on the probability of future insolvency; that is, the probability that debt will become greater than market value. At that point, the property is "bankrupt," and it is likely the lender will suffer a capital loss. The loan-to-value ratio provides a value cushion to minimize the probability and magnitude of such a loss. Another (and related) reason for limiting debt is that as the loan-to-value ratio approaches 100 percent, and the equity investor has little or nothing at risk, the motivation of the equity investor to act in the best interests of the lender may deteriorate. Whether credit rationing is a function of the probability of insolvency, or the potential problems associated with the behavior of the borrower (or a combination of both), the dominant solution in value models has been to limit debt as a function of the loan-to-value ratio.

However, as was discussed earlier in the text, not everyone agrees that observed debt levels are primarily a function of the loan-to-value ratio. As far back as 1931, Babcock suggested that it is current income (and thus a property's ability-to-pay debt service), and not its market value, that is the main determinant of the loan amount.[2] Ratcliff (1972)[3] agreed: "The lender is primarily concerned with the productivity [income] of the property over the term of the loan, and the relationship of the level and pattern of productivity to the cash requirements for operating expenses and debt service . . . It is observable, though not openly admitted by lenders, that many lenders, having determined that the productivity of a property will support a loan of a given amount, will find ways to adjust their appraisal value to a level which will make the loan fall within the legal [loan to value] ratio limit."

Stated differently, this position is grounded in the assumption lenders are equally, if not more, interested in protecting against "technical insolvency" (debt service > income),[4] or default, than against bankruptcy (debt > value). Because payments on debt are assumed to be paid from the property's current production of income, the ability-to-pay debt service, as measured by the relationship of current income to debt service, becomes the focus of concern.

The Debt Service Coverage Ratio: A Review

The relationship of current income to debt service is captured in the debt service coverage ratio (*DSCR*), which is *NOI* divided by annual debt service.

$$DSCR = \frac{NOI}{ADS}$$

The coverage ratio provides a measure of the *NOI* "cushion" before it is equaled or exceeded by debt service; a coverage ratio of 1.0 means that *DS* = *NOI*. Thus, the higher the ratio, the lower the probability of default.

Most lenders set minimum acceptable levels for the coverage ratio, just as they set maximum levels for the loan-to-value ratio. This coverage ratio minimum can be used to estimate the maximum loan amount. Assume the typical coverage ratio is 1.2, with an interest rate of 12 percent over 20 years, amortized monthly. The allowable loan on a property expected to produce first-year *NOI* of $100,000 is found by first calculating the maximum allowable

---

[1] Ellwood, who popularized the use of mortgage-equity models, suggested in an early article that the loan-to-value ratio be set at the maximum ratio available from lenders. L. W. Ellwood, "Appraisal for Mortgage Loan Purposes," *Encyclopedia of Real Estate Appraising,* Edith J. Friedman, ed. (Englewood Cliffs, N.J.: Prentice-Hall), 1959.
[2] Henry A. Babcock, *Real Estate Appraising and Loan Failure,* Henry A. Babcock, ed., NAREB, 1931.
[3] Richard U. Ratcliff, *Valuation for Real Estate Decisions* (Santa Cruz, CA: Democrat Press), 1972, 223.

[4] Nevin D. Baxter, "Leverage, Risk of Ruin, and the Cost of Capital," *The Journal of Finance,* September 1967.

debt service, then capitalizing that debt service by the loan constant.

$$ADS = \frac{NOI}{DSCR}$$

$$= \frac{\$100,000}{1.2}$$

$$= \$83,333$$

$$V_m = \frac{ADS}{R_m}$$

$$= \frac{\$83,333}{.1321}$$

$$= \$630,833$$

This loan will require $83,333 of debt service, which produces the DSCR of 1.2. The two steps can be combined as follows:

$$V_m = \frac{NOI}{(DSCR)(R_m)} \quad (1)$$

$$= \frac{\$100,000}{(1.2)(.1321)}$$

$$= \$630,835$$

Using the DSCR in a Discounted Cash Flow Model[5]

The DSCR, rather than the loan-to-value ratio, is used as the constraint on debt in discounted cash flow models as follows:

$$V = V_m + V_e$$

$$= \frac{NOI_1}{(DSCR)(R_m)} + \sum_{t=1}^{n} \frac{NOI_t - ADS_t}{(1+Y_e)^t}$$

$$+ \frac{[(1-CS)(1+g_v)^n(V)] - MB_n}{(1+Y_e)^n}$$

where NOI_1 is NOI in year one.[6]

---
[5]This section follows Kenneth M. Lusht and Jeffrey D. Fisher, "Anticipated Growth and the Specification of Debt in Real Estate Value Models," *AREUEA Journal* 12, no. 1, 1984.
[6]The DSCR can also be expressed as a function of the current year's NOI.

An Example

To illustrate the mechanics of the DSCR-based discounted cash flow model, assume the following property data:

First-year NOI:	$100,000
NOI growth rate (g_I):	4%
g_v:	3%
DSCR:	1.2
Y_m:	.125
Amortization:	20 years, monthly payments
R_m:	.1363
n:	5 years
Y_e:	15%
CS:	0

$$V = V_m + V_e$$

$$V_m = \frac{NOI}{(DSCR)(R_m)}$$

$$= \frac{\$100,000}{(1.2)(.1363)}$$

$$= \$611,396$$

From this, ADS

$$= (\$611,396)(.1363)$$

$$= \$83,333,$$

which is used to estimate BTCF.

$$V_e = \text{PV of BTCF} + \text{PV of BTER}$$
$$\text{PV of NOI} - \text{PV of ADS} + \text{PV of (NSP} - MB)$$

$$\text{PV of NOI} = NOI_1 \left[\frac{1 - \left(\frac{1+g_I}{1+Y_e}\right)^n}{Y_e - g_I} \right]$$

$$= \$100,000 \left[\frac{1 - \left(\frac{1+.04}{1+.15}\right)^5}{.15 - .04} \right]$$

$$= \$359,190$$

$$\text{PV of ADS} = \$83,333 (3.3522)$$

$$= \$279,349$$

The last step is to estimate PV of BTER.

$$PV \text{ of } BTER = (NSP - MB)(PV \text{ factor})$$

$$NSP = V(1 + g_v)$$
$$= V(1 + .03)^5$$
$$= V(1.1593)$$

$$MB = b(\$611,396)$$
$$= .9218(\$611,396)$$
$$= \$563,585$$

$$PV \text{ of } BTER = [1.1593(V) - \$563,585](.4972)$$
$$= .5764(V) - \$280,214$$

$$V = V_m + V_e$$
$$= \$611,396 + \$359,190 - \$279,349$$
$$+ .5764(V) - \$280,214$$
$$V = \$411,023 + .5764(V)$$
$$.4236(V) = \$411,023$$
$$V = \$970,309$$

This value is composed of $611,396 of debt (calculated in Step 1), and $358,913 of equity.

By constructing the cash flows that result from this valuation, its accuracy can be checked by making certain the resulting y_e is 15 percent.

	1	2	3	4	5
NOI	$100,000	$104,000	$108,160	$112,486	$116,986
ADS	83,333	83,333	83,333	83,333	83,333
BTCF	$16,667	$20,667	$24,827	$29,153	$33,653

$$BTER = NSP - MB$$
$$= \$970,309(1.03)^5 - \$563,585$$
$$= \$561,269$$

If the value estimate of $970,309 is correct, the cash flows to equity, when discounted at 15 percent, should equal the V_e of $358,913. They do.

Should the Appraiser Use the Loan-to-Value Ratio (m), or the DSCR to Constrain Debt?

The proper answer to any question concerning the relative merits of alternative models is to use the model that more closely simulates the behavior of the market. Choosing between the loan-to-value ratio and the debt service coverage ratio is no exception, with the key determinant the anticipated rate of growth in net operating income and property value.

As the anticipated growth rate increases, market value increases, and given some loan-to-value ratio, V_m also increases. This has the effect of pushing the *first-year DSCR* downward. In general, as the proportion of value traceable to growth increases, the current DSCR declines, and the probability of technical insolvency increases. The use of a minimum DSCR does not allow that to happen. During periods when income and values are expected to be more stable, the choice between the loan to value ratio and the DSCR becomes largely academic.

How Does the Market Behave? There is evidence that one important group of mortgage lenders relies heavily on the DSCR. Loan commitments from life insurance companies show a pattern of very stable DSCRs over time, including periods that were characterized by high rates of nominal growth. For example, the average DSCRs for loans made from 1971 through 1981 when inflation was at relatively high levels, were 1.29, 1.29, 1.29, 1.29, 1.33, 1.30, 1.32, 1.29, 1.26, 1.26, 1.30, 1.33, 1.27, and 1.24.[7]

Lusht and Fisher[8] calculated the implied growth rates for the 1971–1981 period using the traditional finance-explicit model, which constrains debt on the basis of the loan-to-value ratio. Table 18–4 shows their results, which compared actual growth rates to

---
[7] American Council of Life Insurance, *Quarterly Investment Bulletins,* Washington, D.C.
[8] Lusht and Fisher, "Anticipated Growth and the Specification of Debt in Real Estate Value Models" *AREUEA Journal.*

TABLE 18-4 Actual versus Simulated Growth Rates Using Traditional Value Models

Year	Actual Growth (Inflation) Rate	Simulated Growth Rate Using Traditional Value Model
1971	.043	−.015
1972	.033	−.019
1973	.062	0
1974	.109	.026
1975	.091	.012
1976	.058	−.003
1977	.065	.002
1978	.077	.019
1979	.113	.033
1980	.135	.046
1981	.103	.055

the growth rates implied by the traditional model, assuming a 5 percent real rate of return.

It is clear from Table 18-4 that during 1971–1981, loan amounts reflected much lower growth expectations than traditional models would imply. That is, given the stability in *DSCR*s during that period, it appears that expected growth was "counted" only to the point it did not violate the target *DSCR*.[9]

The degree to which the *DSCR* specification finds its way into appraisal practice will likely be a function of inflation expectations. As noted, when anticipated inflation is at relatively low levels, the empirical difference between the models is trivial. This explains why, despite support for the *DSCR* approach traceable at least to Babcock in 1931, it was widely ignored until a period when inflation became a valuation issue.

Finally, while the use of *DSCR*s has traditionally been associated with credit rationing by lenders, it can also be used to estimate investment values for equity investors.

---

[9]Some argue that there really isn't a difference in the two models; that by lowering the loan-to-value ratio in the traditional specification, the same result is achieved. This is true, but misses the point of modeling. If m is adjusted in response to changes in the anticipated growth, the question is why? If the answer is to protect the *DSCR*, then it is preferable to use a model that reflects that behavior directly.

CHAPTER 19
Residual Models: Land/Building and Leased Fee/Leasehold

Introduction

There are a number of situations that demand that total property value be separated into components. The finance-explicit model, for example, splits value into the financial components of debt and equity, where $V = V_m + V_E$. Two other commonly encountered separations of value are the subject of this chapter. They are the physical components of land and buildings, where $V = V_L + V_B$, and the contractual components created by a lease, where $V = V_{\text{Leased fee}} + V_{\text{Leasehold}}$. Separating value into land and building components may be necessary when those components are to be sold or leased separately, for property tax purposes where land and buildings are taxed at different rates, or to value land when insufficient data from comparable sales is available.

Fee simple is the name given to the complete bundle of ownership rights. When an owner leases a fee simple, the resulting interest is called a *leased fee*. The tenant's interest, which is possessory but not one of ownership, is called a leasehold interest. Separating value into its leased fee and leasehold components is quite common. Whenever a property is encumbered by a long-term lease, the ownership interest that is being valued is the leased fee. Separate values for the leased fee and leasehold interests may also be needed when selling or financing either interest, or when splitting a condemnation award.

Some clients routinely request separate valuations of land and buildings or leased fees and leaseholds regardless of the purpose of the appraisal. For example, Gibson's (1992) survey of real estate asset managers found that 29 percent of them always requested a separate valuation of land, and 17 percent always requested a separate valuation of leaseholds.[1]

---

[1] Robert Gibson, "Asset Managers' View of the Appraisal of Real Estate Assets," *Appraisal Journal,* January 1989.

The Building and Land Residual Techniques

From the $V = V_B + V_L$ definition, it is clear that the value of the building (or the land) can be estimated when (1) the value of the total property can be estimated using direct sales comparison or the income approach, and (2) the value of the land (or building) can be independently estimated by the direct sales comparison (for land) or cost (for the building) approaches. Thus, the building and land residual (or the physical residual) techniques are "hybrids," because they mix either the direct sales comparison and income approaches, or the cost and income approaches.

The terms *building* and *land residuals* come from the fact that the value of the unknown component is the residual value left when the value of the independently estimated component is subtracted from the estimated total value. Note the similarity to the finance-explicit model discussed previously, where the value of equity is estimated by discounting the residual cash flow after paying debt service (and the mortgage value at sale) to the lender. For that reason, the finance-explicit (or mortgage-equity) model is sometimes called the equity residual model.

An Example of Building Residual Valuation

An investor is considering the purchase of a building (but not its site) and wants an estimate of its value. First-year *NOI* from the entire property is expected to be $50,000, with a 3 percent increase per year. The property's value is expected to increase by 15 percent during the 5-year holding period. The discount rate, Y_o, is 15 percent. Assume there are no costs of sale.

First, the value of the whole property is estimated using the basic value model.

$$V = PV\ NOI + PV\ NSP$$

$$= \sum_{t=1}^{n} \frac{NOI_t}{(1 + Y_o)^t} + \frac{NSP_n}{(1 + Y_o)^n}$$

$$PV\ NOI = \$50,000 \left[\frac{1 - \left(\frac{1 + .03}{1 + .15}\right)^5}{.15 - .03} \right] + 1.15(V)(.4972)$$

$$V = \$412,226$$

Second, the value of the land is estimated using direct sales comparison. Assume the estimate is $112,000. From this, the value of the building is:

$$V = V_L + V_B$$

$$\$412,226 = \$112,000 + V_B$$

$$V_B = \$300,226,\ \text{say},\ \$300,000$$

The Same Example in Reverse: Land Residual Valuation

The same process is used to work from the value of the building to the value of the land. Using the example above to illustrate, suppose that the cost approach indicates the value of the building to be $300,226. All other estimates and inputs remain the same. Therefore $V_L = \$412,226 - \$300,226 = \$112,000$.

Basing the Analysis on Residual Income

The analysis above was based on residual *values:* total value and the value of one of the components (land or buildings) was estimated, with the value of the other component the difference (residual *value*) between the two.

It is also possible to value the unknown component based on residual *income* rather than residual value. To illustrate, return to our example property that is expected to produce first-year income of $50,000, growing at 3 percent per year, with expected appreciation of 15 percent over a 5-year holding period. The discount rate is 15 percent. Suppose it is the value of the land that is to be estimated, and that the building's cost, as before, has been estimated to be $300,000.

To use the residual income approach, the *NOI* necessary to produce the independently estimated building value of $300,000 must be calculated first. That income is then subtracted from total *NOI*, which produces the residual income conceptually attributable to the land value. That residual income is then discounted to estimate the value of the land. The sum of the known building value and the estimated land value is, of course, the estimated value of the total property.

The first-year *NOI* that is necessary to produce the $300,000 of building value is calculated using the basic value model, solving for *NOI*:

$$V_B = \sum_{t=1}^{n} \frac{NOI_t}{(1+Y_o)^t} + \frac{V_B(1+g_v)^n}{(1+Y_o)^n}$$

$$= NOI_1 \left[\frac{1 - \left(\frac{1+g_I}{1+Y_o}\right)^n}{Y_o - g_I} \right] + V_B(1 + \text{apprec.}) \left[\frac{1}{(1+Y_o)^n} \right]$$

$$\$300,000 = NOI_1 \left[\frac{1 - \left(\frac{1+.03}{1+.15}\right)^5}{.15-.03} \right] + \$300,000(1.15)\left[\frac{1}{(1+.15)^5}\right]$$

$$\$300,000 = NOI_1 (3.5303) + \$171,526$$

$$NOI_1 = \$36,392$$

The first-year residual *NOI* attributable to the land is therefore $50,000 − 36,392 = $13,608.

Now the value of the land can be estimated. Given the first-year *NOI* of $13,612, a 3 percent growth rate, and the assumption that the land will be worth 15 percent more in five years than today, land value is:

$$V_L = \$13{,}612 \left[\frac{1 - \left(\frac{1 + .03}{1 + .15}\right)^5}{.15 - .03} \right] + 1.15\,(V_L)\left[\frac{1}{(1 + .15)^5}\right]$$

$$V_L = \$13{,}612\,(3.5303) + .5718\,V_L$$

$$V_L = \$112{,}224 \text{ say, } \$112{,}000, \text{ and total value}$$

$$V = V_B + V_L = \$300{,}000 + \$112{,}000 = \$412{,}000$$

This, of course, agrees with the previous value estimate.

The Reason for the Income Residual Technique: Split Rates

If total market value can be estimated directly, the residual *value* approach can be used and the residual *income* technique (which is computationally more complex) is largely redundant. But if this is so, why is the residual *income* approach widely used? The answer is found in the use of different discount (or capitalization) rates for land and improvements. One rate of return is used to find the income necessary to support the value of the independently valued component, then a different rate is used to discount the residual income attributable to the unknown component.[2] Different rates are used when it is felt that there are different risks associated with the land and building components. When it is assumed that the risks are similar enough to warrant the same discount rate, the residual *income* approach, though conceptually equivalent to the residual value approach, adds complexity without substance.

A Conceptual Problem with the Land Residual Technique

There is a conceptual problem when using the land residual technique. It is best understood by example. Imagine two contiguous sites that are physically and functionally identical. The improvements on the two sites differ,

---

[2] It can also be argued that another reason for using the residual income approach is that the *values* of land and buildings may change at different rates. For example, land may be appreciating while the building is depreciating. This is correct but irrelevant to the discussion, because the value of the independently valued component will reflect whatever change in value the market anticipates.

however, producing total property values, of, say, $1 million and $750,000. Using the cost approach, suppose the improvements are valued at $400,000 and $300,000, respectively. Using the land residual technique, this results in estimated values for the land of $1 million − $400,000 = $600,000 and $750,000 − $300,000 = $450,000. Is there, in fact, a $150,000 difference in the values of the "identical" sites?

The answer is no, for as we learned in an earlier chapter, the value of a site is unaffected by its improvements. If there are adverse effects on value from under- or overdevelopment, those effects are properly reflected in the estimated value of the improvements, not the site. This being the case, great care must be taken when using the land residual technique to estimate market value. Only when the assumed use is the highest and best use (or reasonably close to it) will the process be conceptually correct.

Residual Analysis for Land Development

Land residual analysis is useful for estimating the *investment value* of land for development purposes, that is, to estimate the value of land in a given use. For example, assume that zoning allows 165 multifamily units and 53 single-family units on a 42-acre tract being considered for development. Market analysis suggests a selling price of $45,000 per improved single-family site and $5,700 per improved multifamily unit. The scheduled sellout is over three years, as follows.

Year 1:	12 single-family, 35 multifamily
Year 2:	30 single-family, 75 multifamily
Year 3:	11 single-family, 55 multifamily

Development costs are expected to be $13,200 per single-family site and $2,400 per multifamily unit. These costs will be incurred as follows:

Year 1:	60%
Year 2:	30%
Year 3:	10%

Other expenses will total $72,000 per year, plus 12 percent of yearly sales. If investors expect an 18 percent before-tax return, and the undeveloped land is selling for $23,000 per acre, what do you recommend?

The object is to find the difference between the value of the developed land and the costs of doing the developing. That difference is the residual value left to pay for the undeveloped land. This is then compared to the $23,000 asking price.

TABLE 19–1 Estimate of Annual Cash Flows

	Year 1	Year 2	Year 3
SF	12 ($45,000) = $540,000	30 ($45,000) = $1,350,000	11 ($45,000) = $495,000
MF	35 ($ 5,700) = 199,500	75 ($ 5,700) = 427,500	55 ($ 5,700) = 313,500
	$739,500	$1,777,550	$808,500
−Development costs*	$657,360	328,680	109,560
−Other expenses**	160,740	285,300	169,020
Net cash flow	($78,600)	$1,163,570	$529,920

*Total development costs are 53 ($13,200) + 165 ($2,400) = $1,095,600, which are allocated as follows: Year 1: .60 ($1,095,600) = $657,360; Year 2: .30 ($1,095,600) = $328,680; and Year 3: .10 ($1,095,600) = $109,560.

**Other Expenses: Year 1: $72,000 + .12 ($739,500) = $160,740
Year 2: $72,000 + .12 ($1,777,500) = $285,300
Year 3: $72,000 + .12 ($808,500) = $169,020

We begin by estimating the annual cash flows shown in Table 19–1.

When discounted at 18 percent, the present value of the annual cash flows is $1,091,573. This is the amount that can be spent on land and still produce the expected 18 percent return. Therefore, the developer can pay up to $1,091,573 ÷ 42 = $25,990 per acre. Given an asking price of $23,000 per acre, the net present value is positive. The development seems to make sense.[3]

Residual Analysis and Highest and Best Use

This kind of land development analysis is a direct application of the underlying premise of market value, which is that land value is a function of its highest and best use. In this case, the proposed development seems in line with the market's expectations, as the value of the land in the proposed development is close to its asking price.

On the other hand, if the analysis had indicated an investment value of, say, $40,000 per acre, this would look like a really good deal. Perhaps too good. Whenever you think you've found a free lunch, check your numbers and your assumptions. There are good deals out there, but it is a good bet that the market is right more often than not.

[3] Detailed treatments of valuing development projects are found in William L. Pittinger, "Time/Value Relationships in Development Projects," *The Real Estate Appraiser and Analyst,* Winter 1986, "Future Influences in Development Projects," *The Real Estate Appraiser and Analyst,* Summer 1987, and William Anglyn, Robert Moreya, and John Putman, "Subdivision Analysis–A Profit-Residual Model," *The Appraisal Journal,* January 1988.

Leased Fee/Leasehold Residual Techniques

Another common appraisal assignment that is amenable to solution using a residual value approach is to value either the lessor's interest (the leased fee) or lessee's interest (the leasehold). This request may come from a seller or a buyer of a leasehold or leased fee interest, or to allocate value, say, for an insurance claim or a condemnation settlement.

An Intuitive Explanation of Leasehold Value

Most people have no trouble with the idea that a leased fee ownership interest has a market value. In fact, a high percentage of income properties are leased, and in those cases, it is the leased fee that is typically appraised.[4]

On the other hand, the idea that there may be a market value for a tenant's rights (the leasehold) may seem strange. After all, it is the tenant who is paying the owner. Suppose, however, that the lease agreement calls for rents that are below the market level. In such a case, the rent "savings" have value to the tenant and represents a loss to the owner. The value of the rent savings to the tenant (and the rent loss to the owner) is the difference between what the value of the property would be if it was producing market rents and its value—the value of the leased fee—given that it is encumbered at below-market rents.[5]

Another way to gain insight into the idea that a leasehold interest can have a value is to consider that if the tenant can sublease at market rents, there will be a profit that is equal to the difference between the rent the tenant is collecting from the sublessee and what the tenant must pay the owner of the leased fee under their original lease. Alternatively, the tenant may offer to let the sublessor pay the original (below-market) rent, but in return, demand a lump-sum payment. In theory, this lump sum will be equal to the present value of the rent savings to the sublessor. From this comes an important conclusion: A leasehold has value to the tenant only when there is a difference between market and contract rent. When there is no difference, $V = V_{LF}$, and by definition, $V_{LH} = 0$.

Mechanically, the valuation of leased fees and leaseholds mirrors that of the valuation of all partial interests. From the definition $V = V_{LF} + V_{LH}$, when total value and either the leased fee or leasehold can be independently

---

[4]Which brings up the question of how a fee simple is differentiated from a leased fee. The term *leased fee* is ued to refer to relatively long (for example, more than one year) leases, as opposed to such things as apartment leases. This is because short-term leases turn over quickly, and any gaps between market rent and contract rents are found to be corrected quickly enough to have an insignificant impact on the value of the lessor's interest. However, when such rent gaps occur with a long-term lease, the value impact can be significant. In practice, then, the term *leased fee* refers to the long-term situation.

[5]Lease concessions may also produce a gap. See James D. Venor, "Comparative Lease Analysis Using a Discounted Cash Flow Approach," *The Appraisal Journal*, July 1988.

estimated, the difference between them must be the value of the unknown component.

An Example

A property is leased for a remaining term of 10 years. The tenant pays all operating expenses. First-year *NOI* is expected to be $200,000, with the lease requiring rent increases producing a 2 percent annual increase in *NOI*. Comparable properties are currently renting for $275,000 annually, with rents and values increasing at a rate of 3 percent per year. Investors expect a yield (Y_o) of 11 percent.[6] You are asked to value the leased fee and leasehold interests, assuming no costs of sale.

First, the property is valued as if it were generating market rents. Thus, we begin by estimating the V in the $V = V_{LF} + V_{LH}$ model:

$$V = PV\,NOI + PV\,NSP$$

$$= \$275{,}000 \left[\frac{1 - \left(\frac{1 + .03}{1 + .11}\right)^{10}}{.11 - .03} \right] + V(1 + .03)^{10}\,(.3522)$$

$$V = \$3{,}437{,}474$$

Second, the leased fee is valued based on the contract rent rather than the market rent. Using the basic value model:

$$V_{LF} = PV\,NOI_{LF} + PV\,NSP$$

$$= \$200{,}000 \left[\frac{1 - \left(\frac{1 + .02}{1 + .11}\right)^{10}}{.11 - .02} \right] + \$3{,}437{,}474\,(1 + .03)^{10}\,(.3522)$$

$$V_{LF} = \$2{,}895{,}251$$

Notice that the sale proceeds are estimated based on the current market value estimated above, because when the lease expires it is assumed the property will bring market rents. Thus, the selling price after 10 years will be $3,437,474 $(1 + .03)^{10}$ = $4,619,678.

Given the value estimates made above, V_{LH} = $3,437,474 − $2,895,251 = $542,223. This value may also be estimated by taking the present value of the savings in rent. The annual savings start at $275,000 − $200,000 = $75,000 the first year, and increase slightly each year due to the difference

---

[6]Finance-explicit valuation of leased fees and leasehold interests is covered in the chapter Appendix.

between the market (3 percent) and actual (2 percent) rates of rental increase. These savings have a present value of $542,223 when discounted at 11 percent.

The Use of Split Rates

In the example above, the same discount rate (11 percent) was used to value the fee simple and the leased fee. It can be argued, however, that the discount rate applied to a leased fee at nonmarket rents should be different than the discount rate applied to a fee encumbered at market rents, because: (1) if the contract rent is below market, it is less likely the lessee will break (or attempt to break) the lease, and therefore the risk (and discount rate) should be lower, or (2) if the contract rent is above market, there is a greater chance that the lessee will attempt to break the lease, and the risk (and discount rate) should be higher.

For example, if the risk of the leased fee in the example above was judged to merit, say, a 10 percent rate of return[7] rather than an 11 percent rate of return, its value would have been higher and the residual value of the leasehold would have been lower.

One practical problem with the use of different rates for valuing rents depending on whether they are above, equal to, or below market is that there is little evidence that market participants behave that way, and therefore, there is little evidence on the magnitudes of any such differences.

When different rates are used, there is an important *caveat:* make sure the resulting valuation is internally consistent. If care isn't taken, the following can happen. Assume you are valuing a perpetual flow of net rent at the market level of $10,000, using a discount rate of 10 percent. This gives a market value of the fee simple of $100,000. Suppose now that the fee is leased in perpetuity at a net rent of $9,000, and the appraiser chooses a discount rate of, say, 9 percent. This gives a value of the leased fee of $100,000. This is the same as the value estimated at market rents, and the resulting leasehold value must be zero. Similarly, an $11,000 contract rent discounted at 11 percent also produces a value of $100,000, again with no leasehold value. This would suggest that the lessor (and the lessee) is indifferent between collecting $11,000, $10,000, and $9,000 in net rent, and that

---

[7]This rate was chosen arbitrarily, but in practice, it must be a weighted average of the 11 percent rate applied to that portion of contract rent that represents market rent, and a lower rate applied to the *difference between the market and contract rents.* Distinguishing between the two streams of income is important because *if* a tenant who is paying above-market rents becomes unhappy, the owner may consider an adjustment to the market rent level in order to keep the tenant happy. Similarly, an upward adjustment (to the market) can be agreed to by a tenant in order to appease an unhappy landloard, though this is less likely.

below- and above-market rents produce no leasehold value. This is an illogical result. The correct discount rate for the below-market rent in this case must fall *between* 9–10%. The floor (or ceiling, for above-market rents) under the discount rate can be calculated for any situation by finding the rate which produces the same value as the unencumbered fee. In this simple case the rate floor is

$$\frac{\$9,000}{\$100,000} = 9\%.$$

If a discounted cash flow model is used, solve for the *IRR*. The same is true for above market rents. In this case the ceiling is

$$\frac{\$11,000}{\$100,000} = 11\%,$$

and the correct rate must be between 10–11%. If, for example, the selected rate is 9.5 percent for the $9,000 rent, the value of the leased fee is

$$\frac{\$9,000}{.095} = \$94,737,$$

leaving a residual leasehold value of $100,000 − $94,737 = $5,263.

Sandwich Leases

Tenants sometimes sublease their interest, and as a result, an appraisal assignment may be complicated by a request to value three interests: the fee simple, the leased fee (the original leasehold), and the subleasehold. The original lessee is now both a tenant and a landlord, and his or her interest is commonly referred to as the "sandwich" position.

Suppose a property would have a fee simple market value of $75,000. It was net leased 10 years ago for $50,000 annually for 30 years. The tenant has subleased for $75,000, and there are 20 years remaining on the sublease. The remaining economic life of the improvement is 20 years, and the site is expected to have a value of $1,000,000 at that time. Market evidence suggests that a 10 percent discount rate is applicable to the leased fee, and a 12 percent discount rate is applicable to the "sandwich" interest. Assume that the reversion should be discounted at 11 percent.

$$V_{LF} = V_{Rent} + V_{Reversion}$$

$$= \$50,000 \text{ for 20 yrs. at } 10\% + \$1,000,000 \text{ after 20 yrs. at } 11\%$$

$$= \$425,678 + \$124,034$$

$$= \$550,000 \text{ (rounded)}$$

The value of the sandwich interest is the present value of $25,000 per year ($75,000 − $50,000), discounted at 12 percent, which equals $187,000 (rounded).

The value of the subleasehold by definition should equal $V - (V_{\text{leased fee}} + V_{\text{sandwich}}) = \$700{,}000 - (\$550{,}000 + \$187{,}000) = (\$37{,}000)$. The negative value indicates the sublessee is paying above market rents.

Notice that the relationship among the discount rates is logical. The 10 percent rate for the leased fee is below the 11 percent rate for the reversion because the current $50,000 rent is below market, but at reversion, the lease will have expired and the property will again command market rents. The 12 percent rate on the sandwich interest reflects the higher risk associated with what the negative subleasehold value indicates is an above-market rent being paid by the sublessee.

Lease Options

Some leases contain option clauses allowing the lessee to renew the lease after the current term expires. There may be several options; for example, an original term of 10 years plus two renewal options for 10 years and 5 years, respectively. It is also common for rent and other terms of the lease to change as each option is exercised.

This presents a valuation problem because unless the lease calls for contract rent that is in some way indexed to market rent, the estimate of the current value of the leased fee will be a function of whether the option(s) will be exercised, and it is not known at the time of the appraisal whether that will happen.

One solution to the problem is based on estimating the probability of the option(s) being exercised, with the resulting value estimate a weighted average of the possible outcomes. For example, suppose that a ground lease has five years remaining and that annual rent is $10,000, paid in arrears (at the end of the year). The tenant pays all operating expenses. There is an option to renew the lease for an additional five years at $12,500. Current market rent is $11,000, and it has been increasing at a rate of 4 percent per year. The discount rate is 10 percent.

If the option is *not* exercised, the value of the leased fee is the value of the $10,000 annuity for five years, plus the value of a perpetuity beginning in year six. Mechanically, it is easiest to treat the annuity as a growing perpetuity beginning in year 1, then subtracting the value of years 1–5.

$$V_{LF} = \$10{,}000\,(3.7908) + \frac{\$11{,}440}{.10 - .04} - \left[\frac{1 - \left(\frac{1+.04}{1+.10}\right)^5}{.10 - .04}\right](\$11{,}440)$$

$$= \$181{,}947$$

If the option for years 6–10 *is* exercised, the value of the leased fee is:

$$V_{LF} = \$10{,}000\ (3.7908) + \$12{,}500\ (6.1446 - 3.7908) +$$

$$\frac{\$11{,}440}{.10 - .04} - \left[\frac{1 - \left(\frac{1 + .04}{1 + .10}\right)^{10}}{10 - .04}\right](11{,}440)$$

$$= \$176{,}144$$

In this case, the value of the leased fee is higher if the option is not exercised, because the $12,500 rent at renewal is lower than the market rent is expected to be at that time. The market rent beginning in year 6 is expected to be $11,000 $(1 + .04)^5 = \$13{,}383$.

Suppose now that you assign an 80 percent probability that the option will be exercised. Based on this probability,

$$V_{LF} = .80\ (\$176{,}144) + .20\ (\$181{,}947)$$

$$= \$177{,}305$$

The probabilities assigned to the renewal option(s) are based on the appraiser's judgment, ideally supported by an interview with the tenant(s) to get a feel for the probabilities. Such interviews are more useful as the option date approaches and the tenant has begun to think seriously about the future. If the tenant is not helpful, the appraiser's judgment logically should be based on the relationship between expected market rents and the contract rent at the time the option must be exercised. If market rent is expected to be significantly higher than the contract rent for the option period, the probability the option will be exercised is much higher than if the reverse is expected. In fact, a strong argument could be made that a below-market rent is almost certain to be exercised (producing a 100 percent weighting), while an above-market rent is almost certain not to be exercised. When future rent is tied to market rent, of course, the issue is moot. For the example above, if it is assumed the option is certain to be exercised because $12,500 is well below the expected 6th year rent of $13,383, V_{LF} would be $176,144.

It is also possible there will be more than one option period. That simply extends the string of arithmetic. Remember, however, that as the options extend farther into the future, the discounting process shrinks differences in absolute dollar amounts. Moreover, while there may be cases (like the Empire State Building, which has a declining rent schedule over a lengthy lease period exceeding 100 years) when it is necessary to reflect the almost certain exercise of the option, most modern leases contain some sort of escalation clause. Going beyond one or two option periods in such cases is not likely to be productive, because (1) it is almost impossible to forecast the relationship between contract and market rents that far in the future, and (2) any differences at that point are likely to have a trivial effect on present value.

Does V always = $V_{LF} + V_{LH}$?

The V in the $V = V_{LF} + V_{LH}$ definition is traditionally defined in terms of the fee simple encumbered at market rents. A remaining question is whether those market rents refer to the highest and best use of the property, or to the current use of the property?

The standard assumption is that it is the highest and best use that determines V, and in most cases, that assumption is consistent with the $V = V_{LF} + V_{LH}$ equality. There is one kind of exception, however, and that is when the lease agreement, perhaps written years ago, effectively prevents the current highest and best use. In other words, the lease has extinguished a valuable right.

Suppose, for example, that the *current* highest and best use would produce annual rent of $1, but that the contract rent is $.50. Using a capitalization rate of 10 percent for both the fee simple and leased fee, $V = \$10$ and $V_{LF} = \$5$. According to the $V = V_{LF} + V_{LH}$ equality, V_{LH} must therefore also equal $5. That will be so, however, only if the current highest and best use is allowable under the terms of the lease. If it is not, then V_{LH} will depend on the relationship of the contract rent in the current use, and the rent that could be obtained in the most profitable *allowable* use. If, for example, the best *allowable* use commands a market rent of $.75, then $V_{LH} = \$2.50$, and $V_{LF} + V_{LH} = \$7.50$ rather than $10.

In sum, if the lease extinguishes a valuable property right, the $V = V_{LF} + V_{LH}$ equality will hold only if V is defined in terms of market rent at the best use *allowed* by the lease rather than the highest and best use as determined by the market. We have then the possibility that the value of the sum of the parts may or may not equal the value of the whole, depending on how the whole is defined.

Other Considerations

The leased fee/leasehold residual approach can be applied differently than it was described above. Specifically, the values of the leased fee and the leasehold can be estimated independently, then added to estimate the value of the unencumbered fee. Though this is a conceptually sound approach, it is difficult to find a motivation for using it unless there is reason to believe that the value of the sum of the parts is different than the value of the whole.

Some final considerations in leased fee-leasehold valuation are as follows. First, it is net operating income, and not gross income, that is the proper figure to use in estimating the value of a leased fee. Second, the traditional discounting of leased fee-leasehold rents on a monthly instead of yearly basis is arbitrary. Properties like apartments and offices also produce monthly income, but for analysis purposes their cash flows are discounted annually. There seems no reason to make an exception in the case of leased fees and leaseholds, given that the only difference between what are called "leased fees" and properties like apartments is the typical lengths of the leases. This institutional difference does not affect the timing of cash flows, and if annual discounting is sufficient for other purposes, it should be sufficient for leased fees. However, that is not standard practice. Third, some leases call for payments at the beginning rather than the end of the period. This may have a significant effect on value and should be incorporated.

Your calculator is likely equipped to handle beginning of period payments. If not, calculate the present value as if the payments were at the end of the period, then adjust that value by multiplying it by $(1 + Y)$, where Y is the discount rate. For example, if a lease calls for annual rent of $10,000 in perpetuity, paid in arrears, the value of the leased fee at a 10 percent discount rate is

$$\frac{\$10,000}{.10} = \$100,000.$$

If the rent is to be paid in advance, the value is $100,000 (1.10) = $110,000.

Summary

Total value must often be separated into either physical components or contractual components. In general, the solutions to these valuation problems have in common a reliance on the value additivity rule; that is, the value of the whole is equal to the value of its parts:

$$V = V_L + V_B = V_{LF} + V_{LH}$$

Thus, in order to solve for either land or building value, or leased fee or leasehold value, the other two parts of the formula must be estimated.

In the case of land or buildings, the value of one component is estimated using either the direct sales comparison approach (for land) or the cost approach (for buildings). Total value is estimated by the income approach, and the value of the unknown is the residual value found by subtracting the value of the known component from total value.

The same process works for valuing leaseholds. The values of the leased fee and the fee encumbered at market rents are estimated using standard discounted cash flow models, with the difference between them the residual value of the leasehold interest held by the tenant.

Market value can also be estimated by valuing the components separately and then adding them together. The problem with this approach is not with the theory, but rather that it requires discount rates for components of value that are generally more difficult to estimate than are discount rates for properties as a whole. Moreover, if it is possible to value components separately, it is possible (and likely easier) to value the whole.

The land and building residual approaches have several applications. The most common application is for use in the cost approach. Others are when only one component is to be bought or leased, or where a taxing jurisdiction requires the separation of land and building values. Residual analysis can also be used to estimate an investment value for land to be used for development purposes. Leasehold residual analysis is used for insurance claims and condemnation cases, and increasingly for the splitting of rights for sale (or lease) to various investment clienteles.

Questions and Problems

1. A warehouse is expected to produce $21,500 income the first year. There is a 3 percent annual rent escalation and the tenant pays all expenses. Comparable properties are renting for $19,000 the first year, with 3 percent escalations. The property is expected to appreciate at a rate of 2 percent per year over the remaining lease term of 4 years. Investors expect a 12 percent return.
   a. Value the leased fee.
   b. Value the leasehold.

2. a. What is the argument for using split rates; that is, a different discount rate for the leased fee than for the fee encumbered at market?
   b. What is the difficulty associated with using split rates for fee simples and leased fees?
   c. If you use different rates for fee simple and leased fee interests, what practical constraints are there on the selection of a rate for the leased fee?

3. A 100-acre tract is being considered for development as an industrial park. Sixty percent of the front-end site clearance costs of $1,500 per gross acre will be incurred in year 1, the balance in year 2. Other development costs of $1,600 per gross acre will be incurred as follows: year 1 = 40 percent, year 2 = 30 percent, year 3 = 20 percent, and year 4 = 10 percent. Fixed administrative expenses will be $20,500 per year, and 15 percent of sales will be spent for promotion and selling costs. Fifteen percent of the gross acreage will be set aside for public use, like roads, open space, schools, and church sites.

   Forecasted sales over a projected six-year sell-out are as follows:

Year	
1	5 acres at $18,000/acre
2	5 acres at $18,000/acre
3	20 acres at $22,500/acre
4	25 acres at $25,000/acre
5	20 acres at $25,000/acre
6	10 acres at $17,000/acre

   If a developer expects a 17 percent return, what is the maximum amount that can be paid per acre?

4. The contract rent for the forthcoming year on a leased fee is $26,500, paid in arrears, with a 2.5 percent annual escalation. The tenant pays all expenses. The lease expires in 7 years, but there is an option period of 10 years, with initial rent of $30,000 escalating at a rate of 2 percent per year. The tenant would continue to pay all expenses. The current rent is below market and the rent for the option period is also expected to be below market. At market rents, the value of the leased fee would be $275,000. Property values are expected to increase at a rate of 2 percent per year. The discount rate, Y_o, is 15 percent.

   Value the leased fee, making (and explaining) any necessary assumptions.

5. A fee simple interest encumbered at market rents is often referred to as an unencumbered fee. Comment.

6. The value additivity rule suggests that $V = V_{LF} + V_{LH}$. Define V.

7. Explain how a leasehold can have a negative value.

*Problems 8 and 9 are based on the material in the chapter Appendix.

8. A property is expected to produce $70,000 of rent next year and has 7 years left on the current lease. There is a 4 percent rent escalator in the lease. Comparable properties are (net) leasing for $82,500 the first year, with a 3 percent escalator. Expectations are for 4 percent annual increases in property value over the remaining term of the lease. Typical financing is 75 percent debt, at 13½ percent interest amortized over 15 years with monthly payments. Equity investors in this type property expect a 16 percent before-tax rate of return.
   a. Estimate the value of the fee encumbered at market.
   b. Estimate the value of the leasehold interest.

9. A property is being condemned. It is a 128-unit apartment, with first-year monthly rents expected to be $470 per unit. Vacancy is expected to be 4 percent, with operating expenses at 38 percent of effective gross income. Rents, expenses, and values are expected to decline by 2 percent per year over a projected holding period of 8 years. Typical financing is 70 percent debt, at 14 percent for 15 years with monthly payments. Equity investors expect a 17 percent before-tax rate of return. You have used the cost approach to value the buildings at $2,000,000.
   a. Forecast first-year *NOI*.
   b. Estimate the value of the land.
   c. Do you think your estimate of land value equals its market value? Why or why not?

APPENDIX
USING A FINANCE-EXPLICIT MODEL FOR RESIDUAL VALUATION

In the body of the chapter, value was separated into components without explicit consideration of financing. However, many valuation reports include a finance-explicit model. This appendix demonstrates the use of the finance-explicit model for residual analysis.

An Example of Finance-Explicit Land Residual Valuation

An investor is considering the purchase-leaseback of the land under an existing building and wants an estimate of its value. First-year *NOI* is forecast to be $100,000 and is expected to increase by 3 percent per year over 10 years. Typical terms of debt are 13 percent interest, amortized monthly over 15 years, with a 75 percent loan-to-value ratio. Equity investors expect a 15 percent before-tax yield. The property's value is expected to increase by 25 percent over a 10-year holding period.

Step 1: Estimate the value of a 100 percent interest in the fee simple, using the finance-explicit value model:

$$V = V_m + V_e$$

$$= .75\,(V) + \$100{,}000 \left[\frac{1 - \left(\frac{1 + .03}{1 + .15}\right)^{10}}{.15 - .03} \right]$$

$$- [.75\,(V)\,(.1518)]\,(5.019)$$
$$+ [1.25\,(V) - (.75)\,(V)\,(.5561)]\,(.2472)$$

$$V = \$904{,}149$$

Step 2: Estimate the value of the building using the cost approach. Assume the estimate is $500,000.

Step 3: Estimate the value of the land. This is straightforward. Because $V = V_B + V_L$, and we have estimated V and V_B, we can easily solve for the *residual* value, V_L.

$$\$904{,}149 = \$500{,}000 + V_L$$

$$V_L = \$404{,}149$$

The Same Problem in Reverse: Building Residual Valuation. The same process is used to work from the value of the land to the value of the building. Using the same property to illustrate, suppose that by direct sales comparison, the value of the land had been estimated to be $404,149. All other inputs remain the same. Therefore, $V = \$904{,}149$, and $V_B = \$904{,}149 - \$404{,}149 = \$500{,}000$.

An Example of Finance-Explicit Leased Fee-Leasehold Valuation

A warehouse is currently leased for a remaining term of 10 years at an annual rent of $20,000. The lessor is obligated to pay the first $2,500 in operating expenses, with the lessee paying the balance.

First-year market rent would be $30,000, with a 3 percent yearly graduation and with the lessee paying all operating expenses. A market survey suggests a 5 percent vacancy rate for similar properties. The property is expected to appreciate at a rate of 3 percent per year.

Typical financing is 70 percent debt, at 13 percent interest with a 15-year amortization. Equity investors expect a 15 percent return. The lessee, who is considering subleasing to a third party, asks you to value his or her leasehold interest.

Step 1: Value the fee encumbered at market rent.

Gross rent year 1 =	$30,900
Vacancy (.05)	1,545
EGI	$29,355
Operating expenses (net lease, paid by lessee)	-0-
NOI	$29,355

Using the finance-explicit model, we have

$$V = V_m + V_e$$

$$= .70\,(V) + \$29{,}355 \left(\frac{1 - \left(\frac{1+.03}{1+.15}\right)^{10}}{.15 - .03} \right)$$

$$-\, .70\,(V)\,(.1518)\,(5.0188)$$

$$+\, \frac{V(1+.03)^{10} - .70\,(V)\,(.5561)}{(1+.15)^{10}}$$

$$V = \$273{,}500$$

Step 2: Value the leased fee using the same model. Because rent does not escalate, NOI can be treated as an annuity. Also, because the lease will have expired at the end of the projection period, the forecasted selling price will be at the market. Based on the valuation of the fee encumbered at market rent, the selling price will be $273{,}500\,(1+.03)^{10}$ = \$367,561$.

$$V_{LF} = V_m + V_e$$

$$= .70\,(V_{LF}) + PV\text{ of }NOI$$
$$-\, PV\text{ of }ADS + PV\text{ of }BTER$$

$$= .70\,V_{LF} + (\$20{,}000 - \$2{,}500)\,(5.0188)$$
$$-\, .70\,(V_{LF})\,(.1518)\,(5.0188)$$
$$+\, [\$367{,}561 - .70\,(V_{LF})\,(.5561)]\,(.2472)$$

$$V_{LF} = \$192{,}246$$

Step 3: By definition, the value of the leasehold must be the difference (the residual value) between the values of the unencumbered and leased fees.

$$V_{LH} = V - V_{LF}$$

$$= \$273{,}500 - \$192{,}246$$

$$= \$81{,}254$$

CHAPTER 20

Discounted Cash Flow Model Shortcuts

Introduction

In some situations, the anticipated pattern of cash flows may lend itself to a mathematical shortcut to arrive at a value estimate. A few shortcuts have already been covered; the models used to value level perpetuities, growing perpetuities, and annuities over a finite life. In this chapter they will be reviewed and then other shortcuts will be introduced.

Level Perpetuities

A level income stream expected to be received in perpetuity can be valued by using the discount rate to capitalize annual income, as in Equation (1).

$$V = \frac{NOI}{Y_o} \quad (1)$$

For example, a property expected to produce $10,000 income each year, given a discount rate of 10 percent, has a value of

$$V = \frac{\$10,000}{.10}$$

$$= \$100,000$$

Growing Perpetuity

A perpetuity expected to grow at a constant rate can be valued with a simple adjustment to Equation (1) as follows:

$$V = \frac{NOI_1}{Y_o - g_I} \quad (2)$$

Where g_I is the annual rate of income growth.

For example, a property expected to produce $10,000 income the first year, with a 3 percent annual rate of growth and a discount rate of 10 percent, has a value of

$$V = \frac{\$10,000}{.10 - .03} \tag{3}$$

$$= \$142,857$$

When using Equation (3), it is necessary that $Y > g$.

While the finite life of real estate improvements argues against an assumption that income will be perpetual, recall that (1) if land value is increasing while the improvements are depreciating, a perpetual income stream may in fact be generated, and (2) when the forecasted rates of growth for income and value over the holding period are equal, there is a de facto valuation of a perpetuity.

Annuity With a Finite Life

A stream of income to be received over a given number of years and expected to grow at a constant rate can be valued as follows:

$$V = NOI_1 \left[\frac{1 - \left(\frac{1 + g_I}{1 + Y_o}\right)^n}{Y_o - g_I} \right] \tag{4}$$

For example, a stream of income beginning at $10,000 and growing at an annual rate of 3 percent for 10 years, with a discount rate of 10 percent, is valued as follows:

$$V = \$10,000 \left[\frac{1 - \left(\frac{1 + .03}{1 + .10}\right)^{10}}{.10 - .03} \right] \tag{5}$$

$$= \$68,837$$

In order to arrive at the value of the property, the value of the reversion is added to this value of the income stream.

A Perpetuity with an Escalation Clause

Because income received far in the future typically adds only a trivial amount to present value, we know that long-term income streams can be valued as if they were a perpetuity.

This fact can help us quickly value a stream of income that is expected to increase periodically, a common situation when a property is encumbered with a long-term clause. The overall rate in such a case is:

$$R_o = Y - Y\left[\frac{(1 + g_I)^t - 1}{(1 + Y)^t - 1}\right]$$

where

Y is the expected yield (discount rate)
g_I is the annual growth in rent
t is the time period (number of years) *between* income change

For example, suppose a property is leased at a first-year rent of $100,000 per year. Market rents are expected to increase by 4 percent per year, but the rent under the lease is to be adjusted to market only every 3 years. A 12 percent yield is expected. What is being valued in this case is an income stream that looks like this:

1	2	3	4	5	6	7
100,000	100,000	100,000	112,486*	112,486	112,486	126,532

*$100,000 (1 + .04)^3$

$$R_o = .12 - .12\left[\frac{(1 + .04)^3 - 1}{(1 + .12)^3 - 1}\right]$$

$$= .083$$

$$V = \frac{NOI_1}{R_o}$$

$$= \frac{\$100,000}{.083}$$

$$= \$1,204,819$$

The model assumes end-of-period income. If beginning-of-period income is to be valued, the end-of-period value is simply multiplied by one plus the discount rate. For the example problem above,

$$V = \$1,204,819 \, (1.12) = \$1,349,397$$

"Ellwood"

In 1959, before electronic calculators and widely available computer technology, L. W. Ellwood[1] made the use of the finance-explicit discounted cash

---

[1] L. W. Ellwood, *Ellwood Tables for Real Estate Appraising and Financing*, (Ridgewood, N.J.: L. W. Ellwood), 1959.

flow model practical for the appraiser by precomputing various components of the model so that value could be estimated in a reasonable amount of time with some hope of arithmetic accuracy. Charles Akerson[2] subsequently rearranged Ellwood's model to simplify the arithmetic and make it a bit more intuitive. We will use Akerson's approach to do the calculations in this chapter.

Ellwood/Akerson comes in three packages, the choice of which is dependent on the expected pattern of cash flow and value change. These are the three possibilities:

1. Both annual income and the property value are expected to remain the same during the projected holding period.
2. Annual income is expected to remain the same, but the property value is expected to change over the holding period. (This can occur, for example, when the property is encumbered by a lease at a fixed rental.)
3. Both income and value are expected to change during the holding period.

Regardless of which of the three combinations of income and value change is being valued, the Ellwood model algebraically calculates the overall capitalization rate, R_o, which, as always, is divided into *NOI* to estimate value. The following sections show how the overall capitalization rate is calculated for each of the three combinations of income and value change.[3]

When Income and Value Remain the Same

When both income and the property's value are expected to remain level over the holding period, Akerson's variation of the Ellwood model looks like this:

$$V = \frac{NOI}{R_o}$$

where

$$R_o = (m)(R_m) + (1 - m)(Y_e) - (m)(p)\left(\frac{1}{s_{\overline{n}|}}\right)$$

The first two terms on the right side produce the weighted average of the expected returns to debt and equity. The symbols are already familiar.

---

[2] Charles Akerson, "Ellwood Without Algebra," *The Appraisal Journal,* July 1970.
[3] A detailed analysis of Ellwood's variations is found in Robert J. Martin's, "Ellwood: The Language of Appraisers," *The Real Estate Appraiser and Analyst,* Summer 1981, and Joseph S. Fiore and Paul J. Knepp, "Mortgage-Equity Capitalization," Parts I and II, *The Real Estate Appraiser and Analyst,* Winter 1983, and Spring 1984.

The third term on the right side adjusts the capitalization rate for the effects of mortgage amortization. Two of the symbols in the third term are new: p is the percentage of the debt that will be paid during the projected holding period, and $\frac{1}{s_{\overline{n}|}}$ is the sinking fund factor. You already know how to calculate b, the percentage of the loan outstanding. Therefore, p, the percentage of the loan that has been paid, is simply $1 - b$.

The sinking fund factor, $1/s_{\overline{n}|}$, tells what proportion of a target amount of funds must be set aside in a "sinking fund" each period so that, when compounded at the given interest rate (in this case, Y_e), it will accumulate to the target amount. The sinking fund factor $= i/[1 + i^n - 1]$. Thus, to produce $1 in 5 years, assuming a 6 percent interest rate and end-of-year payments, the required annual deposit into the sinking fund would be $.06/[(1 + .06)^5 - 1]$. If $5,000 was the target, the annual deposit would be $.1774 \times \$5,000 = \$887$.

Using Ellwood: An Example

Assume a property is expected to produce $100,000 of *NOI* each year, with no change in the property's value over a 10-year holding period. The equity yield rate, Y_e, is .15. Debt is available at .13, with a 20-year monthly amortization ($R_m = .1406$) and a 75 percent loan-to-value ratio.

$$V = \frac{NOI}{R_o}$$

$$R_o = (m)(R_m) + (1 - m)(Y_e) - (m)(p)\left(\frac{1}{s_{\overline{n}|}}\right)$$

$$= (.75)(.1406) + (.25)(.15) - (.75)(.2153)(.0493)$$

$$= .1350$$

$$V = \frac{NOI}{R_o}$$

$$V = \frac{\$100,000}{.1350}$$

$$= \$740,741$$

This estimate is shown to be arithmetically correct by constructing the resulting cash flows, and testing whether the yield to equity is 15 percent.

$$V_m = .75(\$740{,}741) = \$555{,}556$$

$$V_e = .25(\$740{,}741) = \$185{,}185$$

$$ADS = .1406(\$555{,}556) = \$78{,}111$$

$$BTCF = \$100{,}000 - \$78{,}111 = \$21{,}889$$

$$BTER = \$740{,}741 - .7847(\$555{,}556) = \$304{,}796$$

An equity investment of $185,185, followed by *BTCF* of $21,889 for 10 years, plus a *BTER* of $304,796, produces a yield (*IRR*) of 15 percent. The value estimate is correct.

When Annual Income Remains the Same, but Property Value Changes

Suppose the $100,000 of *NOI* in the example above is the rent from a net lease which requires the tenant to pay all operating expenses. The lease will expire after 10 years. It is expected that market rents at that time will be above the $100,000 contract rent, by an amount sufficient to make the property's value 25 percent higher than it is today. The Ellwood model with value change becomes:

$$V = \frac{NOI}{R_o}$$

with $R_o = R_o$ as calculated above for no change in value $- (\Delta_o)\left(\dfrac{1}{s_{\overline{n}|}}\right)$

$$= (m)(R_m) + (1 - m)(Y_e) - (m)(p)\left(\frac{1}{s_{\overline{n}|}}\right) - (\Delta_o)\left(\frac{1}{s_{\overline{n}|}}\right)$$

where Δ_o = the percentage change in property value during the holding period.

The value of the example property, assuming 25 percent appreciation over 10 years, is:

$$V = \frac{\$100{,}000}{.1350 - (.25 \times .0493)}$$

$$= \frac{\$100{,}000}{.1227}$$

$$= \$814{,}996$$

Again, the demonstration of mathematical accuracy:

$$V_m = .75\ (\$814{,}996) = \$611{,}247$$
$$V_e = \$203{,}749$$
$$ADS = .1406\ (\$611{,}247) = \$85{,}941$$
$$BTCF = \$100{,}000 - \$85{,}941 = \$14{,}059$$
$$BTER = \$814{,}996\ (1.25) - .7847\ (\$611{,}247) = \$539{,}099$$

An equity investment of \$203,749, followed by $BTCF$ of \$14,059 for 10 years, plus $BTER$ of \$539,099, produces a yield of 15 percent. The value estimate is correct.

Changes in Both Income and Property

Except for net leased properties, both income and property value are likely to change over the holding period of most investments. Ellwood devised what he called a J factor to adjust the capitalization rate for income that changes according to a curvilinear pattern.[4]

Jeffrey Fisher[5] suggested an alternative G factor which uses the familiar model to value an income stream increasing at a given rate, g_I, then adjusts it by an annuity factor so that it can be used to develop the overall capitalization rate. Fisher's G factor is:

$$G = \left[\frac{1 - \left(\frac{1 + g_I}{1 + Y_e}\right)^n}{Y_e - g_I} \right] \div a_{\overline{n}|}$$

Where $a_{\overline{n}|}$ is the annuity factor for n years at a discount rate of Y_e. The value model now becomes

$$V = \frac{NOI}{R_o}$$

where

$$R_o = \frac{(m)(R_m) + (1 - m)(Y_e) - (m)(p)\left(\frac{1}{s_{\overline{n}|}}\right) - (\Delta_o)\left(\frac{1}{s_{\overline{n}|}}\right)}{G}$$

---

[4] The pattern of income change implied by the Ellwood J factor is a complex function which depends on the equity yield rate.

[5] Fisher, Jeffrey D., "Ellwood J Factors: A Further Refinement," *Appraisal Journal* (January 1979).

Notice that the numerator of the R_o calculation is exactly what was developed earlier; that is, the capitalization rate adjusted by the terms which reflect the expected change in property value.

Suppose now that the *NOI* for the example property is expected to be $100,000 the first year, then to increase at a rate of 3 percent per year through year 10. Property value is still expected to increase by a total of 25 percent over the 10-year holding period.

$$V = \frac{\$100,000}{R_o}$$

$$R_o = \frac{.1227 \text{ (the previous example)}}{\left[\dfrac{1 - \left(\dfrac{1+.03}{1+.15}\right)^{10}}{.15-.03}\right] \div 5.0188}$$

$$= \frac{.1227}{5.5650 \div 5.0188}$$

$$= .1107$$

$$V = \frac{\$100,000}{.1107}$$

$$= \$903,342$$

Once more, we demonstrate the estimate is correct.
In this case, the increasing NOI produces increasing BTCF.

$$V_m = .75 \, (\$903,342) = \$677,507$$

$$V_e = .25 \, (\$903,342) = \$225,835$$

$$ADS = \$95,257$$

Year	1	2	3	4	5	6	7	8	9	10
NOI	$100,000	103,000	106,090	109,273	112,551	115,927	119,405	122,987	126,677	130,477
− ADS	95,257	95,257	95,257	95,257	95,257	95,257	95,257	95,257	95,257	95,257
BTCF	$ 4,743	7,743	10,833	14,016	20,294	20,670	24,148	27,730	31,420	35,220

$$BTER = \$903,342 \, (1.25) - .7847 \, (\$677,507) = \$597,538.$$

An equity investment of $225,835, followed by the *BTCF*s and *BTER* calculated above produces a 15 percent yield. The value estimate is correct.

Notice that the Ellwood model is sufficiently flexible to handle all-equity financing (the weighted average return is simply the equity yield rate, with no adjustment for amortization), and/or a change in income without a change in property value ($\Delta_o = 0$). Also, notice that the forecasted changes in the income stream and property value can be different, and that either or both the income and value changes may be negative.

How Precise Is Ellwood?

The Ellwood model is simply an alternate way of estimating value on a finance-explicit basis. Given the same assumptions about cash flows, it gives exactly the same answer as the finance-explicit model introduced in Chapter 18. For example, let's look again at the last example, where the property is expected to produce first-year *NOI* of $100,000, which will increase by 3 percent per year while the property increases in value by 25 percent over the 10-year holding period. Using the general discounted cash flow model learned earlier, the property would be valued as follows:

$$V = V_m + V_e$$

$$= .75\,(V) + \$100{,}000 \left[\frac{1 - \left(\frac{1 + .03}{1 + .15}\right)^{10}}{.15 - .03} \right] -$$

$$(.1406)\,(.75\,V)\,(5.0188) +$$

$$[(1.25\,V - .7847\,(.75\,V)]\,(.2472)$$

$$V = \$903{,}855$$

Allowing for slight rounding along the way, this is exactly the same result. The choice of which model to use is up to you. Regardless of which you choose, you will eventually encounter both in your practice, and therefore it is necessary to understand the workings of both, and appreciate the fact they produce the same results. We will have more to say about the utility of the Ellwood model shortly.

Why Not a Simple Band of Investment?

When learning the band of investment model for use with first-year cash flows, the overall capitalization rate was calculated by weighting the cash returns to debt and equity. When using Ellwood, however, we cannot in most cases simply weight the required yield rates to debt and equity to arrive at the overall yield rate. The reason is that the loan-to-value ratio changes as the loan is amortized and/or the value of the property changes. Thus, a simple weighting of debt and equity yields will work only for an interest-only loan (no amortization), and when income and value will not change over the holding period. From this perspective, it is seen that the "$(m)(p)(1/s_{\overline{n}|})$" term in Ellwood adjusts for loan amortization, and the "$(-\Delta_0)\left(\dfrac{1}{s_{\overline{n}|}}\right)$" term adjusts for value change.

DSCR Model Shortcuts

In the Appendix to Chapter 15, we discussed an alternative specification of debt based on the debt service coverage ratio (*DSCR*). Recall that during periods of inflation, *DSCR*s tend to dominate the loan-to-value ratio as a constraint on debt, particularly for loan valuation purposes. Shortcut models, which utilize the *DSCR* rather than the loan-to-value ratio, are available,[6] but they are exceedingly complex and are most useful when a computer is available. Of course, if a computer is available there is not much need for shortcuts.

Limitations of Shortcuts

Shortcuts often trade simplicity for a loss in flexibility, realism, or information about the cash flows which drive the value estimate. For example, when using Ellwood, and income is expected to change, notice that the model can handle only a *regular* change; that is, the same percentage change each year.[7] No deviation is allowed, so when there is an irregular schedule of lease expirations, as is common for properties like offices and shopping centers, the assumption of regular growth is difficult to defend. Moreover, it is often not obvious what the pattern of cash flow changes will be until explicit forecasts have been made. But once the forecasts have been made, there is no need for a shortcut.

Also, the *reason* these models are shortcuts is because they manipulate the capitalization rate to reflect forecasted changes in cash flow, rather than dealing with the cash flows themselves. This is an important point because it is the informational content of explicit cash flow forecasts that is one of the main reasons to do a discounted cash flow analysis in the first place. Algebraic shortcuts lose both richness and accuracy when lumps are ignored or smoothed.

There are variations of Ellwood that do consider things like transaction costs[8] and taxes.[9] They are very complex, however, and when all is said and

---

[6] Fisher, Jeffrey D., and Kenneth M. Lusht, "Mortgage Equity Analysis with a Debt Coverage Constraint," *The Real Estate Appraiser and Analyst*, Fall 1981.

[7] There is a variation of Ellwood which assumes a regular arithmetic change. That, however, is even less palatable than a regular percentage change.

[8] Colwell, Peter F., and Philip J. Rushing, "To Ellwood and Beyond," *The Appraisal Journal*, July 1979.

[9] Fisher, Jeffrey D., "Ellwood After Tax: New Dimensions," *The Appraisal Journal*, July 1977.

done, they likely save little time compared to the use of explicit cash flow forecasts. In other words they are no longer shortcuts.

In sum, the basic Ellwood model is mathematically precise, but its assumptions about cash flow changes are seldom consistent with market behavior. Thus, in most cases the cost of using Ellwood will be a loss of accuracy. In general, the advantages of all but the most basic mathematical shortcuts, (such as for valuing perpetuities) have been eroded by electronic technology to the point that they are becoming obsolete as valuation tools.[10]

---

[10] See for example, Kelly, W., D. Edley, and D. Mitchell. "A Requiem for Ellwood," *The Appraisal Journal*, July 1995.

Summary

When it is expected that future cash flows will follow a regular pattern of change (including a 0 or a negative change), there are mathematical shortcuts to arrive at a value estimate.

1. For perpetual income streams
   a. For level perpetuities, $V = \dfrac{NOI}{Y_o}$
   b. For growing perpetuities,
   $$V = \dfrac{NOI}{Y_o - g_I},$$
   where g_I is the rate of change in the income stream. To use this model, Y_o must be greater than g.
   c. For perpetuities with an escalation clause, such as periodic rent increases in a long-term lease.
   $$V = \dfrac{NOI_1}{R_o}$$
   where
   $$R_o = Y_o - Y_o \left[\dfrac{(1 + g_I)^t - 1}{(1 + Y_o)^t - 1} \right]$$
   and t is the time period (number of years) between rent escalations.

2. For a finite annuity,
   $$V = NOI_1 \left[\dfrac{1 - \left(\dfrac{1 + g_I}{1 + Y_e}\right)^n}{Y_o - g_I} \right].$$

3. For a finite income stream plus sales proceeds, there are three variations of Ellwood's model:
   a. For no change in income or value over the projected holding period:
   $$V = \dfrac{NOI}{R_o}, \text{ where } R_o = (m)(R_m) + (1 - m)(y_e) - \left(m \times p \times \dfrac{1}{s_{\overline{n}}}\right)$$
   b. With no change in income, but a change in value
   $$V = \dfrac{NOI}{R_o}, \text{ where}$$
   $$R_o = (m)(R_m) + (1 - m)(Y_e) - (m)(p)\left(\dfrac{1}{s_{\overline{n}}}\right) - (\Delta_o)\left(\dfrac{1}{s_{\overline{n}}}\right)$$
   c. With a change in both income and value, and the rate of income change is constant.

$$V = \frac{NOI}{R_o}$$

$$\text{where } R_o = \frac{(m)(R_m) + (1-m)(Y_e) - (m)(p)\left(\frac{1}{s_{\overline{n}}}\right) - (\Delta_o)\left(\frac{1}{s_{\overline{n}}}\right)}{G}$$

$$\text{where } G = \left[\frac{1 - \left(\frac{1+g_I}{1+Y_e}\right)^n}{Y_e - g}\right] \div a_{\overline{n}}$$

There are variations of Ellwood which include transactions costs and income taxes, as well as shortcuts for using debt service coverage ratio models. Their complexity, however, casts doubt as to whether or not they're worth the trouble.

In general, valuation shortcuts can be used only in situations where income is forecasted to change at a regular rate. When that is not the expectation, the results will only approximate true value. Also lost is the necessity to make explicit cash flow forecasts, which is a primary motivation for the use of discounted cash flow analysis in the first place.

Finally, there is the question of whether a menu of models that will handle varying income and value change assumptions is worth the trouble. The models developed earlier based on property productivity and before- and after-tax cash flows are applicable in all cases, regardless of the patterns of income and value changes.

Questions and Problems

1. A site is leased for 99 years at $50,000 per year. Approximate its value, given a discount rate of 12 percent.

2. What is the value of the leased site (in Question 1) if the rent in year 1 is $50,000, and then it increases by 2.5 percent per year through the 99th year.

3. Suppose now that the site (in Questions 1 and 2), which is all-equity financed, produces $50,000 income the first year. The income increases by 2.5 percent per year for 10 years, when it will be sold. Property appreciation during the 10 years will total 48 percent. Value the site using Ellwood.

4. A property is all-equity financed. It is expected to produce $12,500 *NOI* each year over a projected holding period of eight years. The expected equity yield rate is 11 percent. Value is not expected to change over the holding period. What is the property's value?

5. If the property in Question 4 is expected to increase in value by 30 percent over the holding period, what is its value? Use Ellwood.

6. An apartment is expected to produce $105,000 *NOI* the first year, increasing by 3 percent per year each year over a projected 7-year holding period. A 70 percent loan-to-value ratio is typical. Current terms are 13.5 percent interest for 21 years. Equity investors expect a 15 percent yield. The property is expected to depreciate by 20 percent over the holding

period. Value the property using Ellwood.

7. A property is expected to produce *NOI* of $300,000 per year over a 12-year holding period. Value will increase by 2 percent per year. The property is typically financed with an 80 percent loan at 14 percent for 18 years. Equity investors expect a 16.5 percent yield. Value the property using Ellwood. Show that your value estimate is correct.

8. A property is expected to produce $30,000 of *NOI* the first year, increasing by 3 percent and 6 percent in years 2 and 3 of the 3-year holding period. Equity investors expect a 17 percent yield for an all-equity investment, which this is. Property value is expected to increase by 3 percent per year. Costs of sale at reversion will be 5 percent.
   a. Can you use a shortcut to value the property? Why?
   b. Value the property.

9. First-year *NOI* from a long-term net lease is expected to be $50,000. Rent is escalating at a rate of 3 percent per year, but there is a two-year period between adjustments. Thus, the income for years 1 and 2 will be $50,000, increasing to $50,000 $(1 + .03)^2$ = $53,045 in years 3 and 4, and so on. The discount rate is 14 percent. Assuming beginning-of-year payments, estimate the value of the leased fee.

Chapter 21 Relationships among the Income Approach Models

Introduction

Preceding chapters have covered four income approach models: (1) gross income multipliers, (2) directly extracted overall capitalization rates, (3) the band of investment, and (4) discounted cash flow models, including some shortcuts.

In this chapter the historical development of the income approach is discussed, then the relationships among the various income approach models are illustrated by numerical example. Finally, there is a discussion of how the appraiser makes the decision as to which model(s) will be used in a given circumstance.

A Short History of Income Approach Models

Because there is a relationship between the structure of the various models and the investment environment at the time they emerged, some history is helpful as a starting point. In the early real estate appraisal texts published in the 1930s and 1940s, the income approach focused on the use of gross income multipliers and overall capitalization rates, with emphasis on rates that were either extracted directly from the market or built up by beginning with a risk-free rate and adding premiums for such things as business risk and liquidity. For several market-related reasons, neither the finance explicit band of investment model nor the finance-explicit and tax-explicit discounted cash flow models had much impact during this early period. At the time there was relatively more dependence on equity rather than debt, interest rates were at historically low levels, and accelerated depreciation for tax purposes was unknown. Inflation was not a serious issue, so the actual loss in value over time was a major valuation concern. Compared to what followed, it was a relatively uncomplicated investment environment where a property's physical characteristics tended to dominate appraisal theory and technique.

As the financing of property rights began to move toward heavier use of debt in the 1950s and 1960s, the physical criterion of valuation was joined and ultimately dominated by financial and investment criteria. This led to the popularization of the finance-explicit models, initially the band of investment. An allowance for loss in value, once a cornerstone of the income approach, became less important as prices either stabilized or increased over time. Inflation also meant that relatively large portions of value were being contributed by future increases in income and property value and less by the current level of income. The result was the development and adoption of discounted cash flow models.

More recently, there has been an increasing recognition that income tax plays a major role in determining real property values. After-tax models, while still used predominantly for investment valuation, have already begun to carve out a share of the market valuation process, particularly as computer technology makes the calculations more manageable. Computers are doing for after-tax valuation what Ellwood's tables and then electronic calculators did for before-tax valuation.

We find then, that appraisers' attempts to keep pace with changes in the investment environment have been reasonably successful. As investor motivation and behavior has changed, so has the behavior of appraisers.

Another way to view this evolutionary process is based on the observation that as the investment environment has become more complex, the number of variables that may affect value has increased. This translates into greater difficulty locating comparables that are "comparable enough" to use for direct sales comparison. The response to that difficulty is the increasing use of techniques like discounted cash flow models, that allow explicit consideration of individual value-affecting variables, and a decline in the use of less explicit approaches, such as gross income multipliers, which require the extraction of rates from more closely comparable sales.

This is shown in Figure 21–1, which shows the various income approach models (as well as the sales comparison approach) and indicates whether individual variables are implicitly or explicitly recognized.

As we move from left to right in Figure 21–1, the number of implicit variables decreases and the number of explicit variables increases. In terms of appraisal practice, this means that reliance on comparables decreases as we move to the more explicit models. From this perspective it is seen why the use of discounted cash flow models increases as income properties (and transactions) become larger and more complex. In such cases it is difficult to find comparable sales and the subject property must be valued using a model that takes its variables explicitly into consideration.

The relationship between models is illustrated numerically below, where each of the models is applied to the same valuation problem, beginning with the discounted cash flow model, the most explicit model, and working toward the *GIM,* which is the most implicit model.

FIGURE 21-1 Income Approach Models and Treatment of Investment Benefits

Sales Comparison Approach		Income Approach				
		GIMs	Direct Capitalization	Equity Capitalization	Equity Yield, Before Tax	Equity Yield, After Tax
Direct comparison of characteristics, adjusted if necessary	Explicit	Gross income	Gross income Operation expense NOI	NOI Debt service	NOI Debt service Loan amortization Reversion	NOI Debt service Loan amortization Reversion Taxes
	Implicit	Operating expenses Debt service Loan amortization Reversion Taxes	Debt service Loan amortization Reversion Taxes	Loan amortization Reversion Taxes	Taxes	

←————Implicit————————————————————————Explicit————→

←————————————Reliance on comparables————————————

The Relationships among Models: A Numerical Example

The Discounted Cash Flow Model

Suppose you are appraising a property expected to produce first-year *NOI* of:

Potential gross income	$100,000
Vacancy (.05)	5,000
Effective gross income	95,000
Operating expenses (.40)	38,000
NOI	$ 57,000

Typical financing is 60 percent debt, at 13 percent interest, amortized monthly over 20 years. Equity investors expect an 18.75 percent before-tax yield.[1] No change in *NOI* is expected, while property value is expected to

---

[1] To represent the several discounted cash flow model variations, we will use the finance-explicit, before-tax variation.

grow a total of 14 percent over a 3-year holding period. There are no costs of sale.

$$V = V_m + V_e$$

$$V_m = .60\,(V)$$

$$V_e = \sum_{t=1}^{n} \frac{BTCF_t}{(1+Y_e)^t} + \frac{BTER_n}{(1+Y_e)^n}$$

$$PV\ NOI = \$57{,}000\,(2.15) = \$122{,}550$$

$$PV\ ADS = [.6\,(V)\,(.1406)]\,(2.15) = .1814\,(V)$$

$$PV\ BTER = [1.14\,V - .9614\,(.6)\,(V)]\,(.5972) = .3363\,(V)$$

$$V = .6\,(V) + \$122{,}550 - .1814\,(V) + .3363\,(V)$$

$$V = \$499{,}796,\ \text{say},\ \$500{,}000$$

Given the level income assumption, Ellwood (Akerson) could have been used to produce the same result:

$(m)(R_m)$	$= .6 \times .1406$	$= .0844$
$(1-m) \times Y_e$	$= .4 \times .1875$	$= +.0750$
$-(m)(p)\left(\dfrac{1}{s_{\overline{n}}}\right)$	$= .6 \times .0386 \times .2780$	$= -.0064$
$-(\Delta_o)\left(\dfrac{1}{s_{\overline{n}}}\right)$	$= .14 \times .2780$	$= -.0389$
		$R_o = .1141$

$$V = \frac{\$57{,}000}{.1141}$$

$$= \$499{,}562,\ \text{say},\ \$500{,}000$$

The Band of Investment

Given the value of $500,000, we can extract the resulting equity capitalization rate, R_e.

$$V = \$500{,}000$$

$$V_m = .6\,(\$500{,}000) = \$300{,}000$$

$$V_e = .4\,(\$500{,}000) = \$200{,}000$$

$$ADS = .1406\,(\$300{,}000) = \$42{,}180$$

$$BTCF = \$57{,}000 - \$42{,}180 = \$14{,}820$$

$$R_e = \frac{\$14{,}820}{\$200{,}000} = .0741$$

This produces an R_o of:

$$(m)(R_m) = .6 \times .1406 = .0844$$
$$(1 - m)(R_e) = .4 \times .0741 = .0296$$
$$R_o = .1140$$

$$V = \frac{NOI}{R_o}$$
$$= \frac{\$57,000}{.1140}$$
$$= \$500,000$$

What this calculation has shown is that given the variables used in the discounted cash flow model, a first-year equity capitalization rate of .0741 results. Now assume that this property is being used as a comparable from which you have extracted the R_e of .0741. The key question is, when can you use this equity capitalization rate in a band of investment model to value another subject property? The answer is that it can be used only when the *future prospects* for the subject are the same as the future prospects for the comparable, because the level of R_e is a function of those prospects. In terms of Figure 21–1, because only first-year *NOI* and debt service are explicit, prospects for the remaining implicit variables (future *NOI,* amortization, sale proceeds, and taxes) must be the same for the comparable as for the subject. Otherwise, the R_e extracted from the comparable will not be applicable to the subject property.

The Directly Extracted Overall Capitalization Rate

The overall capitalization rate which results from the $500,000 sale price is

$$R_o = \frac{NOI}{\text{Sale price}} = \frac{\$57,000}{\$500,000} = .114.$$

This, of course, is the same result as we got using the band of investment model.

Supposing again that this is a comparable property, the question is when can this overall rate be used? The answer is that it can be used when market financing has not changed *and* when future income and value prospects are reasonably similar. In terms of Figure 21–1, this overall rate can be used when the rather long list of implicit variables (under directly extracted overall rates) are similar.

The Gross Income Multiplier

Given the value of $500,000, the *GIM* from the example property (using *EGI*) is

$$\frac{\$500{,}000}{\$95{,}000} = 5.26.$$

Assuming once more that this property is being used as a comparable, when can this *GIM* be used to value another subject? The answer is that it can be used when the comparable and the subject are reasonably similar in *all* value-affecting variables other than gross income. In terms of Figure 21–1, they must be similar as far as the lengthy list of implicit value-affecting variables under the *GIM*.

Selecting a Model

The discussion above teaches much about when a particular technique *cannot* be used with confidence. That is, when the comparable isn't sufficiently comparable as far as the implicit variables are concerned. As we move from left to right in Figure 21–1, and the number of explicit variables increases, it means the appraiser has more flexibility to account for differences among properties (that is, among the comparables and the subject) in the value estimate. As we move from the sales comparison approach toward discounted cash flow models, the more explicit recognition of value-affecting variables allows the valuation of more heterogeneous properties. Put differently, the further right we move, the less comparable the comparables must be, and vice versa. From yet another perspective, directly extracted rates are the *results* of observable market transactions. Discounted cash flow models, however, are *simulations* of market behavior which produce approximations of market value.

While it is clear that the quantity and quality of sales comparison information will eliminate certain techniques in a given situation, it is also true that the appraiser, if desired, can stray as far right as he or she chooses in any circumstance. The question is how far right should the appraiser move?

The answer is *no further than necessary.* The point is that the appraiser really does not have a choice of approach. Instead, the available data determines the choice. Sales comparison is always preferred a priori, but data deficiencies often force a move to either the income or cost approaches.

Once within the income approach, the same idea is relevant. *GIM*s are closest to sales comparison and are the preferred valuation technique because they are based on objective market evidence. The appraiser is working with objective results of prior transactions. To repeat, however, this is not a sufficient reason to use them. Also necessary for *GIM*s to be used with any degree of confidence is that the properties from which the *GIM* is extracted must be *closely* comparable to the subject. If any of the implicit variables listed under *GIM*s in Figure 21–1 vary significantly among the sample of comparables, or between the comparables and the subject, the *GIM* cannot be used with confidence. The same is true of the directly extracted overall rate. If market terms of financing have changed between the sale of the comparables and the date of the appraisal and/or future expectations are different, the use of the band of investment may be indicated.

Finally, in *any* case, where expectations about the future patterns of cash flows (including sale proceeds) differ significantly among the comparables, and/or between the comparables and the subject, a discounted cash flow model should be used.

Another way to look at this is that the preferred technique is the one which, given the available market information, requires the least manipulation of individual variables. When the appraiser strays further to the right in Figure 21–1 than is dictated by the data, there is a movement away from objectivity toward subjectivity and, by definition, a move away from a value estimate based on observed market behavior. The fact that a lack of data often forces a move to the right is well-taken, but it does not change the conclusion that the cost of such a move will be a decrease in the confidence we have that the resulting estimate of value accurately reflects current market value.

Direct Capitalization and Discounted Cash Flow Models: A Final Comparison

Because in practice both direct capitalization and discounted cash flow models are widely used, it is useful to spend a bit more time on how they are related. We begin with reference to the basic value model.

$$V = V_{NOI} + V_{NSP},$$

which is represented graphically in Figure 21–2.

FIGURE 21–2 Value and Holding Period

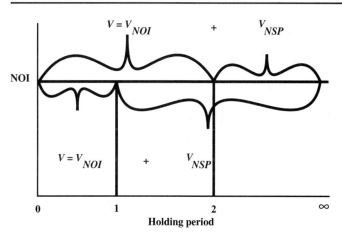

Current market value (time 0) is the present value of the NOI from time 0 through the assumed holding period. Two example holding periods are shown in Figure 21–2; periods 1 and 2. Assuming a holding period of 2, market value would be the sum of the present value of NOI from time 0–2, plus the present value of the NSP (reversion) at that time, which is equal to the present value of NOI beyond 2 through time ∞.

Similarly, assuming a holding period of 1, market value would be the sum of the present value of NOI from time 0–1, plus the present value of the NSP at that time, which is equal to the present value of NOI beyond 1 through time ∞.

Now assume a holding period of 0. In this special case, market value would be the sum of the value of NOI, which with a 0 holding period would be zero, plus the present value of NSP, which is the present value of NOI beyond 0 through time ∞.

Two points to note: (1) As discussed in an earlier chapter, the expected reversion is the expected market value at that time (net of costs of sale), and (2) changing the expected holding period simply rearranges the value estimate between what is attributable to NOI during the holding period and what is attributable to NOI beyond the holding period (which is captured in the reversion estimate). From this perspective, direct capitalization is the special case of the discounted cash flow model where $V_{NOI} = 0$ and the $V_{NSP} = V$.

Summary

The choice of which income approach model to use, like the choice among the three approaches, is not really a choice at all. It is dictated by the available data, and in all cases, the objective is to use the data most efficiently, meaning with the least amount of adjustment or manipulation.

Questions and Problems

1. There are a number of techniques included under the income approach umbrella. The four used most often are GIMs, directly extracted R_os, R_os calculated using the band of investment model, and discounted cash flow models. Define each technique, and discuss when each is properly used for valuation.

2. A property is expected to produce this flow of net operating income:

Year	1	2	3	4	5
NOI	$200,000	$210,000	$220,000	$230,000	$240,000

Typical financing includes 70 percent debt at 13.5 percent interest, amortized monthly over 15 years. Property value is expected to increase by 3 percent per year. Investors expect a 14 percent before-tax yield. Value the property.

3. Suppose now that the property you valued in Question 2 did in fact sell for a price equal to your value estimate, and that it now is being used as a comparable. The subject property is expected to produce first-year income as follows:

PGI	$350,000
Vacancy (.06)	21,000
EGI	$329,000
OE (.35)	115,150
NOI	$213,850

   a. Value the subject using the band of investment model.
   b. What is the directly extracted R_o from the comparable?
   c. Suppose the first-year potential gross income from the comparable was $400,000. What is its *GIM*?
   d. Value the subject using the *GIM*.

4. The values you should have calculated for the subject property in Question 3 are:
   Using the band of investment
   and the directly extracted R_o: $2,086,341
   Using the *GIM*: $1,708,000
   What *might* account for the difference?

5. Which value estimate (from Question 4) would you consider more credible? Why?

6. Suppose you were given the further information that the expected income and value of the subject property analyzed in Questions 3 and 4 was expected to decline by 2 percent per year over the next several years. How would that affect your estimate of value in this case?

7. When "trustable" comparables cannot be located and a discounted cash flow model must be used, how do you describe the resulting appraised value? Specifically, is it market value? Or something else?

8. A property is expected to produce first-year *NOI* of $110,000, which is expected to increase by 2 percent per year over a 5-year holding period. Value is expected to increase by 1 percent per year. Terms of debt are 11.5 percent interest over 21 years. The loan-to-value ratio is 70 percent. The expected yield to equity is 13.5 percent.
   a. Estimate the value of the property
   b. What is the resulting first year R_e?
   c. What is the resulting overall capitalization rate based on first-year *NOI*?

9. "*GIM*s are too crude to use for appraisal." Comment.

CHAPTER 22 Estimating the Discount Rate

Introduction

When the concept of discounting cash flows was introduced, there was a brief discussion of the relationship between risk and the expected return (the discount rate). While this provided a partial explanation for the various discount rates used in succeeding chapters, for the most part the appropriate rates—Y_o for discounting *NOI* and *NSP*, Y_e for use in finance-explicit models, and Y_a for use in tax-explicit models—have been assumed. This strategy was followed so that we could focus on the concepts and mechanics of discounted cash flow models without the complication of learning how to estimate the proper discount rate.

This chapter discusses the theory and practice of making those estimates, beginning with Y_o, then moving to Y_e and finally to Y_a.

Estimating Y_o: Theory

The discount rate reflects the characteristics of an investment that investors expect to be compensated for. As shown in Equation (1), these characteristics are: (1) the "pure" real rate of return, (2) expected inflation, (3) various risks, and (4) the nonrisk costs of investment.

$$Y_o = \text{``Pure'' real rate of return} + \text{Expected inflation} \quad (1)$$
$$+ \text{Risk premium} + \text{Premium for nonrisk costs}.$$

The "pure" real rate of return is the compensation that is expected for waiting for the cash flows. It is compensation only for delaying consumption, not for risk, and therefore it is the same for all investments.

The second factor which affects the discount rate is the expected inflation rate. As the expected rate increases, investors expect higher returns to compensate for the erosion of the purchasing power of future cash flows.

The third factor that affects the discount rate is the risk of the investment. There are three general categories of risk: business risk, unexpected inflation risk, and liquidity risk. Business risk is measured by the degree of variability in operating cash flows. Markets may improve or turn soft. Operating expenses may be higher or lower than expected. Property appreciation rates may vary from expectations. This is unlike, say, a treasury bill, which will always produce exactly the promised cash flow. Because investors do not like uncertainty they expect to be compensated for it. Thus, the expected return on an apartment project will be higher than the expected return on a treasury bill, and the expected return on a warehouse leased to a AAA-credit tenant will be lower than the expected return associated with the development of a motel.

For most real estate investments, business risk has two elements. The first is market risk, the second is residual risk. Market risk is that risk that remains even when the investor is fully diversified. Residual risk is the risk that results from the investor not being diversified. Thus, in a perfectly diversified portfolio of investments, the only risk that is compensated for is market risk; that part of business risk which cannot be diversified away. The standard assumption of models used to value securities, like the capital asset pricing model, is that investors are fully diversified and they are therefore entitled only to a risk premium for the remaining (market) risk.

While we do not know the extent to which typical real estate investors are diversified (or even how to properly diversify), it is clear that they are not *fully* diversified. Thus, there remains a residual business risk which comes from a lack of full diversification, and this risk is reflected in the discount rate. Moreover, unless and until real property rights become completely "securitized" through limited partnerships, it is unlikely that residual risk can ever be completely eliminated, due to the "lumpiness" of the typical investment. This lack of divisibility precludes some diversification by forcing the purchase of suboptimal investment amounts.

The discount rate also reflects compensation for the risk of unexpected inflation. We know that the discount rate reflects inflation expectations to compensate the investor for the loss of purchasing power. Forecasting inflation, however, is a tricky business, and it is unlikely that actual and expected inflation rates will match up. Like other kinds of risk then, the risk of unexpected inflation must also be compensated, and this requires an addition to the discount rate.

Liquidity is a measure of how costly it is to convert an asset to cash. Relatively liquid assets have an advantage over less liquid assets because future opportunities (either consumption or investment) can more easily be captured. Real estate tends to be relatively illiquid (though with securitization this is slowly changing), and the risk that a future opportunity may have to be foregone or taken advantage of only at excessive cost—for example, a sale at a below-market price—must be compensated for by an addition to the discount rate.

The fourth factor that affects the discount rate is the nonrisk cost of investment. There are substantial costs involved in entering and exiting the real estate market. Some of these costs are typically reflected in the cash flow estimates; for example, the expected brokerage commissions when the property is eventually sold. However, other costs such as search costs and some transaction costs typically do not show up in cash flow forecasts and they must therefore be reflected in the discount rate.

Finally, real estate tends to be an active rather than a passive investment, imposing a management burden on the owner. While this burden can be minimized by hiring a professional manager whose compensation is directly reflected in the cash flow statement, there remain the costs of monitoring the activities and performance of the manager. Because these costs do not affect cash flows, they too must be reflected in the discount rate.

In sum, a more detailed model of the discount rate, Y_o, looks like Equation (2).

$$Y_o = \text{``Pure''} + \text{Expected} + \text{Risk premium} + \text{Premium for} \quad (2)$$

real return	inflation	· Business Risk	nonrisk costs
		· Unexpected Inflation	· Search, Information and Transaction Costs
		· Liquidity Risk	· Management

Estimating Y_o: Practice

Moving from the theoretical model of discount rates to estimating the rates in practice is difficult. First, unlike capitalization rates, expected yields cannot be directly observed. Second, while realized yields can be calculated after the fact, they may be only tenuously related to the expected yields which determine current value. Expected yields are based on current conditions and future expectations, not past performance.

Despite these obstacles, there are several approaches to producing a reasonable estimate of the discount rate. They are (1) the "summation" approach, which requires estimates of the expected returns for the individual parts of the theoretical model, (2) the use of observed capitalization rates and forecasts of income and value, (3) the use of historical relationships of the yield from real estate to the yields from other kinds of investments, and (4) the use of surveys of investor expectations. These estimating approaches will be discussed in turn, keeping in mind that regardless of which is used, the process is imprecise and requires a heavy dose of appraiser judgment.

Using the Summation Approach to Estimate Y_o

The property yield, Y_o, can be estimated by making an estimate of the individual terms on the right side of the theoretical model, which include the pure real rate, inflation expectations, and various risk and nonrisk costs.

This summation (or built-up) approach has enjoyed cycles of popularity. After losing favor in the 1960s and 1970s due to the difficulty of making the required estimates, recent empirical work on various elements of return has given it new life.[1]

The summation approach begins with an estimate of the pure real rate of return, which in various studies has been estimated to be between 2 and 3%. Next, inflation expectations and purchasing power risk can be estimated by subtracting the pure real return from the current yield on long-term (10-year) government bonds. The current yield on these bonds is the sum of the pure real return, expected inflation, and the risk of unexpected inflation over an investment horizon (10 years) that is a reasonable proxy for real estate holding periods.

This leaves the appraiser the job of estimating the premiums for risk (other than unexpected inflation risk, which is captured in the 10-year bond rate) and nonrisk costs. While there are no direct measures of these premiums, there is some help available. Bob Zerbst and Barbara Cambon[2] calculated the average real rate of return to real estate to be 5.7 percent, based on studies completed between 1947 and 1984. This is a useful number because it includes the pure rate of return, plus the premiums for risks and nonrisk costs. Only expected inflation is left to estimate, which, as discussed, can be done by subtracting the pure real return (2–3 percent) from the current yield on long-term government bonds.

Therefore, using a pure real return of 2.5 percent and the 5.7 percent average real rate from real estate, the mean nominal yield to real estate can be approximated as:

$$Y_o = 5.7\% + (\text{current yield on 10-year government bonds} - 2.5\%)$$

For example, if the yield on bonds maturing in 10 years is 7.0 percent, then the estimated nominal return to real estate is

$$Y_o = 5.7\% + (7.0\% - 2.5\%)$$

$$= 10.20\%$$

The use of long-term government bond yields as a basis for estimating a discount rate is evidence of the increasingly strong link between the capital and real estate markets. There has been a reasonably consistent difference (1.3–1.5%) between mortgage interest rates and long–term bond rates.[3]

---

[1] It has also been reinvented conceptually. See Roger G. Ibbotson, Jeffrey J. Diermeier, and Lawrence B. Siegel, "The Demand for Capital Market Returns: A New Equilibrium Theory," *Financial Analysts Journal,* January–February, 1984.

[2] Robert Zerbst and Barbara Cambon, "Real Estate: Historical Returns and Risks, *Journal of Portfolio Management,* Spring 1984.

[3] See for example, Gibbons, James E., "Increased Similarity of Real Property Values to Global Money Market Fluctuations," *Appraisal Journal,* October 1988.

Given that the discount rate is heavily influenced by the mortgage interest rate, it is not surprising that bond rates and discount rates are associated.

There are some concerns when using the summation approach. First, it may produce estimates that are slightly high, given the reasonable assumption that the risk of unexpected inflation is reflected in both the historical real return to real property and in the current yield on 10-year bonds.

Second, the real rate of return may not be stable over time. To the extent it changes, (and there is some evidence that it does), historical real returns may not be a reliable proxy for current expectations.

Third, the result of the summation model is an "average" discount rate based on highly aggregated data which will not be representative of all properties. Nevertheless, it represents a starting point from which adjustments for the relative risks of individual properties can be made based on the appraiser's judgment.

Using the Capitalization Rate to Estimate Y_o

Another way to estimate Y_o is to use the capitalization rate(s) extracted from a comparable sale(s), and combine them with forecasts of the expected changes in income and property value for the comparable(s). If for a comparable property it is expected that the growth rates for income and property value will be the same, and will continue into perpetuity (or, in practice, for an extended period), the expected yield rate can be estimated quite simply: $Y_o = R_o$ + Growth rate. For example, if a comparable property sold at a cap rate of 9 percent, and you forecast a 3 percent growth rate, the implied discount rate for the comparable is 12 percent.

If the appraiser does not feel comfortable assuming that income and value will change at the same rate, or that the growth will continue into perpetuity, the discounted cash flow model can be used to estimate Y_o. Assume, for example, that a comparable sale produced an overall capitalization rate of 10 percent, based on first-year *NOI* of $1,000 and a selling price of $10,000. The income and value of the comparable are expected to grow at annual rates of 3 percent and 2 percent, respectively, over a 10-year holding period. From this information, Y_o (the *IRR*) can be solved for using the discounted cash flow model. For the example, it is 12.68 percent. This kind of analysis can be completed for a sample of comparable sales, and the average yield rate used to value similar properties.

There are two potential weaknesses in this approach. The first is common to the use of all discounted cash flow models; the imprecision inherent in forecasting the future. Second, there is the question of whether a calculated yield rate is really needed. Because the rate is based on a market-extracted capitalization rate, the cap rate itself can be used to value properties directly. The counter argument is by now familiar: forecasting income provides information as to where the estimated value comes from.

TABLE 22-1 Yield Rates for Investment Alternatives

	4th Quarter	3rd Quarter	2nd Quarter	1st Quarter
Weighted average				
Real estate yields	11.5%	11.7	11.9	12.6
Retail	11.2	11.2	11.5	11.9
Office	13.8	13.9	13.9	14.0
Industrial	11.8	12.1	12.2	12.4
Yield spread (%)				
(Real estate minus alternative)				
Utilities	1.6%	2.5%	2.7%	3.4%
10-year U.S. bond	2.2%	3.0%	3.1%	3.6%
Stock dividend yields	6.6%	6.8%	6.6%	6.5%

Estimating Y_0 by Using Yields on Alternative Investments

An estimate of the discount rate can be obtained by adding current capital market yields to the historical spread between those yields and the yield to real estate. Table 22-1 below shows yield data by quarters for a hypothetical year. This type of data is available through industry associations and private consulting groups.[4]

Using the data in the table, if the current 10-year U.S. bond rate is 7.5 percent, the current average yield to real estate can be estimated by adding 7.5 percent to the four-quarter average spread of 2.98 percent, giving 10.48 percent.

Note the close relationship between this approach and the summation approach. Using the first-quarter data as an example, the yield on 10-year bonds is estimated to be 12.6 percent − 3.6 percent = 9.0 percent. The summation approach would estimate the yield to real estate as:

$$Y_0 = \text{Pure real return} + (\text{Bond rate} - \text{Pure rate}) + \text{Risk premium}$$

Estimates of the pure rate of return (about 2.5 percent) and the bond rate (9.0 percent) have been described. The risk premium, which includes nonrisk costs, can be estimated by starting with the historical real rate of return to real estate, which recall has averaged 5.7 percent, and subtracting the pure real rate of return average of 2.5 percent. This produces a real estate risk premium of 3.2 percent.

---

[4] An example of an industry publication is *Appraiser News*, published by the Appraisal Institute. An example of a private source is the *Real Estate Investor Survey*, published by Peter F. Korpacz and Associates. A very readable discussion of the linkage money market yields and real estate values is in James E. Gibbons, *Real Estate and the Money Markets*, American Society of Real Estate Counselors, 1989.

We can now estimate Y_0:
$$Y_0 = 2.5\% + (9.0\% - 2.5\%) + 3.2\%$$
$$= 12.2\%$$

This is close to the 12.6 percent reported in the table for the fourth quarter.

Using Surveys to Estimate Y_0: What Do Investors Expect?

Given the fact that expectations drive the market, one way to approximate the discount rate is to ask those close to the market, such as investors, lenders, brokers, and appraisers, what yields they would expect. An advantage of using surveys is that they provide the appraiser with the "bottom line"—the discount rate—without the burden of estimating (and justifying) the various components of the rate.

There are two sources of survey results on expected yields. One source already mentioned are the surveys done regularly and reported in commercial and professional association newsletters. They contain various degrees of disaggregation, most commonly by property type and/or geographic area. They are useful as benchmarks, but are not property specific.

A second source of survey results are those generated by the appraiser within the relevant market area. This has the advantage of being market and even property specific. A disadvantage may be the costs involved, particularly if the survey is done carefully enough to generate reliable results.

One problem with using survey results, regardless of their source, is that empirical studies often find gaps between how people claim they behave and how they actually behave. For example, the average annual expected real return of market participants between 1988 and April 1995 was 7.90 percent.[5] This means that either the real return has jumped by about 38 percent since Zerbst and Cambon's 1984 study or that investors overstate expectations. The latter is more likely.[6] The cause of this expectation-realization gap is not clear. It may be that investors are overoptimistic when forecasting cash flows, or that when asked, investors overstate their yield expectations, but will in fact accept less. Regardless of the cause, the potential for biased survey results exists and must be kept in mind.

Estimating Y_e: The Impact of Financial Risk

The discussion to this point has focused on the determination and estimation of Y_o, the discount rate used to value the net operating income and sale pro-

---

[5]*Korpacz Real Estate Investor Survey,* Peter Korpacz, 1995. Similar results are found in other surveys, such as *The Real Estate Report,* Real Estate Research Corporation, vol. 25, no. 2, 1995.

[6]For example, see Steven Roulac, *Modern Real Estate Investment: An Institutional Approach* (San Francisco CA: Property Press), 1976.

ceeds. When using a finance-explicit model, however, the relevant discount rate is Y_e, the expected yield to the equity investor. Because the use of debt adds financial risk, Y_e will be higher than Y_o, which in turn will be higher than Y_m. Remember that Y_o is simply a (properly) weighted average of Y_e and Y_m.

The bad news for the appraiser attempting to estimate Y_e is that an added layer of risk—financial risk—must be quantified and added to Y_o. The good news, as demonstrated in earlier chapters, is that because the yield to the lender, Y_m, tends to dominate Y_o, any errors in estimating the premium for financial risk, and in turn Y_e, will have a relatively minor impact on the value estimate. Recall the example that showed that given a Y_m of 14 percent and a loan-to-value ratio of 75 percent, an error of 17.5 percent when estimating Y_e would produce only about a 5 percent error in the market value estimate.

Another advantage of estimating Y_e rather than Y_o is that because equity investors tend to think in terms of levered returns, the use of a survey to estimate the expected yield may produce more accurate results when the question is framed in terms of Y_e instead of Y_o.

If an estimate of Y_o has already been made, say by using a capitalization rate and future income expectation as described earlier, an estimate of Y_e can also be calculated. This is done by first estimating value using Y_o. The resulting cash flows to equity are then estimated, and from them the IRR to equity (Y_e) is calculated. This can be tedious without a computer, but there isn't a simple way to algebraically model the relationship between Y_o and Y_e. The closest we can come is to rearrange the Ellwood model to solve for Y_e as follows:

$$Y_e = \frac{Y_o + m\left[(P)(1/s_{\overline{n}} - R_m)\right]}{1 - m}$$

However, this is a limited solution. Recall that this method of estimating Y_e is precise only in the special case of level income and no change in value.

Note that the estimating process can work in reverse; that is, given estimates of Y_e and Y_m, Y_o can be estimated by rearranging the Ellwood formula. Also, a quicker but less precise estimate of Y_o can be obtained by weighting Y_e and Y_m based on the loan-to-value ratio, as in the single-year band of investment model. The error would depend on how much the loan to value changes during the holding period due to loan amortization or to a change in the property's value.

Estimating Y_a: The Impact of Taxes

An increasing number of valuation assignments involve a tax-explicit analysis. This requires an estimate of the after-tax yield to equity, Y_a. For many kinds of investments, once the before-tax yield, (Y_e) is estimated, it is easy to estimate Y_a by adjusting Y_e by the tax rate, as follows:

$$Y_a = Y_e (1 - T)$$

where T is the investor's marginal tax rate. For example, for an investor with a 30 percent marginal tax rate, a before-tax yield of 15 percent translates into an after-tax yield of .15 (1 − .3) = .105.

This straightforward relationship between Y_e and Y_a does not generally hold for investors in real property. First, the amortization of debt affects *BTCF* but not taxable income. Second, depreciation expense affects taxable income but not *BTCF*. From this, and using for illustration a simple one-year investment with the equity reversion equal to the original equity, the relationship between taxable income (*TI*) and *BTCF* looks like this:

$$TI = BTCF - \text{Depreciation expense} + \text{Amortization payment}$$

It is seen that the relationship between taxable income (and therefore, the relationship between Y_e and Y_a) is dependent on the relationship between depreciation expense and amortization. Only when depreciation expense is equal to amortization will $TI = BTCF$ and the $Y_a = Y_e (1 - T)$ relationship hold. This is an infrequent occurrence for real estate.

How then is an estimate of Y_a to be obtained? If Y_o (and/or Y_e) can be estimated (from capitalization rates, the summation approach, or by survey), Y_a can be calculated by estimating value, constructing the resulting after tax cash flows, and solving for Y_a (the after-tax *IRR*). This is the same as the approach used to estimate Y_e based on Y_o.

In addition, it may be useful to develop some general relationships between Y_e and Y_a by constructing hypothetical cash flows, and measuring the resulting before and after-tax yields under various assumptions as to depreciation write-offs and the resulting recapture at reversion. Finally, as in the case of Y_o and Y_e, Y_a can be estimated by surveying investors and other knowledgeable individuals as to their after-tax yield expectations.

Summary

Y_o, the discount rate used to calculate the present value of the expected net operating income and sale proceeds from a real property investment, is the sum of the returns necessary to compensate the investor for both the risks and nonrisk costs associated with the investment. The theoretical model looks like this:

Y_o = "Pure" real return
+ Inflation expectations
+ Premium for risks
+ Premium for nonrisk costs

In practice, it is difficult to estimate Y_o, because unlike capitalization rates, expected yields cannot be extracted from comparable sales. Instead, the appraiser must approximate the expected yield. One way is to begin with the historical mean real rate of return to real property (approximately 5.7 percent), then add to it a premium for inflation expectations, which is the current yield on 10-year government bonds minus the 2.5 percent historical pure real return, and a Premium for nonrisk costs. Using a real rate of 5.7 percent (from Zerbst and Cambon), we have Y_o = 5.7% + (Current 10-year bond yield − 2.5%) + Premium for nonrisk costs. A yield estimated this way must then be adjusted to reflect differences between the subject property and the "average" property.

A second method to estimate Y_o is to solve for the IRR based on observed capitalization rates from comparable sale and forecasts of future income and value changes for the comparable properties. A third method is to begin with the current yields on alternative investments, then add to them the historical spread between those yields and yields to real estate. A fourth method to estimate Y_o is to ask investors and others knowledgeable in the market what yield they would expect from the subject property.

The process is similar for estimating the expected yield to equity, Y_e. When debt is used, $Y_e = Y_o$ + Premium for financial risk. If Y_o can be estimated using one of the methods described above, Y_e can then be estimated by generating the expected cash flows and solving for the IRR to equity. Alternatively, and relying on the fact that Y_o is a weighted average of Y_m and Y_e, the latter can be solved for in an algebraic model like Ellwood. The weakness of this approach is that Ellwood works precisely only with level cash flows and no value change. To incorporate nonlevel cash flows and value change into an algebraic model adds a great deal of complexity, and simply generating the cash flows and solving for Y_e is likely easier. An imprecise but quick estimate of Y_o can be made by simply weighting Y_m and Y_e using the loan-to-value ratio. The result will be in error to the extent loan amortization on a value change affects the loan-to-value ratio over the holding period.

As in the case of Y_o, Y_e can also be estimated by surveying those in the marketplace. Because most investors think in terms of levered yields, the results may prove more accurate than those generated when asking for the expected Y_o.

The approaches used to estimate the after-tax yield to equity, Y_a, are like those used to estimate Y_o and Y_e; that is, by constructing the after-tax cash flows that result from observed capitalization rates and income and value forecasts, and by surveying market participants.

For many kinds of investments, Y_a can be estimated by adjusting Y_e by the tax rate; $Y_a = Y_e (1 − T)$. This approach is unreliable for most real property investments, because the relationship between Y_e and Y_a is distorted by the relationship between loan amortization and the tax impacts of depreciation write-offs.

Questions and Problems

1. What characteristics of real estate investments do investors expect to be compensated for, not including financial risk?
2. Of what use can the appraiser make of the current yield on long-term (such as 10-year) government bonds?
3. Estimating the premiums for various risks

and nonrisk costs is difficult. Is there an alternative way to estimate the average return to real estate, while still utilizing the summation approach?

4. List three possible weaknesses in the approach to estimating the discount rate you described in Question 3.

5. In addition to the summation approach, what are two other ways to estimate a discount rate.

6. When is $Y_e > Y_o$? Why?

7. How can Y_e be estimated? What advantage might the use of a finance-explicit model have over the use of a nonfinance-explicit model?

8. An investment produced $50,000 of taxable income. Depreciation expense was $19,000 and the principal payment on the note was $8,000. What was before-tax cash flow?

9. The relationship between before-tax yield (Y_e) and after-tax yield (Y_a) is often modeled like this: $Y_a = Y_e (1 - T)$, where T is the investor's income tax rate. What does your answer to Question 8 suggest about the use of this model for estimating the Y_a to be used for real estate investments?

10. How can Y_a be estimated?

CHAPTER 23
Partial Interests and Value: Does the Whole Equal the Sum of the Parts?

The purpose of most appraisals is to estimate the value of the complete bundle of property rights. There are many exceptions, however, and some are so common they were given individual treatment earlier in the text. They include the separation of property into the physical components of land and buildings, the financial components of debt and equity, and the contractual components of leased fees and leaseholds. Other partial interests include the conversion of apartments into condominiums or cooperatives, the subdivision of acreage into lots, and the increasingly sophisticated financing instruments used to "securitize" real estate.

A critical issue when considering the value of partial interests is the relationship between the values of the partial interests and the value of the whole. The central question is whether value is (or can be) created or destroyed by dividing the whole. Put differently, is the value of the parts always equal to the value of the whole?

In some cases, the answer is obvious. For example, the total value of the lots exceeds the value of the acreage from which the lots were divided, and the total value of the condominiums exceeds the value of the apartments from which the condominiums were converted. Other situations are less clear cut. Examples include the question of how the financing of a property affects its value and whether the total value of the leasehold and leased fee interests is equal to the value of the fee simple.

Is it proper to assume that the equity value of the underlying real estate is equal to the equity value of the limited partnership units? If not, what accounts for the difference? Similarly, is the value of REIT shares equal to the value of the property interests owned by the REIT?

The appraiser should be able to provide defensible answers to these kinds of questions. The impact on the value estimate can be significant, and at a practical level, what is decided about value relationships is likely to affect appraisal techniques. For example, if it is concluded that the value of the parts is equal to the value of the whole, a residual value approach (like the building residual) can be used. If it is concluded that there is likely to be a difference in the values of the parts and the whole, then the appraisal process becomes more complicated.

The difficulty is that like the search for truth and beauty, the results of a search for a universally applicable answer to the question of whether the value of the whole is equal to the value of its parts is likely to be somewhat disappointing. There is not yet a fully developed theoretical framework for thinking about the issues, and more important, there is insufficient empirical evidence as to how markets actually behave.

This is not unique to real estate markets. For example, there is widespread disagreement about the valuation consequences of a leveraged buyout of a firm, followed by the selling off of bits and pieces. The majority opinion is that such a strategy will increase total value, but we must await more evidence for a definitive answer. A decade or so ago, a similar debate surrounded the opposite phenomenon of the merging of firms. The theory then was that mergers create synergy and ultimately value. That theory did not survive the test of time and we now await judgment on the currently fashionable buy and divide strategy.

In the case of real estate valuation, the problem of valuing partial interests has suffered a bit from benign neglect, because the issues accompanying more traditional value relationships (for example, the relationship between the fee simple and its land and building components) were relatively easier to untangle than those of more recent vintage (for example, the value of limited partnership shares versus the value of the underlying real property). As a result, the development of a theoretical framework has lagged, and there has also been a tendency to treat each kind of partial interest issue separately, instead of as an application of a covering principle. Thus, while most appraisers can correctly identify certain situations where value may be changed by dividing the fee simple, they find it difficult to explain why. This is reflected in the appraisal literature. Most textbooks are either silent on the matter, or, when positions are taken they tend to be quite general. For example, the Federal Home Loan Bank Board's[1] *Statement on Appraisal Policies Practice* contains this advice:

> *Appraisals should reflect, in the valuation of fractional interests in the real estate, the accepted premise that it is inappropriate to arrive at the value of the whole by simply summing the fractional interests.* Similarly, it is also inappropriate to arrive, without market support, at the value of a fractional interest in the real estate by merely subdividing the value of the whole into proportional parts. All analysis involving *fractional interests in the real estate, where the combined value of all interests on estates is not reported,* should establish with market evidence whether the terms and conditions of the agreement creating the estate or fractional interest reflect market rates and terms.

---

[1]*Federal Home Loan Bank Board,* Subchapter D, Chapter V, Table 12, Code of Federal Regulation. 5536.17

Thus, the issue is recognized and the appraiser is told that simplistic formula approaches are inappropriate. However, little insight is given into what *is* appropriate. This is unfortunate, for while a consensus has yet to be reached on many individual issues, some useful lessons have been learned. These lessons can help the appraiser align accepted value theory, standards of principle practice, and common sense.

Our discussion proceeds by first developing a general framework for thinking about the relationship of partial versus whole values, then uses as a more detailed example one of the most widely debated questions—how the value of the property relates to the value of its debt and equity components.

Does the Whole Equal the Sum of the Parts?

Most of the time the answer is yes. The conclusion that the whole equals the sum of the parts is deeply rooted in value theory and in general serves the appraiser well. The question is whether the principle is universally applicable. The answer is that it is not. It is important to understand, however, that there are specific conditions that are necessary for value to be changed by dividing the whole. Further, *if* those conditions are met, and value *is* changed, there remains the question of whether it is the value of the real property or something else that has been changed.

When the Whole *Does Not* Equal the Sum of the Parts

Consider a grocery store, where we find many examples of the whole not equaling the sum of its parts. Whole watermelons sell for less than two halves. A bushel of apples sells for less than an equal amount bought by the pound. Whole chickens and cut-up chickens sit side by side, but at different total prices.

Two conditions are necessary to add value by dividing. First, there must be an unsatisfied demand for the parts. Customers must be willing to pay the added price. Second, from the supply side, it must be costly (including the opportunity cost, which can change if dividing changes the risk) to duplicate the results of the division. Customers will not pay for something they can obtain at little or no cost somewhere else. The most obvious situation where duplication is impossible at any cost is when the product is unique. In the more common case where a duplicate (or a close substitute) can be obtained at trivial cost, competition on the supply side will not allow the price to rise.

The Grocery Store and Real Property

The grocery store lesson can be applied to a number of real property valuation situations. The total value of condominium units does not equal the value of the undivided property because (1) it is more costly to develop (or convert) individual units (including legal and marketing costs) than to build an apartment, and (2) it is less costly for the typical buyer to pay those added costs per unit than to purchase a whole property and attempt to dispose of the unwanted portion.

The same conceptual blanket covers subdivision, which is a costly process that produces a good buy in the sense the consumer does not have the resources to accomplish the same result independently. Conversely, it is equally clear that if the whole is desired, it is not generally prudent to buy it piece by piece. A bakery does not purchase a truckload of apples a pound at a time, nor does one desiring an apartment building acquire it by purchasing all the condominium units in a building and reconverting them.

The point is, if the value of an apartment is at issue, it is not valued by adding the values of the condominiums to which it can be converted, any more than raw acreage is valued by adding the value(s) of the lots to which it may be divided. *After* conversion or subdivision, of course, the question of does "the whole equal the parts" becomes meaningless, as the whole, while it may exist physically, is a legal fiction.

Dividing is not the only way to increase value. Plottage adds value by *combining* individual parcels, assuming again that the process fulfills the necessary conditions that (1) it is costly, and (2) an ultimate purchaser must consider the added cost a good buy relative to the cost of duplication.

When the Whole *Does* Equal the Sum of the Parts

One of the earliest, longest-lasting, and as yet not completely settled debates in the finance literature focuses on the effect of financing (the mix of debt and equity, or in appraisal technology, the loan-to-value ratio) on the value of the firm. There is much to be learned from that debate.

It was at one time thought that the judicial use of debt would increase a firm's value because the use of cheaper debt rather than more expensive equity would drive down the capitalization rate, increasing value. Of course, there was a limit to how high value could be levered. Beyond a certain debt-to-equity (or loan-to-value) ratio, equity investors would become so nervous about the risk of financial distress that they would increase their expected return to a level that would more than offset the effects of the use of the cheaper debt.

In 1958, Modigliani and Miller[2] demonstrated that in perfect markets—without such things as taxes and transaction costs—the use of debt to

---

[2]Franco Modigliani and Merton Miller, "The Cost of Capital, Corporation Finance, and the Theory of Investment," *American Economic Review* (June 1958).

increase value upward is not possible. The reason is that the firm's financing decision can be duplicated by the investor at trivial cost. This violates one of the conditions necessary to add value. Because investors will not pay for something they can get for nothing, in perfect markets the firm's financing decision cannot affect the value of the firm.

Subsequent attention has focused on the more interesting question of how financing affects values in the real world of imperfect markets. Taxes do exist, there are information and transaction costs, and different entities may pay different prices (interest) for credit. Moreover, we notice that debt-equity ratios tend to cluster by industry type, indicating that there may in fact be valuation advantages to certain financing structures. The current wisdom is that the existence of imperfections can affect the choice of financing, and in turn, this can affect the value of the *firm*. However, if financing affects the firm's value because of market imperfections, the value of the firm is increased because it has offered a valuable *financial service*, not because the underlying assets of the firm have changed in value. Thus the value of a firm is:

$$V_{Firm} = V_{Real\ Assets} + V_{Financial\ Services}$$

As an example of a valuable financial service increasing the value of the firm, when zero-coupon bonds were first introduced they met an unsatisfied demand, and bond purchasers were willing to accept a lower interest rate than the rates available on competing securities. This *financial service* was valued in the market, and the interest rate savings to the firm were capitalized into increased market value. Not for long, however. Other firms took notice and offered their own zero-coupon bonds, driving rates up and drying up the temporary value of the financial service.

Financing and Real Estate Value

Now consider real property. If financing affected risk and expected returns only, and didn't matter with respect to value, we would expect a more or less rectangular distribution of loan-to-value ratios corresponding to investors' varying attitudes toward risk. That isn't what we observe, however. Instead, loan-to-value ratios tend to cluster, historically in the 65–80% range. Unless we are willing to assume almost all real estate investors have the same attitude toward risk, there must be another explanation. That explanation is that the existence of typical loan-to-value ratios, like the clustering of debt-equity ratios for certain industries, is likely the result of market imperfections such as taxes, which make certain financing structures more attractive than others, and therefore affect property values *in general*. For example, a rise in interest rates puts downward pressure on prices, just as a more liberal depreciation schedule tends to increase prices. Thus, market values are affected by financing conditions as shown in Equation 1.

$$Value = Value_{unlevered} + Value_{financing\ side\ effects} \quad (1)$$

However, once again this cannot be the whole story, as Equation 1 implies that 100 percent debt is optimal, which is not consistent with what we observe. The rest of the story is that the use of debt carries with it the potential for financial distress—default and perhaps bankruptcy. As the loan-to-value ratio increases, the probability of distress increases. Not only is distress costly when it occurs, but the increased threat of distress is also costly, as it is likely to result in immediate costs, such as a higher interest rate, or more restrictive mortgage covenants.

Therefore, our value model must be modified to reflect these costs, as in Equation 2.

$$Value = Value_{unlevered} + Value_{financing\ side\ effects} - Value_{financial\ distress\ costs} \quad (2)$$

The optimal loan-to-value ratio is at the point when the marginal value added by the use of another dollar of debt equals the marginal value subtracted by the expected value of potential financial distress costs associated with the added dollar. The observed clustering of loan-to-value ratios reflects this optimal level, and is referred to as the typical loan-to-value ratio used in mortgage-equity value models.

This *macro* effect on absolute price levels should not be confused with the *micro* effect of financing on the prices of individual properties. Because typical financing, like run-of-the-mill corporate debt, is widely available, the values of individual properties cannot be affected by how they are financed. Moreover, most financing is extinguished (prepaid) when a property is sold, and the financing of the property is left to the discretion of the purchaser. Given that buyers will not pay for something that can be duplicated at trivial cost, we find that the loan-to-value ratio (unlike chicken parts) does not affect market value. Therefore, the whole of the property must equal the value of the debt and equity parts. In sum, credit conditions help determine property values through the use of optimal loan-to-value ratios. However, once this value is determined, it is not affected by a financing structure different than the optimal.

Optimal Financing and the Market Value Definition

The conclusion that optimal loan-to-value ratios exist and help to determine market values is consistent with the traditional assumption about financing that is found in market value definitions. That is, that the property is typically financed. If we make the assumption that investors behave rationally, it follows that most will choose the optimal, value-maximizing debt/equity ratio. In this way, optimal is typical.

An investor who chooses a nonoptimal debt/equity ratio will likely suffer a suboptimal risk and return relationship. However, the market value of the property will not be affected.

Valuing Creative Financing

There is a second lesson from the valuation of the firm. Like zero-coupon bonds, many real estate financing structures are (at least temporarily) unique. Does this add value? To the *transaction* yes, but not to the real property. As in the case of the firm, transaction prices can be separated into components; one part the value of the real property, the other the value of the financial service provided. Thus,

$$\text{Transaction price} = V_{\text{Real Property}} + V_{\text{Favorable Financing}}$$

This is the conceptual underpinning of techniques like cash equivalency, which are designed to unbundle the value of the favorable interest rate from the value of the real property.

Valuing Limited Partnerships

Another example of value being added to a transaction but not to the real property is the distinction between the market value of initial offerings of limited partnership shares and the value of the underlying real property. Both of the necessary conditions to add value are met by syndication: it is a costly process and there is a demand for the shares. Therefore, the value of the limited partnership shares will typically (but not always) exceed the value of the property. Any added value, however, is properly attributed to the financial service provided by the syndicator, not to a change in the value of the real estate.[3] Thus, the limited partnership's value (V_{LP}) is conceptually the same as that of a firm:

$$V_{LP} = V_{\text{Real Property}} + V_{\text{Financial Services}}$$

Semantics should not be allowed to cloud the issue. When one asks the equity value of, say, General Motors, the proper answer is the market value of the outstanding equity shares. Remember, though, that this value includes more than the value of the real assets owned by General Motors. When asked the value of the equity of a limited partnership, again the proper answer is that it is the market value of the outstanding shares. Like General Motors, however, this value also includes more than the real property. The potential semantic problem comes from the fact that in the real estate business, equity value historically has been used to refer specifically to the equity value of the *real property*. With "securitization" it must be understood that the value of an equity share, for example in an REIT, includes more

---

[3] The value premium may or may not persist in the secondary market, due to factors such as relative illiquidity. See Mark Thompson and Eggert Dagbjartsson, "Market Discounting of Partial Ownership Interests," *Appraisal Journal,* October 1994.

than the value of the real estate, which remains unaffected by the act of syndication.[4]

Allocating a Change in Value: Property or Financing?

It is important to understand the different treatment of the dividing of an apartment into condominiums and the dividing of equity into limited partnership shares. While both must meet the necessary conditions to add value—that it be costly to duplicate, and that there be a demand for the dividend provided—the value added by dividing into condominiums is attributed to real property value while the value added by financing is attributed to the providing of a financial service. The distinction is that when the real property interest is changed, value is added to the interest(s), as in the case of chicken parts and watermelon halves.[5] Conversely, things like the financing decision do not change the form of the property, they refer to how that property is to be paid for.

---

[4] Which is why the "whole equals the parts" rule still can be applied to the *real property value*.

[5] This comes very close to a wholesale versus retail perspective. We hestitate to apply that terminology, however, because it is generally used to refer to differences in amount only. When real property is divided, say acreage into lots, there may result a difference in characteristics (different lots may have different utility) as well as amount.

Summary

There are two issues with respect to partial interests and real estate value: (1) does the value of the parts equal the value of the whole, and (2) if not, to what is the difference in value attributable? The necessary conditions for the value of the parts to exceed the value of the whole are that duplicating the division must be costly and there must be a demand for the final products. The effect of slicing the fee simple into component parts is no exception. That is why the total value of condominium units exceeds the value of the apartment from which they were converted and why the value of lots exceeds the value of the raw acreage.

When the slicing of the fee fails to meet one or both of the necessary conditions, value is not affected. One example is that the value of the fee simple generally equals the value of the leasehold, plus the value of the leased fee, because run-of-the-mill leases are widely available in competitive markets and can be transacted at relatively trivial cost. Readily available debt financing is another example of a valueless division. However, when financing is unique enough to demand a premium, that premium is properly attributed to the value of the financial service offered, not to the value of the property it is used to finance. This is because financing, unlike subdividing, does not affect the real property interest. Similarly, creating a limited partnership is a costly process, and given a demand for the product, a financial service is provided that is valued in the market. This value is attributable to the financial service provided, not to the real property being financed.

Questions and Problems

1. A developer purchases acreage, divides it, and sells the undeveloped lots. An analyst states that the sum of the value of the lots must be equal to the value of the whole parcel. Is the analyst correct?

2. You have convinced the analyst referred to in Question 1 that the total value of the lots exceeds the value of the original parcel. Sometime later, you are reviewing one of his or her reports which suggests that the market value of the real property rights in an office property are affected by the loan-to-value ratio used to finance the property. His rationale is that this is a case where the value of the parts can differ from the value of the whole. Comment.

3. If financing does not affect value, why does the total value of limited partnership shares exceed the value of the fee simple in the underlying real property?

4. Creative financing is to varying degrees unique, and is favorable to the buyer and costly to provide. Why then does it not add value to the real property?

5. What conditions are necessary for total value to be increased by dividing the whole?

6. A subject apartment property is comparable to a recent sale which was subsequently converted to condominiums. The subject is also a good candidate for conversion. Is the value of the subject equal to the price paid for the fee simple in the comparable apartment or to the total value of the condominiums to which it is likely to be converted?

7. If you were asked to value a syndicated property, would its value be equal to the sum of the shares outstanding, on the basis that in order to reacquire the fee simple, those shares must be purchased in the market?

8. If financing "doesn't matter," why do loan-to-value ratios cluster?

CHAPTER 24
Investment Analysis

Investment analysis includes a wide range of client-specific services that the appraiser may be called upon to provide. The difference between doing an investment analysis and estimating market value is that while market value is a same-for-all number that theoretically reflects the average opinion of buyers and sellers, an investment analysis is tailored for an individual whose objectives, attitudes toward risk, ability to borrow, and tax situation may vary considerably from the average. In many cases, the investment analysis begins where the market value appraisal ends, seeking an answer to the question of whether paying at or around the market value makes sense for a given individual.

As is the case for any investment, the attractiveness of a real estate investment depends on its risk/return profile. The analysis is a two-step process. The first step is to forecast income and proceeds of sale. The second step is to apply quantitative performance measures that provide insights into return and risk. These measures are the topic of this chapter, beginning with the expected rate of return.

Measures of Return

The measures of return to be discussed are (1) *NOI/Cost,* (2) *Before-tax cash flow/Cash invested,* (3) *After-tax cash flow/Cash invested,* (4) the reciprocal of the payback period, and (5) discounted cash flow models, including Net present value (NPV) and the *IRR*. Most of these measures are familiar, as they were used in previous chapters to help estimate market value. We will apply them here to an example investment in an apartment property. Forecasts of first year *NOI, BTCF,* and *ATCF* are shown in Table 24–1.

TABLE 24–1 First Year Income and Cash Flow Estimates

Asking price	$800,000	
50 units, renting for $300 per month per unit		
Vacancy	5%	
Operating expenses	Fixed $30,400, Variable $38,000	
Depreciation expense	$36,000	
Debt	$600,000 at 12.5%, interest only amortized monthly	
Annual debt service	$75,000	
Investor's tax rate	35%	

First-Year NOI		**Cash Flows**
Potential gross income	$180,000	BTCF = NOI − DS
(50 units at $300 per month)		
Vacancy (.05)	9,000	= $102,600 − 75,000
Effective gross income	$171,000	= $27,600
Operating expenses		
Fixed $30,400		ATCF = BTCF − Tax
Variable $38,000	68,400	= $27,600 − (2,940)
Net operating income	$102,600	= $30,540
Depreciation expense	36,000	
Interest expense	75,000	
Taxable income	($8,400)	
Tax (.35)	($2,940)	

Measures of Return Based on First-Year Expectations

$$R_o = \frac{NOI}{Cost}$$

The return on investment measured as

$$\frac{NOI}{Cost}, \text{is} \frac{\$102,600}{\$800,000} = 12.8\%.$$

This is the familiar overall capitalization rate, which relates the property's productivity, *NOI*, to the property's cost. While very useful for market valuation, the overall rate has limited utility for making investment decisions. *NOI* explicitly reflects neither tax shelter nor income or value change, nor does it reflect explicitly the impact of financing on the equity investor's expected return. Moreover, the measure of investment used in this rate of return calculation is the property's cost, which represents the equity position only for all cash financing.

In sum, the *NOI/Cost* measure is a very crude decision-making tool for the equity investor, as neither the numerator nor the dominator reflect the investor's actual inflow and outflow of cash.

$$R_e = \frac{\text{Before-Tax Cash Flow}}{\text{Cash Invested}}$$

The *NOI/Cost* measure of return to equity can be improved by considering the effects of debt financing. Subtracting debt service from *NOI*, we get before-tax cash flow, and when the loan amount is subtracted from cost, we get cash invested. Thus,

$$R_e = \frac{NOI - DS}{Cost - Debt} = \frac{BTCF}{Cash\ invested}.$$

For the example property,

$$\frac{BTCF}{Cash} = \frac{\$102{,}600 - 75{,}000}{\$800{,}000 - 600{,}000} = \frac{\$27{,}600}{\$200{,}000} = 13.8\%.$$

This "cash-on-cash" return, or equity-capitalization rate, is more useful than *NOI/Cost* for decision making because it is based on the cash inflows and outflows to equity. However, it must still be considered a rule-of-thumb measure, as it ignores tax shelter, as well as value changes and expected income beyond the first year.

$$R_a = \frac{\text{After Tax Cash Flow}}{\text{Cash Invested}}$$

The impact of taxes on return can be captured by using after-tax rather than before-tax cash flow as the measure of annual cash benefits to the equity investor. This is important for real estate investment, as the opportunity to shelter income is often an important motivation for investing. To get from before-tax to after-tax cash flows, simply subtract the taxes payable from before-tax cash flow. For the example investment, we have

$$R_{\hat{a}} = \frac{BTCF - Tax}{Cash} = \frac{ATCF}{Cash}$$

$$= \frac{\$27{,}600 - (\$2{,}940)}{\$200{,}000} = \frac{\$30{,}540}{\$200{,}000} = 15.3\%.$$

Notice that in this case, the tax shelter covers not only the before-tax cash flow from this investment, but also shelters income from other sources. In other words, the investor will pay $2,940 *less* in taxes with this investment than without it. Therefore, after-tax cash flow is higher than before-tax cash flow. The amount and type of other income that can be sheltered from tax is a function of current tax rules. Whatever those rules happen to be, an after-tax measure of return is of primary importance to the investors.

A summary of first-year return measures shows that as we move from *NOI/Cost*, to *BTCF/Cash* to *ATCF/Cash*, more factors of interest to the equity investor are explicitly included. Put differently, we have worked from a measure of performance that appears near the top of the cash flow statement (*NOI*) to a measure at the bottom (*ATCF*). In the process, an increasingly more useful number has been provided on which to base an investment decision. Nonetheless, all three of these measures of return contain a common weakness—they are all based on first-year expectations. The future is ignored. Thus, in order to make a statement like "the after-tax return (on the example property) is 15.3 percent," it must be assumed (1) that *ATCF* will not change over time, and (2) that the after-tax equity at reversion will equal the original equity investment. This is a highly improbable assumption, and therefore, any return measure based solely on first-year expectations cannot be considered a good estimate of the holding period return.

Measures of Return Based on Expectations beyond the First Year

The remaining measures of return to be discussed are based on forecasts extending beyond the first year and through the projected holding period.

For the same example apartment property, assume the cash flows and sale proceeds shown in Table 24–2 have been forecasted for a projected five-year holding period.

The measures of return that will be discussed are the reciprocal of the payback period, net present value, and the *IRR*.

Reciprocal of the Payback Period $= \dfrac{1}{\textit{Payback Period}}$

The payback period is the length of time it takes to recover the initial investment. For example, a property requiring a $100,000 investment and which produces $10,000 of annual cash flow has a payback period of 10 years. The after-tax payback period for the equity investment in the example property is 5 years, as the initial $200,000 investment is not recovered until the property is sold. The length of the payback period is often used as an indicator of risk, because it is easier to forecast cash flows occurring early in the holding period than those occurring later. Thus, a quicker payback is associated with a less risky investment.

The payback period can also be used as a measure of return by taking its reciprocal. A 10-year payback implies a 1/10 = 10% average annual return, while a five-year payback implies 1/5 = 20% average return. Note that this implies that the initial investment is exactly recovered during the payback period.

A general weakness of the payback reciprocal as a measure of return is that it ignores all cash flows beyond the payback period. For real estate analysis specifically, another difficulty is that the projected holding period is often shorter than the payback period, gutting the utility of the measure.

TABLE 24-2 Holding Period Income and Cash Flow Forecasts

	1	2	3	4	5
Potential gross income	$180,000	$185,000	$191,000	$198,000	$206,000
Vacancy (.05)	9,000	9,250	9,550	9,900	10,300
Effective gross income	$171,000	$175,750	$181,450	$188,100	$195,700
Operating expenses					
Fixed 30,400					
Variable 38,000	68,400	70,300	72,580	75,240	78,280
Net operating income	$102,600	$105,450	$108,870	$112,860	$117,420
Depreciation	36,000	36,000	36,000	36,000	36,000
Interest	75,000	75,000	75,000	75,000	75,000
Taxable income	(8,400)	(5,550)	(2,130)	1,860	6,420
Tax (.35)	($2,940)	($1,943)	($746)	$651	$2,247
NOI	$102,600	$105,450	$108,870	$112,860	$117,420
− DS	75,000	75,000	75,000	75,000	75,000
BTCF	$ 27,600	30,450	33,870	37,860	42,420
BTCF	27,600	30,450	33,870	37,860	42,420
− Tax	+ 2,940	+ 1,943	+ 746	− 651	− 2,247
ATCF	$ 30,540	$ 32,393	$ 34,616	$ 37,209	$ 40,173
Sale Proceeds, end of year 5					
Selling price		$975,000			
Mortgage balance		600,000			
Before-tax equity reversion		375,000			
Taxes		60,000			
After-tax equity reversion		$315,000			

This is, in fact, what happened with the example property; the 20 percent return was driven by the annual 5-year holding period.

Discounted Cash Flow Models: Net Present Value and the Internal Rate of Return

Discounted cash flow models are generally the preferred measures of return, as they explicitly reflect how much cash is expected, and when.[1] Recall that net present value (*NPV*) is the difference between the present value of the future cash flows and the initial equity investment required, and the *NPV* rule is to accept positive *NPV*s because this indicates the expected return exceeds the discount rate (the required return). A negative *NPV* suggests the opposite; that the investment should be rejected (at the assumed price) because the return would fall below the discount rate.

---

[1] The theory and mechanism for discounting cash flows are discussed in Chapter 16.

Chapter 24 Investment Analysis

For example, at a 12 percent discount rate, the cash flows below have a present value of $92,515, and an *NPV* of $92,515 − $85,000 = +$7,515.

0	1	2	3	4	5
($85,000)	10,000	11,000	12,000	15,000	$100,000

The positive present value of $7,515 means this is an acceptable investment, as the expected return exceeds the minimum return of 12 percent used to discount the cash flows. Though sufficient to make an "accept-reject" decision, the *NPV* calculation tells the investor only that the expected return is somewhere above or below the discount rate. A natural question to ask is how much above or below? Or, what is the expected return? What is being asked for is the *internal rate of return* (*IRR*). The *IRR* can be viewed as a special case of *NPV* when the discount rate used produces an *NPV* = 0. The logic is straightforward. If *NPV* < 0, the actual return will be less than the discount rate. If *NPV* > 0, the actual return will be greater than the discount rate. Therefore, if *NPV* = 0, it follows that the discount rate *is* the rate of return, which is called the internal rate of return. The *IRR* for the cash flows immediately above is 14.38 percent. This is consistent with the previous calculation of *NPV* = +$7,515, which meant that the *IRR* > 12 percent.

Therefore, the *IRR* rule is to accept investments which are expected to produce an *IRR* above the minimum acceptable level. Notice the relationship between the *NPV* and the *IRR*. The *NPV* calculation uses the minimum acceptable rate of return as the discount rate, and tests whether the actual rate is higher or lower than that rate. The *IRR* calculates the actual rate to see if it is higher or lower than the minimum.

If *NPV* and the *IRR* seem like alternate routes to the same decision, you are on the right track. In most cases, the *NPV* rule and the *IRR* rule give the same "accept-reject" signal. There are, however, some cases when the *NPV* and *IRR* rules may give conflicting signals, such as when there is more than one negative cash flow. When *NPV* and *IRR* conflict, it is generally thought best to rely on *NPV,* as it enjoys some theoretical advantages over the *IRR*. In practice, however, the instances when conflicting signals are given are quite rare. Thus, the return measure used most often in practice is less a function of theoretical advantage than it is of the specifics of the assignment and the audience for which the analysis is intended.

Returning now to the continuing example of the apartment property (Table 24–2), these after-tax cash flows were estimated:

0	1	2	3	4	5
(200,000)	30,540	32,393	34,616	37,209	40,173 + 315,000

Assuming an expected after-tax return of 15 percent, the *NPV* is +$72,539. The *IRR* is 24.1 percent. As almost always happens, both measures give the same signal, in this case, the investment is acceptable.

A Summary of Rate of Return Measures

Six measures of return have been discussed, and all were applied to the example property shown in Tables 24–1 and 24–2. Table 24–3 is a summary of the results.

Note the large differences among the measures of return. This is not unusual, and is a good example of why it is necessary to understand what is included in the various measures and how much weight they should carry in the decision process.

In this case, the rates of return increase as we move from the crudest measure (*NOI/Cost*) toward the more sophisticated discounted cash flow models. Do not conclude from this that the reason the more sophisticated models are better is because they produce higher estimated returns. The specific pattern of returns will be case-dependent, and it is not uncommon to produce a scattering of relatively high and low returns. However, common sense can help us predict what the pattern might look like for a specific property. If income (and value) is expected to increase over time, those measures that explicitly consider the future (*DCF* models, and to a lesser extent, the payback reciprocal) will capture those increases and give higher return estimates than will measures that are based only on first-year returns. This is what happened for the example property. Conversely, a declining income stream will produce first-year returns that are higher than holding period returns. When relatively level income and value is expected, the differences among the return measures will be relatively smaller.

TABLE 24–3 Summary of Rate of Return Estimates

Return Measure	Estimated Rate of Return
$\dfrac{NOI}{Cost}$	12.8%
$\dfrac{BTCF}{Cash}$	13.8%
$\dfrac{ATCF}{Cash}$	15.3%
$\dfrac{1}{Payback}$	20.0%
NPV (after-tax) at 15%	*NPV* = +$72,539
IRR (after-tax)	24.1%

We conclude this section by pointing out an important conceptual difference between estimating market value and doing an investment analysis. When the various income approach models were compared in an earlier chapter, an important conclusion was that given sales data of sufficient quality, the use of directly extracted rates and ratios (like the GIM and R_o) were perfectly acceptable and even the preferred ways to estimate market value. For investment analysis, however, the opposite is generally true. Seldom will an investor make a decision based solely on a GIM. More likely, a complete discounted cash flow analysis will be done.

Risk Analysis

The investment decision coin has two sides: on one side is the estimated rate of return, on the other side is the estimated risk. In markets that are functioning reasonably efficiently, as the expected return increases, so does the risk, and vice versa.

Historically, while both sides of the coin have been recognized, in practice, the rate of return has dominated the training and thinking of real estate appraisers and analysts. For example, the number of *Appraisal Journal* articles devoted to rate of return measurement far outnumbers those devoted to risk, and appraisal texts (including this one) typically devote much more space to rate of return measurement than to risk analysis.

One reason that risk analysis has lagged is that it tends to be imprecise. While differences of opinion exist with respect to the merits of various return measures, there is little argument about what the numbers mean. Conversely, we are still arguing about what risk is, and how to measure whatever we decide it is. Also, historically, there has not been a pressing need for appraisers to know or do much about risk. In their traditional role as market value estimators, appraisers could rely on market extracted rates and ratios—like GIMs and OARs—realizing these ratios included a premium for whatever risks were present. However, as appraisers expand their services to include more investor-specific analysis, it is not sufficient to refer simply to market-extracted rates.

Several measures of risk will be discussed. They are (1) the breakeven point, (2) risk absorption capacity, (3) IRR partitioning, and (4) sensitivity analysis, scenarios and simulation. These measures are designed to answer questions about the risks of a specific investment, and are applied to the same example property (see Tables 24–1 and 24–2) that was used to estimate rates of return.

The Breakeven Point

The breakeven point is the point at which the $BTCF = 0$. At that point there is exactly enough net operating income to cover operating expenses and debt service, but there is nothing left for the equity investor. Should income fall below the breakeven point the investor must contribute additional equity or fall into default.

The breakeven point can be calculated on the basis of either the necessary occupancy level (given an assumed rent level), or the necessary rent level (given an assumed occupancy level). It is generally calculated based on first-year expectations, reflecting the fact that when default occurs, it is usually early in the investment period.

The *breakeven occupancy level* is the number of units which must be occupied in order to produce enough income to cover operating expenses and debt service. The model is:

$$\text{Breakeven occupancy (BEO)} = \frac{\text{Fixed operating expenses} + \text{Debt service}}{\text{Annual rent per unit} - \text{Variable expenses per unit}}$$

Using the first-year expectations from the property in Tables 24–1 and 24–2, we have:

$$BEO = \frac{\$30{,}400 + \$75{,}000}{\$3{,}600 - \$800}$$

$$= 37.64 \; units^2$$

When 37.64 units are occupied on average, the breakeven point will be reached. This converts to a 37.64/50 = 75.3% occupancy level.

Working backward from the calculated breakeven point shows that it does produce the required zero cash flow to equity.

Rent		$135,504
(37.64 × $300 × 12)		
Operating Expenses		
Fixed	30,400	
Variable	30,112	60,512
(37.64 × $800)		
NOI		$ 74,992
DS		75,000
BTCF		-0- (rounding)

The *breakeven rent level* is calculated using the same logic; dividing operating expenses and debt service by the number of units assumed to be occupied produces the necessary rent per unit. The breakeven rent model is:

---

[2] The $800 of variable expense per unit is calculated by dividing $38,000 of variable expense by the number of units assumed to be occupied as the basis of that estimate, in this case, .95 × 50 = 47.5 units were assumed to be occupied. Thus, $38,000/47.5 = $800.

$$\text{Breakeven Rent} \atop (BER) = \frac{\text{Fixed expenses} + DS + (\text{Units occ.} \times \text{Variable exp. per unit})}{\text{Units occupied}}$$

For example, at an assumed occupancy of 90 percent (45 units occupied), the example property (Tables 24–1 and 24–2) has a breakeven rent of:

$$BER = \frac{\$30{,}400 + \$75{,}000 + (45 \times \$800)}{45}$$

$$= \$3{,}142.22$$

This converts to a monthly rent of $\$3{,}142.22 \div 12 = \$261.85$, say, $262, which is

$$\frac{\$300 - \$262}{\$300} = 12.7\%$$

lower than the expected rent of $300.

Again, it can be shown that this rent produces zero cash flow.

Rent	$141,399
($261.85 × 45 × 12)	
Operating Expenses	
Fixed $30,400	
Variable 30,000	66,400
NOI	74,999
DS	75,000
BTCF	-0- (Rounding)

Breakeven Points and Cash-on-Cash Returns

Another way to describe the breakeven point is that it produces a zero cash-on-cash return (or equity capitalization rate). It follows, then, that if the model can be used to solve for a zero return, it can be used to solve for any target equity capitalization rate by simply adding the required cash flow to the numerator. For example, the occupancy level needed to produce a 10 percent cash return, assuming $300 rents, includes not only the coverage of fixed expense and debt service but also $20,000 of necessary cash flow to equity (.10 × $200,000 equity).

$$\text{Required occupancy} = \frac{\text{Fixed expense} + \text{Debt service} + \text{Required cash flow to equity}}{\text{Rent per unit} - \text{Variable expense per unit}}$$

$$= \frac{\$30{,}400 + \$75{,}000 + \$20{,}000}{\$3{,}600 - \$800}$$

$$= 44.78 \text{ units, } 89.6\% \text{ occupancy}$$

Similarly, the required rent to achieve a 10 percent capitalization rate, assuming 90 percent occupancy, is:

$$\text{Required rent} = \frac{\$30{,}400 + \$75{,}000 + 45(\$800) + \$20{,}000}{45}$$

$$= \$3{,}587, \text{ or } \$299 \text{ per month.}$$

The Debt Service Coverage Ratio[3] (DSCR)

The debt service coverage ratio is defined as *NOI/ADS* (where *ADS* is the annual debt service) and is a simplified form of the breakeven point. It calculates the *NOI* "cushion" before cash flow reaches zero. For the example property (Tables 24–1 and 24–2), the first-year *DSCR* is $102,600/$75,000 = 1.37. That is, *NOI* is 37 percent higher than debt service. Clearly, the higher the expected *DSCR*, the less chance of reaching the breakeven point. Lenders tend to think in terms of the *DSCR* rather than the breakeven point. Historically, *DSCRs* of 1.15–1.30 have been most common for "run-of-the-mill" projects, though they have crept a bit higher lately in response to overbuilt markets. The analyst should be aware of what lenders currently expect as minimum *DSCRs*.

Risk Absorption Capacity

Larry Wofford and Lawrence Gittman[4] developed a measure called risk absorption capacity which answers the question of how large an average decline in annual cash flow can be absorbed before the investor's yield falls below a minimum level. The risk absorption capacity calculation is simple: divide the project's net present value (*NPV*) by the annuity factor at the discount rate. The example property in Table 24–2 was forecasted to produce these after-tax cash flows.

---

[3] The use of the debt service coverage ratio is discussed in the Appendix to Chapter 15.
[4] Larry E. Wofford and Lawrence J. Gittman, "Measuring a Project's Ability to Survive Adversity," *Real Estate Review*, Spring 1978.

0	1	2	3	4	5
($200,000)	30,540	32,393	34,616	37,209	40,173
					+ $315,000 (Reversion)
					355,173

Suppose a 20 percent after-tax yield is expected. Using that discount rate, *NPV* is +$28,658 reflecting the *IRR* of 24.1 percent, and the 5-year annuity factor at 20 percent is 2.9906. Therefore,

$$\text{Risk Absorption Capacity } (RAC) = \frac{NPV}{\text{Annuity Factor}}$$

$$= \frac{\$28,658}{2.9906}$$

$$= \$9,583$$

This means that after-tax cash flow can be $9,583 lower than is forecasted each year, and the equity investor will still receive a 20 percent yield. To test this result, we subtract $9,583 from the expected annual cash flows;

0	1	2	3	4	5
($200,000)	20,957	22,810	25,033	27,626	30,590
					+ $315,000
					345,590,

and as expected, the *IRR* is now 20 percent.

It may be useful to convert the risk absorption capacity figure to the allowable annual decline in *NOI*, as follows: Allowable decline in *NOI* = *RAC*/(1 − *Tax Rate*). This is called the risk absorption ratio (*RAR*). For the example property, with its assumed tax rate of 35 percent, the allowable annual decline in *NOI* is $9,583/(1 − .35) = $14,743. This represents a $14,743/$102,600 = 14.4% decline in first-year *NOI*.

Comparing RACs

When comparing the risk absorption capacities of two (or more) properties, it is not generally correct to conclude that the investment with the highest *RAC* is the least risky, as that would ignore any differences in the sizes of the investments. Instead we use the *RAR*, which was calculated above to be 14.4 percent for the example property.

Suppose now there is an alternative investment with an allowable *NOI* decline of $18,500. This exceeds the allowable decline of $14,743 of the example property, and would appear to be less risky. Suppose, however, that the *expected NOI* of the alternative investment is $190,000. Thus, its *RAR* = $18,500/$190,000 = 9.7%, which is a smaller allowable decline. Thus, the first investment can actually absorb a greater percentage decline in *NOI* and still meet the target yield.

Partitioning the IRR

The good news about the *IRR* is that it is a single number that captures all expected future cash flows. But that can also be bad news, as that single number doesn't tell us where the *IRR* is coming from. It could be any combination of before-tax cash flow, tax shelter, and proceeds of sale. Moreover, annual cash flow and the proceeds of sale can be further divided into the portions attributable to their current levels and the portions attributable to expected future growth.

In order to determine the relative contribution of these various components of return, the *IRR* can be partitioned. This result may be useful in two ways. First, certain clienteles prefer certain sources of return, and partitioning the *IRR* quantifies observations such as "that investment is mainly a tax shelter," while an alternative investment produces "mostly cash flow." Second, it may be the case that certain sources of return are more risky than others. For example, we are usually more certain about the expected first-year level of income than we are about future year's income and property value changes. In other words, by partitioning the *IRR* and identifying its sources, a judgment can be made as to the relative certainty of receiving the expected return.

There are a number of ways the *IRR* can be partitioned. The components selected will change with each situation and depend on the type of property and the clients' needs. To illustrate partitioning, we will use six components: (1) the first-year level of *BTCF*, (2) growth (above year one) of *BTCF*, (3) annual tax savings, (4) the recapture of original equity investment at reversion, (5) the recapture of loan amortization (equity build up) at reversion, and (6) the net increase in equity at reversion.

The mechanics of partitioning are based on what we know about the relationships among present value, net present value, and the *IRR*. Because the *IRR* is the discount rate which sets *NPV* = 0, when the cash flows from an investment are discounted at the investment's *IRR*, their present value must equal the original investment.

Therefore, the *IRR* is partitioned by calculating the present value of each component (by discounting its cash flows at the *IRR*), then calculating the percentage of total present value (the original investment) each component's present value contributes.

Partitioning the IRR of the Example Property

Returning again to Table 24–2, the after-tax *IRR* to the equity investor was calculated earlier to be 24.1 percent. This, then, is the discount rate that will be used to partition the *IRR* into the six components listed above. Below is a short description of each component and how it is calculated.

1. First-year level of *BTCF.* This is the expected *BTCF* in year 1. For the example property, it is $27,600. The present value of $27,600 for 5 years will be calculated.
2. Growth of *BTCF.* This is found by subtracting the *BTCF* of year one from each year's expected *BTCF.* For the 5-year holding period, these amounts (in order) are: $0, $2,850, $6,270, $10,260, and $14,820.[5]
3. Annual tax savings. This is the difference between *BTCF* and *ATCF.* When *ATCF* > *BTCF*, there is a tax savings. When *ATCF* < *BTCF*, there is a tax payment and this reduces the present value of tax savings. In order, the 5 years of tax savings are $2,940, $1,943, $746, ($651), and ($2,247).
4. Recapture of the original equity investment. This is the first of the three components of the after-tax sale proceeds. Of the $315,000 of after-tax proceeds, $200,000 recaptures the original equity investment. It is separated out and its present value calculated.
5. Recapture of loan amortization. Because this is an interest-only loan, there is no amortization. In situations where the loan is amortizing, the amortization is the difference between the original loan amount and the mortgage balance at reversion.
6. Net increase in equity. This is the difference between *ATER* and the sum of the original equity investment and loan amortization. In this case, it is $315,000 − $200,000 − 0 = $115,000.

Table 24–4 shows the calculations of the present values of the components, and what they contribute to the *IRR*.

These results do not mean much in a vacuum. However, like expected rates of return, with experience you will become familiar with typical source-of-return profiles for properties in a given market.

---

[5]For year 1, $27,600 − $27,600 = 0. For year 2, $30,450 − $27,600 = $2,850. For year 3, $33,870 − $27,600 = $6,270, etc.

TABLE 24–4 Contribution of Components to the *IRR*

Components	Amount	PV (at 24.1%)	Percent of PV (and IRR)
First-year level of *BTCF*	$27,600 (each year)	$ 75,615	37.8%*
Growth in *BTCF*	$0, $2,850, $6,270, $10,260, $14,820	$ 14,492	7.2%
Tax savings	$2,940, $1,943, $746, ($651), $2,247	$ 2,983	1.5%
Recapture of original equity	0, 0, 0, 0, $200,000	$ 67,947	34.0%
Loan amortization	-0-	-0-	-0-
Increase in equity	0, 0, 0, 0, $115,000	$ 39,070	19.5%
Totals		$200,107 (rounding)	100.0%

* $\dfrac{\$75{,}615}{\$200{,}107} = 37.8\%$.

Sensitivity Analysis, Scenarios, and Simulation

Some of the most useful information about expected investment performance comes in the form of answers to "what if" questions. Providing answers to "what if" questions may suggest a rethinking of certain aspects of the investment, for example the loan-to-value ratio, and it may also prepare the investor for the consequences if realized results do not match expectations.

"What if" analysis can be roughly divided into three categories. In ascending order of sophistication, they are: sensitivity analysis, scenarios analysis, and simulation. Sensitivity analysis tests the sensitivity of the level of one variable to changes in another variable. For example, if vacancy is 8 percent, what will happen to *NOI*? Or the cash on cash return?

Scenarios complicate things slightly. Instead of tinkering with only one variable, a future situation or scenario is described, likely including the levels of several key variables, and the effect of that combination of variables is calculated. For example, what will happen to a property's value if next year interest rates increase by 2 percent, the vacancy rate declines by 2 percent, and rents remain level? Many appraisers already use scenarios in the form of calculating upside/downside potential. This gives the investor a range of possible outcomes depending on the actual state of the market (scenario) sometime in the future.

Simulation goes one step further. While sensitivity analyzes the effects of changes in a single variable, and scenarios analyze the effect of changes in several key variables, simulation allows simultaneous changes of all variables. In *Monte Carlo* simulation, probability distributions of each variable are developed, and draws are made from each distribution to determine the targeted "bottom line." For example, if *IRR* is being simulated, the distributions of rents, vacancies, operating expense ratios, and value change are developed, and a draw is made from each distribution, resulting in a single *IRR* estimate. This process is repeated many times, resulting in the probability distribution of the *IRR*. The use of *Monte Carlo* simulation for real estate analysis was popularized by Steve Pyhrr[6] and is now available in many software packages.

---

[6] Steve Pyhrr, "A Computer Simulation Model to Measure the Risk in Real Estate Investment," *AREUEA Journal*, June 1973, 57.

Summary

The appraiser's traditional role as an estimator of market value has been joined by an increasing demand for investor-specific services. Like appraisal, investment analysis (or evaluation) is concerned with risk and return. There are a host of rate of return measures available, ranging from the "appraiser return" (the overall capitalization rate) to discounted cash flow models. The most widely used return measures are: (1) *NOI/Cost*, (2) *BTCF/Cash*, (3) *ATCF/Cash*, (4) 1/*Payback Period*, (5) *NPV*, and (6) *IRR*. The measure(s) used in each case will depend on the client's needs and desires, as well as the property and market being analyzed.

Risk analysis can also be tailored to the concerns of the individual, and includes measures of the variability of expected returns, and calculations of critical points at which performance moves from the acceptable range to the unacceptable. These measures include the breakeven point and the debt service coverage ratio, which calculate the point at which cash flow turns negative; the risk absorption capacity, which estimates the allowable decline in cash flow before the rate of return falls below a minimum level; partitioning the *IRR*, which provides information as to the source of the expected return; and sensitivity analysis, scenario writing, and simulation, which answer "what if" questions based on future levels of important variables.

Questions and Problems

1. A 14,000 square-foot office property is being offered for $960,000. An investor is considering financing the purchase with a $750,000 note at 10 percent for 25 years (*ADS* = $81,783). A five-year holding period is projected, with forecasted *NOI*, cash flows and sales proceeds as follows:

	1	2	3	4	5
Potential gross income (1st yr. = $12/ft. × 14,000)	$168,000	171,360	174,787	178,283	181,849
Vacancy (.06)	10,080	10,282	10,487	10,697	10,911
Effective gross income	$157,920	161,078	164,300	167,586	170,938
Operating expenses					
Fixed (1st yr. = $25,000)					
Variable (1st yr. = $40,120)	65,120	66,422	67,751	69,106	70,488
NOI	$ 92,800	94,656	96,549	98,480	100,450
Interest	74,682	73,938	73,114	72,208	71,208
Depreciation	26,315	26,315	26,315	26,315	26,315
Taxable income	(8,197)	(5,597)	(2,880)	(43)	2,927
Tax (.30)	(2,459)	(1,679)	(864)	(13)	878
NOI	$ 92,800	94,656	96,549	98,480	100,450
− DS	81,783	81,783	81,783	81,783	81,783
BTCF	11,017	12,873	14,766	16,697	18,667
− Tax	(2,459)	(1,679)	(864)	(13)	878
ATCF	$ 13,476	$ 14,552	$ 15,630	$ 16,710	$ 17,789

Sales Proceeds

Selling price	$1,075,000
Mortgage balance	706,235
BTER	$ 368,765
Taxes	25,000
ATER	$ 343,765

a. What is the "appraiser's" rate of return $\left(\dfrac{NOI}{Cost}\right)$?

b. What is the before-tax cash-on-cash return $\left(\dfrac{BTCF}{Cash}\right)$?

c. What is the after-tax cash-on-cash return $\left(\dfrac{ATCF}{Cash}\right)$?

d. What is the equity return calculated as the reciprocal of the after-tax payback period?

e. What is the NPV, given expected after-tax yield $(Y_a) = .15$?

f. What is the after-tax IRR?

2. a. What is the break-even occupancy rate for the office property with the expected cash flows shown in Question 1?

   b. Demonstrate your answer is correct.

3. a. What is the breakeven rent for the office property with the expected cash flows shown in Question 1, if occupancy falls to 90 percent?

   b. Demonstrate your answer is correct.

   c. What rent level is necessary,

4. What is the DSCR for the property in Question 1?

5. a. What is the risk absorption capacity for the property in Question 1, if the expected after-tax yield is 14 percent?

b. How does your answer to *a* above translate into an allowable percentage decline in first-year *NOI*?
c. Demonstrate your answer to *a* above is correct.

6. Partition the after-tax *IRR* of the property in Question 1 into these six components: (1) first-year level of *BTCF*, (2) growth of *BTCF*, (3) annual tax savings, (4) recapture of original equity investment at reversion, (5) recapture of amortization at reversion, and (6) increase in equity at reversion.

7. Briefly discuss the differences among the following rates of return: $\dfrac{NOI}{Cost}$; $\dfrac{BTCF}{Cash}$; $\dfrac{ATCF}{Cash}$; $\dfrac{1}{Payback}$; *NPV*; *IRR*.

8. a. What is the *NPV* rule? the *IRR* rule?
   b. Which is preferred, *NPV* or the *IRR*, as the basis for making investment decisions?

9. What is the after-tax risk absorption capacity of the property below, given a discount rate of 15 percent?

Cost:	210,000				
Mortgage:	142,125				
Debt service:	15,500				
	1	*2*	*3*	*Reversion*	
Gross rent	50,000	53,000	54,000	Selling price	250,000
VAC	5,200	5,300	5,500	Cost of sale	12,000
EGI	44,800	47,700	48,500	Mortgage balance	140,000
OE	23,000	23,200	23,500	Taxes	10,000
NOI	21,800	24,500	25,000	ATER	88,000
DEP	7,000	7,000	7,000		
INT	15,000	14,800	14,575		
TI	(200)	2,700	3,425		
Tax	(60)	810	1,028		

PART VI Reconciliation and Appraisal Reporting

CHAPTER 25 Reconciling Value Estimates

Introduction

The main product of an appraisal is typically a single point estimate of value. Therefore, the last analytic hurdle for the appraiser is to arrive at that single point estimate based on the values produced by the approaches used in the appraisal. This part of the appraisal process is called *reconciliation* (or less frequently, *correlation*). Reconciliation is necessary because imperfect real estate markets and imperfect appraisers do not produce perfect estimates and the three approaches are therefore likely to yield different estimates of value.

Each of the approaches presents a different set of estimating problems. Sales comparison is limited by the availability of comparables that are of reasonable quality. The cost approach is limited by the difficulties associated with estimating depreciation, particularly for older improvements, and the problems associated with market disequilibrium. Certain techniques of the income approach require highly subjective forecasts of future income and an estimate of a required return that properly reflects risk.

Given these kinds of uncertainties, in a general sense reconciliation is an ongoing part of the appraisal process. The sales comparison approach, for example, produces a single value estimate that is the result of reconciling the different estimates produced by adjusting each of the comparable sales. The cost approach requires a depreciation estimate, which more often than not is the result of reconciling data which may indicate various rates of depreciation. In the income approach, the net operating income estimate is the result of reconciling ranges of rents, vacancies, and expenses. These kinds of reconciliations were discussed as needed in prior chapters. This chapter is concerned with the reconciliation *step* in the appraisal process that produces the final value estimate.

A proper reconciliation consists of two parts: (1) a review of the technical and conceptual soundness of the analysis, including an explanation of differences among individual value estimates and an evaluation of which among them are most credible, and (2) based on this review, the selection of the final value estimate. Reconciliation, therefore, involves a thorough evaluation of the appraiser's own analysis. It is an "internal" appraisal review.

Despite the importance of reconciliation, there is some evidence that it remains a neglected part of the appraisal process. In a 1977 sample of 640 apartment appraisals,[1] a majority of the reconciliations consisted of either a listing of the individual value estimates and a single statement as to the choice from among them or a listing of the individual estimates, the final choice, and a brief explanation for that choice. One explanation that appeared regularly was that "the income approach value estimate was chosen because it is considered the most useful in valuing income properties."

In almost every instance where the final estimate was the result of the weighting of individual estimates rather than a choice of a single estimate, no explanation was given for the weights chosen. Dividing the reports on the basis of space devoted to the reconciliation, and using one-quarter page increments as a rough measure, the most widely encountered space was one-half page, including a listing of the individual value estimates. This suggests that in most instances, the thought process leading to the final value estimate was not adequately justified and explained.

When writing this chapter, the author gathered a smaller sample of appraisals. The results were similar. Reconciliation tended to be given short shrift, with one-half page again the most common amount of space devoted, and as before, with very little explanation.

Part One: The Review

There are two parts to the review, (1) an evaluation of the overall appropriateness of the appraisal process, given the objectives of the appraisal, and (2) an evaluation of the technical merits of the analysis, including an explanation of differences among the value estimates that were produced by the different appraisal techniques and approaches.

Judging whether the overall appraisal process is appropriate to the defined task is based on how well the appraisal answers the client's question. Is the emphasis on the right approaches? For example, if investment value is the objective, is there a discounted cash flow analysis? If the client needs the value of depreciable improvements for tax purposes, was there sufficient analysis to support the separation of land and improvement values? If market value is the objective, has every effort been made to squeeze the most from the sales comparison approach? And, in general, does the analysis

---

[1] Lusht, Kenneth M. "The Behavior of Appraisers in Valuing Income Properties: A Status Report," *The Real Estate Appraiser and Analyst,* July–August 1979.

conform to any court-mandated procedures, especially if litigation is anticipated? If an appraisal fails these kinds of tests of "appropriateness" it has not accomplished its objective, regardless of its technical merits.

Once the appraiser is satisfied that the appraisal process is appropriate, the technical soundness of the steps in that process must be evaluated. The concerns are for *accuracy* and *explanation*. Examples of the kinds of questions the appraiser should consider include: Is the data reliable? Has it been used properly? Have individual adjustments been made in a logical manner? Is there internal consistency? For example, if a trend analysis is part of the sales comparison approach, is the estimated rate of value change consistent with the rate used to make time adjustments to the prices of comparables? If there was market disequilibrium, was its effect reflected in the depreciation estimate in the cost approach, and is that result consistent with the assumptions and results of the income approach?

Are the measurements for room size, etc., consistent in the sales comparison and cost approaches? In the income approach, is inflation properly reflected in cash flow estimates? If a partial interest is being valued, is the analysis consistent with accepted value theory as far as the relationship of the value of the partial interest and the value of the fee simple? And is the arithmetic correct? It may be useful to have someone else check the numbers.

Part Two: The Final Value Estimate

General Considerations

As the technical review proceeds, what should begin to emerge are explanations for differences among the value estimates and, in turn, a firmer idea of which of the estimates are the most defensible.

It is now time to make the final value estimate. It should be the appraiser's best, most defensible estimate, given the objectives of the appraisal, any legal constraints, and the constraints placed on the appraisal process by the quality of available data. In arriving at the final value, keep in mind that accuracy is a function not only of the number of data manipulations required but also of their size and reliability. Within the sales comparison approach, for example, different sales will produce different estimates of value. It may be that a more reliable estimate is obtained by making a relatively large number of small and relatively certain adjustments, than by making a small number of large and relatively uncertain adjustments.

Sometimes the objective of the appraisal or the client's needs will dictate the primary evidence of value. If insurable value is being sought there may be a bias toward the cost approach. If the objective of the appraisal is investment value the income approach will be emphasized, and so on. The objective of most assignments will be market value. When that is the case, the bias of the appraiser should be toward the results of the sales comparison approach. As has been emphasized, when the market speaks the appraiser should carefully listen. The problem, of course, is that the real estate market may speak infrequently, if at all. That is why appraisers exist, and as far as estimating market value is concerned, why we also have the cost and income approaches. When there is not sales data of sufficient quantity and quality, the appraiser is forced toward the results of either the cost or income approaches as the primary evidence of value. Thus, when estimating market value, the choice among which estimates to weight more heavily is dictated largely by the data. While sales comparison is preferred, it does not always produce the most defensible value estimate because of data limitations.

Recall a similar discussion from a previous chapter about the proper use of the various techniques under the income approach umbrella. The conclusion then, as it is now, is that the appraiser's bias should always be to give primary consideration to the value estimate produced by techniques that reflect direct evidence of value, and therefore, require the least subjective data manipulation by the appraiser.

Where does all of this leave us with respect to choosing the final value estimate? That choice should be made based on two main considerations (1) the objective of the appraisal, and (2) the realities of the marketplace, especially the quantity and quality of data available to estimate market value.

Choosing the Number

Based on the objective of the appraisal and the quantity and quality of data that the appraiser was able to bring to the task, the final value estimate may be the same as one of the value estimates from an approach, or it may result from a weighting of two or more of those estimates.

The weighting process involves consideration of two questions: (1) is it legitimate to average individual value estimates to arrive at the final value estimate?, and (2) is it legitimate during the reconciliation step to reconsider individual value estimates, leading to a compression of the range of those estimates?

Most writers discourage the use of a simple average of the value estimates produced by the three approaches. Boyce and Kinnard's text states that ". . . averages are so unreliable (and possibly unrepresentative as well) that they should not be used."[2] The text of the Appraisal Institute does not rule out averaging explicitly, but does state that "The final value estimate is not derived simply by applying technical and quantitative procedures; rather, it involves the experience of judgment."[3]

Historically, the question of the validity of averaging has been addressed as much from the perspective of the client's demands as on the basis of any

---

[2]Byrl N. Boyce and William N. Kinnard, *Appraising Real Property,* (Lennington: Lennington Books), 1984, 382.
[3]The *Appraisal of Real Estate,* (Chicago: AIREA) 10th ed., 1992, 559.

valuation philosophy. In the 1930s, the Home Owner's Loan Corporation required that all three approaches be used in every appraisal and that the final estimate be the arithmetic mean of the values indicated by the three approaches. While most appraisal texts never endorsed averaging, for a while some did suggest that individual value estimates be reconsidered and the range among them compressed as part of the reconciliation process.[4] While not averaging, this clearly serves much the same purpose. Currently, the practice of compression is not recommended in any widely used text nor by any of the major professional appraisal associations.

While averaging and compressing are not currently socially acceptable, they may in part be getting a bad rap. Consider averaging from the perspective of weighting individual estimates, which is acceptable. As discussed, the appraisal process, and particularly the reconciliation step, will reveal the results of certain approaches to be the most defensible. If the case is clear-cut, for example, when there are a large number of high-quality comparable sales, the final value estimate may be the same as the estimate produced in direct sales comparison. This is the same as giving the sales comparison approach 100 percent weight and the other approaches zero weight. When evidence from sales is thinner and the appraiser feels confident about depreciation estimates, equal weights (50 percent each) may be given to the results of the sales comparison and cost approaches, with the income approach ignored (given zero weight). Conversely, if the subject property produces income and there is little or no evidence from comparable sales, the results of the income approach may be weighted heavily (perhaps 100 percent). This is frequently the case for large or one-of-a-kind properties, like the Pan Am Building in New York or the Sears Tower in Chicago.

Mechanically, the weighting process is simple. Suppose the sales comparison, cost, and income approaches produce estimates of $103,000, $100,000, and $107,000, respectively, and the appraiser's judgment is that the sales comparison estimate should be given a weight of .75, the cost approach .25, and the income approach zero. The final value estimate would be .75($103,000) + .25($100,000) = $102,250.

Suppose now that the appraiser considers the results of the three approaches to be equally valid indicators of value. Assuming equal weights (of .333) produces a value estimate of .333($105,000) + .333($100,000) + .333($107,000) = $104,000. This is the same result we get by averaging the three values. We see then that averaging is simply another way to describe the outcome of assigning equal weights to each value indicator. While the judgment to weight equally may occur infrequently, it is theoretically no more or less valid than any other combination of weights.

Turning now to compression, if we believe that the appraisal process includes more than one technique because individual estimates are not likely

---

[4]See, for example, George L. Schwartz, *The Appraisal Process,* North Hollywood, CA, 1951.

to be 100% accurate, it follows that if there are large differences among the results of two or more techniques, at least one or more (and perhaps all) must be in error. The purpose of reconciliation is in fact to explain and reconcile such differences. If the market evidence supporting an estimate from a given approach is relatively weak, and the value estimate that resulted from that approach is ultimately found to differ significantly from the estimates of the other approaches, which were based on high quality data, is it improper to reconsider the outlier? Or more precisely, is it improper to reconsider the *assumptions* that lead to the outlying value estimate?

It is argued by some that this would violate the spirit of the appraisal process in the sense that the whole idea of different approaches and techniques is to produce independent estimates of value. To simply change those estimates "after the fact" is to ignore what they suggest about value. It is also pointed out that leaving each individual value estimate "as is" provides insight into the range of the expected selling price. The opposing view is that there is nothing sacred about an estimate. As discussed, reconciliation is really an ongoing part of the appraisal process and it is not unusual for individual estimates within an approach to be adjusted. Why then is this not acceptable among the approaches? Put differently, if it is agreed that it is inappropriate to compress or change values for no reason, it would seem to be equally inappropriate to not make changes when there is a reason. Finally, it may be argued that even without explicit compression, the weighting process produces results similar to compression. When using unequal weights, which is typical, the value estimate is forced toward the highest weighted approach(es).

Like many appraisal issues, it is dangerous to set out absolute rules with respect to averaging and compression. A policy to always average or compress seems indefensible, but no more so than a policy to never do so. The use of judgment is necessary throughout the appraisal process, and it should suddenly not be suspended at the last step.

Finally, the idea that all three approaches must be used in every appraisal has been largely abandoned in accepted value theory and by most clients, including government agencies. Similarly, when a given approach is used, but it produces weak evidence of value due to data or analytical problems, there is nothing wrong with ignoring that evidence by giving it a zero weight. At the other extreme, strong evidence of value produced by one approach may be relied on completely (100 percent weight), with the other approaches delegated to supporting roles.

Other Reconciliation Issues

Rounding

Real estate markets are imperfect, as are the value estimates that appraisers produce. Mathematical precision should not be confused with perfect value estimates, and it is accepted, even expected, that the appraiser will round the final value estimate.

Common sense dictates the magnitude of rounding. Rounding a $2,008,000 estimate to $2 million is acceptable; rounding $108,000 to $100,000 is not. As the appraised value increases, so does the acceptable level of absolute rounding.

A Range of Values

While it is recognized that perfect value estimates cannot be produced, single point estimates are nevertheless required by most clients. However, this does not prevent the appraiser from indicating a likely range of value into which the price will fall. This range may be objectively determined by a statistical approach, or it can be a subjectively estimated range, perhaps based on the highest and lowest estimates produced by the three approaches. When a range is indicated, it is helpful to translate the upper and lower bounds into a percentage difference. For example, if the final value estimate is $250,000, with a range of $240,000 to $265,000, the lower bound is 4 percent below and the upper bound 6 percent above the average. In general, a relatively narrow range implies relative confidence in the estimate, while a wider range implies less confidence.

Some Misconceptions about Reconciliation

The reconciliation step is a fertile area for the perpetuation of misconceptions about concepts and techniques. Among the most common are the following:

• "Averaging" and "compressing" are always improper. This has already been discussed.

• The result of the cost approach sets the upper limit on value. For reasons discussed earlier in the text, this is not generally correct. In practice the cost approach is subject to the same margins of error as the other approaches, and thus it cannot be assumed to represent the upper (or lower) limit.

• The more sophisticated the analysis, the more accurate the value estimate. This misconception can be traced largely to the widespread use of discounted cash flow models and the illusion of accuracy that sometimes accompanies complex calculations. In fact, the opposite is often the case. Because it relies heavily on forecasts and subjective judgment, the results of a discounted cash flow analysis will generally be an inferior predictor of selling price as compared to a simple analysis based on direct market evidence, such as overall capitalization rates, assuming the capitalization rates are extracted from truly comparable sales.

• The cost approach is not applicable because it ignores market conditions and expected rates of return. Properly applied, the cost approach reflects both a normal profit level and distortions of the profit level from disequilibrium conditions. The real difficulty with the cost approach is not theoretical, but practical. Estimating depreciation, particularly in disequilibrium and/or for older properties, may be subject to significant error.

• The use of statistics represents a fourth approach, and must be considered independently of the traditional three approaches. Statistical inference is not a fourth approach, but rather a variation of sales comparison generally based on a larger sample size. When mass appraisals are required, as for property tax assessment, statistical models such as regression are commonly used for the sales comparison approach.

Summary

The final analytic step in the appraisal process is the reconciliation of different value estimates to produce the final point estimate of value. Reconciliation consists of two related steps: a review of the conceptual and technical soundness of the analysis and a choice of the final value estimate.

It is important to explain why individual value estimates may differ and which of them are the most defensible, given the objective of the appraisal and the quantity and quality of data that was brought to the task. When estimating market value, the appraiser's bias should be to rely on the sales comparison approach as heavily as the data will allow. Assignments to estimate other kinds of value may suggest primary reliance be placed on either the cost or income approaches.

When the appraiser is satisfied with the conceptual and technical results of his or her work, it is time to choose the number which best represents the value being appraised. This involves a weighting process, whether implicitly or explicitly. The weights assigned to the individual value estimates can range from zero percent, effectively ignoring the estimate, to 100 percent, when the result of one approach is considered extremely convincing evidence of value.

Averaging individual value estimates to arrive at the final estimate is neither right or wrong; averaging is simply the special case of equal weights being assigned to each approach. The same philosophy should guide the appraiser with respect to changing individual value estimates during the reconciliation. While compression for compression's sake is improper, it is equally improper to ignore the fact that a given estimate is likely in error based on the evidence produced by other techniques and approaches.

Research has shown that reconciliation tends to be one of the more poorly presented and explained steps in the appraisal process. This is unfortunate, because it is the reconciliation step that produces the final product of the appraisal process. Therefore, the analysis leading to the final estimate should be thoroughly and clearly explained.

Questions and Problems

1. What is reconciliation?
2. Why is reconciliation necessary?
3. Describe the two related steps in reconciliation.
4. "The appraiser should not average to arrive at the final value estimate." Comment.
5. "The appraiser should not compress individual value estimates during reconciliation." Comment.
6. What impact does the quantity and quality of data used in various approaches have on the choice of the final value estimate?
7. What role does the objective of the appraisal have in the reconciliation?
8. The sales comparison, cost, and income approaches have produced estimates of $300,000, $311,500, and $313,000, respectively. The appraiser weights them 40 percent, 40 percent, and 20 percent. What is the final value estimate?
9. "A general rule of thumb when evaluating the credibility of value estimates from individual comparable sales is that sales requiring a fewer number of adjustments are preferable." Comment.
10. When estimating market value, why should the appraiser be biased toward the results of the sales comparison approach?
11. Does the cost approach set the upper limit on value?
12. An appraiser assigns weights of 40 percent, zero percent, and 60 percent to estimates of $1,500,000, $1,710,000, and $1,770,000. What is the final value estimate? Rounded?

Chapter 26 Professional Practice and Appraisal Reporting

Professional Practice

The primary purpose of appraisal education is to build technical competence. However, while technical competence is necessary for successful practice, it is not sufficient. Also necessary is a high standard of personal and professional conduct. The basic principles applicable to all appraisers are found in the *Uniform Standards of Professional Appraisal Practice* (USPAP). In addition, rules of conduct are set forth in codes of ethics adopted by various appraisal associations. The essential difference between a violation of USPAP and a violation of a code of ethics is whether or not the violation was made knowingly. If it was, then there was an ethics violation. If not, there was a standards violation. Thus, we see that an ethics violation is the more serious.

One of the most influential appraisal associations is the Appraisal Institute, which was formed in 1989 by a merger of the American Institute of Real Estate Appraisers (AIREA), which itself was established in 1932, and the Society of Real Estate Appraisers (SREA), which was established in 1935.

The Institute's Code of Professional Ethics is summarized in six canons:

- A Member or an Affiliate of the Appraisal Institute must refrain from conduct that is detrimental to the Appraisal Institute, the real estate appraisal profession, and the public.
- A Member or an Affiliate must assist the Appraisal Institute in carrying out its responsibilities to the users of appraisal services and the public.
- In the performance of an appraisal assignment, a Member or Affiliate must develop and communicate each analysis and opinion without bias for the client's interest or without accommodation of his or her own interests.
- A Member or Affiliate must not violate the confidential nature of the appraiser-client relationship.

- In promoting an appraisal practice and soliciting appraisal services, a Member or Affiliate must use care to avoid advertising or solicitation that is misleading or otherwise contrary to the public interest.
- A Member or Affiliate must comply with the requirements of the Standards of Professional Practice.

In addition to the six canons, additional guidelines and requirements are set forth in *Supplemental Standards and Guide Notes*. Standards and codes typically apply not only to the appraiser(s) who prepares the report, but also to review appraisers, and in some states, to assessors who value property for property tax purposes.

All rules of technical and ethical conduct have the common objective of protecting the interests of the public, clients, and the appraiser's professional colleagues. An appraisal report may end up being used for a variety of purposes. Thus, the appraiser's duty is to be objective, and to not allow either the client's or his or her own narrow interests to influence the value estimate. It is the appraiser's responsibility to become familiar with the rules of conduct of his or her association and to abide by those rules. Failure to do so can result in sanctions that range from letters of admonishment, to public censure, to expulsion.

The Appraisal Foundation

The Appraisal Foundation was established in 1987. Its members are professional appraisal association and certain academic and related industry associations. The objective of the Foundation is to contribute to the process of establishing standardized appraisal guidelines and appraiser qualifications through the Appraisal Standards Board (ASB) and the Appraiser Qualifications Board (AQB).

It is expected that over time, legislation will give the Foundation an increasing role in establishing appraisal policy, and in developing model bills to guide state licensing and certification.

Licensing and Certification

Federal legislation passed in response to the collapse of real estate markets in the late 1980s (FIRREA, the Financial Institutions Reform, Recovery, and Enforcement Act of 1989) requires appraisers to be either state licensed or certified if they prepare federally related appraisals. The licensing/certification requirement was effective January 1, 1993, with exceptions made for properties below a given minimum value. As of early 1996, the value was set at $250,000 for residential property. Each state is also required to establish minimum education, experience, and examination requirements for licensing and certification. In addition, most states have established continuing education requirements.

The impact of government regulation on appraisal quality has yet to be determined. The argument for licensing is that it raises quality to a minimal acceptable level. The argument against is that, because a license or certification provides widely accepted credentials, the motivation to pursue a more difficult-to-obtain professional designation may be weakened. In fact, as of 1996, many appraisal associations had from 25–40% fewer candidates than they had five years earlier. In the long run, this could lower average appraisal quality.[1]

Appraisal Reporting

The conclusion of most appraisals is an estimate of value. That conclusion is delivered to the client in an appraisal report. Not only must the report be prepared in a manner consistent with standards of professional practice, but on a practical level poorly presented findings are likely to reflect on the credibility of the findings themselves.

There are various kinds of appraisal reports which will be described shortly. Regardless of the kind of report, however, standards of practice require that field notes and other documents used in preparing the appraisal must be retained for a minimum period of time, as they may be necessary to answer questions that arise. Furthermore, they are useful as a source of data for future appraisals.

Whether or not a standard reporting form is used, an appraisal must be complete with respect to its potential use(s). In court proceedings, for example, it is not always possible to introduce supporting evidence, and whatever is in the appraisal report is taken as complete.

Rule 2–1 of the *Uniform Standards of Professional Practice* (USPAP) sets out the following requirements for appraisal reports:

- Clearly and accurately set forth the appraisal in a manner that will not be misleading;
- Contain sufficient information to enable the person(s) who receive or rely on the report to understand it properly;
- Clearly and accurately disclose any extraordinary assumption or limiting condition that directly affects the appraisal and indicate its impact on value.

Standards Rule 2–2 requires that each written appraisal report must:

- Identify and describe the real estate being appraised;
- Identify the real property interest being appraised;

---

[1] This is argued by Robert Evans, "Impact of State Certification on the Commercial Appraisal Market," *Appraisal Journal*, April 1994.

- State the purpose of the appraisal;
- Define the value to be estimated;
- Set forth the effective date of the appraisal and the date of the report;
- Describe the extent of the process of collecting, confirming, and reporting the data;
- Set forth all assumptions and limiting conditions that affect the analyses, opinions, and conclusions;
- Set forth the information considered, the appraisal procedures followed, and the reasoning that supports the analyses, opinions, and conclusions;
- Set forth the appraiser's opinion of the highest and best use of the real estate being appraised, when such an opinion is necessary and appropriate;
- Explain and support the exclusion of any of the usual valuation approaches;
- Set forth any additional information that may be appropriate to show compliance with, or clearly identify and explain permitted departures from, the requirements of Standard 1; and
- Include a signed certification in accordance with Standards Rule 2–3. (For members and affiliates of the Appraisal Institute, the certification must also conform to the Supplemental Standards Rules.)

Types of Appraisal Reports

Complete and Limited

The *Uniform Standards of Professional Appraisal Practice* (USPAP) are intended to guide the appraisal process and the reporting of the results of that process. When there are no departures from USPAP, the product of the appraisal process is called a *complete* appraisal. However, departure from some of the specific guidelines of USPAP are allowed when the assignment suggests that to be appropriate. When the Departure Provision is invoked, the resulting appraisal report is called a *limited* appraisal. The client must agree to the departure and the departure must not result in a report that is misleading or confusing. One practical impact of producing a limited appraisal is that it may not be appropriate to provide a single point estimate of value. A range of values, or even a "more than" or "less than" conclusion may be more in keeping with the spirit of a limited assignment.

Written and Oral

An appraisal may be oral or written. Written reports are the most common, though an oral report may be sufficient when the client's needs do not warrant a written report. Court testimony, for example, is considered an oral report. Oral reports must be responsive to Standards Rule 2–2, and should include enough background information and analysis to support the value conclusion. As in the case of written reports, all notes and data relating to an oral appraisal should be kept on file.

Types of Written Reports

In 1994, the Appraisal Foundation approved the use of three types of written reports: self-contained, summary, and restricted. They differ primarily with respect to the amount of detail provided in the report, and (in the case of a restricted report) with respect to the intended uses of the report.

A self-contained appraisal report contains the most detail. It tells the "who, what, and why" of the appraisal. Summary and restricted reports typically contain less detail. Thus, while a self-contained report may use two pages to provide certain information, a summary or restricted report may combine that information into one or two paragraphs. The restricted report is similar in detail to the summary report, but it differs in the important respect that it is explicitly intended for use by the client only. Any other uses are considered unintended uses.

Note that the type of report produced, whether self-contained, summary, or restricted, does not necessarily imply that the appraisal was complete or limited. The complete versus limited distinction refers to whether or not there was a departure from USPAP, while the type of report is defined by the detail included or the intended use. However, in practice, it is likely that complete appraisals will result more often in self-contained reports, while limited appraisals are more likely to be reported in summary or restricted form.

As of mid 1996, distinctions among the various kinds of reports were just beginning to find their way into appraisal practice, and it is anticipated that further changes and clarifications will be forthcoming. In any case, the appraiser should make clear at or near the beginning of the report which type of report it is.

Other Types of Reports

Over time, various nomenclature has been developed by appraisers and clients to describe different types of assignments and reports. A 1994 Appraisal Standards Board statement attempted to clarify the meaning of some of these terms.

The term *letter opinion of value* has been widely used to describe a short (one-page) report sent to a client that included the value estimate and references to file information as the basis for the estimate. However, this type of report does not comply with USPAP, and it is intended that the restricted report be used in this type of situation.

An *update* of an appraisal is an extension of an existing appraisal. It effectively changes the date of the value estimate. An update is not a *recertification of value*. The latter is a limited appraisal that confirms whether development and market conditions subsequent to an appraisal were consistent with assumptions made in the appraisal based on plans and specifications. Unlike an update, a recertification does not change the effective date of the appraisal.

Finally, an *evaluation of real property* is a term used mainly by financial institutions. An assignment from an institution for an evaluation is to be considered an assignment to provide a summary report based on a limited appraisal. A standard form for evaluations became available in July 1995 from the Federal National Mortgage Association (Fannie Mae). It is called a *Limited One-Family Residential Appraisal and Summary Report*.

Form versus Narrative Reports

Loan originators, government agencies, and secondary mortgage market institutions typically prefer the use of standardized form reports for the routine appraising of one to four family properties being used as loan collateral. The strength of form reports is that their standardization allows rapid processing. Their weakness is the lack of room on the form for descriptive justification of the value estimate, though some do leave space for such things as neighborhood descriptions. Also, some allow the addition of explanatory material by the appraiser. The appraiser should keep in mind that the appraisal is his or her responsibility, and if there is any doubt as to the sufficiency of the information provided on the form, then added explanation is strongly suggested.

The most widely used form, the *Uniform Residential Appraisal Report*, is shown in Figure 26–1. Given the level of detail in the URAR, it seems most consistent with the requirements of a summary report. Form reports are also available for other types of properties, including commercial, industrial, and condominium.

Nonform reports are referred to as narrative reports. They may be self-contained, summary, or restricted. Because the purpose of any appraisal report, and particularly a narrative report, is to effectively communicate with the reader, it follows that the best reports are those which present sound judgments and analysis in a readable, well-written style. Jargon is to be avoided. Remember that the audience for an appraisal is seldom other appraisers.

FIGURE 26–1 Uniform Residential Appraisal Report

X X

Property Description **UNIFORM RESIDENTIAL APPRAISAL REPORT** **File No.**

SUBJECT

Property Address | City | State | Zip Code

Legal Description | County

Assessor's Parcel No. | Tax Year | R.E. Taxes $ | Special Assessments $

Borrower | Current Owner | Occupant ☐ Owner ☐ Tenant ☐ Vacant

Property rights appraised ☐ Fee Simple ☐ Leasehold | Project Type ☐ PUD ☐ Condominium (HUD/VA only) | HOA$ /Mo.

Neighborhood or Project Name | Map Reference | Census Tract

Sales Price $ | Date of Sale | Description and $ amount of loan charges/concessions to be paid by seller

Lender/Client | Address

Appraiser | Address

NEIGHBORHOOD

Location	☐ Urban	☐ Suburban	☐ Rural
Built up	☐ Over 75%	☐ 25-75%	☐ Under 25%
Growth rate	☐ Rapid	☐ Stable	☐ Slow
Property values	☐ Increasing	☐ Stable	☐ Declining
Demand/supply	☐ Shortage	☐ In balance	☐ Over supply
Marketing time	☐ Under 3 mos.	☐ 3-6 mos.	☐ Over 6 mos.

Predominant occupancy: ☐ Owner; ☐ Tenant; ☐ Vacant (0-5%); ☐ Vacant (over 5%)

Single family housing: PRICE $ (000) | AGE (yrs); Low; High; Predominant

Present land use %: One family; 2-4 family; Multi-family; Commercial; ( )

Land use change: ☐ Not likely ☐ Likely; ☐ In process; To:

Note: Race and the racial composition of the neighborhood are not appraisal factors.

Neighborhood boundaries and characteristics:

Factors that affect the marketability of the properties in the neighborhood (proximity to employment and amenities, employment stability, appeal to market, etc.):

Market conditions in the subject neighborhood (including support for the above conclusions related to the trend of property values, demand/supply, and marketing time -- such as data on competitive properties for sale in the neighborhood, description of the prevalence of sales and financing concessions, etc.):

PUD

Project Information for PUDs (If applicable) -- Is the developer/builder in control of the Home Owners' Association (HOA)? ☐ Yes ☐ No

Approximate total number of units in the subject project ______. Approximate total number of units for sale in the subject project ______.

Describe common elements and recreational facilities:

SITE

Dimensions

Site area | Corner Lot ☐ Yes ☐ No

Specific zoning classification and description

Zoning compliance ☐ Legal ☐ Legal nonconforming (Grandfathered use) ☐ Illegal ☐ No zoning

Highest & best use as improved ☐ Present use ☐ Other use (explain)

Utilities	Public	Other
Electricity	☐	
Gas	☐	
Water	☐	
Sanitary sewer	☐	
Storm sewer	☐	

Off-site Improvements	Type	Public	Private
Street		☐	☐
Curb/gutter		☐	☐
Sidewalk		☐	☐
Street lights		☐	☐
Alley		☐	☐

Topography; Size; Shape; Drainage; View; Landscaping; Driveway Surface; Apparent easements

FEMA Special Flood Hazard Area ☐ Yes ☐ No

FEMA Zone ______ Map Date ______

FEMA Map No.

Comments (apparent adverse easements, encroachments, special assessments, slide areas, illegal or legal nonconforming zoning use, etc.):

DESCRIPTION OF IMPROVEMENTS

GENERAL DESCRIPTION	EXTERIOR DESCRIPTION	FOUNDATION	BASEMENT	INSULATION
No. of Units	Foundation	Slab	Area Sq. Ft.	Roof ☐
No. of Stories	Exterior Walls	Crawl Space	% Finished	Ceiling ☐
Type (Det./Att.)	Roof Surface	Basement	Ceiling	Walls ☐
Design (Style)	Gutters & Dwnspts.	Sump Pump	Walls	Floor ☐
Existing/Proposed	Window Type	Dampness	Floor	None ☐
Age (Yrs.)	Storm/Screens	Settlement	Outside Entry	Unknown ☐
Effective Age (Yrs.)	Manufactured House	Infestation		

ROOMS	Foyer	Living	Dining	Kitchen	Den	Family Rm.	Rec. Rm.	Bedrooms	# Baths	Laundry	Other	Area Sq. Ft.
Basement												
Level 1												
Level 2												

Finished area above grade contains: Rooms; Bedroom(s); Bath(s); Square Feet of Gross Living Area

INTERIOR Materials/Condition	HEATING	KITCHEN EQUIP.	ATTIC	AMENITIES	CAR STORAGE:
Floors	Type	Refrigerator ☐	None ☐	Fireplace(s) # ☐	None ☐
Walls	Fuel	Range/Oven ☐	Stairs ☐	Patio ☐	Garage # of cars
Trim/Finish	Condition	Disposal ☐	Drop Stair ☐	Deck ☐	Attached
Bath Floor	COOLING	Dishwasher ☐	Scuttle ☐	Porch ☐	Detached
Bath Wainscot	Central	Fan/Hood ☐	Floor ☐	Fence ☐	Built-In
Doors	Other	Microwave ☐	Heated ☐	Pool ☐	Carport
	Condition	Washer/Dryer ☐	Finished ☐		Driveway

COMMENTS

Additional features (special energy efficient items, etc.):

Condition of the improvements, depreciation (physical, functional, and external), repairs needed, quality of construction, remodeling/additions, etc.:

Adverse environmental conditions (such as, but not limited to, hazardous wastes, toxic substances, etc.) present in the improvements, on the site, or in the immediate vicinity of the subject property:

Freddie Mac Form 70 6-93 | 10 CH. | PAGE 1 OF 2 | Fannie Mae Form 1004 6-93

FIGURE 26–1 Uniform Residential Appraisal Report (concluded)

Valuation Section **UNIFORM RESIDENTIAL APPRAISAL REPORT** **File No.**

COST APPROACH

ESTIMATED SITE VALUE . . . . = $ ______
ESTIMATED REPRODUCTION COST-NEW OF IMPROVEMENTS:
Dwelling ______ Sq. Ft @ $ ______ = $ ______
______ Sq. Ft @ $ ______ = ______
= ______
Garage/Carport ______ Sq. Ft @ $ ______ = ______
Total Estimated Cost-New . . . . = $ ______
Less Physical | Functional | External
Depreciation ______ = $ ______
Depreciated Value of Improvements . . . . = $ ______
"As-is" Value of Site Improvements . . . . = $ ______
INDICATED VALUE BY COST APPROACH . . . . = $ ______

Comments on Cost Approach (such as, source of cost estimate, site value, square foot calculation and, for HUD, VA and FmHA, the estimated remaining economic life of the property): ______

SALES COMPARISON ANALYSIS

ITEM	SUBJECT	COMPARABLE NO. 1		COMPARABLE NO. 2		COMPARABLE NO. 3	
Address							
Proximity to Subject							
Sales Price	$		$		$		$
Price/Gross Liv. Area	$ ⌀	$ ⌀		$ ⌀		$ ⌀	
Data and/or Verification Sources							
VALUE ADJUSTMENTS	DESCRIPTION	DESCRIPTION	+ (-) $ Adjustment	DESCRIPTION	+ (-) $ Adjustment	DESCRIPTION	+ (-) $ Adjustment
Sales or Financing Concessions							
Date of Sale/Time							
Location							
Leasehold/Fee Simple							
Site							
View							
Design and Appeal							
Quality of Construction							
Age							
Condition							
Above Grade Room Count	Total Bdrms Baths	Total Bdrms Baths		Total Bdrms Baths		Total Bdrms Baths	
Gross Living Area	Sq. Ft.	Sq. Ft.		Sq. Ft.		Sq. Ft.	
Basement & Finished Rooms Below Grade							
Functional Utility							
Heating/Cooling							
Energy Efficient Items							
Garage/Carport							
Porch, Patio, Deck, Fireplace(s), etc.							
Fence, Pool, etc.							
Net Adj. (total)		☐ + ☐ -	$	☐ + ☐ -	$	☐ + ☐ -	$
Adjusted Sales Price of Comparable			$		$		$

Comments on Sales Comparison (including the subject property's compatibility to the neighborhood, etc.): ______

ITEM	SUBJECT	COMPARABLE NO. 1	COMPARABLE NO. 2	COMPARABLE NO. 3
Date, Price and Data Source for prior sales within year of appraisal				

Analysis of any current agreement of sale, option, or listing of the subject property and analysis of any prior sales of subject and comparables within one year of the date of appraisal:

INDICATED VALUE BY SALES COMPARISON APPROACH . . . . $ ______
INDICATED VALUE BY INCOME APPROACH (If Applicable) Estimated Market Rent $ ______ /Mo. x Gross Rent Multiplier ______ = $ ______

RECONCILIATION

This appraisal is made ☐ "as is" ☐ subject to the repairs, alterations, inspections, or conditions listed below ☐ subject to completion per plans and specifications.
Conditions of Appraisal: ______

Final Reconciliation: ______

The purpose of this appraisal is to estimate the market value of the real property that is the subject of this report, based on the above conditions and the certification, contingent and limiting conditions, and market value definition that are stated in the attached Freddie Mac Form 439/Fannie Mae Form 1004B (Revised ______).
I (WE) ESTIMATE THE MARKET VALUE, AS DEFINED, OF THE REAL PROPERTY THAT IS THE SUBJECT OF THIS REPORT, AS OF ______ (WHICH IS THE DATE OF INSPECTION AND THE EFFECTIVE DATE OF THIS REPORT) TO BE $ ______.

APPRAISER:		SUPERVISORY APPRAISER (ONLY IF REQUIRED):	
Signature		Signature	☐ Did ☐ Did Not
Name		Name	Inspect Property
Date Report Signed		Date Report Signed	
State Certification #	State	State Certification #	State
Or State License #	State	Or State License #	State

Freddie Mac Form 70 6-93 10 CH. PAGE 2 OF 2 Fannie Mae Form 1004 6-93

Elements of a Narrative Report

There are no rules which mandate the structure of a narrative report, except that it adequately convey the process and reasoning leading to the appraised value. Nonetheless, over time, most appraisers have developed a similar and somewhat standardized format. Standardization minimizes the chance of omitting useful information and provides the appraiser with a familiar "road map" to follow. A self-contained narrative will contain extensive detail, while summary and restricted reports will contain less. A representative narrative report outline is as follow:

1. Preliminary Pages
    a. Title Page
    b. Letter of Transmittal
    c. Table of Contents
2. Introduction
    a. Certification of Value
    b. Purpose of the Appraisal
    c. Value Definition(s)
    d. Property Rights Appraised
3. Descriptions and Data
    a. Area and Neighborhood Description
    b. Site Description
    c. Improvements Description
    d. Summary of Data for Each of the Approaches
4. Analysis of Data
    a. Highest and Best (Expected) Use
    b. Land (or Site) Value
    c. Sales Comparison Approach
    d. Cost Approach
    e. Income Approach
5. Reconciliation and Final Value Estimate
6. Appendices

Summary

The appraiser's task is not finished when a value is estimated. The appraisal process leading to the estimated value must be effectively communicated to the client and other potentially interested parties. This is done in an appraisal report, which may be oral but generally is written. Written reports, in ascending order of detail, are the restricted and summary reports, and the self-contained report. In addition, the restricted report differs in that it is intended for use by the client only. Depending on whether there has been departure from USPAP, a report will be either complete or limited.

During the appraisal process and in preparing the appraisal report, the appraiser should maintain the highest standards of technical competence and personal conduct. Members or associate/candidate members of professional appraisal associations must abide by rules and regulations aimed at protecting the interests of the public, the client, and fellow appraisers. Failure to do so can result in disciplinary action.

In addition, certain users of appraisal reports, most frequently lenders, may require standardized form reports and procedures for preparing those reports. The detail in form reports is such that they are likely to be described as summary reports.

Questions and Problems

1. What is a complete appraisal?
2. What is the appraiser's responsibility to the public?
3. An appraiser is heard to comment, "I don't like to use form reports, because there is no room to explain what I have done." Comment.
4. How does a self-contained report differ from a summary report?
5. An appraiser, after beginning an assignment, takes some shortcuts because the agreed upon fee was not sufficient to justify a more complete analysis. Comment.
6. List the basic parts of a narrative report in a sequence in which they may logically appear. Is a particular sequence required?
7. "A limited report is the same as a restricted report." Comment.

APPENDIX A
DETAILED SOLUTIONS TO ODD-NUMBERED END-OF-CHAPTER PROBLEMS

Chapter 1

1. If you did so, the appraiser's point of reference would be the prices of other unique stones that had sold. However, the relationship between those prices and the value of the Hope Diamond would be tenuous. It is not possible to estimate a market value when neither the product being appraised nor similar products have traded. This is the extreme case of a unique, untraded product, without a reproduction cost, and which produces no income. The utility of the three appraisal approaches in such circumstances is close to zero.

3. The appraiser must know (1) what factors the market associates with value, (2) how much those factors contribute to value, and (3) how to process this knowledge into a value estimate.

5. Reconciling the values produced by the three approaches begins with a review of the appraisal process, a reconsideration of the assumptions made at various points, and a comparison of the relative quality and quantity of information used with each approach. Reconciliation may be viewed as a weighting process, with more weight given to those estimates in which the appraiser has more confidence. The judgment of the appraiser is of paramount importance.

Chapter 2

1. "Value" is a word that resists definition. It tends toward subjectivity, and therefore, imprecise measurement. While market value is a more precise concept, it remains difficult to define in a way that is universally acceptable. Markets are imperfect, meaning the price may not reflect true or equilibrium value. Data may be incorrect and collection tends to be incomplete.

    Finally, there are differing legal and institutional needs which affect the working definition of market value.

3. The recommended definition reflects the probabilistic nature of price setting in real estate markets ("expected price"), it imposes no idealistic assumptions about price setting (no reference to "competitive" markets), it reminds the appraiser and client that market value is the result of an arm's-length transaction, and the reference to "real property" abstracts from the impact of nonreal property, such as favorable financing.

5. Real estate markets have characteristics (heterogeneous products, lack of complete information, costly transactions, slow-moving supply) that are associated with inefficiency. Research indicates that while there may be some inefficiency, it appears to be less severe than previously thought.

Chapter 3

1. Land Value → Rent → Location → Distance

3. Households also bid for land, though their value is a function of amenities rather than of the income the property will produce. Because household incomes are generally lower than the incomes produced by commercial uses in the most accessible locations, they cannot outbid commercial uses for those locations. Thus, the residential gradient is relatively low at distance zero, but because it is flatter than the land-value gradient for commercial uses, it eventually becomes the dominant use.

5. A neighborhood is a geographically contiguous area which is similarly affected by its market setting. Value-affecting components of "neighborhood" are special accessibility, social factors that influence stability, environmental and governmental influences, and the physical and functional characteristics (life cycle) of the neighborhood itself.

7. "District" is the term commonly used to describe a nonsingle-family neighborhood. The main kinds of districts are apartment (multifamily), commercial, and industrial.

9. One way is to compare land values. In the absence of sales of vacant lots, comparing the sales prices of properties with equivalent improvements will provide evidence of different land or locational value.

11. Age is one factor that may be associated with neighborhood quality. The key phrase is "may be associated with," for age is not the *cause* of neighborhood decline but rather is often associated with decline. There are many exceptions. Older neighborhoods that were of higher original quality and have been well-maintained may have more valuable locations than those in younger neighborhoods of lesser inherent quality.

    The lesson is that while all neighborhoods go through a life cycle from development through decline, they do so at widely varying speeds. Thus, age alone cannot be used to categorize neighborhoods.

13. An upwardly sloping value gradient indicates that general accessibility is being dominated by other factors. For example, there may be freedom from noise and congestion, less crime, and proximity to better schools and shopping.

Chapter 4

1. Land is unimproved. When improvements such as utility hookups and curbs are made to the land, it is then called a site.

3. A street name and number description is the street address. A lot and block description generally comes from a recorded plat (map) of a subdivision, and refers to the developer's numbering or lettering of the roads and lots in the subdivision. A metes and bounds description is based on distances and direction starting from a "permanent" marker. Government survey, which is not available in all states, consists of a grid of 36 square-mile townships that are divided into one-square mile sections, which can be further divided as needed.

5. Excess land is land in excess of the size typically needed to support the improvements on the site. The value of any excess land that is marketable is estimated separately from the rest of the site. If the excess is not marketable, a judgment must be made as to how much (if any) it adds to the value "as is."

7. Houses are generally measured in square feet, with the number of rooms also important. Office buildings are measured in terms of gross and net leasable square feet. Warehouses are measured in terms of square feet and cubic feet.

9. The effective age of a structure reflects its general condition. This is analogous to people, where we find some are old at 60, and others going strong at 80. If a structure is assumed to have a total economic life of 50 years, and its condition and functional utility suggests it has 45 years left, its effective age is 5 years, even if its physical or chronological age is more or less than 5 years.

    Effective age is an important variable, as it serves as a proxy for condition, which in turn, is a proxy for utility and therefore value.

11. Size, building materials, condition, design, and compatibility.

Chapter 5

1. A property's value is a function of the use to which it can be put. Thus, the expected selling price, which is what the appraiser estimates when asked to estimate market value, is a function of expected use.

3. The maximum price is unlikely to be received in real estate markets, where prices are determined by a sequential bidding process. Also, most modern market value definitions do not refer to the highest obtainable price, and therefore, they are inconsistent with the highest and best use assumption. Another consideration is that in practice, it is virtually impossible to identify *the* highest and best use when it isn't legally determined by land use regulation, and this puts an unreasonable burden on the appraiser seeking comparables.

5. Succession is justified when the value of the land as though vacant, less demolition costs, exceeds the value of the property as is.

7.

Use	Expected Sale Price	×	Probability of Use	=	
A	$119,000	×	.10	=	$ 11,900
B	$124,000	×	.10	=	$ 12,400
C	$136,000	×	.20	=	$ 22,200
D	$132,500	×	.60	=	$ 79,500
			Expected price	=	$131,000

Alternatively, .05 ($110,000) + .30 ($120,000) + .28 ($130,000) + .24 ($140,000) + .13 ($150,000) = $131,000. The most probable price is $132,500.

9. $185,000, because the current improvement is worth $35,000. It has a positive value and should not be demolished.

11. a.

Use	Probability	×	Expected Sale Price		
1	.70	×	$320,000	=	$224,000
2	.30	×	$330,000	=	99,000
			Expected value		$323,000

The expected use is reported as a 70 percent probability of Use 1, and a 30 percent probability of Use 2.

b. $340,000

Chapter 6

1. Market price is an acceptable proxy for market value, and similar properties will sell for similar prices. Put differently, a buyer will not pay more for a given property right he or she can obtain elsewhere. At the same time, a seller won't accept less than the "going" price. This is sometimes referred to as the principle of substitution; that is, market price is a function of the price of substitutes.

3. This depends on the type and size of the property. Other things equal, the smaller the property, the more important it is to follow the "closer is better" rule, as smaller properties tend to be traded locally. As property size increases, and/or for certain types of properties (like large shopping malls and industrial properties) the market broadens, and the search for comparables may become regional or even national. In addition to the obvious points of comparability between the comparables and the subject, it is necessary that future prospects for the properties also be similar.

5.

	Comparable		
	1	2	3
Transaction price	$350,000	$440,000	$400,000
Financing	—	—	—
Selling price	$350,000	$440,000	$400,000
Time adjustment	38,655	13,200	—
Time adjusted price	$388,655	$453,200	$400,000
Office space value	16,800	22,275	20,900
Price paid for Industrial space	$371,855	$430,925	$379,100
Price per square foot	$29.75	$27.62	$25.27

Assuming equal weighting, the average price per square foot of industrial space is $27.55, giving a value of $27.55 × 13,000 = $358,150 for industrial space, plus $12.50 × 1,600 = $20,000 for office space, plus $55,000 for the excess half acre. The total value is $443,150.

7. The average assessed value/selling price ratio is .40. Valuing the subject using this ratio produces

$$\frac{\$40,500}{.40} = \$101,250.$$

This is considerably below the previously estimated value of $115,500. In such cases, the general rule is to trust the value estimated using traditional approaches, remembering that assessed value/selling price ratio can easily be distorted over time, and that the subject's ratio may be different than other properties in the neighborhood.

Chapter 7

1. Statistical estimation.

3. If the subject property is part of a population of comparables, the estimate of a population parameter can be used to make statements about the selling price of properties that are comparable to the subject. This logic is no different than the use of comparables in traditional direct sales comparison.

5. A normal frequency distribution is the familiar bell-shaped distribution, with equal mean, median, and mode. When a population is approximately normally distributed, sample statistics can be used to make inferences about the population mean, regardless of sample size. When a population is not normally distributed, statistical inferences can be made only if the sample size is relatively large.

7. Using the *t*-table because of the small sample size, the 90 percent confidence interval (with 11 degrees of freedom) is 44.25 ± 1.796 (1.67) = 41.25–47.25%. This tells us that if many samples of equal size were drawn from the population, and confidence intervals constructed around each mean, in 90 percent of the cases the population mean would fall in that interval. This is commonly stated as "90 percent confidence that the mean value of the population falls between 41.25 percent and 47.25 percent."

9. The "traditional" adjustments, that is, those used to make the comparables truly comparable to the subject, should be made. If this is not done, the population is not homogeneous and the results of the analysis will have little utility.

Chapter 8

1. Regression analysis is a statistical tool which uses the association between two or more variables to predict one of the variables (the dependent variable) from the other(s) (the independent variable(s)).

3. When using a qualitative variable, one possible outcome is omitted, and the interpretation of the coefficients in the equation is made relative to the omitted outcome. The example results tell us that a location in a below-average neighborhood is valued at $7,240 less than a location in an average neighborhood, and that an above-average neighborhood is valued at $3,860 more than an average neighborhood. Omitting one state of a qualitative variable saves a degree of freedom and allows interpretation of the coefficients and the intercept.

5. The residuals begin as all positive, then become negative, then positive again. This pattern suggests a curvilinear association between at least one of the independent variables and the dependent variable.

7.
$$Y = 12.72 + 4.3\,(x_1)$$

Conclusions as to causation cannot be drawn based on regression analysis. Only the association between variables is measured.

9. *a.* $Y = \$8,780 + \$34.46\,(2,200)$
    $+ \$18,806.67\,(2) - \$.07\,(32,000)$
    $+ \$7,170.32\,(1) - \$8,999.46\,(0)$
    $+ \$2,204.76\,(1.5)$

    $= \$130,443$

  b. There may be a missing variable that is associated with the number of bathrooms. The number of bathrooms is therefore being credited with the value actually associated with the missing variable.

  c. One approach is to use your experience and judgment to figure out which variable(s) might be missing, and to rerun the regression with the added variables. Inspection of the regression residuals may also be helpful. If they show a pattern of over- and underestimation of the actual prices, and that pattern can be related to a specific difference(s) between the observations, adding an appropriate variable(s) may help.

d. This may be the result of collinearity between house and lot size, in which case, they are "sharing" significance and value impact. The result is that both are insignificant, with an incorrect sign for lot size.

e. If, for example, house size and lot size are linearly related, removing lot size would increase the significance of the house size variable and change its coefficient. Also, because there is likely some degree of collinearity between lot size and the other independent variables, their coefficients and standard errors would also change, though most likely to a lesser extent. Omitting lot size would also reduce r^2, but if it is in fact a largely redundant variable, the drop in r^2 would not be severe.

Chapter 9

1. A site is land that is ready for building. It has been improved with such things as sewers, utilities, and access. Land is unimproved. Therefore, the value difference is the value of the improvements to the site.

3. Their relative values cannot be determined without more information. The first impulse is to choose B, which makes sense considering that front feet are highly valued for commercial use. However, there may be other factors to consider. For example, does B have *excess* frontage? If so, what is the value of the excess?; Is B deep enough to meet setback requirements? And what kinds of properties border A and B?

5. First, there is the relative reliability of actual sales versus asking prices. Other things equal, actual prices are strongly preferred. If both are used, is there a consistency (after adjusting for time) among the actual sale price(s) and the listing price(s)? Second, do any adjustments, including the typical percentage difference between asking and sale prices, need to be made to the prices of the potential comparables? Third, what is the reason for the $2,500 difference in the asking price for the two lots? Hopefully, the adjusted prices of the comparable sale and the listings will be consistent enough to provide the basis for a credible estimate. If not, a decision must be made. Either market value cannot be reported because there is an insufficient quantity of observed prices, or market value must be approximated based on the appraiser's judgment as to which evidence (the time-adjusted comparable sale or the adjusted listings) is more persuasive.

Chapter 10

1. V = Reproduction (or replacement) cost new − Accrued depreciation + Land value

V = Reproduction (or Replacement) Cost New	− Accrued Depreciation	+ Land Value
• Direct costs	• Physical deterioration	• Highest and best use as if vacant
• Indirect costs	• Functional obsolescence	
• Developer's profit	• External obsolescence	

3. Examples of physical deterioration are a leaking roof, loose boards, worn-out linoleum, and a broken window. The estimate of functional obsolescence reflects the effect on property value of characteristics that are out of favor in the marketplace. This often happens in response to technological changes, but sometimes is simply the result of a change in tastes. Examples include a poor floor plan, a lack of sufficient insulation, and an unappealing placement of the improvement on the site.

The estimate of external obsolescence reflects the loss in value from factors external to the subject property. Examples are a poorly maintained neighborhood, a lack of public services, air and noise pollution, excessive traffic in a residential area, and for commercial properties, an oversupply.

5. Reproduction cost is the cost to produce an exact duplicate of the subject's improvements. Replacement cost is the cost to produce utility equal to that provided by the subject's improvements, but using modern materials and building technology.

Reproduction cost has the advantage that it is easier to relate depreciation estimates to a property exactly like the subject. Replacement cost has the advantage that the assumed use of modern materials and workmanship eliminates many (but not necessarily all) elements of functional obsolescence, and thus, they do not have to be estimated.

7. Developers must be compensated for taking risks. Therefore, the expected market value of a completed project must exceed the out-of-pocket costs of getting it completed.

Chapter 11

1. Developers and entrepreneurs are entitled to a return for the risks taken. The market value of a completed building should therefore exceed the direct and indirect costs of development.

3. $\left(\dfrac{101.6}{96.4}\right)(\$171{,}000) = \$180{,}224.$

To the extent the cost of the subject property conformed to the historical cost index when it was built, it can be trusted. However, a cost estimate based on a cost index alone should be viewed with caution. Such estimates are better used to support an estimate made by the comparative unit, unit-in-place, or quantity survey methods.

5. The comparative unit method estimates cost in terms of dollars per foot, per square foot, or per cubic foot. The unit-in-place (or segregated) method uses unit costs for the various building components (installed) using appropriate units of measurement such as lineal feet and square feet. The quantity survey method is based on the quantity and quality of all of the building's materials and labor.

7. $\left(\dfrac{105}{100}\right)(\$90{,}000) = \$94{,}500$

Chapter 12

1. Accrued depreciation is the difference between the reproduction (or replacement) cost new of the improvement on the date of the appraisal and its market value on the same date.

3. Deficiencies, defects, and superadequacies are variations of functional obsolescence. A deficiency is an item that is missing. A defect is an item that is present, but not up to current standards. A superadequacy is an item that is present, but is overadequate by current market standards.

5. The subcategories of external obsolescence are locational obsolescence and economic obsolescence.

7.

	1	2
Selling price	$94,000	$131,000
Land value	18 500	25 000
Improvement value	$75,500	$106,000
Reproduction cost new	90 000	123,500
Accrued depreciation	$14,500	$ 17,500
Percent accrued depreciation	$\dfrac{14{,}500}{90{,}000} = .1611$	$\dfrac{17{,}500}{123{,}500} = .1417$
Annual rate of depreciation	$\dfrac{.16}{13} = 1.24\%$	$\dfrac{.1417}{15} = .94\%$

9.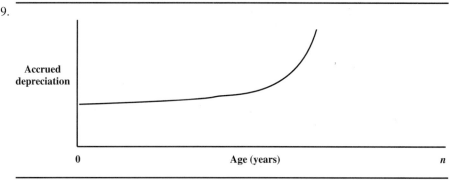

The graph above shows a pattern of an increasing rate of depreciation over time. While this is a pattern found in some empirical studies, there are wide local variations. The depreciation shown for a new building (at an age of 0) is traceable to either built-in functional obsolescence and/or external obsolescence.

11.
Reproduction cost	$115,000
Accrued depreciation =	
12/60 × $115,000 =	
.20 × $115,000 =	23,000
Value of improvements	$ 92,000
Land value	24,000
Market value	$116,000

Chapter 13

1.
Potential gross income		
2 Bedroom: 22 × $275		
× 12	$72,600	
3 Bedroom: 15 × $325		
× 12	58,500	$131,100
Vacancy allowance		
2 Bedroom: (.06)	$ 4,356	
3 Bedroom: (.04)	2,340	6,696
Rents less vacancy		$124,404
Other income		
Laundry: $60 × 12	$ 720	
Parking: $7.50 ×		
20.7 (1.3) × 12	2,422	
$7.50 ×		
14.4 (1.3) × 12	1,685	4,827
Effective gross income		$129,231
Operating expenses		
Fixed:		$ 15,500
Variable: (.35)($129,231)	45,231	$ 60,731
Net operating income		$ 68,500

The mortgage payment and depreciation expense do not appear on the *NOI* statement.

3. *a.* Given typical management, the rents and vacancy rate of the subject are assumed to be at the market until proven otherwise. That is, the appraiser's working assumption is that the subject property's effective gross income is right. When actual rent and vacancy are close to those of the competition, it must be assumed that they are at the market; that is, they are accepted as being market rents. The reason is that no two properties are identical, and small differences in rents and vacancy can be attributed to those differences, even if the reason for the difference is not obvious. You are, in effect, working from the premise that the subject is its own best comparable.

On the other hand, if there are large differences in effective gross income between the subject and its competition, reasons for that difference should be determined. Often they are found in a careful reading of leases. In such cases, market rents (and thus *NOI*) may differ from actual (contractual) rents (and *NOI*). Moreover, in some cases, current rent and vacancy rates can be distorted by hidden rent concessions. A knowledge of the competition and interviews with tenants may help identify such situations.

b. Operating expense ratios (*OER*s) are useful because they give the total picture, and are not seriously affected by the inevitable under- or overestimation of individual operating expenses. A departure from typical *OER* levels suggests either errors in estimating, or that the subject isn't really comparable to the properties whose *OER*s it is being compared to. The *OER* on a property may differ from the "typical" level because it is older (or newer), has different types of tenants, differs in the quality of the original construction, or has been maintained more or less carefully than average. Thus, while an *OER* that differs from the norm is a signal to verify the estimate, it may well be justified by the specifics of the property.

Also, remember that the *OER* can be partially controlled by management. Further, there is not a standard format for reporting operating expenses. Certain expenses, like wages, may be included as part of a general payroll entry in a statement for one property, while for another property, they may have been divided, for example, between maintenance and repair and general payroll.

5. Variable expenses tend to be tied to occupancy and also tend to be relatively more subject to budgetary control. Fixed expenses tend not to be tied to the occupancy level, and cannot be easily controlled by the owner or manager.

7. The major difference can be traced to the terms of existing leases. Apartment leases tend to be relatively short-term, while properties like office buildings tend to be leased for longer periods. In terms of forecasting rents, shorter lease periods largely relieve the appraiser of the problem of scheduling lease expirations and measuring their impact on rents. With short-term leases, it is assumed that any current difference between market and contract rents will be corrected within the one-year period on which income estimates are based.

9. (1) Extrapolate past trends, (2) survey those knowledgeable in the market, (3) do fundamental market analysis, and (4) assume "no change," or that the current level of income will persist.

11. Normal vacancy is 5 percent. First-year market rent is $10.20, which is expected to increase by 4 percent per year. The rent on existing leases graduates at a rate of 2 percent per year. Your assignment is to forecast effective gross income over the next five years.

Year 1
Expiring (New) leases   -0-
Existing leases   12,500 × $ 9.50 $118,750
                 31,000 ×   9.80   303,800
                 8,700 × 10.00   87,000
Contract rent $509,550
Available space   1,800 × 10.20   18,360
Potential gross income $527,910
Less vacancy*   1,800 × $10.20   18,360
Net rent collections $509,550
Other Income   -0-
Effective gross income $509,550

*Vacancy with existing leases is less than 5 percent.

Year 2
Expiring (new) leases   11,600* × $10.61** $123,076
Existing leases   31,000 × 10.00†   310,000
                   8,700 × 10.20†   88,740
Contract rent $521,816
Available space   2,700 × $10.61   28,647
Potential gross income $550,463
Less vacancy   2,700 × $10.61   28,647
Net rent collections $521,816
Other income   -0-
Effective gross income $521,816

*Normal vacancy is .05, or .05 × 54,000 = 2,700 sq. ft. This leaves 54,000 − 2,700 = 51,300 square feet to be rented. Existing leases take 39,700, leaving 11,600 square feet.
**Market rent increases by 4 percent per year.
†Rent on existing leases increases by 2 percent per year.

Year 3
Expiring (new) leases   31,000 × $11.03 $341,930
Existing leases   11,600 × 10.82   125,512
                 8,700 × 10.40   90,480
Contract rent $557,922
Available space   2,700 × 11.03   29,781
Potential gross income $587,703
Less vacancy   2,700 × 11.03   29,781
Net rent collections $557,922
Other income   -0-
Effective gross income $557,922

Year 4
Expiring (new) leases   -0-
Existing leases   31,000 × $11.25 $348,750
               11,600 × 11.04   128,064
               8,700 × 10.61   92,307
Contract rent $569,121
Available space   2,700 × 11.47   30,969
Potential gross income $600,090
Less vacancy   2,700 × 11.47   30,969
Net rent collections $569,121
Other income   -0-
Effective gross income $569,121

Year 5
Expiring leases   8,700 × $11.93 $103,791
Existing leases   31,000 × 11.48   355,880
               11,600 × 11.26   130,616
Contract rent $590,287
Available space   2,700 × 11.93   32,211
Potential gross income $622,498
Less vacancy   2,700 × 11.93   32,211
Net rent collections $590,287
Other income   -0-
Effective gross income $590,287

Chapter 14

1. This is not a generally valid comment. The use of a *GIM* is acceptable when it is extracted from sales that are comparable as far as the operating expense ratios and the prospects for future income and value. Also, the financing of the comparables must be typical or an adjustment must be made to the transaction price before the multiplier is used to value the subject.

3. *a.*

Sale	GIM
1	$\dfrac{\$740{,}000}{\$105{,}500} = 7.01$
2	$\dfrac{\$835{,}000}{\$121{,}700} = 6.86$
3	$\dfrac{\$830{,}000}{\$118{,}000} = 7.03$
4	$\dfrac{\$1{,}445{,}000}{\$170{,}300} = 8.49$

    The average *GIM* is 7.35.

    b. There are several possibilities. It may be that the *GIM*s are a function of property size, or that the operating expense ratio may be lower for Property 4, or that Sale 4 has been favorably financed. Or, Property 4 may not be comparable to Sales 1–3 as far as future income and value change expectations are concerned.

    c. This is a tough call. On one hand, it is dangerous to discard information simply on the basis that it doesn't "look right. "On the other hand, there are three *GIM*s that are quite close, and given the imperfections and inefficiencies of the real estate market, it may be that the sale in question simply isn't representative.

    In such cases, the appraiser must make a decision and be prepared to defend it. That decision may make use of other valuation approaches and techniques. If these techniques produce value estimates consistent with the average *GIM*, including Sale 4, that is evidence in favor of its inclusion.

    Our bias is to include Sale 4, unless there is objective market evidence (like an *OER* difference) that suggests it should be excluded. If it is excluded, the average *GIM* becomes 6.97, and the difference between including and excluding Sale 4 in the final value estimate is about 5 percent
    $$\left(\frac{7.35 - 6.97}{7.35}\right).$$

5. Reserves for replacement are often included as an operating expense entry to reflect an "average" amount that will be spent on renovating or replacing capital items. Though such expenditures tend to occur irregularly, they should not be ignored in the valuation process. When using R_0s, which are based on a single year's income, the average expenditure should be reflected in the reserve account. When using discounted cash flows, the expenditure may be explicitly recognized when it is expected to occur. However, some *NOI* statements will not include a reserve for replacement entry, and the appraiser using an R_0 from such a "comparable" should make appropriate adjustments.

7. The difference between the *GIM* and R_0 is found in the operating expense ratio. $R_0 = 1 - OER/GIM$. For a given *GIM*, the higher the *OER* is, the lower the R_0 will be, and vice versa.

Chapter 15

1. *a.* Ideally from comparable sales. Terms of debt and resulting equity capitalization rates are extracted in the same way *GIM*s and R_0s are extracted.

    b. If the band of investment inputs are obtained from the same comparable sales as were the *GIM*s and R_0s, we may question why the band of investment model is needed for market valuation. In fact, it isn't needed when good comparables are available. However, when sufficiently reliable comparables aren't available from which to directly extract R_0, then the appraiser may choose to estimate R_0 based on a weighted average of returns. Because the majority of funds are generally supplied by lenders, whose expected returns are observable, the appraiser can accurately estimate a big chunk of R_0. Errors made when estimating the expected return to the equity investor will therefore have a relatively small impact on R_0 and the resulting value estimate.

3. While it is correct that equity investors expect higher returns than lenders, it does not follow that the equity capitalization rate must be higher than the interest rate (or loan constant). The key is to remember that the equity capitalization rate is the return from only a single year. A better comparison is between the yields to equity investors and lenders. The lender's yield is the interest rate, while the equity investor's yield is determined by all of the cash flows and changes in property value, which are unlikely to be completely reflected in the equity capitalization rate.

5. Lenders have a preferred claim on *NOI*. After debt service is paid, the residual cash flows goes to the equity position. The band of investment model implicitly capitalizes the residual cash flow into an estimate of the value of the equity position.

7. When relatively high rates of property appreciation are expected. Because in those cases, a relatively high portion of value comes from future increases in income and value, the *DSCR* for the critical early years is forced downward. To protect the ability of the property to service the debt, lenders in such circumstances rely more heavily on the *DSCR*.

9. *a.* .12935
   b. .1308
   c. Monthly payments amortize a loan slightly faster than annual payments. This means the interest paid is lower, which means the loan constant is lower.

Chapter 16

1. The greater the risk, the higher the expected rate of return.

3. You were given a rate of 8 percent for the government bond. The rate for the apartment should be higher, and the rate for the land lease higher still. Using 12 percent for the apartment and 20 percent for the land lease produces the values below. Your estimates, of course, will depend on the exact discount rates you chose.

   a. Government bond:

   $$\frac{1}{(1 + .08)^1} \times \$1,000,000$$

   $$= .9529 \times \$1,000,000 = \$925,900$$

   b. Land lease:

   $$\frac{1}{(1 + .20)^1} \times \$1,000,000$$

   $$= .8333 \times \$1,000,000 = \$833,300$$

   c. Apartment:

   $$\frac{1}{(1 + .12)^1} \times \$1,000,000$$

   $$= .8929 \times \$1,000,000 = \$892,900$$

5. Y can't be negative because that would mean the present value would be more than the expected future value, and a dollar received in the future would be worth more than a dollar received today. You can prove this by inserting a negative y in the formula for the discount factor. You'll get a factor greater than one, which is impossible.

7. *a.* $295,455
   b. $290,179
   c. $285,088

9. *a.*

   $$\frac{1}{(1 + .13)^7} = .4251$$

   b. If you invest about $.4251 today, and receive $1 in 7 years, you will have made 13 percent per year on your $.4251 investment.

11. $$V = \sum_{t=1}^{n} \frac{CF_t}{(1 + Y)^t} + \frac{Proceeds\ of\ Sale_n}{(1 + Y)^n}$$

    This says to sum the present values of the annual cash flows and the sale proceeds to arrive at present value.

13. *a.*

    $$V = \frac{CF}{y}$$

    $$= \frac{\$31,500}{.15}$$

    $$= \$210,000$$

b. They have essentially equivalent present values, because the value of cash flows to be received far in the future approaches zero. (For example, compare your answers to #4 and #5a.) As the discount rate increases, the difference between long-term annuities and perpetuities decreases, and vice versa.

15. Using a calculator, the "true" *IRR* is 8.75 percent. If the *IRR* is estimated by interpolation, the exact answer will depend on the discount rate used. Using 11 percent and 6 percent as the discount rates, the *NPV*s are ($45,129) and $65,418, respectively. The difference between the *NPV*s is $110,547. Using

$$\frac{\$45,129}{\$110,547} = .41,$$

the estimated $IRR = .11 - .41(.11 - .06) = 8.95\%$.

17. a. Compound interest is applied to the beginning investment plus previously earned interest. It earns interest on interest. Simple interest is applied to the beginning investment only. It does not earn interest on interest.

b. *Simple Interest   Compound Interest*

Yearly interest $= .12 \times \$500 = \$60$ $FV = \$500 \times (1 + .12)^{50}$

$50 \times \$60 = \$3,000 + \$500 = \$3,500$ $= \$500 \times 289.0022$

$= \$144,501$

19. As the discount rate is increased, the present value of a given set of cash flows is decreased. This is intuitive: If a higher return is expected, a lower investment must be made per dollar of investment (present value). A positive *NPV*, therefore, indicates a higher return than the discount rate used to calculate the *NPV*.

Chapter 17

1. a. Capitalize expected NOI_{n+1}.
   b. Assume a rate of annual value change during the holding period.

3. a. *NOI* is an annuity for 12 years, and the property can be valued as:

$$V = PV\,NOI + PV\,NSP$$

$$= 5.4206\,(\$15,000) + \frac{V(1.5)}{5.3503}$$

$$V = \$81,309 + .2804\,V$$

$$.7196\,V = \$81,309$$

$$V = \frac{\$81,309}{.7196}$$

$$V = \$112,992$$

b. $1.5\,(\$112,992) = \$169,488$

c. $V = 3.3522\,(\$15,000)$
$+ (5.4206 - 3.3522)\,(18,000)$
$+ \dfrac{V(1.5)}{5.3503}$

$V = \$50,283 + \$37,231 + .2804\,V$

$.7916\,V = \$87,514$

$V = \dfrac{\$87,514}{.7196}$

$= \$121,615$

5. a. $V = \sum\limits_{t=1}^{n} \dfrac{NOI_t}{(1 + Y_o)^t} + \dfrac{NSP_n}{(1 + Y_o)^n}$

b.

	1	2	3	4	5	6	7
NOI	$22,880	$23,795	$24,747	$25,737	$26,766	$27,837	$28,950
PV factor	.893	.797	.712	.636	.567	.507	.452
PV of NOI	$20,432 +	$18,965 +	$17,620 +	$16,369 +	$15,176 +	$14,113 +	$13,085
	= $115,760						

$$V = \$115{,}760 + \frac{V(1+.03)^7}{(1+.12)^7}$$

$$= \$115{,}760 + \frac{V(1.2299)}{2.2107}$$

$$V = \$115{,}760 + .5563\,V$$

$$.4437\,V = \$115{,}760$$

$$V = \$260{,}897$$

c. PV of $NOI = \$115{,}760$

$$V = \$115{,}760 + \frac{V(1.04)^7}{2.2107}$$

$$= \$115{,}760 + \frac{V(1.3159)}{2.2107}$$

$$V = \$115{,}760 + .5952\,(V)$$

$$.4048\,V = \$115{,}760$$

$$V = \$285{,}968$$

7. In the long run, there is a relationship between annual productivity (*NOI*) and value. For example, a property which will *never* produce income (like an office building on the North Pole) will have a market value of zero. Therefore, the appraiser must think carefully about the relationship of the forecasted growth rates for *NOI* and value. Unless a property is encumbered by a lease calling for nonmarket rentals, or is seriously under- or overdeveloped, changes in income without changes in value (and vice versa) should be questioned.

Chapter 18

1. Value models which discount the property's productivity, *NOI* and *NSP,* are not explicitly concerned with who gets what. Finance-explicit models are used to answer questions about the value of the flow of cash to a specific investor, usually the equity investor. Finance-explicit models provide more detail on the assumptions underlying the value estimate.

3. Y_o is a weighted average of Y_m and Y_e. Therefore, $Y_e > Y_o > Y_m$.

5. $V = V_{NOI} + V_{NSP}$

$$= \$307{,}266 + \left(\frac{\$70{,}000\,(1+.03)^6}{.10}\right)(.96)(.5066)$$

$$= \$307{,}266 + \$406{,}497$$

$$= \$713{,}763$$

7. A substantial percentage of institutional investors use finance-explicit models and an even higher percentage use after-tax models. Many use more than one model, suggesting investors may be interested in both before- and after-tax analysis. These conclusions are based on surveys of large investors, and may not be totally representative of all investors.

9. There are two implications. First, a finance-explicit model will provide a valuation that is explicit with respect to the return to equity. Second, the valuation models will be dominated by the yield to the lender, and any errors made when estimating the yield to equity will have a relatively small impact on the value estimate.

11. *a.* The use of a loan-to-value ratio to estimate V_m assumes either lenders or equity investors, or both, limit the amount of debt as a function of the property's market value. The objective is to limit the probability of future insolvency, defined as occurring when debt is greater than value. In such a case, the property is technically bankrupt, and there is a high probability the borrower will allow a foreclosure. The borrower loses equity while the lender may incur a loss of principal, transaction costs, and unearned interest. The lower the loan-to-value ratio, the lower the probability that the amount of debt will ever exceed value.

The use of the debt service coverage ratio is concerned with the probability of technical insolvency ($NOI < ADS$), rather than actual insolvency. Costs are incurred when default occurs, even if foreclosure is avoided. The objective of the use of a debt service coverage ratio is to limit the amount of debt based on the ability to service the debt.

b. $DSCR = \dfrac{NOI}{ADS}$

$NOI = \$108,000$

$ADS = \$1,032,645 \times .158 = \$163,158$

$= \dfrac{\$108,000}{\$163,158}$

$= .66$

c. The *DSCR* is relatively low because a relatively large portion of value is contributed by growth rather than to the current income level. This forces the current *DSCR* downward.

d.
$$V = V_m + V_e$$

$$V = \dfrac{NOI}{(DSCR)(R_m)} + \sum_{t=1}^{n} \dfrac{NOI_t}{(1+Y_e)^t} - \sum_{t=1}^{n} \dfrac{ADS}{(1+Y_e)^t} + \dfrac{V(1+g_v)^n - MB_n}{(1+Y_e)^n}$$

$$V_m = \dfrac{\$100,000}{(1.30)(.158)}$$

$$= \dfrac{\$100,000}{.2054}$$

$$= \$486,855$$

$V_e =$ Step 1: *PV* of *NOI* $= \$661,031$

2: *PV* of *ADS*

$ADS = \$486,855\,(.158) = \$76,923$

PV of *ADS* $= \$76,923\,(A_{\overline{n}|})$

$= \$76,923\,(4.6586)$

$= \$358,353$

3: *PV* of *BTER* $= [2.1589\,(V) - .8162(\$486,855)](.2081)$

$= [2.1589\,(V) - \$397,371](.2081)$

$= .4493\,(V) - \$82,693$

$V_e = \$661,031 - \$358,353 + .4493\,(V) -$

$\$82,693$

$V = V_m + V_e$

$V = \$486,855 + \$661,031 - \$358,353 + .4493\,(V) - \$82,693$

$V = \$706,840 + .4493\,(V)$

$V - .4493\,(V) = \$706,840$

$V = \$1,283,530 \;(V_m = \$486,855,\; V_e = \$796,675)$

e. PROOF: Test if Y_e (IRR) = .17.

Year	NOI	−	ADS	=	BTCF			
1	$108,000	−	$76,923	=	$ 31,077	SP	=	$1,283,530(2.1589)
2	116,640	−	76,923	=	39,717		=	$2,771,013
3	125,971	−	76,923	=	49,048	−MB	=	397,371
4	136,049	−	76,923	=	59,126	BTER	=	$2,373,642
5	146,933	−	76,923	=	70,010			
6	158,687	−	76,923	=	81,764			
7	171,382	−	76,923	=	94,459			
8	185,093	−	76,923	=	108,170			
9	199,900	−	76,923	=	122,977			
10	215,892	−	76,923	=	138,969			

Year	0	1	2	3	4	5	6	7	8	9	10
Cash flow	($796,675)	$31,077	$39,717	$49,048	$59,126	$70,010	$81,764	$94,459	$108,170	$122,977	$ 138,969 + 2,373,642 $2,512,611

Y_e (IRR) = .17

13. a.

$$V = V_m + V_e$$

$$V_m = .70\,(V)$$

$$V_e = \sum_{t=1}^{n} \frac{BTCF_t}{(1+Y_e)^t} + \frac{BTER_n}{(1+Y_e)^n}$$

$$= \sum_{t=1}^{n} \frac{NOI - ADS}{(1+Y_e)^t} + \frac{NSP_n - MB_n}{(1+Y_e)^n}$$

First-Year NOI

Potential gross income		$1,500,000
Vacancy (6%)		90,000
Effective gross income		$1,410,000
Operating expense (38%)		535,800
NOI		$ 874,200

Appendix A

$$PV\ NOI = NOI_1 \left[\frac{1 - \left(\frac{1 + g_I}{1 + Y_e}\right)^n}{Y_e - g_I} \right]$$

$$= \$874,200 \left[\frac{1 - \left(\frac{1 - .03}{1 + .18}\right)^7}{.18 + .03} \right]$$

$$= \$3,106,965$$

$$PV\ ADS = [(.70)(V)(.1518)](3.8115)$$

$$= .1063(3.8115)$$

$$= .4052(V)$$

$$PV\ BTER = (NSP - MB)(PV\ \text{factor})$$

$$= [(1 - .02)^7(V) - .70(V)(.7528)](.3139)$$

$$= .1071(V)$$

$$V = .70(V) + \$3,106,965 - .4052(V) + .1071(V)$$

$$= \$5,194,725$$

b.
$$V = \$5,194,725$$

$$V_m = .7(\$5,194,725) = \$3,636,308$$

$$ADS = \$3,636,308(.1518) = \$551,992$$

$$V_e = \$5,194,725 - \$3,636,308$$
$$= \$1,558,417$$

	1	2	3	4	5	6	7
NOI	$874,200	847,974	822,535	797,859	773,923	750,705	728,184
ADS	551,992	551,992	551,992	551,992	551,992	551,992	551,992
BTCF	$322,208	295,982	270,543	245,867	221,931	198,713	176,192

$$NSP = \$5,194,725(1 - .02)^7$$
$$= \$4,509,673$$

Chapter 19

1. a. Begin by valuing the whole property as if encumbered at market rents.

   $V = PV\ NOI + PV\ NSP$

   $= \$19{,}000 \left[\dfrac{1 - \left(\dfrac{1+.03}{1+.12}\right)^4}{.12 - .03} \right]$

   $+ (1.02)^4\ (V)\ (.6355)$

   $= \$60{,}107 + .6879\ (V)$

   $= \$192{,}589$

   Now value the leased fee, remembering that the sale proceeds will be based on the current *market* value.

   $V_{LF} = \$21{,}500 \left[\dfrac{1 - \left(\dfrac{1+.03}{1+.12}\right)^4}{.12 - .03} \right]$

   $+ \$192{,}589(1.02)^4\ (.6355)$

   $= \$68{,}016 + \$132{,}479$

   $= \$200{,}495$

   b. $V_{LH} = V - V_{LF}$

   $= \$192{,}589 - \$200{,}495$

   $= (\$7{,}906)$

3. Cash Flows

Year	Sales	–	Clearance Costs	–	Development Costs	–	Administrative Expenses	–	Sales and Promotion	=	Cash Flow
1	$90,000	–	$90,000	–	$64,000	–	$20,500	–	$13,500	=	($98,000)
2	$90,000	–	60,000	–	48,000	–	20,500	–	13,500	=	($52,000)
3	$450,000	–	0	–	32,000	–	20,500	–	67,500	=	$330,000
4	$625,000	–	0	–	16,000	–	20,500	–	93,750	=	$494,750
5	$500,000	–	0	–	0	–	20,500	–	75,000	=	$404,500
6	$170,000	–	0	–	0	–	20,500	–	25,500	=	$124,000

At a 17 percent discount rate, the *PV* of these cash flows is $581,155. The developer can pay up to $5,812 per acre.

5. An unencumbered fee and a fee encumbered at market rents have equal values *only* if the unencumbered fee can be immediately and less costly leased at market rents. In the equation $V = V_{LF} + V_{LH}$, V is properly defined in terms of being leased at market rents.

7. A negative leasehold value arises when contract rent exceeds market rent. The excess rent is lost to the tenant and cannot be used for other purposes. If the tenant wanted to sublease, the new tenant would require a lump-sum payment from the current tenant to offset the excess rent that will have to be paid.

9. a.

Potential gross income	$721,920
(128 × $470 × 12)	
Vacancy (.04)	28,877
Effective gross income	$693,043
Operating expenses (.38)	263,356
Net operating income	$429,687

b. $V = V_B + V_L$

$V_B = \$2{,}000{,}000$

$V = V_m + V_e$

$$V_m = .70\,(V)$$

$$V_e = \sum_{t=1}^{n} \frac{NOI_t - DS_t}{(1+Y_e)^t} + \frac{BTER_n}{(1+Y_e)^n}$$

$$PV \text{ of } NOI = \$429{,}687 \left(\frac{1 - \left(\frac{1-.02}{1+.17}\right)^8}{.17 + .02} \right)$$

$$= \$1{,}713{,}592$$

$$PV \text{ of } DS = .70V(.1598)(4.207)$$

$$= .4706V$$

$$PV \text{ of } BTER = [(V)(1-.02)^8 - [.7106(.70)(V)]]$$
$$(.2848)$$

$$= .1006(V)$$

$$V = .70(V) + \$1{,}713{,}592 - .4706(V) + .1006\,(V)$$

$$V = \$2{,}557{,}600$$

$$V = V_L + V_B$$

$$\$2{,}557{,}600 = V_L + \$2{,}000{,}000$$

$$V_L = \$557{,}600$$

c. Land is valued in the market according to its expected use as if vacant. When the land residual technique is used to estimate a justified land price for a given development, the resulting estimate will equal market value only if the given development is reasonably similar to the expected use as if vacant.

Chapter 20

1. This is effectively a perpetuity.

$$V = \frac{NOI}{Y_o}$$

$$= \frac{\$50{,}000}{.12} = \$416{,}667$$

Discounting $50,000 for 99 years produces a value of $416,667. This does not include sale proceeds, but after 99 years, the effect of sale proceeds is trivial. Suppose, for example, that sale proceeds after 99 years were expected to be $50,000,000. At a 12 percent discount rate, this would add only $670 to present value!

3. There is changing income and changing value.

$$V = \frac{NOI}{R_o}$$

$$R_o = \frac{.12 - (.48 \times .0570)}{1 - \left(\frac{1+.025}{1+.12}\right)^{10}} \div 5.6502$$
$$\frac{}{.12 - .025}$$

$$= \frac{.0926}{1.0952}$$

$$= .0846$$

$$V = \frac{\$50{,}000}{.0846}$$

$$= \$591{,}017$$

5.
$$V = \frac{NOI}{R_o}$$

$$R_o = .11 - (\Delta_o)\left(\frac{1}{s_{\overline{n}|}}\right)$$

$$= .11 - (.30 \times .0843)$$

$$= .0847$$

$$V = \frac{\$12{,}500}{.0847}$$

$$= \$147{,}580$$

7. This is level income with value change.

$$V = \frac{NOI}{R_o}$$

$$R_o = (m)(R_m) + (1-m)(Y_e) - (m)(p)\left(\frac{1}{s_{\overline{n}|}}\right)$$
$$ - (\Delta_o)\left(\frac{1}{s_{\overline{n}|}}\right)$$

$$= (.80 \times .1524) + (.20 \times .165)$$
$$ - (.80 \times .3835 \times .0314) - (.27 \times .0314)$$

$$= .1368$$

$$V = \frac{\$300,000}{.1368}$$

$$= \$2,192,982$$

Proof: $V_m = \$2,192,982 \times .80 = \$1,754,386$

$V_e = \$438,596$

$ADS = .1524 \times \$1,754,386 = \$267,368$

$BTCF = \$300,000 - \$267,368 = \$32,632$

$BTER = \$2,192,982 \, (1.27)$

$\qquad - .6165 \, (\$1,754,386) = \$1,703,508$

An equity value of \$438,596, followed by the calculated BTCFs and BTER, produces an equity yield of 16.5 percent. The value estimate is correct.

9. $R_o = Y - Y \left[\dfrac{(1 + g_I)^t - 1}{(1 + Y)^t - 1} \right]$

$\qquad = .14 - .14 \left[\dfrac{(1 + .03)^2 - 1}{(1 + .14)^2 - 1} \right]$

$\qquad = .1115$

$V = \dfrac{\$50,000}{.1115} = \$448,430$

Chapter 21

1. $GIM = \dfrac{\text{Selling price}}{\text{Gross income}}$

$V = GI \times GIM$

$R_o \text{ (directly extracted)} = \dfrac{NOI \text{ (first year)}}{\text{Selling price}}$

$V = \dfrac{NOI}{R_o}$

$R_o \text{ (band of investment)} = (m)(R_m)$
$\qquad\qquad\qquad\qquad\qquad + (1 - m)(R_e)$

$V = V_m + \sum\limits_{t=1}^{n} \dfrac{CF_t}{(1 + Y)^t} + \dfrac{ER}{(1 + Y)^n}$

where CF, ER, and Y can be either on a before- or after-tax basis.

The general rule is to use the most "efficient" technique based on the criteria of least manipulation. GIMs, directly extracted R_os, and the band of investment are (or should be) based on data from market sales. Discounted cash flow models are not. The latter, therefore, should be used as the *primary* estimate of value only when a lack of sales data precludes the use of the others. The choice between GIMs and directly extracted R_os is also data-driven. If OERs differ, R_os are needed. If financing has changed, the use of the band of investment model may be indicated. In any case, when future prospects are different, the use of a discounted cash flow model is indicated.

3. *a.* To use the band of investment, the equity dividend rate must first be extracted from the comparable(s).

$V_m = \$1,952,255 \, (.70) = \$1,366,579$

$ADS = \$1,366,579 \, (.1558) = \$212,913$

$BTCF = \$200,000 - \$212,913 = (\$12,913)$

$R_e = \dfrac{BTCF}{Equity}$

$\qquad = \dfrac{(\$12,913)}{\$585,676} = (.022)$

The equity dividend rate is used in the band of investment model.

$(m)(R_m) = (.70)(.1558) = .1091$

$(1 - m)(R_e) = (.30)(.022) = (.0066)$

$R_o = .1025$

$V = \dfrac{NOI}{R_o}$

$\qquad = \dfrac{\$213,850}{.1025}$

$\qquad = \$2,086,341$

b. $R_o = \dfrac{NOI}{\text{Selling price}}$

$\qquad = \dfrac{\$200,000}{\$1,952,255}$

$\qquad = .1024$

Allowing for a slight rounding difference, this is, of course, the same as the R_o calculated using the band of investment.

c. $$GIM = \frac{Selling\ price}{Gross\ income}$$

$$= \frac{\$1,952,255}{\$400,000}$$

$$= 4.88$$

d. $$V = GI \times GIM$$

$$= (\$350,000)(4.88)$$

$$= \$1,708,000$$

5. The value estimate based on the directly extracted R_o because it explicitly accounts for the difference in the operating expense ratios.

7. Defined strictly, market value must be observed. That is, a market value estimate must be based on the observed prices of comparable properties. Based on that criteria, discounted cash flow models do not produce market values. Rather, they produce *approximations* of market value. Historically, the distinction between market value and approximations of market value has been blurred, and all three income approaches are considered legitimate ways to estimate market value.

9. GIMs are not too crude if there is sufficient comparability between the comparables and the subject property with respect to the operating expense ratio and future income and value changes.

Chapter 22

1. Investors expect compensation for (a) waiting for cash flows (the "pure" real return), (b) inflation expectations, (c) misestimating inflation, (d) business risk (variability of earnings), (e) liquidity risk (the opportunity cost of illiquidity), and (f) nonrisk costs.

3. The mean real rate of return to real estate during the past four decades has been about 5.7 percent. This rate includes the pure real return, as well as premiums for risks and nonrisk costs. To arrive at a discount rate, the inflation expectation must be added, and this can be found by subtracting the pure real return (about 2.5 percent) from the current yield on long-term government bonds.

5. One way to estimate Y_o is to use market-extracted capitalization rates and forecasts of income and value change, and calculate the *IRR*. A second method is to survey those knowledgeable in the market as to their yield expectations.

7. When debt is used, $Y_e = Y_o$ + premium for financial risk. Given an estimate of Y_o, Y_e can be estimated using the Ellwood model if cash flow and value are level, or by constructing the expected cash flows to equity and calculating the IRR (Y_e). Alternatively, Y_e can be estimated based on a survey of investor expectations. The advantage of a finance-explicit model is that the bulk of value (and therefore the bulk of Y_o) is contributed by the loan amount and errors made in estimating Y_e will have a relatively minor impact on value.

9. The relationship between taxable income and before-tax cash flow is dependent on the relationship of depreciation expense to the principal payments. Depreciation write-offs also affect taxes at sale. Thus, the $Y_a = Y_e(1 - T)$ relationship holds only under an unlikely set of assumptions about depreciation, amortization, and sale proceeds.

Chapter 23

1. No. It is costly to divide, and this cost is reflected in the resulting market values of the lots.

3. The reason the shares' value exceeds the fee simple value is that the promoters have provided a financial service to the investor. For example, shares come in small denominations, and may be more liquid than the fee simple. The value of the underlying real property rights is unaffected.

5. The process must be costly and there must be a demand for the parts.

7. It is true that if someone wanted the fee simple of the specific subject property, the only way to get it would be to buy out the limited partners. However, it does not follow that the value of the fee simple is equal to the value of the shares. If someone did purchase all of the shares, what would be paid for is exactly what the original limited partners paid for. That is, the real property value plus the value of financial services.

The value of the latter must be removed from the purchase price to arrive at the value of the real property. On an intuitive level, it is difficult to justify this sort of behavior in a market with reasonably similar alternatives. Why not buy (or develop) a substitute fee simple and avoid paying for financial services that won't be used? Recall the analogy to the supermarket. A consumer desiring a whole chicken does not buy the package of parts, but rather buys the less expensive whole chicken.

Chapter 24

1. a. $$R_o = \frac{NOI}{Cost}$$

    $$= \frac{\$92,800}{\$960,000}$$

    $$= 9.7\%$$

   b. $$R_e = \frac{BTCF}{Cash}$$

    $$= \frac{\$11,017}{\$210,000}$$

    $$= 5.2\%$$

   c. $$R_a = \frac{ATCF}{Cash}$$

    $$= \frac{\$13,476}{\$210,000}$$

    $$= 6.4\%$$

   d. $$\frac{1}{5} = 20\%$$

   e. The after-tax NPV at .15 = +$12,309
   f. The after-tax IRR = 16.47%

3. a. $$BER = \frac{FE + ADS + (VE/\text{unit} \times \text{\# units})}{\text{\# units}}$$

    $$= \frac{\$25,000 + \$81,783 + (3.05)(.90)(14,000)}{.90(14,000)}$$

    $$= \frac{\$145,213}{12,600}$$

    $$= \$11.52 \text{ square foot}$$

   b.
Rent ($11.52 × 12,600)	$145,152
Operating expenses	
Fixed $25,000	
Variable $38,430	63,430
($3.05 × 12,600)	
NOI	81,722
DS	81,783
	-0- (rounding)

c. Necessary Rent

$$= \frac{\$25{,}000 + \$81{,}783 + (3.05)(.9)(14{,}000) + .10(\$210{,}000)}{(.9)(14{,}000)}$$

$$= \frac{\$166{,}213}{\$12{,}600}$$

$$= \$13.19$$

5. a. $$RAC = \frac{NPV \text{ at } .14}{Annuity\ factor\ at\ .14}$$

$$= \frac{+\$21{,}242}{3.43}$$

$$= \$6{,}193$$

b. Allowable decline in $NOI = \dfrac{RAC}{1 - Tax\ rate}$

$$= \frac{\$6{,}193}{.7}$$

$$= \$8{,}847$$

Percent decline $= \dfrac{\$8{,}847}{\$92{,}800}$

$$= 9.5\%$$

c. Subtracting $6,193 from each year's expected ATCF produces these cash flows:

0	1	2	3	4	5
($210,000)	$7,283	$8,359	$9,437	$10,517	$ 11,596
					+ $343,765
					$355,361

The IRR is 14 percent.

7. $\dfrac{NOI}{Cost}$ is the "appraiser's" return (the capitalization rate) and is not explicit regarding the effects (on the equity return) of financing, taxes, future cash flows, and value change. $\dfrac{BTCE}{Cash}$ captures the effects of financing, but only on a first-year basis.

$\dfrac{ATCF}{Cash}$ captures the effects of financing and taxes, but again only on a first-year basis.

The reciprocal of the payback period, $\dfrac{1}{Payback\ period}$ considers more than a single year, but nothing beyond the payback period.

Equally troubling is that if a sale is projected prior to the payback period, the return will be overestimated.

Net present value and the *IRR* are the result of discounting all expected cash flows and explicitly consider the amount, the timing, and the risk of an investment. While they produce mathematically precise estimates of return, discounted cash flow models require forecasts which carry varying degrees of uncertainty.

9.

	1	2	3
NOI	21,800	24,500	25,000
DS	15,500	15,500	15,500
BTCF	6,300	9,000	9,500
TAX	(60)	810	1,028
ATCF	6,360	8,190	8,472 + ATER of 88,000

$$RAC = \frac{NPV}{\text{Annuity factor}} = \frac{\$5,155}{2.28} = \$2,261$$

Chapter 25

1. Reconciliation is the process of evaluating various indicators of value on the basis of their relative strengths and weaknesses, and choosing a final value estimate from those indicators.

3. The review allows the appraiser to evaluate his or her own work. Was the general approach and emphasis of this appraisal process consistent with the objective of the appraisal as reflected in the definition of value being appraised? Technically, are the data reliable and arithmetic calculations correct, and are the applications of the different approaches internally consistent? After the review is completed, the appraiser must then choose a final value estimate, based on a weighting of the estimates produced by the various techniques.

5. The appraiser should not compress simply to create the appearance of a tighter range of estimates. However, if the review produces evidence that the results of a given approach should be changed, and when changed it results in compression, so be it.

7. The objective of the appraisal will guide the appraiser toward certain approaches that may be theoretically preferable or that are required by the client or the courts. These approaches should be emphasized (within the constraints of the available data) throughout the appraisal process, including reconciliation.

9. Other things being equal, this statement is correct. However, in each case the number of adjustments must be balanced against the size of adjustments and the confidence the appraiser has in the adjustments. Therefore, it is possible that the estimated value resulting from a comparable sale requiring a small number of large and uncertain adjustments may be less reliable than the estimates from a comparable requiring a larger number of small and relatively certain adjustments.

11. This is theoretically incorrect, and in practice, it is no more or less likely than any other approach to produce the highest estimate.

Chapter 26

1. A complete appraisal is one that makes no departure from USPAP.

3. The appraiser is more wrong than right. It is true that certain forms have limited space for description, and that some clients discourage the use of information beyond that allowed on the body of the form. Nonetheless, the appraiser is ultimately responsible for the appraisal, and if added information is considered necessary, it should be included, possibly in an appendix.

5. This is unacceptable behavior. The time to determine the fee is *prior* to accepting the assignment. Once the fee is agreed upon, the appraiser's behavior must be independent of the size of the fee.

7. No. A restricted report is a report that contains relatively little detail and is intended for the client's use only. A limited report is one that departs from USPAP.

Index

A

Accessibility; *see* Location factors, accessibility
Accrued depreciation; *see also* Depreciation
  age and, 205–206, 207, 212–214
  categories of, 183, 203–205, 219
  described, 199–200, 206–207
  economic obsolescence, 184, 188, 204–205
  estimation of, 183–184, 208–230
  external obsolescence; *see* External obsolescence
  functional obsolescence; *see* Functional obsolescence
  locational obsolescence, 184, 188, 204
  physical deterioration; *see* Physical deterioration
After-tax model; *see* Tax-explicit models
After-tax yield to equity (Y_a), 399–400
Age-depreciation relationship, 205–206, 207, 212–214
Age-value relationship, 88
  actual *vs.* effective age, 62–63
Airports, value impact of, 37–38
Akerson, Charles, 373, 373n
Albers, Heide, 37n
Alonso, W., 25n
American Institute of Real Estate Appraisers (AIREA), 441
American Real Estate and Urban Economics Association, 13
Anderson, John E., 156n
Andrews, R., 40n
Anglyn, William, 195n, 357n
Annuities, level, 303–304
Apartments
  residential districts, location factors of, 41
  units of comparison example, 110–111
Appraisal Foundation, 15, 442, 445
Appraisal Institute, 13, 19, 435
  Code of Professional Ethics, 441–442
  highest and best use premise, 75
  price adjustments, order of, 94
Appraisal Journal, 419
Appraisal process, 2–12; *see also* Appraisals
  approaches to, 7–10
  cost approach; *see* Cost approach
  income approach; *see* Income approach
  introduction to, 6–7
  market results and, 10–11, 90
  one-price rule, 7–8
  principle of substitution, 8–9
  reconciliation phase; *see* Reconciliation phase, of appraisals
  reports; *see* Appraisal reports
  sales comparison approach; *see* Sales comparison approach
Appraisal Qualifications Board (AQB), 442
Appraisal reports; *see also* Appraisal process; Appraisals; *Uniform Residential Appraisal Report* (URAR)
  complete, 444, 445
  evaluation of real property, 446
  form reports, 446–448
  letter opinion of value, 446
  limited, 444, 445
  Limited One-Family Appraisal and Summary Report, 446
  narrative reports, 446, 449
  neighborhoods and, 44–45
  oral, 445
  recertification of value, 446
  restricted, 445
  self-contained, 445
  standards for, 443–444
  summary, 445
  updates, 446
  written, 445
Appraisals; *see also* Appraisal process; Appraisal reports
  defined, 2
  expected use analysis; *see* Expected use analysis
  limited or no-market, 180–181
  market information and, 4
  need for, 3–6
  neighborhood categorization, 43–44
  reliability of, 4–6
  uses of, 2–3
Appraisal Standards Board (ASB), 442
Asabere, Paul K., 27n, 52n, 54, 54n, 55, 55n, 104n
Asbestos, 62
Asking (list) price, comparable selection and, 90–91
Assessed value, 22
  value impact of, 50
Assessment ratios, 114–115, 172
Average absolute deviation, 126–128
Averages
  types of, 124–126
  of value estimates, 435–437

B

Babcock, Frederick N., 69, 69n
Babcock, Henry A., 348, 348n, 351
Band of investment model, 277–291
  alternative, 289–291
  debt service coverage ratio (DSCR) and, 289–291
  described, 278–279
  Ellwood model and, 378–379
  equity capitalization rate; *see* Equity capitalization rate (R_e)
  examples, 278–279, 386–387
  loan constant; *see* Loan constant (R_m)
  loan-to-value ratio, 282–283
  multiple mortgages and, 284
  rationale of, 277, 279
  reliability of, 283–284
  usefulness of, 285–286
  variables in, 282–283

473

Bar graphs, 122
Barkham, Richard, 18n
Bathrooms, value impact of, 61–62
Baxter, Nevin D., 348n
Beasley, Ben T., 273, 273n
Bednarz, Robert J., 41n
Before-tax cash flow (BTCF), 326
Before-tax equity reversion (BTER), 326
Benchmark buildings, 188, 190
Benjamin, J., 103n
Berens, 64n
Bernes, Gary L., 266, 266n
Berry, Brian J. L., 27n, 41n
Black, Roy, 43n
Bland, Robert L., 52n
Bleich, Donald, 38
Bloom, George F., 60, 60n
Boeckh Co., 189
Born, Waldo, 18n
Bottum, MacKenzie S., 217n
Boyce, Byrl N., 33, 33n, 203n, 435, 435n
Breakdown method, of accrued depreciation estimation, 217–230
  application of, 217–218
  benefit of, 218
  curable depreciation; see Curable depreciation
  defects, 220, 224
  deficiencies, 220, 223–224
  example, 220–230
  incurable depreciation; see Incurable depreciation
  long-lived items, 219–220, 226–228
  sequence for, 220–230
  short-lived items, 219–220, 225–226
  superadequacies, 220, 224–225
  total value estimate, 229–230
  utility of, 218
Breakeven points, 419–422
  occupancy level (BEO), 420
  rent level, 420–421
Brown, H. James, 36, 36n, 54, 54n, 57, 57n
Brueggeman, Bill, 30n
Building costs, 187–198
  data sources, 188–189
Building materials, value impact of, 59–60
Building Owners and Managers Association, 59
Building value factors, 58–64
  adequacy, 61–62
  age, 62–63
  building materials, types and quality, 59–60

compatibility and conformity, 63–64
condition, 62–63
design, 60–61
effective age, 63
of other property types, 64
proportion, 61–62
size, 58–59
Business risk, 393
Business value, of real estate, 104–105

C
Cambon, Barbara, 395, 395n, 398
Cannaday, Roger E., 92, 92n, 94n, 102n, 151n, 212n
Capital expenditures, *NOI* estimates and, 248
Carman, Kenneth, 337, 337n
Carruthers, C., 38, 38n
Cash equivalency model, 100–103
Cash flow analysis
  finance-explicit models, 331–333
  land residual technique, 357
  multiple cash flow valuation, 300–302
  tax-explicit models, 339–340
Cash-on-cash returns, 421–422
Central business districts (CBDs)
  accessibility, 25–29
  location factors, 41–42
Central limit theorem, 136
Central tendency, measures of, 124–126
Cerf, Alan R., 337, 337n
Cho, Chien-Ching, 156n
Citibank, 32, 100
Cities
  "edge," 30
  growth of, 29
Clapp, John M., 254n
Clean and Green laws, 50
Coate, Douglas, 37n
Code of Professional Ethics, 441–442
Coefficient of determination (r^2), 144–145, 147, 151–152
  multicollinearity and, 155–156
  surprising, missing variables and, 157–158
Cole, R., 5n
Colwell, Peter F., 20n, 26n, 27n, 35, 35n, 38n, 52n, 54, 54n, 92n, 102n, 171n, 379n
Commercial districts, location factors of, 41–42

Community shopping centers, 42
Comparables (income property); *see also* Direct sales comparison
  potential gross income (PGI) estimation, 235–237
  price adjustment of, 107–112
  rent comparisons, 235–237
  selection of, 106, 112, 267–268
Comparables (single-family residential)
  price adjustment of, 91–100
  selection of
    age differentials, 88
    financing considerations, 103
    geographical considerations, 85–86
    list prices, use of, 90–91
    marketing time, 88–89
    physical characteristics, 86–87
    quantity, optimum, 89–90
    time considerations, 86
    three-comparable rule of thumb, 89
Comparative unit method, of cost estimation, 189–192, 194–196
Competitive markets, 15–16
Complete appraisal report, 444, 445
Compound interest, 298–300
Compression, of estimates, 436–437
Computer software
  for finance-explicit models, 332–333
  The Real Estate Applications Software Directory, 333n
  for simulation risk analysis, 427
Confidence intervals
  more precise, 165–166
  in regression analysis, 146
  in statistical inference sales comparison, 132–136
Conformity, structural, 63–64
Consistent use requirement, 76
Contingency clauses, mortgage, 103–104
Corgel, John B., 88, 88n, 212n
Corner lots, 55
Correlation; *see* Reconciliation phase, of appraisals
Correlation analysis, 144–147; *see also* Regression analysis
  coefficient of determination (r^2), 144–145, 147, 151–152

limitations, 146–147
Correlation matrix, 154
Cost approach, 8–9, 177–231
  accrued depreciation; *see* Accrued depreciation
  advantages, 180
  building costs; *see* Building costs
  historical background, 184–185
  land value, estimation of, 184, 202–203
  limitations, 180
  misconceptions, 200–203, 438, 439
  model for, 179
  other uses, 180–181
  reproduction/replacement costs; *see* Reproduction/replacement cost new
  residual models; *see* Residual models
  sales comparison approach *vs.*, 177
  steps in, 181
  underlying assumption of, 179
  utility of, 201–202
Cost(s); *see also* Expense(s)
  building; *see* Building costs
  demolition, and site value, 173
  direct, 183, 187
  indirect, 183, 187
  of investment, nonrisk, 394
  reproduction/replacement; *see* Reproduction/replacement cost new
Cost trending, 197
Coughlin, Robert E., 37n
Crecine, J. P., 36n
Cul-de-sac lots, 55
Cultural characteristics, of neighborhoods, 37
Curable depreciation, 211–212
  breakdown method and, 219
  measurement of
    functional obsolescence, 223–225
    physical deterioration, 222–223
Curb appeal, 61
Curcio, Richard J., 156n

D
Dagbjartsson, Eggert, 409n
Davis, O. A., 36n
Debt, constraint of, 350
Debt service coverage ratio (DSCR), 289–291, 348–351
  in discounted cash flow model, 349–350
  loan-to-value ratio *vs.*, 350

Debt service coverage ratio (DSCR) *(Cont.)*
  mortgage lender use of, 350–351
  risk analysis and, 422
  shortcuts using, 379
Deed restrictions, 49–50
Defects, functional obsolescence, 220, 224
Deficiencies, functional obsolescence, 220, 223–224
Demographics, of neighborhoods, 39–40
Dependent variables, 140, 144–145
Depreciation
  accrued; *see* Accrued depreciation
  age and, 205–206, 207, 212–214
  curable; *see* Curable depreciation
  expense of, 247
  incurable; *see* Incurable depreciation
  local patterns of, 212
  types of, 188
Derbes, Max, Jr., 70n, 75, 75n
Description, property; *see* Property description
Design, value impact of, 60–61
Devaney, Michael, 18n, 37n
Deviation
  average absolute, 126–128
  standard (σ), 128–131
Diermeier, Jeffrey J., 395n
Direct costs, 183, 187
Direct sales comparison, 83–118, 388
  data sources, 113
  of income properties, 106–115
  residual models; *see* Residual models
  of single-family residential properties, 84–106
  site value estimation, 169–172
  supporting estimates, 113–115
Discounted cash flow models; *see also* Present value
  compound interest and, 298–300
  and direct capitalization, compared, 389–390
  discounting net operating income/net selling price, 292–322
  finance-explicit; *see* Finance-explicit models
  income estimation; *see* Multiple-year income forecasts; Net operating income (*NOI*)
  for investment analysis, 344, 416–418
  misconceptions, 438–439
  mortgage-equity; *see* Finance-explicit models
  ratio models *vs.*, 233
  selection of, 342–344
  shortcuts
    "Ellwood"; *see* Ellwood model
    level annuities, 303–304, 371
    limitations of, 379–380
    perpetuities
      with escalation clause, 371–372
      growing, 370–371
      level, 304–306, 370
    tax-explicit; *see* Tax-explicit models
    types of, 323–324
Discount factor, 293–295; *see also* Discount rate (Y_o)
  time and, 297–298
Discount rate (Y_o), 336
  discount factor and, 293–294
  estimation of, 392–400
  inflation and, 256–259
  nominal *vs.* real, 256–259
  overall capitalization rate (OAR) and, 336
  and risk, 295–297, 393
  split rate usage, 360–362
Dispersion, measures of, 126–128
Districts; *see* Location factors, districts
Do, A. Quang, 35n
Dotzour, Mark G., 5n
Doutzour, Mark, 185n
Duben, Robin, 37n

E
Easements, value impact of, 50
Economic obsolescence, 184, 188, 204–205
"Edge cities," 30
Edley, D., 380n
Effective age
  economic life variation, 208–211
  modified, 211–212
  vs. actual age, 62–63
Efficient markets, 16–17
Ellwood, L. W., 348n, 372n, 372–373, 376
Ellwood model, 373–379
  band of investment model and, 378–379
  G factor, 376–377
  income/value both change, 376–378
  income/value remain same, 373–374
  limitations of, 379–380
  precision of, 378
  value changes, 375
Emerson, Frank C., 213n
Encroachments, value impact of, 50
Environmental influences
  laws/regulations, 57–58
  on neighborhoods, 37–39
  property assessments, 58
  value impact, estimating, 57–58
Epley, Donald, 85n, 208, 208n, 210n
Equity capitalization rate (R_e), 278
  equity yield rate (Y_e) and, 335–336
  estimation of, 282–283
  for investment analysis, 414
  loan constant and, 279–280
Equity residual models
  band of investment model; *see* Band of investment model
  finance-explicit model; *see* Finance-explicit models
Equity yield rate (Y_e)
  equity capitalization rate (R_e) and, 335–336
  estimation of, 398–399
Escape clause, lease, 251
Ethical standards, of appraisal practice, 441–442
Evaluation of real property, 446
Evans, Richard, 18n
Evans, Robert, 443n
Excess land
  and expected use analysis, 77, 78
  as site factor, 56–57, 171–172
Expected rate of return; *see* Discount rate (Y_o)
Expected use analysis, 67–79
  additions and, 77–78
  comparables and, 70–71
  consistent use requirement, 76
  criteria for, 68–69
  example, 71–73
  excess land and, 77, 78
  expected use premise, 70–71
  highest and best use; *see* Highest and best use premise
  for improved properties, 73–74
  interim uses, 75–76
  of land, as if vacant, 69–71
  mixed uses, 76–77
  more efficient use and, 77–78
  most probable use premise, 73
  premises, compared, 74–75
  renovations and, 77–78
Expected use premise, 70–71
Expense(s); *see also* Cost(s)
  capitalizing, 248
  depreciation, 247
  division of, in leases, 251
  interest, 247
  maintenance/repair, 244
  operating; *see* Operating expenses
  reserve accounts, 244–245, 274
Exposure time, 15
External obsolescence, 183–184, 188, 204–205
  incurable, 228–229

F
Fanning, Steve, 69n
Farragher, Edward J., 343, 343n
Farrell, Michael D., 149, 149n
Federal Home Bank Board, 404
Federal Housing Administration, 171, 173
Federal National Mortgage Association (Fannie Mae), 446
Fee simple, 352, 358n
Ferrerra, E. J., 102n
Ferri, Michael G., 213n
Finance-explicit models, 325–336
  cash flow analysis, 331–333
  computer software for, 332–333
  debt service coverage ratio-based, 349–350
  equity yield rate (Y_e) estimation, 398–399
  examples, 326–330, 385–386
  income participation and, 334
  interest only loans and, 334
  for market value estimation, 341–342
  property taxes and, 334–335
  for residual valuation, 368–369
  utility of, 330–331
  variable rate loans and, 334
Financial Institutions Reform, Recovery, and Enforcement Act of 1989 (FIRREA), 442
Financial risk, 398–399
Financing; *see also* Loans; Mortgages
  adjusting for, 100–104

Financing *(Cont.)*
  creative, 409
  favorable, estimating value of, 102
  favorable, market value of, 409
  GIMs and, 269
  optimal, 408
  and value, 285, 407–410
Findlay, Chapman, 38n
Fiore, Joseph S., 373n
Fisher, Jeffrey D., 62n, 337, 337n, 349n, 350, 350n, 376, 376n, 379n
Fixed operating expenses, 242–243
Flat rental leases, 250
Floor plans, utility of, 60–61
Frankel, Marvin, 34n, 38n
Freitag, Mark, 185n
Friedman, Edith J., 41n
Frontage-to-depth ratio, 54
F-statistic, 152n
Functional obsolescence, 183, 188, 203–204
  curable, 223–225
  deficiencies, defects, and superadequacies, 220, 223–225
  incurable, 228
F. W. Dodge, 189

G
Galleshaw, Mark, 75n
Galton, Sir Francis, 140
Garreau, Joel, 30n
Garrod, G. D., 155n
Gatzlaff, Dean, 18n
Gau, George W., 18n, 155n, 156n
Geltner, David, 18n
General Electric, 83
General Motors, 272, 409
General payroll expenses, 243
Geography, and land-value gradients, 32
Gibbons, James E., 395n, 397n
Gibson, Robert, 168n, 352, 352n
Gittman, Lawrence J., 422, 422n
Goldberg, Michael A., 31n, 31–32, 154n
Goodheim, Brian, 72, 72n
Government (rectangular) survey, as property description, 48
Government restrictions; *see also* Legal issues
  environmental, 57–58
  excess land, 57, 171–172
  and land-value gradients, 32–33
  and neighborhoods, 37–39
  zoning; *see* Zoning

Graaskamp, James, 72n
Graduated-rental leases, 251
Gray, J. Brian, 99n, 139n
Green, Richard, 74n, 165n
Grether, D. M., 36n
Grissom, Terry V., 252n
Gross income multiplier (GIM), 107–111, 233, 264–269
  application, consistent, 269
  application of, 388
  comparable selection, 267–268
  defined, 265
  example, comparative, 387–388
  financing and, 269
  inflation and, 268
  logic of, 266–267
  mechanics of, 265–266
  operating expense ratios (OERs) and, 269–270
  potential *vs.* effective gross income, 268
  property size and, 267, 268
  real changes in, 268–269
Gross rent multiplier (GRM), 265
Grudnitski, Gary, 35n
Guilkey, D., 5n
Guntermann, Karl L., 35, 35n, 55, 55n

H
Hall, Peter, 25n
Hamilton, S., 38, 38n
Hanford, Lloyd D., 286n
Hansz, Andrew, 104n
Harner, Thomas R., 37n
Harris, Jack, 18n
Harris, Matthew, 27, 27n
Harrison, Henry S., 60, 60n
Hartzell, David, 212, 212n
Hazardous waste sites, and land value, 38
Hendershott, Pat, 5n
Heuson, Andrea, 41n
Highest and best use premise, 69–70, 75, 77–78, 168
  interim uses, 75–76
  and residual land analysis, 357
Highway noise, value impact of, 38
Histograms, 122
Hoch, Irving, 27n
Home Owner's Loan Corporation, 436
Horn, Edward T., 37n
Hotels, value factors, 64; *see also* Building value factors
Hough, Douglas E., 61n
Huffman, Forrest H., 104n
Hurd, Richard M., 25, 25n

I
Ibbotson, Roger G., 395n
Improvements
  condition of, and value, 62–63
  demolition costs, and site value, 173
  land value and, 51
  tenant, 252
Income approach, 9–10, 233–429
  discounted cash flow models; *see* Discounted cash flow models
  history of, 383–385
  implicit *vs.* explicit variables, 385
  income forecasts; *see* Multiple-year income forecasts; Net operating income (*NOI*)
  investment analysis; *see* Investment analysis
  model comparison examples, 385–388
  model selection considerations, 388–389
  net operating income; *see* Net operating income (*NOI*)
  ratio models, 233
  residual models; *see* Residual models
Income properties; *see also* Income approach
  direct sales comparison of; *see* Direct sales comparison, of income properties
  market disequilibrium and, 216–217
Incurable depreciation, 211–212, 219–220
  breakdown method and, 219–220
  measurement of, 225–229
Independent variables, 140, 140–145
  missing, 157–159
  multicollinearity and, 154–157
  significance of, 151
Indexed leases, 250
Indirect costs, 183, 187
Industrial districts, location factors of, 42–43
Industrial properties
  appraisal reliability, 5
  proximity and, 34
  value factors, 64; *see also* Building value factors
Inflation
  debt service coverage ratio and, 351
  GIMs and, 268

income forecasts and, 256–259
  unexpected, risk of, 393
Institute of Real Estate Management (IREM), 237
Insurable value, 22, 181
Interest
  compound, 298–300
  simple, 299–300
Interest expense, 247
Interim uses, 75–76
Internal rate of return (IRR), 307–308
  investment analysis and, 417–418
  partitioning of, 424–426
Investment analysis
  cost approach for, 181
  and market value estimation, compared, 419
  rate of return measures, 412–419
  risk and; *see* Risk analysis
Investment value, 21
  estimating; *see* Investment analysis
Isakson, Hans R., 89n

J
Jackson, J. E., 36n
Janssen, C. T. L., 55n
January, David, 162n
Jud, G. Donald, 36n

K
Kain, J. F., 36n
Kane, Edward, 5n
Kang, Han-Bin, 99n, 266, 266n
Kapplin, Steve, 195n
Kau, James, 27, 27n
Kazdin, S. Edwin, 277n
Keith, Tom J., 52n
Kelley Blue Book, 189
Kelly, W., 380n
Kinnard, William N., 13, 435, 435n
Kish, Leslie, 4n
Knepp, Paul J., 373n
Knos, Duane S., 27, 27n, 28n
Kohlhepp, Dan, 155n, 156n
Kohlhose, J. E., 39n
Kolbe, Phillip, 266, 266n
Korpacz, Peter F., 252n, 397n, 398n
Kratz, Charles G., 61n
Kroll, Mark, 237n
Kuhle, James C., 252n

L
Land fills, and land value, 38
Land residual technique; *see* Residual models, land

Land value; *see also* Market value; Site value
  accessibility and, 25–29
  estimated, for
    cost approach, 184, 202–203
  expected use analysis; *see* Expected use analysis
  land-value gradients, 26–27
  geography and, 32
  government regulation and, 32–33
  lumps in, 30–33
  neighborhood effects on, 40–41
  technology improvements and, 32
  transportation improvements and, 30–33
  land vs. site, 168
  and total property value, percentage of, 167–168
  urban, empirical evidence for, 27–29
Lansing, John B., 4n
Laundry machines, income from, 240–242
Leased fee, 249
  defined, 352
  simple fee vs., 358n
Leasehold interest, 352
  value of, 358–360
Leases; *see also* Rent
  analysis of, 250
  division of expenses in, 251
  escape clause, 251
  flat rental, 250
  graduated rental, 251
  indexed, 250
  net, 251
  nonrental clauses, 251–252
  percentage, 251
  renewal/purchase options, 252, 362–363
  rental clauses, 250–251
  sandwich, 361–362
  tenant improvements, 252
  value impact of, 50
Least-squared error, 142
Legal issues; *see also* Government restrictions
  Clean and Green laws, 50
  de minimus level for residential properties, 6
  environmental laws/regulations, 57–58
Lenk, M., 160n
Lentz, George, 62n
Lessor's interest; *see* Leased fee
Letter opinion of value, 446
Level annuities, 371
Li, Mingche M., 36, 36n, 54, 54n, 57, 57n

Limited appraisal reports, 444, 445
Limited One-Family Appraisal and Summary Report, 446
Limited partnerships, 409–410
Limited-use properties, 21
Linneman, Peter, 18n
Lipscomb, Joseph, 99n, 139n
Liquidity risk, 393
Loan constant (R_m), 278, 280–281
  equity capitalization and, 279–280
  estimation of, 282–283
Loans; *see also* Mortgages
  interest only, 334
  present value of, 302–303
  variable rate, 334
Loan-to-value ratio (m), 282–283, 348
  debt service coverage ratio vs., 350
  market value and, 407–408
Locational obsolescence, 184, 188, 204
Location factors, 24–46
  accessibility
    land value and, 25–29
    special, 34–35
  transportation improvements, 30–33
  districts
    commercial, 41–42
    industrial, 42–43
    multifamily residential, 41
  neighborhoods; *see* Neighborhoods
Long-lived depreciation items, 219–220, 226–228
Lot and block numbers, as property description, 48
Louargand, Marc, 343, 343n
Love, A. Scruggs, 15n
Lumps, in land-value gradient, 30–33
Lusht, Kenneth M., 60n, 86n, 89n, 104n, 244n, 267n, 285n, 292n, 349n, 350, 350n, 379n, 433n

M
McDonald, John F., 36, 36n
McDonald's, 21
MacKenzie, D. M., 30, 30n
MacLean, D. G., 55n
McMillen, Daniel P., 36, 36n
McQualin, J., 27n
Maintenance/repair expenses, 244
Malizia, 64n
Malpezzi, Stephen, 212n
Management fees, 243, 248
Marchitelli, Richard, 202n

Mark, Jonathan, 154n
Market conditions factor (MCF), 215–216
Market disequilibrium
  and accrued depreciation estimation, 214–217
  rent adjustment for, 259–260
Marketing time, 15
  and comparable selection, 88–89
Market results, appraisal process and, 10–11
Market risk, 393
Market setting, 33
Market value; *see also* Land value
  cash flow models for, 341–344
  defined, 13–18
  financing and, 407–410
  favorable, 102, 409
  location and; *see* Location factors
  most probable price, 14–15
  non-ownership impacts on, 48–50
  present value and, 294–295
  reasonable exposure and, 15
Marquette, R. Penny, 156n
Marshall Valuation Services, 189, 191n, 196n
Marshall Valuation Services Manual, 190
Martin, Robert J., 333n, 373n
Maser, S. M., 52n
Mason, James J., 15n
Matched pairs analysis, for comparable price adjustment, 94–98
  example, 96–98
  in practice, 98
  sequence for, 95–96
Mean (M), 124–126
Measures of central tendency, 124–126
Median, 125–126
Medici, G., 15, 15n
Mehdian, Seyed, 104n
Messner, Stephen D., 254n
Metes and bounds, as property description, 48
Mieszkowski, D., 36n
Miles, 64n
Miles, M., 5n
Miller, Merton, 406, 406n
Miller, Norman G., 18, 18n, 88–89, 89n
Mills, Edwin S., 51n
Mitchell, D., 380n
Mitchell, Phillip S., 266, 266n
Mode, 125
Modigliani, Franco, 406, 406n
Monte Carlo simulation, 427
Moore, James S., 156n, 157n
Moreya, Robert, 357n

Mortgage constant; *see* Loan constant (R_m)
Mortgage-equity models; *see* Finance-explicit models
Mortgages; *see also* Loans; Loan-to-value ratio (m)
  cash equivalency model, 101–103
  contingency clauses, 103–104
  mortgage constant; *see* Loan constant (R_m)
  multiple, 284
Most probable price, 14–15
Most probable use premise, 73
Muller, Anders, 53n
Multicollinearity, 154–157
Multifamily residential districts, location factors of, 41
Multiple nuclei, of urban areas, 30
Multiple regression, 149–151; *see also* Regression analysis
Multiple-year income forecasts, 249–260
  example, 252–256
  forecasting strategies, 253–254
  inflation expectations and, 256–259
  leases and, 250–252
  market disequilibrium and, 259–260
  real vs. nominal discount rates, 256–259
  rent forecasts, 255–256
Munneke, Henry, 26n
Murdoch, James, 39n

N
Natural hazards, and land value, 39
Neighborhoods
  categorization of, 43–44
  components of, 33–40
  defined, 33
  demographics, 39–40
  environmental influences, 37–39
  governmental influences, 37–39
  life cycles of, 40
  "micro-neighborhood," 57
  non-single-family; *see* Location factors, districts
  proximity, 34–35
  stability, 36–37
Neighborhood shopping centers, 42
Nelson, A. C., 38, 38n
Nelson, Jon P., 4n, 38, 38n
Net income multiplier (NIM), 272

Net leases, 251
Net operating income (*NOI*), 234–249
　capital expenditures and, 248
　capitalization of, 314
　declining, 316–317
　deferred maintenance and, 248–249
　depreciation expense and, 247
　discounted; *see* Discounted cash flow models
　distortions in, 247–249
　example statement, 245–246
　existing leases and, 249
　interest expense and, 247
　market *vs.* actual, 249
　multiyear; *see* Multiple-year income forecasts
　and net selling price estimation, 314
　operating expense ratio (OER), 246–247
　operating expenses; *see* Operating expenses
　other income, 240–242
　potential gross income; *see* Potential gross income (PGI)
　property taxes and, 248
　rent/vacancy levels and, 248
　vacancy allowance, 239–240
Net present value (NPV), 308
　investment analysis and, 416–418
Net selling price (NSP)
　estimation, 313–315
　two-period model, 321–322
New Shelter, 99
Newsome, Bobby, 338n
Nominal discount rate, 256–259
Nonlinear relationships, 160–162
Non-ownership property rights, 48–50
　assessed value, 50
　deed restrictions, 49–50
　discovery of, 49
　easements/encroachments, 50
　leases; *see* Leases
　property taxes, 50
　zoning; *see* Zoning
Non-residential property, appraisal reliability, 5

O
Office buildings
　units of comparison example, 107–110
　value factors, 64; *see also* Building value factors
One-price rule, 7–8
Operating expense ratio (OER), 246–247, 269–270
Operating expenses
　division of, in net leases, 251
　fixed, 242–243
　maintenance and repair, 244, 248
　operating expense ratio (OER), 246–247, 269–270
　reserve for replacements, 244–245, 274
　variable, 243
Oral appraisal report, 444
Other income, of rental properties, 240–242
Overall capitalization rate (OAR or R_o); *see also* Ellwood model
　band of investment model; *see* Band of investment model
　directly extracted, 270–274
　and discount rate (Y_o), 336, 396
　for investment analysis, 413
Overhead power lines, and land value, 38
Ozorne, Larry, 212n

P
Page, Dan, 343, 343n
Palmquist, Raymond B., 38, 38n, 212n, 213n
Parameters, of a population, 129
Partial interests, 403–410; *see also* Residual models
　financing and value, 407–410
　limited partnerships, 409–410
　value of whole equal to, 406–407
　value of whole increased by, 405–406, 410
Patchin, Peter, 39n
Payback reciprocal, 415–416
Pearson, Thomas D., 69n
Peiser, Richard, 39, 39n
Pension Real Estate Association, 173
Percentage leases, 251
Periodic revaluation leases, 250
Perpetuities
　with escalation clause, 371–372
　growing, 370–371
　level, 304–306, 370
Phillips, G. Michael, 38n
Physical deterioration, 183, 188, 203, 219
　measurement of
　　curable, 222–223
　　incurable, 225–228
Pindyck, 160n
Pittinger, William L., 357n
Pittman, Robert, 43n
Plattage, 56, 171
Plottage, 56, 171, 406
Point estimate, of value, 119
Potential gross income (PGI), 235–239; *see also* Net operating income (NOI)
　estimation of
　　using competitive properties, 235–237
　　mixed uses/sizes and, 238
　　quoted *vs.* effective rent, 239
　　using regression analysis, 262–263
　　search area, for comparable rents, 238–239
　　using subject property, 237
　　using surveys, 237
　　units of comparison, 238
Present value, 293–295; *see also* Discounted cash flow models
　concept of, 293–294
　of loans, 302–303
　market value and, 294–295
　of multiple cash flows, 300–302
　net (NPV), 308, 416–418
　and net selling price estimation, 314–315
Price-bracketing, 111–112
Principle components method, 156
Principle of substitution, 8–9
Professional practice
　environmental problems, 58
　ethical standards, 441–442
　licensing and certification, 442–443
　Supplemental Standards and Guide Notes, 442
　Uniform Standards of Professional Appraisal Practice (USPAP), 58, 441
Profit, developer's, 183, 187
Property analysis
　expected use and; *see* Expected use analysis
　location; *see* Location factors
　property-specific characteristics; *see* Building value factors; Site value
Property description, 47–48
Property insurance, cost approach for, 181
Property taxes
　assessed value and, 22
　and finance-explicit models, 334–335
　NOI statements and, 248
　overall capitalization rate (R_o) and, 274
　value impact of, 50
Proportion, value impact of, 61–62
Proximity, 34–35, 41
Pugh, Frederick, 86n, 89n
Purchase options, lease, 252
Putman, John, 357n
Pyhrr, Steve, 427, 427n

Q
Qualitative (dummy) variables, 152–153
Quantity-survey method, of building cost estimation, 192
Quigley, J.M., 36n

R
Rabianski, Joseph, 105n
Radon gas, 62
Rahmatian, Mortega, 37n
Randle, Paul A., 337, 337n
Ratcliff, Richard U., 15, 15n, 266, 266n, 292, 292n, 348, 348n
Rates of return
　expected; *see* Discount rate (Y_o)
　internal; *see* Internal rate of return (IRR)
　to lender; *see* Loan constant (R_m)
Rayburn, William, 18n, 37n
Real discount rate, 256–259
The Real Estate Applications Software Directory, 333n
The Real Estate Appraiser and Analyst, 85n
Real estate market
　appraisal process and, 2–12
　competitiveness of, 15–16
　efficiency of, 17–18
　price and value in, 13–22
　value trends, 113–114
Recertification of value, 446
Reconciliation phase, of appraisals, 10, 432–439
　final value estimate, 434–437
　misconceptions, 438–439
　review, 433–434
Regional shopping centers, 42
Regression analysis, 82, 139–163; *see also* Correlation analysis; Sales comparison approach
　for comparable price adjustment, 99

Regression analysis *(Cont.)*
  multiple regression
    adjusted coefficient of determination (r^2), 151–152
    confidence intervals, 165–166
    correlation matrix, 154
    default variable, 152
    errors, potential, 154–157
    F-statistic, 152n
    independent variables, 151
    multicollinearity, 154–157
    nonlinear relationships, 160–162
    principle components method, 156
    qualitative (dummy) variables, 152–153
    regression residuals, 158–159
    rent prediction, 153
    results, improving, 154–162
    ridge regression, 156–157
    scatter diagrams, 141–142
    stepwise, 155–156
    for PGI estimation, 262–263
  simple regression, 140–149
Regression coefficient (b), 145
Regression residuals, 158–159
Reichert, Alan K., 99n, 156n, 157n, 266, 266n
Remodeling Contractor, 100
Renewal options, lease, 252, 362–363
Rent; *see also* Leases
  for comparable properties, 235–237
    quoted *vs.* effective, 239
    search area for, 238–239
  future, estimation of, 259–260
  land, capitalization of, 173
  predicting, regression analysis and, 153
Reproduction/replacement cost
  new
    categories of, 183, 187
    compared, 182
    components of, single-family house, 222
  defined, 182, 183
  estimation of, 183–184; *see also* Building costs
Reserve expense accounts, 244–245, 274
Residential properties, single-family
  appraisal reliability, 4–5
  de minimus level for, 6
  direct sales comparison of; *see* Direct sales

comparison
  value of; *see also* Building value factors
Residual models, 352–365; *see also* Partial interests
  building, 353–354
  equity; *see* Band of investment model; Finance-explicit models
  income-based, 354–355
  land, 354
    conceptual problem of, 355–356
    finance-explicit example, 368
    for land development, 356–357
    leased fee/leasehold, 358–365
Residual risk, 393
Restricted appraisal report, 445
Reuter, F. H., 52n
Reversion, 313; *see also* Net selling price (NSP) estimation
  before-tax equity (BTER), 326
Ridge regression, 156–157
Riker, W. H., 52n
Risk
  analysis of; *see* Risk analysis
  business, 393
  discount rate (Y_o) and, 295–297, 393
  financial, 398–399
  of inflation, unexpected, 393
  liquidity, 393
  market, 393
  residual, 393
Risk analysis, 419–426
  breakeven points, 419–422
  cash-on-cash returns, 421–422
  computer software for, 427
  debt service coverage ratio (DSCR), 422
  partitioning IRR, 424–426
  risk absorption capacity (RAC), 422–424
  scenarios, 426
  sensitivity analysis, 426
  simulation, 426–427
Robins, Philip K., 4n
Rose, Louis A., 27n
Rosen, Kenneth T., 102n
Rosett, R. N., 52n
Roth, Mark I., 252n
Roulac, Steven, 398n
Rowe, N. A., 155n
R. S. Means, 189
Rubinfeld, 160n
Rushing, Philip J., 379n
Ryan, James P., 15n

S
Sabella, Edward, 212n
Sadevion, Z., 149n
Sales comparison approach, 7–8, 81–175
  direct; *see* Direct sales comparison
  regression analysis; *see* Regression analysis
  using statistical inference; *see* Statistical inference sales comparison
Salomon Brothers, 32
Scatter diagrams, 141–142
Scenarios, for risk analysis, 426
Scheu, Tim, 54, 54n
Schwann, G., 38, 38n
Segregated cost method, 192, 193
Self-contained appraisal report, 445
Sensitivity analysis, 426
Shenkel, William M., 266, 266n
Shilling, J., 103n
Shopping centers, 42
Short-lived depreciation items, 219–220, 225–226
Siegel, Lawrence B., 395n
Silva, A., 160n
Simple interest, 299–300
Simulation, for risk analysis, 426–427
Singh, Harinder, 39n
Single-family properties; *see* Residential properties, single-family
Sirmans, C. F., 27, 27n, 52n, 102n, 103n, 113n, 171n, 173n, 273, 273n, 338n
Sirmans, G. Stacy, 102n, 273, 273n
Site components, 51
Site value, 50–58, 167–175; *see also* Expected use analysis; Land value
  comparable price adjustment, 169–171
  contour, 56
  corner lots, 55
  cul-de-sacs, 55
  data sources, 173
  demolition costs and, 173
  environmental laws/regulations, 57–58
  estimation, methods of allocation, 172
    capitalization of land rent, 173
    direct sales comparison, 169–172
    land residual approach, 172
    tax assessment ratios, 172
  excess land, 56–57,

171–172
  highest and best use premise, 168
  "micro-neighborhood," 57
  plottage and plattage, 56, 171–172
  shape, 53–54
  site, defined, 168
  size, 51–53, 54
  soil quality, 56
  topography, 56
  value-determining factors, 168–169
Size-value relationship
  buildings, 58–59, 87
  land, 51–53, 54
Sklacz, Michael, 18n
Sklarz, Michael A., 89, 89n
Smith, Adam, 24
Smith, Bruce H., 35n, 149n
Smith, Charles A., 149n, 237n
Smith, Halbert C., 88, 88n, 212n
Smith, Stanley D., 102n
Social characteristics, of neighborhoods, 37
Society of Real Estate Appraisers (SREA), 441
Special accessibility (proximity), 34–35
Special purpose properties, 181
Spinks, James A., 27, 27n
Stability, of neighborhoods, 36–37
Stallings, Dick, 217n
Standard deviation (σ), 128–131
Standard error of the coefficient (s_b), 145–146
Standard error of the estimate (s_e), 143
Standard error of the mean, 134–136
Statement on Appraisal Policies Practice, 404
Statement on Appraisal Standards Number 6, 15
Statistical inference sales comparison, 81, 119–138; *see also* Sales comparison approach
  average absolute deviation, 126–128
  bar graphs, 122
  central limit theorem, 136
  confidence intervals, 132–136
  frequency distributions, 121–128
  histograms, 122
  mean (M), 124–126
  median, 125–126
  misconceptions, 439
  mode, 125
  populations, 119–122
    parameters of, 129

Statistical inference sales comparison *(Cont.)*
  samples, 131–134
  standard deviation (σ), 128–131
  t-values, 132–134, 145
  Z-values, 129–131, 133–134
Statistics, defined, 132
Stenejhem, Eric, 33n
Step-up/step-down leases, 251
Stepwise regression, 155–156
Stigler, George J., 18n
Stratification, narrow, 159
Street address, as property description, 48
Stull, W. J., 36n
Summary appraisal report, 445
Summation approach, discount rate (Y_o) estimation, 394–396
Sunderman, Mark A., 102n, 212n
Sung, Chein-Hsing, 37n
Superadequacies, functional obsolescence, 220, 224–225
Super-regional shopping centers, 42
Supplemental Standards and Guide Notes, 442
Surveys, comparable price adjustment, 100
Swensen, Philip R., 337, 337n

T
Taxes; *see also* Tax-explicit models
  impact on yield to equity, 399–400
  property; *see* Property taxes
Tax-explicit models, 336–340
  cash flow analysis, 339–340
  example, 338–340
  for investment value estimation, 344
  for market value estimation, 342
Taylor, Chris, 39, 39n
Tenant improvements, 252
Thayer, Mark, 37n, 39n
Thibodeau, Thomas G., 36n, 212n
Thompson, Mark, 409n
Three-comparable rule of thumb, 89
Tirtiroglu, Dogan, 18n
Transactional audits, 58
Transportation, land-value gradients and, 30–33
Travis, 64n
Trend analysis, 113–114
Tse, K. C. Maurice, 62n
Turnbull, G., 103n
t-values, 132–134, 145

U
Uniform Residential Appraisal Report (URAR), 44–45, 182, 189, 201, 264, 446–448
Uniform Residential Report Form, 107
Uniform Standards of Professional Appraisal Practice (USPAP), 441
  appraisal report standards, 443–444
  environmental influences, estimation of, 58
Unique properties, 181
Unit-in-place (segregated) method, of cost estimation, 192, 193
Unit(s) of comparison
  for income properties, 106–107, 238
  apartment example, 110–111
  gross income multiplier (GIM), 107–111
  office building example, 107–110
  for residential properties, 105–106
  for site valuation, 169
Unit(s) of measurement
  for buildings, 59
  for land, 51
Updates, of appraisals, 446
Use-value, 21
  expected; *see* Expected use analysis
Utility expenses, 243

V
Vacancy allowance, 239–240
Value
  age and, 88
  assessed, 22
  business, 104–105
  financing and, 285
  future, 313–315, 321–322
  insurable, 22, 181
  investment, 21
  land; *see* Land value
  market; *see* Market value
  use-value, 21
Vandell, Kerry D., 71, 71n, 74, 74n, 89n
Vanderhoff, James, 37n
Variable operating expenses, 243
Variables
  default, 152
  dependent, 140, 144–145
  implicit *vs.* explicit, 385
  independent; *see* Independent variables
  qualitative (dummy), 152–153
Vending machines, income from, 240–241
Venor, James D., 358n
Vernor, James, 105n
Veterans Administration, 173
Visual appeal, 61
Voith, Richard, 30n
Von Thunen, 25n

W
Waddell, Paul, 27, 27n
Wade, Charles E., 55n
Walden, Michael, 35n
Wal-Mart, 42
Walsh, Thomas J., 33n
Warden, John, 43n
Webb, James R., 156n, 343, 343n
Weicher, John C., 212, 212n
Weiss, 64n
Wendt, Paul F., 31n, 31–32, 264, 264n, 337, 337n
West, Richard W., 4n
West, Robert J., 38n
White, Robert P., 6n, 67n
Wiley, Robert J., 343, 343n
Willis, K. G., 155n
Wofford, Larry E., 422, 422n
Worzala, E., 160n
Written appraisal report, 444
Wu, Chunchi, 92n

Z
Zawati, A. K., 5n
Zerbst, Robert, 395, 395n, 398
Zones, home interior, 60–61
Zoning
  excess land and, 57
  and expected use analysis, 68
  industrial districts and, 43
  and land-value gradients, 32–33
  value impact of, 49–50
Z-values, 129–131, 133–134